Web Developer's Cookbook

MORE THAN 300 READY-MADE PHP, JAVASCRIPT, AND CSS RECIPES

Robin Nixon

New York Chicago San Francisco
Lisbon London Madrid Mexico City
Milan New Delhi San Juan
Seoul Singapore Sydney Toronto

The *McGraw·Hill* Companies

Cataloging-in-Publication Data is on file with the Library of Congress

McGraw-Hill books are available at special quantity discounts to use as premiums and sales promotions, or for use in corporate training programs. To contact a representative, please e-mail us at bulksales@mcgraw-hill.com.

Web Developer's Cookbook:
More Than 300 Ready-Made PHP, JavaScript, and CSS Recipes

1234567890   DOC DOC   1098765432

ISBN   978-0-07-179431-2
MHID   0-07-179431-X

Sponsoring Editor Roger Stewart	**Acquisitions Coordinator** Ryan Willard	**Production Supervisor** George Anderson
Editorial Supervisor Jody McKenzie	**Copy Editor** Mike McGee	**Composition** Cenveo Publisher Services
Project Manager Anupriya Tyagi, Cenveo Publisher Services	**Proofreader** Lisa McCoy	**Illustration** Cenveo Publisher Services
	Indexer Claire Splan	**Art Director, Cover** Jeff Weeks

For Julie

About the Author

Robin Nixon has worked with and written about computers since the early 1980s (his first computer was a Tandy TRS 80 Model 1 with a massive 4KB of RAM!). During this time, he has written in excess of 500 articles for many of the UK's top computer magazines. *Web Developer's Cookbook* is his eleventh book.

Robin lives on the southeast coast of England (where he writes full time), along with his five children and wife Julie (a trained nurse and university lecturer)—between them they also foster three disabled children.

Other Web Development Books by Robin Nixon

Learning PHP, MySQL, and JavaScript, O'Reilly 2009, ISBN 978-0596157135
HTML5 for iOS and Android, McGraw-Hill 2010, 978-0071756334
HTML & HTML5 Crash Course, Nixon 2011, 978-0956895615
CSS & CSS3 Crash Course, Nixon 2011, 978-0956895622

Contents

Part III   JavaScript Recipes

Acknowledgments

I would like to thank Wendy Rinaldi for giving me the opportunity to put this large collection of personal recipes I use in my everyday web development together into a form I can share with other developers. I also want to thank my commissioning editor Roger Stewart, as well as Jody, Anupriya, Ryan, Mike, Lisa, Claire, George, and Jeff, and everyone else who helped create this book, without whom it would not have been the same. McGraw-Hill is always an exceptionally professional and friendly company to work with.

Introduction

When the World Wide Web was first invented by Sir Tim Berners-Lee, simply having a means to create hypertext links to other documents (including ones on remote computers), and to combine text and images using basic formatting, was a revolutionary concept that we take for granted today.

But slowly, web developers started getting used to the initial 20 elements provided by HTML (Hypertext Markup Language) 1, and began adding more and more features in each new specification of the language. Luckily, though, the people driving this development realized early on that if these extensions to the language were not handled sensibly, they could end up as an unwieldy tangled web of tags. Thus, HTML was created using the Document Object Model (DOM), meaning that all elements of a web page would be uniquely addressable from both JavaScript and CSS.

More than that, it made it easy to insert PHP script commands into web pages, and even integrate them with a database such as MySQL to provide powerful back-end functionality, and form the backbone of the Ajax process of behind-the-scenes communications between a web server and web browser.

In these days of widely varying browser capabilities and screen dimensions, developing code for a growing range of platforms such as iPhones, iPads, Android devices, PCs, Macs, tablets, and so on is more complicated than ever. Thankfully, this book is here to help take some of that development off your shoulders and to save you from "reinventing the wheel" by rewriting commonly used processes yourself.

What this Book Provides

This book provides over 300 ready-to-use PHP, JavaScript, and CSS functions, as well as classes and groups of classes that you can simply drop into your web pages. They are fully documented and their functionalities clearly explained, often with tips on how you can further tailor them to your requirements. In addition, each one you use in your project will save you much development and debugging time, because all this has been done for you already.

There's also no lack of documentation either, because each variable, property, class, and pseudo-class, as well as every other element of each recipe, is explained as it is encountered, and is included in easy-to-follow tables. Afterward, each recipe is broken down section by section so you know exactly what it will do for you, how to use it, and how to tailor it to your own requirements.

Includes CSS3 and HTML5 Features

Since many CSS3 features are now adopted in all modern browsers, this book also provides plug-ins to take advantage of this latest version of CSS, including examples of native text and box shadowing, rounded borders, and even web fonts, so you can break away from the same old fonts the Web has put up with for so many years.

Also, all the plug-ins come with HTML examples and screen shots showing you exactly how to use them in real-world situations. What's more, where possible the recipes also offer support for the emerging HTML5 standard to make your web pages even more interactive and dynamic, helping you create more cutting-edge web sites.

About the Recipes

All the recipes in this book are revised and updated from ones published separately in my books *Plug-in PHP, Plug-in JavaScript,* and *Plug-in CSS.* They have been brought fully up to date to ensure that where they are supposed to integrate with other web sites, they continue to do so correctly. They have also been improved as a result of additional testing since the previous books were published, incorporating feedback and suggestions from readers.

In the process, the recipes have been optimized down to just three main files that are each easily includable with a single command, and all have been modified so they will work synergistically with each other. They represent an enormous wealth of ready-made code and features on which you can draw.

Although the first aim of this book is to provide a comprehensive resource of recipes to draw on, it has a secondary goal: to help you move up to the next level and create your own web development toolkit.

And while this book isn't a design manual or teaching guide, I do hope that by reading through the explanations, rather than just including the plug-ins in your projects, you'll pick up a number of tips and tricks that many developers take years to discover.

You are free to use any of the recipes in this book in your own projects, and may modify them as necessary, without attributing this book—although if you do attribute them, it will always be appreciated.

A companion web site (*webdeveloperscookbook.com*) accompanies this book, where all 300+ recipes are available for download, along with example PHP, JavaScript, and HTML (and several accompanying) files for you to experiment with.

PART I
Introduction

CHAPTER 1

Getting Started

There are over 300 handcrafted recipes spread across three sections in this book. They are divided into three collections, each in their own file (*WDC.php, WDC.js,* and *WDC.css*). Using the recipes is a matter of including the relevant files in your programs or web pages and simply calling the functions or applying the classes you need.

But before unleashing your new code on the world at large, it makes sense to first thoroughly test it on a local web development server so you can iron out all the bugs.

This chapter points you in the right direction to get started with downloading the web browsers you need so you can test your code on all the different browsers currently in use, select a program editor so you have a lot more power than simply using a plain notepad, install a local PHP server if you need one, and deal with older versions of the Internet Explorer web browser, which vary substantially in how they process web pages.

Downloading and Installing Web Browsers

If you are going to test all your programs and web development projects thoroughly, you will need to see how they run on all the different browsers currently in use. Table 1-1 lists the five major web browsers and their Internet download locations. While all of them can be installed on a Windows PC, some are not available for OS X or Linux. The web pages at these URLs are smart and offer up the correct version to download according to your operating system, if available.

Before proceeding with this book, I recommend that you ensure you have installed as many of these browsers on your computer as you can.

If you're running any version of Windows from XP onwards, you will be able to install all of them, but on other operating systems it's not quite so easy. For example, on Mac OS X, because the development of IE for the Mac was halted many years ago when it reached version 5, you can install all the browsers except for Microsoft Internet Explorer.

Plus, although it's possible to install the Wine windows application interface on a Mac and run Internet Explorer using it, I have found it to be a laborious process with inconsistent results, and therefore wouldn't recommend that method. Neither would I suggest you rely on those web sites that take screen shots of a web page in different browsers, because they can't tell you whether the mouse, keyboard, and other features are working well, or even at all.

TABLE 1-1   Web
Browsers and Their
Download URLs

Web Browser	Download URL
Apple Safari	apple.com/safari
Google Chrome	google.com/chrome
Microsoft Internet Explorer	microsoft.com/ie
Mozilla Firefox	mozilla.com/firefox
Opera	opera.com/download

Instead, your best option is to either perform a dual install of Windows alongside Mac OS X, or ensure you have access to a Windows PC. After all, unless you intend to only develop for Mac computers, people using a Windows operating system will represent most of your users.

As for Linux, not only does it not have access to Internet Explorer, there is no version of Safari either, although all the other browsers do come in Linux flavors. Also, as with OS X, while various solutions exist that incorporate Wine for running Internet Explorer, they only seem to work with some distributions and not others, so it can be a bit of a minefield trying to find a bulletproof way for you to run Windows browsers on Linux.

So what it all comes down to is that, if you will be developing on a non-Windows computer, I recommend you arrange to have access to a Windows PC, or have Windows installed as a dual boot (or a virtual machine) alongside your main operating system, so you can fully test your programs before publishing them to the Web at large.

Don't forget that nowadays you also need to check your projects on iOS and/or Android phones, and even on tablets if you are targeting that market. For this, you will need access to at least an iPhone 3GS and an iPad 1, as well as a decent Android phone and tablet. And with Microsoft now pushing the Metro front-end to both Windows Phone 7 and Windows 8, it seems likely that you will also want to arrange access to a Windows Phone 7 phone, and also a tablet that runs Windows 8. Yes, unfortunately web development is getting more expensive for small developers. Still, you can probably write off the purchase cost against tax.

Choosing a Program Editor

Long gone are the days of relying on a simple notepad program for coding. Software for writing program code has progressed by leaps and bounds in recent years, with text editors having been replaced by powerful program editors that highlight your syntax using different colors, and which can quickly locate things for you like matching (and missing) brackets and braces, and so on.

Table 1-2 lists a number of free program editors that will all do a great job of helping you write code quickly and efficiently. Which one you choose is largely a matter of personal preference—in my case, I have settled on Notepad++ (see Figure 1-1).

When using a program editor, you will usually find that by moving the cursor to different parts of a program you can highlight sections of the code. For example, placing the cursor next to any bracket in Notepad++ automatically highlights the matching one.

Program	URL	Windows	Mac	Linux
Bluefish	*bluefish.openoffice.nl*		✓	✓
Cream	*cream.sourceforge.net*	✓		✓
Editra	*editra.org*	✓	✓	✓
Free HTML Editor	*coffeecup.com/free-editor*	✓		
jEdit	*jedit.org*	✓	✓	✓
Notepad++	*notepad-plus.sourceforge.net*	✓		

TABLE 1-2   A Selection of Free Program Editors

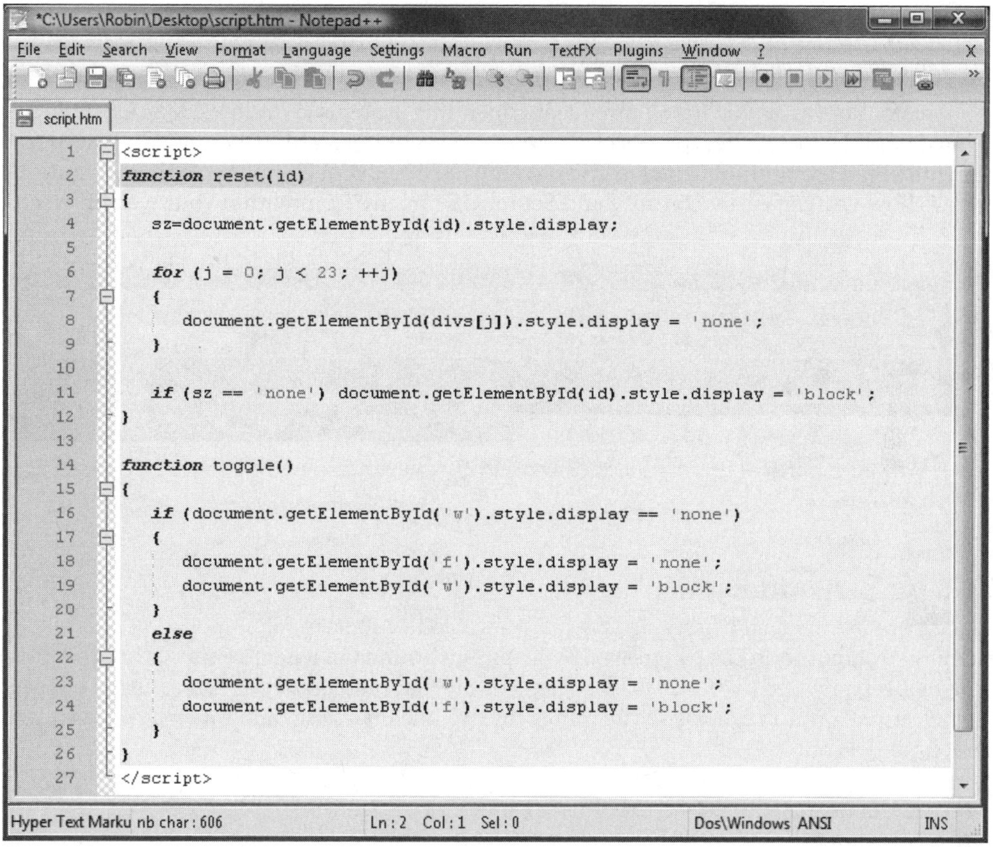

FIGURE 1-1   The Notepad++ program editor

They also commonly support multiple tabs, folding away sections of code that aren't being worked on, multiple views of the same document, doing search and replace across multiple documents, and so on. These are all features you would miss once you have grown used to using them.

Installing a PHP Server

If you wish to test the PHP recipes on a local development computer before uploading them to a web server elsewhere, you'll need to install a web server and PHP processor. This means you can instantly try out any code changes you make without having to upload them to the Internet first, thus speeding up the development process.

Installing a PHP web server is relatively simple because the developers of PHP have released an all-in-one application called Zend Server Community Edition (or CE for short) that includes all of PHP, an Apache web server, and a MySQL database, and which you can download from the following URL:

zend.com/products/server-ce

Versions are available for all three main operating systems (Windows, Mac OS X, and Linux), and the installation process is reasonably straightforward, although you'll need to carefully read the prompts you are given and make intelligent responses to them. Figure 1-2 shows how you can easily control Zend Server CE directly from within your web browser.

FIGURE 1-2   The Zend Server CE dashboard

	Operating System	Document Root
TABLE 1-3 The Zend Server CE Document Root on Various Platforms	Windows	*C:/Program Files/Zend/Apache2/htdocs*
	Mac OS X	*/usr/local/zend/apache2/htdocs*
	Debian/Ubuntu Linux	*/var/www*
	Fedora Linux	*/var/www/html*
	Generic Linux	*/usr/local/zend/apache2/htdocs*

The place where you will store all your PHP files and from where they will run is known as the server's document root, and you will need to know where this is. Table 1-3 details the default locations of the document root that Zend Server CE creates on different operating systems. If you keep your various HTML, JavaScript, and PHP files in that folder (and subfolders), they can all be served up by the Apache web server.

Unfortunately, there's no room to go into further details about Zend Server CE in this book, but there is a very good online user guide, which you can access at the following URL:

files.zend.com/help/Zend-Server-Community-Edition/welcome.htm

Older Versions of Microsoft Internet Explorer

The latest version of Internet Explorer (IE9 at the time of writing) has made tremendous strides toward compatibility with the other major browsers, but there are still large numbers of users running IE8, IE7, and even IE6. According to *statcounter.com*, as of late 2011 the breakdown of browsers by use was as shown in Figure 1-3.

Because each version of Internet Explorer works differently, and because IE6 through IE8 have over 40 percent of all users between them (IE9 has under 3 percent), you need to test your web pages in these older versions, too, not just in the latest versions of the main browsers. I know, it's a pain, but it has to be done. Luckily, though, there's a trick to make this easier than it might otherwise be.

Emulating Earlier Internet Explorer Versions

To aid developers who have designed websites to work specifically with older versions, the developers of Internet Explorer created a meta tab that you can add to the head of a web page to make IE think it is an earlier version of itself. Here is the meta tag to use, in which you must replace the v with a 5, or either 7 or 8:

```
<meta http-equiv="X-UA-Compatible" content="IE=v" />
```

Here's how you would incorporate the tag to emulate Internet Explorer 7:

```
<html>
   <head>
      <meta http-equiv="X-UA-Compatible" content="IE=7" />
      <title>My Website</title>
   </head>
   <body>
      ... Website Contents ...
```

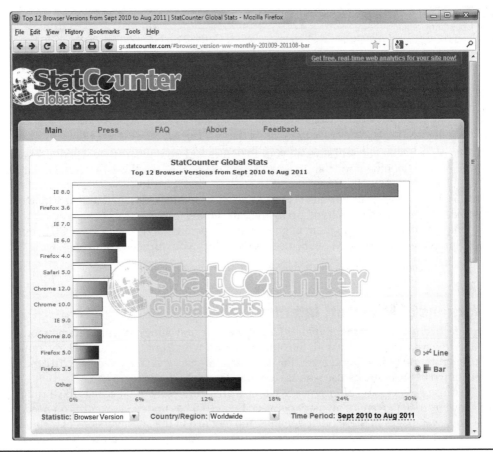

FIGURE 1-3   Browser market share as of August 2011

There is no IE=6 option (presumably because the rendering engines for IE5 and IE6 are so similar), so using the IE=5 option makes Internet Explorer enter what is known as "quirks" mode, in which it behaves like both IE5 and IE6.

Incidentally, if you wish to force Internet Explorer into full standards mode (to be as compatible as possible with other browsers), you can use the option IE=8. Or, without the meta tag, Internet Explorer will use its own proprietary and optimal settings, known as "edge" mode—which you can also select with the option IE=edge.

Of course, once you have finished testing you should remove or comment out these meta tags.

Fortunately, with Internet Explorer 9, Microsoft has mostly caught up on its compatibility issues, and the browser is about as good as any out there. But its takeup right now is still quite low. Hopefully this will change fairly soon, especially when Windows 8 is released, which will come with IE10—an improved version that's fully compatible with IE9.

Generally, you will not need to test older versions of other browsers because they have mostly been compatible with each other for some years now.

PART I

> ***TIP*** *If you are interested in the subject of browser compatibility and its various nuances, I recommend visiting the Quirks Mode web site at* quirksmode.org.

The Companion Web Site

To save you the effort of typing them all in, you can download the plug-ins from this book's companion web site at *webdeveloperscookbook.com*.

Click the Download link to download the file *examples.zip*, which is an archive file (easily extractable on all operating systems) containing all the recipes and associated example files. Once extracted, you'll find all the recipe files in the main folder of the archive, saved as *WDC.php*, *WDC.js*, and *WDC.css*. Additionally, there are three subfolders called *PHP*, *JS*, and *CSS* that each contain *example.php*, *example.js*, or *example.htm* files illustrating the use of every recipe, along with various images and other accompanying files.

> ***CAUTION*** *By default, Windows computers may not show the file extensions unless you have enabled this facility, in which case the files will simply show as* index *(instead of* index.html*) or* WDC *(instead of* WDC.css*) and so on—you will therefore need to identify them by their icons:* WDC.PHP *will probably display as a blank page if no PHP web server is installed,* WDC.js *will appear as a scroll icon, and* WDC.css *will show a cog wheel over a ruled page.*

CHAPTER 2

Using the Recipes

Including the recipes from this book is as easy as downloading the three main files (*WDC.php, WDV.js,* and *WDC.css*) and extracting them from the *examples.zip* file you can get by clicking the *Downloads* link at *webdeveloperscookbook.com*. You can then use a single, simple instruction in either a PHP program or web page to include a complete set of recipes as if you had written them into the program or page yourself.

This means that, apart from the single line, you can forget that they are there and concentrate on writing your own code or developing your own web pages. Whenever you need to implement a common routine that might distract you from the main creativity of your development process, chances are there is a recipe you can call on that will save you from being distracted and having to reinvent the wheel.

So this short chapter is divided into three sections, showing how to incorporate the different sets of recipes, and ending with a quick refresher on the Document Object Model (DOM) and how it relates to both JavaScript and CSS.

Inserting the PHP Recipes

To insert the PHP functions into a PHP program, use the `require _ once()` function. This is a built-in PHP function that prevents a PHP program from continuing execution unless the specified file is first loaded in. It also performs checks to ensure that the file is not inadvertently loaded more than once by ignoring multiple calls.

Loading in the recipes is as simple as using the function right at the start of a PHP program, like this:

```php
<?php

require_once('WDC.php');

// Your program goes here

?>
```

You can safely include this call in all your PHP program files because even if one of your program files includes another call and both attempt to load in the *WDC.php* recipes, only the first call will succeed—subsequent calls will be ignored.

If you keep the *WDC.php* file anywhere other than the local directory (such as in the folder */includes*), you must provide a path to the call, like this:

```
require _ once('/includes/WDC.php');
```

You may also load the file in from another server, like this:

```
require _ once('http://anotherserver.com/WDC.php');
```

Inserting the JavaScript Recipes

Inserting the JavaScript recipes is just as straightforward as PHP—you simply provide an src attribute and a value to a pair of <script> tags to load in the *WDC.js* file, like this:

```
<script src='WDC.js'></script>
```

You should generally include this line of HTML within a document's <head> section, like this (shown in bold):

```
<html>
   <head>
      <title>Page Title</title>
      <script src='WDC.js'></script>
   </head>
   <body>
      Body contents
   </body>
</html>
```

You may also load the file in from another sever elsewhere on the Web, as follows:

```
<script src='http://anotherserver.com/WDC.js'></script>
```

The *WDC.js* file contains all the recipes from Part II of this book, as well as the JavaScript functions that power the dynamic CSS classes from Part III.

There is also another version of the *WDC.js* file called *WDCsmall.js*. It's identical in use but is much smaller and therefore will load in more quickly and save bandwidth on busy sites. Because of its compression, however, the file cannot be modified.

To load it instead of *WDC.js,* use code such as either of the following lines, depending on whether the file is in the current folder or elsewhere:

```
<script src='WDCsmall.js'></script>
<script src='http://anotherserver.com/WDCsmall.js'></script>
```

Inserting the CSS Recipes

To add all the CSS recipes to a web page, you should use the <link rel=... /> tag to link to the *WDC.css* file from within the <head> of your document, like this (shown in bold):

```html
<html>
  <head>
    <title>Page Title</title>
    <link rel='stylesheet' type='text/css' href='WDC.css' />
    <script src='WDC.js'></script>
  </head>
  <body>
    Body contents
  </body>
</html>
```

If you will be using any of the dynamic CSS recipes from Part III of this book (CSS Recipes 59–100), or if you will be using the JavaScript recipes, you must also ensure that you have loaded in the *WDC.js* file, too (shown in the previous example).

You may also include the style sheet from another server elsewhere on the Web, like this:

```html
<link rel='stylesheet' type='text/css'
    href='http://anotherserver.com/WDC.css' />
```

A Quick Refresher on the DOM

Before moving on to the recipes, I think it's important to quickly offer a recap of the DOM (Document Object Model), since so many of these recipes interact with it.

When HTML was invented, one of the fundamental design decisions was to base it around a DOM as a means of separating out all the different elements within a web page into discrete objects, each with their own properties and values. It was a very smart decision because it led to the introduction of style sheets, enabling a web page's content to be completely separated from its styling, and it also made HTML documents easily modifiable by languages such as JavaScript, providing dynamic user interaction.

When a web page is placed into a DOM, it is a simple matter for you to access individual elements with JavaScript or style them with CSS. For example, each heading will be within pairs of tags such as `<h1>` ... `</h1>` and a single CSS instruction can set the styling of all such occurrences within a document, changing the font used, its size, any font decoration, and so on. This lets you completely change the design of a page without altering the HTML and, as you'll see in some of the later plug-ins, some style settings can even apply dynamic effects to page elements such as changing their color and other properties when the mouse passes over them, or even create transition effects by using proprietary browser extensions.

How the DOM Works

The Document Object Model separates the different parts of an HTML document into a hierarchy of objects, each one having its own properties. The term *property* is used to refer to an attribute of an object such as the HTML it contains, its width and height, and so on.

The outermost object possible is the *window* object, which is the current browser window, tab, iframe, or popped-up window. Underneath this is the *document* object, of which there can be more than one (such as several documents loaded into different iframes within a page). And inside a document there are other objects such as the head and body of a page.

Within the head, there can be other objects such as the title and meta objects, while the body object can contain numerous other objects, including HTML tags containing headings, anchors, forms, and so forth.

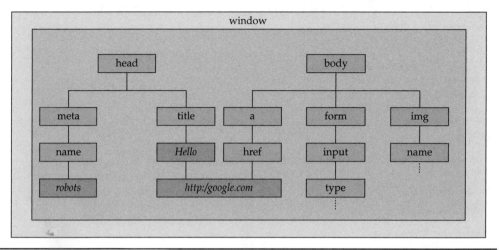

FIGURE 2-1 Example of a DOM showing head and body sections

Figure 2-1 shows a representation of the DOM of an example document, with the title "Hello" and a meta tag in the head section, and three HTML elements (a link, a form, and an image) in the body section. Of course, even the simplest of web pages has more structure than is shown here, but it serves to illustrate how the DOM works—starting from the very outside is the window, inside which there's a single document, and within the document are the various elements or objects, which connect to each other.

In the figure, properties are shown with a darker background and in italics. For example, the value "robots" is a property of name, which is a property of meta, and so on. Although it isn't shown in the figure, the meta tag should have another matching property called content, which would contain a string specifying which robots (such as search engine crawlers) may access the web page.

Other properties are "http://google.com," which is a property of the href tag (itself a property of a, and so on), and "Hello," which is a property of title. All the other items are objects or object argument names. If the figure were to extend further down and sideways, other objects and properties attached to the ones shown would come into view. A couple of the places where these would appear are shown by unconnected dotted lines.

Representing this as HTML code, the structure of the head section looks like this:

```
<head>
    <meta name="robots" content="index, follow" />
    <title>Hello</title>
</head>
```

And the body section of HTML might look like this:

```
<body>
    <img src="/images/welcome.jpg" />
    <a href="http://google.com">Visit Google</a>
    or enter your username and password to continue...
    <form id="login" method="post" action="login.php">
        <input type="text" name="name" />
```

```
      <input type="password" name="password" />
      <input type="submit" />
   </form>
</body>
```

Remembering that these two sections of HTML are part of the same document, we would bring them both together inside an `<html>` tag, like this:

```
<html>
   <head>
      <meta name="robots" content="index, follow" />
      <title>Hello</title>
   </head>
   <body>
      <img src="/images/welcome.jpg" />
      <a href="http://google.com">Visit Google</a>,
      or enter your username and password to continue...
      <form id="login" method="post" action="login.php">
         <input type="text" name="name" />
         <input type="password" name="password" />
         <input type="submit" />
      </form>
   </body>
</html>
```

Of course, a web page can look quite different from this, but it will usually follow the same form, although that's not always the case because most browsers are very forgiving and allow you to omit many things, such as the closing tags at the end and the opening ones too if you choose. I don't recommend you do this, though, because one day you might want to convert your page to XHTML, which is a lot stricter. So it's always a good idea to close every tag and make sure you do so in the right order. For example, you shouldn't close a document by issuing `</html>` followed by `</body>` because the proper nesting of tags would be broken by this reversal.

For the same reason, you should also get into the habit of self-closing any tags that do not have a closing version, such as `<img src="..." />`, which does not have a matching `</img>` tag, and therefore requires a / character right before the final > in order to properly close it. In the same way, `<br>` becomes `<br />`, and so on.

You should also remember that arguments within tags must have either single or double quotation marks to be XHTML-compatible, even though nearly all browsers allow you to omit them.

NOTE *In the early days of the Web, when most users had very slow dial-up modems, it was common to see all manner of things such as quotation marks and various tags omitted from web pages. But nowadays, most of your users will have fairly decent bandwidth speeds, and there's no longer any reason to do this.*

Accessing the DOM from JavaScript

JavaScript handles all of this DOM nesting quite easily with the use of the period character. For example, some standard properties, such as the document title, can be read like this:

```
title = document.title
```

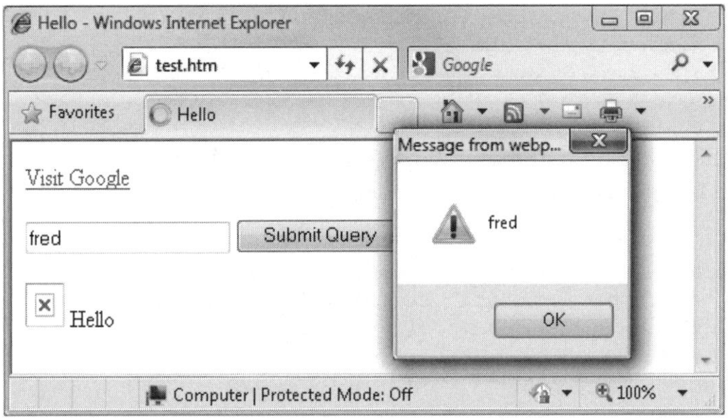

FIGURE 2-2 A popup window showing the input value

But in order to access most other object properties, you need to assign an ID to the object. For example, once the value "name" is assigned to the input field, you can find its current value (if any), in the following manner, which assigns the value to the variable `username`:

```
username = document.forms.login.name.value
```

To retrieve a value, for example, the following code will pop up an alert box displaying the current value of the same element (as shown in Figure 2-2):

```
<script>
   alert(document.forms.login.name.value)
</script>
```

About Cascading Style Sheets

Using CSS, you can apply styles to your web pages to make them look exactly how you want. This works because CSS is connected to the DOM so that you can quickly and easily restyle any element. For example, if you don't like the default look of the <h1>, <h2>, and other heading tags, you can assign new styles to override the default settings for the font family and size used, or whether bold or italics should be set, and many more properties, too.

One way you can add styling to a web page is by inserting the required statements into the head of a web page between the <head> and </head> tags. So, to change the style of the <h1> tag, you might use the following code:

```
<style>
   h1 { color:red; font-size:3em; font-family:Arial; }
</style>
```

Within an HTML page, this might look like the following (see Figure 2-3):

```
<html>
   <head>
      <style>
```

```
        h1 { color:red; font-size:3em; font-family:Arial; }
    </style>
</head>
<title>Hello World</title>
<body>
    <h1>Hello there</h1>
</body>
</html>
```

Importing a Style Sheet from Within HTML

You can include a style sheet with the HTML `<link>` tag like this:

```
<link rel="stylesheet" type="text/css" href="/css/styles.css" />
```

Remember that `<link>` is an HTML-only tag and is not a valid style directive, so it cannot be used from within one style sheet to pull in another, and also cannot be placed within a pair of `<style>` ... `</style>` tags.

You can also use as many `<link>` statements as you like in your HTML.

Importing a Style Sheet from Another Style Sheet

You can also import a style sheet from within another style sheet using the CSS `@import` directive like this:

```
<style>
    @import url("/css/styles.css");
</style>
```

This statement tells the browser to fetch a style sheet with the name *styles.css* from the */css* folder. The `@import` command is quite flexible in that you can create style sheets that themselves pull in other style sheets, and so on. Just make sure that there are no `<style>` or `</style>` tags in any of your external style sheets or they will not work.

FIGURE 2-3
Styling the <h1>
tag, with the
original style
shown in the small
window

Local Style Settings

There's also nothing stopping you from individually setting or overriding certain styles for the current page on a case-by-case basis by inserting style statements directly within HTML, like this (which results in italic blue text within the tags):

```
<div style="font-style:italic; color:blue;">Hello</div>
```

But this should be reserved only for the most exceptional circumstances, because it breaks the separation of content and layout.

About IDs and Classes

A better solution for setting the style of an element is to assign an *ID* to it in the HTML, like this:

```
<div id='iblue'>Hello</div>
```

What this does is state that the contents of the div with the ID "iblue" should have the style defined in the "iblue" style setting applied to it. The matching CSS statement for this might look like the following:

```
#iblue { font-style:italic; color:blue; }
```

Note the use of the # symbol, which specifies that only the ID with the name "iblue" should be styled with this statement.

If you would like to apply the same style to many elements, you do not have to give each one a different ID because you can specify a *class* to manage them all, like this:

```
<div class="iblue">Hello</div>
```

What this does is state that the contents of this element (and any others that use the class) should have the style defined in the "iblue" class applied to it. Once a class is applied, you can use the following style setting, either in the page header or within an external style sheet for setting the styles for the class:

```
.iblue { font-style:italic; color:blue; }
```

Instead of using a # symbol, which is reserved for IDs, class statements are prefaced with a . (period) symbol.

Summary

How to insert the recipes and the best ways to use them either on a web server or in a web client accessing the DOM is also explained in each of the following parts of the book, and is illustrated with numerous working examples.

PART II
PHP Recipes

CHAPTER 3

Text Processing

Although many web sites have video and other multimedia capabilities, the most fundamental part of almost all web sites remains the information contained within their text. This first batch of recipes concentrates on providing a range of functions to facilitate manipulating and presenting text in the most suitable way.

Whether you wish to control word wrapping, use of upper- and lowercase, spelling and grammar, text length, unwanted words and characters, or other textual features, there's a recipe here that will do the job. Some of these recipes are so useful they are themselves used by other recipes in this book.

RECIPE 1

WrapText( )

You can make text wrap in a browser in various ways, including using tables, iframes, and textareas, but sometimes you need absolute control over the wrapping in terms of the number of characters at which the wrap should occur, regardless of whether the user resizes their browser window.

Using this recipe, it's easy to pass a string of text and have it wrapped using `<br />` tags. What's more, it can also indent the start of each new paragraph by an amount of your choosing. Figure 3-1 shows the opening paragraphs of Charles Dickens' *Oliver Twist*, with a wrap width of 71 characters and a paragraph indent setting of 5 characters.

About the Recipe

This recipe takes a string variable containing any text and then adds `<br />` and ` ` tags in the right places to make the text wrap and indent paragraphs. It takes these arguments:

- **$text**   A string variable containing the text to be wrapped.
- **$width**   An integer representing the character at which to force word wrapping.
- **$indent**   An integer representing the number of characters by which to indent each paragraph start.

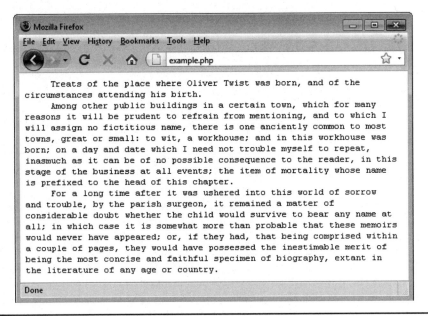

FIGURE 3-1   Setting text to wrap at a fixed width is a breeze with this recipe.

Variables, Arrays, and Functions

$wrapped	String variable containing the wrapped text to be returned
$paragraphs	Array containing the separate paragraphs as determined by \n characters
$paragraph	String containing an individual paragraph being processed
$words	Array of all words in a paragraph
$word	String containing the current word being processed
$len	Numeric variable containing the length of the current line
$wlen	Numeric variable containing the length of the next word to be processed

How It Works

The code works by first splitting the text it is passed into separate paragraphs using the PHP explode() function with an argument of \n, which is the newline character. What this function does is return an array of substrings based on splitting the original string each time a \n is encountered. The function returns these paragraphs in the array $paragraphs, like this:

```
$paragraphs = explode("\n", $text);
```

A `foreach` loop is then entered passing $paragraphs as the input, and then each iteration of the loop places one paragraph at a time into the string variable $paragraph, like this:

```
foreach($paragraphs as $paragraph)
```

PART II

NOTE *Notice the singular form of the variable name $paragraph, with no s on the end. This is a convention I use throughout this book—the plural form of a name being for an array, and the singular form of the same name used for an element extracted from that array.*

Next, a check is made to see whether paragraphs must be indented. If so, $indent will have a value greater than zero and so the `str_repeat()` function is used to add $indent number of nonblank spaces to the string $wrapped, which contains the wrapped text to be returned, like this:

```
if ($indent > 0) $wrapped .= str_repeat(" ", $indent);
```

Now it's time to extract all the words in the current paragraph by using the `explode()` function again, but this time splitting the text up at each space. The resulting list of words is placed in the array $words. Then, before proceeding into processing the words, the variable $len, which monitors the length of the current line, is set to whatever value $indent has, so that the length of the first line is correctly initialized, like this:

```
$words = explode(" ", $paragraph);
$len   = $indent;
```

Another `foreach` loop is now used to iterate through the words, assigning each element in the array $words in turn to the string variable $word. Then, the first action taken in the loop is to make a note of the length of the word in the variable $wlen, as follows:

```
foreach($words as $word)
{
    $wlen = strlen($word);
```

Next, an `if … else` pair of tests check whether, if added together, the current line length, $len, plus the current word length, $wlen, would be less than the required width, $width. If so, then the word is appended to $wrapped, followed by a space, and then $len is updated accordingly, like this:

```
if (($len + $wlen) < $width)
{
    $wrapped .= "$word ";
    $len     += $wlen + 1;
}
```

If adding the word to the current line would have made it too long, then the `else` part of the test is executed. Here, any space character previously added to $wrapped is now unnecessary and is removed by a quick call to `rtrim()`, which removes whitespace from a string's tail. Then, a `<br />` tag followed by a newline character (to help make viewing the page source clearer) and a space are appended to $wrapped, followed by $word (which is now on a new line). The <br /> is used because a \n does not add a line break to HTML output. The value of $len is then updated to reflect this, as follows:

```
else
{
    $wrapped    = rtrim($wrapped);
    $wrapped   .= "<br />\n$word ";
    $len        = $wlen;
}
```

Once the inner loop has completed executing, rtrim() is again called to remove any extra space that was added (but isn't now needed), and a <br /> tag and newline are appended to $wrapped to signify reaching the end of a paragraph, like this:

```
$wrapped = rtrim($wrapped);
$wrapped .= "<br />\n";
```

Once the outer loop has also completed, the text has been fully processed and so the value in $wrapped is returned to the calling code like this:

```
return $wrapped;
```

How to Use It

To transform unwrapped text into wrapped, call the function like this:

```
echo WrapText($news_item, 80, 5);
```

Here $news_item is the text to be wrapped, 80 is the character at which to force the wrapping, and 5 is the number of characters by which to indent the start of each paragraph. If you don't want indenting, just set the third parameter to zero.

The Recipe

```
function WrapText($text, $width, $indent)
{
    $wrapped    = "";
    $paragraphs = explode("\n", $text);

    foreach($paragraphs as $paragraph)
    {
        if ($indent > 0) $wrapped .= str_repeat(" ", $indent);

        $words = explode(" ", $paragraph);
        $len   = $indent;

        foreach($words as $word)
        {
            $wlen = strlen($word);

            if (($len + $wlen) < $width)
```

```
        {
            $wrapped .= "$word ";
            $len     += $wlen + 1;
        }
        else
        {
            $wrapped  = rtrim($wrapped);
            $wrapped .= "<br />\n$word ";
            $len      = $wlen;
        }
    }

    $wrapped = rtrim($wrapped);
    $wrapped .= "<br />\n";
    }

    return $wrapped;
}
```

RECIPE 2 CapsControl()

When dealing with user input, you will often come across people who keep their CAPSLOCK key permanently enabled, which can make reading what they write difficult on the eye. It also looks like they are shouting. To diminish or entirely remove this problem, use this recipe, which also supports three other upper- and lowercase text transformations. Figure 3-2 shows these four transformations applied to a poem by Lewis Carroll.

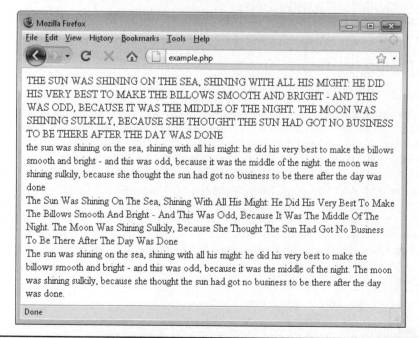

FIGURE 3-2   Converting all caps or other nonstandard text to a more readable form using this recipe

About the Recipe

This code takes a string variable containing any text and then transforms its case according to the second parameter. It takes these arguments:

- **$text**   A string variable containing the text to be transformed.
- **$type**   A string containing the type of transformation to make:

  u - capitalize all letters

  l - set all letters to lowercase

  w - capitalize the first letter of every word

  s - capitalize the first letter of every sentence

Variables, Arrays, and Functions

$newtext	String variable containing transformed text
$words	Array of all words in the text
$word	String containing the current word being processed
$sentences	Array of all sentences in the text
$sentence	String containing the current sentence being processed

How It Works

This recipe is based around a four-way `switch` statement, the first two of which are extremely simple in that if the style of transform requested (passed in the $type variable) is either u or l, then the text to transform is simply passed through either the `strtoupper()` or `strtolower()` functions and then returned, as follows:

```
switch($type)
{
    case "u": return strtoupper($text);
    case "l": return strtolower($text);
```

If the transformation type is w, then the string variable $newtext is initialized to the empty string; it will be used to build the transformed string to be returned. Then all the words in the text are extracted into the array $words using the function `explode()`, which is set to split $text into smaller strings at each space character and return the result in an array.

Next, a foreach loop iterates through all the elements in $words, placing them one at a time in the string variable $word, from where they are first converted to lowercase using `strtolower()`, and then the first letter of the word is converted to uppercase using the `ucfirst()` function. After this, a space is added back to the end of each word. Once $newtext has been constructed, any extra space that was appended is removed using the `rtrim()` function and the string is returned. Here is the code for this case:

```
case "w":
    $newtext = "";
    $words   = explode(" ", $text);
    foreach($words as $word)
      $newtext .= ucfirst(strtolower($word)) . " ";
    return rtrim($newtext);
```

If the transformation type is s, then $newtext is initialized to the empty string and all the sentences are extracted into the array $sentences using the explode() function. From here, they are processed one at a time using a foreach loop into the string variable $sentence, which is then converted to lowercase using strtolower(), any preceding whitespace is removed using ltrim(), and then the first character of the sentence is set to uppercase using the ucfirst() function. After building $newtext, any trailing space is removed and the string is returned, as follows:

```
case "s":
   $newtext    = "";
   $sentences = explode(".", $text);
   foreach($sentences as $sentence)
      $newtext .= ucfirst(ltrim(strtolower($sentence))) . ". ";
   return rtrim($newtext);
```

In the case of an unknown type being passed to this function, the final line will return the original string unchanged:

```
return $text;
```

How to Use It

You use the recipe by calling it up in one of the four following ways:

```
echo CapsControl($text, "u");
echo CapsControl($text, "l");
echo CapsControl($text, "w");
echo CapsControl($text, "s");
```

The $text argument should contain the string to transform, while the second argument should be one of the four letters shown (in lowercase).

The Recipe

```
function CapsControl($text, $type)
{
   switch($type)
   {
      case "u": return strtoupper($text);
      case "l": return strtolower($text);

      case "w":
         $newtext = "";
         $words    = explode(" ", $text);
         foreach($words as $word)
            $newtext .= ucfirst(strtolower($word)) . " ";
         return rtrim($newtext);

      case "s":
         $newtext    = "";
         $sentences = explode(".", $text);
         foreach($sentences as $sentence)
```

```
        $newtext .= ucfirst(ltrim(strtolower($sentence))) . ". ";
    return rtrim($newtext);
}

  return $text;
}
```

RECIPE 3 — FriendlyText()

Sometimes when you have text to post on a web site, it can be quite dry and unexciting. Although there's not much you can do about that (apart from completely rewriting it), at least you can make it read better by converting it into as friendly a form as possible by making it flow better by using contractions. For example, replacing *you have* with *you've* or *it is* with *it's* is easier to read and more like the way we speak in everyday life, and this code takes that concept to the extreme.

Figure 3-3 shows an excerpt from one of Winston Churchill's speeches, which now flows a lot better, although I admit, the original has a certain punchiness and power that's lost in the conversion. Still, it shows you can leave this recipe running on your server and it will almost always produce proper, readable English.

This is also a good example of why these recipes are so useful, because you probably could write this code quite easily yourself, but actually sitting down and working out all

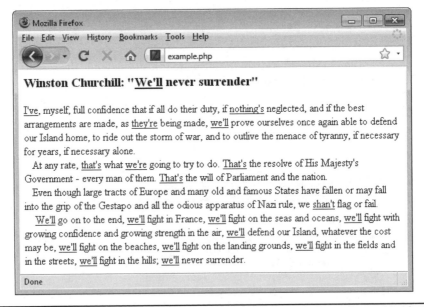

FIGURE 3-3   This recipe is used to convert a famous speech with the underline option enabled for testing.

the various parts of the rules of the English language (and all its exceptions) is quite time-consuming. Thankfully, though, I've done all that work for you.

About the Recipe

This recipe takes a string variable containing English text, processes it into a "friendly" form of speech, and returns the modified text. It takes these arguments:

- **$text** A string variable containing the text to be modified.
- **$emphasis** A Boolean value that, if TRUE, underlines all modifications.

Variables, Arrays, and Functions

$misc	Array containing pairs of strings to find and substitute
$nots	Array of words that can preface the word *not*
$haves	Array of words that can preface the word *have*
$who	Array of pronouns and question words
$what	Array of common verbs that can be contracted
$contractions	Array of the contracted forms of $what
$j, $k	Integer loop counters
$from, $to	Strings to convert from and to
$u1, $u2	Strings containing start and end underline tags if $emphasis is true
$f, $t, $s, $e	Various arguments passed to the function FT_FN1()
$uf, $ut	String variable copies of $f and $t, with their initial letters capitalized
$1, $2	String variables containing the matches found by preg_replace()
FT_FN1()	Function to perform the string replacements

How It Works

This recipe takes as an argument a string of text, which it then modifies and returns. The original text is not changed by the process. It performs five passes through the text to change different types of English.

The first pass iterates through the $misc array, stepping two elements at a time. It then searches for the first element and, if found, replaces it with the second. The $misc array contains a set of unusual contractions that don't follow the normal English rules, which is one reason why the program gets them out of the way first, like this:

```
for ($j = 0 ; $j < sizeof($misc) ; $j += 2)
{
    $from = $misc[$j];
    $to   = $misc[$j+1];
    $text = FT_FN1($from, $to, $text, $emphasis);
}
```

The second pass works through the $nots array and checks whether any of the words in it are followed by the word *not*. If so, it contracts them so that, for example, *did not* becomes *didn't*, as follows:

```
for ($j = 0 ; $j < sizeof($nots) ; ++$j)
{
    $from = $nots[$j] . " not";
    $to   = $nots[$j] . "n't";
    $text = FT_FN1($from, $to, $text, $emphasis);
}
```

In the third pass, the $haves array is processed in an identical manner to the $nots array, except that pairs of words such as *should have* become *should've*, like this:

```
for ($j = 0 ; $j < sizeof($haves) ; ++$j)
{
    $from = $haves[$j] . " have";
    $to   = $haves[$j] . "'ve";
    $text = FT_FN1($from, $to, $text, $emphasis);
}
```

Pass four uses a pair of nested loops to iterate through the $who array of pronouns and similar words and then iterate through the $what array of words that follow them and can be contracted. If matches are made, then the contraction to use is looked up in $contractions and applied. So, for example, *he has* will become *he's*, like this:

```
for ($j = 0 ; $j < sizeof($who) ; ++$j)
{
    for ($k = 0 ; $k < sizeof($what) ; ++$k)
    {
        $from = "$who[$j] $what[$k]";
        $to   = "$who[$j]'$contraction[$k]";
        $text = FT_FN1($from, $to, $text, $emphasis);
    }
}
```

The final pass, at the end of the main function, looks for all instances of the word *is* with another word and a space in front of it, and when it finds any, it contracts the two together so that, for example, *Paul is* would become *Paul's*, like this:

```
return preg_replace("/([\w]*) is([^\w]+)/", "$u1$1$to$u2$2", $text);
```

The second function in this code, FT_FN1(), is only used by the recipe. It takes the four arguments $f, $t, $s, and $e, which (in order) contain a string to change from, what to change it to if found, the string to search within, and whether to emphasize any changes by making them underlined. It does all this by using regular expressions within the PHP preg_replace() function. It repeats each match and replace twice; the second time to catch strings beginning with capital letters.

NOTE *The function* FT_FN1() *uses an obscure name since it has no real use anywhere other than as a partner function to* FriendlyText(). *Where partner functions can be useful in their own right, they are given a more memorable name, such as the ones for* SpellCheck(), SpellCheckLoadDictionary(), *and* SpellCheckWord(), *a little further on in this chapter, in PHP Recipe 8.*

How to Use It

To transform any text (including text with HTML) using this code, call the main function in the following way:

```
$oldtext = "Let us go for a picnic. I hope it will not rain.";
$newtext = FriendlyText($oldtext, TRUE);
```

The first parameter holds the string to be modified. This will not be changed. Instead, a new string containing the transformed text will be returned by the function. The second parameter can be either FALSE or TRUE, which will cause all changes to be underlined. This can be useful for debugging purposes.

In this example, the value of $newtext becomes "Let's go for a picnic. I hope it won't rain."

The Recipe

```
function FriendlyText($text, $emphasis)
{
    $misc = array("let us", "let's", "i\.e\.", "for example",
        "e\.g\.", "for example", "cannot", "can't", "can not",
        "can't", "shall not", "shan't", "will not", "won't");
    $nots = array("are", "could", "did", "do", "does", "is",
        "had", "has", "have", "might", "must", "should", "was",
        "were", "would");
    $haves = array("could", "might", "must", "should", "would");
    $who = array("he", "here", "how", "I", "it", "she", "that",
        "there", "they", "we", "who", "what", "when", "where",
        "why", "you");
    $what = array("am", "are", "had", "has", "have", "shall",
        "will", "would");
    $contractions = array("m", "re", "d", "s", "ve", "ll", "ll",
        "d");

    for ($j = 0 ; $j < sizeof($misc) ; $j += 2)
    {
        $from = $misc[$j];
        $to   = $misc[$j+1];
        $text = FT_FN1($from, $to, $text, $emphasis);
    }

    for ($j = 0 ; $j < sizeof($nots) ; ++$j)
    {
        $from = $nots[$j] . " not";
        $to   = $nots[$j] . "n't";
        $text = FT_FN1($from, $to, $text, $emphasis);
    }
```

```php
for ($j = 0 ; $j < sizeof($haves) ; ++$j)

{
    $from = $haves[$j] . " have";
    $to   = $haves[$j] . "'ve";
    $text = FT_FN1($from, $to, $text, $emphasis);
}

for ($j = 0 ; $j < sizeof($who) ; ++$j)
{
    for ($k = 0 ; $k < sizeof($what) ; ++$k)
    {
        $from = "$who[$j] $what[$k]";
        $to   = "$who[$j]'$contractions[$k]";
        $text = FT_FN1($from, $to, $text, $emphasis);
    }
}

$to = "'s";
$u1 = $u2 = "";

if ($emphasis)
{
    $u1 = "<u>";
    $u2 = "</u>";
}

    return preg_replace("/([\w]*) is([^\w]+)/", "$u1$1$to$u2$2", $text);
}

function FT_FN1($f, $t, $s, $e)
{
    $uf = ucfirst($f);
    $ut = ucfirst($t);

    if ($e)
    {
        $t  = "<u>$t</u>";
        $ut = "<u>$ut</u>";
    }


    $s   = preg_replace("/([^\w]+)$f([^\w]+)/", "$1$t$2",  $s);
    return preg_replace("/([^\w]+)$uf([^\w]+)/", "$1$ut$2", $s);
}
```

RECIPE 4 StripWhitespace()

A few of the recipes in this book are really short and sweet and, at just a single line of code, this is one of them. But although it's tiny, it packs a punch because it can clean up the messiest text by removing all the whitespace in a string, such as extra spaces, tabs, newlines, and so on.

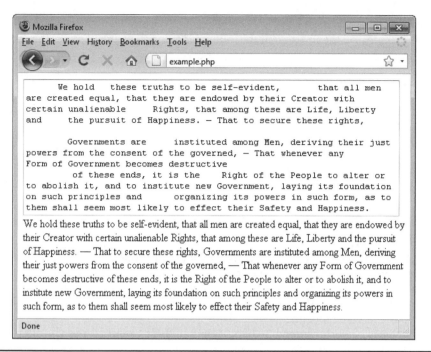

FIGURE 3-4   Unsightly whitespace can seriously mess up some text, but this recipe will remove it for you.

Figure 3-4 shows part of the U.S. Declaration of Independence as it might appear if read from a poor-quality reprint by some optical character recognition software, followed by it being run through this recipe.

Although browsers generally ignore whitespace, if the text is displayed using the `<pre>` tag or is placed in a form element such as a `<textarea>` (as used in Figure 3-4), then all the whitespace will be apparent.

About the Recipe

This recipe takes a string variable containing any text and removes all whitespace. It requires a single argument:

- **$text**   A string variable containing the text to be modified.

How It Works

This code makes use of the regular expression feature built into PHP. What it does is search for the text within the two forward slash characters (/) and then replaces any it finds with a single space. Between the slashes is the simple string \s+, which means find any section of whitespace that is one or more characters in length. The \s stands for a whitespace character, and the + indicates that the preceding character should appear one or more times in the search. The actual string passed to the `preg_replace()` function is modified and then returned to the calling code.

How to Use It

To use this recipe, call the function in the following manner, where $text is the string to be cleaned up:

```
echo StripWhitespace($text);
```

The Recipe

```
function StripWhitespace($text)
{
    return preg_replace('/\s+/', ' ', $text);
}
```

5 WordSelector()

Quite often, you will find you need to somehow highlight chosen words within a web page—for example, when a user arrives from a search engine, you may wish to highlight the search terms they used to help them find what they are looking for. Other times, you might *not* want certain words to appear, such as profanities or other terms you wish to prevent your users from posting.

This recipe is powerful enough to handle both of these cases because you simply decide on the relevant words and what should happen to them. Figure 3-5 shows a few words highlighted within a section of the U.S. Declaration of Independence.

About the Recipe

This recipe takes a string variable containing the text to process and an array containing words to be highlighted, as well as a parameter defining the type of highlighting. These are the arguments:

- **$text**   A string variable containing the text to be modified.
- **$matches**   An array containing words to highlight.

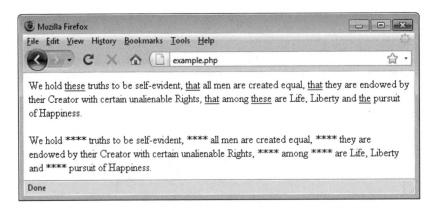

FIGURE 3-5   Using this recipe, you can highlight selected words or censor unwanted ones.

- **$replace** A string representing the action to perform on matching words. If it is any of u, b, or i, then the matching words will be highlighted using one of underline, italic, or bold face—otherwise, matching words are replaced with its value.

Variables, Arrays, and Functions

$match	String containing the current word being matched

How It Works

The code starts iterating through the $matches array of supplied words one at a time, using a switch statement to decide whether any matches found should be highlighted in underline, bold, or italic font (if $replace contains one of u, b, or i).

In the case of highlighting a word, the preg_replace() function is called, passing three elements to it:

1. ([^\w]+) Looks for any sequence of one or more non-word characters, followed by...
2. ($match) ... the current word being matched, followed by...
3. ([^\w]+) ... another sequence of one or more non-word characters

Using this pattern, it's possible to extract individual words by checking for one or more non-word characters on either side of the second parameter ($match).

The brackets enclosing each of these parts tell PHP to save the matches found for use in the replace part of the function, where they can be inserted using the values $1, $2, and $3, each representing the values in the order they appear in the brackets.

When a match is found, the replace string inserts the non-word characters before the match ($1), followed by <$replace>, which will be one of <u>, <b>, or <i>, followed by the word found ($2), followed by </$replace> to close the tag that was opened, finally followed by the non-word characters after the match ($3).

In the case of a string of text having been passed in $replace, rather than one of u, b, or i, the same initial match is made, except that $match doesn't have brackets around it because we won't be needing to save a copy of the match, as it will be replaced. Therefore, the replace section is simpler in that it just replaces the entire match with the value in $replace.

How to Use It

To use this function, you should provide the text to be checked, an array of words to match, and a string to either replace or highlight matched words. For example, to underline a given set of words, you could use the following line of code:

```
echo WordSelector($text, array("cat", "dog"), "u");
```

If the list of words is long, you probably would not want to create an array on the fly, and instead would pre-populate an array first, using code such as these two lines:

```
$words = array("rat", "fish", "cat", "dog", "rabbit");

echo WordSelector($text, $words, "u");
```

To blank out or censor a set of words, you specify a replace string that is none of "b",
"u", or "i". For example, the following line replaces all the words in the array $words that
are found in $text with four asterisks:

```
echo WordSelector($text, $words, "****");
```

The Recipe

```
function WordSelector($text, $matches, $replace)
{
    foreach($matches as $match)
    {
        switch($replace)
        {
            case "u":
            case "b":
            case "i":
                $text = preg_replace("/([^\w]+)($match)([^\w]+)/",
                    "$1<$replace>$2</$replace>$3", $text);
                break;

            default:
                $text = preg_replace("/([^\w]+)$match([^\w]+)/",
                    "$1$replace$2", $text);
                break;
        }
    }

    return $text;
}
```

CountTail()

Displaying a date in the format "23 November" or "March 12" isn't really that friendly and
you may wish to use the better flowing "23rd November" and "March 12th." In fact, there
are many places where you use numbers and they would look better displayed with one of
"st," "nd," "rd," or "th" following, such as in the sentence "You're our 124,362nd" visitor,
rather than "You are visitor 124,362," and so on. Figure 3-6 shows how to use this recipe to
add the correct suffix to all the numbers between 0 and 100.

About the Recipe

This recipe takes a number as input and then returns that number with a possible suffix of
"st," "nd," "rd," or "th." It takes a single argument:

- **$number**   The number on which to append a suffix.

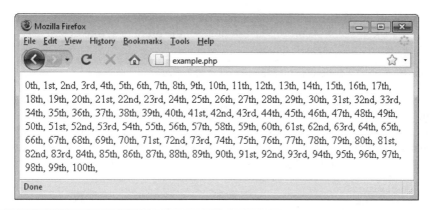

Figure 3-6 Using this recipe makes it easy to add "st," "nd," "rd," and "th" automatically to numbers.

Variables, Arrays, and Functions

`$nstring`	String variable created from `$number`
`$pointer`	Numeric variable that points into `$nstring`
`$digit`	Single character string extracted from `$nstring`
`$suffix`	String representing the suffix to append

How It Works

In order to operate on individual digits of the given number, it is first turned into a string using the *cast* keyword (`string`) and is then stored in `$nstring`. This is because, although PHP is a loosely typed language and does its best to automatically change the type of a variable according to how it is accessed, it cannot be relied upon to make the change correctly in this instance, where numbers would have to be treated as strings, which are then treated as arrays. Thus, the forced change of type using the cast statement.

Next, the numeric variable `$pointer` is defined with a value derived from the length of `$nstring - 1`. This means it will also point at (or index into) the final character in `$nstring`. Using `$pointer`, the variable `$digit` is then set to the value of the final digit in the number. The string variable `$suffix` is then set to the default value "th", the most common suffix. The first four of lines that do these things are as follows:

```
$nstring = (string) $number;
$pointer = strlen($nstring) - 1;
$digit   = $nstring[$pointer];
$suffix  = "th";
```

With all the variables initialized, a test is made to see whether `$pointer` has a value of 0. In other words, is `$number` a single-digit number less than 10? A second part of the test then takes the case of $pointer being greater than zero (therefore $number is 10 or higher), and if it is, it tests whether the second-to-last digit is *not* the number 1, like this:

```
if ($pointer == 0 ||
   ($pointer > 0 && $nstring[$pointer - 1] != 1))
```

The reason for this test is that any number ending in 1, 2, or 3 usually requires the suffix "st," "nd," or "rd," *unless* the previous digit is a 1, in which case the suffix must be "th," as in 11th, 12th, and 13th. If it isn't an exception case, the switch statement sets $suffix to one of the three lesser common suffixes if the last digit is a 1, 2, or 3. Otherwise, you will recall, $suffix was already set to "th" by default, using this code:

```
switch ($nstring[$pointer])
{
   case 1: $suffix = "st"; break;
   case 2: $suffix = "nd"; break;
   case 3: $suffix = "rd"; break;
}
```

Finally, the number is returned with the correct suffix appended.

How to Use It

To add a suffix to a number, just call the code passing the number, like this:

```
echo CountTail(123);
```

So, for example, to create the output shown in Figure 3-6, you could use the following:

```
for ($j = 0 ; $j < 101 ; ++$j) echo CountTail($j) . ", ";
```

The Recipe

```
function CountTail($number)
{
   $nstring = (string) $number;
   $pointer = strlen($nstring) - 1;
   $digit   = $nstring[$pointer];
   $suffix  = "th";

   if ($pointer == 0 ||
      ($pointer > 0 && $nstring[$pointer - 1] != 1))
   {
      switch ($nstring[$pointer])
      {
         case 1: $suffix = "st"; break;
         case 2: $suffix = "nd"; break;
         case 3: $suffix = "rd"; break;
      }
   }

   return $number . $suffix;
}
```

TextTruncate()

Have you noticed how the results provided by the Google search engine always neatly display snippets of information from each web site without truncating the text midword? Now you can cut long strings short in a similar manner using this recipe, as shown by the screen shot in Figure 3-7, which illustrates three snippets from the first paragraph of Charles Dickens' *A Tale of Two Cities.*

About the Recipe

This recipe takes a string variable containing text to truncate, the maximum number of characters to allow in the new string, and a symbol or string to follow the truncated text—to show what has been done. It takes these arguments:

- **$text**   A string variable containing the text to be modified.
- **$max**   A numeric variable representing the maximum number of characters allowed.
- **$symbol**   A string variable to follow the new text.

Variables, Arrays, and Functions

$temp	Temporary copy of the string variable $text after initial truncating
$last	Numeric variable pointing to the final space character in $temp

How It Works

The truncation process has several parts. The first is a hard truncation down to the maximum size allowed by $max. This is done using the substr() function. Next, the strrpos() function is used to find the final space in the newly truncated string. Once determined, the new string is again truncated at this new position.

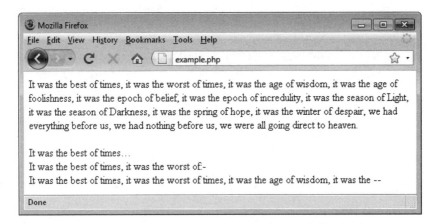

FIGURE 3-7   Using this recipe, it's easy to truncate text automatically at a word break.

In the case of the Google search engine, this would be most of the process, but I decided it's unsightly to leave punctuation or another non-word character as the final character in the new string, so `preg_replace()` is called up to remove any non-word character that may be there. Only then is the new string returned, with the value of `$symbol` attached to its end.

How to Use It

To use this recipe, pass it some text to truncate, the maximum number of allowed characters, and a symbol or string to attach to the end of the truncated string, like this:

```
echo TextTruncate($text, 90, " --");
```

You can choose any character or string for `$symbol` (or even the empty string), such as the useful HTML entity `&hellip;`, which displays an ellipsis made up of three periods—the standard notation to indicate that some text is missing.

The Recipe

```
function TextTruncate($text, $max, $symbol)
{
    $temp = substr($text, 0, $max);
    $last = strrpos($temp, " ");
    $temp = substr($temp, 0, $last);
    $temp = preg_replace("/([^\w])$/", "", $temp);
    return "$temp$symbol";
}
```

SpellCheck()

There's a spell-checking module available for PHP called *pspell*, but if it's not already installed on your server, it needs to be downloaded, installed, and configured before you can use it. But if you want to ensure your code will work on any server, this recipe provides a reasonably fast spell checker based on a dictionary of over 80,000 words, which is supplied on the companion web site (*http://webdeveloperscookbook.com*), along with the recipes.

Figure 3-8 again shows a paragraph from Dickens' *A Tale of Two Cities*, but this time some deliberate spelling errors have been introduced, which have been caught by the recipe.

About the Recipe

This recipe takes a string variable containing text to spell check, along with a variable to determine how the resulting text should be displayed. It requires these arguments:

- **$text** A string variable containing the text to be modified.
- **$action** A string variable that should contain a single-letter text formatting tag.

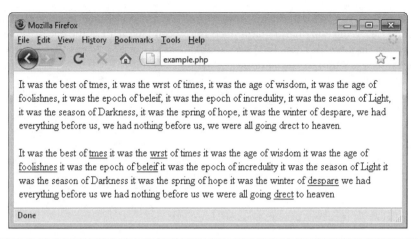

Figure 3-8   Checking user input for spell checking is easily accomplished with this recipe.

Variables, Arrays, and Functions

`$filename`	String variable containing the path and name of the dictionary file to load
`$dictionary`	Array containing all the dictionary words
`$newtext`	String variable containing the transformed text
`$matches`	Array containing the results from the `preg_match()` calls
`$offset`	Numeric variable pointer to the next word to check
`$word`	String variable containing the current word
`SpellCheckLoadDictionary()`	Function to load in the dictionary
`SpellCheckWord()`	Function to check a single word
`$top, $bot, $p`	Temporary variables used by `SpellCheckWord()` to perform a binary search of the dictionary

How It Works

With this recipe, you get two for the price of one, because the main function, `SpellCheck()`, relies on another function, `SpellCheckWord()`, to check individual words, and you can call it on its own, too.

The very first thing the main function does is load the dictionary file into the array `$dictionary`, like this:

```
$dictionary = SpellCheckLoadDictionary("dictionary.txt");
```

This file is on the web site and will be downloaded along with the recipe. It comprises over 80,000 words separated by \r\n (carriage return and linefeed) pairs. If you have your own collection of words, you can also use it, as long as you make sure there's a \r\n pair between each. This is also why you are provided with the function `SpellCheckLoadDictionary()`, so you can specify the path and filename to such a file.

With the dictionary loaded into an array, $text has a space character appended to it. This is so the following code has a guaranteed non-word character at the end so a match can be made on the final word. Then, the two variables $newtext and $offset are initialized. Respectively, they contain the transformed text and a pointer to the next word to be checked in the string $text, as follows:

```
$text       .= ' ';
$newtext    = "";
$offset     = 0;
```

The heart of the system comprises a while loop, which continues iterating through each word in $text until it reaches the end of the string. It knows this by checking $offset and seeing whether it is still less than the length of $text, and looks like this:

```
while ($offset < strlen($text))
{
    preg_match('/[^\w]*([\w]+)[^\w]+/',
        $text, $matches, PREG_OFFSET_CAPTURE, $offset);
    $word   = $matches[1][0];
    $offset = $matches[0][1] + strlen($matches[0][0]);

    if (!SpellCheckWord($word, $dictionary))
        $newtext .= "<$action>$word</$action> ";
    else $newtext .= "$word ";
}
```

Within the loop, each word is extracted in turn using the preg_match() function with a three-part regular expression:

1. [^\w]*   This looks for zero or more non-word characters, followed by...
2. ([\w]+)   ... one or more word characters (a–z, A–Z, or 0–9), followed by...
3. [^\w]+   ... one or more non-word characters.

In part 2 earlier, the regular expression segment is surrounded by brackets, which means that particular value will be saved in the array element $matches[1][0], and its length in $matches[1][1]. The whole matched string, comprising all three parts, is saved in the array element $matches[0][1], and the length of this value is saved in $matches[0][1].

Provided with these values, the string variable $word is assigned just the part 2 match, which is the word to be spell checked, then $offset, the pointer to the next word to be checked, is incremented by the length of the full matched string, so as to jump over any non-word characters. The code is then ready to process the following word the next time around the loop.

In the meantime, the newly extracted word is passed to the function SpellCheckWord(), along with the dictionary array to use, in $dictionary. The return value from this function is either TRUE, if the word is found, or FALSE if it isn't. Depending on the value returned, the word is added to $newtext, either with or without highlighting tags. Once execution exits from the loop, the text has been fully checked and so $newtext is returned, after passing it through the `rtrim()` function to remove the final space that was added at the function start, like this:

```
return rtrim($newtext);
```

The function `SpellCheckLoadDictionary()` is next. It simply loads in the specified text file, explodes it into an array by splitting it at all the \r\n pairs, and then returns the new array, like this:

```
return explode("\r\n", file_get_contents($filename));
```

Finally, there's the function `SpellCheckWord()`. This takes the arguments $word and $dictionary and then returns either TRUE or FALSE, depending on whether or not the word is in the dictionary.

This is done by means of a binary search in which the $dictionary array is continually bisected until a word is found, or is found to be missing. In a dictionary of 80,000 words or so, it will take no more than about 17 iterations maximum to drill down to where a word is (or should be), which is an order of magnitude faster than checking every word in the dictionary. By the way, this search relies on having a fully sorted list of words, so if you use your own word list, make sure you sort it alphabetically first.

The way the code performs the binary search is to say, "Is the word I am looking for in the top or the bottom half of this section of words?" Then, the loop goes around again splitting whichever half it determines the word to be in, asking the same question. This continues until the word is either found or determined not to be in the dictionary.

The variables that control this divide-and-conquer method are $bot and $top, which represent the start and end positions to search between within the $dictionary array. Initially, they are set to the first and last elements, like this:

```
$top = sizeof($dictionary) -1;
$bot = 0;
```

Then, $bot is moved up or $top is moved down by taking the midway point between the two values and assigning that to a pivotal numeric variable called $p, right in the middle. If the word is greater than the one at position $p, then $bot is moved up past that word. If the word is lower than the one at position $p, then $top is dropped below that position, using this code:

```
while($top >= $bot)
{
    $p =    floor(($top + $bot) / 2);
    if      ($dictionary[$p] < $word) $bot = $p + 1;
    elseif  ($dictionary[$p] > $word) $top = $p - 1;
    else    return TRUE;
}
```

If at any point the word at position $p in the $dictionary array is the same as $word, then a match has been found and the value TRUE is returned. Otherwise, the process continues and eventually $top and $bot will pass each other and $bot will have a value

PART II

higher than $top, because all the words in the dictionary have been checked, at which point the loop exits and the value FALSE is returned because no match was made.

How to Use It

To use the main function and have any misspelled words highlighted with underlines, you call it like this:

```
echo SpellCheck($text, "u");
```

This will check the words in $text against all the dictionary words and highlight any that are not recognized. You can replace the u with i or b for italic or bold if you prefer.

If you wish to spell check a single word, perhaps to support interactive spell checking, you must make sure you have loaded the dictionary in before calling the SpellCheckWord() function. Ideally, place the call to the function to do this somewhere at the start of your PHP file so you know for sure it has been loaded when you make a call. To load a dictionary file, use a command such as this:

```
$dictionary = SpellCheckLoadDictionary("dictionary.txt");
```

Make sure you provide the correct file and pathname. If you are using the supplied code from the web site, then *dictionary.txt* will be in the same directory. Then, to spell check an individual word, call the function like this:

```
$result = SpellCheckWord($word, $dictionary);
```

It will return TRUE if the word is recognized or FALSE if it isn't.

The Recipe

```
function SpellCheck($text, $action)
{
    $dictionary = SpellCheckLoadDictionary("dictionary.txt");
    $text       .= ' ';
    $newtext    = "";
    $offset     = 0;

    while ($offset < strlen($text))


    {
        $result = preg_match('/[^\w]*([\w]+)[^\w]+/',
            $text, $matches, PREG_OFFSET_CAPTURE, $offset);
        $word   = $matches[1][0];
        $offset = $matches[0][1] + strlen($matches[0][0]);

        if (!SpellCheckWord($word, $dictionary))
            $newtext .= "<$action>$word</$action> ";
        else $newtext .= "$word ";
    }

    return rtrim($newtext);
}
```

```
function SpellCheckLoadDictionary($filename)
{
   return explode("\r\n", file_get_contents($filename));
}

function SpellCheckWord($word, $dictionary)
{
   $top = sizeof($dictionary) -1;
   $bot  = 0;
   $word = strtolower($word);

   while($top >= $bot)
   {
      $p =    floor(($top + $bot) / 2);
      if      ($dictionary[$p] < $word) $bot = $p + 1;
      elseif  ($dictionary[$p] > $word) $top = $p - 1;
      else    return TRUE;
   }

   return FALSE;
}
```

RemoveAccents( )

When you have data that's accented with diacritics (such as é), you sometimes need to convert this data to plain ASCII but still be able to read it. The solution is to replace all the diacritic characters with standard ones using this recipe. Figure 3-9 shows some French text before and after running the recipe.

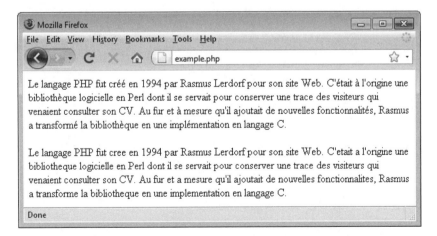

FIGURE 3-9   Part of the French Wikipedia entry for PHP before and after running it through this recipe.

About the Recipe

This recipe takes a string variable containing accented text and returns a nonaccented version. It requires this argument:

- **$text** A string variable containing the text to be modified.

Variables, Arrays, and Functions

$from	Array containing a list of accented characters
$to	Array containing nonaccented versions of $from

How It Works

This recipe uses the str_replace() function to replace the characters in the string $text that match those in the array $from with their nonaccented counterparts in the array $to.

In PHP, you can use str_replace() either to substitute single items or, as here, with arrays. There are 55 characters in each array. If, for example, character 23 is matched in the array $from, then character 23 from array $to is substituted. The substituted text is then returned.

How to Use It

To transform accented text to nonaccented text, call up the code as follows:

```
echo RemoveAccents($text);
```

The Recipe

```
function RemoveAccents($text)
{
    $from = array("ç", "æ", "œ", "á", "é", "í", "ó", "ú", "à", "è",
                  "ì", "ò", "ù", "ä", "ë", "ï", "ö", "ü", "ÿ", "â",
                  "ê", "î", "ô", "û", "å", "e", "i", "ø", "u", "Ç",
                  "Æ", "Œ", "Á", "É", "Í", "Ó", "Ú", "À", "È", "Ì",
                  "Ò", "Ù", "Ä", "Ë", "Ï", "Ö", "Ü", "Ÿ", "Â", "Ê",
                  "Î", "Ô", "Û", "Å", "Ø");

    $to  =  array("c", "ae", "oe", "a", "e", "i", "o", "u", "a", "e",
                  "i", "o", "u", "a", "e", "i", "o", "u", "y", "a",
                  "e", "i", "o", "u", "a", "e", "i", "o", "u", "C",
                  "AE", "OE", "A", "E", "I", "O", "U", "A", "E", "I",
                  "O", "U", "A", "E", "I", "O", "U", "Y", "A", "E",
                  "I", "O", "U", "A", "O");

    return str_replace($from, $to, $text);
}
```

ShortenText( )

Sometimes, when you want to display the URL on a web page, it can be so long it looks untidy and messes up your layout. Of course, you can come up with suitable text for a hyperlink instead of showing the URL, but what about when a user posts a web address to your web site?

This recipe has a simple solution because it shortens any long URLS (or other strings) by removing the middle and only keeping the two ends. Figure 3-10 shows a long URL text string, followed by a version shortened by this recipe.

You should note that when used on URLs, the shortened text is *only* for the displayed part of an HTML link and not the actual link itself, which must remain unchanged. The code's main use is for reducing the space that the text of a link takes up on a web page.

About the Recipe

This recipe takes a string variable containing a long URL (or other string) and returns a shortened version. It takes these arguments:

- **$text**   A string variable containing the text to be modified.
- **$size**   A numeric variable containing the new string size.
- **$mark**   A string variable containing a character sequence to mark the part that was removed.

Variables, Arrays, and Functions

$len	Numeric variable containing the length of the original string
$a	String variable containing the left-hand part of the new string
$b	String variable containing the right-hand part of the new string

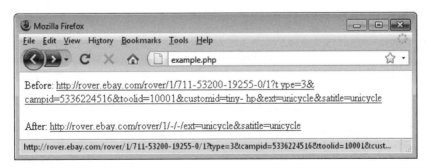

FIGURE 3-10   Shortening URLs or other strings is easily done with this recipe.

How It Works

This recipe first notes the length of the original string and, if the new required length is not smaller, simply returns the original string since there's no shortening to do, like this:

```
$len = strlen($text);
if ($size >= $len) return $text;
```

Otherwise, the left portion of the new string is created by copying half the number of characters that are to be in the new string from the left of the original string using the substr() function. The result is then stored in $a. The right-hand portion is similarly derived by taking half the number of characters required for the new string from the right of the original string, as follows:

```
$a = substr($text, 0, $size / 2 -1);
$b = substr($text, $len - $size / 2 + 1, $size/ 2 -1);
```

This is not quite true. Actually, the left and right halves are each one character less than half the required size of the new string to allow for inserting the $mark string to signify the part of the string that has been removed.

The three parts—$a, $mark, and $b—are then assembled and returned:

```
return $a . $mark . $b;
```

How to Use It

To shorten a URL (or other string), call the code like this, where $text is the string to shorten, 60 is the new maximum size, and /-/-/ is the marker to signify the portion of the string that was removed:

```
echo ShortenText($text, 60, "/-/-/");
```

The new shorter string will be displayed. You can replace the marker shown with any string of your choosing.

The Recipe

```
function ShortenText($text, $size, $mark)
{
    $len = strlen($text);
    if ($size >= $len) return $text;

    $a = substr($text, 0, $size / 2 -1);
    $b = substr($text, $len - $size / 2 + 1, $size/ 2 -1);
    return $a . $mark . $b;
}
```

CHAPTER 4

Image Handling

HTML and CSS have developed to such an extent that the depth and variety of features available to a web developer have never been greater. But when it comes to images and manipulating them, there's not a lot you can do other than resize them in-browser (not a true resize, more of a squash or a stretch) and add borders. True, using JavaScript you can overlay one image on another and blend them by making one image semitransparent, but that's about the extent of it.

That's where PHP comes to the rescue, thanks to the GD library of image functions, which most implementations of PHP now include by default. For example, the recommended Zend Server CE from Chapter 1 already has GD enabled.

For further details on the GD library, including installation and usage, please visit *http://php.net/manual/en/book.image.php*. Otherwise, let's get started on the next batch of 10 recipes.

RECIPE 11 UploadFile( )

A major service offered by many web sites is the facility for users to upload files and images. For example, you may wish to let your users create avatars or upload photos they have taken. Or perhaps you need to support the uploading of Word, Excel, or other types of files. Using this recipe, you can enable this feature while retaining the security of your web site. Figure 4-1 shows the result of uploading an image file called *test.jpg* using it.

FIGURE 4-1   This recipe is easy to use and provides lots of information and error checking.

About the Recipe

This recipe takes the name of a form field used to upload a file to a web server and returns the uploaded file in a string. Upon success, it returns a two-element array, the first value of which is zero and the second is the uploaded file. On failure, a single-element array is returned with one of these values:

- −1 = upload failed
- −2 = wrong file type
- −3 = file too large
- 1 = file exceeds `upload_max_filesize` as defined in *php.ini*
- 2 = file exceeds the `MAX_FILE_SIZE` directive in the HTML form
- 3 = file was only partially uploaded
- 4 = no file was uploaded
- 6 = PHP is missing a temporary folder
- 7 = failed to write file to disk
- 8 = file upload stopped by extension

There is no returned value of either 0 or 5, and the code takes these arguments:

- **$name**   String containing the form field name given to the uploaded file.
- **$filetypes**   Array containing the supported file (mime) types.
- **$maxlen**   Integer representing the maximum allowable file size.

Variables, Arrays, and Functions

`$_FILES`	System array containing the uploaded file information
`$temp`	String containing a temporary copy of the uploaded file

How It Works

Once a file has been received by the web server, it's stored in a temporary location and a system array called `$_FILES` is populated with various details about the file, as follows:

- **`$_FILES['file']['name']`**   The original name of the file on the client machine.
- **`$_FILES['file']['type']`**   The mime type of the file (such as "image/jpeg").
- **`$_FILES['file']['size']`**   The size, in bytes, of the uploaded file.
- **`$_FILES['file']['tmp_name']`**   The temporary filename of the file in which the uploaded file was stored on the server.
- **`$_FILES['file']['error']`**   Any error code associated with this file upload.

In this code, the form field name used to upload the file is passed to the function in $name, which is used in place of 'file' as shown earlier. To check whether a file was successfully uploaded, the first thing the recipe does is see whether `$_FILES[$name]['name']` has a value. If so, a file has been uploaded. Otherwise, an error value of −1 is returned.

Next, the `$filetypes` array of allowable file (or mime) types is compared with the type in `$_FILES[$name]['type']`, using the `in_array()` function. If it isn't one of the allowed types, then the recipe returns a value of −2.

Then, the maximum allowed file length in `$maxlen` is compared with `$_FILES[$name]['size']` and, if the file is too large, an error value of −3 is returned. After this, `$_FILES[$name]['error']` is tested and if it has a value greater than 0, there was an error and that error value is returned.

In all these cases, the function actually returns an array of three elements, only the first of which contains the error value. The second two elements are set to NULL since they will only return data upon successful file upload.

After passing all the tests, the uploaded file is loaded into the variable `$temp` from its temporary location, pointed to by `$_FILES[$name]['tmp_name']`, and a value of 0 is returned in the first element of the array (meaning the function was successful). Then, the file type and the file itself are returned in the other two elements.

How to Use It

To use this recipe, you need to offer an HTML upload form similar to this:

```
<form method="post"  action="upload.php"
    enctype="multipart/form-data">
<input  type="file"    name="test" />
<input  type="submit" value="Upload" /></form>
```

Here, the form has been set to post its input to the PHP program *upload.php* using the encoding type of `multipart/form-data`. The program uploaded to can be any of your choosing, even the current PHP program, but the encoding type must be as shown; otherwise, the upload will fail.

The second line tells the browser that a file needs to be uploaded and that its name, as sent to the server, should be `test`. In fact, the web browser will normally also send the name of the file as it is stored on the local computer too, but, as explained a little later, it's a security risk to rely on that information since a malicious person could create a web form of their own, with altered details planned to send spoof filenames to your web server in the hope of saving a file on it with which they can compromise it. This recipe therefore totally ignores the original filename and uses only the form field name as an identifier.

The final line creates a submit button with the label "Upload" and closes the form. When they click the Browse button created by the form, users can then navigate their local file system to locate and upload a file to the server.

When you call up the code, all you need to do is pass it the field name used in the form, an array of acceptable file (or mime) types, and the maximum allowable file length. Everything else is taken care of for you. When the function returns to the calling code, it will either pass an error code, or it will return the uploaded file, from where you can save it (if you wish) to the server's hard disk.

The following code creates an array of two mime types in `$allowed`—for the regular and progressive kinds of JPEG images. Then, the recipe is called and the returned array is stored in `$result`. If the first element of `$result`, `$result[0]`, is non-zero, there was an error and a message will be displayed; otherwise, the returned file, stored in $result [2], is saved to the disk as *test.jpg*. If you need to know it, the type of the uploaded file is also available in $result [1].

```
$allowed = array("image/jpeg", "image/pjpeg");
$result  = UploadFile("test", $allowed, 100000);
if ($result != 0) echo "There was an error"
else               file_put_contents($result[2], "test.jpg");
```

If the recipe had accepted the supplied filename instead (in $_FILES['file']['name']), then users could upload a name such us *c:\windows\system32\calc.exe*, which, if you simply saved it as is, could overwrite your calculator program. The same goes for Linux systems where, for example, a filename of */bin/sh* could overwrite your Bourne shell. A secure system will try and step in to prevent this happening, but not always. And what if the uploaded filename was a PHP file? Your system could then easily be compromised and taken control of.

Following is a full example of the type of code you might write to make use of this recipe:

```
echo <<<_END
<form method="post"  action="$_SERVER[PHP_SELF]"
    enctype="multipart/form-data">
<input  type="hidden"  name="flag" value="1" />
<input  type="file"    name="test" />
<input  type="submit" value="Upload" /></form>
_END;

if (isset($_POST['flag']))
{
   $result = UploadFile("test",
       array("image/jpeg", "image/pjpeg"), 100000);

   if ($result[0] == 0)
   {
       file_put_contents("test.jpg", $result[2]);
       echo "File received with the type '$result[1]' and saved ";
       echo "as <a href='test.jpg'>test.jpg</a><br />";
   }
   else
   {
       if ($result[0] == -2) echo "Wrong file type<br />";
       if ($result[0] == -3) echo "Maximum length exceeded<br />";
       if ($result[0] > 0)   echo "Error code: $result<br />";
       echo "File upload failed<br />";
   }
}
```

The first section is a multiline echo that displays an HTML web form for uploading images. After that, the POST variable $_POST['flag'] is checked. This is a hidden form field that will have the value 1 only if the form is submitted. If this happens, something was uploaded and the rest of the code is executed.

First, $result is assigned the file returned from the call to UploadFile(). Then, if $result [0] has a value of 0, the upload succeeded and the contents of the file are saved as *test.jpg*. A message is then displayed, along with a link to the file.

If $result[0] is non-zero, then there was an error and its value is the error number, as detailed in the *About the Recipe* section.

The Recipe

```
function UploadFile($name, $filetypes, $maxlen)
{
    if (!isset($_FILES[$name]['name']))
        return array(-1, NULL, NULL);

    if (!in_array($_FILES[$name]['type'], $filetypes))
        return array(-2, NULL, NULL);

    if ($_FILES[$name]['size'] > $maxlen)
        return array(-3, NULL, NULL);

    if ($_FILES[$name]['error'] > 0)
        return array($_FILES[$name]['error'], NULL, NULL);

    $temp = file_get_contents($_FILES[$name]['tmp_name']);
    return array(0, $_FILES[$name]['type'], $temp);
}
```

12 ImageResize()

Although you can easily resize an image using HTML by specifying the width and height at which to display it, the way the image will appear depends entirely on the browser being used, and whether the original is resampled rather than simply pixel resized. Also, if you wish an image to be reduced in size, changing its dimensions from within HTML won't reduce the amount of data transferred from the server to the browser.

Instead, try using this recipe to resize images first. With it, you can choose whether to resize an image on the fly before sending it to a browser, or you can save the resized image to the hard disk. Figure 4-2 shows a 313 × 317–pixel image that has been resized to 500 × 100 pixels.

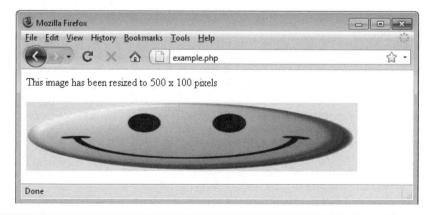

FIGURE 4-2   Using this function, you can reduce, enlarge, and change the ratio of image dimensions.

Although it is now squashed, the resampling used has ensured that the new image remains smooth, without the jagged edges a pixel resize would create.

About the Recipe

This recipe accepts an image to be resized and the new dimensions required. It takes these arguments:

- **$image**   An image to be transformed, as a GD library object.
- **$w**   The new required width.
- **$h**   The new height.

Variables, Arrays, and Functions

$oldw	Integer representing the image's current width
$oldh	Integer representing the image's current height
$temp	Temporary copy of the new GD image

How It Works

This recipe first looks up the image's current width and height and places these values in the variables $oldw and $oldh. It then creates a new GD image object of the new width and height, as supplied in $w and $h, like this:

```
$oldw = imagesx($image);
$oldh = imagesy($image);
$temp = imagecreatetruecolor($w, $h);
```

The imagecopyresampled() function is then called, passing these values to it. It takes the old image, resamples it to the new width and height, and the new image is then placed in the $temp GD image object, which is returned by the function, as follows:

```
imagecopyresampled($temp, $image, 0, 0, 0, 0, $w, $h, $oldw, $oldh);
return $temp;
```

How to Use It

The way you use this recipe is to have an image already created or loaded into a GD image object, which you then pass to the function, along with two arguments stating the new width and height needed. Once the new image has been created, it's returned by the function.

So, for example, the following code loads in the image $image from the file *test.jpg*, resizes it into the new image object $newim using ImageResize(), and saves it as the new image *squashed.jpg* using the imagejpeg() function:

```
$image = imagecreatefromjpeg("test.jpg");
$newim = ImageResize($image, 500, 100);
imagejpeg($newim, "squashed.jpg");
```

If you prefer, you can have your PHP program act as if it were the new image itself by outputting it directly to the browser, like this:

```
$image = imagecreatefromjpeg("test.jpg");
header("Content-type: image/jpeg");
imagejpeg(ImageResize($image, 500, 100));
```

Here, after loading the image into `$image`, a special header is sent to the browser, `"Content-type: image/jpeg"`, which tells it that the next data to arrive will be a JPEG image. Then, the `imagejpeg()` function is called using the value returned from the recipe, but without a filename argument, so the resulting JPEG is sent straight to the browser, rather than saved to disk.

The Recipe

```
function ImageResize($image, $w, $h)
{
    $oldw = imagesx($image);
    $oldh = imagesy($image);
    $temp = imagecreatetruecolor($w, $h);
    imagecopyresampled($temp, $image, 0, 0, 0, 0,
        $w, $h, $oldw, $oldh);
    return $temp;
}
```

RECIPE 13 MakeThumbnail()

Many thumbnail programs exist that will take a large image and reduce it to a thumbnail for you, often supporting working in batches. But what about turning user-uploaded images into thumbnails? Obviously, you don't want to simply send a large image to the browser and have HTML resize it, because the quality wouldn't be great, and your bandwidth would go through the roof. So you need something to handle this process on the fly, which is where this recipe comes in handy.

With it, you specify a source image and the maximum dimensions allowed for the new thumbnail. The function will then resize the image, retaining the aspect ratio, so that whichever is larger—the height or width dimension—is then set to the new maximum size, and the other is reduced in proportion. Figure 4-3 shows the smiley face image from the previous recipe, here used as a thumbnail source for two smaller thumbnail images.

About the Recipe

This recipe accepts an image to be converted into a thumbnail and the new maximum width or height. It takes these arguments:

- **$image** A GD image to be transformed.
- **$max** The new maximum width or height (whichever is the greater dimension).

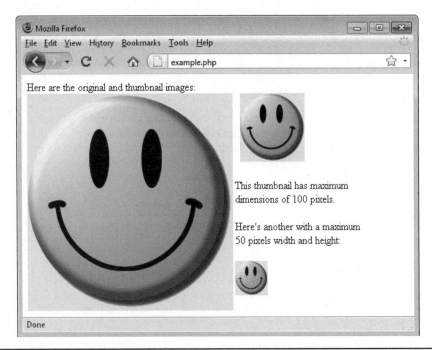

FIGURE 4-3   This recipe has been used to make two different thumbnails of a smiley face.

Variables, Arrays, and Functions

$w	Integer representing the image's current width
$h	Integer representing the image's current height
$thumbw	Integer representing the thumbnail's new width
$thumbh	Integer representing the thumbnail's new height

How It Works

To create the new thumbnail image, this recipe accepts a GD image object and then sets $w and $thumbw to its width, and $h and $thumbh to its height, like this:

```
$thumbw = $w = imagesx($image);
$thumbh = $h = imagesy($image);
```

Next, it looks at these values to find out which dimension is the larger. If $w is greater than $h, then the image is wider than it is high, so the new width will take the value in $max. $thumbh, the smaller thumbnail height, is then set to the maximum dimension value of $max divided by the original image's width, in $w, and multiplied by its height, in $h, as follows:

```
if ($w > $h && $max < $w)
{
    $thumbh = $max / $w * $h;
    $thumbw = $max;
}
```

So, for example, if the original image's width is 1200 pixels, the height is 1000 and the new maximum dimension size is 100 pixels, the following formula is applied:

```
Thumbnail Height = 100 / 1200 × 1000
```

This becomes:

```
Thumbnail Height = 0.0833 × 1000
```

which results in:

```
Thumbnail Height = 83.33
```

Therefore, if the new width is to be 100 pixels, the new height must be 83.33 pixels (which will be rounded down to 83).

Similarly, if the height is greater than the width, then the height will be set to the value in $max, and the width will be set to a percentage of that height, like this:

```
elseif ($h > $w && $max < $h)
{
    $thumbw = $max / $h * $w;
    $thumbh = $max;
}
```

In both cases, a test is made to see whether $max isn't already smaller than the new height or width, because if it's not, then the image is already of thumbnail size.

Finally, a last test checks whether the previous two tests failed but $max *is* less than $h. If so, then both the width and the height must have the same value and so the tests would have failed, as no dimension was larger. In this case, the thumbnail will be square and so both $thumbw and $thumbh are assigned the value in $max, like this:

```
elseif ($max < $w)
{
    $thumbw = $thumbh = $max;
}
```

With all the calculations over, the previous recipe, `ImageResize()`, is called to perform the resizing, the returned image from which is itself returned to the calling code:

```
return ImageResize($image, $thumbw, $thumbh);
```

How to Use It

To create a thumbnail, you pass the function `MakeThumbnail()` a GD image object and the maximum value of the greater dimension for the thumbnail. For example, the following code loads in the image in *test.jpg* using the `imagecreatefromjpeg()` function, and then passes it to the recipe, along with a maximum dimension of 100. The function then returns the new thumbnail to the string variable $thumb, which is then saved to the file *thumb.jpg* using the imagejpeg() function.

```
$image = imagecreatefromjpeg("test.jpg");
$thumb = MakeThumbnail($image, 100);
imagejpeg($thumb, "thumb.jpg");
```

You can also output the thumbnail straight to the browser by first sending the correct header, like this:

```
$image = imagecreatefromjpeg("test.jpg");
header("Content-type: image/jpeg");
imagejpeg(MakeThumbnail($image, 100));
```

The Recipe

```
function MakeThumbnail($image, $max)
{
    $thumbw = $w = imagesx($image);
    $thumbh = $h = imagesy($image);

    if ($w > $h && $max < $w)
    {
        $thumbh = $max / $w * $h;
        $thumbw = $max;
    }
    elseif ($h > $w && $max < $h)
    {
        $thumbw = $max / $h * $w;
        $thumbh = $max;
    }
    elseif ($max < $w)
    {
        $thumbw = $thumbh = $max;
    }

    return ImageResize($image, $thumbw, $thumbh);
}
```

RECIPE 14 ImageAlter()

The PHP GD library is so powerful that it can perform a variety of image manipulations you would normally only find in a graphics program. In fact, you could probably build quite an advanced image editor using them. This recipe goes some way toward that by providing 14 different image transformations you can apply to your graphics, and Figure 4-4 shows just one of these, Edge Detect, in use.

FIGURE **4-4**   The photograph has been modified by passing it through this recipe.

About the Recipe

This recipe accepts an image to be converted into a thumbnail, along with the transformation required. It takes these arguments:

- **$image**   A GD image to be transformed.
- **$effect**   The transformation to apply, between 1 and 14:

$effect	Action
1	Sharpen
2	Blur
3	Brighten
4	Darken
5	Increase contrast
6	Decrease contrast
7	Grayscale
8	Invert
9	Increase red
10	Increase green
11	Increase blue
12	Edge detect
13	Emboss
14	Sketchify

How It Works

To select between the available transformation effects, the recipe uses a large `switch` statement that supports 14 different cases to apply to the supplied GD image object. It then calls the relevant function with the required parameters and returns the new image.

How to Use It

To perform an Edge Detect transformation on a file called *photo.jpg,* as shown in Figure 4-4, you could use the following code, which will load a GD image object using the `imagecreatefromjpeg()` function, and save the transformed image with the function `imagejpeg()`, using the filename *photo2.jpg:*

```
$image = imagecreatefromjpeg("photo.jpg");
$copy  = ImageAlter($image, 12);
imagejpeg($copy, "photo2.jpg");
```

Or to output the transformed image directly to a browser, you could use the following code to output the correct header first:

```
$image = imagecreatefromjpeg("photo.jpg");
header("Content-type: image/jpeg");
imagejpeg(ImageAlter($image, 12));
```

The Recipe

```
function ImageAlter($image, $effect)
{
    switch($effect)
    {
        case 1:  imageconvolution($image, array(array(-1, -1, -1),
                    array(-1, 16, -1), array(-1, -1, -1)), 8, 0);
                 break;
        case 2:  imagefilter($image,
                    IMG_FILTER_GAUSSIAN_BLUR); break;
        case 3:  imagefilter($image,
                    IMG_FILTER_BRIGHTNESS, 20); break;
        case 4:  imagefilter($image,
                    IMG_FILTER_BRIGHTNESS, -20); break;
        case 5:  imagefilter($image,
                    IMG_FILTER_CONTRAST, -20); break;
        case 6:  imagefilter($image,
                    IMG_FILTER_CONTRAST, 20); break;
        case 7:  imagefilter($image,
                    IMG_FILTER_GRAYSCALE); break;
        case 8:  imagefilter($image,
                    IMG_FILTER_NEGATE); break;
        case 9:  imagefilter($image,
                    IMG_FILTER_COLORIZE, 128, 0, 0, 50); break;
        case 10: imagefilter($image,
                    IMG_FILTER_COLORIZE, 0, 128, 0, 50); break;
        case 11: imagefilter($image,
                    IMG_FILTER_COLORIZE, 0, 0, 128, 50); break;
```

```
        case 12: imagefilter($image,
                IMG_FILTER_EDGEDETECT); break;
        case 13: imagefilter($image,
                IMG_FILTER_EMBOSS); break;
        case 14: imagefilter($image,
                IMG_FILTER_MEAN_REMOVAL); break;
    }

    return $image;
}
```

ImageCrop()

This recipe lets you crop a portion from an image by passing it as a GD image object, along with the top-left *x* and *y* coordinates and the width and height to crop. Figure 4-5 shows a 285 × 214–pixel image, which has been cropped starting 100 pixels in from the left and 0 pixels from the top, with dimensions of 110 × 140 pixels.

About the Recipe

This recipe accepts a GD image from which a portion is to be cropped, along with details about the crop offset and dimensions. If any arguments are out of the image bounds, then FALSE is returned. It takes these arguments:

- **$image** A GD image to be transformed.
- **$x** Offset from the left of the image.
- **$y** Offset from the top of the image.
- **$w** The width to crop.
- **$h** The height to crop.

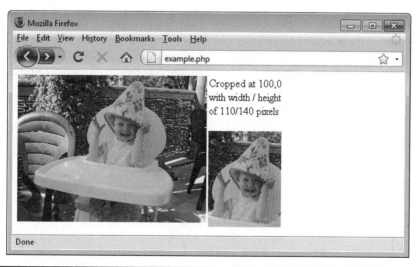

FIGURE 4-5 Images are easily cut down to size using this recipe.

Variables, Arrays, and Functions

$temp	GD image copy of the cropped image
$tw	Integer containing the width of the passed image
$th	Integer containing the height of the passed image

How It Works

This recipe works by creating a new GD image object of the dimensions supplied in $w and $h using the `imagecreatetruecolor()` function. This blank image is stored in $temp, like this:

```
$temp = imagecreatetruecolor($w, $h);
```

Then, the `imagecopyresampled()` function is called, passing the required arguments to copy a portion of the image supplied in $image, starting at the offset $x pixels in and $y pixels down (and with a width and height of $w by $h), into the image held in $temp, which is then returned:

```
imagecopyresampled($temp, $image, 0, 0, $x, $y, $w, $h, $w, $h);
return $temp;
```

How to Use It

To crop a section out of an image, you need to first place the image in a GD image object and then call the `ImageCrop()` function with the required parameters, like this:

```
$image = imagecreatefromjpeg("photo.jpg");
$copy  = ImageCrop($image, 100, 0, 110, 140);
if (!$copy) echo "Crop failed: Argument(s) out of bounds";
else        imagejpeg($copy, "photo1.jpg");
```

This code creates a GD image object in $image by loading it in from the file *photo.jpg* using the `imagecreatefromjpeg()` function. Then, the recipe is called with the top-left corner of the crop and the dimensions to use, the returned result of which is assigned to $copy. The cropped image is then saved as the file *photo1.jpg* using the `imagejpeg()` function. Note that arguments passed with values outside the image bounds will result in FALSE being returned, so you can check for this and issue an appropriate message.

To output the resulting cropped image to a browser, you can use the following code instead, which, as long as there wasn't an error, first sends the correct header:

```
$image = imagecreatefromjpeg("photo.jpg");
$copy  = ImageCrop($image, 100, 0, 110, 140);

if ($copy != FALSE)
{
    header("Content-type: image/jpeg");
    imagejpeg();
}
```

The Recipe

```
function ImageCrop($image, $x, $y, $w, $h)
{
    $tw = imagesx($image);
    $th = imagesy($image);

    if ($x > $tw || $y > $th || $w > $tw || $h > $th)
        return FALSE;

    $temp = imagecreatetruecolor($w, $h);
    imagecopyresampled($temp, $image, 0, 0, $x, $y,
        $w, $h, $w, $h);
    return $temp;
}
```

ImageEnlarge()

RECIPE 16

I've already covered a couple of image resizing recipes in this chapter, including
ImageResize() and MakeThumbnail(). So, you may wonder, why the need for yet
another? The reason is that a standard enlargement, even if it resamples the original image
(rather than merely resizing the pixels), will still result in a pixelated blow-up. And the
more you enlarge an image, the more it will pixelate. For example, imagine increasing the
size of an image by a factor of 10 in each dimension, which results in the contents of every
original pixel now occupying 100 pixels.

Even with resampling the pixels nearby, this will still result in an exceedingly blocky
enlargement with only the edges of each block of 100 pixels showing any differences.
However, now imagine resizing by just doubling each dimension, which results in the
data from each original pixel now only occupying four pixels. With resampling of the
surrounding pixels, this new group of four will contain averaged values from similar
pixels, and therefore pixelation will be minimized as the color and brightness information
is spread out smoothly.

And that's how this recipe works. To achieve a smoother enlargement, it resamples an
original image upwards just a little at a time, spreading the color and brightness smoothly
at each enlargement, until the desired final dimensions are reached.

If you look closely at Figure 4-6, you'll see that an original thumbnail of 100×75 pixels
has been resampled in a single pass to 285×214 pixels, and that this eightfold increase in
size has introduced substantial pixelation into the left-hand enlargement. The increase in
size is calculated by multiplying each pair of dimensions together and then dividing the
larger result by the smaller. Therefore, 100 × 75 is 7,500, and 285 × 214 is 60,990, and
so 60,990/7,500 gives an enlargement amount of 8.132 times.

However, because the image on the right was passed through the ImageEnlarge()
recipe (as you can see from the insets), there is almost no pixelation. Instead, the blockiness
has been replaced with even transitions of color and brightness. Of course, the image
appears a little blurry, but what do you expect from creating picture data out of thin air?
The new picture is eight times the size and therefore comprises over 85 percent made-up
(or interpolated) data. But this recipe even gives you control over that because you can
specify the amount of smoothing to apply to get just the right balance between pixelation
and blurring.

FIGURE 4-6   Even with resampling, enlarging a picture causes pixelation—but this recipe helps reduce it, as shown by the zoomed-in insets.

About the Recipe

This recipe accepts a GD image to enlarge, along with details about the new dimensions and amount of smoothing. It takes these arguments:

- **$image**   A GD image to be enlarged.
- **$w**   The new width.
- **$h**   The new height.
- **$smoothing**   The amount of smoothing (0 = minimum, 90 = maximum).

Variables, Arrays, and Functions

$oldw	Integer representing the image's current width
$oldh	Integer representing the image's current height
$step	Float representing the amount of each enlargement
$max	Integer representing the number of steps to take
$ratio	Float representing the new width relative to the height
$j	Temporary counter to track iterations

How It Works

This recipe first makes a note of the image's current dimensions, placing them in $oldw and $oldh, and then calculates the step size between each of the enlargements. This is derived by multiplying the value of π (3.1415927) by the amount of smoothing required, as follows:

```
$oldw  = imagesx($image);
$oldh  = imagesy($image);
$step  = 3.1415927 * ((100 - $smoothing) / 100);
```

You may ask "Why this formula?" Well, I have to be honest here. I tried dozens of different step sizes until it occurred to me to enter π, and then the amount of smoothing increased substantially. Without being able to explain why, I suspect it has something to do with sines and cosines and the resampling routines used by the GD library.

Anyway, armed with these values, a `for` loop then iterates through all the steps, enlarging the original image a little at a time by passing it to recipe number 12, *Image Resize*, like this:

```
$max   = $w / $step;
$ratio = $h / $w;

for ($j = $oldw ; $j < $max; $j += $step)
   $image = ImageResize($image, $j * $step,
      $j * $step * $ratio);
```

Because each step is a floating point number, the final image will be close to but rarely exactly the new dimensions required. Therefore, before returning the final enlargement, `ImageResize()` is called one last time to ensure the exact size needed is returned:

```
return ImageResize($image, $w, $h);
```

How to Use It

To enlarge an image with this recipe, you must already have it stored as a GD image object, which you then pass to `ImageEnlarge()`, along with the new width and height, and a smoothing level, like this:

```
$image = imagecreatefromjpeg("icon.jpg");
$image = ImageEnlarge($image, 285, 214, 15);
imagejpeg($image, "enlarged.jpg");
```

Here, the image *icon.jpg* is loaded into memory using `imagecreatefromjpeg()` and then passed to the recipe, with requested new dimensions of 285 × 214 pixels and a smoothing level of 15. The returned enlargement is then saved using the filename *enlarged .jpg* with the `imagejpeg()` function. The enlargement could equally be output directly to the browser like this:

```
$image = imagecreatefromjpeg("icon.jpg");
header("Content-type: image/jpeg");
imagejpeg(ImageEnlarge($image, 285, 214, 15));
```

Because the recipe `ImageResize()` is called by this recipe, you will need to ensure you have it already copied to, or included by, your program.

CAUTION *Because this recipe requires multiple iterations of a time-intensive resampling function it's not recommended for on-the fly conversion of images on a production server, and is much better suited for running as part of a background or housekeeping image management process, or for use on a personal PHP installation.*

The Recipe

```
function ImageEnlarge($image, $w, $h, $smoothing)
{
    $oldw  = imagesx($image);
    $oldh  = imagesy($image);
    $step  = 3.1415927 * ((100 - $smoothing) / 100);
    $max   = $w / $step;
    $ratio = $h / $w;

    for ($j = $oldw ; $j < $max; $j += $step)
        $image = ImageResize($image, $j * $step,
            $j * $step * $ratio);

    return ImageResize($image, $w, $h);
}
```

ImageDisplay()

I've already shown you how to output a JPEG image directly to a browser by sending the correct header. But here's a recipe that will output any GIF, JPEG, or PNG image and, if it's a JPEG or PNG, at whatever quality you choose to achieve the optimum balance between bandwidth use and image quality. For example, Figure 4-7 shows a JPEG image displayed by a PHP program at the default quality setting of 75.

About the Recipe

This recipe accepts a filename to display, the image type, and the quality required. It takes these arguments:

- **$filename** A string containing the path/filename of an image.
- **$type** The file type of the image (one of *gif, jpeg* or *png*).
- **$quality** The display quality if a *jpeg* or *png* (0 = lowest, up to 99 = best quality).

Variables, Arrays, and Functions

$contents	Temporary copy of the image loaded from file
$filetype	Array containing details about the file
$mime	String containing the image's type (such as "image/png")
$image	GD image object created from $contents

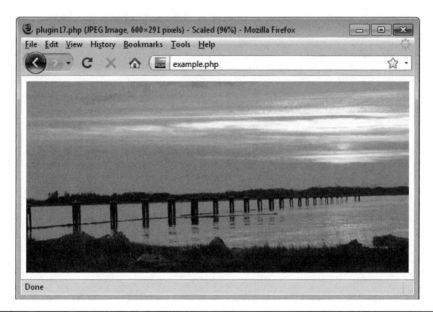

FIGURE 4-7 Using this recipe, you can display images in a variety of formats and quality settings.

How It Works

The first thing this recipe does is load the contents of the file pointed to by $filename into the string variable $contents. Next, if the $type parameter hasn't been given a value, the calling code wants the output type to remain unchanged, so it's looked up by calling the imagegetsize() function and saving the result in the array $filetype. The third element of this array is a string containing the mime file type, so that is extracted and placed in the variable $mime. The correct header is then output, followed by the image, stored in $contents. The die() function is used to send the image, because it combines an echo and exit statement in one, so it's more efficient. Here's the code that does these things:

```
$contents = file_get_contents($filename);

if ($type == "")
{
    $filetype = getimagesize($filename);
    $mime     = image_type_to_mime_type($filetype[2]);
    header("Content-type: $mime");
    die($contents);
}
```

The rest of the code is only executed if $type has a value, and so the output type has been fixed. In this case, a GD image is created from the file stored in $contents using imagecreatefromstring(), and the chosen mime type header is sent to the browser, like this:

```
$image = imagecreatefromstring($contents);
header("Content-type: image/$type");
```

Next, a `switch` statement tests $type to see whether it refers to a GIF, JPEG, or PNG image and calls the correct function to display it out of `imagegif()`, `imagejpeg()`, and `imagepng()`, as follows:

```
switch($type)
{
    case "gif":   imagegif($image); break;
    case "jpeg":  imagejpeg($image, NULL, $quality); break;
    case "png":   imagepng($image,  NULL,
                      round(9 - $quality * .09)); break;
}
```

If the file is a JPEG or a PNG file, then the quality setting is applied. For a JPEG, the value passed needs to be between 0 and 99, with 0 being the worst and 99 the best. This is exactly how the `imagejpeg` function expects to receive this value, so the value of $quality is passed as is. But the `imagepng()` function requires a quality value between 0 and 9, where 0 is the best and 9 the worst, which is the inverse of the former and also one-tenth of the value. Therefore, a quick formula is applied to $quality to conform.

Using a lower-quality setting results in the sent image being smaller and a corresponding saving in bandwidth, whereas a higher setting uses more bandwidth but results in better quality.

How to Use It

To display a file directly to a browser, just call the recipe passing the filename, file type, and quality setting like the following, which outputs a JPEG image in PNG format, at a compression level of 50:

```
ImageDisplay("pic.jpg", "png",  50);
```

To display an image in its native format, you can omit the file type argument, as you can with the quality, by replacing the parameter with NULL:

```
ImageDisplay("pic.jpg", NULL, NULL);
```

The Recipe

```
function ImageDisplay($filename, $type, $quality)
{
    $contents = file_get_contents($filename);

    if ($type == "")
    {
        $filetype = getimagesize($filename);
        $mime     = image_type_to_mime_type($filetype[2]);
        header("Content-type: $mime");
        die($contents);
    }

    $image = imagecreatefromstring($contents);
    header("Content-type: image/$type");
```

```
switch($type)
{
   case "gif":   imagegif($image); break;
   case "jpeg":  imagejpeg($image, NULL, $quality); break;
   case "png":   imagepng($image,  NULL,
                 round(9 - $quality * .09)); break;
}
}
```

RECIPE 18 ImageConvert()

This recipe is similar to the previous one, `ImageDisplay()`, but it saves the new image to disk. Wrapped in suitable code, it's very handy for automatically changing image type (and quality) either singly or in batches. Figure 4-8 shows a 42KB JPEG image that has been converted to another JPEG of only 8KB by using a quality setting of 25.

The second image is discernibly degraded, but the conversion achieves an 80 percent savings on bandwidth. You can specify the quality setting yourself so, at the expense of saving so much bandwidth, you can increase the quality of the converted images, although you can't increase the original quality.

About the Recipe

This recipe accepts the name of a file to convert, the name of the file to be saved as, the image type, and the quality required. It takes these arguments:

- **$fromfile**   String containing the path/filename of an image.

- **$tofile**   String containing the path/filename to save the new image.

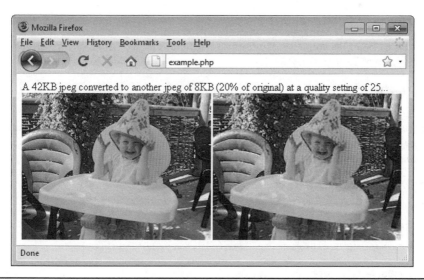

FIGURE 4-8   This recipe converts images between JPEG, GIF, and PNG, and can change the quality setting, too.

- **$type**   The file type of the image (one of *gif*, *jpeg*, or *png*).
- **$quality**   The image quality if JPEG or PNG (0 = lowest, up to 99 = best quality).

Variables, Arrays, and Functions

$contents	Temporary copy of the image loaded from file
$image	GD image object created from $contents

How It Works

This recipe loads in the contents of the image referred to by $fromfile into the string variable $contents, from where it creates a GD image object using the imagecreatefromstring() function, as follows:

```
$contents = file_get_contents($fromfile);
$image    = imagecreatefromstring($contents);
```

Then, a switch statement is used to check whether the new image type required is GIF, JPEG, or PNG and accordingly calls the imagegif(), imagejpeg(), or imagepng() function, passing the value of $tofile, which holds the path and name of the file to save, and $quality, which describes the quality setting if the image is a JPEG or PNG, like this:

```
switch($type)
{
    case "gif":  imagegif($image,  $tofile); break;
    case "jpeg": imagejpeg($image, $tofile, $quality); break;
    case "png":  imagepng($image,  $tofile,
                    round(9 - $quality * .09)); break;
}
```

As with the previous recipe, ImageDisplay(), the quality setting has to be specially calculated for PNG files since the imagepng() function expects the compression setting in a different format from imagejpeg().

How to Use It

To convert an image type, call ImageConvert() with the source and destination path and/or filenames, along with the type to convert to and the quality setting to use, like in the following line of code, which converts the image in *photo.jpg* to a PNG file, and saves it as *photo.png*, using a compression value of 50:

```
ImageConvert("photo.jpg", "photo.png", "png", 50);
```

The Recipe

```
function ImageConvert($fromfile, $tofile, $type, $quality)
{
    $contents = file_get_contents($fromfile);
    $image    = imagecreatefromstring($contents);
```

```
switch($type)
{
   case "gif":  imagegif($image,  $tofile); break;
   case "jpeg": imagejpeg($image, $tofile, $quality); break;
   case "png":  imagepng($image,  $tofile,
                   round(9 - $quality * .09)); break;
}
}
```

Note that GIF images do not have a quality setting, so this value will make no difference to the resulting image. Also, to see the differences between before and after, make sure you reload any converted images into your browser so that previous unconverted images are not served up from the cache in place of the converted ones.

RECIPE 19 GifText()

Although web browsers come with a reasonable range of default fonts, they don't always provide the look you need for a particular web site. In such cases, you usually must resort to calling up a graphic editor and creating logos or headlines there.

However, with this recipe all you have to do is upload the TrueType fonts you wish to use to your web site and you can then display text in these fonts by having the GD library convert it on the fly to GIF images. Figure 4-9 shows the text "Old English Font" displayed at four different sizes using an Old English TrueType font.

About the Recipe

This recipe takes the name of a file to save as a finished GIF, the text and font to use in it, and various details such as color, size, and shadowing. It takes these arguments:

- **$file**   The path/filename to save the image.
- **$text**   The text to create.

FIGURE 4-9   Now you can use any fonts you like on your web pages thanks to this recipe.

- **$font**   The path/filename of the TrueType font to use.
- **$size**   The font size.
- **$fore**   The foreground color in hexadecimal (such as "000000").
- **$back**   The background color (such as "FFFFFF").
- **$shadow**   The number of pixels to offset a shadow underneath the text (0 = no shadow).
- **$shadowcolor**   The shadow color (such as "444444").

Variables, Arrays, and Functions

$bound	Array containing the boundaries required to make room for the text
$width	Integer containing the text width in pixels calculated from $bound
$height	Integer containing the text height in pixels calculated from $bound
$image	Temporary copy of the final image
$bgcol	The background color identifier created from $back
$fgcol	The foreground color identifier created from $fore
$shcol	The shadow color identifier created from $shadowcolor
GD_FN1()	Function to create color identifiers

How It Works

To create a GIF image of the correct dimensions to hold the text, the function `imagettfbbox()` is called with the font, its size, and the text to display as arguments. The result, which contains the *x* and *y* coordinates of all four corners, is then stored in the array $bound. Using these, the variables $width and $height are assigned values sufficiently large to accommodate the text and any shadow, as well as a few pixels of space all around. Then, a new GD image is created in $image using this width and height, as follows:

```
$bound  = imagettfbbox($size, 0, $font, $text);
$width  = $bound[2] + $bound[0] + 6 + $shadow;
$height = abs($bound[1]) + abs($bound[7]) + 5 + $shadow;
$image  = imagecreatetruecolor($width, $height);
```

Next, three color identifiers are created in $bgcol, $fgcol, and $shcol using the string values supplied in $fore, $back, and $shadowcolor by calling the function GD_FN1(), which takes a six-character hexadecimal string and converts it to a color identifier. These identifiers are unique to the $image object and are used to set colors in it. This function is just a helper function to the main recipe and is not documented because it's not intended to be called directly by any other code. And with the colors prepared, the image is then filled with the background color using the `imagefilledrectangle()` function, like this:

```
$bgcol = GD_FN1($image, $back);
$fgcol = GD_FN1($image, $fore);
$shcol = GD_FN1($image, $shadowcolor);
imagefilledrectangle($image, 0, 0, $width, $height, $bgcol);
```

Next, if $shadow is greater than 0, then a shadow needs to be displayed so the imagettftext() function is called to display the text at an offset (down and to the right) of $shadow + 2 pixels, and in the correct shadow color, like this:

```
if ($shadow > 0) imagettftext($image, $size, 0, $shadow + 2,
    abs($bound[5]) + $shadow + 2, $shcol, $font, $text);
```

After that, the code for adding the main text itself is called. This is the same as for the shadow text except that no offset is used and the text is created in the foreground color, like this:

```
imagettftext($image, $size, 0, 2, abs($bound[5]) + 2, $fgcol,
    $font, $text);
```

Finally, the imagegif() function is called to save the finished image using the path/filename stored in $file:

```
imagegif($image, $file);
```

How to Use It

To use this recipe, upload the TrueType file(s) you want to the same folder as the PHP program. In this case, it's assumed you have uploaded a font called *oldenglish.ttf*. You can then create a GIF containing the text of your choice, like this:

```
GifText("greeting.gif", "Hello there!", "oldenglish.ttf",
    26, "ff0000", "ffffff", 1, "444444");
```

To display the image, you then only need to output some HTML code, like this:

```
echo "<img src='greeting.gif' />";
```

However, to ensure the image is only created the first time it is needed, you will probably want to wrap the call to GifText() within an if statement, like this:

```
if (!file_exists("greeting.gif"))
{
    GifText("greeting.gif", "Hello there!", "oldenglish.ttf",
        26, "ff0000", "ffffff", 1, "444444");
}
```

The Recipe

```
function GifText($file, $text, $font, $size, $fore, $back,
    $shadow, $shadowcolor)
{
    $bound  = imagettfbbox($size, 0, $font, $text);
    $width  = $bound[2] + $bound[0] + 6 + $shadow;
    $height = abs($bound[1]) + abs($bound[7]) + 5 + $shadow;
    $image  = imagecreatetruecolor($width, $height);
    $bgcol  = GD_FN1($image, $back);
```

```
$fgcol  = GD_FN1($image, $fore);
$shcol  = GD_FN1($image, $shadowcolor);
imagefilledrectangle($image, 0, 0, $width, $height, $bgcol);

if ($shadow > 0) imagettftext($image, $size, 0, $shadow + 2,
   abs($bound[5]) + $shadow + 2, $shcol, $font, $text);

imagettftext($image, $size, 0, 2, abs($bound[5]) + 2, $fgcol,
   $font, $text);
imagegif($image, $file);
}

function GD_FN1($image, $color)
{
   return imagecolorallocate($image,
      hexdec(substr($color, 0, 2)),
      hexdec(substr($color, 2, 2)),
      hexdec(substr($color, 4, 2)));
}
```

RECIPE 20 ImageWatermark()

In a similar way to creating GIF images of text, you can also overlay text on an existing image to create watermarks. With the amount of copying and pasting of images across the Web, when you have one you would like to protect, sometimes watermarking is the best way, and this recipe provides a variety of options. For example, Figure 4-10 shows a photograph with the word *Watermark* overlaid in white at a transparency setting of 10 percent.

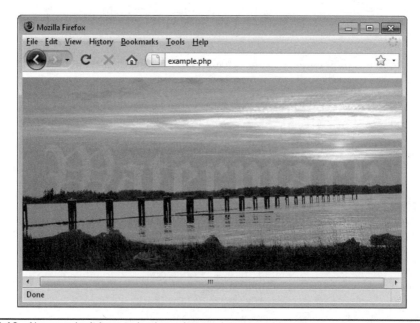

FIGURE 4-10   Now you don't have to load your images into a graphic editor to add watermarks.

About the Recipe

This recipe takes the name of a file in which to save a finished GIF, the text and font to use, and various details such as color, size, and shadowing. It takes these arguments:

- **$fromfile** The path/filename of the original image.
- **$tofile** The path/filename to save the image.
- **$type** One of *gif*, *jpeg*, or *png*.
- **$quality** Quality setting of final image (0 = worst, up to 99 = best).
- **$text** The text to create.
- **$font** The path/filename of the TrueType font to use.
- **$size** The font size.
- **$fore** The foreground color in hexadecimal (such as "000000").
- **$opacity** The opacity of the watermark (0 = transparent, up to 100 = opaque).

Variables, Arrays, and Functions

$contents	The image contents loaded in from $fromfile
$image1	GD image object created from $contents
$bound	Array containing the boundaries required to make room for the text
$width	Integer containing the text width in pixels calculated from $bound
$height	Integer containing the text height in pixels calculated from $bound
$image2	GD image object created to hold watermarking text
$bgcol	The background color identifier, from the string "fedcba" (see the *How It Works* section)
$fgcol	The foreground color identifier created from $fore
GD_FN1()	Function to create color identifiers

How It Works

This recipe starts by loading the image referred to by $fromfile into $contents, from where it's changed to a GD image object and stored in $image1. Then, the array $bound is populated with the result of calling imagettfbbox() to get the coordinates of all the corners needed to create a space big enough to store the watermark text, like this:

```
$contents = file_get_contents($fromfile);
$image1   = imagecreatefromstring($contents);
$bound    = imagettfbbox($size, 0, $font, $text);
```

The width and height of this box are then extracted from $bound into $width and $height, with a few pixels leeway being left in all dimensions. Using this width and height, a new GD image object is created in $image2. Then, two color identifiers are created for the background and foreground colors in $bgcol and $fgcol. This is done using the function GD_FN1(), which is designed for use only by these recipes and is not intended to be called directly from your programs, like this:

```
$width  = $bound[2] + $bound[0] + 6;
$height = abs($bound[1]) + abs($bound[7]) + 5;
$image2 = imagecreatetruecolor($width, $height);
$bgcol  = GD_FN1($image2, "fedcba");
$fgcol  = GD_FN1($image2, $fore);
```

Because the text for watermarking will be transparent, I selected a background color of "fedcba", which is unlikely to be used as the foreground color. If you do need that as a foreground color, I'm sure you could get away with using "fedcb9" or "fedcbb", and so on instead.

As I said, the background color must be transparent, so it's passed to the function imagecolortransparent(), and then the entire $image2 rectangle is filled in that color using imagefilledrectangle(). With the background canvas prepared, the text is then written to it in the foreground color, using the font and size specified, as follows:

```
imagecolortransparent($image2, $bgcol);
imagefilledrectangle($image2, 0, 0, $width, $height, $bgcol);
imagettftext($image2, $size, 0, 2, abs($bound[5]) + 2,
    $fgcol, $font, $text);
```

At this point, the function now has two separate images—the original, and the watermark to add—so it calls the imagecopymerge() function to merge the watermark onto the original image, exactly in the middle, and with an opacity of $opacity, like this:

```
imagecopymerge($image1, $image2,
    (imagesx($image1) - $width) / 2,
    (imagesy($image1) - $height) / 2,
    0, 0, $width, $height, $opacity);
```

Finally, a switch statement is used to check the image type for being one of GIF, JPEG, or PNG, and then calls one of imagegif(), imagejpeg(), or imagepng() accordingly to save the image, using the path/filename in $tofile. If the type you wish to save it as is a PNG or JPEG, then the quality setting in $quality is also applied, although a little math is required to manipulate it into the correct form required for the imagepng() function:

```
switch($type)
{
    case "gif":  imagegif($image1,  $tofile); break;
    case "jpeg": imagejpeg($image1, $tofile, $quality); break;
    case "png":  imagepng($image1,  $tofile,
                    round(9 - $quality * .09)); break;
}
```

How to Use It

To watermark an image, you supply the function ImageWatermark() with the names of a source and destination file, the image type, and the parameters required for font, size, color, and transparency, like this:

```
ImageWatermark("pic.jpg", "wmark.png", "png", 75,
   "Watermark", "oldenglish.ttf", 90, "ffffff", 10);
```

Here, the file *pic.jpg* is overlaid with a watermark containing the text "Watermark", using the *oldenglish.ttf* font with a size of 90, a color of "ffffff", and an opacity value of 10. The file is saved as a PNG image, at a quality setting of 75, using the filename *wmark.png*.

The Recipe

```
function ImageWatermark($fromfile, $tofile, $type,
   $quality, $text, $font, $size, $fore, $opacity)
{
   $contents = file_get_contents($fromfile);
   $image1   = imagecreatefromstring($contents);
   $bound    = imagettfbbox($size, 0, $font, $text);
   $width    = $bound[2] + $bound[0] + 6;
   $height   = abs($bound[1]) + abs($bound[7]) + 5;
   $image2   = imagecreatetruecolor($width, $height);
   $bgcol    = GD_FN1($image2, "fedcba");
   $fgcol    = GD_FN1($image2, $fore);

   imagecolortransparent($image2, $bgcol);
   imagefilledrectangle($image2, 0, 0, $width, $height, $bgcol);
   imagettftext($image2, $size, 0, 2, abs($bound[5]) + 2,
      $fgcol, $font, $text);
   imagecopymerge($image1, $image2,
      (imagesx($image1) - $width) / 2,
      (imagesy($image1) - $height) / 2,
      0, 0, $width, $height, $opacity);

   switch($type)
   {
      case "gif":  imagegif($image1,  $tofile); break;
      case "jpeg": imagejpeg($image1, $tofile, $quality); break;
      case "png":  imagepng($image1,  $tofile,
                      round(9 - $quality * .09)); break;
   }
}

function GD_FN1($image, $color)
{
   return imagecolorallocate($image,
      hexdec(substr($color, 0, 2)),
      hexdec(substr($color, 2, 2)),
      hexdec(substr($color, 4, 2)));
}
```

PART II

CHAPTER 5

Content Management

When developing web projects, there are certain content management processes that are so common it can save you a great deal of programming to have ready-made recipes available. Some examples include converting relative to absolute URLs, checking for broken links, tracking web visitors, and more.

This chapter explores 10 of these types of functions that you can add to your toolbox, and explains how they work so you can further tailor them to your own requirements. Along the way, it covers parsing URLs, extracting information from web pages (even on other servers), reading the contents of local files and directories, accessing query strings that result from search engine referrals, embedding YouTube videos, counting raw and unique web visits, and tracking where users are coming from.

RelToAbsURL()

Any project that needs to crawl web pages, whether their own or a third party's, needs a way to convert relative URLs into absolute URLs that can be called up on their own, without reference to the page in which they are located. For example, the URL */sport/index .html* means nothing at all when looked at on its own, and there is no way of knowing the URL was extracted from the web page *http://server.com/news/*.

Using this recipe, relative URLs can be combined with the referring page to create stand-alone, absolute URLs, such as *http://server.com/sport/index.html*. Figure 5-1 shows a variety of links being converted to absolute.

About the Recipe

This recipe takes the URL of a web page, along with a link from within that page, and then returns the link in a form that can be accessed without reference to the calling page—in other words, an absolute URL. It takes these arguments:

- **$page** A web page URL, including the *http://* preface and domain name.
- **$url** A link extracted from $page.

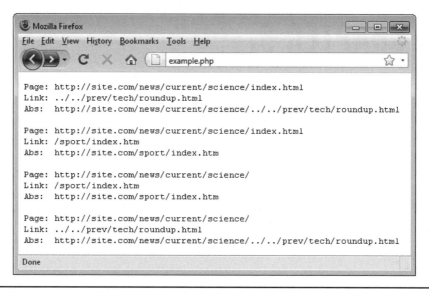

Figure 5-1 This recipe provides the solution to a common problem encountered in web development—converting a relative URL to absolute.

Variables, Arrays, and Functions

$parse	Associative array derived from parsing $page
$root	String comprising the first part of $page, up to and including the host domain name
$p	Integer pointer to final "/" in $page
$base	The current directory where $page is located

How It Works

In order to convert a URL from relative to absolute, it's necessary to know *where* the relative URL is relative *to*. This is why the main page URL is passed along with the relative URL. In fact, not all the URLs passed may be relative, and they could even all be absolute, depending on how $page has been written. But what this recipe does is process a URL anyway, and if it's determined to be relative, then it's turned into an absolute URL.

It does this by first parsing the original URL, passed in $page, and extracting the scheme (for example, *http://* or *ftp://*, and so on) and host (such as *myserver.com*) and combining just these two parts together into the string variable $root to create, for example, the string *http://myserver.com*, like this:

```
if (substr($page, 0, 7) != "http://") return $url;

$parse = parse_url($page);
$root  = $parse['scheme'] . "://" . $parse['host'];
```

Then $page is examined to see if there are any / characters after the initial http://. If so, the final one is located and its position is placed in $p, as follows:

```
$p = strrpos(substr($page, 7), '/');
```

If there isn't one, then $p is set to 0. Using this value, $base is assigned either the substring of $page all the way up to, and including, the final /, or if there wasn't one, $base is assigned the value of $page itself, but with a final / appended to it. Either way, $base now represents the location of the directory containing $page, like this:

```
if ($p) $base = substr($page, 0, $p + 8);
else    $base = "$page/";
```

Next, $url is examined, and if it starts with a "/", then it must be a relative URL—referring to an offset from the domain's document root. In which case, $url is replaced with a value comprising the concatenation of $root and $url. So, for example, *http:// myserver.com* and */news/index.html* would combine to become *http://myserver.com/news/index .html*, as follows:

```
if (substr($url, 0, 1) == '/') $url = $root . $url;
```

If $url doesn't start with a /, then a test is made to see whether it begins with http://. If not, the URL must also be relative, but this time it is relative to the directory location of $page, so $url is replaced with a value comprising the concatenation of $base and $url. So, for example, *http://myserver.com/sport* and *results.html* would combine to become *http:// myserver.com/sport/results.html*, like this:

```
elseif (substr($url, 0, 7) != "http://") $url = $base . $url;
```

If both these tests fail, then $url commences with http:// and therefore is an absolute URL and cannot be converted; it is returned unchanged.

NOTE *For the sake of speed and simplicity, a complete relative-to-absolute URL conversion is not made. For example, the URL ../news/index.html in the page http://myserver.com/ sport/ is not converted to http://myserver.com/news/index.html. Instead it becomes http://myserver.com/sport/../news/index.html. This saves the code having to further parse a URL, locating examples of ../ and then removing the directory immediately previous to it. There's no need, because this longer form of absolute URL is perfectly valid and works just fine.*

How to Use It

To use this recipe, pass it the full URL of a page that contains a relative link, along with the relative link itself, like this:

```
$page = "http://site.com/news/current/science/index.html";
$link = "../../prev/tech/roundup.html";
echo RelToAbsURL($page, $link);
```

The value returned will be an absolute URL that can be used to access the destination page without recourse to the original web page. In the preceding case, the following URL will be returned:

```
http://site.com/news/current/science/../../prev/tech/roundup.html
```

The Recipe

```
function RelToAbsURL($page, $url)
{
    if (substr($page, 0, 7) != "http://") return $url;

    $parse = parse_url($page);
    $root  = $parse['scheme'] . "://" . $parse['host'];
    $p     = strrpos(substr($page, 7), '/');

    if ($p) $base = substr($page, 0, $p + 8);
    else    $base = "$page/";

    if (substr($url, 0, 1) == '/')            $url = $root . $url;
    elseif (substr($url, 0, 7) != "http://") $url = $base . $url;

    return $url;
}
```

GetLinksFromURL()

When you first need to extract HTML links from a web page (even your own), it looks almost impossible and seems quite a daunting task. And it's true, parsing HTML is quite complex. But with this recipe, all you need to do is pass it the URL of a web page, and all the links found within it will be returned. Figure 5-2 shows links being extracted from a web page.

About the Recipe

This recipe takes the URL of a web page and parses it, looking only for <a href links, and returns all that it finds in an array. It takes a single argument:

- **$page**   A web page URL, including the *http://* preface and domain name.

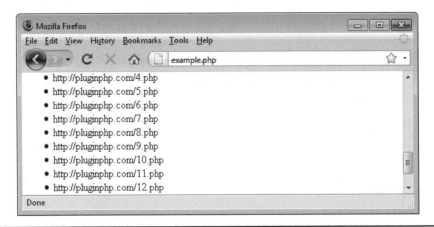

FIGURE 5-2   Using this recipe, you can extract and return all the links in a web page.

Variables, Arrays, and Functions

`$contents`	String containing the HTML contents of `$page`
`$urls`	Array holding the discovered URLs
`$dom`	Document object of `$contents`
`$xpath`	Xpath object for traversing `$dom`
`$hrefs`	Object containing all `href` link elements in `$dom`
`$j`	Integer loop counter for iterating through `$hrefs`
`RelToAbsURL()`	Function to convert relative URLs to absolute

How It Works

This recipe first reads the contents of $page into the string $contents (returning NULL if there's an error). Then, it creates a new Document Object Model (DOM) of $contents in $dom using the loadhtml() method. The statement is prefaced with an @ character to suppress any warning or error messages. Even poorly formatted HTML is generally useable with this method, because it finds the URLs easy to extract and parse, like this:

```
$contents = @file_get_contents($page);
if (!$contents) return NULL;

$urls = array();
$dom  = new domdocument();
@$dom ->loadhtml($contents);
```

Then, a new XPath object is created in $xpath with which to search $dom for all instances of href elements, and all those discovered are then placed in the $hrefs object, like this:

```
$xpath = new domxpath($dom);
$hrefs = $xpath->evaluate("/html/body//a");
```

Next, a for loop is used to iterate through the $hrefs object and extract all the attributes, which in this case are the links we want. Prior to storing the URLs in $urls, each one is passed through the RelToAbsURL() function to ensure they are converted to absolute URLs (if not already), as follows:

```
for ($j = 0 ; $j < $hrefs->length ; $j++)
   $urls[$j] = RelToAbsURL($page,
      $hrefs->item($j)->getAttribute('href'));
```

Once extracted, the links are then returned as an array:

```
return $urls;
```

How to Use It

To extract all the URLs from a page and receive them in absolute form, just call GetLinksFromURL() like this:

```
$result = GetLinksFromURL("http://webdeveloperscookbook.com");
```

You can then display (or otherwise make use of) the returned array like this:

```
for ($j = 0 ; $j < count($result) ; ++$j)
    echo "$result[$j]<br />";
```

The Recipe

```
function GetLinksFromURL($page)
{
    $contents = @file_get_contents($page);
    if (!$contents) return NULL;

    $urls  = array();
    $dom   = new domdocument();
    @$dom  ->loadhtml($contents);
    $xpath = new domxpath($dom);
    $hrefs = $xpath->evaluate("/html/body//a");

    for ($j = 0 ; $j < $hrefs->length ; $j++)
        $urls[$j] = RelToAbsURL($page,
            $hrefs->item($j)->getAttribute('href'));

    return $urls;
}
```

CheckLinks()

The two previous recipes provide the foundation for being able to crawl the Internet by:

1. Reading in a third-party web page
2. Extracting all URLs from the page
3. Converting all the URLs to absolute

Armed with these abilities, it's now a simple matter for this recipe to offer the facility to check all links on a web page and test whether the pages they refer to actually load or not (this is a great way to alleviate the frustration of your users upon encountering dead links or mistyped URLs). Figure 5-3 shows this plug-in being used to check the links on the *alexa.com* home page.

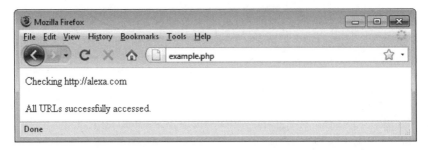

FIGURE 5-3   The recipe has been run on the alexa.com home page, with all URLs reported present and correct.

About the Recipe

This recipe takes the URL of a web page (yours or a third party's) and then tests all the links found within it to see whether they resolve to valid pages. It takes these three arguments:

- **$page**   A web page URL, including the *http://* preface and domain name.
- **$timeout**   The number of seconds to wait for a web page before considering it unavailable.
- **$runtime**   The maximum number of seconds your script should run before timing out.

Variables, Arrays, and Functions

$contents	String containing the HTML contents of $page
$checked	Array of URLs that have been checked
$failed	Array of URLs that could not be retrieved
$fail	Integer containing the number of failed URLs
$urls	Array of URLs extracted from $page
$context	Stream context to set the URL load timeout
GetLinksFromURL()	Function to retrieve all links from a page
RelToAbsURL()	Function to convert relative URLs to absolute

How It Works

The first thing this recipe does is set the maximum execution time of the script using the ini_set() function, like this:

```
ini_set('max_execution_time', $runtime);
```

This is necessary because crawling a set of web pages can take a considerable amount of time. I recommend you experiment with maximums of up to 180 seconds or more. If the script ends without returning anything, try increasing the value

The contents of $page are then loaded into $contents. After that, two arrays are initialized. The first, $checked, will contain all the URLs that have been checked so that, where a page links to another more than once, a second check is not made for that URL. The second array, $failed, will contain all the URLs that couldn't be loaded, while the counter $fail is also set to 0 (when any URL fails to load, it will be incremented), as follows:

```
$contents = @file_get_contents($page);
if (!$contents) return array(1, array($page));

$checked = array();
$failed  = array();
$fail    = 0;
```

Next, the array $urls is populated with all the URLs from $page using the GetLinksFromURL() recipe, and $context is assigned the correct values to set the timeout for each checked page to the value that was supplied to the function in the variable $timeout. This will be used shortly by the file_get_contents() function, like this:

```
$urls    = GetLinksFromURL($page);
$context = stream_context_create(array('http' =>
   array('timeout' => $timeout)));
```

With all the variables, objects, and arrays initialized, a for loop is entered in which each URL is tested in turn, but only if it hasn't been already. This is determined by testing whether the current URL already exists in $checked, the array of checked URLs. If it doesn't, the URL is added to the $checked array and the file_get_contents() function is called (with the $context object) to attempt to fetch the first 256 bytes of the web page. If that fails, the URL is added to the $failed array and $fail is incremented, as follows:

```
for ($j = 0 ; $j < count($urls); $j++)
{
    if (!in_array($urls[$j], $checked))
    {
        $checked[] = $urls[$j];

        if (!@file_get_contents($urls[$j], 0, $context, 0, 256))
            $failed[$fail++] = $urls[$j];
    }
}
```

Once the loop has completed, an array is returned with the first element containing 0 if there were no failed URLs, otherwise it contains the number of failures, while the second element contains an array listing all the failed URLs.

How to Use It

To check all the links on a web page, you can call the function using code such as this:

```
$page   = "http://myserver.com";
$result = CheckLinks($page, 2, 180);
```

To then view or otherwise use the returned values, use code such as the following, which either displays a success message or lists the failed URLs:

```
if ($result[0] == 0) echo "All URLs successfully accessed.";
else for ($j = 0 ; $j < $result[0] ; ++$j)
    echo $result[1][$j] . "<br />";
```

HINT Because crawling like this can take time, you may wonder whether your program is actually working when nothing is displayed to the screen. So if you wish to view the plug-in's progress, you can uncomment the line shown to have each URL displayed as it's processed.

The Recipe

```
function CheckLinks($page, $timeout, $runtime)
{
   ini_set('max_execution_time', $runtime);
   $contents = @file_get_contents($page);
   if (!$contents) return array(1, array($page));

   $checked = array();
   $failed  = array();
   $fail    = 0;
   $urls    = GetLinksFromURL($page);

   $context = stream_context_create(array('http' =>
      array('timeout' => $timeout)));

   for ($j = 0 ; $j < count($urls); $j++)
   {
      if (!in_array($urls[$j], $checked))
      {
         $checked[] = $urls[$j];

         // Uncomment the following line to view progress
         // echo " $urls[$j]<br />\n"; ob_flush(); flush();

         if (!@file_get_contents($urls[$j], 0, $context, 0, 256))
            $failed[$fail++] = $urls[$j];
      }
   }

   return array($fail, $failed);
}
```

DirectoryList()

24

When you need to know the contents of a directory on your server—for example, because you support file uploads and need to keep tabs on them—this recipe returns all the filenames using a single function call. Figure 5-4 shows the plug-in in action.

About the Recipe

This recipe takes the location of a directory on your server and returns all the files within it in an array. Upon success, it returns a four-element array, the first of which is the number of directories found. The second is the number of files found, the third is an array of directory names, and the fourth is an array of filenames. On failure, it returns a single-element array with the value FALSE. It requires this argument:

- **$path** The path of a directory on the server.

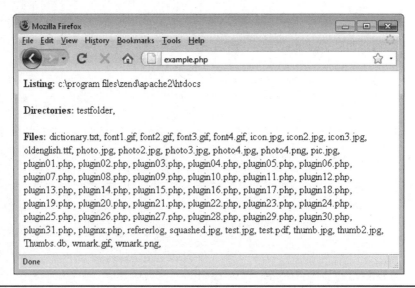

FIGURE 5-4   Using this recipe under Windows to return the contents of Zend Server CE's document root

Variables, Arrays, and Functions

$files	Array containing the files encountered
$dirs	Array containing the directories encountered
$fnum	Integer containing the number of files
$dnum	Integer containing the number of directories
$dh	Handle to identify the directory
$item	String containing each encountered item in turn

How It Works

This program initializes the two arrays, $files and $dirs, which will contain the files and directories encountered in $path, and sets the two counters for the numbers of files and directories, $fnum and $dnum, to 0, like this:

```
$files = array();
$dirs  = array();
$fnum  = $dnum = 0;
```

Then, $path is checked to ensure it's a valid directory. If it is, the directory is opened using opendir() and a handle to it is placed in $dh, as follows:

```
if (is_dir($path))
{
   $dh = opendir($path);
```

Then, a do loop is entered in which each item in the directory is read in turn into the string $item. If the value of $item is FALSE at any time, the end of the directory listing has been encountered. However, there's a slight problem because a file or subdirectory could have the name "0", which would be interpreted as having the value FALSE by PHP. To avoid this, instead of comparing using the != operator, !== is used. This tells PHP not to try to evaluate anything before making the comparison, and only to compare exact values. The filenames . and .. are also ignored, as follows:

```
Do
{
   $item = readdir($dh);

   if ($item !== FALSE && $item != "." && $item != "..")
```

Next, the current item is tested to see whether it's a file or a directory. If it's a directory, it is placed in the $dirs array and $dnum is incremented. If it's a file, it is placed in the $files array and $fnum is incremented, like this:

```
if ($item !== FALSE && $item != "." && $item != "..")
{
   if (is_dir($item)) $dirs[$dnum++]  = $item;
   else               $files[$fnum++] = $item;
}
```

The do loop then continues until $item has a value of FALSE, at which point the $dh handle is closed, as follows:

```
} while($item !== FALSE);

closedir($dh);
```

At the end of the code the results are returned in an array of four elements as follows:

- Element 0: The number of directories found
- Element 1: The number of files found
- Element 2: Array containing the directory names
- Element 3: Array containing the filenames

The return code looks like this:

```
return array($dnum, $fnum, $dirs, $files);
```

If $path was not a valid directory, the return statement will simply return zeros and empty array values.

How to Use It

You call up the recipe using code such as this, setting $directory to the folder whose contents you are interested in:

```
$directory = "c:\windows";
$result    = DirectoryList($directory);
```

You can then use the returned values like this to display the directories found:

```
if ($result[0] == 0) echo "No Directories found";
else for ($j=0 ; $j < $result[0] ; ++$j)
   echo $result[2][$j] . "<br />";
```

Or like this to list the files:

```
if ($result[1] == 0) echo "No files found";
else for ($j=0 ; $j < $result[1] ; ++$j)
   echo $result[3][$j] . "<br />";
```

Or you might prefer to use foreach instead of for loops, like this:

```
if ($result[0] == 0) echo "No Directories found";
else foreach($result[2] as $directory)
   echo "$directory<br />";

if ($result[1] == 0) echo "No files found";
else foreach($result[3] as $file)
   echo "$file<br />";
```

The Recipe

```
function DirectoryList($path)
{
    $files = array();
    $dirs  = array();
    $fnum  = $dnum = 0;

    if (is_dir($path))
    {
        $dh = opendir($path);

        do
        {
            $item = readdir($dh);

            if ($item !== FALSE && $item != "." && $item != "..")
            {
                if (is_dir("$path/$item")) $dirs[$dnum++] = $item;
                else $files[$fnum++] = $item;
            }
        } while($item !== FALSE);

        closedir($dh);
    }

    return array($dnum, $fnum, $dirs, $files);
}
```

QueryHighlight( )

When a visitor comes to your web site from a search engine result, you can use this recipe to be helpful and highlight all the items from their search in your text, deciding whether to highlight these terms with either boldface, italics, or an underline. Figure 5-5 shows some words from a Shakespeare play being highlighted using this plug-in.

About the Recipe

This recipe takes the text to display and the type of highlighting required for any search terms encountered. It requires these arguments:

- **$text**   The text to highlight.
- **$highlight**   The type of highlight to use, from a choice of b, i, or u for bold, italic, or underline.

Variables, Arrays, and Functions

$refer	The referring web page, if any
$parse	Array containing the parts of $refer
$queries	String containing queries extracted from $refer
$key	String containing the first half of a key/value pair
$value	String containing the second half of a key/value pair
$matches	Array containing search words
WordSelector()	Function used to highlight selected words in text

How It Works

The URL of the referring page is placed in $refer, and the array $parse is set to the component parts of $refer. If there was no referring page, the text supplied in $text is returned unmodified. This is also the case if there *was* a referring page but *no* search string query.

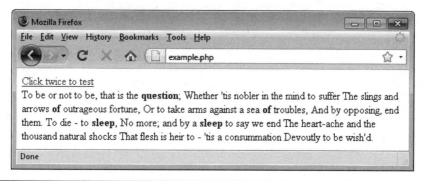

Figure 5-5   If a page has been arrived at from a search engine, you can highlight all the words matching the query with this recipe.

Otherwise, the array $queries is filled with the various queries that can follow a URL, and which are separated by & characters, as follows:

```
$refer = getenv('HTTP_REFERER');
$parse = parse_url($refer);

if ($refer == "") return $text;
elseif (!isset($parse['query'])) return $text;

$queries = explode('&', $parse['query']);
```

A foreach loop is then entered, which iterates through each of the strings in the $queries array, setting $key and $value to the left and right halves of each. If any of the $key values is either q or p, chances are the code is looking at the result of a search query made with one of the major search engines (Yahoo!, Bing, Google, or Ask Jeeves), and so the contents of $value will be passed to urldecode() to turn any unusual characters into regular ones, and then all words found in this string will be split out into the array $matches.

Provided with this array of search words, WordSelector() is then called to highlight any of these words that appear within the string $text. The result of this is then returned. The following is the loop's code:

```
foreach($queries as $query)
{
    list($key, $value) = explode('=', $query);

    if ($key == "q" || $key == "p")
    {
        $matches = explode(' ', preg_replace('/[^\w ]/', '',
            urldecode($value)));
        return WordSelector($text, $matches, $highlight);
    }
}
```

How to Use It

To highlight search terms within some text, you call the recipe like this:

```
$text = "To be or not to be, that is the question; " .
        "whether 'tis nobler in the mind to suffer " .
        "the slings and arrows of outrageous fortune, " .
        "or to take arms against a sea of troubles, " .
        "and by opposing, end them. To die - to sleep, " .
        "no more; and by a sleep to say we end " .
        "the heart-ache and the thousand natural shocks " .
        "that flesh is heir to - 'tis a consummation " .
        "devoutly to be wish'd.";

echo QueryHighlight($text, "b");
```

In this example, any words in the string $text, which were used as a search term at a major search engine to discover the current page, will be highlighted in bold face. So, for example, if the user searched for "question of sleep," then the previous text would be highlighted like this:

To be or not to be, that is the **question***; whether 'tis nobler in the mind to suffer the slings and arrows* **of** *outrageous fortune, or to take arms against a sea* **of** *troubles, and by opposing, end them. To die - to* **sleep***, no more; and by a* **sleep** *to say we end the heart-ache and the thousand natural shocks that flesh is heir to - 'tis a consummation devoutly to be wish'd.*

You can include any text or HTML you like and the recipe will still work correctly. Punctuation is also fully supported, so you don't have to ensure spaces exist on either side of keywords for them to be recognized.

On its own, if you just type in the preceding example and call it up in a browser, you will not see any highlighting because there is no referring page; you will have entered the page directly. So, to simulate a referred visit from a search engine, you can add the following code to the example:

```
echo "<br /><a href=\"" . $_SERVER['PHP_SELF'] .
    "?q=" . rawurlencode("question of sleep") .
    "\">Click twice to test</a><br />";
```

This displays an HTML link that will cause the PHP program to call itself up when the link is clicked on, acting as its own referring page. You need to do this twice, though, in order to properly simulate a visit referred from a search engine. The first click adds the referrer information to the tail of the URL (as displayed in the browser address field), and the second passes that tail to the program where it can be processed. After the second click, you'll see that the text has been highlighted.

The Recipe

```
function QueryHighlight($text, $highlight)
{
    $refer = getenv('HTTP_REFERER');
    $parse = parse_url($refer);

    if ($refer == "") return $text;
    elseif (!isset($parse['query'])) return $text;

    $queries = explode('&', $parse['query']);

    foreach($queries as $query)
    {

        list($key, $value) = explode('=', $query);

        if ($key == "q" || $key == "p")
        {
            $matches = explode(' ', preg_replace('/[^\w ]/', '',
                urldecode($value)));
            return WordSelector($text, $matches, $highlight);
        }
    }
}
```

RollingCopyright()

If you've developed for the Web for more than a couple of years, you're bound to have encountered the problem whereby every January you have to wade in and locate all the copyright statements to bring them up to date with the new year. Well, with this short and sweet recipe, that never need be a problem again, since it will ensure your web sites always show the current year, as shown in Figure 5-6.

About the Recipe

This recipe takes a copyright message and the first year the copyright began. It requires these arguments:

- **$message**   The copyright message.
- **$year**   The year the copyright began.

How It Works

Although this is a very short recipe, it's well worth using because it can save you no end of time. What it does is return the message supplied in $message, along with a copyright sign, the start year in $year, and the current year, as returned by the date() function.

Note the use of the date_default_timezone_set() function. This is required by more recent versions of PHP to ensure that a time zone has been chosen.

How to Use It

To add an always up-to-date copyright message to your web site, use code such as this:

```
echo RollingCopyright("All rights reserved", 2012);
```

The Recipe

```
function RollingCopyright($message, $year)
{
   date_default_timezone_set('UTC');
   return "$message &copy;$year-" . date("Y");
}
```

FIGURE 5-6   Ensuring your copyright message is always up to date is easy with this recipe.

EmbedYouTubeVideo()

How often have you grabbed the embed code for a YouTube video only to find you have to tweak it to get the right dimensions for your web site or select high-quality video or make it auto start? With this recipe, you can replace all that with a single function call whenever you need to embed a video, and it handles browsers that only support HTML5 video (and disallow the Flash plug-in). Figure 5-7 shows such a video displayed with a single call to this code.

About the Recipe

This recipe takes the YouTube ID of a video and the parameters required to display it to your requirements. It accepts these arguments:

- $id   A YouTube video ID, such as "VjnygQ02aW4".
- $width   The display width.
- $height   The display height.
- $high   If set to 1, enable high-quality display, if available.
- $full   If set to 1, enable the video to play in full-screen mode.
- $auto   If set to 1, start the video playing automatically on page load.

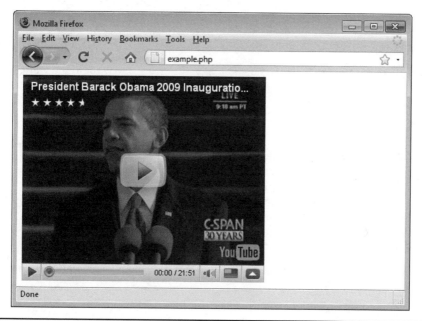

FIGURE 5-7   This recipe facilitates embedding a YouTube video with various options such as video quality and auto start.

Variables, Arrays, and Functions

$fs	Variable set to the string allowfullscreen if $full is 1, otherwise set to the empty string
$hd	Variable set to the string ?hd=1 if $high is 1, otherwise set to the empty string
$as	Variable set to the string ? if $full is not 1, otherwise set to the string &
$ap	Variable set to the value in $as followed by the string autoplay=1 if $auto is 1, otherwise set to the empty string

How It Works

This code first ensures that the video has valid width and height dimensions, like this:

```
if ($width && !$height) $height = $width  * 0.7500
if (!$width && $height) $width  = $height * 1.3333
if (!$width)            $width  = 480
if (!$height)           $height = 385
```

If only one dimension is entered, the other is scaled accordingly to keep the average ratio of 4:3, while if no dimensions are passed, defaults of 480 by 385 pixels are chosen. If you know the dimensions of a video, it's always best to use them to ensure the best playback quality.

After this, the code checks whether $full has a value of 1, and if so, it sets $fs to the value allowfullscreen, which will be appended to the end of the <iframe> tag to enable full-screen playback, like this:

```
$fs = ($full) ? 'allowfullscreen' : '';
```

Then, if the parameter $high has a value of 1, the string $hd is set to the value ?hd=1, which is later tacked onto the URL of the video to enable it to be played in high-quality video (if available), as follows:

```
$hd = ($high) ? '?hd=1' : '';
```

After this, the string variable $as is set either to ? if $high is not 1, or to & if it is. This prepares the correct symbol to place before the part of the query string used to make a video auto play. If it is the first argument in the query string, it must be prefaced by a ? symbol, otherwise a & symbol should be used. It will be the first argument if there is no argument to set high definition, otherwise it will be the second argument, like this:

```
$as = ($hd) ? '?' : '&';
```

The $ap variable is then set to either the null string or the relevant value to cause the video to auto play, like this:

```
$ap = ($auto) ? "$as" . 'autoplay=1' : '';
```

The result is that the recipe returns the HTML required to display a YouTube video exactly to your requirements, and even if a web browser doesn't have the Flash plug-in, as long as it supports HTML5, the video will still play, as follows:

```
return "<iframe class='youtube-player' type='text/html' " .
"width='$width' height='$height' " .
"src='http://www.youtube.com/embed/$id$hd$ap' $fs></iframe>";
```

How to Use It

To embed a YouTube video in a web page, you call the recipe like this:

```
echo EmbedYouTubeVideo("VjnygQ02aW4", 370, 300, 1, 1, 0);
```

Here a video showing President Obama's inauguration has been selected to be displayed at a width of 370 and height of 300 pixels, with both the high-quality and full-screen options enabled, but with auto start disabled.

HINT *If you wish to display videos using YouTube's recommended default dimensions, select a width and height of 480 × 385 for a 4:3 video, or 640 × 385 for a 16:9 video.*

The Recipe

```
function EmbedYouTubeVideo($id, $width, $height,
    $high, $full, $auto)
{
    if ($width && !$height) $height = $width  * 0.7500
    if (!$width && $height) $width  = $height * 1.3333
    if (!$width)            $width  = 480
    if (!$height)           $height = 385

    $fs = ($full == 1 ) ? 'allowfullscreen'    : '';
    $hd = ($high == 1 ) ? '?hd=1'              : '';
    $as = ($hd   == '') ? '?'                  : '&';
    $ap = ($auto == 1 ) ? "$as" . 'autoplay=1' : '';

    return "<iframe class='youtube-player' type='text/html' " .
    "width='$width' height='$height' " .
    "src='http://www.youtube.com/embed/$id$hd$ap' $fs></iframe>";

}
```

CreateList()

Displaying lists is one of the most common elements of a web page. Whether for lists of related blog entry URLs, headlines, navigation, or others, lists provide an instant visual cue and are easy to use. With this recipe, you can easily create the HTML for eight different types of lists using a single function call. Figure 5-8 shows the types of list this recipe supports.

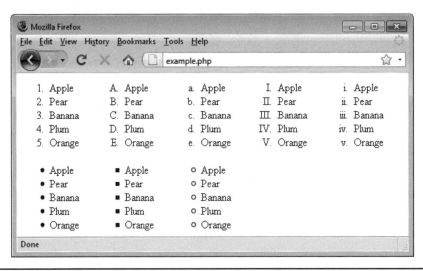

FIGURE 5-8   Using this recipe, you can automatically create the HTML for eight different types of lists.

About the Recipe

This recipe takes an array containing all the items in a list, along with parameters to control the display formatting. It accepts these arguments:

- **$items**   An array containing all the items in the list.
- **$start**   The start number for ordered lists.
- **$type**   The type of list: ul for unordered, and ol for ordered.
- **$bullet**   The type of bullet. For unordered lists: square, circle, or disc. For ordered lists: 1, A, a, I, or i.

Variables, Arrays, and Functions

$list	String variable containing HTML to be returned

How It Works

This recipe starts by opening a new HTML list tag, which can be one of <ol or <ul, depending on the value in $type. It also sets the start value to $start and the bullet type to $bullet.

A foreach loop is then entered to iterate through every element in the $items array, temporarily placing each in the string variable $item, which is then enclosed by <li> and </li> tags. The result is then appended to the string $list, which, once the loop completes, is returned to the calling code, along with a closing </ol> or </ul> tag.

How to Use It

To create the HTML for a list, pass it an array containing the list of elements, along with the formatting arguments required, like the following, which creates the HTML for an unordered list using the circle character as a bullet:

```
$fruits = array("Apple", "Pear", "Banana", "Plum", "Orange");
echo CreateList($fruits, NULL, "ul", "circle");
```

If you wish, with ordered lists you can change the start value to any numerical value you like, instead of the default of 1. But note how the start argument in the preceding code is set to NULL because it's not required. In this case, you could actually set it to any value since it will be ignored, but using NULL will remind you when browsing your code that no value is being passed.

The types of bullet you can use depend on the type of list being created. For an ordered list, five different bullet types are available:

- **1** Numerical: From 1 onwards in decimal.
- **A** Alphabetic: A–Z, then AA–AZ, then BA–BZ, and so on.
- **a** Alphabetic: a–z, then aa–az, then ba–bz, and so on.
- **I** Roman: I, II, III, IV, V, and so on.
- **i** Roman: i, ii, iii, iv, v, and so on.

For unordered lists, there are three types of bullets you can use:

- **square** A filled-in square.
- **circle** An open circle.
- **disc** A filled-in circle.

The Recipe

```
function CreateList($items, $start, $type, $bullet)
{
    $list = "<$type start='$start' type='$bullet'>";
    foreach ($items as $item) $list .= "<li>$item</li>\n";
    return $list . "</$type>";
}
```

HitCounter()

RECIPE 29

For long-term statistical information, you can always use a service such as Google Analytics to keep track of your web visitors. However, when you have a brand new page and need to know instantly whether and how much traffic it is attracting, your normal recourse is to look at the server log files. But now you can use this recipe to add a simple invisible counter to your web pages in order to get a quick snapshot of raw and unique hits, as shown in Figure 5-9.

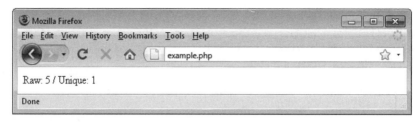

FIGURE 5-9   When you need instant stats from your web site, this recipe will provide them.

About the Recipe

This recipe takes the name of a file to hold the counts for the current page, as well as details on what to do with it. It accepts these arguments:

- **$filename**   A path/filename to use for storing hit count data.
- **$action**   What to do with the data: reset = reset all counts, add = add the current visit to the data, get = retrieve hit stats, delete = delete the counter file.

Variables, Arrays, and Functions

$data	String containing user's IP address and browser details
$fp	File pointer to the counter file
$file	String containing contents of $filename
$lines	Array containing all lines extracted from $file
$raw	Numeric variable containing the total number of hits saved in the file
$unique	Numeric variable containing the number of hits with unique IP/browser details

How It Works

The first thing this code does is make a note of the current visitor's IP address, which is a four-part number that directly identifies that user, and looks something like 209.85.169.103. Then, because IP addresses can be shared—for example, across a business or home network—the browser's User Agent string is also noted. This is a string that identifies the type and version of a browser and varies widely in use but may look something like "Mozilla/4.0 (compatible; MSIE 8.0; Windows NT 6.1; Media Center PC 6.0)". These two strings are then combined and placed in the string variable $data, followed by a \n newline character, like this:

```
$data = getenv("REMOTE_ADDR") .
        getenv("HTTP_USER_AGENT") . "\n";
```

Next, a switch statement with four sections is entered. The first section is processed if $action is set to reset. It opens the file $filename for writing, using an argument of "w", and then calls the function flock(). This is PHP's file locking mechanism, and what this call does is request an exclusive lock on the file by passing the argument LOCK_EX.

The function waits until any and all other processes have finished using the file, and then releases the lock using flock() with an argument of LOCK_UN, and closes the file. This has the effect of truncating the file to zero bytes. Had a lock not been set and the program not waited its turn, then if two requests came through at the same time, one to append to the file and one to truncate it, there would be no way of knowing which process might "win." This way, all accesses to the file are queued up and all processes take their turn. This code looks like the following:

```
switch ($action)
{
    case "reset":
        $fp = fopen($filename, "w");
        if (flock($fp, LOCK_EX))
            ;
        flock($fp, LOCK_UN);
        fclose($fp);
        return;
```

The second section is executed if $action is set to add. Here the file is opened in a similar way to the previous example, except that the argument "a+" is used, which stands for "append to." Again, the flock() function is called and, when control over the file is gained, the data in $data is appended to the file, the lock is released, and the file closed, as follows:

```
case "add":
    $fp = fopen($filename, "a+");
    if (flock($fp, LOCK_EX))
        fwrite($fp, $data);
    flock($fp, LOCK_UN);
    fclose($fp);
    return;
```

The third section is executed if $action is set to get, in which case the file is opened just for reading using an argument of "r". Then, flock() is called and, after control is gained, the fread() function is called to read the entire contents of $filename into $file, except for the final character, which will be a \n newline, and is not needed. The file lock is then released and the file closed. With the file contents in $file, it is extracted into the array $lines by using the explode() function to split it at every \n linefeed character. Then, the number of elements is counted using count() and assigned to the variable $raw. To obtain the unique counts (the number of hits made by different IP/browser combinations, ignoring multiple hits by the same user), the array_unique() function is called before using count() and passing the result to $unique. Afterward, a two-element array containing these raw and unique values is returned, as follows:

```
case "get":
    $fp = fopen($filename, "r");
    if (flock($fp, LOCK_EX))
        $file = fread($fp, filesize($filename) - 1);
    flock($fp, LOCK_UN);
    fclose($fp);
```

```
$lines  = explode("\n", $file);
$raw    = count($lines);
$unique = count(array_unique($lines));
return array($raw, $unique);
```

The final section is executed when $action is set to delete and simply uses the unlink()
function to delete the file pointed to by $filename:

```
case "delete":
   unlink($filename);
   return;
```

How to Use It

Most times, you will use this recipe as follows:

```
HitCounter("counter.txt", "add");
```

This code passes the filename *counter.txt* and the parameter add to the function
HitCounter(), which then appends the IP address and User Agent of the current user to
the file. It's not necessary to first create the file, because if it doesn't already exist, it will
be created.

Should you wish to reset the file data and start over, you can issue the following
command, which truncates the data file back to zero bytes in length:

```
HitCounter("counter.txt", "reset");
```

To delete the counter, use this command:

```
HitCounter("counter.txt", "delete");
```

To get an instant hit count report, use code such as this:

```
$result = HitCounter("counter.txt", "get");
echo "Raw: $result[0] / Unique: $result[1]";
```

You can give the counter any name you like, but if you use the *.txt* extension, as in these
examples, you'll be able to load it into a text editor and browse through it.

The Recipe

```
function HitCounter($filename, $action)
{
   $data = getenv("REMOTE_ADDR") .
           getenv("HTTP_USER_AGENT") . "\n";

   switch ($action)
   {
      case "reset":
         $fp = fopen($filename, "w");
         if (flock($fp, LOCK_EX))
            ;
```

```
        flock($fp, LOCK_UN);
        fclose($fp);
        return;

    case "add":
        $fp = fopen($filename, "a+");
        if (flock($fp, LOCK_EX))
            fwrite($fp, $data);
        flock($fp, LOCK_UN);
        fclose($fp);
        return;

    case "get":
        $fp = fopen($filename, "r");
        if (flock($fp, LOCK_EX))
            $file = fread($fp, filesize($filename));
        flock($fp, LOCK_UN);
        fclose($fp);
        $lines  = explode("\n", $file);
        $raw    = count($lines) - 1;
        $unique = count(array_unique($lines)) - 1;
        return array($raw, $unique);

    case "delete":
        unlink($filename);
        return;
    }
}
```

RECIPE 30 — RefererLog()

In a similar way to being able to instantly track visitor hits, this recipe keeps constant track of the URLs from which your users are being sent. Again, this is something you can track with a service such as Google Analytics or by processing your log files, but neither of these methods is as quick and easy to use as this recipe for providing instant data, as shown in Figure 5-10.

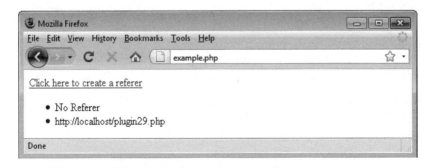

FIGURE 5-10 Keeping track of pages referring to your site is easy using this recipe.

About the Recipe

This recipe takes the name of a file to hold the referring data for the current page, as well as details on what to do with it. Upon success, it either updates or returns details from the data file. It accepts these arguments:

- **$filename**   A path/filename to use for storing referring page data.
- **$action**   What to do with the data: reset = reset all data, add = add the current visit to the data, get = retrieve referrer stats, delete = delete the file.

Variables, Arrays, and Functions

$data	String containing the referring page URL
$fp	File pointer to the referrer file
$file	String containing contents of $filename
$temp	Temporary array containing unique referring URLs

How It Works

The first thing this recipe does is make a note of the referring page's URL, if there is one, placing it in $date, followed by a \n newline character. If no referring page was passed to the current program, perhaps because the URL was typed in directly, then $data is assigned the string "No Referrer", followed by a \n newline, like this:

```
$data = getenv("HTTP_REFERER") . "\n";
if ($data == "\n") $data = " No Referrer\n";
```

Next, a switch statement with four sections is entered. The first section is processed if $action is set to reset. It opens the file $filename for writing, using an argument of "w", and then calls the function flock(). The function waits until all other processes have finished using the file and then releases the lock and closes the file, truncating it to zero bytes, as follows:

```
switch ($action)
{
    case "reset":
        $fp = fopen($filename, "w");
        if (flock($fp, LOCK_EX))
            ;
        flock($fp, LOCK_UN);
        fclose($fp);
        return;
```

The second section is executed if $action is set to add. Here, the argument "a+" is used to open the file for appending. Again, the flock() function is called and, when control over the file is gained, the data in $data is appended to the file, the lock is released, and the file closed, like this:

```
case "add":
    $fp = fopen($filename, "a+");
    if (flock($fp, LOCK_EX))
        fwrite($fp, $data);
    flock($fp, LOCK_UN);
    fclose($fp);
    return;
```

The third section is executed if $action is set to get, in which case the file is opened for reading using an argument of "r". Then, flock() is called and, after control is gained, the fread() function is called to read the entire contents of $filename into $file, all except the final character, which will be a \n newline, and is therefore not needed. The file lock is then released and the file closed. With the file contents in $file, the explode() function is used to extract it into the array $temp, splitting it at every \n linefeed character. Then, all nonunique entries are removed from the array, which is then sorted to remove the gaps, and the resulting array is returned, as follows:

```
case "get":
    $fp = fopen($filename, "r");
    if (flock($fp, LOCK_EX))
        $file = fread($fp, filesize($filename) -1);
    flock($fp, LOCK_UN);
    fclose($fp);
    $temp = array_unique(explode("\n", $file));
    sort($temp);
    return $temp;
```

The final section is executed when $action is set to delete and simply uses the unlink() function to delete the file pointed to by $filename:

```
case "delete":
    unlink($filename);
    return;
```

How to Use It

You will normally call the recipe with code such as the following, which creates the file *refer .log* if it doesn't already exist and writes the contents of $data to it. If the file does exist, the data is appended to it:

```
RefererLog("refer.log", "add");
```

To delete this log file, use this command:

```
RefererLog("refer.log", "delete");
```

Or to reset the log file by truncating it back to zero length, use:

```
RefererLog("refer.log", "reset");
```

To display all the entries in the log file, you could use code such as the following, which uses a `for` loop to iterate through all the entries in the returned array and display them:

```
$result = RefererLog("refer.log", "get");
for ($j = 0 ; $j < count($result) ; ++$j)
   echo "$result[$j]<br />";
```

The Recipe

```
function RefererLog($filename, $action)
{

    $data = getenv("HTTP_REFERER") . "\n";
    if ($data == "\n") $data = " No Referrer\n";

    switch ($action)
    {
       case "reset":
          $fp = fopen($filename, "w");
          if (flock($fp, LOCK_EX))
             ;
          flock($fp, LOCK_UN);
          fclose($fp);
          return;

       case "add":
          $fp = fopen($filename, "a+");
          if (flock($fp, LOCK_EX))
             fwrite($fp, $data);
          flock($fp, LOCK_UN);
          fclose($fp);
          return;

       case "get":
          $fp = fopen($filename, "r");
          if (flock($fp, LOCK_EX))
             $file = fread($fp, filesize($filename) -1);
          flock($fp, LOCK_UN);
          fclose($fp);
          $temp = array_unique(explode("\n", $file));
          sort($temp);
          return $temp;

       case "delete":
          unlink($filename);
          return;
    }
}
```

CHAPTER 6

Forms and User Input

Even with the growth in Web 2.0 Ajax techniques, most people still interact with web sites using forms. They are a tried and tested means of obtaining user input and are likely to retain an important position for a long time to come.

Receiving user input is all well and good—that's the easy part. But turning that input into usable and secure data is another matter. In this chapter, you'll find a collection of solutions for helping you with expression evaluation, validation of credit card details, e-mail addresses and text strings, identifying spam, preventing automated input from "bots," and ways of supporting user-supplied text formatting.

31 EvaluateExpression()

You might think that offering support for evaluating expressions would be a simple matter of calling the PHP `eval()` function with a user-supplied input. Unfortunately, though, `eval()` is an extremely powerful function that will interpret any string supplied to it as if it were a PHP program; using it could completely open up your web site to any intruder with a minimum of PHP knowledge.

However, with this recipe the user input is completely sanitized by stripping out any characters and functions that are not safe, leaving only a selection of 22 mathematical functions and the basic math operators (plus, minus, multiply, and divide), and only then is the input passed to `eval()`. Figure 6-1 shows a variety of expressions being calculated.

About the Recipe

This recipe accepts a string containing a mathematical expression and returns the result of evaluating it. It takes this argument:

- **$expr**   A string containing an expression.

Variables, Arrays, and Functions

$f1	Array containing the 22 mathematical function names supported
$f2	Array containing tokens the function names are temporarily converted to

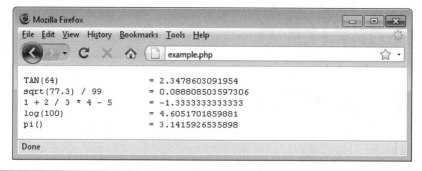

FIGURE 6-1   This recipe enables powerful calculator functionality on your web site.

How It Works

To allow the use of PHP's built-in eval() function, it is necessary to remove any harmful expressions before passing them to it. To achieve this, the array $f1 contains 22 function names (out of the hundreds supported by PHP) that are considered safe. Using the $f2 array, which contains a matching set of tokens, any of the 22 functions found in the argument $expr are converted to a corresponding token. This means that any remaining alphabetical characters may form other function names, and therefore are stripped out. Here are the two arrays:

```
$f1 = array ('abs',    'acos',  'acosh', 'asin',  'asinh',
             'atan',   'atan2', 'atanh', 'cos',   'cosh',
             'exp',    'expm1', 'log',   'log10', 'log1p',
             'pi',     'pow',   'sin',   'sinh',  'sqrt',
             'tan',    'tanh');

$f2 = array ('!01!',   '!02!',  '!03!',  '!04!',  '!05!',
             '!06!',   '!07!',  '!08!',  '!09!',  '!10!',
             '!11!',   '!12!',  '!13!',  '!14!',  '!15!',
             '!16!',   '!17!',  '!18!',  '!19!',  '!20!',
             '!21!',   '!22!');
```

The preceding is achieved by first converting the string $expr to lowercase using the function strtolower(), and then employing str_replace() to replace all occurrences of the allowed function names with their tokens, like this:

```
$expr = strtolower($expr);
$expr = str_replace($f1, $f2, $expr);
```

Next, preg_replace() is called to strip out anything remaining that is not required, using the regular expression /[^\d+*\/\-\.()!]/. Okay, I know it looks like I just dropped the keyboard on the floor, but this is actually a powerful expression that I'll now break up for you, like this:

```
$expr = preg_replace("/[^\d+\*\/\-\.(),! ]/", '', $expr);
```

The outer / characters denote the start and end of a regular expression.

The square brackets, [], state that a match should be made against any single character enclosed within them.

The ^ symbol, when immediately following a [symbol, forces negation so that the expression will match anything that is *not* one of the characters following.

Next comes a sequence of characters, which are all escaped by prefacing them with a \ symbol, because otherwise they would be interpreted as special regular expression operators:

- \d   Any digit (0–9).
- \+   An addition symbol.
- *   A multiplication symbol.
- \/   A division symbol.
- \-   A subtraction symbol.
- \.   A decimal point symbol.

So, if any symbol is not one of these escaped symbols, it will be considered a match and the second argument to preg_replace(), '', will replace it with nothing—in other words, the symbol will be removed. Finally, a few other symbols are also allowed through. These are the left and right brackets, the comma, the exclamation mark, and a space.

You might wonder why the exclamation mark is allowed within a mathematical expression. Well, the answer is that it isn't allowed in order to support certain expression types. Instead, it's there because it forms part of each of the 22 tokens in the array $f2. I chose the exclamation mark at random and could equally have used any one of many other symbols. Once the mathematical functions have been converted to tokens, the ! symbols remain there so that the tokens can be converted back again after stripping the remaining unwanted characters out, which is done using another call to the str_replace() function, as follows:

```
$expr = str_replace($f2, $f1, $expr);
```

After all this processing, the resulting sanitized string is passed to the eval() function, the result of which is returned to the calling statement, like this:

```
return eval("return $expr;");
```

If you wish to see what the sanitized expression looks like, you can uncomment the line shown in the source code.

How to Use It

To evaluate a user-supplied expression, just call the function EvaluateExpression(), passing the expression to be calculated in the following manner, which calculates the area of a circle with a radius of 4:

```
echo EvaluateExpression("pi() * pow(4, 2)");
```

The Recipe

```
function EvaluateExpression($expr)
{
    $f1 = array ('abs',   'acos',  'acosh', 'asin',  'asinh',
                 'atan',  'atan2', 'atanh', 'cos',   'cosh',
                 'exp',   'expm1', 'log',   'log10', 'log1p',
                 'pi',    'pow',   'sin',   'sinh',  'sqrt',
                 'tan',   'tanh');

    $f2 = array ('!01!',  '!02!',  '!03!',  '!04!',  '!05!',
                 '!06!',  '!07!',  '!08!',  '!09!',  '!10!',
                 '!11!',  '!12!',  '!13!',  '!14!',  '!15!',
                 '!16!',  '!17!',  '!18!',  '!19!',  '!20!',
                 '!21!',  '!22!');

    $expr = strtolower($expr);
    $expr = str_replace($f1, $f2, $expr);
    $expr = preg_replace("/[^\d\+\*\/\-\.(),! ]/", '', $expr);
    $expr = str_replace($f2, $f1, $expr);

    // Uncomment the line below to see the sanitized expression
    // echo "$expr<br />\n";

    return eval("return $expr;");
}
```

RECIPE 32 ValidateCC()

Sometimes people make mistakes when entering credit card numbers in web forms, or even just make numbers up to see what will happen. Using this recipe, you can at least ensure that a credit card number and expiration date you have been provided with has an acceptable number sequence, a correct checksum, and a valid expiry date.

This enables you to only pass on sensible-looking details to your card processing organization, and possibly limit any additional fees that may be charged. In Figure 6-2, you can see a made-up card number that has not validated.

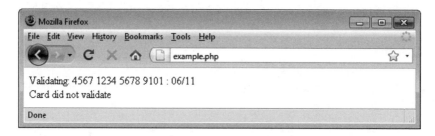

FIGURE 6-2   Credit card numbers have a built-in checksum that this recipe will validate.

About the Recipe

This recipe accepts a credit card number and expiry date and returns TRUE if they validate, and FALSE otherwise. It takes these arguments:

- **$number** A string containing a credit card number.
- **$expiry** A credit card expiry date in the form 07/12 or 0712.

Variables, Arrays, and Functions

$left	String containing the left four digits of $number
$cclen	Integer containing the number of characters in $number
$chksum	Integer containing the credit card checksum
$j	Loop counter
$d	Character containing individual digits extracted from $number

How It Works

In the 1950s, Hans Peter Luhn, a scientist working at IBM, created the Luhn checksum algorithm, also known as the *modulus 10* or *mod 10* algorithm. It will detect any single-digit error, as well as almost all transpositions of adjacent digits in a string of digits. This makes it very useful for verifying whether a credit card number has been successfully entered by using the simple method of adding a checksum digit at the number's end. All major credit companies use this system and so can we.

The first thing the recipe does is remove any non-digit characters from $number; the same is done for the expiry date in $expiry. Then, the contents of the first four digits of $number are placed in the variable $left, the length of $number is placed in $cclen, and $checksum is initialized to 0, like this:

```
$number = preg_replace('/[^\d]/', '', $number);
$expiry = preg_replace('/[^\d]/', '', $expiry);
$left   = substr($number, 0, 4);
$cclen  = strlen($number);
$chksum = 0;
```

Each card issuer has their own initial sequences of numbers, and card number length can vary between 13 and 16 digits depending on the issuer. So, using the contents of $left, the next main section of code looks up the type of card using a sequence of if and elseif statements and, based on the result, returns FALSE if $number does not contain the correct number of digits for that card.

Once all the known sequences of initial digits have been processed, if no card has yet been matched, then FALSE is returned because $number represents the number for a card type the program is unaware of—most likely it's a made-up number.

Otherwise, the card type has been identified and $number has been found to have the right number of digits, so the next portion of code runs the Luhn algorithm to see whether the sequence of numbers appears valid. It does this by checking alternate digits and adding them together in a pre-set manner. If the result is exactly divisible by 10, then the sequence is valid. If not, FALSE is returned, as follows:

```
for ($j = 1 - ($cclen % 2); $j < $cclen; $j += 2)
    $chksum += substr($number, $j, 1);

for ($j = $cclen % 2; $j < $cclen; $j += 2)
{
    $d = substr($number, $j, 1) * 2;
    $chksum += $d < 10 ? $d : $d - 9;
}

if ($chksum % 10 != 0) return FALSE;
```

Lastly, the expiry date is checked against the date of the last day of the current month and, if the card has expired, FALSE is returned. Otherwise, if all these tests pass, a value of TRUE is returned, like this:

```
if (mktime(0, 0, 0, substr($expiry, 0, 2), date("t"),
    substr($expiry, 2, 2)) < time()) return FALSE;

return TRUE;
```

TIP *If you are interested in exactly how the Luhn algorithm works, there's an explanation at en.wikipedia.org/wiki/Luhn_algorithm.*

How to Use It

To verify a credit card's details prior to submitting it to a credit card processing organization, you could use code such as this:

```
$card   = "4567 1234 5678 9101";
$exp    = "06/14";
$result = ValidateCC($card, $exp);
if (!$result)
{
    // Re-ask for details or an alternate payment method
}
else
{
    // Debit the card
}
```

In the preceding example, if the card doesn't validate, the details are re-requested. Or, if it does, the card is processed.

CAUTION *All this recipe does is check whether the credit card details entered meet the issuer identity, checksum, and date requirements for a valid card. It should only be used as a quick test to ensure that a user has not made a typographical error when entering their details. Also, you should keep yourself informed about all the latest card numbers allocated so that you can update this validator and not incorrectly reject any cards. You can keep track of the major credit card issuers at wikipedia.org/wiki/Credit_card_numbers.*

The Recipe

```
function ValidateCC($number, $expiry)
{
    $ccnum  = preg_replace('/[^\d]/', '', $number);
    $expiry = preg_replace('/[^\d]/', '', $expiry);
    $left   = substr($ccnum, 0, 4);
    $cclen  = strlen($ccnum);
    $chksum = 0;

    // Diners Club
    if (($left >= 3000) && ($left <= 3059) ||
        ($left >= 3600) && ($left <= 3699) ||
        ($left >= 3800) && ($left <= 3889))
        if ($cclen != 14) return FALSE;

    // JCB
    if (($left >= 3088) && ($left <= 3094) ||
        ($left >= 3096) && ($left <= 3102) ||
        ($left >= 3112) && ($left <= 3120) ||
        ($left >= 3158) && ($left <= 3159) ||
        ($left >= 3337) && ($left <= 3349) ||
        ($left >= 3528) && ($left <= 3589))
        if ($cclen != 16) return FALSE;

    // American Express
    elseif (($left >= 3400) && ($left <= 3499) ||
            ($left >= 3700) && ($left <= 3799))
        if ($cclen != 15) return FALSE;

    // Carte Blanche
    elseif (($left >= 3890) && ($left <= 3899))
        if ($cclen != 14) return FALSE;

    // Visa
    elseif (($left >= 4000) && ($left <= 4999))
        if ($cclen != 13 && $cclen != 16) return FALSE;

    // MasterCard
    elseif (($left >= 5100) && ($left <= 5599))
        if ($cclen != 16) return FALSE;
```

```
// Australian BankCard
elseif ($left == 5610)
   if ($cclen != 16) return FALSE;

// Discover
elseif ($left == 6011)
   if ($cclen != 16) return FALSE;

// Unknown
else return FALSE;

for ($j = 1 - ($cclen % 2); $j < $cclen; $j += 2)
   $chksum += substr($ccnum, $j, 1);

for ($j = $cclen % 2; $j < $cclen; $j += 2)
{
   $d = substr($ccnum, $j, 1) * 2;
   $chksum += $d < 10 ? $d : $d - 9;
}

if ($chksum % 10 != 0) return FALSE;

if (mktime(0, 0, 0, substr($expiry, 0, 2), date("t"),
   substr($expiry, 2, 2)) < time()) return FALSE;

return TRUE;
}
```

RECIPE 33 CreateCaptcha()

Spam is everywhere these days, and not just in our e-mail inboxes. The Internet is saturated with "bots" (automated programs) trawling web pages in search of web forms that will let them drop their payload into a comment or other field. Usually they try to drop in a link leading to a knock-off product they are trying to sell. But worse than that, many of these bots inject pornographic links, or attempt to get users to visit phishing sites where their bank, credit card, or other personal details may be stolen.

One of the most successful ways to prevent this is the Captcha, a type of challenge-response test used in computing to ensure that the response is not generated by a computer. The word is a highly contrived acronym that stands for "Completely Automatic Public Turing Test to Tell Computers and Humans Apart."

With a Captcha, you are asked to reenter some text displayed in a graphic image. If the image is complex enough, a bot will not be able to decipher it and so only human input is able to get through. This still doesn't guarantee you will be spam-free, but with this recipe you'll prevent the majority of it from getting through. Figure 6-3 shows the plug-in generating a Captcha.

About the Recipe

This recipe creates a temporary image containing a word that must be typed in to verify a user is human. It returns a three-element array in which the first element is the Captcha text

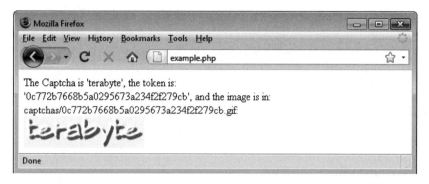

Figure 6-3   Ensuring that users are humans and not "bots" is easy with this recipe.

to be entered, the second is a unique 32-character token, and the third is the location of the Captcha image. It takes these arguments:

- **$size**   The font size of a TrueType font.
- **$length**   The number of characters in the Captcha word.
- **$font**   The location of a TrueType font to use.
- **$folder**   The location of a folder to store the Captcha images. This must be web-accessible and end with a trailing / character; or to use the current folder, use a value of NULL..
- **$salt1**   A string to make the Captcha hard to crack.
- **$salt2**   A string to make cracking even harder.

Variables, Arrays, and Functions

$file	String containing the contents of the file *dictionary.txt*
$temps	Array of all words extracted from $file
$temp	String containing each value in turn from $temps
$dict	Array of all correct-length words extracted from $temps
$captcha	String containing the Captcha word
$token	String containing an md5() hash based on $captcha, $salt1, and $salt2
$fname	String containing the Captcha image location
$image	GD library image of the Captcha image
$j	Loop counter
GifText()	PHP Recipe 19 function: converts text to a GIF image
GD_FN1()	Function used by Recipe 19
ImageAlter()	PHP Recipe 14 function: modifies an image

PART II

How It Works

Rather than simply supplying a selection of random letters for the Captcha, I decided it's much more natural to enter an English word, and so this recipe requires a file called *dictionary* *.txt* to be in the same directory. This file should be a list of words with one per line and each line separated by a \r\n carriage return\linefeed pair. On the companion web site to this book at *webdeveloperscookbook.com*, there's an 80,000-word *dictionary.txt* file already saved in the same Zip file as this recipe. Or you can choose to use your own sorted list of words.

Either way, the first thing the function does is load the contents of *dictionary.txt* into the variable $temps, from where all the words with a length of the value in $length are extracted into the array $dict using a foreach loop, and the Captcha word is then selected from this subset of words, as follows:

```
$file   = file_get_contents('dictionary.txt');
$temps  = explode("\r\n", $file);
$dict   = array();

foreach ($temps as $temp)
   if (strlen($temp) == $length)
      $dict[] = $temp;

$captcha = $dict[rand(0, count($dict) - 1)];
```

Next, a token is created with which the Captcha can be uniquely connected, like this:

```
$token = md5("$salt1$captcha$salt2");
```

The PHP md5() function is a one-way function that converts the input into a 32-character string in such a way that the algorithm cannot be reversed. This is why it's called a one-way function. However, instead of simply taking the dictionary word and creating an md5() hash of it, it's necessary to obfuscate things a little. This is because some people have spent a lot of time assembling dictionaries containing the hashes of every single word. Therefore, for example, the md5() hash of the word "hello" is easily looked up and is known to be the following:

```
5d41402abc4b2a76b9719d911017c592
```

Wherever this particular hash is encountered, the chances are very high indeed that it was created from the string "hello", and so it would be a cinch to crack this Captcha system. So, like I said, it's necessary to be a little sneaky by making it impossible for a dictionary crack to work.

We do this by adding additional characters to the Captcha word that only we know. Such strings of characters are called *salts*, and this recipe uses two of them for good measure. When you call the recipe, you will have to provide values for $salt1 and $salt2, which will be inserted on either side of the Captcha word chosen. For example, if you choose the strings 3$a7* and dk%%d, and the Captcha word is hello, then the string that will be passed to md5() is 3$a7*hellodk%%d, which results in the following hash:

```
99ccb37e57e885ac76b0145246ef7e8e
```

As you can see, this is a totally different string and, without knowing the two salt values, it is utterly impossible to crack without attempting brute force (multiple attempts), which would take an inconceivably long time, even using a modern supercomputer.

So, the result of creating the hash token is placed in $token, and $fname is set to point to the location where the resulting Captcha GIF file will be stored. This is based on concatenating the value supplied in $folder, the md5() token in $token, and the file extension *.gif*, as follows:

```
$fname = "$folder$token.gif";
```

The function then creates the graphic image by calling GifText() (PHP Recipe 19 from Chapter 4), with the correct values to form a shadowed word. This function also saves the image to disk when done, like this:

```
GifText($fname, $captcha, $font, $size, "444444",
    "ffffff", $size / 10, "666666");
```

To complete the Captcha creation, the image is reloaded into memory and ImageAlter() (PHP Recipe 14 from Chapter 4) is called in four different ways (and in a couple of instances multiple times) to blur, emboss, brighten, and increase its contrast. The result is then resaved back into the GIF image and an array containing three elements is returned. These are:

1. The captcha text

2. The md5() token

3. The location of the Captcha image

The code to do this is as follows, starting with loading the image and altering it in the first three lines, followed by multiple alterations, saving the image, and then returning the Captcha data:

```
$image = imagecreatefromgif($fname);
$image = ImageAlter($image, 2);
$image = ImageAlter($image, 13);

for ($j = 0 ; $j < 3 ; ++$j)
    $image = ImageAlter($image, 3);
for ($j = 0 ; $j < 2 ; ++$j)
    $image = ImageAlter($image, 5);

imagegif($image, $fname);
return array($captcha, $token, $fname);
```

How to Use It

To create a Captcha, you call up CreateCaptcha(), passing it the required values, like this:

```
$result = CreateCaptcha(26, 8, 'captcha.ttf', '',
    '!*a&K', '.fs£!+');
```

In this example, the passed values are 26 for the font size, 8 for the length of the Captcha word required, captcha.ttf for the name of a TrueType file to use, '' for the image folder to use, and !*a&K and .fs£!+ for the two salt values. You should have already uploaded a suitable TrueType font file, named *captcha.ttf*, to your server—preferably a nonstandard or script type font.

The recipe will return an array of three values with which you can display the Captcha image and create a form to request the Captcha word as text input. The first of the returned values is the Captcha word itself, and you don't actually need it other than for testing purposes. So at this point, let's forget it and concentrate on the other two returned values. The first of these is the image you need to display, like this:

```
<img src="$result[2]" />
```

You also need to embed the value of the token in a hidden field, like this:

```
<input type="hidden" name="token" value="$result[1]" />
```

Taking all this into account, the following example code creates a Captcha and then displays the Captcha image along with a form for requesting the Captcha word to be entered:

```
<?php
$result = CreateCaptcha(26, 8, 'captcha.ttf', '',
    '!*a&K', '.fs£!+');
echo <<<_END
<img src="$result[2]" /><br />
Please enter the word shown<br />
<form method="post" action="checkcaptcha.php">
<input type="hidden" name="token" value="$result[1]" />
<input type="text" name="captcha" />
<input type="submit" />
</form>
_END;
```

You may wish to save this example (giving it a filename such as *testcaptcha.php*), as you'll able to test it with an example from the following recipe. Or you can download the file using the *Download* link at *webdeveloperscookbook.com*.

If you would like to have random-length words in your Captchas, you can achieve this by modifying the function call to use the rand() function, as in the following, which will generate a Captcha of between 4 and 10 letters in length:

```
$result = CreateCaptcha(26, rand(4,10), 'captcha.ttf', '',
    '!*a&K', '.fs£!+');
```

TIP *If you ever find your Captchas are not preventing all bots anymore, perhaps because their image recognition has improved, I suggest you upload a different TrueType font and start using that. You could also modify* CreateCaptcha() *itself and introduce a few more (or use different) image manipulations.*

The Recipe

```
function CreateCaptcha($size, $length, $font,
   $folder, $salt1, $salt2)
{
   $file    = file_get_contents('dictionary.txt');
   $temps   = explode("\r\n", $file);
   $dict    = array();

   foreach ($temps as $temp)
      if (strlen($temp) == $length)
         $dict[] = $temp;

   $captcha = $dict[rand(0, count($dict) - 1)];
   $token   = md5("$salt1$captcha$salt2");
   $fname   = "$folder" . $token . ".gif";
   GifText($fname, $captcha, $font, $size, "444444",
      "ffffff", $size / 10, "666666");
   $image   = imagecreatefromgif($fname);
   $image   = ImageAlter($image, 2);
   $image   = ImageAlter($image, 13);

   for ($j = 0 ; $j < 3 ; ++$j)
      $image = ImageAlter($image, 3);
   for ($j = 0 ; $j < 2 ; ++$j)
      $image = ImageAlter($image, 5);

   imagegif($image, $fname);
   return array($captcha, $token, $fname);}
```

RECIPE 34 CheckCaptcha()

Once you have created a Captcha image and asked a user to type it in, you can use this recipe to verify their input, and determine whether they entered the correct word. Figure 6-4 shows the plug-in being used.

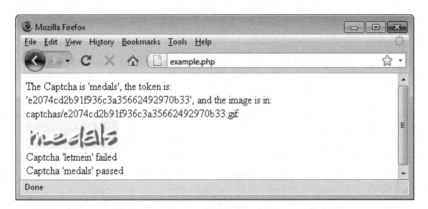

FIGURE 6-4   This recipe verifies a Captcha word entered by a user.

About the Recipe

This recipe verifies the Captcha word input by a user, in response to a request made using a Captcha created with PHP Recipe 33, CreateCaptcha(). It takes these arguments:

- **$captcha**   The Captcha as typed in by a user.
- **$token**   The token representing the current Captcha.
- **$image**   The image location of the GIF file.
- **$salt1**   The first salt string.
- **$salt2**   The second salt string.

How It Works

This function returns the result of re-creating the md5() hash from PHP Recipe 33, based on the user string provided in $captcha, and the two salts in $salt1 and $salt2, like this:

```
return $token == md5("$salt1$captcha$salt2");
```

As long as the salts are the same as when the Captcha was created, if the user has typed in the correct hash word, then the result of concatenating all three and passing them to the md5() function will be the same as the value stored in $token—in which case, a value of TRUE is returned. Otherwise, the correct word was not entered and FALSE is returned.

How to Use It

After a Captcha has been created using the previous recipe, you will have been provided with the location of a GIF image and a token representing the Captcha. Using these, you will then have displayed the image and provided a web form requesting that the user type in the word in the Captcha image. This form will now have been posted to your server, and the three items of data received will be:

- **$_POST['captcha']**   The Captcha text entered by the user.
- **$_POST['token']**   The token embedded in the hidden form field.

Using these values, the following example code will verify the Captcha word as entered by the user:

```
if (CheckCaptcha($_POST['captcha'], $_POST['token'],
   '!*a&K', '.fs£!+')) echo "Captcha verified";
else echo "Captcha failed";
```

Note that the two salts are not passed as arguments because they are a secret and only your code should know them. Just ensure that you use the same salts for both CreateCaptcha() and CheckCaptcha(); otherwise, the recipes won't work.

If you wish to test the example code (*testcaptcha.php*) in the previous recipe, type in the preceding example and save it as *checkcaptcha.php*, and it will verify the result of using the Captcha. Both of these programs can be found in the accompanying files available from the *Download* link at *webdeveloperscookbook.com*.

After using this facility for a while, you will find that your folder of Captcha images gets quite full. You may therefore wish to use code, such as the following, to clear these files out every now and then:

```
foreach (glob("*.gif") as $file)
   if (time() - filectime($file) > 300)
      unlink($file);
```

What the code does is use the glob() function to search for all files with a *.gif* extension, and if they are more than five minutes (300 seconds) old, they are removed using the unlink() function. If the files are in a different folder, you should ensure that you have first assigned that name to a variable called $folder, and that it has a trailing / (for example, using a value such as images/ if your folder is called *images*). Then, you can use the following code instead:

```
foreach (glob($folder . "*.gif") as $file)
   if (time() - filectime($file) > 300)
      unlink($file);
```

The Recipe

```
function CheckCaptcha($captcha, $token, $salt1, $salt2)
{
   return $token == md5("$salt1$captcha$salt2");
}
```

35 ValidateText()

Processing user input takes a lot of work, especially when you need data to be in a certain format or to fit within various constraints. Using this recipe, you can check user input to ensure it is the right length and contains the right types of data, whether alphabetical, numeric, or another form.

It's also highly versatile, allowing you to specify the allowed characters (and therefore those that are disallowed), and also types of characters that must be used. Figure 6-5 shows two different strings being validated.

About the Recipe

This recipe accepts a string to be validated, along with parameters describing what is and isn't allowed in the string. The function returns a two-element array on failure, the first of which is the value FALSE, and the second is an array of error messages. On success, it returns a single element with the value TRUE. It takes these arguments:

- **$text**   The text to be validated.
- **$minlength**   The minimum acceptable length.
- **$maxlength**   The maximum acceptable length.
- **$allowed**   The characters that are allowed in the text. Any characters can be entered here, including ranges indicated by using a - character, such as a-zA-Z.

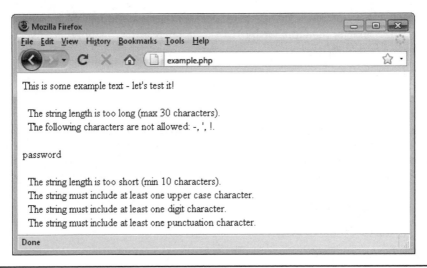

Figure 6-5   Processing form input is now easier than ever using this recipe.

- **$required**   Types of characters of which at least one of each must be in the text, out of a, 1, u, d, w, and p, which (in order) stand for <u>a</u>ny letter, <u>l</u>owercase, <u>u</u>ppercase, <u>d</u>igit, <u>w</u>ord (any letter or number), or <u>p</u>unctuation.

Variables, Arrays, and Functions

$len	Integer containing the length of $text
$error	Array of all error message strings
$result	Integer result of matching the $allowed characters
$caught	String containing matched characters from $allowed
$plural	String with the value " is", or "s are" if there is more than one match
$j	Loop counter

How It Works

This recipe sets the value of $len to the length of $text and, after initializing the array $error so it is ready to hold any error messages, checks whether $len is smaller or larger than the required minimum and maximum lengths. If either is the case, a suitable error message is added to the $error array, as follows:

```php
$len   = strlen($text);
$error = array();

if ($len < $minlength)
   $error[] = "The string length is too short " .
      "(min $minlength characters)";
```

```
elseif ($len > $maxlength)
    $error[] = "The string length is too long " .
        "(max $maxlength characters)";
```

Next, the `preg_match_all()` function is called to check for the existence of any characters *not* in the string $allowed, which contains a list of all allowed characters, including supporting ranges created using the - character so that, instead of having to use the string abcde, the equivalent of a-e is allowed. So, for example, to accept all upper- and lowercase letters, the string a-zA-Z could be used. Those characters that do not match are placed in the array $matches by the function and, from there, are then placed in the string $caught, separated by a comma/space pair so that they can be added to an error message, like this:

```
$result = preg_match_all("/([^$allowed])/", $text, $matches);
$caught = implode(array_unique($matches[1]), ', ');
```

The string variable $plural is then assigned the value " is" if there is a single match, or "s are" if there is more than one. This is then used when constructing the error message so that it reads grammatically, using one or other of the forms (the value of $plural is shown in bold): "The following character **is** not allowed", "The following characters **are** not allowed", as follows:

```
$plural = strlen($caught) > 1 ? $plural = "s are" : " is";

if ($result) $error[] = "The following character$plural " .
    "not allowed: " . $caught;
```

Then, a `for` loop is entered for iterating through all the characters in the variable $required, which can contain any or all of the letters a, l, u, d, w, or p, which stand for any letter, lowercase, uppercase, digit, word (any letter or number), or punctuation. This is all handled within a `switch` statement, as follows:

```
for ($j = 0 ; $j < strlen($required) ; ++$j)
{
    switch(substr(strtolower($required), $j, 1))
    {
        case "a": $regex = "a-zA-Z"; $str = "letter";
                break;
        case "l": $regex = "a-z";    $str = "lower case";
                break;
        case "u": $regex = "A-Z";    $str = "upper case";
                break;
        case "d": $regex = "0-9";    $str = "digit";
                break;
        case "w": $regex = "\w";     $str = "letter, number or _";
                break;
        case "p": $regex = "\W";     $str = "punctuation";
                break;
    }
```

Depending on which letter is being processed, the variable $regex is assigned the correct value to enable the following preg_match() call to ensure that at least one of that character type is included in the string:

```
if (!preg_match("/[$regex]/", $text))
    $error[] = "The string must include at least one " .
      "$str character";
```

This feature is very useful in cases where a certain type of input is required, such as a number, or maybe a password that must have at least one each of a letter, number, and punctuation character.

As the variable's name indicates, all characters in $required must exist in the string being validated. Therefore, if any one of the types of characters described by $required is not encountered, another error message is added to the $error array.

Finally, if $error has no messages in it, then no errors were encountered, so a single-element array containing the value TRUE is returned. Otherwise, a two-element array is returned, the first of which is the value FALSE and the second is the array of error messages:

```
if (count($error)) return array(FALSE, $error);
else                return array(TRUE);
```

How to Use It

To validate a user-supplied string, call the ValidateText() function, giving it the string to validate and various parameters indicating which characters are both allowed and required.

For example, to ensure that a string to be used for a password has one each of a lowercase, uppercase, digit, and punctuation character, and is at least 6 and no more than 16 characters long, you could use code such as the following, where $text is extracted from the form input password:

```
echo "<form method='post' action='$_SERVER[PHP_SELF]'>";
echo "<input  type='text'   name='password' />";
echo "<input  type='submit' /></form>";

if (isset($_POST['password']))
{
    $text     = $_POST['password'];
    $allowed  = "a-zA-Z0-9 !&*+=:;@~#";
    $required = "ludp";
    $result   = ValidateText($text, 10, 16, $allowed, $required);

    if ($result[0] == FALSE)
        for ($j = 0 ; $j < count($result[1]) ; ++$j)
            echo $result[1][$j] . ".<br>";
    else  echo "Password validated";
}
```

You may wish to save this file with a filename such as *validate.php,* then you can call it up in your browser and view the result of entering different values. A copy of this file is also in the download archive, available at *webdeveloperscookbook.com.*

In this code, the string variable $allowed sets the recipe to accept any of the letters of any case, digits, the space character, and any characters out of ! &*+=: ;@~ and #. The $required string simultaneously tells the code that there must be at least one lowercase letter, one uppercase letter, one digit, and one punctuation character.

Upon the function's return, if the first element of the array $result is FALSE, then validation failed and so the strings in the array stored in the second element are displayed— they are the error messages returned by the recipe. But if the first element is TRUE, validation succeeded.

Here's another example. Because $allowed may include regular expression operators such as \w (which means any letter or digit, or the _ character), you could use the recipe to ensure that a username (determined by you) may only include letters, digits, underlines, periods, and hyphens (and cannot be comprised only of punctuation), and has been correctly entered, like this:

```
$result = ValidateText($username, 4, 20,  "\w\.\-", "w");
```

In this case, the $allowed argument of \w means "allow letters, digits, and the underline," while \ . and \ - also allow the period and hyphen. The $required parameter of a ensures there is at least one letter, which can be of either case.

The Recipe

```
function ValidateText($text, $minlength, $maxlength,
   $allowed, $required)
{
   $len   = strlen($text);
   $error = array();

   if ($len < $minlength)
      $error[] = "The string length is too short " .
         "(min $minlength characters)";
   elseif ($len > $maxlength)
      $error[] = "The string length is too long " .
         "(max $maxlength characters)";

   $result = preg_match_all("/([^$allowed])/", $text, $matches);
   $caught = implode(array_unique($matches[1]), ', ');
   $plural = strlen($caught) > 1 ? $plural = "s are" : " is";

   if ($result) $error[] = "The following character$plural " .
      "not allowed: " . $caught;

   for ($j = 0 ; $j < strlen($required) ; ++$j)
   {
      switch(substr(strtolower($required), $j, 1))
      {
         case "a": $regex = "a-zA-Z"; $str = "letter";
               break;
```

```
        case "l": $regex = "a-z";    $str = "lower case";
                break;
        case "u": $regex = "A-Z";    $str = "upper case";
                break;
        case "d": $regex = "0-9";    $str = "digit";
                break;
        case "w": $regex = "\w";     $str = "letter or number";
                break;
        case "p": $regex = "\W";     $str = "punctuation";
                break;
    }

    if (!preg_match("/[$regex]/", $text))
        $error[] = "The string must include at least one " .
            "$str character";
    }

if (count($error)) return array(FALSE, $error);
else                return array(TRUE);
}
```

36 ValidateEmail()

Quite often people will make mistakes when entering their e-mail address into a web form. This is also another common area where some users just enter rubbish to see what happens. To catch these things, you can use this recipe to at least check whether the format of an e-mail address supplied to you is valid, as shown in Figure 6-6.

About the Recipe

This recipe accepts an e-mail address whose format requires validating. On success, it returns TRUE; otherwise, it returns FALSE. It takes this argument:

- **$email**   The e-mail address to be validated.

The email address: 'paul.smith@smithandson.com' validates
The email address: 'jdoe@usacom' does not validate

Figure 6-6   Using this recipe, you can ensure that the format of an e-mail address is valid.

Variables, Arrays, and Functions

`$at`	Integer pointing to the position of the @ sign
`$left`	String containing the left half of the e-mail address
`$right`	String containing the right half of the e-mail address
`$res1`	Array result from validating `$left`
`$res2`	Array result from validating `$right`
`ValidateText()`	PHP Recipe 35: function to validate a string

How It Works

The most obvious required part of an e-mail address is the @ symbol, so the first thing this recipe does is locate its position and store it in the variable $at. If $at is given the value FALSE, or if the length of $email is less than the minimum of six characters that an e-mail address can have (*a@b.cc*), then the value FALSE is returned because the address is already found to be invalid, as follows:

```
$at = strrpos($email, '@');

if (!$at || strlen($email) < 6) return FALSE;
```

Next, the e-mail address is split into the two halves either side of the position pointed to by $at using the substr() function. The left portion is assigned to the variable $left and the right to the variable $right, like this:

```
$left  = substr($email, 0, $at);
$right = substr($email, $at + 1);
```

Then, Recipe 35, ValidateText(), is called to evaluate each half. The left half must be between 1 and 64 characters in length and may comprise any letters, digits, underlines, periods, and + or - symbols. This is enforced using the argument of \w\.\+\-. Also, at least one letter must be included, so the second argument of a checks for that.

The right half of an e-mail address must be between 1 and 255 characters in length and may be comprised of any mix of letters, digits, hyphens, or periods. This validation is accomplished using the argument \a-zA-Z0-9\.\-. And to ensure at least one letter appears in the domain, a second argument of a is supplied. The results of these two validations are placed in the arrays $res1 and $res2, like this:

```
$res1 = ValidateText($left,  1, 64,  "\w\.\+\-",       "a");
$res2 = ValidateText($right, 1, 255, "\a-zA-Z0-9\.\-", "a");
```

Final validation is achieved by ensuring there is at least one period in the right half of the e-mail address and that both the previous two validations were also successful. If so, then TRUE is returned; otherwise, FALSE is returned:

```
if (!strpos($right, '.') || !$res1[0] || !$res2[0])
    return FALSE;
else return TRUE;
```

How to Use It

To validate an e-mail address, just pass it to ValidateEmail(), which will return TRUE if successful; otherwise, it will return FALSE, like this:

```
if (ValidateEmail($email)) echo "Validation succeeded";
```

The Recipe

```
function ValidateEmail($email)
{
    $at = strrpos($email, '@');

    if (!$at || strlen($email) < 3) return FALSE;

    $left  = substr($email, 0, $at);
    $right = substr($email, $at + 1);
    $res1  = ValidateText($left,  1, 64,  "\w\.\+\-",      "a");
    $res2  = ValidateText($right, 1, 255, "\a-zA-Z0-9\.\-", "a");

    if (!strpos($right, '.') || !$res1[0] || !$res2[0])
        return FALSE;
    else return TRUE;
}
```

RECIPE 37 SpamCatch()

Even with a strong Captcha system in place, you will still find users trying to manually spam your web site. They tend to be people who discover your site through a very specific search engine query, for which they would like their own site to also rank well, and they hope that by adding a link back to their site from yours this will happen.

Using this recipe, you can specify a set of keywords that will trigger spam detection, and then use the level of spam certainty returned by the function to decide whether to ignore a user post. Figure 6-7 illustrates the plug-in in action.

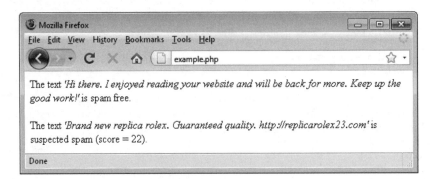

FIGURE 6-7 This recipe will go a long way toward further reducing spam on your web site.

About the Recipe

This recipe accepts a user-supplied string and matches it against a list of keywords to determine the likelihood that the string contains spam. It takes these arguments:

- `$text` The e-mail address to be validated.
- `$words` An array of keywords against which to check.

How It Works

This is another of those extremely short and sweet, yet exceedingly powerful, recipes. What it does is take the text you supply it, along with the array of keywords, and calls PHP Recipe 5, `WordSelector()`, with a blank replace string. This has the effect of removing every matching word from the string. It's then a simple matter to subtract the length of the new string from the original one and return the difference, like this:

```
return strlen($text) - strlen(WordSelector($text, $words, ''));
```

The larger the difference, the more words are removed from the string, and so the more the keywords that have matched, the more likely it is that the string contained spam. If there is no difference, then no words matched and the string is considered spam-free.

How to Use It

To use this recipe well, you need to first create your array of trigger keywords. You should base this on words unique to user spam that you have already received, with code such as the following to filter user posts:

```
$words  = array('rolex', 'replica', 'loan', 'mortgage', 'viagra',
                'cialis', 'acai', 'free', 'stock', 'guaranteed',
                'refinancing', 'cartier', 'manhood', 'drugs');
if (SpamCatch($text, $words) < 15) echo "Probably not spam";
else                               echo "Probably spam";
```

Of course, this is a very small set of keywords and you will very likely need to come up with your own much larger list, which you will probably compile over time, and which may include large numbers of keywords unsuitable for publication in this book.

You may also wish to experiment with the spam score of 15 used earlier to distinguish between spam and non-spam. Set it lower if too much is getting through, or higher if too many non-spams are being rejected.

The Recipe

```
function SpamCatch($text, $words)
{
    return strlen($text) - strlen(WordSelector($text, $words, ''));
}
```

38 SendEmail()

Often after receiving user input, you need to send an e-mail, perhaps to yourself, to a colleague, or maybe to the e-mail submitter, thanking them for their input.

Sending an e-mail from your server isn't too hard using PHP's built-in `mail()` function. But if you want to send CCs or BCCs, you have to start assembling a header, which starts getting complicated. Using this recipe, all of that is handled for you. You just supply the message, subject lines, and e-mail addresses of all recipients and it gets on with sending the e-mail for you. You can even specify a different reply-to address if needed. Figure 6-8 shows the code in use.

About the Recipe

This recipe accepts a string containing the text of an e-mail to send, along with another for a subject line, and various other arguments specifying the e-mail addresses of people to whom it should also be sent. It takes these arguments:

- **$message**   The text of the e-mail.
- **$subject**   The e-mail's subject.
- **$priority**   The message's priority: 1 (high) – 5 (low), or leave it blank for none.
- **$from**   The e-mail address of the sender.
- **$replyto**   The e-mail address to which replies should be addressed.
- **$to**   The e-mail address of the recipient.
- **$cc**   An array of e-mail addresses for CC copies.
- **$bcc**   An array of e-mail addresses for Blind CC copies (no recipient will see any BCC e-mail addresses in the message they receive).
- **$type**   If set to "HTML," the e-mail will be sent in HTML format; otherwise, it will be sent as text.

Variables, Arrays, and Functions

$headers	String containing additional headers to be sent

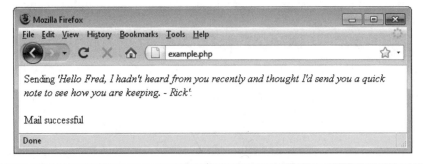

FIGURE 6-8   Sending an e-mail with this recipe is a single-line function call.

How It Works

A lot of the work is handled by the `mail()` function built into PHP, but it needs help constructing additional headers because it only supports arguments of *recipient, subject, message,* and *headers.*

Therefore, this recipe starts by assigning the string variable $headers the value *From:,* followed by the value in $from and a \r\n carriage return\linefeed pair, like this:

```
$headers = "From: $from\r\n";
```

If this is not done, the e-mail could be sent as if the sender were the web server itself. Next, if the value of $type is set to "HTML", the correct headers to send the e-mail using HTML are appended to $headers:

```
if (strtolower($type) == "html")
{
    $headers .= "MIME-Version: 1.0\r\n";
    $headers .= "Content-type: text/html; charset=iso-8859-1\r\n";
}
```

After that, if $priority has a value greater than 0, then an *X-Priority:* header is appended to $headers. Also, if the $replyto variable has a value, then the correct *Reply-To:* header is appended to $headers, as follows:

```
if ($priority > 0)   $headers .= "X-Priority: $priority\r\n";
if ($replyto != "")  $headers .= "Reply-To: $replyto\r\n";
```

Then, the CC and BCC headers are created by iterating through the arrays of e-mail addresses in $cc and $bcc (if any), appending each to the relevant header line, like this:

```
if (count($cc))
{
    $headers .= "Cc: ";
       for ($j = 0 ; $j < count($cc) ; ++$j)
           $headers .= $cc[$j] . ",";
    $headers = substr($headers, 0, -1) . "\r\n";
}

if (count($bcc))
{
    $headers .= "Bcc: ";
       for ($j = 0 ; $j < count($bcc) ; ++$j)
           $headers .= $bcc[$j] . ",";
    $headers = substr($headers, 0, -1) . "\r\n";
}
```

Finally, the `mail()` function is called with the values in $to, $subject, and $message, but now with a properly formatted sequence of headers in $headers to handle the other parameters:

```
return mail($to, $subject, $message, $headers);
```

How to Use It

Sending an e-mail with this code is as easy as the following example, in which *me@myserver*
.com is the sender's e-mail address, and *rick@otherserver.net* is the recipient's:

```
if (SendEmail($message, $subject, '', 'me@myserver.com', '',
    'rick@otherserver.net', NULL, NULL, ''))
        echo "Mail successful";
```

Or, to add a CC line, this might change to the following, noting that the CC and BCC
arguments must be passed as arrays of e-mail addresses:

```
if (SendEmail($message, $subject, '', 'me@myserver.com', '',
    'rick@otherserver.net', array('bill@test12.com'), NULL, ''))
        echo "Mail successful";
```

Tip *If, when you use this recipe, you get an error such as* Warning: mail() [function.mail]: Failed
to connect to mailserver at "localhost" port 25, *then you don't have your server properly
configured for e-mail. In fact, if you are using Zend Server CE and/or a web development server,
you may not actually want to run a mail server on that machine anyway, and should probably
test this code on a server already configured for mail.*

The Recipe

```
function SendEmail($message, $subject, $priority, $from,
    $replyto, $to, $cc, $bcc, $type)
{
    $headers = "From: $from\r\n";

    if (strtolower($type) == "html")
    {
        $headers .= "MIME-Version: 1.0\r\n";
        $headers .= "Content-type: text/html; charset=iso-8859-1\r\n";
    }

    if ($priority > 0)  $headers .= "X-Priority: $priority\r\n";
    if ($replyto != "") $headers .= "Reply-To: $replyto\r\n";

    if (count($cc))
    {
        $headers .= "Cc: ";
            for ($j = 0 ; $j < count($cc) ; ++$j)
                $headers .= $cc[$j] . ",";
        $headers = substr($headers, 0, -1) . "\r\n";
    }

    if (count($bcc))
    {
        $headers .= "Bcc: ";
            for ($j = 0 ; $j < count($bcc) ; ++$j)
```

```
            $headers .= $bcc[$j] . ",";
        $headers = substr($headers, 0, -1) . "\r\n";
    }

    return mail($to, $subject, $message, $headers);
}
```

BBCode( )

Because of the risks involved with allowing users to enter HTML via a web form, alternatives had to be invented that would offer freedom of textual formatting without the risk of server hacking. One of the first and most popular of these systems was BB Code, which stands for Bulletin Board Code.

Because it is used on web forums all over the Internet, your users will be very familiar with BB Code, and using this recipe, you can now fully support it on your web site—including making URLs clickable, as you can see in Figure 6-9.

About the Recipe

This recipe accepts a string containing BB Code and returns it translated into safe HTML. It takes this argument:

- **$string**   The string to translate.

Variables, Arrays, and Functions

$from	Array containing the supported BB Codes
$to	Array containing the HTML equivalents to BB Code

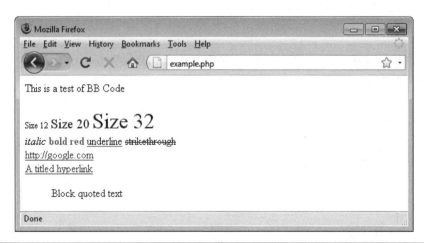

FIGURE 6-9   BB Code is a great way to allow users the ability to control their HTML layout without worrying about getting hacked.

How It Works

This recipe starts by replacing all occurrences found in the string $string from the array $from with those in the array $to using the str_replace() function. Here are the two arrays and the str_replace() call:

```
$from    = array('[b]', '[/b]',    '[i]', '[/i]',
                  '[u]', '[/u]',    '[s]', '[/s]',
                  '[quote]',        '[/quote]',
                  '[code]',         '[/code]',
                  '[img]',          '[/img]',
                  '[/size]',        '[/color]',
                  '[/url]');
$to      = array('<b>', '</b>',    '<i>', '</i>',
                  '<u>', '</u>',    '<s>', '</s>',
                  '<blockquote>', '</blockquote>',
                  '<pre>',          '</pre>',
                  '<img src="',     '" />',
                  '</span>',        '</font>',
                  '</a>');
$string = str_replace($from, $to, $string);
```

It then uses the preg_replace() function four times to perform slightly more complex translations, like this:

```
$string = str_replace($from, $to, $string);
$string = preg_replace("/\[size=([\d]+)\]/",
    "<span style=\"font-size:$1px\">", $string);
$string = preg_replace("/\[color=([^\]]+)\]/",
    "<font color='$1'>", $string);
$string = preg_replace("/\[url\]([^\[]*)<\/a>/",
    "<a href='$1'>$1</a>", $string);
$string = preg_replace("/\[url=([^\]]*)]/",
    "<a href='$1'>", $string);
```

These lines of code perform the following actions:

- Convert any [size=??] codes to CSS font-size:??px tags
- Convert any [color=??] codes to <font color='??'> HTML tags
- Convert any [url]??[/url] codes to <a href='??'>??</a> HTML tags
- Convert any [url=??] codes to <a href='??'> HTML tags

With all translations completed, the modified string is returned. If no modifications were made, then the original string is returned:

```
return $string;
```

How to Use It

To use this recipe, just pass the function BBCode() some text to be translated and it will be returned to the calling code. If there is BB Code in the text, it will be replaced with matching

HTML and/or CSS tags otherwise, it will be returned unchanged. The following example populates $text with some text, including BB Code, and then calls the recipe to display it:

```
$text = <<<_END
This is a test of BB Code
[size=12]Size 12[/size]
[size=20]Size 20[/size]
[size=32]Size 32[/size]
[i]italic[/i]
[color=red][b]bold red[/b][/color]
[u]underline[/u]
[s]strikethrough[/s]
[url]http://google.com[/url]
[url=http://yahoo.com]A titled hyperlink[/url]
[quote]Block quoted text[/quote]
_END;

echo BBCode($text);
```

The list of BB Codes supported by this recipe and the actions they perform are shown in Table 6-1.

I should mention that I believe BB Code's support for images and URLs represents a potential security risk and I would recommend using Pound Code (the next recipe) instead. Or, on a site that makes use of GET requests, if you must support BB Code, you should consider removing or commenting out the sections supporting images and URLs. I have more to say on this matter in the "How to Use It" section of the Pound Code recipe, following.

You must also remember that this recipe provides support for BB Code but *does not* reject HTML code. For that, you need to first run inputted text through functions to strip out HTML and JavaScript, which would probably look like this:

```
$text = htmlentities(strip_tags($text));
```

Opening BB Code	Closing BB Code	Action
[b]	[/b]	Bold face on and off
[i]	[/i]	Italics on and off
[u]	[/u]	Underline on and off
[s]	[/s]	Strikethrough on and off
[quote]	[/quote]	Blockquote on and off
[code]	[/code]	Preformatted text on and off
[img] *url*	[/img]	Start and end of an image URL
[url] *url*	[/url]	Start and end of a hyperlink
[url=*url*] *text*	[/url]	Start and end of a hyperlink (display *text* not *url*)
[size=??]	[/size]	Font size = ?? and End font size
[color=??]	[/size]	Font color = ?? and End font color

TABLE 6-1 List of BB Codes Supported by this Recipe

The strip_tags() function removes all HTML tags from a string, and htmlentities() turns all quotation marks and other punctuation into harmless entities that will be displayed and not acted upon.

The Recipe

```
function BBCode($string)
{
    $from   = array('[b]', '[/b]',   '[i]', '[/i]',
                    '[u]', '[/u]',   '[s]', '[/s]',
                    '[quote]',       '[/quote]',
                    '[code]',        '[/code]',
                    '[img]',         '[/img]',
                    '[/size]',       '[/color]',
                    '[/url]');
    $to     = array('<b>', '</b>',   '<i>', '</i>',
                    '<u>', '</u>',   '<s>', '</s>',
                    '<blockquote>', '</blockquote>',
                    '<pre>',        '</pre>',
                    '<img src="',    '" />',
                    '</span>',      '</font>',
                    '</a>');
    $string = str_replace($from, $to, $string);
    $string = preg_replace("/\[size=((\d)+)\]/",
        "<span style=\"font-size:$1px\">", $string);
    $string = preg_replace("/\[color=([^\]]+)\]/",
        "<font color='$1'>", $string);
    $string = preg_replace("/\[url\]([^\[]*)<\/a>/",
        "<a href='$1'>$1</a>", $string);
    $string = preg_replace("/\[url=([^\]]*)]/",
        "<a href='$1'>", $string);
    return $string;
}
```

PoundCode()

BB Code is all well and good, but in my opinion it makes for a lot of typing of square brackets. So I invented a sleeker and simpler code called Pound Code (or Hash Code outside of the USA). With it, you don't need to surround a code with brackets, instead you just type a # symbol, followed by the action you want to achieve, and the recipe works out the rest for you. Figure 6-10 shows the result.

About the Recipe

This recipe accepts a string containing Pound Code and returns it translated into safe HTML. It takes this argument:

- **$text** The string to translate.

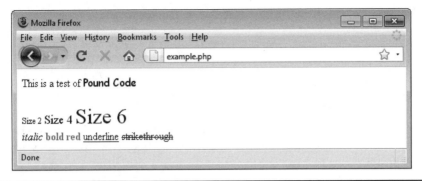

FIGURE 6-10   Pound Code is easier than BB Code and offers more flexibility.

Variables, Arrays, and Functions

$names	Array containing the supported short font names
$fonts	Array containing the HTML long names of $names
$to	Array containing the strings required to translate the short font codes to HTML

How It Works

This recipe performs in a similar way to the BB Code recipe, but starts off by offering nine different font styles. It takes the short codes in $names and, using the long names of each stored in $fonts, creates <font face='fontname'> strings for all of them using a for loop to iterate through them, placing the results in the array $to, as follows:

```
$names = array('#georgia', '#arial',   '#courier',
               '#script',  '#impact',  '#comic',
               '#chicago', '#verdana', '#times');
$fonts = array('Georgia',  'Arial',    'Courier New',
               'Script',   'Impact',   'Comic Sans MS',
               'Chicago',  'Verdana',  'Times New Roman');
$to    = array();

for ($j = 0 ; $j < count($names) ; ++$j)
   $to[] = "<font face='$fonts[$j]'>";
```

Then, the function str_ireplace() is called to replace all occurrences found, regardless of whether they are in upper- or lowercase, and the preg_replace() function is called four times to perform the more complex translations, like this:

```
$text = str_ireplace($names,             $to,                      $text);
$text = preg_replace('/#([bius])-/i', "</$1>",                    $text);
$text = preg_replace('/#([bius])/i',  "<$1>",                     $text);
$text = preg_replace('/#([1-7])/',     "<font size='$1'>",  $text);
$text = preg_replace('/#([a-z]+)/i',   "<font color='$1'>", $text);
$text = str_replace( '#-',             "</font>",                $text);
```

The actions of the preg_replace() calls are as follows:

- Convert any #b-, #i-, #u-, or #s- codes into , </i>, </u>, or </s>
- Convert any #b, #i, #u, or #s codes into , <i>, <u>, or <s>
- Convert any of #1 to #7 into <font size='1'> through <font size='7'>
- Convert any other #code into <font color='code'>

Finally, any instances of #- are translated into </font>. Then, with all translations completed, the modified string is returned. If no modifications were made, the original string is returned:

```
$text = str_replace( '#-', "</font>", $text);
return $text;
```

How to Use It

To use this recipe, just pass it the code that needs to be translated. If it includes any Pound Code, the returned result will be modified accordingly; otherwise, it will be the same as the original. In the following example, $string is populated with some text and Pound Code, and then passed to the recipe:

```
$string = <<<_END
This is a test of #comicPound Code#-
#2Size 2#-
#4Size 4#-
#6Size 6#-
#iitalic#i-
#red#bbold red#b-#-
#uunderline#u-
#sstrikethrough#s-
_END;

echo PoundCode($string);
```

The list of Pound Codes supported by this recipe and the actions they perform are shown in Table 6-2. If your users are new to it, you might wish to copy this table to your web site.

Note that I have deliberately not offered the facility for users to include either image or hyperlink URLs, and that's for very good security reasons. Based on many years of experience in writing chat room software, you'd be amazed how often programmers put things in GET requests (tails of posted data appended to URLs, also known as a *query string*), thinking only the user can see them. This can sometimes even include password or other login details!

Opening # Code	Closing # Code	Action
#b	#b-	Bold face on and off.
#i	#i-	Italics on and off.
#u	#u-	Underline on and off.
#s	#s-	Strikethrough on and off.
#*font*	#-	Change to the *font* name provided (out of #arial, #chicago, #comic, #courier, #georgia, #impact, #script, #times, and #verdana). The #- code reverts to the previous font.
#*color*	#-	Change to any legitimate HTML *color* name (such as #red or #purple, and so on). The #- code reverts to the previous font color.
#1-#7	#-	Change to an HTML font size between 1 and 7. The #- code reverts to the previous font size.

TABLE 6-2   List of Pound Codes Supported by this Recipe

The problem with this is that if you allow an image to be displayed on that web site from a third-party server, then the current page's URL will be sent to the other server where it can be saved in the log files. The same goes for any users clicking links to third-party sites. The full details of the page they are on will be sent to the other server by their browser, and if either of these includes login details or a session ID embedded in a GET query string, the other server will gain access to it.

So, if your site uses GET requests, the proper way to do this is to write a routine to retrieve the image from the other server and then display it from a local cache on your own server without any GET query string appended to the URL. While for URLs, you should create a redirection link on your web site and send your users off via that, also ensuring there is no GET query string. This is one reason why (apart from the fact that I wrote it and think it's easier to use) I would generally recommend Pound Code over BB Code.

In a similar way to the previous one, this recipe *does not* reject HTML code, and so you will probably first want to run inputted text through functions to strip out HTML and JavaScript such as these:

```
$string = htmlentities(strip_tags($string));
```

The strip_tags() function removes all HTML tags from a string, and htmlentities() turns all quotation marks and other punctuation into harmless entities that will be displayed and not acted upon.

The Recipe

```
function PoundCode($text)
{
    $names = array('#georgia', '#arial',   '#courier',
                   '#script',  '#impact',  '#comic',
                   '#chicago', '#verdana', '#times');
    $fonts = array('Georgia',  'Arial',    'Courier New',
                   'Script',   'Impact',   'Comic Sans MS',
                   'Chicago',  'Verdana',  'Times New Roman');
    $to    = array();

    for ($j = 0 ; $j < count($names) ; ++$j)
       $to[] = "<font face='$fonts[$j]'>";

    $text = str_ireplace($names,            $to,                 $text);
    $text = preg_replace('/#([bius])-/i',   "</$1>",             $text);
    $text = preg_replace('/#([bius])/i',    "<$1>",              $text);
    $text = preg_replace('/#([1-7])/',      "<font size='$1'>",  $text);
    $text = preg_replace('/#([a-z]+)/i',    "<font color='$1'>", $text);
    $text = str_replace( '#-',              "</font>",           $text);

    return $text;
}
```

CHAPTER 7

The Internet

When you create a web site, rather than existing on its own, it becomes part of the wider Internet as a whole. This means people will interact with it in many ways, from bookmarking pages they like to subscribing to RSS feeds. While other web sites may wish to exchange links with you to help pool and build traffic, Twitter users may want to tweet about something on your site and so on.

This chapter provides a range of recipes to help integrate your new property into the Internet community at large, including link management, creating short URLs, converting between HTML and RSS, adapting a site to mobile browsers, and more.

RECIPE 41 · LookupLinks( )

When building up a web site, and especially if the marketing budget is tight, you often have to embark on a campaign of link exchanges with other sites. But tracking all those link exchanges to ensure the other sites keep their end of the deal is time-consuming. However, with this recipe you simply pass an array of one or more links that should be present on a particular web page and you will be informed whether those links are all in place. Figure 7-1

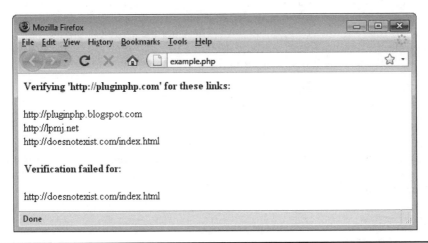

FIGURE 7-1   This recipe tests whether certain links are present on a particular web page.

shows the recipe in action; two of the links have passed, but a link to *http://doesnotexist.com/ index.html* is not found on a web page.

About the Recipe

This recipe accepts the URL of a web page to check, along with a set of links that ought to be present on it. If all the links are present, it returns an array with the single value TRUE; otherwise, it returns a two-element array of which the first element is FALSE. The second is an array containing all the links that were not present. It takes these arguments:

- **$url**   A string containing the URL of a page to check.
- **$links**   An array of links to look for on the page at $url.

Variables, Arrays, and Functions

$results	Array containing all the links found at $url
$missing	Array containing any links passed in $links that are not present in $results
$failed	Integer counter that indexes into $missing, incrementing on each failed match
$link	String containing the current link being processed, as extracted from $links
GetLinksFromURL()	PHP Recipe 22: This function returns all the links at a given URL
RelToAbsURL()	PHP Recipe 21: This function converts a relative to an absolute URL and is used by Recipe 22

How It Works

The first thing this recipe does is call PHP Recipe 22, GetLinksFromURL(), to fetch all the links within the page supplied in the variable $url. All links found are then placed in the array $results. Next, a couple of variables are initialized ready for checking, whether these links include the ones being looked for. These are the array $missing, which will hold any links that are not found, and the integer $failed, which is set to zero and will be incremented when any link is determined to not be present, as follows:

```
$results = GetLinksFromURL($url);
$missing = array();
$failed  = 0;
```

Then, a foreach loop iterates through all the returned links, temporarily placing each in the string variable $link, where it is then checked against the array of all links in $results, using the function in_array(). Any that are not found are placed in $missing and the array pointer $failed is incremented, like this:

```
foreach($links as $link)
   if (!in_array($link, $results))
      $missing[$failed++] = $link;
```

After this checking, if any links are not found, then a two-element array is returned, the first element of which is FALSE, and the second is an array containing all the links that failed the check. Otherwise, a single-element array is returned, containing the value TRUE, as follows:

```
if ($failed == 0) return array(TRUE);
else return array(FALSE, $missing);
```

How to Use It

To use this recipe, you should supply a URL to be checked and a list of links that should be included within the page at that URL, like this:

```
$url    = "http://webdeveloperscookbook.com";
$links  = array("http://html5formobile.com",
                "http://lpmj.net",
                "http://doesnotexist.com/index.html");
$result = LookupLinks($url, $links);
```

If the value in $result[0] is TRUE, then all the links are present and correct. But if $result[0] is FALSE, then $result[1] will contain an array of all failed links. You can check for these conditions using code such as the following, which employs a for loop to iterate through the failed links:

```
if ($result[0]) echo "All links verified";
else
{
   echo "<br /><b>Verification failed for:<br />";
   for ($j = 0 ; $j < count($result[1]) ; ++$j)
      echo $result[1][$j] . "<br />";
}
```

The Recipe

```
function LookupLinks($url, $links)
{
   $results = GetLinksFromURL($url);
   $missing = array();
   $failed  = 0;

   foreach($links as $link)
      if (!in_array($link, $results))
         $missing[$failed++] = $link;

   if ($failed == 0) return array(TRUE);
   else return array(FALSE, $missing);
}
```

GetTitleFromURL()

Sometimes you want to know what the title of a web page is. The following recipe, PHP Recipe 43 (following), can be used to automatically link back to referring web sites. Using this code in combination with it, it's possible to link back using the page's title. Figure 7-2 shows the title being fetched from the Yahoo! News home page.

About the Recipe

This recipe accepts the URL of a web page whose title is to be extracted and returns the title. It takes this argument:

- **$page** A string containing the URL of a page to check.

Variables, Arrays, and Functions

$contents	String containing the contents of $page

How It Works

This simple recipe calls get_file_contents() to load the contents of $page into the string variable $contents. If for any reason the page could not be read in, then FALSE is returned, like this:

```
$contents = @file_get_contents($page);
if (!$contents) return FALSE;
```

Otherwise, preg_match() is called to extract the contents between the page's <title> and </title> tags. This is denoted by the (.*) in the expression passed to the function, like this:

```
preg_match("/<title>(.*)<\/title>/i", $contents, $matches);
```

Of course, some pages may not include a title, meaning this recipe may fail, so before returning, it checks whether a title has been successfully extracted, and if so, the information

FIGURE 7-2 When you need to know the title of a web page, you can call this recipe.

needed as a result of calling the function is placed in the second element of the array
$matches, which is then returned. Otherwise, FALSE is returned, as follows:

```
if (count($matches)) return $matches[1];
else return FALSE;
```

How to Use It
To extract the title from a page, you can call this recipe in the following way:

```
$page   = "http://news.yahoo.com";
$result = GetTitleFromURL($page);
```

Then, to act on the value returned, use code such as this:

```
if (!$result) echo "The URL could not be accessed";
else          echo "The title is: $result";
```

The Recipe
```
function GetTitleFromURL($page)
{
   $contents = @file_get_contents($page);
   if (!$contents) return FALSE;

   preg_match("/<title>(.*)<\/title>/i", $contents, $matches);

   if (count($matches)) return $matches[1];
   else return FALSE;
}
```

AutoBackLinks( )
A traffic-building technique that is known to work is to offer automatic back-links to sites
that link to yours. Using this program, providing that facility is extremely easy and will
help you build more traffic with a minimum of extra work. Figure 7-3 shows example
output from this recipe.

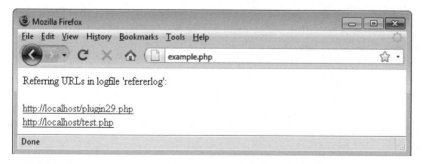

FIGURE 7-3   With this recipe, you can automatically link back to sites that link to yours.

About the Recipe

This recipe accepts the name of a file used as a data file for storing details about sites linking to the current web page. This will be a file created by PHP Recipe 30, RefererLog(). It takes this argument:

- **$filename**   The file and/or path name to read.

Variables, Arrays, and Functions

$inbound	Array containing all the inbound links in the log file
$logfile	String containing the contents of $filename
$links	Array of data extracted from $logfile
$key	String containing a link extracted from $links
$val	String containing the number of visitors who came from $key

How It Works

This recipe assumes you are already using PHP Recipe 30, RefererLog(), to track inbound links to a web page and that you've already specified a data file where the data is being stored, which you have also passed to this function in $filename.

What it does is then read the data file into the string variable $logfile. If the file is unreadable (perhaps because it doesn't yet exist), a single-element array is returned with the value FALSE by this line:

```
if (!file_exists($filename)) return array(FALSE);
```

Otherwise, $logfile is split into lines at the linefeed characters, \n, using the explode() function, and then the lines are placed in the array $links. At this point, many of the links in $links will be repeated due to multiple visitors coming from a referring page, so the array_count_values() function is called, which returns an array using the values of $links as keys, and each unique key's frequency as values. The following three lines perform these actions:

```
$logfile = file_get_contents($filename);
$links   = explode("\n", rtrim($logfile));
$links   = array_count_values($links);
```

So far, this code has the effect of determining the popularity of each referring page by counting the number of occurrences of each. Afterward, the result is placed back in the array $links, and then arsort() is called to sort the array numerically in *reverse* order, so that those referring URLs with the most counts come first, like this:

```
arsort($links, SORT_NUMERIC);
```

Next, a foreach loop is initiated to iterate through all the elements of $links, which are placed in $key and $val ($key for the link and $val for its count, although the latter is no longer needed and is ignored), removing all the entries listed as " No Referer", since they must also be ignored. All other links are added to the array $inbound, like this:

```
foreach ($links as $key => $val)
   if ($key != " No Referer")
      $inbound[] = $key;
```

At this point, the $inbound array now contains a list of all the referring URLs in order of numbers of visitors sent by each, so a two-element array is returned by the final line of code. The first element of this is TRUE, while the second is the array $inbound.

How to Use It

To extract all referring pages from the log file, use code such as this:

```
$logfile = "refer.log";
$results = AutoBackLinks($logfile);
```

$results will now be an array with either one element, FALSE, in which case no referring links were found, or it will be a two-element array, the first value of which will be TRUE, while the second element will be an array of referring URLs in the order of visitors referred. You can act on this data like this:

```
if (!$results[0]) echo "No referring URLs";
else foreach ($results[1] as $result) echo "$result<br />";
```

This provides you with useful data, but you can also provide automatic back-links for your users to follow by using this code instead:

```
echo "The following sites kindly link to us:<br />";
foreach ($results[1] as $result)
   echo "<a href='$result'>$result</a><br />";
```

However, we can do better than that, because PHP Recipe 42, GetTitleFromURL(), can also be brought into the equation to link back to the referring site by name, so that if a referring page has a title, it will be used in the link back (otherwise, the page URL will be used), like this:

```
foreach ($results[1] as $result)
{
   $title = GetTitleFromURL($result);
   echo "<a href='$result'>";
   echo $title ? $title : $result;
   echo "</a><br />";
}
```

The Recipe

```
function AutoBackLinks($filename)
{
   if (!file_exists($filename)) return array(FALSE);

   $inbound = array();
```

```
$logfile = file_get_contents($filename);
$links   = explode("\n", rtrim($logfile));
$links   = array_count_values($links);
arsort($links, SORT_NUMERIC);

foreach ($links as $key => $val)
    if ($key != " No Referer")
        $inbound[] = $key;

return array(TRUE, $inbound);
}
```

RECIPE 44 CreateShortURL()

With the rapid growth of Twitter and its short message lengths, many services have sprung up offering short URL services. These are all well and good except that they tend to also be used by spammers to disguise links that might reveal their destination. Consequently, some of these services are slow, while others disappear overnight. What's more, users can be wary of entering a short URL, even from an established service, because they are never sure where the URL may lead.

To help diminish all these negatives, this recipe lets you offer your own short URLs using your own domain name, not a third party's, which should mean it is more trusted. For example, which of the two following URLs would you rather click?

microsoft.com/go.php?u=12345
asite.net/go.php?u=12345

Personally, I would be far less worried about visiting the former. Figure 7-4 shows a long URL being shortened with this recipe.

About the Recipe

This recipe accepts a URL to be shortened, along with some other data, and returns a short URL. It takes these arguments:

- **$url**   The URL to be shortened.
- **$redirect**   The name of a PHP file on your server that will make the redirects from short URLs to their original destinations.

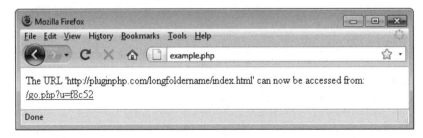

FIGURE 7-4   Use this recipe to create short aliases for long URLs on your web site.

- **$len** The number of characters to use in the token part of a short URL. The more you use them, the more URLs are supported. For example, three characters will support 4,096 URLs since this recipe uses the hexadecimal digits 0–9 and a–f.
- **$file** The name of a file in which to store the short URL data.

Variables, Arrays, and Functions

$contents	String variable containing the contents of $file
$lines	Array containing all the separate lines from $contents
$shorts	Array of short token versions of $longs
$longs	Array of full URL versions of $shorts
$line	String containing a single line extracted from $lines
$j	Integer counter for iterating through $longs
$str	String containing a newly created short token

How It Works

This recipe reads the contents of $file into the variable $contents, from where all the individual lines are extracted into the array $lines. Then, two arrays ($shorts and $longs) are initialized to hold the short tokens and their long URL equivalents, as extracted from $lines, using these four lines of code:

```
$contents = @file_get_contents($file);
$lines    = explode("\n", $contents);
$shorts   = array();
$longs    = array();
```

Then, if $contents actually contains anything—in other words, there was data in $file and it was successfully loaded—an if statement is entered. In this case, a foreach loop iterates through all the lines in $lines and assigns the left and right items of data on either side of the | symbol, which divides them into the $shorts and $longs arrays. The function list() is used to neatly extract both halves at once. When complete, for example, $shorts[1] will contain a token that represents the URL in $longs[1], like this:

```
if (strlen($contents))
   foreach ($lines as $line)
      if (strlen($line))
         list($shorts[], $longs[]) = explode('|', $line);
```

Next, the in_array() function is called to see whether $url already exists in the data file. If so, the $longs array, which contains the list of URLs, is stepped through, incrementing the pointer $j until the matching URL is found, at which point $j is used to index into $shorts and extract the equivalent token from there. This token is then returned, along with some other details, as follows:

The variable $redirect is passed to the function and represents the name of a PHP program you will use to handle the short URL redirects. Suppose this is called go.php.

Therefore, when the function returns, it will pass back the string `go.php?u=nnnn` where nnnn is the short token equivalent to the URL in `$url`. The code to do this is as follows:

```
if (in_array($url, $longs))
   for ($j = 0 ; $j < count($longs) ; ++$j)
      if ($longs[$j] == $url) return $redirect .
         "?u=" . $shorts[$j];
```

If `$url` is not already in the data file, a do loop is entered to randomly construct a new token `$len` characters in length, which is stored in `$str`. The loop repeats until the value of `$str` is unique to the data file, so that no two URLs can have the same short token, using these lines of code:

```
do $str = substr(md5(rand(0, 1000000)), 0, $len);
while (in_array($str, $shorts));
```

With a short token now created in `$str`, the `file_put_contents()` function is called to save the new details into the data file. It does this by saving `$contents` (the data previously read from the file), followed by `$str`, a | symbol, and `$url`. It is terminated with a `\n`, (newline character), like this:

```
file_put_contents($file, "$contents$str|$url\n");
```

So, an example line from this file would look like this:

```
f8c52|http://webdevelopmentcookbook.com/foldername/index.html
```

Finally, in the last line of code, a redirect URL is returned, comprising the values of `$redirect`, `?u=` and `$str`, such as go.php?u=xxxx.

How to Use It

To create a short URL, use this recipe. The following one (PHP Recipe 45) is for using the short URLs you create. To create a short URL, you need to pass four arguments to the function, like this:

```
$long     = "http://webdeveloperscookbook.com/foldername/index.html";
$redirect = "go.php";
$len      = 5;
$file     = "shorturls.txt";
$result   = CreateShortURL($long, $redirect, $len, $file);
```

Now you can display the link to this shortened URL using code such as this:

```
echo " http://mysite.com/$result";
```

In the preceding case, this will display a link looking like the following:

```
http://mysite.com/go.php?u=abcde
```

This is much shorter than the original of:

```
http://webdeveloperscookbook.com/foldername/index.html
```

You will use the following recipe to create go.php. You'll also see how you can use the *mod rewrite* facility in an *.htaccess* file to make the shortened URL even smaller, like the following, which is half the length of the original:

```
http://mysite.com/abcde
```

Or, even more simply, all that users will have to type into their browser's address bar is the following 16-character string (39 fewer characters than the original 55-character URL):

```
mysite.com/abcde
```

The Recipe

```php
function CreateShortURL($url, $redirect, $len, $file)
{
    $contents = @file_get_contents($file);
    $lines    = explode("\n", $contents);
    $shorts   = array();
    $longs    = array();

    if (strlen($contents))
        foreach ($lines as $line)
            if (strlen($line))
                list($shorts[], $longs[]) = explode('|', $line);

    if (in_array($url, $longs))
        for ($j = 0 ; $j < count($longs) ; ++$j)
            if ($longs[$j] == $url) return $redirect .
                "?u=" . $shorts[$j];

    do $str = substr(md5(rand(0, 1000000)), 0, $len);
    while (in_array($str, $shorts));

    file_put_contents($file, "$contents$str|$url\n");
    return $redirect . "?u=$str";
}
```

45 UseShortURL()

Once you've created a short URL, you need a means to access it. You do this via this recipe, which accepts a short token in a GET tail, known as a query string, and then redirects the user to the equivalent longer URL. Figure 7-5 shows the function being used just to decode a short token, without redirecting.

About the Recipe

This recipe accepts a short token and returns its longer URL equivalent. It takes these arguments:

- **$token**   A short token with which to look up the equivalent URL.
- **$file**   The data file for this recipe.

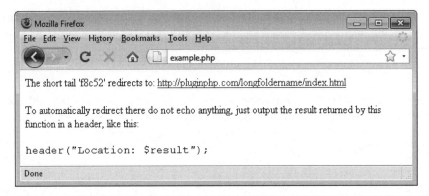

FIGURE 7-5   Creating short URLs using your own domain is easy with this recipe.

Variables, Arrays, and Functions

`$contents`	String variable containing the contents of `$file`
`$lines`	Array containing all the separate lines from `$contents`
`$shorts`	Array of short token versions of `$longs`
`$longs`	Array of full URL versions of `$shorts`
`$line`	String containing a single line extracted from `$lines`
`$j`	Integer counter for iterating through `$longs`

How It Works

This recipe must be passed a short token as created by the previous recipe, `CreateShortURL()`. It then returns the associated URL. It does this by reading the contents of `$file` into the variable `$contents`, from where all the individual lines are extracted into the array `$lines`. Then, two arrays (`$shorts` and `$longs`) are initialized to hold the short tokens and their long URL equivalents, as extracted from `$lines`, like this:

```
$contents = @file_get_contents($file);
$lines    = explode("\n", $contents);
$shorts   = array();
$longs    = array();
```

Then, an `if` statement is entered if the data in `$file` was successfully loaded into `$contents`. In which case, a `foreach` loop iterates through all the lines in `$lines` and assigns the left and right items of data on either side of the | symbol, which divides them into the `$shorts` and `$longs` arrays. The function `list()` is called to extract both halves at once, as follows:

```
if (strlen($contents))
   foreach ($lines as $line)
      if (strlen($line))
         list($shorts[], $longs[]) = explode('|', $line);
```

Next, the `in_array()` function is called to see whether `$token` already exists in the data file. If so, the `$shorts` array, which contains the list of tokens, is stepped through, incrementing the pointer `$j` until the matching URL is found, at which point `$j` is used to index into `$longs` and extract the equivalent URL from there. This URL is then returned, like this:

```
if (in_array($token, $shorts))
   for ($j = 0 ; $j < count($longs) ; ++$j)
      if ($shorts[$j] == $token)
         return $longs[$j];
```

If the token is not found in the data file, FALSE is returned in the final line.

How to Use It

In the previous section I discussed a program called *go.php*. This is what we will write here. It's very short and simple:

```
$file   = "shorturls.txt";
$result = UseShortURL($_GET['u'], $file);
if ($result) header("Location: $result");
else         echo "That short URL is unrecognized";
```

What this code does is fetch the argument passed to it in the GET variable `'u'` and run it through `UseShortURL()`, which then looks up the associated URL and returns it to the string variable `$result`. The `header()` function is then called to issue a `Location:` header, informing the browser where the contents it is requesting can be found.

All you need to do is save the preceding four lines of code (along with the `UseShortURL()` recipe) to your server's document root as *go.php* (remembering to add the surrounding `<?php` and `?>` tags), and it can be called up as follows (assuming your server has the domain name *myserver.com*):

```
http://myserver.com/go.php?u=nnnn
```

As long as nnnn is a valid short token, as created by PHP Recipe 44, then this program will look up the associated URL and redirect the browser to it.

But there's a very neat trick you can employ to make this recipe even more effective, and that's to use *mod rewrite* to further modify the short URL, making it even shorter. You do this by creating (or editing) a file called *.htaccess* in the same directory as *go.php*.

If you are using Windows, you will not be able to create the *.htaccess* file by right-clicking and selecting New because Windows will tell you that you need a filename before the period. Instead, you must use a program editor to save the file, as most of these understand what an *.htaccess* file is and can correctly create it. If you are using Windows Notepad or a program that doesn't allow you to save an *.htaccess* file, just place double quotes around it (like this: `".htaccess"`) when saving to tell Windows to save it as is.

Once you have the *.htaccess* file, add the following two lines of code to it:

```
RewriteEngine On
RewriteRule ^([a-zA-Z0-9]+)$ go.php?u=$1 [L]
```

What this does is tell the Apache web server that when it can't find a file or folder on your server, it should translate the filename requested (which can be any combination of letters and numbers) into the following form, where *request* is the original location requested:

```
go.php?u=request
```

So, for example, assume your web domain is *myserver.com* and you already have the short token `12345`, which redirects to a valid URL, and you have entered the following short URL into your browser:

```
http://myserver.com/12345
```

The mod rewrite module in the Apache web server will notice there is no file or folder named `12345` and therefore will translate the request into the following:

```
http://myserver.com/go.php?u=12345
```

And, hey presto, this is a valid URL pointing to the *go.php* program, which has been arrived at using the smallest possible short URL for your domain.

If you find using mod rewrite and *.htaccess* don't work for you, it may be because your *httpd.conf* configuration file doesn't have `AllowOverride` enabled. If this is the case, you'll need to modify the relevant line and restart Apache. Under Windows, using Zend Server CE, you will find *httpd.conf* at *c:\program files\zend\apache2\conf\httpd.conf*. On Linux/Mac, you should find the file at */usr/local/zend/apache2/conf/httpd.conf*. On other Apache installations, the file may be elsewhere and you should consult the relevant documentation.

You can open *httpd.conf* with any text editor and at (or somewhere near) line 211 you should see `AllowOverride None`, which should be changed to `AllowOverride All`. Then, resave the file. If you are not allowed to save the file, you may need to adjust the file and/or folder permissions first.

You should now restart Apache by clicking the Apache icon in your system tray and selecting Restart. Or, on Linux/Mac, using Zend Server CE, you would type `/usr/local/zend/bin/zendctl.sh restart` into a Terminal window.

For more about the mod rewrite program and *.htaccess* files on the Apache web server, please visit *tinyurl.com/modrewriteguide*.

The Recipe

```php
function UseShortURL($token, $file)
{
    $contents = @file_get_contents($file);
    $lines    = explode("\n", $contents);
    $shorts   = array();
    $longs    = array();

    if (strlen($contents))
        foreach ($lines as $line)
            if (strlen($line))
                list($shorts[], $longs[]) = explode('|', $line);
```

```
    if (in_array($token, $shorts))
        for ($j = 0 ; $j < count($longs) ; ++$j)
            if ($shorts[$j] == $token)
                return $longs[$j];

    return FALSE;
}
```

SimpleWebProxy( )

There are times when you are unable to browse to a site from one location but you can ping it from a server at another location, so you know the site should be up and running, but your connection to it is probably temporarily blocked. When this happens, you can use this recipe to act as a simple web proxy to browse right through to that site from your web server. Or, if you wish, you can use this code as a basis for your own web proxy service, which could be free, or you could even drop in a small advertisement to cover bandwidth costs—although you'd have to add that code yourself.

Figure 7-6 shows the *news.com* web site as browsed through to using this recipe. You can see from the status bar that all URLs in the page have been updated to call up linked pages through the proxy, too. And, yes, even the images have been served via the proxy.

FIGURE 7-6   This small recipe provides powerful web proxy functionality, including web images.

About the Recipe

This recipe accepts a URL to fetch and returns it with all URLs and links to images altered to run through the proxy. It takes these arguments:

- **$url** The URL to fetch.
- **$redirect** The filename of a PHP program to act as the web proxy.

Variables, Arrays, and Functions

$contents	String containing the contents of $url
$dom	Document object of $contents
$xpath	XPath object for traversing $dom
$hrefs	Object containing all a href= link elements in $dom
$sources	Object containing all img src= link elements in $dom
$iframes	Object containing all iframe src= link elements in $dom
$scripts	Object containing all script src= link elements in $dom
$css	Object containing all link href= link elements in $dom
$links	Array of all the links discovered in $contents
$to	Array containing the version of what each $link should be changed to in order to ensure it is absolute
$count	Integer containing the number of elements in $to
$link	Each link in turn extracted from $links
$j	Integer counter for iterating through $to
RelToAbsURL()	PHP Recipe 21: This function converts a relative URL to absolute

How It Works

This recipe fetches the contents of $url and places it in $contents. If it cannot load the page at $url, FALSE is returned, like this:

```
$contents = @file_get_contents($url);
if (!$contents) return NULL;
```

Next, if $url refers to any image file such as *.jpg, .gif, .png,* or *.ico,* or any *.css, .js,* or *.xml* file, then a switch statement is implemented to return the contents of the file unaltered (since there is no need to attempt to convert relative links to absolute in these types of files because they are not HTML), using this code:

```
switch(strtolower(substr($url, -4)))
{
   case ".jpg": case ".gif": case ".png": case ".ico":
   case ".css": case ".js": case ".xml":
      return $contents;
}
```

However, any file that is not one of those mentioned is assumed to be HTML. If you wish to improve on this recipe, here's one area for a start where you could add support for many other file types. HTML will be assumed from here on, however.

So the next thing that happens is all instances of & (the XML and XHTML required form of the & symbol) are converted to just the & symbol and then all & symbols are changed to a special token with the value !!**1**!!. You may wonder what on earth is going on here. Well, I can report that after a huge amount of time testing the str_replace() function built into PHP, I believe it has an obscure, and hard-to-catch, bug when it comes to processing the & symbol. In the end, I gave up trying to find out why and simply chose to convert all occurrences of & to a sequence of characters I could be pretty sure would not appear in any HTML document, hence the string !!**1**!!. This is the code I used:

```
$contents = str_replace('&amp;', '&',          $contents);
$contents = str_replace('&',     '!!**1**!!', $contents);
```

So, having got the & problem out of the way, a new Document object is created in $dom, and the document in $contents is loaded into it. This makes the whole HTML page easily searchable using the $xpath object, which is created from $dom, like this:

```
$dom   = new domdocument();
@$dom  ->loadhtml($contents);
$xpath = new domxpath($dom);
```

Next, five types of tags are searched for using the $xpath object; a href=, img src=, iframe src=, script src=, and link src=. All the associated strings for each tag are then placed in the objects $hrefs, $sources, $iframes, $scripts, and $css, like this:

```
$hrefs   = $xpath->evaluate("/html/body//a");
$sources = $xpath->evaluate("/html/body//img");
$iframes = $xpath->evaluate("/html/body//iframe");
$scripts = $xpath->evaluate("/html//script");
$css     = $xpath->evaluate("/html/head/link");
```

The reason for this is that it is necessary to ensure that all links within a page are of the absolute type, so that the page this recipe returns can be served up from any server and, by grabbing all the links, it will be possible to perform a relative URL to absolute URL conversion on each.

To facilitate this, all the separate objects are then traversed, and the links found in each are extracted into the array $links, as follows:

```
for ($j = 0 ; $j < $hrefs->length ; ++$j)
    $links[] = $hrefs->item($j)->getAttribute('href');

for ($j = 0 ; $j < $sources->length ; ++$j)
    $links[] = $sources->item($j)->getAttribute('src');

for ($j = 0 ; $j < $iframes->length ; ++$j)
    $links[] = $iframes->item($j)->getAttribute('src');
```

```
for ($j = 0 ; $j < $scripts->length ; ++$j)
   $links[] = $scripts->item($j)->getAttribute('src');

for ($j = 0 ; $j < $css->length ; ++$j)
   $links[] = $css->item($j)->getAttribute('href');
```

Then, to ensure there is no duplication of conversions, the `array_unique()` function is called to remove all duplicates, and the resulting set of unique URLs is then saved back into the `$links` array, like this:

```
$links = array_unique($links);
$to    = array();
$count = 0;
sort($links);
```

After the links are sorted alphabetically and resaved in the `$links` array, a `foreach` loop is used to iterate through each. The first part of the loop ensures there was actually a URL supplied in a link before continuing, and if so, the string variable `$temp` is assigned the contents of each link, but with the & symbols replaced. Here is the code that achieves this:

```
foreach ($links as $link)
{
   if ($link != "")
   {
      $temp = str_replace('!!**1**!!', '&', $link);
```

This is so that the array `$to` can be assigned an untokenized URL in the next step, in which the value /`$redirect?u=` is assigned to the current element of `$to`, as indexed by `$count`, which will later be incremented for each iteration of the loop. But before that, after the /`$redirect?u=`, the URL itself is attached to the end of the element, after first running it through the `RelToAbsURL()` function to ensure it is absolute. So, if the value in `$redirect` is `webproxy.php`, and the link to add is `http://google.com`, then `$to[$count]` will be assigned the string /`webproxy.php?u=http://google.com`. Here's the code to do this:

```
$to[$count] = "/$redirect?u=" .
   urlencode(RelToAbsURL($url, $temp));
```

Now it's time to make the link replacements within the document itself, which as you'll recall, is stored in `$contents`. This is done by two sets of `str_replace()` calls to cover the three types of links allowed in an HTML document:

- Single quoted
- Double quoted
- Without quotes

To do this, all `href="link"`, `href='link'`, and `href=link` statements are replaced with a unique token comprising the value of `$count` surrounded by two pairs of exclamation marks. The first link is replaced with `!!0!!`, the second with `!!1!!`, and so on. Again, I chose this as being unlikely to appear within an HTML document. This process is then repeated with all occurrences of `src="link"`, `src='link'`, and `src=link`, as follows:

```
$contents = str_replace("href=\"$link\"",
    "href=\"!!$count!!\"", $contents);
$contents = str_replace("href='$link'",
    "href='!!$count!!'",   $contents);
$contents = str_replace("href=$link",
    "href=!!$count!!",     $contents);
$contents = str_replace("src=\"$link\"",
    "src=\"!!$count!!\"",  $contents);
$contents = str_replace("src='$link'",
    "src='!!$count!!'",    $contents);
$contents = str_replace("src=$link",
    "src=!!$count!!",      $contents);
```

At the end of the loop, there will be no URLs remaining in the document, only the exclamation mark tokens representing them. And there's a very good reason for all these shenanigans, which is that the final part of this recipe needs to convert all the links to absolute, but if it tried to do this with all the links still in place it would seriously mess up.

To explain why, imagine that the server being proxied is http://server.com, and therefore all occurrences of /news/index.html must be replaced with http://server.com/news/index.html. This is all fine and dandy, but what if all occurrences of /news/ need changing, too? When this happens, it will also impact the previous change because the newly converted http://server.com/news/index.html strings will get changed to http://server.com/http://server.com/news/index.html. Do you see the problem? The changes will get changed.

This is why all the links that need converting are first pre-processed into tokens. Then, all the tokens can be safely processed into the absolute URLs, without new changes modifying previous ones.

And that's what the next bit of code does. It's a for loop that iterates through all the entries in $to (the absolute URLs) and changes each of the tokens in turn to each of the values in $to, as follows:

```
for ($j = 0 ; $j < $count ; ++$j)
    $contents = str_replace("!!$j!!", $to[$j],
        $contents);
```

Once all that has been achieved, then all the links in the document will now be in absolute format, so it's safe to make a final conversion, changing any remaining !!**1**!! tokens back into & symbols, the result of which is then returned by the recipe, like this:

```
return str_replace('!!**1**!!', '&', $contents);
```

How to Use It

At its simplest, all you need to do to use this recipe is to create a program, perhaps called *webproxy.php*, looking like this:

```
$url = urldecode($_GET['u']);
echo SimpleWebProxy($url, "webproxy.php");
```

This program should be saved in the document root of your server.

The first line simply extracts the contents following the `?u=` part of a `GET` request (the query string) into the variable `$url`, and the second makes the call to the recipe.

You can call up the web proxy by typing a command such as the following into your browser's address bar (making sure you always enter the `http://` part of the URL; otherwise, the program won't work):

```
webproxy.php?u=http://google.com
```

Or, more likely, if your server domain is *myserver.com*:

```
http://myserver.com/webproxy.php?u=http://google.com
```

Your new web proxy will now work, including sending images, because each link in a document has been converted to run through the web proxy, and therefore all images do so, too.

However, to make the program work as well as possible, you will probably want to support all the content types checked for near the start of the code, and send the correct headers for each prior to sending the data. Therefore, your program should probably look more like this:

```
$url    = urldecode($_GET['u']);
$result = SimpleWebProxy($url, "webproxy.php");

switch(strtolower(substr($url, -4)))
{
    case ".jpg": header("Content-type: image/jpeg");    die($result);
    case ".gif": header("Content-type: image/gif");     die($result);
    case ".png": header("Content-type: image/png");     die($result);
    case ".ico": header("Content-type: image/x-icon");  die($result);
    case ".css": header("Content-type: text/css");      die($result);
    case ".xml": header("Content-type: text/xml");      die($result);
    case ".htm": case "html": case ".php":
        header("Content-type: text/html"); die($result);
    default:
        if (strtolower(substr($url, -3)) == ".js")
            header("Content-type: application/x-javascript");
        die($result);
}
```

In the preceding code, a `switch` statement is used to determine the current file type, and then the appropriate header for each is sent to the browser, followed by the contents, as returned in `$result`. This is sent using the `die()` function since it combines both an `echo` and an `exit` statement in one. In the case of HTML files, they are allowed for the extensions *.htm* and *.php*, as well as *.html*.

Under the `default` section *.js*, JavaScript files are caught. They are handled separately since their extensions are only two characters long, instead of three. Finally, if nothing else matches, `$contents` is simply sent without a header, and it is hoped this will be good enough (generally it is).

Not including whitespace and comments, you will now have a web proxy program in under 100 lines of code that will work quite well, but you should realize that it only likes properly formed pages and is not forgiving of badly formatted HTML. Therefore, some pages will display strangely, if at all. But now that you know how it all works, you can easily tweak the code to your preferences.

The Recipe

```
function SimpleWebProxy($url, $redirect)
{
    $contents = @file_get_contents($url);
    if (!$contents) return NULL;

    switch(strtolower(substr($url, -4)))
    {
        case ".jpg": case ".gif": case ".png": case ".ico":
        case ".css": case ".js": case ".xml":
            return $contents;
    }

    $contents = str_replace('&amp;', '&',          $contents);
    $contents = str_replace('&',     '!!**1**!!', $contents);

    $dom      = new domdocument();
    @$dom     ->loadhtml($contents);
    $xpath    = new domxpath($dom);
    $hrefs    = $xpath->evaluate("/html/body//a");
    $sources  = $xpath->evaluate("/html/body//img");
    $iframes  = $xpath->evaluate("/html/body//iframe");
    $scripts  = $xpath->evaluate("/html//script");
    $css      = $xpath->evaluate("/html/head/link");
    $links    = array();

    for ($j = 0 ; $j < $hrefs->length ; ++$j)
        $links[] = $hrefs->item($j)->getAttribute('href');


    for ($j = 0 ; $j < $sources->length ; ++$j)
        $links[] = $sources->item($j)->getAttribute('src');

    for ($j = 0 ; $j < $iframes->length ; ++$j)
        $links[] = $iframes->item($j)->getAttribute('src');

    for ($j = 0 ; $j < $scripts->length ; ++$j)
        $links[] = $scripts->item($j)->getAttribute('src');

    for ($j = 0 ; $j < $css->length ; ++$j)
        $links[] = $css->item($j)->getAttribute('href');

    $links = array_unique($links);
    $to    = array();
    $count = 0;
    sort($links);
```

```
foreach ($links as $link)
{
    if ($link != "")
    {
        $temp = str_replace('!!**1**!!', '&', $link);

        $to[$count] = "/$redirect?u=" .
          urlencode(RelToAbsURL($url, $temp));
        $contents = str_replace("href=\"$link\"",
            "href=\"!!$count!!\"", $contents);
        $contents = str_replace("href='$link'",
            "href='!!$count!!'",   $contents);
        $contents = str_replace("href=$link",
            "href=!!$count!!",     $contents);
        $contents = str_replace("src=\"$link\"",
            "src=\"!!$count!!\"",  $contents);
        $contents = str_replace("src='$link'",
            "src='!!$count!!'",    $contents);
        $contents = str_replace("src=$link",
            "src=!!$count!!",      $contents);
        ++$count;
    }


}

for ($j = 0 ; $j < $count ; ++$j)
    $contents = str_replace("!!$j!!", $to[$j],
        $contents);

return str_replace('!!**1**!!', '&', $contents);
}
```

PageUpdated()

If you want to allow your users to be notified whenever one of your pages is updated, or perhaps you would like to be informed when a web page that interests you has been changed, all you need is this recipe. For example, Figure 7-7 shows a web page being monitored for changes.

FIGURE 7-7   Monitoring changes to web pages is automatic with this recipe.

About the Recipe

This recipe accepts the URL of a web page to monitor and lets you know whether it has been changed. It returns 1 if the page has changed, 0 if it is unchanged, –1 if the page is a new one not yet in the data file, or –2 if the page was inaccessible. It takes these arguments:

- **$url** The URL to check.
- **$datafile** The filename of a file containing the data file.

Variables, Arrays, and Functions

$contents	String containing the contents of $url
$checksum	String containing the result of passing $contents through the md5() function
$rawfile	String containing the contents of $datafile
$data	Array containing the lines extracted from $rawfile
$left	Array of all the left halves of $data
$right	Array of all the right halves of $data
$exists	Integer pointer to the location in $left of $page if it is already in the data file
$j	Integer counter for iterating through $left
PU_F1()	Function to extract the left half of a supplied string
PU_F2()	Function to extract the right half of a supplied string

How It Works

This recipe loads the contents of $page into $contents, returning the value FALSE if it could not be fetched. Otherwise, an md5() checksum is made of the page's contents. This is a one-way function that creates a 32-character unique string. Should even one letter change on a web page, the resulting md5() string will be substantially different, so it's the perfect way to detect changes in a web page. Here are those opening three lines:

```
$contents = @file_get_contents($page);
if (!$contents) return FALSE;
$checksum = md5($contents);
```

Next, a check is made to see whether $datafile already exists. If it does, then its contents are loaded into $rawfile, which is then split line by line into the array $data by using the explode() function based around the \n linefeeds in the file. Then, instead of using a loop to iterate through each element of $data, the much faster and more efficient array_map() function is called. This does the same thing, only requiring the name of a function to call for each element, like this:

```
if (file_exists($datafile))
{
    $rawfile  = file_get_contents($datafile);
    $data     = explode("\n", rtrim($rawfile));
    $left     = array_map("PU_F1", $data);
    $right    = array_map("PU_F2", $data);
```

In the case of populating the $left array, which will be assigned all the left halves of each line, the function PU_F1() is called, for the $right array, PU_F2() is called. These functions separate the strings passed to them into two substrings at the !1! tokens, then one returns the left half of the passed string, and the other the right, as follows.

```
function PU_F1($s)
{
    list($a, $b) = explode("!1!", $s);
    return $a;
}

function PU_F2($s)
{
    list($a, $b) = explode("!1!", $s);
    return $b;
}
```

The reason for the split is that the checksum and URL are stored side by side on a line, separated only by the token !1!, which is unlikely to appear in any URL.

A for loop is then started to iterate through the $left array and check whether $page already exists in the data file. If so, $exists is set to point to the element number within the array where it is located. Using this pointer, the matching element in $right is compared with the value of $checksum and, if it is the same, zero is returned to indicate that the page is still the same as last time the program checked. Here is the code for the loop:

```
for ($j = 0 ; $j < count($left) ; ++$j)
{
    if ($left[$j] == $page)
    {
        $exists = $j;
        if ($right[$j] == $checksum) return 0;
    }
}
```

If, on the other hand, $page exists in the data file but $checksum does not match the saved value, then the page contents must have changed. In which case, the old checksum value in the data file is overwritten with the new value in $checksum using the str_replace() function, the data file is saved back to disk, and a value of 1 is returned to indicate that the web page has changed, like this:

```
    if ($exists > -1)
    {
        $rawfile = str_replace($right[$exists],
            $checksum, $rawfile);
        file_put_contents($datafile, $rawfile);
        return 1;
    }
}
else $rawfile = "";
```

At the end of the `if (file_exists($datafile))` set of statements, if the file does not already exist, then the string `$rawfile` is assigned the empty string.

Finally, whether or not the file exists, the contents of `$rawfile` are saved to disk, along with the values of `$page` and `$checksum`, separated by the token `!1!`. This has the effect of either creating the data file if it doesn't exist, or if it does, it appends a new line of data to it, followed by a `\n` newline character. Either way, a value of –1 is returned to indicate that the URL in `$page` was new to the data file and has now been saved, as follows:

```
file_put_contents($datafile, "rawfile$page!1!$checksum\n");

return -1;
```

Note that the two functions `PU_F1()` and `PU_F2()` are for the exclusive use of the main code and are not intended to be called elsewhere.

How to Use It

To use this recipe, call it like this:

```
$page     = "http://pluginphp.com";
$datafile = "urldata.txt";
$result   = PageUpdated($page, $datafile);
```

Then, to act on the value in `$result`, you might use code such as this:

```
echo    "<pre>(1st call) The URL '$page' is ";
if      ($result == -1) echo "New";
elseif  ($result == 1)  echo "Changed";
elseif  ($result == 0)  echo "Unchanged";
else                    echo "Inaccessible";
```

This will tell you (or your users) whether the index page at *pluginphp.com* has changed since the last time it was checked, or whether it is new to the data file, or even inaccessible. The first time you make the call regarding a new page, it will always report that the page is new. If you try an additional call (such as via the following code) immediately after on a site that is not dynamically generated, you will then be informed that the page is unchanged; otherwise, you'll be told it has changed:

```
$result = PageUpdated($page, $datafile);
echo    "<br />(2nd call) The URL '$page' is ";
if      ($result == -1) echo "New";
elseif  ($result == 1)  echo "Changed";
elseif  ($result == 0)  echo "Unchanged";
else                    echo "Inaccessible";
```

You might prefer to send an e-mail instead of displaying this information to a browser, in which case just replace the `echo` statements with a call to PHP Recipe 38, `SendEmail()`, sending the contents of the `echo` statements in the `$message` argument.

The Recipe

```php
function PageUpdated($page, $datafile)

{
   $contents = @file_get_contents($page);
   if (!$contents) return FALSE;

   $checksum = md5($contents);

   if (file_exists($datafile))
   {
      $rawfile  = file_get_contents($datafile);
      $data     = explode("\n", rtrim($rawfile));
      $left     = array_map("PU_F1", $data);
      $right    = array_map("PU_F2", $data);
      $exists   = -1;

      for ($j = 0 ; $j < count($left) ; ++$j)
      {
         if ($left[$j] == $page)
         {
            $exists = $j;
            if ($right[$j] == $checksum) return 0;
         }
      }

      if ($exists > -1)
      {
         $rawfile = str_replace($right[$exists],
            $checksum, $rawfile);
         file_put_contents($datafile, $rawfile);
         return 1;
      }
   }
   else $rawfile = "";

   file_put_contents($datafile, "$rawfile$page!1!$checksum\n");
   return -1;
}

function PU_F1($s)
{
   list($a, $b) = explode("!1!", $s);
   return $a;
}

function PU_F2($s)
{
   list($a, $b) = explode("!1!", $s);
   return $b;
}
```

HTMLToRSS()

The popularity of RSS (Really Simple Syndication) feeds is still growing due to the ease with which you can subscribe to a feed, which then have updates automatically sent to the feed reader. In fact, most decent browsers also offer RSS reading facilities. But what if you're too busy developing the HTML portion of your site to start building RSS feeds? Or what if you'd like to be able to view other web sites in RSS?

The solution comes with this recipe, which will fetch a web page, analyze it (stripping out non-essential and formatting items), and reformat it into RSS (see Figure 7-8 for an example).

About the Recipe

This recipe accepts a string containing the HTML to be converted, along with other required arguments, and returns a properly formatted RSS document. It takes these arguments:

- **$html**   The HTML to convert.
- **$title**   The RSS feed title to use.
- **$description**   The RSS description to use.
- **$url**   The URL to which the feed should link.
- **$webmaster**   The e-mail address of the responsible webmaster.
- **$copyright**   The copyright details.

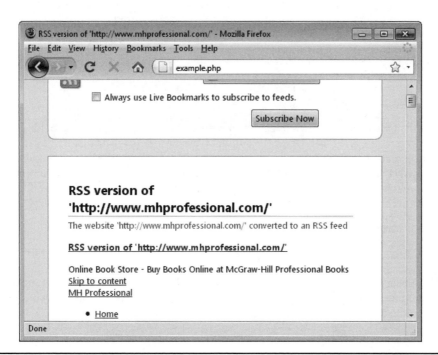

FIGURE 7-8   The recipe is used to output the McGraw-Hill web site as an RSS feed.

Variables, Arrays, and Functions

`$date`	String containing the date in RSS-compatible form
`$dom`	Document object of `$contents`
`$xpath`	XPath object for traversing `$dom`
`$hrefs`	Object containing all `a href=` link elements in `$dom`
`$links`	Array of all the links discovered in `$url`
`$to`	Array containing the version of what each `$link` should be changed to in order to ensure it is absolute
`$count`	Integer containing the number of elements in `$to`
`$j`	Integer counter for iterating through `$hrefs` and `$to`
`$link`	Each link in turn extracted from `$links`
`$temp`	Nontokenized copy of `$link`
`RelToAbsURL()`	PHP Recipe 21: Converts a relative URL to absolute

How It Works

This recipe starts by setting the string variable `$date` to the current date and time (after first specifying the time zone) in a format that is acceptable to RSS readers. Then, all instances of `&amp;` (the XML and XHTML required form of the `&` symbol) are converted to just the `&` symbol, and then all `&` symbols are changed to a special token with the value `!!**1**!!`. As described in Recipe 46, this is done because the `str_replace()` function seems to have a bug relating to the use of the `&` symbol, so the token is substituted to avoid it. The `&` symbols will be swapped back later, as follows:

```
date_default_timezone_set('utc');
$date  = date("D, d M Y H:i:s e");
$html  = str_replace('&amp;', '&',          $html);
$html  = str_replace('&',       '!!**1**!!', $html);
```

After that, the code has much in common with many of the other recipes in this chapter in that it must traverse an HTML DOM (Document Object Model), ensuring all `a href=` links are in absolute format. It does this by creating a new DOM object in `$dom` and then loading it up with the HTML tags from `$html`. Then, a new XPath object is created in `$xpath`. This is used by `$xpath->evaluate` to extract all the `a href=` tags into the `$hrefs` array, like this:

```
$dom   = new domdocument();
@$dom  ->loadhtml($html);
$xpath = new domxpath($dom);
$hrefs = $xpath->evaluate("/html/body//a");
```

Next, the arrays `$links` and `$to` are initialized. These will respectively contain all the encountered links and the absolute forms to which they should be changed. A counter that will index into these arrays, `$count`, is also initialized, like this:

```
$links = array();
$to    = array();
$count = 0;
```

A `for` loop is then used to extract the links from each a `href=` tag into the array `$links`, which then has all duplicates removed using the `array_unique()` function. This simply removes any duplicates so the array is then sorted with all elements stored contiguously, as follows:

```
for ($j = 0 ; $j < $hrefs->length ; ++$j)
    $links[] = $hrefs->item($j)->getAttribute('href');

$links = array_unique($links);
sort($links);
```

A `foreach` loop is then used to iterate through each link, first checking that a link actually has been assigned a value. If it has, the string variable `$temp` is assigned a version of `$link` *without* any `!!**1**!!` tokens that may have replaced any & symbols. This ensures a properly formed URL is ready for converting to absolute format using the `RelToAbsURL()` function, for assigning to an element in the `$to` array.

Again, as in PHP Recipe 46, tokens are then substituted for all links within the main document to prevent potential clashes during multiple replace operations. Every form of link allowable is substituted, whether single, double, or unquoted: `href="link"`, `href='link'`, and `href=link`. The tokens take the form `!!$count!!`, and therefore start at `!!0!!` and proceed on through `!!1!!` and so on each time a new link is substituted. Here is the relevant code:

```
foreach ($links as $link)
{
    if ($link != "")
    {
        $temp = str_replace('!!**1**!!', '&', $link);
        $to[$count] = urlencode(RelToAbsURL($url, $temp));
        $html = str_replace("href=\"$link\"",
            "href=\"!!$count!!\"", $html);
        $html = str_replace("href='$link'",
            "href='!!$count!!'",    $html);
        $html = str_replace("href=$link",
            "href=!!$count!!",      $html);
        ++$count;
    }
}
```

Once all the tokens are in place in the document and there is no chance of clashes during string substitutions, a `for` loop is used to convert them into the absolute URLs held in the `$to` array, like this:

```
for ($j = 0 ; $j < $count ; ++$j)
    $html = str_replace("!!$j!!", $to[$j],
        $html);
```

Next, any encoded URLs in which `http://` has been turned into `http%3A%2F%2F` are restored back to `http://`, any & symbols are restored back from the token `!!**1**!!`, and all whitespace is removed from the document using the `preg_replace()` function with a parameter of /[\s]+/. This forces all consecutive strings of one or more whitespace characters to be replaced with a single space, like this:

```
$html = str_replace('http%3A%2F%2F', 'http://', $html);
$html = str_replace('!!**1**!!', '&', $html);
$html = preg_replace('/[\s]+/', ' ', $html);
```

The next lines strip out any <script> and <style> tags and their contents, ensuring that all <h> tags have their contents removed. This is done so a conversion can easily be made later into RSS headers. With those tags removed, all remaining tags are also stripped out, with the exception of those listed in the string $ok. This process is handled by the function strip_tags(). In case you're wondering, I tried to also remove the <script> and <style> tags using strip_tags(), but the function seems buggy and would not always remove them, so that's why these are handled separately, like this:

```
$html = preg_replace('/<script[^>]*>.*?<\/script>/i', '', $html);
$html = preg_replace('/<style[^>]*>.*?<\/style>/i', '', $html);
$ok   = '<a><i><b><u><s><h><img><div><span><table><tr>' .
        '<th><tr><td><br><p><ul><ol><li>';
$html = strip_tags($html, $ok);
$html = preg_replace('/<h[1-7][^>]*?>/i', '<h>', $html);
$html = htmlentities($html);
```

After that, all remaining HTML characters are replaced with their RSS equivalents—for example, the < symbol becomes <, the > becomes >, and so on—and the final two preg_replace() calls substitute the two opening and closing forms of the <h> tag (which previously had any contents stripped out) into the XML required for properly formatted RSS headers. In other words, this recipe assumes that anything between <h> and </h> tags should be treated as RSS headers, as follows:

```
$html = preg_replace("/&lt;h&gt;/si",
    "</description></item>\n<item><title>", $html);
$html = preg_replace("/&lt;\/h[1-7]&gt;/si",
    "</title><guid>$url</guid><description>", $html);
```

Finally, the RSS itself is returned within a return <<<_END ... _END construct, where you can see $title, $url, $description, and all the other variables in their correct places, all the way down to $html, the main contents of the feed on which this recipe has performed all the processing. The code to do this is as follows:

```
  return <<<_END
<?xml version="1.0" encoding="UTF-8"?>
<rss version="2.0"><channel>
<generator>webdevelopmentcookbook.com: recipe 48</generator>
<title>$title</title><link>$url</link>
<description>$description</description>
<language>en</language>
<webMaster>$webmaster</webMaster>
<copyright>$copyright</copyright>
<pubDate>$date</pubDate>
<lastBuildDate>$date</lastBuildDate>
```

```
<item><title>$title</title>
<guid>$url</guid>
<description>$html</description></item></channel></rss>
_END;
```

How to Use It

When you want to convert HTML to RSS, use code such as the following, in which your web site domain is assumed to be *myserver.com*:

```
$html        = "Your HTML content goes here";
$title       = "RSS version of my webpage";
$description = "This feed was converted from HTML";
$url         = "http://myserver.com";
$webmaster   = "webmaster@myserver.com";
$copyright   = "Copyright 2010 myserver.com";
header('Content-Type: text/xml');
echo HTMLToRSS($html, $title, $description, $url,
   $webmaster, $copyright);
```

Or, you can convert almost any HTML page on the Web by using code such as this:

```
$url         = "http://www.mhprofessional.com/";
$html        = file_get_contents($url);
$title       = "RSS version of '$url'";
$description = "The website '$url' converted to an RSS feed";
$webmaster   = "nobody@nowhere.com";
$copyright   = "Copyright $url";
header('Content-Type: text/xml');
echo HTMLToRSS($html, $title, $description, $url,
   $webmaster, $copyright);
```

The Recipe

```
function HTMLToRSS($html, $title, $description, $url,
   $webmaster, $copyright)
{
   $date   = date("D, d M Y H:i:s e");
   $html   = str_replace('&amp;', '&',         $html);
   $html   = str_replace('&',     '!!**1**!!', $html);
   $dom    = new domdocument();
   @$dom   ->loadhtml($html);
   $xpath  = new domxpath($dom);
   $hrefs  = $xpath->evaluate("/html/body//a");
   $links  = array();
   $to     = array();
   $count  = 0;

   for ($j = 0 ; $j < $hrefs->length ; ++$j)
      $links[] = $hrefs->item($j)->getAttribute('href');
```

```php
    $links = array_unique($links);
    sort($links);

    foreach ($links as $link)
    {
        if ($link != "")
        {
            $temp = str_replace('!!**1**!!', '&', $link);
            $to[$count] = urlencode(RelToAbsURL($url, $temp));
            $html = str_replace("href=\"$link\"",
                "href=\"!!$count!!\"", $html);
            $html = str_replace("href='$link'",
                "href='!!$count!!'",    $html);
            $html = str_replace("href=$link",
                "href=!!$count!!",        $html);
            ++$count;
        }
    }

    for ($j = 0 ; $j < $count ; ++$j)
        $html = str_replace("!!$j!!", $to[$j],
            $html);

    $html = str_replace('http%3A%2F%2F', 'http://', $html);
    $html = str_replace('!!**1**!!', '&', $html);
    $html = preg_replace('/[\s]+/', ' ', $html);
    $html = preg_replace('/<script[^>]*>.*?<\/script>/i', '', $html);
    $html = preg_replace('/<style[^>]*>.*?<\/style>/i', '', $html);
    $ok   = '<a><i><b><u><s><h><img><div><span><table><tr>' .
            '<th><tr><td><br><p><ul><ol><li>';
    $html = strip_tags($html, $ok);
    $html = preg_replace('/<h[1-7][^>]*?>/i', '<h>', $html);
    $html = htmlentities($html);
    $html = preg_replace("/&lt;h&gt;/si",
        "</description></item>\n<item><title>", $html);
    $html = preg_replace("/&lt;\/h[1-7]&gt;/si",
        "</title><guid>$url</guid><description>", $html);

  return <<<_END
<?xml version="1.0" encoding="UTF-8"?>
<rss version="2.0"><channel>
<generator>Pluginphp.com: recipe 48</generator>
<title>$title</title><link>$url</link>
<description>$description</description>
<language>en</language>
<webMaster>$webmaster</webMaster>
<copyright>$copyright</copyright>
<pubDate>$date</pubDate>
<lastBuildDate>$date</lastBuildDate>
<item><title>$title</title>
<guid>$url</guid>
<description>$html</description></item></channel></rss>
_END;
}
```

RSSToHTML()

This recipe provides the inverse functionality of PHP Recipe 48—it converts an RSS feed into standard HTML format. It's perfect for when you don't have a feed reader on hand or wish to grab some syndicated content and put it in one of your own web pages (make sure you have any required permissions if you do, though).

Figure 7-9 shows the NASA Image of the Day RSS feed after converting it to HTML. You can access this feed at *www.nasa.gov/rss/image_of_the_day.rss*.

About the Recipe

This recipe accepts a string containing the contents of an RSS feed to be converted and returns that string transformed into HTML. It takes this argument:

- **$rss** The contents of an RSS feed to convert.

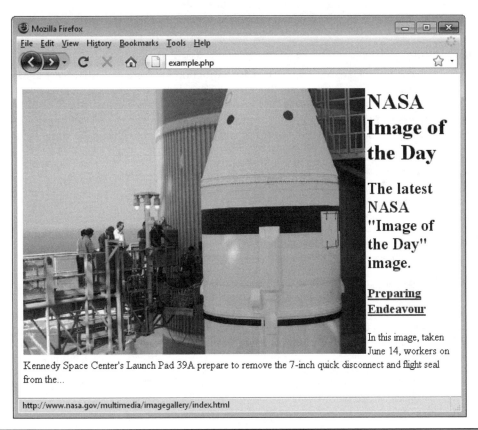

FIGURE 7-9 This recipe will convert RSS feeds into regular HTML web pages.

Variables, Arrays, and Functions

`$xml`	XML object created from `$rss`
`$title`	String extracted from the RSS title tag
`$link`	String extracted from the RSS link tag
`$desc`	String extracted from the RSS description tag
`$copyr`	String extracted from the RSS copyright tag
`$ilink`	String extracted from the RSS image link tag
`$ititle`	String extracted from the RSS image title tag
`$iurl`	String extracted from the RSS image url tag
`$out`	String containing converted HTML
`$tlink`	String containing link of current item
`$tdate`	String containing publication date of current item
`$ttitle`	String containing title of current item
`$tdesc`	String containing description of current item

How It Works

This recipe uses the `simplexml_load_string()` function to create an XML object in `$xml` from the RSS feed in `$rss`. From there, the string variables `$title`, `$link`, `$desc`, `$copyr`, `$ilink`, `$ititle`, and `$iurl` are easily assigned by extracting the various items from `$xml->channel`. In case any items do not exist in the RSS feed, each of these extractions is prefaced by an @ symbol, which will suppress any error messages. This is the code used:

```
$xml    = simplexml_load_string($rss);
$title  = @$xml->channel->title;
$link   = @$xml->channel->link;
$desc   = @$xml->channel->description;
$copyr  = @$xml->channel->copyright;
$ilink  = @$xml->channel->image->link;
$ititle = @$xml->channel->image->title;
$iurl   = @$xml->channel->image->url;
```

Next, the string variable `$out` is initialized with the opening tags for a standard HTML document, and then if an image was specified in the feed, the image and its associated title and description are also added. I have decided to align the image to the left and allow the description to butt up to the right of it because the main image in an RSS feed is generally a logo. This seems to work well with most other main images, too. This is achieved as follows:

```
$out = "<html><head><style> img {border: 1px solid " .
       "#444444}</style>\n<body>";

if ($ilink != "")
   $out      .= "<a href='$ilink'><img src='$iurl' title=" .
                "'$ititle' alt='$ititle' border='0' style=" .
                "'border: 0px' align='left' /></a>\n";
```

After that, `<h1>` and `<h2>` headings containing the main RSS feed title and description are added to $out, like this:

```
$out .= "<h1>$title</h1>\n<h2>$desc</h2>\n";
```

Then, a `foreach` loop is used to iterate through every item within the feed. As each is extracted, its details are placed in the variables $tlink, $tdate, $ttitle, and $tdesc, from where they are appended to $out, within suitable HTML heading and paragraph tags, as follows:

```
foreach($xml->channel->item as $item)
{
    $tlink  = @$item->link;
    $tdate  = @$item->pubDate;
    $ttitle = @$item->title;
    $tdesc  = @$item->description;

    $out    .= "<h3><a href='$tlink' title='$tdate'>" .
               "$ttitle</a></h3>\n<p>$tdesc</p>\n";
}
```

And that's it. All that remains is to return $out, along with the copyright string in $copyr and the closing HTML tags, like this:

```
return "$out<a href='$link'>$copyr</a></body></html>";
```

How to Use It

To convert an RSS feed to HTML, just pass it to the recipe, like this:

```
$url = "http://www.nasa.gov/rss/image_of_the_day.rss";
$rss = file_get_contents($url);
echo   RSSToHTML($rss);
```

As you can see, the feed can be pulled in from anywhere on the Web, or it can be a feed from your own site. All you need to do is pass the feed itself (not the URL it came from) to the recipe and display the result returned.

Alternatively, to insert the HTML version of the feed into your own web pages, just use the string returned by the recipe, like this:

```
$result = RSSToHTML($rss);
echo        "<h1>Here's NASA's image of the day</h1>$result";
```

The Recipe

```
function RSSToHTML($rss)
{
    $xml    = simplexml_load_string($rss);
    $title  = @$xml->channel->title;
    $link   = @$xml->channel->link;
    $desc   = @$xml->channel->description;
```

```
$copyr  = @$xml->channel->copyright;
$ilink  = @$xml->channel->image->link;
$ititle = @$xml->channel->image->title;
$iurl   = @$xml->channel->image->url;

$out = "<html><head><style> img {border: 1px solid " .
       "#444444}</style>\n<body>";

if ($ilink != "")
    $out    .= "<a href='$ilink'><img src='$iurl' title=" .
               "'$ititle' alt='$ititle' border='0' style=" .
               "'border: 0px' align='left' /></a>\n";

$out .= "<h1>$title</h1>\n<h2>$desc</h2>\n";

foreach($xml->channel->item as $item)
{
    $tlink  = @$item->link;
    $tdate  = @$item->pubDate;
    $ttitle = @$item->title;
    $tdesc  = @$item->description;

    $out    .= "<h3><a href='$tlink' title='$tdate'>" .
               "$ttitle</a></h3>\n<p>$tdesc</p>\n";
}

return "$out<a href='$link'>$copyr</a></body></html>";
}
```

HTMLToMobile( )

The final recipe in this chapter will take an HTML page and format it in such a way that it will load faster on a mobile browser that may have limited download speeds, and also display better due to removing a lot of style and formatting information.

Figure 7-10 shows the *yahoo.com* web page after being processed by this recipe. As you can see, the recipe has substantially reduced the original web page, shown in Figure 7-11.

About the Recipe

This recipe accepts a string containing the HTML to be converted, along with other required arguments, and returns a properly formatted HTML document with various formatting elements removed. It takes these arguments:

- **$html** The HTML to convert.
- **$url** The URL of the page being converted.
- **$style** If "yes", style and JavaScript elements are retained; otherwise, they are stripped out.
- **$images** If "yes", images are kept; otherwise, they are removed.

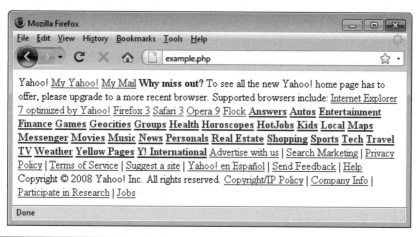

FIGURE 7-10   With this recipe, you can make the busiest of web pages load quickly on a mobile browser.

FIGURE 7-11   This is the original Yahoo! home page before the recipe is applied.

Variables, Arrays, and Functions

$dom	Document object of $contents
$xpath	XPath object for traversing $dom
$hrefs	Object containing all a href= link elements in $dom
$links	Array of all the links discovered in $url
$to	Array containing the version of what each $link should be changed to in order to ensure it is absolute
$count	Integer containing the number of elements in $to
$link	Each link in turn extracted from $links
$j	Integer counter for iterating through $to
RelToAbsURL()	PHP Recipe 21: Converts a relative URL to absolute

How It Works

This function starts off by creating a DOM object that is loaded with the HTML from $html. Then, an XPath object is created from this, with which all a href= tags are extracted and placed in the object $hrefs. After initializing the arrays $links and $to, which will contain the links before and after converting to absolute format, all occurrences of & are converted to & symbols, and then all & symbols to the token !!**1**!!, to avoid the suspected str_replace() bug that doesn't handle & symbols well, as follows:

```
$dom    = new domdocument();
@$dom   ->loadhtml($html);
$xpath  = new domxpath($dom);
$hrefs  = $xpath->evaluate("/html/body//a");
$links  = array();
$to     = array();
$count  = 0;
$html   = str_replace('&amp;', '&',          $html);
$html   = str_replace('&',     '!!**1**!!', $html);
```

Next, the link parts of the tags are pulled out from $hrefs and placed into the array $links using a for loop, and all duplicate links are removed from the array, which is then sorted, like this:

```
for ($j = 0 ; $j < $hrefs->length ; ++$j)
   $links[] = $hrefs->item($j)->getAttribute('href');

$links = array_unique($links);
sort($links);
```

After this, the technique used in PHP Recipes 46 and 48 is implemented to swap all links in $html with numbered tokens. This ensures that multiple replaces don't interfere with each other. Although, first, the $to array is loaded with a proper URL that has had any !!**1**!! tokens changed back to & symbols, after running them through RelToAbsURL()

to ensure they are absolute. This makes sure that legal URLs will be substituted when the tokens are later changed back.

To be flexible, the recipe supports three types of links—double quoted, single quoted, and unquoted—each case being handled by one of the following `str_replace()` calls, in which links within $html are substituted for the token `!!$count!!`. This means that the first link becomes `!!0!!`, the second `!!1!!`, and so on, as $count is incremented at each pass. Here's the code to do it:

```
foreach ($links as $link)
{
    if ($link != "")
    {
        $temp = str_replace('!!**1**!!', '&', $link);
        $to[$count] = urlencode(RelToAbsURL($url, $temp));
        $html = str_replace("href=\"$link\"",
            "href=\"!!$count!!\"", $html);
        $html = str_replace("href='$link'",
            "href='!!$count!!'",    $html);
        $html = str_replace("href=$link",
            "href=!!$count!!",    $html);
        ++$count;
    }
}
```

With all the tokens having been substituted, they can now be swapped with their associated links from the $to array. This is achieved using the following `for` loop:

```
for ($j = 0 ; $j < $count ; ++$j)
    $html = str_replace("!!$j!!", $to[$j], $html);
```

Then, any remaining occurrences of the URL-encoded format `http%3A%2F%2F` are rectified to `http://`, and any `!!**1**!!` tokens are returned to being & symbols, like this:

```
$html = str_replace('http%3A%2F%2F', 'http://', $html);
$html = str_replace('!!**1**!!', '&', $html);
```

Next, if $style does not have the value "yes", then whitespace, styling, and JavaScript are removed from $html, like this:

```
if (strtolower($style) != "yes")
{
    $html = preg_replace('/[\s]+/', ' ', $html);
    $html = preg_replace('/<script[^>]*>.*?<\/script>/i', '', $html);
    $html = preg_replace('/<style[^>]*>.*?<\/style>/i', '', $html);
}
```

After this, $images is also tested, and if it's equal to "yes", then images are allowed to remain in place. This is achieved, along with removing all remaining tags, by appending the tag `<img>` to the list of allowed tags in $allowed, which is then passed to the `strip_tags()` function, along with $html. If $images is not equal to "yes", then the `<img>` tag will not be appended to $allowed and consequently all image tags will also be removed by this function. Upon completing all the processing, the result (in $html) is returned. Here is the code that achieves these remaining actions:

```
$allowed = "<a><p><h><i><b><u><s>";
if (strtolower($images) == "yes") $allowed .= "<img>";
return strip_tags($html, $allowed);
```

How to Use It

To convert HTML to a format more suitable for mobile browsers, use the recipe like this:

```
$url    = "http://yahoo.com";
$html   = file_get_contents($url);
$style  = "no";
$images = "no";
echo      HTMLToMobile($html, $url, $style, $images);
```

This loads in the HTML from the index page at *yahoo.com* and passes it to the recipe with both $style and $images set to "no". This means that neither styling nor JavaScript will be allowed in the converted HTML, and neither will images.

If $style is set to "yes", then style tags and JavaScript are retained in the HTML. If $images is also equal to "yes", then some images will be retained—but not all, due to a lot of the page's content being removed.

If you play with this recipe, you'll find you can often set both $style and $images to "yes" and many web pages will still return a lot less information because the strip_tags() function removes plenty of HTML not strictly needed to use a web page.

The Recipe

```
function HTMLToMobile($html, $url, $style, $images)
{
    $dom    = new domdocument();
    @$dom   ->loadhtml($html);
    $xpath  = new domxpath($dom);
    $hrefs  = $xpath->evaluate("/html/body//a");
    $links  = array();
    $to     = array();
    $count  = 0;
    $html   = str_replace('&amp;', '&',          $html);
    $html   = str_replace('&',     '!!**1**!!', $html);

    for ($j = 0 ; $j < $hrefs->length ; ++$j)
        $links[] = $hrefs->item($j)->getAttribute('href');

    $links = array_unique($links);
    sort($links);
```

```
foreach ($links as $link)
{
   if ($link != "")
   {
      $temp = str_replace('!!**1**!!', '&', $link);
      $to[$count] = urlencode(RelToAbsURL($url, $temp));
      $html = str_replace("href=\"$link\"",
         "href=\"!!$count!!\"", $html);
      $html = str_replace("href='$link'",
         "href='!!$count!!'",   $html);
      $html = str_replace("href=$link",
         "href=!!$count!!",       $html);
      ++$count;
   }
}

for ($j = 0 ; $j < $count ; ++$j)
   $html = str_replace("!!$j!!", $to[$j],
      $html);

$html = str_replace('http%3A%2F%2F', 'http://', $html);
$html = str_replace('!!**1**!!', '&', $html);

if (strtolower($style) != "yes")
{
   $html = preg_replace('/[\s]+/', ' ', $html);
   $html = preg_replace('/<script[^>]*>.*?<\/script>/i', '', $html);
   $html = preg_replace('/<style[^>]*>.*?<\/style>/i', '', $html);
}

$allowed = "<a><p><h><i><b><u><s>";
if (strtolower($images) == "yes") $allowed .= "<img>";
return strip_tags($html, $allowed);
}
```

CHAPTER 8

Chat and Messaging

Offering chat, messaging, and user interaction features are fundamental ways to create addictive content and build up traffic to a site. The phenomenal growth of sites such as MySpace, Facebook, and Twitter (as well as the huge increase in use of instant messaging software) all serve to show that what Internet users love to do more than anything else is communicate with other users.

Whether leaving messages, commenting on blogs or web sites, e-mailing, or Twittering, if you provide the right services, your users will not only take to them, they'll invite their friends along, too. And presto, you'll now have free compelling content, as long as you treat your users well and make your web site easy to use.

And that's the aim of this batch of recipes: to provide a collection of ready-made functions you can draw on to add the user-interaction features your web site needs.

UsersOnline()

One of the things that drives webmasters crazy is the fact that getting the ball rolling and building up a user base is very hard, but the more users you have, the easier it is to get more. Why? One answer has to be that people don't want to feel alone on a web site. So what better way to reassure them than to display the number of users currently using your web site? And that's what this recipe will do for you. It lists the total number of people who have used your web site within a recent period decided by you.

Of course, at times when you don't have many active users you may want to disable this code, or maybe increase the time span during which a visitor is considered recent. But if you do have a few visitors online, discretely displaying the number in a sensible place will reassure them that your web site has something going on. Figure 8-1 shows a web page with five active users.

About the Recipe

This recipe reports the number of users who have recently been active. It takes the following arguments.

- **$datafile** A string containing the location of a file for storing the data.
- **$seconds** The period of time, in seconds, during which a recent user is considered active.

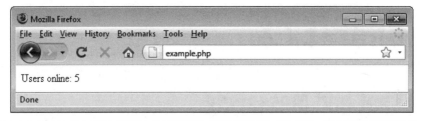

Figure 8-1   This recipe provides a quick snapshot of your site's usage and popularity.

Variables, Arrays, and Functions

$ip	String containing the IP address and the User Agent of the current user
$out	String containing the contents of the datafile to be written back to the server
$online	Integer counter containing the number of users online
$users	Array containing unique user details
$usertime	String containing time the user being processed last accessed the web site
$userip	String containing the IP and User Agent string of the user being processed

How It Works

This code starts by determining the current user's IP address and User Agent string, as provided by their browser, and then assigning the result to the string $ip. Afterward, a couple of variables are initialized: $out, the contents of the datafile that will be written back, is set to the empty string; and $online, the number of users online, is set to 1 (since the program knows that at least the current user is active), as follows:

```
$ip     = getenv("REMOTE_ADDR") .
          getenv("HTTP_USER_AGENT");
$out    = "";
$online = 1;
```

If the file $datafile already exists, then there may be previous users who have been active within the last number of seconds specified by $seconds. In which case, the contents of $datafile are loaded in, with the last character (a \n linefeed) being removed by the rtrim() function since it is not needed. The result is then split at each remaining \n linefeed into the array $users, so that $users will now have one entry for each user, like this:

```
if (file_exists($datafile))
{
    $users = explode("\n", rtrim(file_get_contents($datafile)));
```

A foreach loop is then used to iterate through $users, with the details of each one being processed stored in $user, like this:

```
foreach($users as $user)
{
    list($usertime, $userip) = explode('|', $user);

    if ((time() - $usertime) < $seconds && $userip != $ip)
    {
        $out .= $usertime . '|' . $userip . "\n";
        ++$online;
    }
}
```

Inside the loop, the list() function is used to assign $usertime and $userip the time and IP/User Agent details for the user being processed. These are split out of $user using the explode() function with an argument of | (the | symbol being the separator I chose for this code's data).

Then, the current time is looked up using the time() function, and if that value minus the value stored in $usertime is less than the number of seconds stored in $seconds, then that user is considered to still be active and so their details are appended to the string $out, causing the count of active users in $online to be incremented.

However, if more seconds than the value in $seconds have elapsed since their last access, then they are assumed to no longer be active and their details are forgotten by not appending them to $out.

Note how a test is made to ensure the *current* user's details are always ignored using the code && $userip != $ip, so that the IP/User Agent details of the user being processed are not the same as the current user's. This is to ensure those details are removed so they will not be duplicated when the datafile is written back to disk.

After completing the loop, $out has the current time and IP/User Agent details appended to it, from the function time() and the variable $ip, separated by a | character, and terminated with a \n newline. The contents of $out are then saved to the file $datafile and the number of active users in $online is returned, like this:

```
$out .= time() . '|' . $ip . "\n";
file_put_contents($datafile, $out);
return $online;
```

How to Use It

When you want to keep a count of the active users on your web site, you should include a call to this code on all your pages where the count is wanted. Doing so is as simple as using the following code:

```
UsersOnline('users.txt', 300);
```

Here, the 300 represents 300 seconds (or five minutes), which is probably a reasonable time window to start with. Whenever you want to know the number of active users, you assign the result returned by the function to a variable, or simply echo it, like this:

```
echo "Users online: " . UsersOnline('users.txt', 300);
```

You can replace the datafile name *users.txt* with whatever name you prefer.

The Recipe

```
function UsersOnline($datafile, $seconds)
{
    $ip     = getenv("REMOTE_ADDR") .
              getenv("HTTP_USER_AGENT");
    $out    = "";
    $online = 1;

    if (file_exists($datafile))
    {
        $users = explode("\n", rtrim(file_get_contents($datafile)));

        foreach($users as $user)
        {
            list($usertime, $userip) = explode('|', $user);

            if ((time() - $usertime) < $seconds && $userip != $ip)
            {
                $out .= $usertime . '|' . $userip . "\n";
                ++$online;
            }
        }
    }

    $out .= time() . '|' . $ip . "\n";
    file_put_contents($datafile, $out);
    return $online;
}
```

PostToGuestBook()

No self-respecting web site is complete without some means of providing feedback, so here's a simple recipe to enable you to offer a Guestbook feature in just a few lines of PHP code. Figure 8-2 shows the same information posted twice, but because flooding control is enabled, the second post is not added to the Guestbook.

About the Recipe

This recipe posts a message to a Guestbook. It takes these arguments:

- **$datafile**   A string containing the location of a file for storing the data.
- **$name**   The name of the poster.
- **$email**   The poster's e-mail address.
- **$website**   The poster's web site.
- **$message**   The message to be posted.

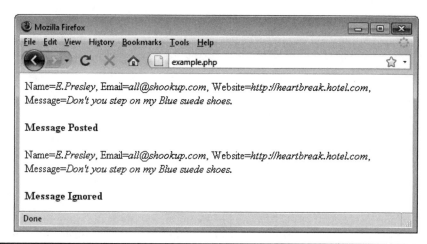

FIGURE 8-2 This recipe provides easy posting to a Guestbook with flood control.

Variables, Arrays, and Functions

$data	String containing a concatenation of $name, $email, $website, and $message, separated by the token !1!
$lines	Array containing the messages extracted from $datafile
$fh	File handle into the file $datafile

How It Works

This code takes all the data supplied to it and, if it's not a duplicate of an existing entry, adds it to the datafile. It begins by first creating the line of data to add to $datafile by concatenating the values of $name, $email, $website, and $message, separating them all by the token !1!, which I chose since it's unlikely to ever be used in a message, name, and so on. It places the result in the string $data, like this:

```
$data = "$name!1!$email!1!$website!1!$message";
```

Then if the file $datafile already exists, it is opened and its contents extracted into the array $lines, after removing the final character, which is a \n newline character and is not required. The extraction is performed using the explode() function with an argument of \n, newline, containing the points at which to perform the splitting. Then, using the function in_array(), each element of $lines is checked to see whether it already contains the contents of $data. If so, then this would be a duplicate entry and so a value of 0 would be returned to indicate the fact, and the post would not be added, as shown next:

```
if (file_exists($datafile))
{
    $lines = explode("\n", rtrim(file_get_contents($datafile)));

    if (in_array($data, $lines)) return 0;
}
```

Otherwise, the entry is not a duplicate, so the file handle $fh is assigned the value returned upon opening $datafile for appending, with the fopen() function and an argument of 'a'. If $fh is set to FALSE, then the file can't be opened and –1 is returned to indicate that fact, like this:

```
$fh = fopen($datafile, 'a');
if (!$fh) return -1;
```

Then, the flock() function is called with a parameter of LOCK_EX (for EXclusive lock), which forces the function to wait until all other processes have finished accessing the file, like this:

```
if (flock($fh, LOCK_EX)) fwrite($fh, $data . "\n");
```

This is done because other users could be posting to the file at the same time and could end up corrupting it. So, once flock() gains control over the file, all other functions that access $datafile using the flock() method will now have to wait their turn.

Once the flock() function allows execution to proceed, the fwrite() function is called to write the data in $data to $datafile, followed by a \n newline. This is to separate each line from the next. Because the parameter of 'a' was used with fopen(), this data is appended to the end of the file's existing contents.

Finally, the lock is released using flock() with a parameter of LOCK_UN (for UNlock) and the file is closed, like this:

```
flock($fh, LOCK_UN);
fclose($fh);
```

At this point, the write has been made successfully and so a value of 1 is returned.

CAUTION *The flock() function will not work on NFS and many other networked file systems, or on FAT and its derivatives. Also, when using a multithreaded server API like ISAPI, you may not be able to rely on flock() to protect files against other PHP scripts running in parallel threads of the same server instance.*

How to Use It

To add a post to your Guestbook, you just have to decide on the name of a file in which to store the data and pass that and the post details to the function PostToGuestBook(), like this:

```
$name    = 'F. Gump';
$email   = 'run@forestrun.com';
$website = 'http://www.mymommaalwayssaid.com';
$message = 'Life is like a box of chocolates';
$result  = PostToGuestBook('guestbook.txt', $name, $email,
    $website, $message);
```

Of course, when handling user-submitted data you will probably also want to sanitize the input using other recipes from this book, such as *Caps Control* or *Spell Check* from Chapter 3, or some of the form and user input recipes from Chapter 6, before saving data to the Guestbook.

The Recipe

```
function PostToGuestBook($datafile, $name, $email,
   $website, $message)
{
   $data = "$name!1!$email!1!$website!1!$message";

   if (file_exists($datafile))
   {
      $lines = explode("\n", rtrim(file_get_contents($datafile)));

      if (in_array($data, $lines)) return 0;
   }

   $fh = fopen($datafile, 'a');
   if (!$fh) return -1;

   if (flock($fh, LOCK_EX)) fwrite($fh, $data . "\n");
   flock($fh, LOCK_UN);
   fclose($fh);
   return 1;
}
```

RECIPE 53 GetGuestBook()

Once you have a Guestbook and the facility to post messages to it, you'll also want to be able to display the messages. This function goes most of the way toward that by fetching all the messages from the datafile and returning them in an array.

It does this rather than display them directly so as to leave you in complete control over how you want the output to appear. Figure 8-3 shows posts from a Guestbook simply being displayed as regular text with no special formatting.

About the Recipe

This recipe accepts the name of a datafile containing Guestbook data and returns all the messages from that file. Upon success, it returns a two-element array, the first of which contains the number of posts. The second element is a further array containing all the posts.

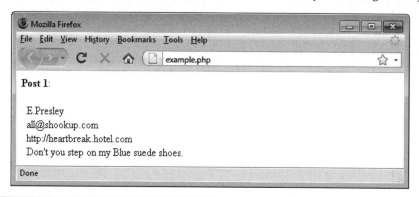

FIGURE 8-3   Using this recipe, it's easy to list all your Guestbook posts.

Or, upon failure it returns a single-element array with the value FALSE. It takes the following arguments.

- **$datafile** A string containing the location of a Guestbook datafile.
- **$order** The order in which to return the messages. If its value is "r", then posts are returned in reverse order, with the newest posts first; otherwise, posts are returned in order from oldest to newest.

Variables, Arrays, and Functions

$data	Array containing sub-arrays, each with all the items extracted from a post
$posts	Array containing the messages extracted from $datafile
$post	The current post being processed

How It Works

This code reads in a previously created-and-posted-to-Guestbook datafile and returns all the messages it contains. If the file cannot be read, it returns a single-element array with the value FALSE. Once read in, the array $posts is populated with the contents of $datafile, which is split into separate entries using the explode() function with an argument of \n, making the newline character the split boundary. The rtrim() function is also used to remove the final character, which is a \n newline, and is not required, as shown next:

```
if (!file_exists($datafile)) return array(0);

$data  = array();
$posts = explode("\n", rtrim(file_get_contents($datafile)));
```

Next, the argument $order is tested. If it contains the value "r", then the order of messages returned needs to be reversed so the function array_reverse() is applied to $posts, like this:

```
if (strtolower($order) == 'r')
   $posts = array_reverse($posts);
```

With $posts now in the order required, a foreach loop steps through the array, placing each element in turn into the variable $post. From here, the array $data (which was previously initialized as an empty array) has another element added to it, comprising an array extracted from the data in $post. This is done using the explode() function with an argument of !1!, which is the token I chose to split fields in a record. This separates out all the parts (name, e-mail, web site, and message) and returns an array, which is assigned to the current element of the $data array, as follows:

```
foreach ($posts as $post)
   $data[] = explode('!1!', $post);
```

Finally, a two-element array is returned, of which the first element contains the number of messages returned, while the second contains an array of arrays, each sub-array containing the parts of a single message:

```
return array(count($posts), $data);
```

How to Use It

To use this recipe, you only need to pass it the name of a datafile containing Guestbook data and an argument telling it which order to use when returning the messages, like this:

```
$result = GetGuestBook('guestbook.txt', 'f');
```

Then, you test $result[0] to see whether it contains the value FALSE. If it does, the function call failed and there are no messages to display. You can check for it like this:

```
if (!$result[0]) echo "Could not read file";
```

Otherwise, it contains a value representing the number of messages returned by the function. You can display this number like this:

```
echo "There are $result[0] posts";
```

If posts exits, the second element will then contain an array of arrays, each main array element containing a sub-array of four elements that represent, in order, the name, e-mail, web site, and message of a post. You can therefore act on this data like this:

```
for ($j = 0 ; $j < $result[0] ; ++$j)
{
    for ($k = 0 ; $k < 4 ; ++$k)
        echo $result[1][$j][$k] . "<br />";
    echo "<br />";
}
```

This code loops through all main elements in the array $result[1] with $result[1][0] being the first element of this array, and itself being an array with the following elements:

```
$result[1][0][0]
$result[1][0][1]
$result[1][0][2]
$result[1][0][3]
```

These four values represent the name, e-mail, web site, and message of the first post. The second post (if there is one) is returned in these four array elements (and so on):

```
$result[1][1][0]
$result[1][1][1]
$result[1][1][2]
$result[1][1][3]
```

Using these values, it's now up to you to create the styling and layout needed to make your Guestbook look just how you want it. Displaying them is as easy as placing them after echo statements, like this:

```
echo $result[1][1][0];
echo $result[1][1][1];
echo $result[1][1][2];
echo $result[1][1][3];
```

The Recipe

```php
function GetGuestBook($datafile, $order)
{
    if (!file_exists($datafile)) return array(0);

    $data  = array();
    $posts = explode("\n", rtrim(file_get_contents($datafile)));

    if (strtolower($order) == 'r')
        $posts = array_reverse($posts);

    foreach ($posts as $post)
        $data[] = explode('!1!', $post);

    return array(count($posts), $data);
}
```

PostToChat()

Some of the more popular features of a web site are messaging and chat facilities, particularly if they are fast and easy to use, which this recipe is—even though it's only about 30 lines of actual code, without a sign of Java or Flash in sight.

I first wrote the predecessor of this chat in 1996 using PERL scripts, and then later transported it to compiled C code. With the advent of PHP—due to its tremendous speed (even though it's not compiled)—I rewrote it again. But the code's format has remained pretty much the same: a simple text file that is continuously read from and written to, using file locking to prevent file corruption.

It also uses a feature that predates Ajax (the sending of background requests to a server to exchange data) but provides a similar functionality, in that messages appear in the browser when posted, without having to refresh the page. Figure 8-4 shows this post part of the chat engine being used to post a message, with and without flood control.

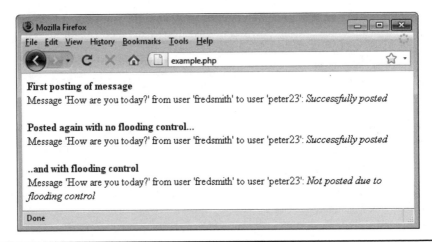

FIGURE 8-4   You can operate your own chatroom using this recipe.

About the Recipe

This recipe posts a message to a live chatroom and supports a number of parameters. Upon success, the code returns a value of 1. If the file cannot be written to, then –1 is returned, or if flooding control is on and a duplicate post has been prevented, 0 is returned. If $message is empty or there are illegal | symbols in either $to or $from, then –2 is returned. The recipe takes these arguments:

- **$datafile**   A string containing the location of a chatroom datafile.
- **$maxposts**   The maximum number of messages to retain at a time.
- **$maxlength**   The maximum message length in characters.
- **$from**   The username of the message poster.
- **$to**   The message recipient's username—leave blank if the message is public.
- **$message**   The contents of the message.
- **$floodctrl**   If this has the value "on", the same message cannot be reposted by the same user within $maxposts messages.

Variables, Arrays, and Functions

$data	Array used to populate $datafile with blank messages
$fh	File handle used to reference $datafile
$text	String containing all but the first message in $datafile
$lines	Array containing posts extracted from $text
$temp	String containing the post number of the final post in the file

How It Works

The object of this recipe is to remove the oldest message from the datafile and add the new message—if, that is, the new message is not a repeat, and flood control has not been enabled. So the first thing it does if the datafile doesn't exist is create it by putting together a collection of dummy blank posts in $data, like this:

```
if (!file_exists($datafile))
{
    $data = "";
    for ($j = 0 ; $j < $maxposts ; ++$j) $data .= "$j|||\n";
    file_put_contents($datafile, $data);
}
```

Each post is of the form: number|recipient|sender|message. The | symbols serve to separate the parts. Therefore, if the value in $maxposts is 20, for example, then $data will be populated with 20 |||\n strings. This ensures that, for an initial chat file, all fields in each post are blank and that each is terminated with a \n newline to separate records from each other. This whole string is then saved to $datafile using the file_put_contents() function.

At this point, there is definitely a datafile of posts, either one just created or one that was preexisting. So now the arguments passed to the code are checked. If $message is blank, or either $from or $to contains a banned | symbol, then there was a problem. In the former case, there is nothing to post, and in the latter the | symbols would corrupt the datafile and therefore would not be allowed. Ideally, when users enter your chatroom you will already have weeded out any such occurrences, but if not, this check will catch them. A value of –2 is returned in either case:

```
if ($message == "" || strpos($from, '|') ||
    strpos($to, '|')) return -2;
```

The | symbol can actually be useful in messages, so if any are encountered in $message, they are converted to their HTML entity equivalent of |. Also, if $message has more characters than the value specified in $maxlength, then $message is passed through the substr() function to truncate it to the maximum length allowed, like this:

```
$message = str_replace('|', '&#124;', $message);
$message = substr($message, 0, $maxlength);
```

With all the fields now prepared, the datafile is opened using the fopen() function and the file handle for manipulating it is assigned to $fh. If $fh is FALSE, the file couldn't be opened and so –1 is returned:

```
$fh = fopen($datafile, 'r+');
if (!$fh) return -1;
```

Otherwise, the flock() function is called (see PHP Recipe 52, *Post to Guestbook*, for further details) to ensure the program has exclusive access to the file, so there will be no clashes of concurrent writes. With the file lock obtained, the very first line of the file is returned using fgets(). This is the oldest post and therefore will be discarded—so the value returned is not used and is simply ignored, like this:

```
flock($fh, LOCK_EX);
fgets($fh);
```

Next, the string variable $text is assigned the remaining contents of the file using the fread() function, with an argument of 100000. This tells the function to read in at most, 100,000 characters from the file, up to the file's end. This should be more than you are likely to need because, for example, 20 messages of 1,000 characters each would only occupy 20,000 bytes. But you can easily change this value if you need to:

```
$text = fread($fh, 100000);
```

Next, the argument $floodctrl is checked, and if it has the value "on", no repeated posts are allowed. To check for this, the function strpos() is called, which returns a value of 0 or greater if a match is found, or FALSE if not. The string being checked for is |$to|$from|$message\n, which will ensure that only repeated posts from the same poster to the same recipient, with the same message, will be ignored.

If the post is a duplicate and flood control is on, then the file lock is released, the file is closed, and a value of 0 is returned, as follows:

```
if (strtolower($floodctrl) == 'on' &&
    strpos($text, "|$to|$from|$message\n"))
{
    flock($fh, LOCK_UN);
    fclose($fh);
    return 0;
}
```

Otherwise, the posts in the string variable $text are extracted into the array $lines using the explode() function to split them all out at \n newlines:

```
$lines = explode("\n", $text);
```

Next, the counter at the start of the last line of chat is extracted into the array $temp. This is done by referencing the correct element of $lines and then using explode() to pull out all the parts into $temp. The code is only interested in the first element of $temp, so that value is looked up and the number 1 is added to increment it. This gives the value to use for the message number of the new post being appended—the next in sequence. Therefore, $text (which contains the remaining chat posts, after ignoring the first one) has that number appended to it, followed by the contents of $to, $from, and $message, separated by | symbols, and terminated with a \n newline character. Here's the code that does this:

```
$temp = explode('|', $lines[$maxposts - 2]);
$text .= ($temp[0] + 1) . "|$to|$from|$message\n";
```

To update the file's contents, the fseek() command is now called to move the read and write pointer into $datafile to the very start. You remember that the first post was discarded? Well, now all the following posts must be moved back accordingly, so after seeking, the contents of $text are written to the file starting at position 0, as follows:

```
fseek($fh, 0);
fwrite($fh, $text);
```

Lastly, because the file is readable and writeable and we have been treating it like random access memory, if the size of the new set of posts is smaller than the previous set, the file will have some spurious text remaining at its end, which has to be discarded by issuing a call to the truncate() function, passing it the exact size of $text. The file lock is then released, the file closed, and a value of 1, representing success, is returned:

```
ftruncate($fh, strlen($text));
flock($fh, LOCK_UN);
fclose($fh);
return 1;
```

How to Use It

Generally, you will use this recipe as part of an HTML form submission and processing program. To allow the chat to be viewed without interruption, you will also probably place the program within an <iframe> tag so it takes up just a portion of the screen and works independently from the rest of the chat.

A good way to do this is to create a simple web form like the following, but embedded within your PHP code:

```
echo <<<_END
<form method=post action="$_SERVER[PHP_SELF]"><pre>
   From: <input type=text name='from' />
     To: <input type=text name='to' />
Message: <input type=text name='message' />
         <input type=submit value='Post Message' />
</pre></form>
_END;
```

Instead of using a program name for the action of the form, this script uses the PHP system variable $_SERVER[PHP_SELF], which simply refers to the program currently running, whatever name it may have. This means you can call the program anything you like.

For simplicity of layout, I have used a <pre> tag here to force a monospaced font. You will probably want a much more interesting layout for your own program. Also, you will most likely have already asked for the user's name, and if so, could use the following From: input line instead:

```
<input type=hidden name='from' value='$from' />
```

This means that the only two items you will ask your users for are the recipient's name and the message to post. To simplify things even further for your users, you might even replace the To: input line with a <select> tag and a dropdown list of all current users—but with the default name being blank, for public posts.

In other words, you should think about how your users will initially enter their usernames, which you will then store if you are going to offer pull-down lists of names for private messaging. So when about to call this recipe, your program should be armed with three pieces of information:

- The poster's username
- The recipient's name (or blank if a post is public)
- The message to post

If these have been posted to your program, they will appear in the $_POST array and can be referenced like this (not forgetting that you may wish to also use some other recipes in this book to sanitize user input):

```
$from    = $_POST['from'];
$to      = $_POST['to'];
$message = $_POST['message'];
```

You can then add the post to the chat by calling the code like this:

```
$result = PostToChat('chatroom.txt', 20, 1000, $from, $to,
    $message, 'off');
```

Here, the chatroom datafile is *chatroom.txt*, the maximum number of posts to keep stored is 20, the maximum length allowed for each post is 1000 characters, and flood control is set to "off".

If $result contains the value 1, then the message has been successfully posted. Otherwise, see the preceding section, *About the Recipe,* for the list of error codes and their meanings.

Bringing this all together, a program to display a single line input, residing in an iframe, that continually allows posting of public messages to the chat might look like this:

```php
<?php
if (isset($_POST['message']))
{
    $from    = $_POST['from'];
    $to      = $_POST['to'];
    $message = $_POST['message'];
    PostToChat('chatroom.txt', 20, 1000, $from, $to,
        $message, 'off');
}
else $from = 'username'; // Enter the poster's username here

echo <<<_END
<form method=post action="$_SERVER[PHP_SELF]">
<input type=hidden name='from' value='$from' />
<input type=hidden name='to' value='' />
Message: <input type=text name='message' />
<input type=submit value='Post Message' />
</form>
_END;


?>
```

This code will keep displaying a prompt similar to the following, and whenever a message is entered, it will post it to the chat datafile and redisplay the prompt:

Message: _____ **[Post Message]**

As discussed previously, posting private messages to other users is a little more complicated, but *only* a little, in that you simply have to set $to to the recipient's username. To do this, you would probably change the input form display to look something like the following, in which the first entry of a dropdown list is *ALL*, and then, if the variable $to ever has the value *ALL*, you would simply set it to the empty string before calling the code.

Message: _____ **To: [*All*] [Post Message]**

Or you may wish to offer other ways of sending private messages, such as listing all current users in a side panel and making them clickable to pull up a private messaging input prompt. That's why I have left the code fully flexible, so you can choose exactly how your chat should look and work.

The following recipe, *View Chat,* will be used to display the messages in real time with auto scrolling.

The Recipe

```php
function PostToChat($datafile, $maxposts, $maxlength,
    $from, $to, $message, $floodctrl)
{
    if (!file_exists($datafile))
```

```
{
    $data = "";
    for ($j = 0 ; $j < $maxposts ; ++$j) $data .= "$j|||\n";
    file_put_contents($datafile, $data);
}

if ($message == "" || strpos($from, '|') ||
    strpos($to, '|')) return -2;

$message = str_replace('|',  '&#124;', $message);
$message = substr($message, 0, $maxlength);
$fh      = fopen($datafile, 'r+');
if (!$fh) return -1;

flock($fh, LOCK_EX);
fgets($fh);
$text = fread($fh, 100000);

if (strtolower($floodctrl) == 'on' &&
    strpos($text, "|$to|$from|$message\n"))
{
    flock($fh, LOCK_UN);
    fclose($fh);
    return 0;
}

$lines = explode("\n", $text);
$temp  = explode('|', $lines[$maxposts - 2]);
$text .= ($temp[0] + 1) . "|$to|$from|$message\n";
fseek($fh, 0);
fwrite($fh, $text);
ftruncate($fh, strlen($text));
flock($fh, LOCK_UN);
fclose($fh);
return 1;
}
```

ViewChat()

This recipe is surprisingly small considering the power it packs, providing a continuously open connection to a chat server using just HTML, so that new messages appear as posted, without having to refresh the page. With some nifty JavaScript, it also auto scrolls the page when new messages display at the page bottom, and it can distinguish between a private and a public message, displaying each to the correct people.

Figure 8-5 shows half a dozen users chatting as viewed from the user *fredsmith*'s perspective. You can see all the public messages in regular typeface, while the private ones from and to *fredsmith,* are shown in italic font, and prefaced by the string (PM to *username*).

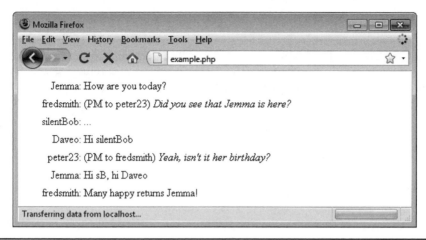

FIGURE 8-5   This recipe handles viewing of public and private messages and includes auto scrolling.

About the Recipe

This recipe takes a chatroom datafile and displays all the messages the current user is allowed to see—either public or private ones to or from that user. It takes the following arguments:

- **$datafile**   A string containing the location of a chatroom datafile.
- **$username**   The username of the current user viewing the chat.
- **$maxtime**   The maximum time in seconds a connection will stay open to the server. This needs to be a large value to prevent the chat reloading too often. About 300 seconds (5 minutes) is a good start point.

Variables, Arrays, and Functions

$tn	String containing the current time as a timestamp
$tstart	String containing the HTML table start tags
$tmiddle	String containing the HTML table middle tags
$tend	String containing the HTML table end tags
$oldpnum	Integer containing the value of the highest read post number
$lines	Array containing the posts extracted from $datafile
$line	String containing a single line of data from $lines
$thisline	Array containing all the elements extracted from $line
$postnum	Integer containing the number of the current post being read
$to	String containing the recipient name of the current post being read
$from	String containing the sender name of the current post being read
$message	String containing the message of the current post being read

How It Works

This recipe is really one big loop that goes round and round checking the contents of $datafile and displaying any new posts it finds that the user is authorized to view. It starts by trying to load in the chatroom datafile $datafile, and returns FALSE if it can't be read. Otherwise, the time the program is allowed to run (in seconds) is set using the set_time_limit() function and the argument $maxtime + 5. The extra five seconds are added to ensure the code will return gracefully, without displaying any warning message about the program having timed out, as shown next:

```
if (!file_exists($datafile)) return FALSE;

set_time_limit($maxtime + 5);
$tn      = time();
```

Tables are used to isolate the messages from each other so the next three string variables are initialized, $tstart, $tmiddle, and $tend. These contain HTML tags suitable for building a table in which to place each displayed message. This is a particularly useful trick, for example, when you offer the use of BB Code or Pound Code (PHP Recipes 39 and 40) and the user doesn't properly close tags. By placing the strings in a table, all tags will be fully closed regardless of which ones are left open, and the formatting from any one message won't affect any other. The final variable to initialize is $oldpnum. This is set to 0 to start with, but will be increased to the value of the highest numbered post so far read. This way, the program can tell when a new post comes in by noting whether it has a higher post number, like this:

```
$tstart  = "<table width='100%' border='0'><tr><td " .
           "width='15%' align='right'>";
$tmiddle = "</td><td width='85%'>";
$tend    = "</td></tr></table><script>scrollBy(0,1000);" .
           "</script>\n";
$oldpnum = 0;
```

Now the main while loop begins. It is set to loop forever by being passed an argument of 1. Each time around the loop the contents of $datafile are read in, the final character, an unwanted \n newline, is removed using rtrim(), and the posts are extracted into the array $lines using the explode() function, with an argument of \n to split all lines at the newline characters:

```
$lines = explode("\n", rtrim(file_get_contents($datafile)));
```

Next, a foreach loop is entered in which each post in the $lines array is placed into $line and then the parts of that post's details are extracted into the array $thisline using the explode() function, with the argument |, the separator I chose to signify field boundaries. These four items of information are then saved in $postnum, $to, $from, and $message, as follows:

```
$thisline = explode("|", $line);
$postnum  = $thisline[0];
$to       = $thisline[1];
$from     = $thisline[2];
$message  = $thisline[3];
```

Next, a test is made to see whether the number of the current post being processed is greater than the value stored in $oldpnum. If it is, then a post that has not been read yet has been encountered and so it must be examined to see if it should be displayed. Within this if statement, decisions on what to display are made, like this:

```
if ($postnum > $oldpnum)
{
   if ($to == "")
   {
      echo "$tstart$from:$tmiddle$message$tend";
   }
   elseif ($to == $username || $from == $username)
   {
      echo "$tstart$from:$tmiddle(PM to $to) " .
      "<i>$message</i>$tend";
   }
```

So, if the contents of $to is the empty string, then the post is public, in which case it is displayed using the echo command, by being placed into the correct position between the table-building strings $tstart, $tmiddle, and $tend. The $from string is also inserted to show who posted the message. The output will look something like the following (taken from the movie *Home Alone*):

Kevin: You guys give up, or are you thirsty for more?

If $to is not empty, then the message is private, so tests are made to determine whether the post is either *to* or *from* the current user. If either is the case, then the message is displayed in the correct place within the array strings, along with the $from string. In addition, the string (PM to *username*) is inserted to make it clear that the message is private, and the message itself is displayed in italics as a further indication. It will look something like this:

Marv: (PM to Harry) He's only a kid, Harry. We can take him.

Once the post has been processed, $oldpnum is set to the value of the post's number so it won't be looked at again. Then, two functions are called, ob_flush() and flush(), to ensure that all the text is sent to the browser, like this:

```
$oldpnum = $postnum;
ob_flush();
flush();
```

If they were not called, PHP would try to be helpful and hold back on sending all the posts until the script ended. Generally, this is the behavior you want from a web page—all the data in one block. But for chat, where you want to see messages in real time, and particularly in this case where a program could run for some minutes, the output needs to be flushed out after each post is displayed.

After processing all the posts in $datafile, the sleep() function is called with a parameter of 2:

```
sleep(2);
```

This makes the PHP program sit and do nothing for two seconds. It's necessary to do this because a delay of up to two seconds (and therefore an average of only one second) before seeing a new post is not very noticeable, but it does wonders for ensuring that the server runs smoothly. Otherwise, `$datafile` would be constantly called by all the chat view processes, when most of the time there would be no new posts to display, while the server's processor and hard disk would be getting thrashed.

Finally, a check is made to see whether the current time, as returned by the function `time()`, less the time stored in `$tn` when the program was started, is greater than the value of `$maxtime`. If it is, then the program has exceeded the maximum number of seconds it is allowed to run for, and the function returns with the value TRUE:

```
if ((time() - $tn) > $maxtime) return TRUE;
```

Now, you may ask why I don't simply allow the program to run for as long as the user is chatting. Well, the answer is that many chatters leave the chat running when they go off to make cups of coffee, or do the shopping, or even when they go to bed. Unfortunately, leaving a program running in such cases can very soon tie up even a powerful server.

One solution to this is to use an Ajax call to fetch all new posts instead of retaining an open connection to the server. This way, the server would only be polled every now and then. But the solution I have used here, as you'll see in the following section, is to exit from displaying the chat after a given length of time and then ask the user to click a link to reload the chat—it's a really simple way of ensuring the user is still active.

How to Use It

Using this recipe can be as simple as the following code, which restarts the script when the user clicks a link:

```
if (!ViewChat('chatroom.txt', 'fredsmith', 300))
   echo "Error. Could not open the chat data file";
else echo "<a href='" . $_SERVER['PHP_SELF'] .
   "'>Click here to continue</a>";
```

It requires just three arguments: the name of the chatroom datafile, the username of the person viewing the chat, and the timeout in seconds of the program. By using the PHP variable `$_SERVER['PHP_SELF']`, it doesn't matter what your program is called, because this variable will refer to it correctly.

If you know that the current user is still active—for example, because they have recently posted a message—you could restart the script automatically for them. In this case, you needn't impose a `Click here` message on them. One way to do this would be to load in the `$datafile` file and process it looking for any *From* fields with the user's username. If you find one, then the user posted recently and you can auto renew the chat using a bit of JavaScript, like this:

```
die("<script>self.location='" . $_SERVER['PHP_SELF'] . "'</script>");
```

The `die()` function acts as a combined `echo` and `exit` statement, and the JavaScript in it will cause the current page to be reloaded.

Of course, when you run your own chat server, you'll soon see the kinds of loads it is under, and the amount of time you can afford to leave the code running for in order to get the best uninterrupted user experience. For example, you may find that 15 minutes is more appropriate, particularly when fewer users are active.

The main thing, though, is that you can quickly and easily offer a fast and flexible chat service in a few lines of PHP code, without having to install large programs, or rely on Java or Flash programs, and you don't need to be stuck with a look and feel someone else has designed. The fact that this chat is only a few lines of code means you can tailor it exactly to your requirements, without delving through hundreds or thousands of lines of code.

TIP *Of course, going the Ajax route (where background calls are made behind the scenes to send and retrieve data to and from the server) is an even better solution to providing a smooth and flexible chat service, and you wouldn't need to change a lot to implement it. However, it can be tricky to get just right and would be too large a project for this book. That said, in Chapter 11 I do show you the principles of making Ajax calls and provide you with the code you will need.*

The Recipe

```php
function ViewChat ($datafile, $username, $maxtime)
{
    if (!file_exists($datafile)) return FALSE;

    set_time_limit($maxtime + 5);
    $tn      = time();
    $tstart  = "<table width='100%' border='0'><tr><td " .
               "width='15%' align='right'>";
    $tmiddle = "</td><td width='85%'>";
    $tend    = "</td></tr></table><script>scrollBy(0,1000);" .
               "</script>\n";
    $oldpnum = 0;

    while (1)
    {
        $lines = explode("\n", rtrim(file_get_contents($datafile)));

        foreach ($lines as $line)
        {
            $thisline = explode("|", $line);
            $postnum  = $thisline[0];
            $to       = $thisline[1];
            $from     = $thisline[2];
            $message  = $thisline[3];

            if ($postnum > $oldpnum)
            {
                if ($to == "")
                {
                    echo "$tstart$from:$tmiddle$message$tend";
                }
                elseif ($to == $username || $from == $username)
```

```
        {
            echo "$tstart$from:$tmiddle(PM to $to) " .
        "<i>$message</i>$tend";
        }

        $oldpnum = $postnum;
        ob_flush();
        flush();
    }
    }

    sleep(2);
    if ((time() - $tn) > $maxtime) return TRUE;
    }
}
```

SendTweet()

I have to admit that Twitter baffled me when it first came out. I asked myself, "What good was a micro blogging service supporting only 140 characters? And what kind of people would use it?"

The message length restriction was obviously based around the constraints of the mobile text messaging system, which is also limited to 140 characters, so if there was going to be a huge crossover between the two, that would make sense.

On the other hand, it soon became obvious to me when one day Google Mail went down for a few hours that Twitter was valuable because I could perform a search at *search. twitter.com* to instantly see whether it was just me, or if others were affected. Pretty soon, I got into the habit of checking Twitter for updates on major news stories—and that, as they say, was the start of that.

So now I believe Twitter to be an amazingly powerful tool for performing almost real-time research, interacting with colleagues and customers, and generally keeping up to date on the world in general (as well as keeping others up to date with your world). Therefore, it was a given that I would write a recipe for it. In fact, this is the first of three recipes for Twitter in this book.

Using this one, you can send a Tweet to your own account, the result of which is shown in Figure 8-6.

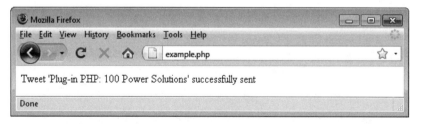

FIGURE 8-6 Posting a Tweet to Twitter is easy with this recipe.

About the Recipe

This recipe accepts the name and password for a Twitter account, along with a message to be Tweeted, and then sends the message to that user's account. Upon success, it returns TRUE. On failure, FALSE is returned. It takes these arguments:

- **$user**   A Twitter username.
- **$pass**   The matching password for $user.
- **$text**   Up to 140 characters of text to Tweet.

Variables, Arrays, and Functions

$url	String containing the URL of Twitter's status update API
$curl_handle	Handle returned by curl_init()
$result	XML result of calling curl_exec()
$xml	XML object created from $result

How It Works

Sometimes you can fetch web pages from other servers quite easily using the file_get_contents() function, but it only works for pages that can be fetched with a GET request. When a POST request is required, you either have to use a web form and submit it to the page in question or, more simply, you can use *mod curl,* as in this code.

This code starts off by using the substr() function to truncate the string $text to 140 characters (the maximum number of characters supported by Twitter), if it's longer than that. It does this to ensure that the string won't be truncated by Twitter, because later the code will check to see whether the status string of the user's most recent message is the same as $text. If so, then a status update has occurred. If $text were ever greater than 140 characters in length, then Twitter would truncate it before posting the Tweet, and so the returned status message would not be the same as the original $text. Therefore, the code ensures that Twitter never has to truncate $text:

```
$text = substr($text, 0, 140);
```

Next, the variable $url is set to the Twitter status update API page, and then all the parameters required for the call to curl_exec() are assigned their correct values, starting with setting the CURLOPT_URL option to $url and the CURLOP_CONNECTTIMEOUT option to 2, like this:

```
$url  = 'http://twitter.com/statuses/update.xml';
$curl_handle = curl_init();
curl_setopt($curl_handle, CURLOPT_URL, "$url");
curl_setopt($curl_handle, CURLOPT_CONNECTTIMEOUT, 2);
curl_setopt($curl_handle, CURLOPT_RETURNTRANSFER, 1);
curl_setopt($curl_handle, CURLOPT_POST, 1);
curl_setopt($curl_handle, CURLOPT_POSTFIELDS, "status=$text");
curl_setopt($curl_handle, CURLOPT_USERPWD, "$user:$pass");
```

The CURLOPT_RETURNTRANSFER option is set to 1 to prevent curl_exec() from directly outputting the result of making the POST request. Instead, the result is returned by the function in place of the normal success value of TRUE. The CURLOP_POST option is set to 1, indicating that a POST request is to be made, and the CURLOPT_POSTFIELDS option is given the string "status=$text", while CURLOPT_USERPWD is given the value "$user:$pass" to set up the login details.

Finally, curl_exec() is called, passing the handle $curl_handle, which was created at the start, and then curl_close() is called to close the connection. The result of the call is now in $result and will be FALSE for failure, or on success it will be a string of XML data containing the result returned by the called URL. If the Tweet was successful, there will be various elements in the XML, but notably the <text> field will contain the contents of the most recent status update (or Tweet):

```
$result = curl_exec($curl_handle);
curl_close($curl_handle);
```

To examine this field, a new XML object is created from $result in $xml using the simplexml_load_string() function. If it cannot be created, then the value FALSE is returned; otherwise, the object property $xml->text is compared with the value of $text, and if they are the same, the Tweet was successful and a value of TRUE is returned. Otherwise, FALSE is returned to indicate failure:

```
$xml = simplexml_load_string($result);
if      ($xml == FALSE)        return FALSE;
elseif ($xml->text == $text) return TRUE;
else                         return FALSE;
```

How to Use It

To send a Tweet to your Twitter account, just call the code like this:

```
$user   = 'twitteruser';
$pass   = 'twitterpass';
$text   = 'Hello world';
$result = SendTweet($user, $pass, $text);
```

The variables $user and $pass must be a valid Twitter username and password pair, and $text the text to Tweet. If the Tweet was successfully sent, $result will be TRUE; otherwise, it will have a value of FALSE, and you can use this variable to display a message, like this:

```
if ($result) echo "Tweet '$text' sent";
else         echo "Tweet '$text' failed";
```

The Recipe

```
function SendTweet($user, $pass, $text)
{
    $url = 'http://twitter.com/statuses/update.xml';
    $curl_handle = curl_init();
```

```
curl_setopt($curl_handle, CURLOPT_URL, "$url");
curl_setopt($curl_handle, CURLOPT_CONNECTTIMEOUT, 2);
curl_setopt($curl_handle, CURLOPT_RETURNTRANSFER, 1);
curl_setopt($curl_handle, CURLOPT_POST, 1);
curl_setopt($curl_handle, CURLOPT_POSTFIELDS, "status=$text");
curl_setopt($curl_handle, CURLOPT_USERPWD, "$user:$pass");
$result = curl_exec($curl_handle);
curl_close($curl_handle);

$xml = simplexml_load_string($result);
if     ($xml == FALSE)          return FALSE;
elseif ($xml->text == $text)    return TRUE;
else                            return FALSE;
}
```

SendDirectTweet( )

You can also send direct messages to other Twitter users as long as you are both following each other. It's an invaluable way to chat with other Twitter users without clogging up your public Twitter feed. Figure 8-7 shows the result of sending a direct message to the Twitter user *otheruser*.

About the Recipe

This recipe accepts the name and password for a Twitter account, along with the name of the Twitter user being sent the direct message and the message to Tweet. It then sends the message to that user's account. Upon success, it returns TRUE; otherwise, FALSE. It takes the following arguments:

- **$user**   A Twitter username.
- **$pass**   The matching password for $user.
- **$to**   The direct Tweet's recipient.
- **$text**   Up to 140 characters of text to Tweet.

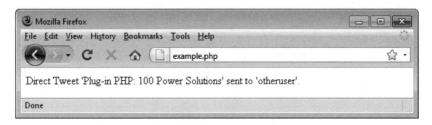

FIGURE 8-7   You can also send direct Tweets to other Twitter users.

Variables, Arrays, and Functions

`$url`	String containing the URL of Twitter's status update API
`$curl_handle`	Handle returned by `curl_init()`
`$result`	XML result of calling `curl_exec()`
`$xml`	XML object created from `$result`

How It Works

This recipe is substantially similar to the previous one, with just a few minor differences. So rather than explain its workings in full, I'll just cover the differences, which are that an additional argument, `$to`, is required by the code, which then gets appended to the `CURLOPT_POSTFIELDS` option as `&user=$to`, and the message now takes the different format of `text=$text` instead of `status=$text`. So the full string passed to `CURLOPT_POSTFIELDS` now becomes `user=$to&text=$text`.

Also, the API URL is different for sending a direct message and is now `/direct_messages/new.xml` instead of `/statuses/update.xml`. But apart from that, it's essentially the same code.

It's true, you *can* send a direct Tweet to another Twitter user by starting it with the letter d, followed by a space and then the person's username, but the data returned by `curl_exec()` would then only be that of the most recent Tweet because of using the `/statuses/update.xml` API URL.

However, by using the API URL of `/direct_messages/new.xml`, and passing the recipient to it as well as the message, Twitter will return the most recent direct message data when the Tweet is sent. You can then check this to see if the value in `$test` was actually posted, and therefore whether the direct message was successfully sent.

How to Use It

To send a direct Tweet, ensure that both the sending and recipient Twitter accounts follow each other and then call the code, like this:

```
$user   = 'twitteruser';
$pass   = 'twitterpass';
$to     = 'otheruser';
$text   = 'This is a direct Tweet';
$result = SendDirectTweet($user, $pass, $to, $text);
```

If all is well, `$result` will be set to a value of TRUE; otherwise, it will be FALSE upon failure. You can use this value as follows to display a success or failure message:

```
if ($result) echo "Direct Tweet '$text' sent";
else         echo "Direct Tweet '$text' failed";
```

The Recipe

```
function SendDirectTweet($user, $pass, $to, $text)
{
   $text = substr($text, 0, 140);
   $url  = 'http://twitter.com/direct_messages/new.xml';
```

```
$curl_handle = curl_init();
curl_setopt($curl_handle, CURLOPT_URL, "$url");
curl_setopt($curl_handle, CURLOPT_CONNECTTIMEOUT, 2);
curl_setopt($curl_handle, CURLOPT_RETURNTRANSFER, 1);
curl_setopt($curl_handle, CURLOPT_POST, 1);
curl_setopt($curl_handle, CURLOPT_POSTFIELDS,
    "user=$to&text=$text");
curl_setopt($curl_handle, CURLOPT_USERPWD, "$user:$pass");
$result = curl_exec($curl_handle);
curl_close($curl_handle);

$xml = simplexml_load_string($result);
if      ($xml == FALSE)        return FALSE;
elseif ($xml->text == $text) return TRUE;
else                          return FALSE;
}
```

RECIPE 58 GetTweets()

Here's the last of the triumvirate of Twitter treats. It's a recipe to fetch up to the last 20 posts of any Twitter user whose profile isn't private. Figure 8-8 shows the result of pointing the code at Eminem's Twitter feed.

About the Recipe

This recipe accepts the username of a Twitter account and, as long as it's not private, it returns the most recent Tweets. Upon success, it returns a two-element array, the first of which is the number of Tweets found, and the second is an array containing the Tweets. On failure, it returns a single-element array with the value FALSE. It takes this argument:

- **$user**   A Twitter username.

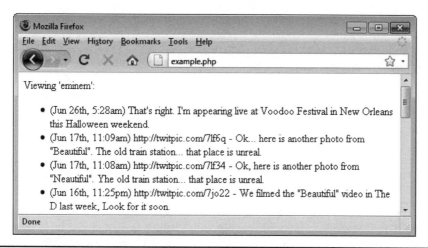

FIGURE 8-8   With this recipe, you can fetch the 20 most recent posts of a Twitter user.

Variables, Arrays, and Functions

$url	String containing the URL of Twitter's user timeline API
$file	String containing the data returned by $url
$xml	XML object created from $file
$tweets	Array of up to the 20 most recent Tweets from $user
$tweet	String containing each property of $xml->status as it is processed
$timestamp	Unix timestamp extracted from the date and time of a Tweet

How It Works

This recipe fetches a Twitter user's timeline feed from the following URL, where *username* is the name of the user:

http://twitter.com/statuses/user_timeline/username.xml

If the account is not set to private, the feed is returned in XML format. First of all, the time zone is set for reliable date information, then $url is assigned the URL to be retrieved and passes it to the file_get_contents() function, from where the XML is loaded into the string $file. If $file is zero characters in length, a single-element array with the value FALSE is returned because the feed could not be retrieved, or the username was invalid, as shown next:

```
date_default_timezone_set('utc');
$url  = "http://twitter.com/statuses/user_timeline/$user.xml";
$file = @file_get_contents($url);
if (!strlen($file)) return array(FALSE);
```

Otherwise, a new XML object called $xml is created from the contents of $file using the simplexml_load_string() function. If the object's value is FALSE, then the XML was invalid or otherwise unusable, so again an array with the value FALSE is returned, like this:

```
$xml  = @simplexml_load_string($file);
if ($xml == FALSE) return array(FALSE);
```

Now the code is ready to extract the Tweets from a feed, so the array $tweets is initialized and a foreach loop steps through each $xml->status property in the object, passing it into the object $tweet, as follows:

```
$tweets = array();

foreach ($xml->status as $tweet)
{
    $timestamp = strtotime($tweet->created_at);
    $tweets[] = "(" . date("M jS, g:ia", $timestamp) . ") " .
        $tweet->text;
}
```

The strtotime() function is used to convert the time stored in the property $tweet->created_at into a standard Unix timestamp value, which is then stored in $timestamp. This allows the code to replace the very awkward and overly precise dates and times used by Twitter, such as Thu Jun 5 21:28:18 +0000 2014, with much more friendly and readable strings, like Jun 5th, 9:28pm. This is done using the date() function with a formatting argument of "M jS, g:ia".

This new version of the date and time is then surrounded by brackets and followed by the Tweet itself, as retrieved from the property $tweet->text, and the resulting string is assigned to the next available element of the array $tweets.

Once all the Tweets have been processed, a two-element array is returned, the first element of which contains the number of Tweets returned, and the second an array containing all the Tweets:

```
return array(count($tweets), $tweets);
```

Incidentally, the @ symbols are in the code to suppress any warning error messages that might otherwise be displayed.

How to Use It

To use the recipe, just call it, passing the name of a Twitter user with a public account, like this:

```
$user   = 'stephenhawking';
$result = GetTweets($user);
```

You can then test the value(s) returned by checking $result[0], like this:

```
if (!$result[0]) echo 'Failed';
```

If $result[0] doesn't contain the value FALSE, then $result[1] will contain an array of all the Tweets, which can be displayed like this:

```
for ($j = 0 ; $j < $result[0] ; ++$j)
    echo $result[1][$j] . "<br />";
```

As with most of the recipes in this book, this one handles the task of manipulating the data and returning it to you in a sensible format. It's then up to you how you choose to display the result, but the preceding code will, at the very least, provide the information you want.

The Recipe

```
function GetTweets($user)
{
    date_default_timezone_set('utc');
    $url  = "http://twitter.com/statuses/user_timeline/$user.xml";
    $file = @file_get_contents($url);
    if (!strlen($file)) return array(FALSE);

    $xml  = @simplexml_load_string($file);
    if ($xml == FALSE) return array(FALSE);

    $tweets = array();

    foreach ($xml->status as $tweet)
    {
```

```
    $timestamp = strtotime($tweet->created_at);

    $tweets[] = "(" . date("M jS, g:ia", $timestamp) . ") " .
        $tweet->text;
}

    return array(count($tweets), $tweets);
}
```

ReplaceSmileys()

In the early days of bulletin boards, emoticons were invented as a means of expressing emotions not quickly conveyable in brief messages. These included the familiar :) and : (happy and unhappy faces, as well as dozens more. Nowadays, you still see them, but they are more often replaced with icons such as smileys.

In fact, many e-mail programs and other applications such as Microsoft Word will substitute emoticons for smileys automatically for you. And that's exactly the functionality that this recipe offers. Figure 8-9 shows the set of 20 smileys provided by it, a few of which (such as the kiss smiley) are animated to better convey their meaning.

About the Recipe

This recipe accepts a string of text to search for emoticons to replace with smiley GIF images. It takes the following arguments:

- **$text**   The text to process for emoticons.
- **$folder**   The folder in which you have saved the smiley GIFs.

Variables, Arrays, and Functions

$chars	Array of emoticons to search for
$gifs	Array of GIF filenames without the .gif extensions
$j	Integer index for iterating through the arrays

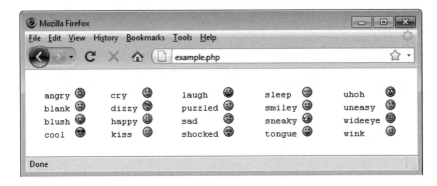

FIGURE 8-9   Use this recipe to replace text emoticons with smiley GIF images.

How It Works

This recipe supports 20 different types of emoticons and their associated GIF smileys. The emoticons are stored in the array $chars, and the GIF filenames (minus the *.gif* extensions) are housed in the array $gifs. They are all in groups to make the code easy to modify. For example, the first four elements of each array are the *angry* emoticons and smileys. Here are the supported emoticons and image filenames (minus their file extensions):

```
$chars = array('>:-(', '>:(', 'X-(',  'X(',
               ':-)*', ':)*', ':-*',  ':*', '=*',
               ':)',   ':]',
               ':-)',  ':-]',
               ':(',   ':C',   ':[',
               ':-(',  ':\'(', ':_(',
               ':O',   ':-O',
               ':P',   ':b',   ':-P', ':-b',
               ':D',   'XD',
               ';)',   ';-)',
               ':/',   ':\\',  ':-/', ':-\\',
               ':|',
               'B-)',  'B)',
               'I-)',  'I)',
               ':->',  ':>',
               ':X',   ':-X',
               '8)',   '8-)',
               '=-O',  '=O',
               'O.o',  ':S',   ':-S',
               '*-*',  '*_*');
```

```
$gifs = array( 'angry',   'angry',   'angry',   'angry',
               'kiss',    'kiss',    'kiss',    'kiss', 'kiss',
               'smiley',  'smiley',
               'happy',   'happy',
               'sad',     'sad',     'sad',
               'cry',     'cry',     'cry',
               'shocked', 'shocked',
               'tongue',  'tongue',  'tongue', 'tongue',
               'laugh',   'laugh',
               'wink',    'wink',
               'uneasy',  'uneasy',  'uneasy', 'uneasy',
               'blank',
               'cool',    'cool',
               'sleep',   'sleep',
               'sneaky',  'sneaky',
               'blush',   'blush',
               'wideeye', 'wideeye',
               'uhoh',    'uhoh',
               'puzzled', 'puzzled', 'puzzled',
               'dizzy',   'dizzy');
```

The emoticons need to be replaced with the correct HTML with which to display an associated GIF image, so the argument $folder is used to provide the correct path to the images. To ensure that paths (either with or without trailing slashes) are accepted, the code first removes any such slashes, before then adding one later where required, like this:

```
if (substr($folder, -1) == '/')
   $folder = substr($folder, 0, -1);
```

Then, a for loop is entered to iterate through all of the names in $gifs, replacing each element with the HTML that will reference each GIF, and providing its *width, height, alt,* and *title* attributes, as follows:

```
for ($j = 0 ; $j < count($gifs) ; ++$j)
   $gifs[$j] = "<image src='$folder/$gifs[$j].gif' " .
      "width='15' height='15' border='0' alt='$gifs[$j]' " .
      "title='$gifs[$j]' />";
```

With the $gifs array now suitably processed, both arrays are passed to the str_ireplace() function, which then replaces all occurrences of any emoticons in the $chars array, with the replacement code in the $gifs array. It does this while ignoring the case of each character so that, for example, both :S and :s will be replaced with the HTML for displaying the *puzzled.gif* smiley:

```
return str_ireplace($chars, $gifs, $text);
```

How to Use It

Before you call this recipe, you must download the folder of GIFs from the companion web site at *webdevelopmentcookbook.com*. Once downloaded and extracted, you'll find the GIFs in the folder *smileys*. To use them, copy the smileys to your web server and into a folder within your document root so they are accessible by a web browser.

If you wish, you can replace some or all of the icons as long as you keep the same filenames for the same smiley type. But remember, you may need to alter the *width* and *height* attributes in the code if your new smileys have different dimensions (or just leave those attributes out if the dimensions vary). The provided set of GIFs are all 15 × 15 pixels in size. Also make sure you don't rename or delete any of the files; otherwise, the code will not work correctly because it will assume all the files have the names specified in the array $gifs.

You use the code by passing it the text to process, as well as the path to the folder of the GIFs, like this (where *smileys* is the name of the folder):

```
echo ReplaceSmileys($text, 'smileys');
```

To test it, make sure $text contains a few emoticons, like ':) :] :D XD', and so on.

If you prefer, you can also assign the result of calling the recipe to a string variable, where it can then be used elsewhere in your program, like this:

```
$html = ReplaceSmileys($text, 'smileys');
```

The Recipe

```
function ReplaceSmileys($text, $folder)
{
   $chars = array('>:-(', '>:(', 'X-(',   'X(',
                  ':-)*', ':)*', ':-*',   ':*', '=*',
```

```
                    ':)',    ':]',
                    ':-)',   ':-]',
                    ':(',    ':C',    ':[',
                    ':-(',   ':\'(',  ':_(',
                    ':O',    ':-O',
                    ':P',    ':b',    ':-P', ':-b',
                    ':D',    'XD',
                    ';)',    ';-)',
                    ':/',    ':\\',   ':-/', ':-\\',
                    ':|',
                    'B-)',   'B)',
                    'I-)',   'I)',
                    ':->',   ':>',
                    ':X',    ':-X',
                    '8)',    '8-)',
                    '=-O',   '=O',
                    'O.o',   ':S',    ':-S',
                    '*-*',   '*_*');

    $gifs = array( 'angry',   'angry',   'angry',  'angry',
                   'kiss',    'kiss',    'kiss',   'kiss',   'kiss',
                   'smiley',  'smiley',
                   'happy',   'happy',
                   'sad',     'sad',     'sad',
                   'cry',     'cry',     'cry',
                   'shocked', 'shocked',
                   'tongue',  'tongue',  'tongue', 'tongue',
                   'laugh',   'laugh',
                   'wink',    'wink',
                   'uneasy',  'uneasy',  'uneasy', 'uneasy',
                   'blank',
                   'cool',    'cool',
                   'sleep',   'sleep',
                   'sneaky',  'sneaky',
                   'blush',   'blush',
                   'wideeye', 'wideeye',
                   'uhoh',    'uhoh',
                   'puzzled', 'puzzled', 'puzzled',
                   'dizzy',   'dizzy');


    if (substr($folder, -1) == '/')
        $folder = substr($folder, 0, -1);


    for ($j = 0 ; $j < count($gifs) ; ++$j)
        $gifs[$j] = "<image src='$folder/$gifs[$j].gif' " .
            "width='15' height='15' border='0' alt='$gifs[$j]' " .
            "title='$gifs[$j]' />";

    return str_ireplace($chars, $gifs, $text);
}
```

60 ReplaceSMSTalk( )

Sometimes your users will use *text speak* in their posts, so called because it evolved through the use of texting messages on mobile phones. It's a more compact and less time-consuming way of communicating that's also often used on Twitter, due to its similar restriction on message length.

But one thing it isn't is pretty. So if you would like to clean up posts a little before adding them to your site, this recipe will do the trick. Figure 8-10 shows the result of passing a string containing several text speak acronyms to the code, which it suitably corrects.

About the Recipe

This recipe accepts a string which, if it contains recognized text speak acronyms, is converted to standard English and returned. It takes this argument:

- **$text**   The text to be processed.

Variables, Arrays, and Functions

$sms	Array of text speak acronyms to be replaced and their equivalents in standard English
$from1	Array based on the $sms array with regular expression operators for processing uppercase
$to1	Array containing the standard English replacements for $from1
$from2	Array based on the $sms array with regular expression operators for processing lowercase
$to2	Array containing the standard English replacements for $from2
$j	Integer index for iterating through the arrays

How It Works

This function is based around the array $sms, which contains pairs of data: a text speak SMS acronym and its equivalent in standard English. I built the code this way to make it very

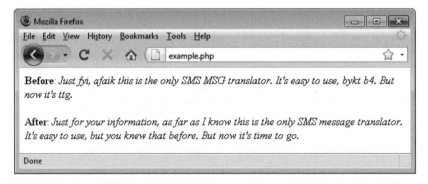

Figure 8-10   Want to translate your users' text speak? Do it with this recipe.

easy for you to change any pairs or add more of your own. Just remember to precede any apostrophes with a \ escape character (like this: \') to avoid getting an error message.

Because of the way these pairs are stored, they do need a little massaging to get them into a state with which $text can be processed. This is done by first initializing two pairs of *from* and *to* arrays: $from1 / $to1 and $from2 / $to2, like this:

```
$from1 = array(); $from2 = array();
$to1   = array(); $to2   = array();
```

Then, a for loop iterates through the $sms array, extracting the *from* and *to* halves of each pair, as follows:

```
for ($j = 0 ; $j < count($sms) ; $j += 2)
{
    $from1[$j] = "/\b$sms[$j]\b/";
    $to1[$j]   = ucfirst($sms[$j + 1]);

    $from2[$j] = "/\b$sms[$j]\b/i";
    $to2[$j]   = $sms[$j + 1];
}
```

This is done twice so all the uppercase text speak acronyms can have a different effect than lowercase ones. For example, the acronym BTW should be replaced with By the way (note the initial capital letter), but the acronym btw should be replaced with by the way (with no initial capital letter).

To achieve this, the $from1 array is populated with the correct regular expression to match only the uppercase acronyms. It does this using the \b operator, which marks the boundary between a word and a non-word character, so that only acronyms are matched and not groups of the same letters that may occur within words.

Next, $to1 has each replacement string passed through the ucfirst() function, which forces the initial letter of a string to uppercase, before being assigned the resulting value.

On the other hand, $from2 uses the same regular expression as $from1, except that a letter i is added after the closing / of the expression. This tells the preg_replace() function that matching should take place regardless of whether the acronyms are upper- or lowercase (or even a combination). The $to2 array doesn't have the replacements run through the ucfirst() function, so they will remain unchanged.

When the loop has completed, the arrays will all be correctly populated and so the preg_replace() function will be called twice to perform the replacements. The first time, $from1 acronyms are replaced with $to1 standard English and their first letters are capitalized. The second time, $from2 acronyms are replaced with $to2 standard English equivalents. The result of all these translations is then returned:

```
$text = preg_replace($from1, $to1, $text);
return  preg_replace($from2, $to2, $text);
```

How to Use It

To use this recipe, pass a string of text that you think may contain text speak to it, like this:

```
$text = "FYI, afaik imho this is a cool recipe. LOL.";
echo ReplaceSMSTalk($text);
```

The code will then make any required substitutions and return the result, which in the preceding case would be "For your information, as far as I know in my humble opinion this is a cool recipe. Laughing out loud."

The Recipe

```
function ReplaceSMSTalk($text)
{
    $sms = array('ABT2', 'about to',
                 'AFAIC', 'as far as I\'m concerned',
                 'AFAIK', 'as far as I know',
                 'AML', 'all my love',
                 'ATST', 'at the same time',
                 'AWOL', 'absent without leave',
                 'AYK', 'as you know',
                 'AYTMTB', 'and you\'re telling me this because?',
                 'B4', 'before',
                 'B4N', 'bye for now',
                 'BBT', 'be back tomorrow',
                 'BRB', 'be right back',
                 'BTW', 'by the way',
                 'BW', 'best wishes',
                 'BYKT', 'but you knew that',
                 'CID', 'consider it done',
                 'CSL', 'can\'t stop laughing',
                 'CYL', 'see you later',
                 'CYT', 'see you tomorrow',
                 'DGA ', 'don\'t go anywhere',
                 'DIKU', 'do I know you?',
                 'DLTM', 'don\'t lie to me',
                 'FF', 'friends forever',
                 'FYI', 'for your information',
                 'GBH', 'great big hug',
                 'GG', 'good game',
                 'GL', 'good luck',
                 'GR8', 'great',
                 'GTG', 'got to go',
                 'HAK', 'hugs and kisses',
                 'ILU', 'I love you',
                 'IM', 'instant message',
                 'IMHO', 'in my humble opinion',
                 'IMO', 'in my opinion',
                 'IMS', 'I\'m sorry',
                 'IOH', 'I\'m outta here',
                 'JK', 'just kidding',
                 'KISS', 'Keep it simple silly',
                 'L8R', 'later',
                 'LOL', 'laughing out loud',
                 'M8 ', 'mate',
                 'MSG', 'message',
                 'N1', 'nice one',
                 'NE1', 'anyone?',
                 'NMP', 'not my problem',
```

```
            'NOYB', 'none of your business',
            'NP', 'no problem',
            'OMDB', 'over my dead body',
            'OMG', 'oh my gosh',
            'ONNA', 'oh no, not again',
            'OOTO', 'out of the office',
            'OT', 'off topic',
            'OTT', 'over the top',
            'PLS', 'please',
            'PM', 'personal message',
            'POOF', 'goodbye',
            'QL', 'quit laughing',
            'QT', 'cutie',
            'RBTL ', 'reading between the lines',
            'ROLF', 'rolling on the floor laughing',
            'SMEM', 'send me an email',
            'SMIM', 'send me an instant message',
            'SO', 'significant other',
            'SOHF', 'sense of humor failure',
            'STR8', 'straight',
            'SYS', 'see you soon',
            'TAH', 'take a hike',
            'TBC', 'to be continued',
            'TFH', 'thread from hell',
            'TGIF', 'thank goodness it\'s Friday',
            'THX', 'thanks',
            'TM', 'trust me',
            'TOM', 'tomorrow',
            'TTG', 'time to go',
            'TVM', 'thank you very much',
            'VM', 'voice mail',
            'WC', 'who cares?',
            'WFM', 'Works for me',
            'WTG', 'way to go',
            'WYP', 'what\'s your problem?',
            'WYWH', 'wish you were here',
            'XOXO', 'hugs and kisses',
            'ZZZ', 'sleeping, bored');

    $from1 = array(); $from2 = array();
    $to1   = array(); $to2   = array();

    for ($j = 0 ; $j < count($sms) ; $j += 2)
    {
        $from1[$j] = "/\b$sms[$j]\b/";
        $to1[$j]   = ucfirst($sms[$j + 1]);

        $from2[$j] = "/\b$sms[$j]\b/i";
        $to2[$j]   = $sms[$j + 1];
    }

    $text = preg_replace($from1, $to1, $text);
    return  preg_replace($from2, $to2, $text);
}
```

CHAPTER 9

MySQL, Sessions, and Cookies

This chapter covers a lot of different topics, ranging from using MySQL to working with PHP sessions, and from applying basic security measures to handling cookies. Although at first sight these topics may not seem too closely related, they actually are because they're mostly to do with the processing, storage, and recall of data.

The three MySQL recipes provide a means of creating a database to hold various details about a user, the facility to add new users, and a recipe to verify a user against their username and password, while the PHP session recipes provide the ability to hold a user's details across multiple instances of the same or different web pages or PHP programs. Finally, the cookie recipes provide similar functionality to the session variables, except that you can set cookies to live for a shorter or longer time than the current session.

Along the way, you'll also learn how to build your own variations of these recipes, or how to extract the basic functionality from them to create totally new functions.

AddUserToDB( )

This recipe saves a user's details in a MySQL database. If the data table used doesn't already exist, it even creates it for you, so that there's minimum setup required.

So why MySQL? Well, so far in this book I've concentrated on using "flat" text files for storing data on the server. This is a quite adequate solution for small applications and utilities and it saves on having to configure and maintain a database such as MySQL. Indeed, had I gone the database route (and if you've been experimenting with the recipes), you'd probably have dozens of databases residing within MySQL. Instead, you should only have a collection of text files that you can simply delete when you don't want them any more.

However, the time will eventually come when the benefits of using a database begin to outweigh those of not doing so, and this recipe, which allows thousands of users and several fields per user, will help you deal with this issue. Yes, I could have used a text file and split all records at line breaks, separating out the fields with a special token, but the code required to support such a system would never run as fast as, or be as flexible as, using a database.

Figure 9-1 shows this recipe in action with a user being added twice to the database, the duplicate checking ensuring that the second insertion is ignored.

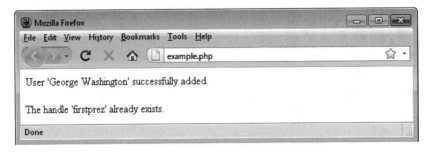

FIGURE 9-1   This recipe creates a user database and adds users to it.

About the Recipe

This recipe inserts a record into a MySQL database. If the database table does not already exist, it creates it first. Upon success, a value of 1 is returned. Otherwise, –1 is returned if the insert failed, or –2 if the handle already exists. It requires these arguments:

- **\$table**   The name of the data table.
- **\$nmax**   The maximum length allowed for \$name.
- **\$hmax**   The maximum length allowed for \$handle.
- **\$salt1**   Semi-random string to help secure the password.
- **\$salt2**   A second string to go with \$salt1.
- **\$name**   The user's full name to add to the database.
- **\$handle**   The user's username.
- **\$pass**   The user's password.
- **\$email**   The user's e-mail address.

Variables, Arrays, and Functions

\$query	String containing the query to pass to the MySQL database

How It Works

At the start of this recipe, the query required to create the table named by \$table is put together. For example, assuming that names are allowed 32 characters and handles 16, then the command-line MySQL statements in the query would be as follows:

```
CREATE TABLE IF NOT EXISTS Users
(
    name VARCHAR(32),
    handle VARCHAR(16),
    pass CHAR(32),
    email VARCHAR(256),
    INDEX(name(6)),
```

```
     INDEX(handle(6)),
     INDEX(email(6))
);
```

As you may know, when entered at its command-line interface, MySQL allows you to input a line at a time, and only sends the completed instructions when a final semicolon is encountered. So the preceding is valid MySQL syntax that you could type in. If you were to then enter:

```
DESCRIBE Users;
```

MySQL would show you the format of the table by displaying the following, which shows that the table *Users* has four fields (also known as columns), with *name, handle,* and *email* being variable-length character fields of up to 32, 16, or 256 characters, respectively, and *pass* being a fixed-length field of exactly 32 characters:

```
+--------+--------------+------+-----+---------+-------+
| Field  | Type         | Null | Key | Default | Extra |
+--------+--------------+------+-----+---------+-------+
| name   | varchar(32)  | YES  | MUL | NULL    |       |
| handle | varchar(16)  | YES  | MUL | NULL    |       |
| pass   | char(32)     | YES  |     | NULL    |       |
| email  | varchar(256) | YES  | MUL | NULL    |       |
+--------+--------------+------+-----+---------+-------+
```

This output also shows another thing worth pointing out, which is that all of *name, handle,* and *email* have been given indexes by the MySQL INDEX() statement, as shown by the word MUL under the Key heading. This means that, just like using a card index in a library, they will be quick to search.

Back to the PHP, though. No semicolon is required (or even allowed) when using the mysql_query() function, so all the preceding commands are run together into a single string stored in $query, which is then passed onto the mysql_query() function. If the call fails, then something has gone very wrong and so the code exits, returning an error message. This will enable you to properly debug your program, but on a production server you may wish to replace the die() function call with error handling of your own.

By the way, did you notice the IF NOT EXISTS clause at the start of the query? Using this means that the CREATE TABLE instruction will only ever be called once. Thereafter, the table will already exist and the command will be ignored. It's a neat way of avoiding having to issue an additional MySQL call to see whether a table exists before creating it. Note that this code assumes you have already created a suitable database and a user to access it (there's more on this in the following section).

So, having ensured that the table named by $table exists, a new query is placed in $query with which to check whether the user already exists in the table. We need to do this to avoid filling it up with duplicates. The query takes the following form (although *tablename* and *handle* will be different):

```
SELECT * FROM tablename WHERE handle='handle';
```

Again, the preceding is a MySQL command as you would type it into the command line—just leaving off the final semicolon makes it work with mysql_query(), to which the query is passed. Upon success, the mysql_query() function always returns a resource after a SELECT command, which can be used to examine the result of the query. In this case, the resource is returned directly to the mysql_num_rows() function, which returns a count representing the number of times the search is found in the database.

In this case, only a single entry of any handle is allowed so this value will be either 0 or 1. If the returned value is 1, then an entry already exists and so the function returns with a value of –2 to indicate the fact. Otherwise, it is all right to proceed with inserting the data into the database.

First, however, the password needs to be obfuscated to protect all the users should the database get into the wrong hands. This is done by converting the password into a special string called a *hash* using the md5() function. This is a type of function that only goes one way, and so the input cannot be derived from the output. In addition, to prevent attempts at dictionary hash cracking, a semi-random sequence of characters called a *salt* is added to both ends of the password before passing it to md5(). There's more on passwords and salting in the *Create Captcha* recipe section of Chapter 6, but suffice it to say that you must decide on the values of $salt1 and $salt2 and stick to them for as long as you use your database. These two values will be used for all stored password hashes.

The hash created by concatenating the password and two salts, and passing them to md5() is then assigned back to the variable $pass, which means that from this point onward even the program doesn't know the value of the user's password.

A final query string is then assembled in $query along the lines of this MySQL command-line statement:

```
INSERT INTO tablename VALUES
(
    name,
    handle,
    pass,
    email
);
```

Of course, these values are replaced with the actual contents of the variables $table, $name, $handle, $pass, and $email, and the semicolon is omitted. The string is then passed to mysql_query() and, if the result of the call is TRUE, a value of 1 is returned; otherwise, –1 is returned to indicate failure.

More experienced MySQL users may wonder why I didn't make the *handle* field UNIQUE and simply try to apply the INSERT INTO regardless, which would automatically fail if a handle of the same name already exists. The answer is that mysql_query() only returns either TRUE or FALSE for an INSERT command. Therefore, it would not be possible to distinguish between a call that failed due to a record already existing, or one that failed from a syntax or other error. As well as being perfect for preventing duplicate entries, the former case is important to check for so that a user can be told whether or not the handle they have chosen has already been taken.

TIP *MySQL doesn't mind whether you enter commands in upper- or lowercase. Neither does it worry about the case of database, table, or field names; it is case-insensitive. However, the convention for SQL queries is to use uppercase for commands and lowercase (or mixed upper- and lowercase) for everything else, but it's up to you whether or not to follow this suggested style. Note that this does not affect the contents of fields, which are usually stored exactly as provided.*

How to Use It

Before using this recipe, you will need to have created a MySQL database and a MySQL user that has access to that database. If you are using Zend Server CE, you should log in to the Command Line Client, which you can do as follows, according to the operating system upon which you installed it:

- **Windows**
  Select Start | All Programs | Zend Server Community Edition | MySQL Server 5.1 | MySQL Command Line Client. When the terminal window appears, as long as you haven't yet set up a password, just press RETURN.

- **Linux**
  Open up a terminal window and enter the following, followed by your MySQL root password (which should be the same as your Linux root password):
  ```
  mysql -uroot -p
  ```

- **Mac OS X**
  Open up a terminal window and enter the following (assuming you have not yet created a root password for MySQL):
  ```
  /usr/local/zend/mysql/bin/mysql -uroot
  ```

If you aren't using Zend Server CE or have a different installation of MySQL, you will need to refer to the documentation that came with your version to see how to enter the MySQL command-line prompt as user *root*.

Whatever setup you have, you should now be able to create a new database so, for example, let's create one called *mydb* by entering the following MySQL command:

```
CREATE DATABASE mydb;
```

Now you need to create a user that has access to this new database so, for example, to create the user *testing* with the password *testing,* you would enter the following:

```
GRANT ALL ON mydb.* TO 'testing'@'localhost' IDENTIFIED BY 'passwd';
```

The GRANT command is the standard way to create a MySQL user, and the qualifier ALL tells MySQL to allow the user to do anything with the database piphp and any of its objects, such as tables, denoted by the .* part. The user is given the @'localhost' suffix because that is where the PHP program that will access MySQL will reside. The IDENTIFIED BY 'passwd' portion sets the password for the user.

Note that you must use the full form of 'testing'@'localhost', in which quotes are placed around the user and host names because, although it may sometimes work when you omit these quotes, that is not always the case.

Some of the examples on the *webdeveloperscookbook.com* web site use a user/password pair of *testing/testing* by default, so you may want to issue the preceding command exactly as you see it, as well as creating any other users you think you will need. When you've finished with the *testing* user account, you can always delete it by entering:

```
DROP USER 'testing'@'localhost';
```

With the database and a user now created, let's get onto using the recipe. The first thing you must do before using it is establish a connection to the MySQL database. To do this, you need to provide the details given in the following code:

```
$dbhost = 'localhost';
$dbname = 'mydb';
$dbuser = 'testing';
$dbpass = 'passwd';
```

Because the web server will generally be running on the same computer as the MySQL database, $dbhost will usually require the value localhost. If you were using a different server for your database, you would replace this with its domain name or IP address.

The name of the database to use is placed in $dbname—if you followed the earlier instructions, you will have created a database called *mydb* that you can use. You will also have created a MySQL user called *testing* with a password of *passwd*, so $dbuser and $dbpass can be set to those values. Otherwise, assign values for another user you have created with access to the database referred to by $dbname.

You are now ready to establish a connection to MySQL by issuing a mysql_connect() call, like this:

```
mysql_connect($dbhost, $dbuser, $dbpass) or die(mysql_error());
```

Because success of this call is fundamental to the recipe, if it fails, an error is instantly output and the program quits. This will enable you to fully debug your code before using it on a production server. However, you will probably want to replace the call to die() with your own error management when you do so.

Once the connection has been made, you can then select the database to be used by the program employing the mysql_select_db() function, like this:

```
mysql_select_db($dbname) or die(mysql_error());
```

Again, failure will generate an error and cause the program to exit. But, all being well, execution will then move onto the remainder of your program which, for illustration of the use of this recipe, needs to prepare a selection of variables, as follows:

```
$table  = 'Users';
$nmax   = 32;
$hmax   = 16;
$name   = "George Washington";
$handle = "firstprez";
$pass   = "GW022232";
$email  = "george@washington.com";
$salt1  = "F^&£g";
$salt2  = "9*hz!";
```

The string value of *Users* in $table is the name of the MySQL table to create and use within the database *mydb* (or whatever you called it). Although I have shown it with an initial capital letter to differentiate it from a field name, it could have the value *users* or *USERS* and so on, because table names are case-insensitive.

The numeric variables $nmax and $hmax, respectively, represent the maximum number of characters allowed in the strings $name and $handle. You will very likely decide to use different values in your own programs.

The $name, $handle, $pass, and $email string variables contain the name, username, password, and e-mail details for the current user, while $salt1 and $salt2 are semi-random strings you should create to help make it next to impossible to deduce a password from the md5() hash, which will be created from the concatenation of the password with these strings.

We are now ready to insert a new record into the database using code such as this:

```
$result = AddUserToDB($table, $nmax, $hmax, $salt1, $salt2,
   $name, $handle, $pass, $email);
```

If this is the first record to add, then a table with the name in $table will be created before the record is inserted. If the insert was successful, $result will now contain a value of 1; otherwise, it will be –1 if the insert failed, or –2 if a record containing the string in $handle already exists in the database. You can therefore test this value as follows to decide what to do next:

```
if ($result == -2) echo "The handle '$handle' already exists." .
   "Please choose a different handle.";
elseif ($result == 1) echo "User '$name' successfully added.";
else echo "Failed to add user '$name'.";
```

The Recipe

```
function AddUserToDB($table, $nmax, $hmax, $salt1, $salt2,
   $name, $handle, $pass, $email)
{
   $query = "CREATE TABLE IF NOT EXISTS $table(" .
           "name VARCHAR($nmax), handle VARCHAR($hmax), " .
           "pass CHAR(32), email VARCHAR(256), " .
           "INDEX(name(6)), INDEX(handle(6)), " .
           "INDEX(email(6)))";
   mysql_query($query) or die(mysql_error());

   $query = "SELECT * FROM $table WHERE handle='$handle'";
   if (mysql_num_rows(mysql_query($query)) == 1) return -2;

   $pass  = md5($salt1 . $pass . $salt2);


   $query = "INSERT INTO $table VALUES('$name', '$handle', " .
           "'$pass', '$email')";
   if (mysql_query($query)) return 1;
   else return -1;
}
```

PART II

62 GetUserFromDB()

Using this recipe, you can look up a user's details as entered using the previous recipe, AddUserToDB(), by passing just their handle (username) and the name of the table in which the database details are stored. Figure 9-2 shows the items returned, including the obfuscated password, which cannot be used to determine the original password.

About the Recipe

Provided with a table name and handle, this recipe retrieves a user's details and returns them. Upon success, it returns a two-element array with the first element having the value TRUE and the second being an array containing the user's details (in turn: *name, handle, pass,* and *email*). On failure, it returns a single-element array with the value FALSE. It requires these arguments:

- **$table**   The name of the data table.
- **$handle**   The user's username.

Variables, Arrays, and Functions

$query	String containing the query to pass to the MySQL database
$result	Integer result of performing the query in $query

How It Works

This recipe expects a database and associated table to have already been created and to contain the user's details being looked up. Because a connection to MySQL should already be open and the database selected, it takes just the arguments $table and $handle, from which it constructs a query to make to MySQL, which it assigns to $query. In standard command-line MySQL syntax, the query looks like this:

```
SELECT * FROM tablename WHERE handle='username';
```

This tells MySQL to search through the table *tablename* and make a note of every record in which the field (also known as the column) called *handle* contains the string *username*. When sent to the mysql_query() function, the semicolon is omitted and the variables

FIGURE 9-2   Four items of information are stored for each user.

`$table` and `$handle` are substituted with their contents. The result of making the function call is then assigned to `$result`.

TIP *The * symbol tells MySQL to fetch all the fields in a record and is shorthand for providing all the field names individually, separated with commas. However, when you only want some of the fields to be returned, using a * would be wasteful of both memory and CPU cycles, and therefore in such a case naming each one would be more efficient.*

Then, the `mysql_num_rows()` function is called using `$result` as its argument. Because no handle is allowed to be duplicated, this function can only ever return 0 if the handle doesn't already exist, or 1 if it does. So, if a value of 0 is returned, then the recipe returns FALSE to indicate no matching record exists in the database.

Otherwise, a matching record has been found and the recipe returns a two-element array, the first of which contains the value TRUE to indicate success, and the second holds a four-element array containing all the fields in the record.

How to Use It

To use this recipe, it is assumed you have already created a MySQL database and a MySQL user that has been allowed access to it (as in the previous recipe, *Add User to DB*). You will therefore have to provide these details to your program so it can connect to MySQL and select the database. You can do this with the following code:

```
$dbhost = 'localhost';
$dbname = 'mydb';
$dbuser = 'testing';
$dbpass = 'passwd';
mysql_connect($dbhost, $dbuser, $dbpass) or die(mysql_error());
mysql_select_db($dbname) or die(mysql_error());
```

These six lines define the database host and name (as well as a MySQL username and password), connect to MySQL, and select the database. If any errors occur in this process program, execution is terminated and an error message is displayed. On a production server, you may wish to replace the calls to the `die()` function with your own, more user-friendly error handling.

Next, you need to define the table name and the handle of the user whose details you wish to look up, and then call the recipe, like this:

```
$table  = 'Users';
$handle = 'firstprez';
$result = GetUserFromDB($table, $handle);
```

After the call, if `$result[0]` is FALSE, then the lookup failed and no matching user was found. Otherwise, `$result[0]` will have a value of TRUE and `$result[1]` will contain a sub-array with the user's details, which you can access using code such as this:

```
if ($result[0] == FALSE) echo "Lookup failed.";
else echo "Name        = " . $result[1][0] . "<br />" .
          "Handle      = " . $result[1][1] . "<br />" .
          "Pass(salted) = " . $result[1][2] . "<br />" .
          "Email       = " . $result[1][3];
```

The Recipe

```
function GetUserFromDB($table, $handle)
{
    $query  = "SELECT * FROM $table WHERE handle='$handle'";
    $result = mysql_query($query);
    if (mysql_num_rows($result) == 0) return array(FALSE);
    else return array(TRUE, mysql_fetch_array($result, MYSQL_NUM));
}
```

VerifyUserInDB()

Using this recipe, you can pass a username (also known as a handle) and password, as entered by a user and, without needing to look up any details, just pass on these to the recipe, which will then report whether they verify or not. In Figure 9-3, the handle *firstprez* is checked against two similar but different passwords. Only the correct one of *GW022232* verifies.

Incidentally, *GW022232* is not a very secure password, and the user would be well advised *not* to use his birthday of February 22nd '32 in future passwords.

About the Recipe

This recipe compares a supplied handle (username) and password to those stored in the database. If they match, it returns TRUE; otherwise, it returns FALSE. It requires these arguments:

- **$table**   The name of the data table.
- **$salt1**   The first salt as supplied to AddUserToDB().
- **$salt2**   The second salt value.
- **$handle**   The user's username as entered by them.
- **$pass**   The user's password.

Variables, Arrays, and Functions

$result	Array result of calling GetUserFromDB()

FIGURE 9-3   A username (handle) and password must match exactly to be verified.

How It Works

This function takes the handle supplied to it, which will in turn have been provided by a user, and passes it to the GetUserFromDB() recipe to retrieve the accompanying user details from the database.

If the call fails, signified by the return value $result[0] having a value of FALSE, then the handle in $handle was not found in the database, and so a value of FALSE is returned. Otherwise, the value in $result[1][2], which is the stored salted and md5() processed password, is compared with the result of performing the identical salting and md5() transformation on the supplied password.

If the results are the same, then the password supplied is the same as the one originally used to create the account, and so a value of TRUE is returned. Otherwise, FALSE is returned.

How to Use It

To use this recipe, you need to have opened a connection to MySQL and selected the database to use, with code such as this:

```
$dbhost = 'localhost';
$dbname = 'piphp';
$dbuser = 'testing';
$dbpass = 'passwd';
mysql_connect($dbhost, $dbuser, $dbpass) or die(mysql_error());
mysql_select_db($dbname) or die(mysql_error());
```

In the preceding, $dbhost is likely to remain with a value of localhost, since the web server and PHP processor will be running on the same computer as the MySQL database. The variable $dbname is the database you should have created, as advised in the earlier recipe in this chapter, AddUserToDB(). The variables $dbuser and $dbpass should be the username and password of a MySQL user that has been granted access to the database.

The remaining two lines connect to MySQL and select the database. If either action fails, an error message is displayed and program execution stops. Therefore, on a production server, you may wish to replace the die() call with an error handling function of your own.

Next, you need to assign values for the table and two salts used, as well as the handle and password to be verified, like this:

```
$table   = 'Users';
$salt1   = "F^&£g";
$salt2   = "9*hz!";
$handle  = 'firstprez';
$pass    = 'GW022231';
```

The two salts, $salt1 and $salt2, must be the same semi-random strings you assigned when using AddUserToDB().

You are now ready to verify the user's details in the following way:

```
$result = VerifyUserInDB($table, $salt1, $salt2,
   $handle, $pass);
```

Upon success, $result will have the value TRUE; otherwise, it will be FALSE. You can use this return value in the following manner:

```
if ($result) echo "Login details $handle/$pass verified.";
else echo "Login details $handle/$pass could not be verified.";
```

Other than for testing the recipe, this code isn't actually useful. Instead, your code will likely re-present a form to the user if verification failed; otherwise, it will probably log a user in, possibly using PHP sessions (described a little later on in this chapter, starting at the CreateSession() recipe).

Incidentally, if you entered the details for this sample user earlier on in this chapter, this example will not verify unless you change the password from *GW022231* to *GW022232*.

The Recipe

```
function VerifyUserInDB($table, $salt1, $salt2,
   $handle, $pass)
{
   $result = GetUserFromDB($table, $handle);
   if ($result[0] == FALSE) return FALSE;
   elseif ($result[1][2] == md5($salt1 . $pass . $salt2))
      return TRUE;
   else return FALSE;
}
```

SanitizeString() and MySQLSanitizeString()

When accepting user input for redisplay, and particularly if it will be inserted into a database, it's important that you sanitize the input to remove any malicious attempts at hijacking your server, or otherwise injecting unwanted MySQL commands, HTML, or JavaScript. Figure 9-4 shows each of the recipes in this section being used to sanitize a string.

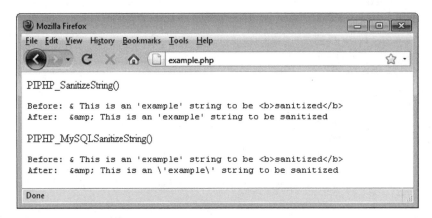

FIGURE 9-4 This pair of recipes will protect your web site from hacking attempts.

The function SanitizeString() has removed the HTML <b> and </b> tags from it and converted the & symbol to the & HTML entity, while MySQLSanitizeString() has also added escape characters before the single quotation marks so that they will be inserted into a field by MySQL, rather than possibly being interpreted.

About the Recipes

These recipes take a string and sanitize it for reuse on your web site and/or in a MySQL database. They require this argument:

- **$string**   A string to be sanitized.

Variables, Arrays, and Functions

SanitizeString()	The function MySQLSanitizeString calls the function SanitizeString() to prevent code duplication

How They Work

Let's start with the SanitizeString() function, which calls two PHP functions: strip_tags() and htmlentities(). The former removes all HTML tags from a string, while the latter converts all instances of characters such as < and > to < and >, & to &, and so on, like this:

```
$string = strip_tags($string);
return htmlentities($string);
```

Between them, they will remove any attempts at inserting any HTML tags into your web site, whether they are simple tags such as <b> for bold or more dangerous <script> tags. They also see to it that no special characters are allowed by replacing any with HTML entities that will not perform an action, only displaying in a browser as the characters they represent.

The MySQLSanitizeString() function does the same by calling the SanitizeString() function, but in addition it deals with potential problems relating to MySQL.

First, it checks whether the *Magic Quotes* setting of PHP is enabled, which is a method of dealing with quotation marks supplied by the user. When Magic Quotes is on, all single- and double-quote characters, as well as backslashes and NULL characters are escaped automatically by preceding them with a backslash. However, the feature is now deprecated and should not be used since there are better ways of sanitizing data (such as using the two recipes presented in this section), as follows:

```
if (get_magic_quotes_gpc())
    $string = stripslashes($string);
```

Therefore, if Magic Quotes is enabled, then the first thing this recipe does is call the stripslashes() function to remove any that may have been added. Next, it calls the SanitizeString() function, and finally it calls the mysql_real_escape_string() function, which renders a string totally harmless to MySQL injection attacks, which are where a user enters a quotation mark in the hope that it will close a MySQL statement, enabling MySQL commands they add after the quote to be executed.

For example, the following MySQL command, resulting from a user having entered the handle `jjones`, looks quite safe:

```
SELECT * FROM Users WHERE handle='jjones' AND pass='secret';
```

But what if, when asked for their handle, a user were to input a value of `Admin'#` and it wasn't sanitized? Well, if this string was allowed through to MySQL, the complete command would become:

```
SELECT * FROM Users WHERE handle='Admin'#' AND pass='secret';
```

What has happened here is that the user closed the quotation mark and then supplied a # symbol, which is treated by MySQL as the start of a comment. Therefore, everything from the # onwards (highlighted in the preceding code in italics) gets ignored and so users find themselves logged in as the user *Admin*. Obviously, this is not good, to say the least.

However, a simple call to `mysql_real_escape_string()` replaces all such possible hacks with escaped versions of the characters, so that the string can only ever be used as data and never treated as a command to be executed. Combining all these security measures into these new functions ensures you never forget any when coding your web sites.

How to Use Them

To use either of these functions, simply call them up by passing a string to be sanitized, like this:

```
$string = "& This is an 'example' string to be <b>sanitized</b>";
echo "Using Sanitize String<xmp>";
echo "Before: " . $string . "\n";
echo "After:  " . SanitizeString($string);
echo "</xmp>";
$dbhost = 'localhost';
$dbname = 'mydb';
$dbuser = 'testing';
$dbpass = 'testing';
mysql_connect($dbhost, $dbuser, $dbpass) or die(mysql_error());
echo "Using MySQL Sanitize String<xmp>";
echo "Before: " . $string . "\n";
echo "After:  " . MySQLSanitizeString($string);
echo "</xmp>";
```

The `<xmp>` tag sets the typeface to a form that indicates example text. The `SanitizeString()` function is quite straightforward, but there are two important things to note about the `MySQLSanitizeString()` function, which are that it will generate an error if it is called when a connection to a database is not already open (which is why the preceding example creates a database connection before calling it), and you must make sure that `SanitizeString()` is also pasted into your program, or otherwise included by it, because it is referenced.

The Recipes

```
function SanitizeString($string)
{
    $string = strip_tags($string);
    return htmlentities($string);
}

function MySQLSanitizeString($string)
{
    if (get_magic_quotes_gpc())
        $string = stripslashes($string);
    $string = SanitizeString($string);
    return mysql_real_escape_string($string);
}
```

CreateSession()

If you have a web site that a user can join, then you need a way to keep track of that person as they navigate through the site. Not for reasons of spying on them or anything like that, but purely in order to keep them logged in and to offer them all the benefits that membership provides. Figure 9-5 shows this recipe being used to create a session and read back one of the session variables.

About the Recipe

This recipe takes all the same details about a user we have previously been storing in a MySQL database and saves them in PHP session variables. It requires these arguments:

- **$handle**   A username.
- **$pass**   A matching password.
- **$name**   The user's real name.
- **$email**   The user's e-mail address.

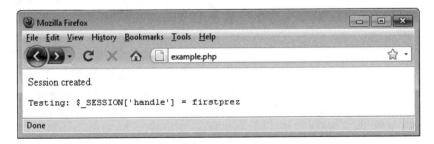

FIGURE 9-5   Creating a PHP session allows you to maintain a user's details across multiple pages.

Variables, Arrays, and Functions

$_SESSION['handle']	The user's handle stored in a session variable
$_SESSION['pass']	The user's password stored in a session variable
$_SESSION['name']	The user's name stored in a session variable
$_SESSION['email']	The user's e-mail address stored in a session variable
$_SESSION['ipnum']	The user's IP number stored in a session variable
$_SESSION['agent']	The user's web browser User Agent string stored in a session variable

How It Works

This is a recipe that provides convenience more than anything else, because it simply starts a new PHP session using the session_start() function and then assigns the values passed to the recipe to the various session variables. If the session can't be started, then FALSE is returned; otherwise, TRUE is returned, as follows:

```
if (!session_start()) return FALSE;

$_SESSION['handle'] = $handle;
$_SESSION['pass']   = $pass;
$_SESSION['name']   = $name;
$_SESSION['email']  = $email;
$_SESSION['ipnum']  = getenv("REMOTE_ADDR");
$_SESSION['agent']  = getenv("HTTP_USER_AGENT");
```

One reason the call may fail is if any text has already been output by your program. This is because session details are often stored in cookies (unless the user has cookies disabled, in which case they are stored in the query string), and therefore they must be exchanged between the server and browser before any other data.

Note how the user's IP address and the User Agent string supplied by their browser are also saved as session variables. They will be used later in this chapter in the *Secure Session* recipe.

Don't worry about this system possibly storing private details (for example, a username and password) anywhere unsafe, because it doesn't. PHP stores these details internally and they are never sent to the browser. Instead, an identifying token is all that is ever passed back and forth between the server and browser.

How to Use It

In order to use this recipe, you already need to have available the four items of data about a user to store in the session variables. These may have been input by the user or retrieved from a MySQL database, but in the following example they are simply assigned to some variables and then the CreateSession() function is called:

```
$handle = "firstprez";
$pass   = "GW022232";
$name   = "George Washington";
$email  = "george@washington.com";
$result = CreateSession($handle, $pass, $name, $email);
```

Upon success, $result will have the value TRUE; otherwise, it will be FALSE. You can act on this value in the following manner, which displays the contents of one of the session variables to demonstrate that the call succeeded:

```
if (!$result) echo "Could not create session.";
else
{
    echo 'Session created.<br /><pre>';
    echo 'Testing: $_SESSION[\'handle\'] = ' .
        $_SESSION['handle'];
}
```

For correct results, make sure you only call this recipe before you output any text; otherwise, session creation and variable assignment may fail.

The Recipe

```
function CreateSession($handle, $pass, $name, $email)
{
    if (!session_start()) return FALSE;

    $_SESSION['handle'] = $handle;
    $_SESSION['pass']   = $pass;
    $_SESSION['name']   = $name;
    $_SESSION['email']  = $email;
    $_SESSION['ipnum']  = getenv("REMOTE_ADDR");
    $_SESSION['agent']  = getenv("HTTP_USER_AGENT");

    return TRUE;
}
```

RECIPE 66   OpenSession()

Once you have used CreateSession() to store a user's details, any other pages (or even the same one if called up separately) can easily retrieve these values using this recipe. Figure 9-6 shows data that has been saved in a session before being recalled.

FIGURE 9-6   With this recipe, a single function call will retrieve a range of user details, even across different web pages.

About the Recipe

This recipe opens a previously created PHP session and returns the session variables stored in it. It does not require any arguments.

Variables, Arrays, and Functions

$vars	Array containing the various session variables' values

How It Works

This recipe first attempts to start a session using the session_start() function. If that fails for any reason, a single-element array with the value FALSE is returned. One reason it could fail is if a session is already open, which is why the @ symbol prefaces the function call; it is there to suppress any error messages, like this:

```
if (!@session_start()) return array(FALSE);
```

If a session is successfully opened, a check is then made for one of the session variables that ought to be set, namely $_SESSION['handle']. If it's not set, an error has occurred and a single-element array with the value FALSE is returned, like this:

```
if (!isset($_SESSION['handle'])) return array(FALSE);
```

Otherwise, everything seems to be in order, so the array $vars is initialized and then the four main user-session variables are inserted in it and a two-element array is returned, the first of which has the value TRUE, while the second contains the $vars array:

```
$vars = array();
$vars[] = $_SESSION['handle'];
$vars[] = $_SESSION['pass'];
$vars[] = $_SESSION['name'];
$vars[] = $_SESSION['email'];
return array(TRUE, $vars);
```

How to Use It

Using this recipe is as easy as making a short function call, like this:

```
$result = OpenSession();
```

If $result[0] has the value FALSE, an error occurred; otherwise, $result[1] contains a sub-array that will itself contain the four main items of user details. You can use code such as the following to act on the value of $result[0] and retrieve the details:

```
if (!$result[0]) echo "Could not open session.";
else list($handle, $pass, $name, $email) = $result[1];
```

Here, use has been made of the list() function, which takes an array and assigns its elements to the variables passed to it, providing an excellent means of quickly retrieving the four values. It could be considered shorthand code for the following:

```
$handle = $result[1][0];
$pass   = $result[1][1];
$name   = $result[1][2];
$email  = $result[1][3];
```

Whichever method you use, you will now have retrieved four items of data about the user without them having to enter those details again, and by placing a call to this recipe on each page where these details may be needed, you will always have access to them.

The Recipe

```
function OpenSession()
{
    if (!@session_start()) return array(FALSE);
    if (!isset($_SESSION['handle'])) return array(FALSE);

    $vars = array();
    $vars[] = $_SESSION['handle'];
    $vars[] = $_SESSION['pass'];
    $vars[] = $_SESSION['name'];
    $vars[] = $_SESSION['email'];
    return array(TRUE, $vars);
}
```

67 CloseSession()

When a user has finished with your web site, it's a good idea to provide them with a logout button or link, with which they can close the current session in order to prevent another user on their PC from coming back to it. With this recipe, not only can you close the session, but all associated data is also destroyed, leaving no potential security risk behind. Figure 9-7 shows the result of first opening a session with OpenSession() and then closing it again.

FIGURE 9-7   Closing a session will completely log a user out of your web site.

After closing it, you will not be able to open the session again since all its data was destroyed. Your only option is to create a new one.

About the Recipe

This recipe closes a previously created and/or opened PHP session and destroys any associated data. It does not require any arguments.

Variables, Arrays, and Functions

$_SESSION	The PHP main session array, which is reinitialized to an empty array to delete its data

How It Works

This recipe ensures that any data stored in the PHP $_SESSION array is destroyed by reinitializing the array, which it does by assigning it the value array():

```
$_SESSION = array();
```

Next, a couple of tests are made. These check whether the value returned by session_id() is not FALSE, in which case a session does exist (and that value will be the session ID), and whether a cookie exists with the name returned by session_name(), like this:

```
if (session_id() != "" ||
 isset($_COOKIE[session_name()]))
   setcookie(session_name(), '', time() - 2592000, '/');
```

If either of these cases is TRUE, then it's necessary to destroy any session cookie that may exist on the user's computer. This is done by issuing a setcookie() call with the same details that will have been used to create it, but with an expiry date of 30 days in the past. Being a month ago, the browser will automatically delete the cookie as having expired already. Any time in the past will do. I chose a month just to be sure.

Finally, the session_destroy() function is called and the value returned by it is returned by the recipe. The @ symbol prefacing the call is there to suppress any error messages that might occur, particularly if the call fails due to the session already having been destroyed, or the recipe having been called with no session in existence:

```
return @session_destroy();
```

How to Use It

To terminate a session, place a call to this recipe before any text is output, like this:

```
$result = CloseSession();
```

The variable $result will have the value TRUE if the call succeeded; otherwise, it will be FALSE. You generally don't need to worry if the call fails, since it usually only happens if there is no session to close, which is the situation you wanted anyway.

The Recipe

```
function CloseSession()
{
  $_SESSION = array();

  if (session_id() != "" ||
      isset($_COOKIE[session_name()]))
    setcookie(session_name(), '', time() - 2592000, '/');

  return @session_destroy();
}
```

SecureSession()

If there's a way a hacker can break into your web site, you can bet they'll try. One trick they use is to hijack PHP sessions. This might be achieved in different ways, but the main security hole is when a hacker locates a site that passes the session ID in a GET URL tail.

Given this information, a hacker could start a session and then pass on the URL (including the session ID) in spam or other links. They could then go back and look for evidence of any of these links being followed, and if the user hasn't logged out, they may be able to hijack the session and assume the user's identity.

But by using this simple recipe, tricks of that nature are rendered completely useless. Figure 9-8 shows a session that is opened with OpenSession() and then tested with this recipe for being secure.

About the Recipe

This recipe checks whether a session appears to not be secure, and if not, it closes the session. It does not require any arguments.

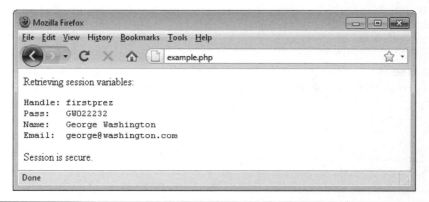

FIGURE 9-8 This recipe helps secure against hackers hijacking a user's session.

Variables, Arrays, and Functions

$ipnum	String variable containing the IP number of the current user
$agent	String variable containing the browser User Agent string of the current user

How It Works

In Recipe 65, `CreateSession()`, I mentioned the session variables containing the IP number and browser User Agent string, which are set up when a session is created using the `CreateSession()` recipe. Well, this recipe is where they come into use.

What it does is check the current browser's User Agent and IP number against those saved in the session variables, as follows:

```
$ipnum = getenv("REMOTE_ADDR");
$agent = getenv("HTTP_USER_AGENT");
```

If either is different, the session is closed using `CloseSession()`, and a value of FALSE is returned. This is done to ensure that only the user who was online and present when the session was created can continue to use it, neatly avoiding any attempts by hackers to either poison a new session or take over an existing one, like this:

```
if (isset($_SESSION['ipnum']))
{
    if ($ipnum != $_SESSION['ipnum'] ||
        $agent != $_SESSION['agent'])
    {
        CloseSession();
        return FALSE;
    }
    else return TRUE;
}
else return FALSE;
```

If the strings do match, it is assumed the user is the same person, and so TRUE is returned. Oh, and if there appears to be no session active (tested by seeing whether `$_SESSION['ipnum']` has a value), then FALSE is returned.

How to Use It

To use the function, you would probably call it immediately after a call to `OpenSession()`, like this:

```
if (!SecureSession())
{
    // Login code goes here to log the
    // user back into a secure session
}
```

It may be extra work but it's worth implementing this feature for your users' protection.

The Recipe

```
function SecureSession()
{
    $ipnum = getenv("REMOTE_ADDR");
    $agent = getenv("HTTP_USER_AGENT");

    if (isset($_SESSION['ipnum']))
    {
        if ($ipnum != $_SESSION['ipnum'] ||
            $agent != $_SESSION['agent'])
        {
            CloseSession();
            return FALSE;
        }
        else return TRUE;
    }
    else return FALSE;
}
```

RECIPE 69 ManageCookie()

Cookies are a great way to provide additional functionality to your users, and contrary to the impression that some news reports might give, they have other more beneficial functions besides tracking users for advertising purposes. For example, you can save a token representing a person's username and password in a cookie to keep them logged in to a site, something PHP sessions do unless cookies are disabled, in which case the query string is used for this.

Cookies are also great for associating variables directly with a user via the browser they use, so you could use them, for example, to note that a user has already completed a questionnaire on your site and should not be asked again.

Figure 9-9 shows the cookie *Test* being given the value *3.1415927* by this recipe. The cookie is sent to the browser but has not been returned by it because cookies are only transferred in the header exchange that takes place before the contents of a web page are transferred. After reloading the page, the cookie is passed back to the web server by the browser, and so the cookie returns the assigned value, as the figure inset shows.

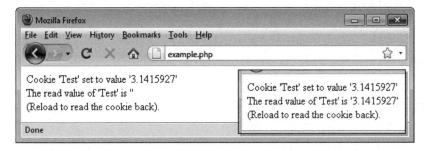

FIGURE 9-9   This recipe lets you set, read, and delete cookies in a user's browser.

About the Recipe

This recipe sets, reads, and deletes cookies. It requires the following arguments:

- **$action** The action to take: set, read, or delete.
- **$cookie** The name to use for the cookie.
- **$value** The value to give the cookie.
- **$expire** The number of seconds after which the cookie will expire.
- **$path** The path to the cookie on the server.

Variables, Arrays, and Functions

- None

How It Works

This recipe comprises three parts, separated by the case qualifiers of a switch statement, based on the value of $action after converting it to lowercase, like this:

```
switch(strtolower($action))
```

If the value is set, then the number of seconds passed in $expire is added to the value returned by time() to create a timestamp $expire seconds into the future. Or, if $expire is NULL, it is left alone. When this value is passed to the setcookie() function, the expiry date of that cookie will either be $expire seconds in the future, or if $expire is NULL, the cookie will expire when the browser is closed. Next, the setcookie() call is made, passing the name of the cookie in $cookie, the value to assign to it in $value, the value in $expire, and the path to the server in $path. The latter defines the scope over which a cookie is valid. For example, if $path has the value /news/, then only that folder (and its subfolders) can access the cookie. But if it is /, then the cookie can be accessed by all folders on that web domain. Here is the code that performs this:

```
case 'set':
   if ($expire) $expire += time();
   return setcookie($cookie, $value, $expire, $path);
```

If $action has the value read then, using the function isset(), a test is made to see whether a cookie of the name stored in $cookie exists. If so, that value is returned; otherwise, FALSE is returned, as follows:

```
case 'read':
   if (isset($_COOKIE[$cookie]))
      return $_COOKIE[$cookie];
   else return FALSE;
```

If $action contains the word delete, then if the cookie with the name in $cookie is found to exist, using isset(), the cookie is resent to the browser using its current name and an expiry date of a month in the past, as calculated by subtracting 30 days' worth of seconds from the value returned by a call to `time()`. This has the effect of making the cookie instantly expire, like this:

```
case 'delete':
   if (isset($_COOKIE[$cookie]))
      return setcookie($cookie, NULL,
         time() - 60 * 60 * 24 * 30, NULL);
   else return FALSE;
```

If `$action` is none of the preceding words, then FALSE is returned:

```
return FALSE;
```

How to Use It

To set a browser cookie, you could use code such as this:

```
$cookie = 'Test';
$val    = '3.1415927';
$exp    = 300;
$path   = '/';
$result = ManageCookie('set', $cookie, $val, $exp, $path);
```

If `$result` has a value of TRUE, then the cookie was successfully set. To then read back the value of a cookie (which would have to occur the subsequent time the page loads), you would then use code like this:

```
$result = ManageCookie('read', $cookie, NULL, NULL, NULL);
```

Upon success, `$result` will contain the contents of the cookie; otherwise, it will have the value FALSE.

To delete the cookie, issue the following command:

```
$result = ManageCookie('delete', $cookie, NULL, NULL, NULL);
```

Successful deletion will give `$result` a value of TRUE; otherwise, it will be FALSE. Possible reasons for the call failing are if the cookie is already deleted or it doesn't exist.

The Recipe

```
function ManageCookie($action, $cookie, $value, $expire,
   $path)
{
   switch(strtolower($action))
   {
      case 'set':
         if ($expire) $expire += time();
         return setcookie($cookie, $value, $expire, $path);
```

```
    case 'read':
        if (isset($_COOKIE[$cookie]))
            return $_COOKIE[$cookie];
        else return FALSE;

    case 'delete':
        if (isset($_COOKIE[$cookie]))
            return setcookie($cookie, NULL,
                time() - 60 * 60 * 24 * 30, NULL);
        else return FALSE;
    }

    return FALSE;
}
```

BlockUserByCookie()

If you've ever done any chat-related programming, you'll have come across *trolls*: downright nasty individuals who you don't want on your site. You may even have banned them via their IP address. If you have, you may also have encountered the problem of these individuals restarting their web connections to obtain new IP addresses with which to harass you and your users. You will also possibly have noticed that some "bad" users share their IP address with "good" ones, generally because they work in the same building and share a DSL or similar Internet connection. So blocking a "bad" user by IP would also block "good" ones.

But there is a way you can ban unwanted users more permanently and precisely, and that's to leave a cookie on their computer, as this recipe does. For example, Figure 9-10 shows a session being opened with the OpenSession() recipe, and then this recipe, BlockUserByCookie(), being called to send a blocking cookie to the user's browser.

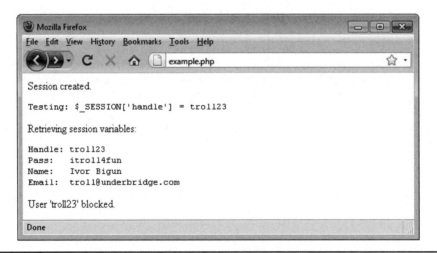

FIGURE 9-10 Some users can be a pest, but this recipe can help you block them.

About the Recipe

This recipe sets a cookie in a user's browser with which you can tell whether or not they have been blocked from using your site. It requires the following arguments:

- **$action**   The action to take.
- **$handle**   The handle of the user to block.
- **$expire**   The number of seconds after which the cookie will expire.

Variables, Arrays, and Functions

ManageCookie()	The recipe for setting, reading, and deleting cookies

How It Works

This function checks the value of the argument $action after converting it to lowercase. If it is block, then a special cookie is saved on the user's web browser. Because we don't want to alert the user to the fact that they have a blocking cookie, I chose to call it simply *user*. To make it even more innocuous, I give it the value of their handle (or username) so that, at a brief rummage through their cookies, most users will assume this is a simple username cookie for your web site. The cookie is set to expire after $expire seconds, so you can choose how long to lock a user out for, as follows:

```
if (strtolower($action) == 'block')
{
   if ($_SESSION['handle'] != $handle) return FALSE;
   else return manageCookie('set', 'user', $handle,
      $expire, '/');
}
```

If $action doesn't have the value block, then the value of the cookie named *user* is looked up. If it has a value, then that is returned; otherwise, FALSE is returned:

```
return manageCookie('read', 'user', NULL, NULL, NULL);
```

Figure 9-11 shows the cookie *user* with the value *troll23* as sent to a Firefox browser.

Note how the cookie's details such as the Host, Path, and Expires fields are all available for the user to look up, hence the deviousness. You can call up this window on Firefox versions prior to 3.5 using the Tools menu followed by Options | Privacy | Show Cookies. On Firefox 3.5 and later, you need to select Tools | Page Info | Security | View Cookies. Other major browsers also allow you to view their cookies.

How to Use It

The beauty of this recipe (as long as the user has cookies enabled, which most do) is that it doesn't matter what handle (or username) you ban someone under, because the cookie will still work. So even if they manage to sign up for another account, a quick call of this recipe will still tell you whether the person has already been blocked. What's more, it will reveal to

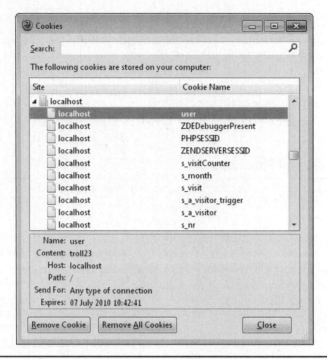

Figure 9-11   The cookie "user" with the value "troll23" as sent to a Firefox browser.

you the handle of the original account that got them blocked in the first place. The only downside is that all users on the same computer account using the same web browser will be denied access.

To use the recipe, you will likely already have a PHP session running and will pass a few arguments to the recipe taken from the session variables. So here are some lines of example code to set up a session with which the recipe can be tested:

```
$handle = "troll23";
$pass   = "itroll4fun";
$name   = "Ivor Bigun";
$email  = "troll@underbridge.com";
$result = CreateSession($handle, $pass, $name, $email);
```

If you run this code and there are no errors, you should now have a session created with the various values assigned to session variables, so you can now simulate being a user to be blocked like this:

```
$result = BlockUserByCookie('block', $handle, 60*60*24*365);
```

This line of code will set the block cookie on the computer belonging to the owner of $handle, which, in this case, will only expire after one year. If you now use the following line of code in a new program (or after reloading the same one) to ensure the cookie has been passed back from the user's web browser, you will see that the user has been blocked:

```
$result = BlockUserByCookie(NULL, $handle, NULL);
```

By passing a value of NULL instead of block as the first parameter, this tells the recipe to return either the value of the block cookie (which will be the user's original handle), or the value FALSE if the user has not been blocked. Thus, if $result is not FALSE, then the user has been blocked. You can therefore use the value of $result like this:

```
if ($result)
{
   // User is blocked so place code here
   // to provide limited or zero functionality
}
else
{
   // User is not blocked so place code here
   // to provide full functionality
}
```

Rather than letting a user know they are blocked, I have found it a good idea *not* to tell them, as they will then try everything in their power to circumvent the block. Instead, I tend to resort to tactics such as blocking a user for an hour or a day and then unblocking and reblocking them randomly. And in place of telling them about this I will do things such as continuing to display their own posts to the screen but not to any other user, so they will assume they are simply being ignored.

They will never be able to work out exactly what is going on. Sometimes their trolling will work; other times it won't. In most cases the user will eventually drift away from your site and find another one to bother. Sneaky? Yes. Effective? Also yes. But now you have the means to deal with unwanted users, I leave it up to you to devise your own methods of blocking or banning them.

By the way, when using this recipe, make sure you have also copied ManageCookie() into your program, or otherwise included it, as it is called by the code.

The Recipe

```
function BlockUserByCookie($action, $handle, $expire)
{
   if (strtolower($action) == 'block')
   {
      if ($_SESSION['handle'] != $handle) return FALSE;
      else return manageCookie('set', 'user', $handle,
         $expire, '/');
   }

   return manageCookie('read', 'user', NULL, NULL, NULL);
}
```

PART II

CHAPTER 10

APIs, RSS, and XML

One of the most interesting recent developments on the Web is the trend of providing Application Programming Interfaces (APIs) to web sites, with which you can integrate content from other sites into your own. Generally such APIs accept standard POST or GET requests as might be sent from an HTML form or hyperlink, and then return data in the form of XML (Extensible Markup Language), JSON (JavaScript Object Notation), or other easy-to-process formats.

For example, both Google and Yahoo! provide a range of APIs for many of their web properties, such as Google Book Search and Charts, or Yahoo! Search, Answers, and Stocks, for all of which there are recipes in this chapter. There are also recipes for handling Wikipedia entries, Flickr photo streams, and currency conversion from the European Central Bank.

However, although these recipes provide the functionality to process the information supplied by those companies, it's your responsibility to ensure you follow each service's rules and guidelines and have sufficient permission to reuse or republish data extracted from their sites.

CreateGoogleChart( )

Google Charts is a great API that not too many people seem to know about yet. With it, you can create a huge variety of charts to display on your web site or incorporate in your documents, and so on. However, it is quite complex and requires using a number of different command strings, which is where this recipe comes in.

With this recipe, you only have to supply the data to be charted and (optionally) various widths, heights, colors, and other details. The recipe then interfaces with Google Charts and returns a ready-made image (as a GD object) containing the chart. You can then display the image straightaway or save it to disk for future use. Figure 10-1 shows a 3D pie chart created from seven items of data, representing types of cheese.

About the Recipe

This recipe returns a GD image containing a chart created using the supplied data. Upon failure, it returns FALSE. It requires the following arguments, all of which (except for $width, $height, and $data) may be passed as NULL or the empty string to use default values:

- **$title** The chart's title.
- **$tcolor** The title's color.

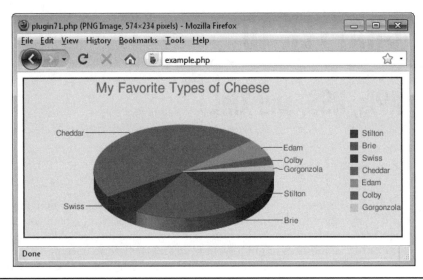

FIGURE 10-1   Leverage the power of the Google Charts API with this recipe.

- **$tsize**   The title's font size.
- **$type**   The chart type to create out of:

    line   A line chart.
    vbar   A vertical bar chart.
    hbar   A horizontal bar chart.
    gometer   A Google-O-Meter chart.
    pie   A pie chart (the default).
    pie3d   A 3D pie chart.
    venn   A Venn chart.
    radar   A radar chart.

- **$bwidth**   Bar width (only applies for bar charts).
- **$labels**   The data labels, separated by | symbols.
- **$legends**   The data legends, separated by | symbols.
- **$colors**   The data colors, separated by commas.
- **$bgfill**   The background fill color (six hex digits).
- **$border**   The border width in pixels.
- **$bcolor**   The border color (six hex digits).
- **$width**   The chart width in pixels.
- **$height**   The chart height in pixels.
- **$data**   The chart data, separated by commas.

Variables, Arrays, and Functions

$types	Associative array containing the chart type names and Google Chart command equivalents
$tail	String containing the command tail to add to the Google Charts URL
$url	String containing the Google Charts URL
$image	GD image containing the returned Google Chart
$w	The width of $image in pixels
$h	The height of $image in pixels
$image2	GD image containing the final image to return after adding any border
$clr	GD color object created from the $bcolor border color

How It Works

This recipe starts by populating the $types associative array so that the chart types passed in the argument $type can be quickly converted to the types Google Charts requires. For example, a 3D pie chart is represented by a $type of pie3d, which must be translated to p3 for Google. To facilitate this, the array element $types['pie3d'] has been given the value p3 so that simply looking up the value of $types[$type] will return p3 when $type is pie3d. All the other types will also be similarly translated, like this:

```
$types = array('line'    => 'lc',
               'vbar'    => 'bvg',
               'hbar'    => 'bhg',
               'gometer' => 'gom',
               'pie'     => 'p',
               'pie3d'   => 'p3',
               'venn'    => 'v',
               'radar'   => 'r');
```

So, next the value of $types[$type] is tested with the isset() function to see whether it has a value. If not, then an unknown value was passed in $type and so $type is set to pie, making it the default:

```
if (!isset($types[$type])) $type = 'pie';
```

Next, $tail is built up using the various parameters passed to the recipe such as the title, type, width, height, and so on. The contents of $tail will be appended to the base API URL for Google Charts to make a query string, which is sent as a GET request to the server, like this:

```
$tail  = "chtt=" . urlencode($title);
$tail .= "&cht=$types[$type]";
$tail .= "&chs=$width" . "x" . "$height";
$tail .= "&chbh=$bwidth";
$tail .= "&chxt=x,y";
$tail .= "&chd=t:$data";
```

After the main values have been placed in $tail, if they were passed in the function call, the next five if statements add further values. For example, in the fifth line of code below, if $colors is NULL or the empty string, then no color information will be appended to $tail. Otherwise, the Google Charts command &chco= will be appended to $tail, followed by the colors supplied, as follows:

```
if ($tcolor)
    if ($tsize) $tail .= "&chts=$tcolor,$tsize";
if ($labels)    $tail .= "&chl=$labels";
if ($legends)   $tail .= "&chdl=$legends";
if ($colors)    $tail .= "&chco=$colors";
if ($bgfill)    $tail .= "&chf=bg,s,$bgfill";
```

Next, the tail is appended to the Google Charts API URL and the result is placed in $url, which is then passed to the imagecreatefrompng() function to call up the API, which (on success) returns a chart as a PNG image. This image is then placed in the GD image object $image:

```
$url   = "http://chart.apis.google.com/chart?$tail";
$image = imagecreatefrompng($url);
```

Now that an image has been created, the width and height of it are placed in the variables $w and $h so that a new image can be created by passing these values to imagecreatetruecolor(), like this:

```
$w = imagesx($image);
$h = imagesy($image);
```

Then, if $border has a value, it will define the width of a border to be added to the image, and the new image is made slightly larger than the original to allow for the borders. The new image is then stored in $image2, and a GD color object is created in $clr from the color in $bcolor, like this:

```
$image2 = imagecreatetruecolor($w + $border * 2,
    $h + $border * 2);
$clr = imagecolorallocate($image,
    hexdec(substr($bcolor, 0, 2)),
    hexdec(substr($bcolor, 2, 2)),
    hexdec(substr($bcolor, 4, 2)));
```

This color is then passed to the imagefilledrectangle() function to fill in the new image with the specified color:

```
imagefilledrectangle($image2, 0, 0, $w + $border * 2,
    $h + $border * 2, $clr);
```

Finally, the original image is copied to the exact center of the new image so that, if the new image is larger, the image will now be a bordered version of the original. If no border width is specified, then the copy will simply overwrite the fill color and the new image will be identical to the original:

```
imagecopy($image2, $image, $border, $border, 0, 0, $w, $h);
```

Now that it is no longer required, the original image object is removed from memory using the `imagedestroy()` function, returning the memory back to the system. The new image is then returned by the recipe:

```
imagedestroy($image);
return $image2;
```

TIP *The Google Charts API actually includes many more features than there is room to include in this recipe. If you visit* tinyurl.com/googlecharts, *you will see more options you may wish to add to the recipe for your own use. You should be able to slot them in without too much difficulty.*

How to Use It

To obtain a Google Chart using this recipe, you should prepare all the parameters you want in it and then pass them to the recipe, like this:

```
$title   = 'My Favorite Types of Cheese';
$tcolor  = 'FF0000';
$tsize   = '20';
$type    = 'pie3d';
$width   = '570';
$height  = '230';
$bwidth  = NULL;
$labels  = 'Stilton|Brie|Swiss|Cheddar|Edam|Colby|Gorgonzola';
$legends = $labels;
$colors  = 'BD0000,DE6B00,284B89,008951,9D9D9D,A5AB4B,8C70A4,FFD200';
$bgfill  = 'EEEEFF';
$border  = '2';
$bcolor  = '444444';
$data    = '14.9,18.7,7.1,47.3,6.0,3.1,2.1';
$result  = CreateGoogleChart( $title,   $tcolor, $tsize,
    $type,   $bwidth, $labels, $legends, $colors, $bgfill,
    $border, $bcolor, $width,  $height,  $data);
```

The preceding lines of code will re-create the chart shown in Figure 10-1, which is returned in $result as a GD image object, and which you can then output to a browser by first sending the correct PNG image header, followed by the image data, like this:

```
header('Content-type: image/png');
imagepng($result);
```

According to the Google Charts Usage Policy at *code.google.com/apis/chart/:* "*There's no limit to the number of calls per day you can make to the Google Chart API. However, we reserve the right to block any use that we regard as abusive. If you think your service will make more than 250,000 API calls per day, please let us know."* Therefore, you may prefer to employ caching techniques by saving the chart to disk (if it hasn't already been saved), and then serving it from there. You can save the image using one of these commands where `path/filename` `.ext` is the filename, including path and extension:

```
imagepng($result,  'path/filename.png');
imagegif($result,  'path/filename.gif');
imagejpeg($result, 'path/filename.jpg');
```

Just choose the type of file you wish to save the image as, and select one of these three commands accordingly.

On the other hand, if your usage will not be high enough to get your program blocked, you may wish to save on your own bandwidth and use Google's by uncommenting the `return $url;` command about two-thirds of the way into the recipe. You will now only need code such as the following to display the chart directly from Google's servers:

```
echo "<img src='$result' />";
```

However, the border options will be ignored and you'll therefore have to use CSS (Cascading Style Sheets) if you need borders.

The Recipe

```
function CreateGoogleChart($title, $tcolor, $tsize,
    $type, $bwidth, $labels, $legends, $colors, $bgfill,
    $border, $bcolor, $width, $height, $data)
{
    $types = array('line'    => 'lc',
                   'vbar'    => 'bvg',
                   'hbar'    => 'bhg',
                   'gometer' => 'gom',
                   'pie'     => 'p',
                   'pie3d'   => 'p3',
                   'venn'    => 'v',
                   'radar'   => 'r');

    if (!isset($types[$type])) $type = 'pie';

    $tail  = "chtt=" . urlencode($title);
    $tail .= "&cht=$types[$type]";
    $tail .= "&chs=$width" . "x" . "$height";
    $tail .= "&chbh=$bwidth";
    $tail .= "&chxt=x,y";
    $tail .= "&chd=t:$data";

    if ($tcolor)
        if ($tsize) $tail .= "&chts=$tcolor,$tsize";
    if ($labels)    $tail .= "&chl=$labels";
    if ($legends)   $tail .= "&chdl=$legends";
```

```
if ($colors)    $tail .= "&chco=$colors";
if ($bgfill)    $tail .= "&chf=bg,s,$bgfill";

$url = "http://chart.apis.google.com/chart?$tail";

// Uncomment the line below to return a URL to
// the chart image instead of the image itself
// return $url;

$image = imagecreatefrompng($url);

$w = imagesx($image);
$h = imagesy($image);
$image2 = imagecreatetruecolor($w + $border * 2,
    $h + $border * 2);
$clr = imagecolorallocate($image,
    hexdec(substr($bcolor, 0, 2)),
    hexdec(substr($bcolor, 2, 2)),
    hexdec(substr($bcolor, 4, 2)));
imagefilledrectangle($image2, 0, 0, $w + $border * 2,
    $h + $border * 2, $clr);
imagecopy($image2, $image, $border, $border, 0, 0, $w, $h);
imagedestroy($image);
return $image2;
}
```

RECIPE 72 CurlGetContents()

Some web sites don't like to be accessed by anything other than a web browser, which can make it difficult to fetch data from them with a PHP program using a function such as file_get_contents(). Such sites generally block your program by checking for a User Agent string, which is something all browsers send to web sites they visit, and which can vary widely. They look something like this:

```
Mozilla/5.0 (Windows; U; Windows NT 6.1; en-GB; rv:1.9.1)
Gecko/20090624 Firefox/3.5 (.NET CLR 3.5.30729)
```

Therefore, to access these sites it is necessary to simulate being a browser, which, as shown in Figure 10-2, this recipe will do for you.

About the Recipe

This recipe is intended to replace the PHP file_get_contents() function when used to fetch a web page. It accepts the URL of a page and a browser User Agent to emulate, and on success it returns the contents of the page at the given URL. On failure, it returns FALSE. It requires these arguments:

- **$url** The URL to fetch.
- **$agent** The User Agent string of a browser.

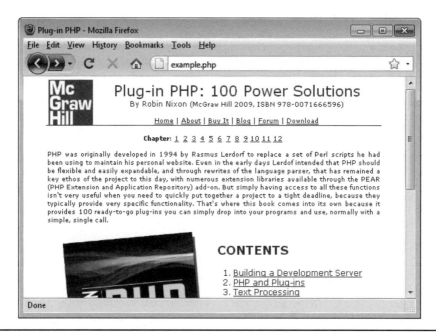

FIGURE **10-2** This recipe is used to fetch and display the *pluginphp.com* home page.

Variables, Arrays, and Functions

$ch	Curl handle to an opened `curl_init()` session
$result	The returned result from the `curl_exec()` call

How It Works

This recipe uses the Mod CURL (Client URL) library extension to PHP. If it fails, then you need to read your server and/or PHP installation instructions or consult your server administrator about enabling Mod CURL. What it does is open a session with `curl_init()`, passing a handle to the session to $ch. But first it checks whether a browser User Agent string has been passed to the function and, if not, creates one:

```
$agent = ($agent != '') ? $agent :
   'Mozilla/5.0 (compatible; MSIE 9.0; Windows' .
   ' NT 6.1; Win64; x64; Trident/5.0)';
```

A CURL session can perform a wide range of URL-related tasks by specifying options with a call to `curl_setopt()` to set up the various options required prior to making the `curl_exec()` call, like this:

```
$ch = curl_init();
curl_setopt($ch, CURLOPT_URL,          $url);
curl_setopt($ch, CURLOPT_USERAGENT,    $agent);
curl_setopt($ch, CURLOPT_HEADER,       0);
curl_setopt($ch, CURLOPT_ENCODING,     "gzip");
```

```
curl_setopt($ch, CURLOPT_RETURNTRANSFER, 1);
curl_setopt($ch, CURLOPT_FOLLOWLOCATION, 1);
curl_setopt($ch, CURLOPT_FAILONERROR,    1);
curl_setopt($ch, CURLOPT_CONNECTTIMEOUT, 8);
curl_setopt($ch, CURLOPT_TIMEOUT,        8);
```

These include setting CURLOPT_URL to the value of $url and CURLOPT_USERAGENT to the value of $agent. Additionally, a number of other options are set to sensible values.

The curl_exec() function is then called, with the result of the call being placed in $result. The session is then closed with a call to curl_close(), and the value in $result is returned:

```
$result = curl_exec($ch);
curl_close($ch);
return $result;
```

How to Use It

Using this recipe is as easy as replacing calls to file_get_contents() with CurlGetContents(). As long as you have passed the code a sensible-looking User Agent string, the recipe will be able to return some pages that could not be retrieved using the former function call. If you fail to provide one, it will make one up for you. For example, you can load in and display the contents of a web page like this (using a standard Windows 7 / Internet Explorer 9 / 64-bit architecture User Agent string):

```
$agent = 'Mozilla/5.0 (compatible; MSIE 9.0; Windows' .
         ' NT 6.1; Win64; x64; Trident/5.0)';
$url   = 'http://webdeveloperscookbook.com';
echo CurlGetContents($url, $agent);
```

Or you can simply use:

```
echo CurlGetContents('http://webdeveloperscookbook.com');
```

This will display the main page of the *webdevelopmentcookbook.com* web site.

CAUTION *Sometimes the reason a web site only allows a browser access to a web page is because other programs are not permitted from accessing it. So please check how you are allowed to access information, and what you are allowed to do with it, at such a web site before using this recipe. There's a comprehensive explanation (and collection) of User Agent strings at* useragentstring *.com.*

The Recipe

```
function CurlGetContents($url, $agent)
{
    $agent = ($agent != '') ? $agent :
        'Mozilla/5.0 (compatible; MSIE 9.0; Windows' .
        ' NT 6.1; Win64; x64; Trident/5.0)';
```

```
$ch = curl_init();
curl_setopt($ch, CURLOPT_URL,             $url);
curl_setopt($ch, CURLOPT_USERAGENT,       $agent);
curl_setopt($ch, CURLOPT_HEADER,          0);
curl_setopt($ch, CURLOPT_ENCODING,        "gzip");
curl_setopt($ch, CURLOPT_RETURNTRANSFER,  1);
curl_setopt($ch, CURLOPT_FOLLOWLOCATION,  1);
curl_setopt($ch, CURLOPT_FAILONERROR,     1);
curl_setopt($ch, CURLOPT_CONNECTTIMEOUT,  8);
curl_setopt($ch, CURLOPT_TIMEOUT,         8);
$result = curl_exec($ch);
curl_close($ch);
return $result;
}
```

73 FetchWikiPage()

Wikipedia is an excellent resource, with several million articles. Even if you take into account that some of the information may not always be correct due to any user being able to edit a page, on the whole most of the web site is factual and it contains a summary of almost the whole depth and breadth of human knowledge.

What's even better is that Wikipedia is published under the GNU Free Documentation License—see *www.gnu.org/copyleft/fdl.html*. Essentially this means that you can use any text from it as long you give full attribution of the source, and also offer the text (with any amendments) under the same license. As a consequence, I now have the entire Wikipedia database stored in my iPhone so that I can instantly look up any entry, even when mobile connectivity is limited. By using data compression techniques and keeping only the main article text, it takes up just 2GB of space.

The GFDL license used also means you can use programs such as this recipe to reformat and reuse articles from Wikipedia, as shown in Figure 10-3, in which just the text has been extracted from its article on PHP.

If you also take a look at Figure 10-4, you'll see the original article at Wikipedia and, comparing the two, you'll notice that the recipe has completely ignored all the formatting, graphics, tables, and other extras, leaving behind just the text of the article.

Using it, you could create your own reduced-size local copy of Wikipedia, or perhaps use it to add hyperlinks to words or terms you may wish to explain to your readers. I have used this code to add short encyclopedia entries to searches returned by a customized Google search engine I wrote.

Combined with other recipes from this book, you could reformat articles into RSS feeds, translate them into "friendly" text, or, well, once you have access to the Wikipedia text, it's really only up to your imagination what you choose to do with it.

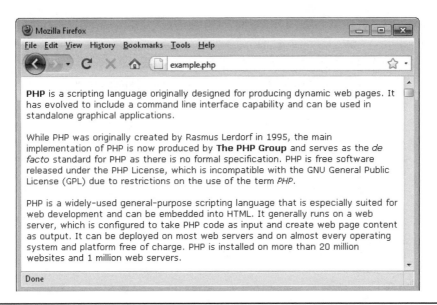

Figure 10-3   Using this recipe, you can extract just the text from a Wikipedia entry.

About the Recipe

This recipe takes the title of a Wikipedia entry and returns just the text of the article, or on failure it returns FALSE. It requires this argument:

- **$entry**   A Wikipedia article title.

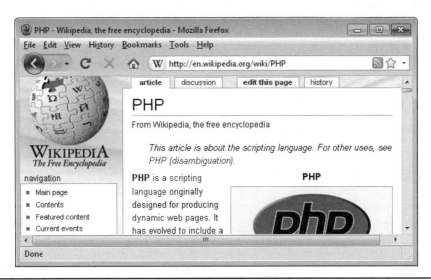

Figure 10-4   The original article about PHP on the Wikipedia web site

Variables, Arrays, and Functions

$agent	String containing a browser User Agent string
$url	String containing the URL of Wikipedia's XML export API
$page	String containing the result of fetching the Wikipedia entry
$xml	SimpleXML object created from $page
$title	String containing the article title as returned by Wikipedia
$text	String containing the article text
$sections	Array of four section headings at which to truncate the text
$section	String containing each element of $sections in turn
$ptr	Integer offset into $text indicating start of $section
$data	Array of search and replace strings for converting raw Wikipedia data
$j	Integer loop counter for processing search-and-replaces
$url	String containing the URL of the original Wikipedia article

How It Works

Wikipedia has kindly created an API with which you can export selected articles from their database. You can access it at:

```
http://en.wikipedia.org/wiki/Special:Export
```

Unfortunately, they have set this API to deny access to programs that do not present it with a browser User Agent string. Luckily, the previous recipe provides just that functionality, so using it, along with this recipe, it's possible to export any Wikipedia page as XML, which can then be transformed into just the raw text.

This is done by setting up a browser User Agent string and then calling the Export API using CurlGetContents(), passing the Export API URL, along with the article title and the browser agent. Before making the call, though, $entry is passed though the rawurlencode() function to convert non-URL-compatible characters into acceptable equivalents, such as spaces into %20 codes, as follows:

```
$agent = 'Mozilla/5.0 (compatible; MSIE 9.0; Windows' .
         ' NT 6.1; Win64; x64; Trident/5.0)';
$text  = '';

while ($text == '' || substr($text, 0, 9) == '#REDIRECT')
{
   $entry = rawurlencode($entry);
   $url   = "http://en.wikipedia.org/wiki/Special:Export/$entry";
   $page  = CurlGetContents($url, $agent);
```

The XML page returned from this call is then parsed into an XML object using the simplexml_load_string() function, the result being placed in $xml, and then the only two items of information that are required (the article title and its text) are extracted from $xml->page->title and $xml->page->text into $title and $text:

```
$xml   = simplexml_load_string($page);
$title = $xml->page->title;
$text  = $xml->page->revision->text;
```

Notice that all of this occurs inside a while loop. This is because by far the majority of Wikipedia articles are redirects from misspellings or different capitalizations. What the loop does is look for the string #REDIRECT in a response and, if one is discovered, the loop goes around again using the redirected article title, which is placed in $entry by using preg_match() to extract it from between a pair of double square parentheses. The loop can handle multiple redirects (which are not as infrequent as you might think given the age of Wikipedia and the amount of times many articles have been moved by now) as follows:

```
if (substr($text, 0, 9) == '#REDIRECT')
{
   preg_match('/\[\[(.+)\]\]/', $text, $matches);
   $entry = $matches[1];
}
```

So, with the raw Wikipedia text now loaded into $text, the next section truncates the string at whichever of five headings out of *References, See Also, External Links, Notes,* or *Further reading* (if any) appears first, because those entries are not part of the main article and are to be ignored, like this:

```
$sections = array('References', 'See also', 'External links',
   'Notes', 'Further reading');

foreach($sections as $section)
{
   $ptr = stripos($text, "==$section==");
   if ($ptr) $text = substr($text, 0, $ptr);
   $ptr = stripos($text, "== $section ==");
   if ($ptr) $text = substr($text, 0, $ptr);
}
```

This is done by using a foreach loop to iterate through the headings, which are enclosed by pairs of = symbols, Wikipedia's markup to indicate an <h2> heading. Because some Wikipedia authors use spaces inside the ==, both cases (with and without spaces) are tested. Each heading in turn is searched for using the stripos() function and, if a heading is found in $text, $ptr will point to its start and so $text is then truncated to end at that position.

Now that $text has the raw article we want, it's time to convert Wikipedia's special markup into the text and basic HTML this recipe supports. Before writing this recipe, I searched for hours trying to find other code already doing the job. And while there were a few examples, they were all quite long-winded and seemed overly complicated, which is why I chose to write my own routine.

In the end, it turned out that less than a couple of dozen rules were enough to make sense of most of Wikipedia's markup. For example, you've already seen how ==Heading== stands for <h2>Heading</h2>. Similarly, ===Subheading=== stands for <h3>Subheading</h3>, and so on, while '''word''' (three single quotes on either side of some text) stands for <i>word</i>, and ''word'' (two single quotes on either side of some text) stands for word. Ordered and unordered lists are also indicated by starting a new line with a

or a * symbol for each item, so for simplicity, I choose to convert both into the HTML bullet entity, ●, and treat nested lists as if they are on the same level.

Tables begin by starting a newline with a { symbol, so the code ignores everything from \n{ up to a closing } symbol, and double newlines, \n\n, are converted into <p> tags. And there's also some more complicated markup such as [[Article]], meaning "Place a hyperlink here to Wikipedia's article entitled Article," or [[Article|Look at this]], which means "Add a hyperlink to Wikipedia's article entitled Article here, but display the hyperlink text *Look at this*." A few more variations on a theme exist here, plus there are several types of markup I chose to ignore such as [[Image...]], [[File...]] and [[Category...]], which contain additional material to the main text, and [http...], which contains hyperlinks I didn't want to use.

What's more, there are also sections such as <gallery> and <ref>, which I decided should also be ignored, and some major sections appearing within the {{ and }} pairs of symbols that are often nested with sub- and sub-sub-sections. Again, all of these provide more rich content to a standard Wikipedia article, but are not necessary when we simply want the main text.

Therefore, the following $data array contains a sequence of regular expressions to be searched for, accompanied by strings with which to replace the matches:

```
$data = array('\[{2}Imag(\[{2})*.*(\]{2})*\]{2}', '',
              '\[{2}File(\[{2})*.*(\]{2})*\]{2}', '',
              '\[{2}Cate(\[{2})*.*(\]{2})*\]{2}', '',
              '\{{2}([^\{\}]+|(?R))*\}{2}',
              '\'{3}(.*?)\'{3}',                '<b>$1</b>',
              '\'{2}(.*?)\'{2}',                '<i>$1</i>',
              '\[{2}[^\|\]]+\|((^\]]*)\]{2}',    '$1',
              '\[{2}(.*?)\]{2}',                '$1',
              '\[(http[^\]]+)\]',               '  ',
              '\n(\*|#)+',    '<br /> &#x25cf; ',
              '\n:.*?\n',                       '',
              '\n\{[^\}]+\}',                   '',
              '\n={7}([^=]+)={7}',     '<h7>$1</h7>',
              '\n={6}([^=]+)={6}',     '<h6>$1</h6>',
              '\n={5}([^=]+)={5}',     '<h5>$1</h5>',
              '\n={4}([^=]+)={4}',     '<h4>$1</h4>',
              '\n={3}([^=]+)={3}',     '<h3>$1</h3>',
              '\n={2}([^=]+)={2}',     '<h2>$1</h2>',
              '\n={1}([^=]+)={1}',     '<h1>$1</h1>',
              '\n{2}',                          '<p>',
              '<gallery>([^<]+?)<\/gallery>',   '',
              '<ref>([^<]+?)<\/ref>',           '',
              '<ref [^>]+>',                    '');
```

Now, using a for loop, the array is iterated through a pair at a time, passing each pair of strings to the preg_replace() function:

```
for ($j = 0 ; $j < count($data) ; $j += 2)
   $text = preg_replace("/$data[$j]/", $data[$j+1], $text);
```

TIP *If you want to learn more about the regular expressions used, there's a lot of information at* wikipedia.org/wiki/Regular_expression.

Having massaged the text into almost plain text (with the exception of `<h1>` through `<h7>` headings, and the `<p>`, `<br>`, `<b>`, and `<i>` tags), the `strip_tags()` function is called to remove any other tags (except those just mentioned) that remain:

```
$text = strip_tags($text, '<h1><h2><h3><h4><h5><h6><h7>' .
                          '<p><br><b><i>');
```

Finally, before returning the article text, a notice and hyperlink are appended to it showing the original Wikipedia article from which the text was derived:

```
$url   = "http://en.wikipedia.org/wiki/$title";
$text .= "<p>Source: <a href='$url'>Wikipedia ($title)</a>";
return trim($text);
```

In all, I think you'll find that these rules handle the vast majority of Wikipedia pages very well, although you will encounter the odd page that doesn't come out quite right. In such cases, you should be able to spot the markup responsible and add a translation for it into the `$data` array.

If you use this recipe on a production server, you'll also need to comply with Wikipedia's licensing requirements by adding a link to the GNU Free Documentation License, and indicating that your version of the article is also released under this license. For details, please see *en.wikipedia.org/wiki/Wikipedia_Copyright*.

How to Use It

To use this recipe, just pass it a Wikipedia article title and you can display the result returned, like this:

```
$result = FetchWikiPage('Climate Change');
if (!$result) echo "Could not fetch article.";
else echo $result;
```

Incidentally, I chose this article because it is one of those that returns the previously mentioned `#REDIRECT` string. In this case, `Climate Change` is redirected to `Climate change` (with a lowercase c in the second word), and serves to show that the code correctly handles redirects.

Because Wikipedia makes use of the UTF-8 character set to enable all the different languages it supports, you may also need to ensure you include the following HTML `<meta>` tag in the `<head>` section of your HTML output to ensure that all characters display correctly:

```
<meta http-equiv="Content-Type" content="text/html; charset=utf-8"/>
```

To save on thrashing Wikipedia's servers and to also cut down on the programming power required on your own, you should definitely consider saving the result from each call to this recipe, either as a text file or, preferably, in a MySQL database, and then serve up the cached copy whenever future requests are made for the same article.

If you wish to compile your own database of Wikipedia articles using this recipe, you can find all the various indexes at *en.wikipedia.org/wiki/Portal:Contents*.

The Recipe

```
function FetchWikiPage($entry)
{
    $agent = 'Mozilla/5.0 (compatible; MSIE 9.0; Windows' .
             ' NT 6.1; Win64; x64; Trident/5.0)';
    $text  = '';

    while ($text == '' || substr($text, 0, 9) == '#REDIRECT')
    {
        $entry = rawurlencode($entry);
        $url   = "http://en.wikipedia.org/wiki/Special:Export/$entry";
        $page  = CurlGetContents($url, $agent);
        $xml   = simplexml_load_string($page);
        $title = $xml->page->title;
        $text  = $xml->page->revision->text;

        if (substr($text, 0, 9) == '#REDIRECT')
        {
            preg_match('/\[\[(.+)\]\]/', $text, $matches);
            $entry = $matches[1];
        }
    }

    $sections = array('References', 'See also', 'External links',
        'Notes', 'Further reading');

    foreach($sections as $section)
    {
        $ptr = stripos($text, "==$section==");
        if ($ptr) $text = substr($text, 0, $ptr);
        $ptr = stripos($text, "== $section ==");
        if ($ptr) $text = substr($text, 0, $ptr);
    }

    $data = array('\[{2}Imag(\[{2})*.*(\]{2})*\]{2}', '',
                  '\[{2}File(\[{2})*.*(\]{2})*\]{2}', '',
                  '\[{2}Cate(\[{2})*.*(\]{2})*\]{2}', '',
                  '\{{2}([^\{\}]+|(?R))*\}{2}',        '',
                  '\'{3}(.*?)\'{3}',          '<b>$1</b>',
                  '\'{2}(.*?)\'{2}',          '<i>$1</i>',
                  '\[{2}[^\|\]]+\|(([^\]]*)\]{2}',     '$1',
                  '\[{2}(.*?)\]{2}',          '$1',
                  '\[(http[^\]]+)\]',         ' ',
                  '\n(\*|#)+',     '<br /> &#x25cf; ',
                  '\n:.*?\n',                 '',
                  '\n\{([^\}]+\}',            '',
                  '\n={7}([^=]+)={7}',        '<h7>$1</h7>',
                  '\n={6}([^=]+)={6}',        '<h6>$1</h6>',
                  '\n={5}([^=]+)={5}',        '<h5>$1</h5>',
                  '\n={4}([^=]+)={4}',        '<h4>$1</h4>',
                  '\n={3}([^=]+)={3}',        '<h3>$1</h3>',
                  '\n={2}([^=]+)={2}',        '<h2>$1</h2>',
                  '\n={1}([^=]+)={1}',        '<h1>$1</h1>',
```

```
                    '\n{2}',                               '<p>',
                    '<gallery>([^<]+?)<\/gallery>',         '',
                    '<ref>([^<]+?)<\/ref>',                 '',
                    '<ref [^>]+>',                          '');

    for ($j = 0 ; $j < count($data) ; $j += 2)
        $text = preg_replace("/$data[$j]/", $data[$j+1], $text);

    $text  = strip_tags($text, '<h1><h2><h3><h4><h5><h6><h7>' .
                              '<p><br><b><i>');
    $url   = "http://en.wikipedia.org/wiki/$title";
    $text .= "<p>Source: <a href='$url'>Wikipedia ($title)</a>";
    return trim($text);

}
```

74 FetchFlickrStream( )

If you enjoy looking at photographs, chances are you have used the Flickr photo sharing service and may also have discovered a few photographers whose Flickr streams you like to follow. Well, now you can offer the same facility to your users with this recipe.

Using it, you can look up any public Flickr stream and return the (up to) 20 most recent photographs from it. Figure 10-5 shows the result of pointing the recipe at a new account I created at Flickr. In this instance, I chose to display links to the photos, but you can also embed them in your web pages if you wish.

About the Recipe

This recipe takes the name of a public Flickr account and returns the most recent photos. Upon success, it returns a two-element array, the first of which is the number of photos returned, and the second is an array containing URLs for each photo. On failure, it returns a single-element array with the value FALSE. It requires this argument:

- **$account**   A Flickr account name such as *xxxxxxxx@Nxx* (where the *x* symbols represent digits), or the more friendly Flickr usernames such as mine, which is *robinfnixon*.

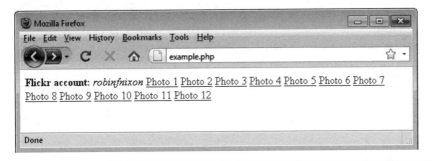

Figure 10-5   With this recipe, you can view the stream of a public Flickr user.

Variables, Arrays, and Functions

`$url`	String containing the Flickr photo stream base URL
`$page`	String containing the Flickr stream HTML page contents
`$rss`	String containing the location of the RSS feed for `$page`
`$xml`	String containing the contents of `$rss`
`$sxml`	SimpleXML object created from `$xml`
`$pics`	Array containing the image URLs
`$item`	SimpleXML object extracted from item in `$sxml`
`$j`	Integer loop variable for iterating through image URLs
`$t`	String used for transforming URLs into the form required

How It Works

This recipe takes the base Flickr stream URL and appends the account name in `$account` to it. This HTML page is then returned using the `file_get_contents()` function, and its contents are stored in `$page`. The `@` symbol prefacing the function suppresses any error messages should the call fail. And, if it does fail, a value of `FALSE` is returned in a single-element array, as follows:

```
$url  = 'http://flickr.com/photos';
$page = @file_get_contents("$url/$account/");
if (!$page) return array(FALSE);
```

Next, the array that will hold the image URLs, `$pics`, is initialized and the program *screen scrapes* the HTML page to locate the position of the RSS link within it. Screen scraping is the term given to the process of extracting information from HTML pages that hasn't been explicitly provided to you in an API or via another method. Actually, there are Flickr APIs to do this, but these three lines of code are simpler and represent all the coding required to find the RSS feed on the page and return its URL to the variable `$rss`, like this:

```
$pics = array();
$rss  = strstr($page, 'rss+xml');
$rss  = strstr($rss, 'http://');
$rss  = substr($rss, 0, strpos($rss, '"'));
```

Using this URL, the RSS feed is fetched and placed in the string `$xml`, from where it is transformed into a SimpleXML object in `$sxml`. This is a DOM (Document Object Model) object that can be easily traversed. To do this, a `foreach` loop iterates through the items in `$sxml->entry`, placing each in a new object called `$item`:

```
$xml  = file_get_contents($rss);
$sxml = simplexml_load_string($xml);

foreach($sxml->entry as $item)
```

Then, a `for` loop is used to iterate though all the items in `$item->link`, which contains the URLs we are interested in. If `$item->link[$j]['type']` has the value `image`, then `$item->link[$j]['href']` will contain a URL, so this is extracted into the variable `$t`, first removing any `_t` or `_m` sequences from the URL since they represent different sizes of the photo that we are not interested in. Once `$t` contains the URL wanted, its value is assigned to the next available element of the `$pics` array, and the `foreach` loop continues, as follows:

```
for ($j=0 ; $j < sizeof($item->link) ; ++$j)
{
   if (strstr($item->link[$j]['type'], 'image'))
   {
      $t=str_replace('_m', '', $item->link[$j]['href']);
      $t=str_replace('_t', '', $t);
      $pics[]=$t;
   }
}
```

The recipe returns a two-element array with the first element containing the number of photos found, calculated using the `count()` function, and the second contains an array of the photo URLs:

```
return array(count($pics), $pics);
```

Figure 10-6 shows a photo taken at random from the list returned and entered into a browser. In this case, it has the following Flickr URL:

```
http://farm3.static.flickr.com/2522/3708788611_5a9964f24d_o.jpg
```

FIGURE 10-6   The recipe determines the exact URL required for each photo.

How to Use It

To return the most recent photos in a public Flickr stream, just pass the Flickr account name to the recipe, like this:

```
$result = FetchFlickrStream('robinfnixon');
```

You can then choose how to proceed depending on the value of $result, like this:

```
if (!$result[0]) echo 'No photos found.';
else foreach($result[1] as $photo)
   echo "<a href='$photo'>Photo</a> ";
```

Or to display the images, you could use code such as this:

```
foreach($result[1] as $photo)
   echo "<img src='$photo' /><br />";
```

Users of Flickr's API are requested to make polling requests such as this no more than once per hour, so you are recommended to save the stream to file or a database and serve it from the cache in the future, only looking for new photos if 60 minutes have expired.

The Recipe

```
function FetchFlickrStream($account)
{
   $url  = 'http://flickr.com/photos';
   $rss  = @file_get_contents("$url/$account/");
   if (!$rss) return array(FALSE);

   $rss  = strstr($rss, 'rss+xml');
   $rss  = strstr($rss, 'http://');
   $rss  = substr($rss, 0, strpos($rss, '"'));
   $xml  = file_get_contents($rss);
   $sxml = simplexml_load_string($xml);
   $pics = array();

   foreach($sxml->entry as $item)
   {
      for ($j=0 ; $j < sizeof($item->link) ; ++$j)
      {
         if (strstr($item->link[$j]['type'], 'image'))


         {
            $t=str_replace('_m', '', $item->link[$j]['href']);
            $t=str_replace('_t', '', $t);
            $pics[]=$t;
         }
      }
   }

   return array(count($pics), $pics);
}
```

GetYahooAnswers()

The Yahoo! Answers web site contains questions and answers on just about any subject you can imagine, all supplied by users of the service. Sometimes this can mean that both the questions and the answers can be foolish or humorous, but equally they can also provide just the answer you are looking for to a problem or question you have.

That makes them ideal to drop in alongside informational web pages, in much the same way as you might link to or display dictionary definitions or encyclopedia entries. Figure 10-7 shows one of the Q&As returned by this recipe in response to a search for the term *gardening*.

About the Recipe

This recipe takes a search term and returns any matches for it found at Yahoo! Answers. Upon success, it returns a two-element array with the first value being the number of question/answer pairs returned, and the second an array of the Q&As, containing a sub-array in each element, with the following five values:

- The subject
- A Unix timestamp representing the date the question was posted
- The question
- The answer
- A URL pointing to the original Q&A

On failure, it returns a single-element array with the value FALSE. It requires this argument:

- **$search**   A search string.

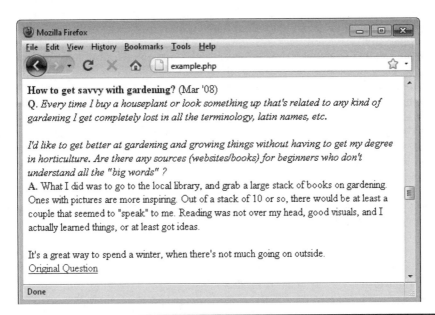

FIGURE 10-7   With this recipe, you can add the wealth of knowledge from Yahoo! Answers to your web site.

Variables, Arrays, and Functions

$id	String containing a Yahoo! Answers API key
$url	String containing the API URL with the $id and $search appended
$xml	String containing the contents of $url
$sxml	SimpleXML object created from $xml
$qandas	Array containing the questions and answers returned
$question	SimpleXML object extracted from $sxml->Question
$s	String containing the current subject
$t	String containing the current timestamp
$q	String containing the current question
$a	String containing the current answer
$l	String containing the current link

How It Works

This recipe calls the Yahoo! Answers API URL in $url, which has been preconfigured with the search query in $search (after ensuring it is suitably encoded for use in a URL by passing it through the rawurlencode() function), and a valid Yahoo! Answers API key, taken from $id, like this:

```
$search = rawurlencode($search);
$id     = 'This-is-a-very-long-string-of-letters-and-numbers';
$url    = 'http://answers.yahooapis.com' .
          '/AnswersService/V1/questionSearch' .
          "?appid=$id&query=$search";
```

In the code provided, the API key shown must be replaced with your own API key that you will obtain from *developer.yahoo.com/wsregapp*. Check the box that says *Generic, No user authentication required*, enter your details, and click the Continue button to be provided with your new API key. Or, if you already have any Yahoo! API keys, you can view them at *developer.yahoo.com/wsregapp/?view*. If you see generic IDs, then any of those will work.

Once the API has been successfully called with the required arguments using the file_get_contents() function (prefaced by an @ symbol to suppress any error messages if it fails), the result is returned to the string $xml. If $xml is empty or has the value FALSE, then FALSE is returned. Otherwise, the contents of $xml are converted into a SimpleXML object and placed in $sxml. An array to hold the questions and answers returned, $qandas, is also initialized, like this:

```
$xml    = @file_get_contents($url);
if (!$xml) return array(FALSE);

$sxml   = simplexml_load_string($xml);
$qandas = array();
```

Now all the Q&As are extracted from $sxml using a foreach loop, with each element of $sxml->Question being assigned to the object $question. From there, the actual parts of

each Q&A—the subject, timestamp, question, answer, and link—are retrieved and placed in
the variables $s, $t, $q, $a, and $l, as follows:

```
foreach($sxml->Question as $question)
{
    $s = trim($question->Subject);
    $t = $question->Timestamp + 0;
    $q = trim($question->Content);
    $a = trim($question->ChosenAnswer);
    $l = $question->Link;

    $s = str_replace("\n", '<br />', htmlentities($s));
    $q = str_replace("\n", '<br />', htmlentities($q));
    $a = str_replace("\n", '<br />', htmlentities($a));

}
```

The link in $l is a URL pointing to the original question and answer at Yahoo! Answers,
as shown in Figure 10-8.

The variables $s, $q, and $a then have any HTML tag symbols such as <, >, or &
replaced with their entity equivalents of <, >, &, and so on:

```
if (strlen($a)) $qandas[] = array($s, $t, $q, $a, $l);
```

At the same time, any \n newline characters are replaced with <br /> tags. If those
strings weren't converted to use HTML entities, then any tags posted in those fields would
be treated as HTML markup, rather than displayed. We want to keep the tags viewable, as
sometimes they are needed to help provide HTML or other programming and web
development–related answers.

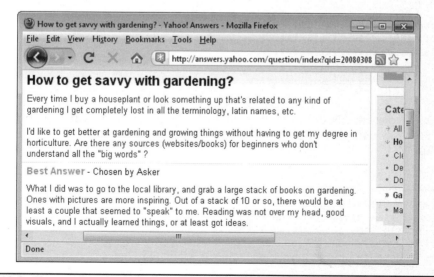

Figure 10-8 The question about savvy gardening as displayed on the Yahoo! Answers web site.

The five short variables are then grouped into an array and assigned to the next available element of $qandas. Once all have been processed, a two-element array is returned, the first of which is the number of Q&As returned, and the second is an array of sub-arrays, containing all the details:

```
if (strlen($a)) $qandas[] = array($s, $t, $q, $a, $l);

return array(count($qandas), $qandas);
```

How to Use It

Using this recipe is as easy as ensuring you have created and set up an API key for it (as described in the previous section) and then simply calling the recipe, passing it a search query, like this:

```
$search = 'gardening';
$result = GetYahooAnswers($search);
if (!$result[0]) echo "No matching questions found for $search.";
```

An error message is displayed if $result [0] has the value FALSE. Otherwise, the returned results are all contained in sub-arrays, each within an element of $result [1], and which you could access like this for the first Q&A:

```
$subject   = $result[1][0][0];
$timestamp = $result[1][0][1];
$question  = $result[1][0][2];
$answer    = $result[1][0][3];
$link      = $result[1][0][4];
```

The second Q&A is then accessible like this (and so on):

```
$subject   = $result[1][1][0];
$timestamp = $result[1][1][1];
$question  = $result[1][1][2];
$answer    = $result[1][1][3];
$link      = $result[1][1][4];
```

However, it's much better to use a foreach loop to iterate through all the elements of $result [1], placing each one in another variable such as $qa. From there, the various values are easily retrieved, like this (in which the time zone is first set to ensure valid dates and times):

```
date_default_timezone_set('utc');

foreach($result[1] as $qa)
    echo "<b>$qa[0]</b> (" . date('M \'y', $qa[1]) . ')<br />'.
        "<b>Q.</b> <i>$qa[2]</i><br />" .
        "<b>A.</b> $qa[3]<br />" .
        "<a href='$qa[4]'>Original Question</a><br /><br />";
```

The only unusual thing of note here is the use of the date() function on $qa[1]. Because this value is a Unix timestamp, you can reformat it any way you like using date(). So, by passing date() the argument 'M \'y', the three-letter month abbreviation, and the shorthand for the year appear next to each message.

The Recipe

```
function GetYahooAnswers($search)
{
    $search = rawurlencode($search);
    $id     = 'This-is-Your-API-key-you-must-get-for-yourself';
    $url    = 'http://answers.yahooapis.com' .
              '/AnswersService/V1/questionSearch' .
              "?appid=$id&query=$search";
    $xml    = @file_get_contents($url);
    if (!$xml) return array(FALSE);

    $sxml   = simplexml_load_string($xml);
    $qandas = array();

    foreach($sxml->Question as $question)
    {
        $s = trim($question->Subject);
        $t = $question->Timestamp + 0;
        $q = trim($question->Content);
        $a = trim($question->ChosenAnswer);
        $l = $question->Link;

        $s = str_replace("\n", '<br />', htmlentities($s));
        $q = str_replace("\n", '<br />', htmlentities($q));
        $a = str_replace("\n", '<br />', htmlentities($a));

        if (strlen($a)) $qandas[] = array($s, $t, $q, $a, $l);
    }

    return array(count($qandas), $qandas);
}
```

SearchYahoo()

Yahoo! has opened up its search engine to third-party developers using an API. This means you can have your applications search for relevant information in the Yahoo! database and then act on it accordingly.

However, before using this API you should be aware that you will need a valid Yahoo! API key, and that Yahoo! now charges for the results it returns. The pricing schedule (in U.S. dollars) is at *developer.yahoo.com/search/boss/#pricing*, and currently starts at 0.04 cents per search made (or 25 searches per cent/1,000 searches for 40 cents). For details on signing up for the service, please refer to *developer.yahoo.com/search/boss*. Figure 10-9 shows this recipe being used to find web sites relating to the query *yahoo search api*.

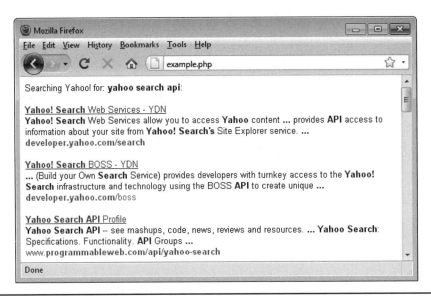

FIGURE 10-9 Use this recipe to add Yahoo! search results to your web site.

About the Recipe

This recipe takes a search term and returns results from the Yahoo! search engine. Upon success, it returns a two-element array with the first value being the number of results returned, and the second an array of result details, containing a sub-array in each element, with the following values:

- The title
- The abstract
- The URL to be displayed
- The URL for clicking through to

On failure, it returns a single-element array with the value FALSE. It requires these arguments:

- **$search**   A search string.
- **$start**   The first result to return.
- **$count**   The maximum number of results to return.

Variables, Arrays, and Functions

$id	String containing a Yahoo! search API key
$url	String containing the API URL with $id and $search appended
$xml	String containing the contents of $url
$sxml	SimpleXML object created from $xml

$data	Array containing the results returned
$result	SimpleXML object extracted from `$sxml->resultset_web->result`
$t	String containing the current title
$a	String containing the current abstract
$d	String containing the current display URL
$c	String containing the current click-through URL

How It Works

Because the search query in $search will be passed to the API as part of a URL, it is first encoded using the `rawurlencode()` function. Then $search, along with a valid Yahoo! search API key, in $id, is incorporated with the API URL to create the string $url, which is then passed to the `file_get_contents()` function to retrieve the results into the variable $xml, as follows:

```
$search = rawurlencode($search);
$id     = ' Your-own-unique-Yahoo!-search-API-key-goes-here ';
$url    = 'http://boss.yahooapis.com/ysearch/web/v1/' .
          "$search?appid=$id&format=xml&start=$start" .
          "&count=$count";
```

It's important to remember that the string $id must contain your own unique Yahoo! search API key, as explained in the previous recipe.

Once these details have been sent to the API, it will return its result in $xml. If it contains the empty string or the value FALSE, then FALSE is returned. An @ symbol is also placed in front of the `file_get_contents()` call to suppress any error messages:

```
$xml = @file_get_contents($url);

if (!$xml) return array(FALSE);
```

A bit of work then needs to be done to transform the contents of $xml because the function that will be used to process the XML data, `simplexml_load_string()`, doesn't seem to like the CDATA that Yahoo! sometimes returns. In XML, a CDATA section is a piece of content that is marked for the parser to interpret as only character data, not markup. So the next few lines of code remove the <![CDATA[and]]> tags, leaving behind just the contents:

```
$xml = str_replace('<![CDATA[', '', $xml);
$xml = str_replace(']]>',       '', $xml);
```

Then these contents are made XML-safe by saving all examples of & by converting them to the string [ampersand] and then changing any & symbols that remain into & entities. The [ampersand] strings are then changed back to & entities. After that, all , , and <wbr> tags (the only ones Yahoo! search seems to employ) are changed into their HTML entity equivalents:

```
$xml = str_replace('&amp;', '[ampersand]', $xml);
$xml = str_replace('&',            '&amp;', $xml);
$xml = str_replace('[ampersand]', '&amp;', $xml);
```

```
$xml = str_replace('<b>',    '&lt;b&gt;', $xml);
$xml = str_replace('</b>',   '&lt;/b&gt;', $xml);
$xml = str_replace('<wbr>', '&lt;wbr&gt;', $xml);
```

At this point, the XML data should be in a format acceptable to SimpleXML, so the contents of $xml are then processed into a SimpleXML object and placed in the object $sxml, and the array that will be used to store all the result details, $data, is also initialized, like this:

```
$sxml = simplexml_load_string($xml);
$data = array();
```

Now, to retrieve all the results, a foreach loop is used to iterate through $sxml->resultset_web->result, placing each element into the object $result. From here, the title, abstract, display URL, and click-through URL are retrieved into the variables $t, $a, $d, and $c. If $a, the abstract, has a value, then these four variables are grouped into an array and inserted into the next available element of $data. This check is made because sometimes Yahoo! search results don't have an abstract, and I choose to ignore such results. Here are the contents of the loop:

```
foreach($sxml->resultset_web->result as $result)
{
    $t = html_entity_decode($result->title);
    $a = html_entity_decode($result->abstract);
    $d = html_entity_decode($result->dispurl);
    $c = $result->clickurl;

    if (strlen($a)) $data[] = array($t, $a, $d, $c);
}
```

Once $data has been populated, a two-element array is returned, with the first element being the number of results returned and the second an array, each element of which is a sub-array containing the parts of each result:

```
return array(count($data), $data);
```

How to Use It

As long as you have assigned a valid Yahoo! search API key to $id in the recipe, you can call it by passing a query string, the number of the first result to return, and the maximum number of results to return, like this:

```
$search  = "yahoo search api";
$results = SearchYahoo($search, 1, 10);
if (!$results[0]) echo "No matching results found for $search.";
```

In this case, the first result requested is 1, and up to 10 results are wanted. If $results[0] is FALSE or has the value 0, then no results were retrieved. Otherwise, the first result is accessible in the following way:

```
$title    = $results[1][0][0];
$abstract = $results[1][0][1];
```

```
$dispurl  = $results[1][0][2];
$clickurl = $results[1][0][3];
```

And the second result, like this (and so on):

```
$title    = $results[1][1][0];
$abstract = $results[1][1][1];
$dispurl  = $results[1][1][2];
$clickurl = $results[1][1][3];
```

The best way to process these results, though, is with a foreach loop, placing each array of results temporarily in a new array such as $result, and then accessing them from there, like this:

```
foreach($results[1] as $result)
    echo "<a href='$result[3]'>$result[0]<a/><br />".
        "$result[1]<br />" .
        "<font color='green'>$result[2]</font><br /><br />";
```

Yahoo! requires that you observe their terms and only ever offer the click-through URL to your users so that their click tracking will be applied. So make sure you don't use the Display URL in an <a href='...'> tag.

If you wish to allow your users to page through the results, you can change the value of the start argument and re-call the recipe.

The Recipe

```
function SearchYahoo($search, $start, $count)
{
    $search = rawurlencode($search);
    $id     = 'Your-own-unique-Yahoo!-search-API-key-goes-here';
    $url    = 'http://boss.yahooapis.com/ysearch/web/v1/' .
              "$search?appid=$id&format=xml&start=$start" .
              "&count=$count";

    $xml = @file_get_contents($url);
    if (!$xml) return array(FALSE);

    $xml = str_replace('<![CDATA[',            '', $xml);
    $xml = str_replace(']]>',                  '', $xml);
    $xml = str_replace('&amp;', '[ampersand]', $xml);
    $xml = str_replace('&',            '&amp;', $xml);
    $xml = str_replace('[ampersand]', '&amp;', $xml);
    $xml = str_replace('<b>',      '&lt;b&gt;', $xml);
    $xml = str_replace('</b>',    '&lt;/b&gt;', $xml);
    $xml = str_replace('<wbr>', '&lt;wbr&gt;', $xml);
    $sxml = simplexml_load_string($xml);
    $data = array();

    foreach($sxml->resultset_web->result as $result)
    {
        $t = html_entity_decode($result->title);
        $a = html_entity_decode($result->abstract);
```

```
    $d = html_entity_decode($result->dispurl);
    $c = $result->clickurl;

    if (strlen($a)) $data[] = array($t, $a, $d, $c);
  }

  return array(count($data), $data);
}
```

GetYahooStockNews()

If you offer any finance-related services, you can add some great content to your site by using this recipe to retrieve stock information from the Yahoo! Finance web site. With it, you can fetch the latest chart for a ticker symbol, along with all the latest news about that stock. Figure 10-10 shows it being used to display information for Apple Computer, Ticker Symbol: AAPL.

About the Recipe

This recipe takes a stock ticker such as AAPL or MSFT and returns news and information about the stock. Upon success, it returns a three-element array (the first of which is the number of news items returned) and a sub-array of two URLs (the first of which is a small— and the second a large—intraday chart for the stock), while the third element is a sub-array containing the following report details:

- Title
- Publishing site

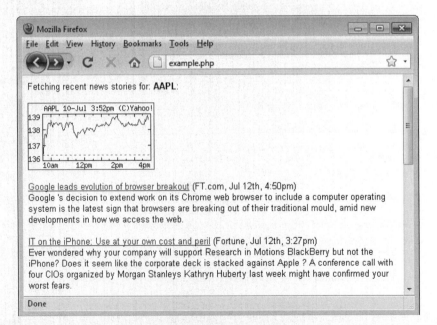

FIGURE 10-10   Add the latest stock news and charts to your web site with this recipe.

- Date
- Story summary/description
- URL to the original story

On failure, it returns a single-element array with the value FALSE. It requires this argument:

- **$stock**   A valid stock ticker symbol such as YHOO or JPM.

Variables, Arrays, and Functions

$url	String containing the Yahoo! Stocks URL
$check	String containing the result of checking whether a ticker symbol exists
$reports	Array containing returned news reports
$xml	String containing news reports in RSS format
$sxml	SimpleXML object created from $xml
$flag	Boolean value set if a story title is too similar to another
$title	String containing the current title
$temp	Array used to extract the publishing site from the title
$site	String containing the current publisher of the story
$desc	String containing the current description/summary
$date	String containing the current story date
$percent	Integer representing how similar one title is to another
$url1	String containing the URL of a small stock chart
$url2	String containing the URL of a large stock chart

How It Works

This recipe starts by ensuring the value entered for the stock ticker symbol in $stock is in uppercase using the strtoupper() function. Then file_get_contents() is called, passing the values in $url (the main Yahoo! Finance URL) and $stock to see whether any information is returned. If the string *Invalid Ticker Symbol* appears anywhere in the returned text saved in $check, then there is no such stock and so a single-element array with the value FALSE is returned as follows (in which the time zone is first set to ensure valid dates and times):

```
date_default_timezone_set('utc');
$stock = strtoupper($stock);
$url   = 'http://finance.yahoo.com';
$check = @file_get_contents("$url/q?s=$stock");

if (stristr($check, 'Invalid Ticker Symbol') || $check == '')
    return array(FALSE);
```

Otherwise, the array $reports, which will hold the news reports returned later, is initialized and $xml is loaded with the XML string returned from calling the RSS feed for the ticker in $stock. Next, because the SimpleXML routines that will be used to process the

XML don't seem to like CDATA (character data; see the previous recipe, SearchYahoo() for more details), the next few lines of code massage the data into a format it will accept by removing or translating certain tags, replacing them with entities it understands. Here's the code that performs these actions:

```
$xml = file_get_contents("$url/rss/headline?s=$stock");
$xml = preg_replace('/&lt;\/?summary&gt;/', '', $xml);
$xml = preg_replace('/&lt;\/?image&gt;/', '', $xml);
$xml = preg_replace('/&lt;\/?guid&gt;/', '', $xml);
$xml = preg_replace('/&lt;\/?p?link&gt;/', '', $xml);
$xml = str_replace('&lt;![CDATA[', '', $xml);
$xml = str_replace(']]&gt;', '', $xml);
$xml = str_replace('&amp;', '[ampersand]', $xml);
$xml = str_replace('&', '&amp;', $xml);
$xml = str_replace('[ampersand]', '&amp;', $xml);
$xml = str_replace('<b>', '&lt;b&gt;', $xml);
$xml = str_replace('</b>', '&lt;/b&gt;', $xml);
$xml = str_replace('<wbr>', '&lt;wbr&gt;', $xml);
```

After this, $xml is passed to simplexml_load_string() and the resulting object created from it is placed in $sxml:

```
$sxml = simplexml_load_string($xml);
```

From here, a foreach loop iterates through all the elements in $sxml->channel->item, each time storing them in the object $item to make them easier to access, as follows:

```
foreach($sxml->channel->item as $item)
```

Inside the loop, the Boolean variable $flag is set to FALSE at the start of each iteration. Later on, if a story title appears too similar to a previously returned title, this flag will be changed to the value TRUE, then the URL of the original story is extracted into $url, and the title is also retrieved in $title. However, because the title also contains the name of the publishing web site in brackets, the explode() function is used to split the title into two elements of an array in $temp. The first now contains just the title, so that is saved back to the variable $title. The second then has the brackets and the word at removed, and the resulting publishing site name is placed in $site. These are the lines of code responsible:

```
$flag  = FALSE;
$url   = $item->link;
$title = $item->title;
$temp  = explode(' (', $title);
$title = $temp[0];
$site  = str_replace(')', '', $temp[1]);
$site  = str_replace('at ', '', $site);
```

The description (or summary) is then placed in $desc and the date, which is returned as a timestamp, is converted to a friendly string using the strtotime() and date() functions, and saved in $date:

```
$desc = $item->description;
$date = date('M jS, g:ia',
   strtotime(substr($item->pubDate, 0, 25)));
```

Next, a `for` loop checks through all the news reports so far saved in the `$reports` array. Using the `similar_text()` function, each title is compared to the current one (first converting both to lowercase using the `strtolower()` function), with a score of between 0 and 100 percent being allocated to the variable $percent, depending on how similar the strings are to each other. A score of 0 means totally different, and 100 means identical:

```
for ($j = 0 ; $j < count($reports) ; ++$j)
{
   similar_text(strtolower($reports[$j][0]),
      strtolower($title), $percent);

   if ($percent > 70)
   {
      $flag = TRUE;
      break;
   }
}
```

After some testing, I chose a value of 70 percent or greater to mean that the same or a similar story has already been saved in the array and, if so, the variable $flag is set to TRUE and a break command is issued to exit the loop.

Finally, within the main loop, the value of $flag is checked. If it's not TRUE and if the story summary doesn't relate to an item on a paid-for subscription site (indicated by the string [$$] in the title), and if the value in $desc isn't the empty string, then the story details are grouped together into an array that is inserted into the next available element in the $reports array:

```
if (!$flag && !strstr($title, '[$$]') && strlen($desc))
   $reports[] = array($title, $site, $date, $desc, $url);
```

Lastly, the two variables $url1 and $url2 are assigned the URLs of a small (192 × 96 pixels) and a large (512 × 288 pixels) chart of the most recent (or current) day's trading of $stock:

```
$url1 = "http://ichart.finance.yahoo.com/t?s=$stock";
$url2 = "http://ichart.finance.yahoo.com/b?s=$stock";
```

A three-element array is then returned by the recipe, the first of which is the number of news items returned, the second is a sub-array of two elements containing the small and large chart URLs, and the third element is the $reports array containing all the news stories:

```
return array(count($reports), array($url1, $url2), $reports);
```

How to Use It

To retrieve stock data using this recipe, all you have to do is pass the name of a valid stock ticker symbol to it, like this:

```
$stock   = "AAPL";
$results = GetYahooStockNews($stock);
if (!$results[0]) echo "No stories found for $stock.";
```

If $results[0] is FALSE, then an error message is displayed. Otherwise, it contains the number of news stories returned, and the value of $results[1] will be an array containing a pair of URLs for a small and a large chart of the stock, which you can display using one or the other of the following lines of code:

```
echo "<img src='" . $results[1][0] . "' />"; // Small chart
echo "<img src='" . $results[1][1] . "' />"; // Large chart
```

Each of the news stories will be supplied with separate details, which can be accessed like this for the first story:

```
$title = $results[2][0][0];
$site  = $results[2][0][1];
$date  = $results[2][0][2];
$story = $results[2][0][3];
$url   = $results[2][0][4];
```

And the second story's details can be accessed like this (and so on):

```
$title = $results[2][1][0];
$site  = $results[2][1][1];
$date  = $results[2][1][2];
$story = $results[2][1][3];
$url   = $results[2][1][4];
```

But the best way to iterate through the array of stories is to use a foreach loop, assigning the value of each element of $results[2] to another array such as $result (singular as opposed to plural), like this:

```
foreach($results[2] as $result)
    echo "<a href='$result[4]'>$result[0]</a> " .
        "($result[1], $result[2])<br />$result[3]<br /><br />';
```

Because all the individual parts of the story are returned separately, you can rearrange and display each story exactly the way you want. In the preceding code, each title in $result[0] is displayed as part of a link to the original story in $result[4], then the originating site in $result[1] and the date in $result[2] are placed inside brackets, and a <br /> tag is displayed. Finally, the story in $result[3] is displayed, followed by a couple more <br /> tags.

As with some of the other similar recipes to this, please be aware that you are using servers and data belonging to other organizations, so make sure you have the relevant permissions required to republish any data. Please also respect the bandwidth and CPU cycles of these companies by caching the results returned, and only requesting updates when necessary.

The Recipe

```
function GetYahooStockNews($stock)
{
    date_default_timezone_set('utc');
    $stock = strtoupper($stock);
    $url   = 'http://finance.yahoo.com';
```

```php
$check = @file_get_contents("$url/q?s=$stock");

if (stristr($check, 'Invalid Ticker Symbol') || $check == '')
    return FALSE;

$reports = array();
$xml     = file_get_contents("$url/rss/headline?s=$stock");
$xml     = preg_replace('/&lt;\/?summary&gt;/', '', $xml);
$xml     = preg_replace('/&lt;\/?image&gt;/',   '', $xml);
$xml     = preg_replace('/&lt;\/?guid&gt;/',    '', $xml);
$xml     = preg_replace('/&lt;\/?p?link&gt;/',  '', $xml);
$xml     = str_replace('&lt;![CDATA[',          '', $xml);
$xml     = str_replace(']]&gt;',                '', $xml);
$xml     = str_replace('&amp;',        '[ampersand]', $xml);
$xml     = str_replace('&',                  '&amp;', $xml);
$xml     = str_replace('[ampersand]',        '&amp;', $xml);
$xml     = str_replace('<b>',            '&lt;b&gt;', $xml);
$xml     = str_replace('</b>',          '&lt;/b&gt;', $xml);
$xml     = str_replace('<wbr>',        '&lt;wbr&gt;', $xml);
$sxml    = simplexml_load_string($xml);

foreach($sxml->channel->item as $item)
{
    $flag  = FALSE;
    $url   = $item->link;
    $title = $item->title;
    $temp  = explode(' (', $title);
    $title = $temp[0];
    $site  = str_replace(')',    '', $temp[1]);
    $site  = str_replace('at ', '', $site);
    $desc  = $item->description;
    $date  = date("M jS, g:ia",
        strtotime(substr($item->pubDate, 0, 25)));

    for ($j = 0 ; $j < count($reports) ; ++$j)
    {
        similar_text(strtolower($reports[$j][0]),
            strtolower($title), $percent);

        if ($percent > 70)
        {
            $flag = TRUE;
            break;
        }
    }

    if (!$flag && !strstr($title, '[$$]') && strlen($desc))
        $reports[] = array($title, $site, $date, $desc, $url);
}

$url1 = "http://ichart.finance.yahoo.com/t?s=$stock";
$url2 = "http://ichart.finance.yahoo.com/b?s=$stock";
return array(count($reports), array($url1, $url2), $reports);
}
```

GetYahooNews()

In the last of this chapter's Yahoo! related recipes, you can request the latest news results for a given search query. What this recipe does is load in the Yahoo! News RSS feed for a query and extract the various elements into arrays, which are then returned to your program. Figure 10-11 shows it being used to retrieve all the latest news for the query *climate change*.

About the Recipe

This recipe takes a search query and returns news items from *news.yahoo.com* based on it. Upon success, it returns a two-element array, the first of which is the number of news items returned, and the second is a sub-array containing the following details:

- Title
- Publishing site
- Date
- Story summary/description
- URL to the original story

On failure, it returns a single-element array with the value FALSE. It requires this argument:

- **$search**   A standard search query.

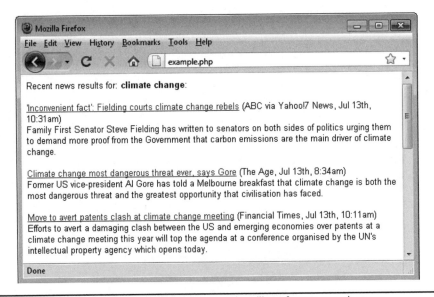

FIGURE 10-11   With this recipe, you can fetch the news headlines for any search query.

Variables, Arrays, and Functions

$reports	Array containing returned news reports
$url	String containing the Yahoo! News URL
$xml	String containing news reports in RSS format
$sxml	SimpleXML object created from $xml
$flag	Boolean value set if a story title is too similar to another
$date	String containing the current date
$title	String containing the current title
$temp	Array used to extract the publishing site from the title
$site	String containing the current publisher of the story
$desc	String containing the current description/summary
$percent	Integer representing how similar one title is to another

How It Works

This program starts by initializing $reports, the array that will hold all the news reports. Then, $url is assigned the location of the Yahoo! News RSS feed for the search term in $search—after $search has been converted to a form that can be passed in a URL using the rawurlencode() function. The feed is then called up using the file_get_contents() function, preceded by an @ symbol to suppress any error messages. The result is then placed in $xml. If it is FALSE or the empty string, then a single-element array containing the value FALSE is returned, as follows (with the time zone first set to ensure valid dates and times):

```
date_default_timezone_set('utc');
$reports = array();
$url      = 'http://news.search.yahoo.com/news/rss?' .
            'ei=UTF-8&fl=0&x=wrt&p=' . rawurlencode($search);
$xml      = @file_get_contents($url);
if (!strlen($xml)) return array(FALSE);
```

Then, because the SimpleXML routines to be used later don't appear to work with CDATA (XML character data; see the earlier recipe, SearchYahoo(), for details), the next few lines remove the CDATA tags and convert characters that might clash with SimpleXML into entities it understands. Finally, $xml is converted into a SimpleXML object using the simplexml_load_string() function, and the result is stored in $sxml, as follows:

```
$xml = str_replace('<![CDATA[',         '',  $xml);
$xml = str_replace(']]>',               '',  $xml);
$xml = str_replace('&amp;', '[ampersand]',   $xml);
$xml = str_replace('&',             '&amp;',  $xml);
$xml = str_replace('[ampersand]',   '&amp;',  $xml);
$xml = str_replace('<b>',        '&lt;b&gt;', $xml);
$xml = str_replace('</b>',      '&lt;/b&gt;', $xml);
$xml = str_replace('<wbr>',    '&lt;wbr&gt;', $xml);
$sxml = simplexml_load_string($xml);
```

Next, a foreach loop is used to iterate through all the elements of $sxml->channel->item, assigning each in turn to the object $item. Inside the loop, the first thing that happens is the variable $flag is set to FALSE. If it is later set to TRUE, then a title was found that was too similar to a previous one. The variable $url is then extracted and the string $date is created from a timestamp by using the strtotime() and date() functions. After that, the title and publishing site name are extracted into $title and $site, after exploding the title into the array $temp to split $site out of the title, where it was stored inside a pair of brackets. The news story is then saved into the variable $desc, like this:

```
foreach ($sxml->channel->item as $item)
{
    $flag   = FALSE;
    $url    = $item->link;
    $date   = date('M jS, g:ia', strtotime($item->pubDate));
    $title  = $item->title;
    $temp   = explode(' (', $title);
    $title  = $temp[0];
    $site   = str_replace(')', '', $temp[1]);
    $desc   = $item->description;
```

To prevent similar stories being returned, a for loop is then used to iterate through all the saved stories in the $reports array. Using the similar_text() function, each previous title is compared to the current one, and if it is more than 70 percent similar, the variable $flag is set to TRUE and a break command is issued to break out of the loop, as no further duplication checking is necessary, like this:

```
for ($j = 0 ; $j < count($reports) ; ++$j)
{
    similar_text(strtolower($reports[$j][0]),
        strtolower($title), $percent);

    if ($percent > 70)
    {
        $flag = TRUE;
        break;
    }
}
```

At the tail end of the loop, as long as $flag doesn't have a value of TRUE and $desc actually contains some text, then the story parts are grouped into an array that is then assigned to the next available element of $reports:

```
if (!$flag && strlen($desc))
    $reports[] = array($title, $site, $date, $desc, $url);
```

The recipe returns a two-element array in which the first element is the number of news stories returned and the second is the $reports array:

```
return array(count($reports), $reports);
```

How to Use It

To use this recipe, you pass it a search term, like this:

```
$search = "climate change";
$results = GetYahooNews($search);
if (!$results[0]) echo "No news found for $search.";
```

If `$results[0]` has the value FALSE or zero, then no stories were returned. Otherwise, you can access the stories in the following manner, which retrieves all the parts of the first story:

```
$title = $results[1][0][0];
$site  = $results[1][0][1];
$date  = $results[1][0][2];
$story = $results[1][0][3];
$url   = $results[1][0][4];
```

And the second result, like this (and so on):

```
$title = $results[1][1][0];
$site  = $results[1][1][1];
$date  = $results[1][1][2];
$story = $results[1][1][3];
$url   = $results[1][1][4];
```

The best way to display the results, though, is to use a `foreach` loop to iterate through each element of `$results[1]`, placing each in another array such as `$result` (using the singular version of the variable name for single items extracted from the array), like this:

```
foreach($results[1] as $result)
   echo "<a href='$result[4]'>$result[0]</a> ($result[1], " .
        "$result[2])<br />$result[3]<br /><br />";
```

In this example, each title in `$result[0]` is made the text of a hyperlink to the story's original URL in `$result[4]`, and the site and date in the variables `$result[1]` and `$result[2]` are displayed next to it in brackets. After a `<br />` tag, the story in `$result[3]` is then displayed, followed by a couple more `<br />` tags.

To display Yahoo! News results to their best effect, you will probably also want to first echo or print a UTF-8 `<meta>` tag in the `<head>` section of your web page so that any unusual characters display correctly. The correct meta tag looks like this:

```
<meta http-equiv="Content-Type" content="text/html; charset=utf-8"/>
```

The Recipe

```
function GetYahooNews($search)
{
   date_default_timezone_set('utc');
   $reports = array();
   $url     = 'http://news.search.yahoo.com/news/rss?' .
```

```
                     'ei=UTF-8&fl=0&x=wrt&p=' . urlencode($search);
    $xml      = @file_get_contents($url);
    if (!strlen($xml)) return array(FALSE);

    $xml  = str_replace('<![CDATA[',            '', $xml);
    $xml  = str_replace(']]>',                  '', $xml);
    $xml  = str_replace('&amp;', '[ampersand]', $xml);
    $xml  = str_replace('&',           '&amp;', $xml);
    $xml  = str_replace('[ampersand]', '&amp;', $xml);
    $xml  = str_replace('<b>',      '&lt;b&gt;', $xml);
    $xml  = str_replace('</b>',    '&lt;/b&gt;', $xml);
    $xml  = str_replace('<wbr>', '&lt;wbr&gt;', $xml);
    $sxml = simplexml_load_string($xml);

    foreach($sxml->channel->item as $item)
    {
        $flag  = FALSE;
        $url   = $item->link;
        $date  = date('M jS, g:ia', strtotime($item->pubDate));
        $title = $item->title;
        $temp  = explode(' (', $title);
        $title = $temp[0];
        $site  = str_replace(')', '', $temp[1]);
        $desc  = $item->description;

        for ($j = 0 ; $j < count($reports) ; ++$j)
        {
            similar_text(strtolower($reports[$j][0]),
                strtolower($title), $percent);

            if ($percent > 70)
            {
                $flag = TRUE;
                break;
            }
        }

        if (!$flag && strlen($desc))
            $reports[] = array($title, $site, $date, $desc, $url);
    }

    return array(count($reports), $reports);
}
```

SearchGoogleBooks()

As well as having already scanned in hundreds of thousands of out-of-copyright books, as I write this, Google is in the process of making agreements with several book publishers over digitizing their in-copyright publications. This means that Google Books is likely to become an ever more useful research source that we can add to our toolkit. Figure 10-12 shows this recipe being used to query the database for the term *Mark Twain*.

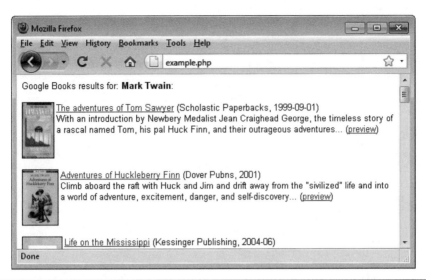

FIGURE 10-12   Add the vast resource of Google Book Search to your web site with this recipe.

About the Recipe

This recipe takes a search query and returns matching books found in the Google Books database. Upon success, it returns a two-element array, the first of which is the number of books returned and the second being an array containing details about those books. On failure, it returns a single-element array with the value FALSE. It requires these arguments:

- **$search**   A standard search query.
- **$start**   The first result to return.
- **$count**   The maximum number of results to return.
- **$type**   The type of result to return. If this is 'none', then all books are returned; if 'partial', then books with partial previews are returned; or if 'full', then only books with full previews are returned.

Variables, Arrays, and Functions

$results	Array containing returned book details
$url	String containing the Google Books API URL
$xml	String containing the result of loading in $url
$sxml	SimpleXML object created from $xml
$title	String containing the current book's title
$author	String containing the current book's author
$pub	String containing the current book's publisher

$date	String containing the current book's publication date
$desc	String containing the current book's description/summary
$thumb	String containing the URL of the current book's cover thumbnail
$info	String containing the URL of the current book's information
$preview	String containing the URL for previewing the current book

How It Works

This recipe starts off by initializing the array $results, which will be used to store the details of any books returned. Then, $url is built up from the URL of the Google Books API, $search, converted into a form that can be passed in a URL using rawurlencode(), and the values of $start, $count, and $type, like this:

```
$results = array();
$url     = 'http://books.google.com/books/feeds/volumes?' .
           'q=' . rawurlencode($search) . '&start-index=' .
           "$start&max-results=$count&min-viewability=" .
           "$type";
```

The result of calling this URL using file_get_contents(), prefaced by an @ symbol to suppress error messages, is placed in the string variable $xml, which is then passed to simplexml_load_string() to be converted into the object $sxml. But, just before this, all occurrences of the string dc: in $xml have the colon removed for the benefit of the SimpleXML routines, which don't seem to like colons in XML field names:

```
$xml     = @file_get_contents($url);
if (!strlen($xml)) return array(FALSE);

$xml  = str_replace('dc:', 'dc', $xml);
$sxml = simplexml_load_string($xml);
```

The $sxml object is then iterated through using a foreach loop, with each element in $sxml->entry being assigned to the object $item for ease of access, as follows:

```
foreach($sxml->entry as $item)
{
    $title   = $item->title;
    $author  = $item->dccreator;
    $pub     = $item->dcpublisher;
    $date    = $item->dcdate;
    $desc    = $item->dcdescription;
    $thumb   = $item->link[0]['href'];
    $info    = $item->link[1]['href'];
    $preview = $item->link[2]['href'];
```

The title, author, publisher, date, and description are all retrieved and placed in the variables $title, $author, $pub, $date, and $desc. Then there are three URLs to fetch, which are the thumbnail image, a link to the information page at Google Books, and the link to the preview page at Google Books. These are placed in $thumb, $info, and $preview.

Next, a few bits of sorting out need to occur. First, if $pub doesn't have a value, then the value in $author is given to it. Similarly, if $preview is found to not link to an actual preview of the book, then it is set to FALSE. If the description in $desc is missing, it is assigned the value *(No description)*, and if it is determined that there is no thumbnail image specific to this book, a link to a generic cover image at Google Books is assigned to $thumb. Here are the lines of code that perform these actions:

```
if (!strlen($pub))
    $pub = $author;
if ($preview ==
    'http://www.google.com/books/feeds/users/me/volumes')
    $preview = FALSE;
if (!strlen($desc))
    $desc = '(No description)';
if (!strstr($thumb, '&sig='))
    $thumb = 'http://books.google.com/googlebooks/' .
        'images/no_cover_thumb.gif';
```

At the tail end of the loop, all these items of information are grouped together into an array, which is then assigned to the next available element in $results:

```
$results[] = array($title, $author, $pub, $date, $desc,
    $thumb, $info, $preview);
```

The recipe returns a two-element array in which the first element is the number of books returned and the second is the $results array:

```
return array(count($results), $results);
```

How to Use It

To use this recipe, pass it a search query and arguments telling it which number result to start returning details from, the maximum number of results, and the type of results. For example, to return up to 20 books relating to the search *Mark Twain,* starting at the first result, and where any or no summary is available, you would use code such as this:

```
$search = "Mark Twain";
$result = SearchGoogleBooks($search, 1, 20, 'none');
if (!$result[0]) echo "No books found for $search.";
```

If $result[0] is FALSE or zero, then no results were returned. Otherwise, the details returned for the first book will be in the array $result[1] and can be accessed like this:

```
$title       = $result[1][0][0];
$author      = $result[1][0][1];
$publisher   = $result[1][0][2];
$date        = $result[1][0][3];
$description = $result[1][0][4];
$thumbnail   = $result[1][0][5];
$information = $result[1][0][6];
$preview     = $result[1][0][7];
```

The second book's details can therefore be accessed like this (and so on):

```
$title       = $result[1][1][0];
$author      = $result[1][1][1];
$publisher   = $result[1][1][2];
$date        = $result[1][1][3];
$description = $result[1][1][4];
$thumbnail   = $result[1][1][5];
$information = $result[1][1][6];
$preview     = $result[1][1][7];
```

However, you will probably want to use a `foreach` loop to iterate through the `$result[1]` array, passing each element to another array with a name such as `$book`, like this:

```
foreach($result[1] as $book)
{
    echo "<img src='$book[5]' align='left' border='1'>";
    echo "<a href='$book[6]'>$book[0]</a> ($book[2], " .
        "$book[3])<br />$book[4]";
    if ($book[7]) echo " (<a href='$book[7]'>preview</a>)";
    echo "<br clear='left' /><br />";
}
```

Because all eight items are provided separately, you can choose exactly how you wish to lay out a book's details. In the preceding code, the thumbnail image in `$book[5]` is displayed aligned to the left and with a one-pixel border. Then, the book title in `$book[0]` is used as a text hyperlink for the book's information page in `$book[6]`. Alongside this, the book's publisher and publication date in `$book[2]` and `$book[3]` are added within brackets, followed by a `<br />` tag and the book's description in `$book[4]`.

After this, if the book has a preview, identified by `$book[7]` having a value, then a link is provided to it, enclosed in brackets. Finally, the book thumbnail's left alignment is cleared using the tag `<br clear='left' />`, and then another `<br />` tag is used to separate book details from each other.

If you want to only return results for books where the whole text is available in the summary, generally because they are out of copyright control or because their authors have allowed the entire contents to be released, just replace the preceding call to the recipe with this one:

```
$result = SearchGoogleBooks($search, 1, 20, 'full');
```

Or, to allow results with either partial or full previews, you could use:

```
$result = SearchGoogleBooks($search, 1, 20, 'partial');
```

You can also support paging through the search results by changing the start argument for the book number at which returned results should begin, and re-calling the recipe.

The Recipe

```
function SearchGoogleBooks($search, $start, $count, $type)
{
    $results = array();
    $url     = 'http://books.google.com/books/feeds/volumes?' .
```

```
                'q=' . rawurlencode($search) . '&start-index=' .
                "$start&max-results=$count&min-viewability=" .
                "$type";
    $xml      = @file_get_contents($url);
    if (!strlen($xml)) return array(FALSE);

    $xml  = str_replace('dc:', 'dc', $xml);
    $sxml = simplexml_load_string($xml);

    foreach($sxml->entry as $item)
    {
        $title    = $item->title;
        $author   = $item->dccreator;
        $pub      = $item->dcpublisher;
        $date     = $item->dcdate;
        $desc     = $item->dcdescription;
        $thumb    = $item->link[0]['href'];
        $info     = $item->link[1]['href'];
        $preview  = $item->link[2]['href'];

        if (!strlen($pub))
            $pub = $author;
        if ($preview ==
            'http://www.google.com/books/feeds/users/me/volumes')
            $preview = FALSE;
        if (!strlen($desc))
            $desc = '(No description)';
        if (!strstr($thumb, '&sig='))
            $thumb = 'http://books.google.com/googlebooks/' .
                'images/no_cover_thumb.gif';

        $results[] = array($title, $author, $pub, $date, $desc,
            $thumb, $info, $preview);
    }

    return array(count($results), $results);
}
```

ConvertCurrency()

The final recipe in this chapter allows you to produce up-to-date currency conversions between 34 major currencies. The data used is supplied by the European Central Bank and is based on the prices of each currency relative to the euro at the previous trading session's close of business. Figure 10-13 shows the recipe being used to convert 100 U.S. dollars into UK pounds.

About the Recipe

This recipe takes a value and currencies to convert it from and to. Upon success, it returns a floating point number, accurate to two decimal places, representing the value of the amount

FIGURE 10-13   Using this recipe, you can instantly convert between 34 currencies.

given when converted to the new currency. On failure, it returns the value FALSE. It requires these arguments:

- **$amount**   The amount of money to convert.
- **$from**   The abbreviation for the source currency.
- **$to**   The abbreviation for the destination currency.

The available currencies and their abbreviations are:

AUD = Australian Dollar   HRK = Croatian Kuna   PHP = Philippine Peso
BGN = Bulgarian Lev   HUF = Hungarian Forint   PLN = Polish Zloty
BRL = Brazilian Real   IDR = Indonesian Rupiah   RON = Romanian Lei
CAD = Canadian Dollar   INR = Indian Rupee   RUB = Russian Ruble
CHF = Swiss Frank   JPY = Japanese Yen   SEK = Swedish Krona
CNY = Chinese Yuan   KRW = South Korean Won   SGD = Singapore Dollar
CZK = Czech Koruna   LTL = Lithuanian Litas   THB = Thai Baht
DKK = Danish Krone   LVL = Latvian Lats   TRY = Turkish Lira
EEK = Estonian Kroon   MXN = Mexican Peso   USD = U.S. Dollar
EUR = European Euro   MYR = Malaysian Ringgit   ZAR = South African Rand
GBP = British Pound   NOK = Norwegian Krone
HKD = Hong Kong Dollar   NZD = New Zealand Dollar

Variables, Arrays, and Functions

$url	String containing the URL for the European Central Bank exchange rates page
$data	String containing the result of loading in $url
$ptr1	Integer pointer to the start of the currency data
$ptr2	Integer pointer to the end of the currency data
$main	Array in which the currencies and prices are stored
$lines	Array of data lines extracted from $data
$line	String containing a line of data from $lines
$l	String containing the left half of a currency/value pair
$r	String containing the right half of a currency/value pair

How It Works

This recipe loads into the variable $data the XML page that the European Central Bank maintains of currency rates compared to the euro. If no data is returned, then there was an error and FALSE is returned, like this:

```
$url  = 'http://www.ecb.europa.eu/stats/eurofxref/' .
        'eurofxref-daily.xml';
$data = file_get_contents($url);
if (!strlen($data)) return FALSE;
```

Otherwise, instead of converting the XML data into an object as some of the other recipes do, the information needed is easily extracted with just a few PHP commands. First, the start and end of the section of XML of interest are put in the variables $ptr1 and $ptr2. This is done using the strpos() function to search for certain strings in the file. The contents of $data are then cropped down to just that section using the substr() function, then a few keywords, tags, and other pieces of XML are replaced with values of more use to the recipe, and whitespace is also removed, like this:

```
$ptr1 = strpos($data, '<Cube currency');
$ptr2 = strpos($data, '</Cube>');
$data = substr($data, $ptr1, $ptr2 - $ptr1);
$data = str_replace("<Cube currency='", '', $data);
$data = str_replace("' rate='",        '|', $data);
$data = str_replace("'/>",             '@', $data);
$data = preg_replace("/\s/",           '', $data);
```

This leaves $data containing just 33 lines, each of which is a currency/value pair in relation to the euro at the time of closing of the previous day's trading session. Each line is separated from the others with an @ symbol, and the currency abbreviations are separated from their values by | symbols. Using these as separators, the contents of $data are split into the array $lines at each of the @ symbols using the explode() function, while prior to this the array $main is created, ready for storing the results of the data extraction:

```
$main  = array();
$lines = explode('@', substr($data, 0, -1));
```

Then, using a foreach loop, each individual line is processed into the associative array $main by using explode() to separate the currencies from their values at the | symbols. The parts are placed in $l and $r using the list() function, and from there the values are assigned to the $main array:

```
foreach($lines as $line)
{
    list($l, $r) = explode('|', $line);
    $main[$l]    = $r;
}
```

At this point, the $main array has 33 currencies, each one accessible by its abbreviation. For example, $main['DKK'] will return the value of the Danish krone against the euro. But there is one currency missing because all the other values are set against it, and that's the euro, with an abbreviation of EUR. Therefore, that gets added to the $main array with a value of 1, because that is its value in relation to itself:

```
$main['EUR'] = 1;
```

Next, both the values in $from and $to are set to uppercase (if they aren't already) using the strtoupper() function, and then they are also checked to ensure they both have an associated value in the $main array. If either of them doesn't, then an unknown abbreviation was used and so the value FALSE is returned, as follows:

```
$from = strtoupper($from);
$to   = strtoupper($to);

if (!isset($main[$from]) || !isset($main[$to])) return FALSE;
```

Otherwise, a quick calculation converts one currency to another using the formula *New value = Original value / From value * To value*. The result is then passed through the sprintf() function to ensure it has exactly two decimal places and the final result is then returned:

```
return sprintf('%.02f', $amount / $main[$from] * $main[$to]);
```

If you need more decimal places in your returned values, you can change the %.02f to another string such as %.04f for four decimal places, and so on.

How to Use It

To use the recipe, you pass it a value to convert, along with abbreviations representing currencies from and to which the value should be converted, like this:

```
$amount = 100;
$from   = 'USD';
$to     = 'GBP';
$result = ConvertCurrency(100, $from, $to);
if (!$result) echo "Conversion failed.";
else          echo "$amount $from is $result $to";
```

If you plan to call this function a lot, you would be well advised to save the contents of $data once per day and return conversions based on the saved values. This will stop your program from excessively calling the ECB server, which is not necessary anyway because the data there is only updated daily.

The Recipe

```
function ConvertCurrency($amount, $from, $to)
{
    $url    = 'http://www.ecb.europa.eu/stats/eurofxref/' .
              'eurofxref-daily.xml';
    $data   = file_get_contents($url);
    if (!strlen($data)) return FALSE;
```

```
$ptr1  = strpos($data, '<Cube currency');
$ptr2  = strpos($data, '</Cube>');
$data  = substr($data, $ptr1, $ptr2 - $ptr1);
$data  = str_replace("<Cube currency='", '', $data);
$data  = str_replace("' rate='",           '|', $data);
$data  = str_replace("'/>",                 '@', $data);
$data  = preg_replace("/\s/",               '', $data);
$main  = array();
$lines = explode('@', substr($data, 0, -1));

foreach($lines as $line)
{
    list($l, $r) = explode('|', $line);
    $main[$l]    = $r;
}

$main['EUR'] = 1;
$from        = strtoupper($from);
$to          = strtoupper($to);

if (!isset($main[$from]) || !isset($main[$to])) return FALSE;
return sprintf('%.04f', $amount / $main[$from] * $main[$to]);
}
```

PART II

CHAPTER 11

Incorporating JavaScript

JavaScript is a powerful programming language in its own right. Most of the things you can do with other languages like Java, C, and PHP can also be done with it (although obviously you can't create compiled programs such as device drivers and the like). Its great utility lies in the fact that it runs inside a web browser, and so if you interact with it, you can substantially increase the dynamic features of your web site by adding Web 2.0 functionality such as Ajax calls, the manipulating of elements within a web page, assisting user input, and a whole lot more.

Although Part III of this book is dedicated solely to JavaScript, the recipes in this chapter are closely related to PHP, which is why they appear here. Even if you have never used JavaScript before, you should at least understand what is going on, and see how to modify the recipes for your own purposes.

In particular, including a few JavaScript recipes in this PHP section of the book illustrates how to embed JavaScript within or alongside PHP code, something you will frequently find yourself having to do on more complex web projects.

CreateAjaxObject()

Ajax is the power behind the vastly improved user interaction of Web 2.0. It stands for Asynchronous JavaScript and XML, which is really a contrived acronym for a background call made to a web server. Using this recipe, you can easily create a new Ajax object that can be used to send and request information to and from a web server in the background, without the user being aware of it.

Unlike in the past, when a POST or GET stopped action in the browser until it completed, with Ajax the browser handles the request without disrupting the web application.

Figure 11-1 shows a simple HTML file that has been fetched from the web server and inserted into a div element, using this recipe in conjunction with the next one, GetAjaxRequest(). This recipe is repeated as JavaScript Recipe 85 because JavaScript is the other half of the Ajax equation to PHP.

About the Recipe

This recipe doesn't take any arguments but returns an XMLHttpRequest object upon success; otherwise, it returns false.

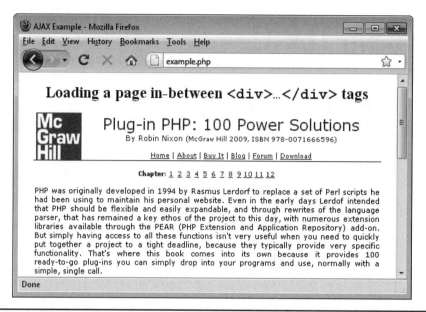

FIGURE 11-1   Using Ajax techniques, you can load new elements into a page in the background.

Variables, Arrays, and Functions

request	XMLHttpRequest object or the value `false` on failure

This recipe creates an Ajax object ready for making background calls to the web server. It requires the following argument:

- **callback**   The function to pass the returned data to once it has been retrieved.

Variables, Arrays, and Functions

Ajax	Local Ajax object
readyState	Property of `ajax` containing its state
Status	Property of `ajax` containing its status
responseText	Property of `ajax` containing the text returned by the Ajax call
XMLHttpRequest()	Function used by non-Microsoft browsers to create an Ajax object
ActiveXObject()	Function used by Microsoft browsers to create an Ajax object

How It Works

Since the Ajax request object has to be created in different ways for different browsers, this recipe uses pairs of `try ... catch()` statements to try each method in turn until one works or until all have been tried and `false` is returned, like this:

```
try
{
   var ajax = new XMLHttpRequest()
}
catch(e1)
{
   try
   {
      ajax = new ActiveXObject("Msxml2.XMLHTTP")
   }
   catch(e2)
   {
      try
      {
         ajax = new ActiveXObject("Microsoft.XMLHTTP")
      }
      catch(e3)
      {
         ajax = false
      }
   }
}
```

The first `try` works with any browser but Internet Explorer version 6 or earlier, the second is for Internet Explorer 6, and the third is for Internet Explorer 5. Therefore, the tests are made roughly in order of popular browser usage.

Assuming one of the `try` statements succeeds, `ajax` is a new Ajax object; otherwise, it contains the value `false`. If it isn't an object, then the recipe will return `false`; otherwise, the following code attaches an inline anonymous function to the `onreadystatechange` event of `ajax`, as follows:

```
if (ajax) ajax.onreadystatechange = function()
{
   if (this.readyState    == 4   &&
       this.status        == 200 &&
       this.responseText != null)
      callback.call(this.responseText)
}

return ajax
```

This subfunction is called every time the `readyState` property of `ajax` changes, and checks whether it has a value of 4, the `status` property has a value of 200, and the `responseText` property is not `null`. If all these tests are satisfied, it means an Ajax request was successful, so the function passed in the `callback` argument is called, passing it the data returned in `this.responseText`.

The actual Ajax call is not made by this recipe. It merely catches the event ready to populate `id` with the value that is returned by an Ajax call. The Ajax call itself is made in the next two recipes: `GetAjaxRequest()` and `PostAjaxRequest()`.

How to Use It

Generally, you will not use this function directly if you call either GetAjaxRequest() or PostAjaxRequest() to handle your Ajax calls, because they will call it for you—as in the following code, which loads some data into a div element:

```
<div id='a'>The data returned by Ajax will replace this text</div>

<script>
OnDOMReady(function()
{
   url = 'ajaxtest.htm'
   GetAjaxRequest(todiv, url, '')

   function todiv()
   {
      Html('a', this)
   }
})
</script>
```

The function todiv() is passed to the recipe (note that parentheses have been omitted from the function; otherwise, only the value returned by it would be passed) and is later called back by it when the returned data is ready. At that point, it retrieves the data using the this keyword and assigns it to the innerHTML property of the div using the Html() recipe.

You need to know that Ajax is a tightly controlled process to prevent hackers using it to inject malevolent code from other servers. Therefore, only files or programs on the same server as the one containing the Ajax can be accessed. For example, if you wanted to pull a copy of the Google home page into a div element on your web site, it would not be possible and the Ajax call would fail.

This code is the same as JavaScript Recipe 84, and you will need to load in the file *WDC. js* to the <head> section of your web page (including adding any server and/or path prefix) as follows in order to use this function:

```
<script src='WDC.js'></script>
```

The Recipe

```
function CreateAjaxObject(callback)
{
   try
   {
      var ajax = new XMLHttpRequest()
   }
   catch(e1)
   {
      try
      {
         ajax = new ActiveXObject("Msxml2.XMLHTTP")
      }
      catch(e2)
      {
         try
```

```
        {
            ajax = new ActiveXObject("Microsoft.XMLHTTP")
        }
        catch(e3)
        {
            ajax = false
        }
      }
  }

  if (ajax) ajax.onreadystatechange = function()
  {
     if (this.readyState    == 4   &&
         this.status        == 200 &&
         this.responseText != null)
         callback.call(this.responseText)
  }

  return ajax
}
```

RECIPE 82 GetAjaxRequest()

The previous recipe provides a means of creating an XMLHttpRequest object, with which this recipe makes a POST request to the server to request some data to be transferred back to the browser. Both of these requests happen seamlessly in the background with the user generally unaware that such things are taking place. A POST request is where data is sent to the server within header messages, rather than as part of a URL tail (or query string), as is the case with GET requests.

Figure 11-2 shows this recipe being used to load Facebook's mobile web site main page at *m.facebook.com*, replacing the contents of a <div>...</div> pair of tags.

About the Recipe

This recipe fetches data from a web site in the background. It requires the following arguments:

- **callback**   The function to pass the returned data to once it has been retrieved.
- **url**   The URL with which to communicate.
- **args**   Any arguments to pass to the URL.

Variables, Arrays, and Functions

nocache	Local variable assigned a random string to prevent caching
ajax	Local variable assigned an Ajax object
CreateAjaxObject()	Function to return a new Ajax object
open()	Method of ajax for opening a request
send()	Method of ajax for sending a request
Math.random()	Function to return a random number

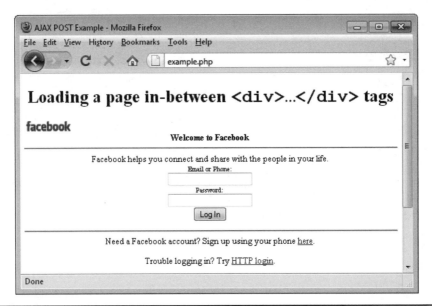

Figure 11-2 A one-line PHP program interfaces with a browser via Ajax to insert a web page into an HTML element.

How It Works

This recipe uses the GET method to communicate with a server, which passes data in the tail of the URL called a query string. However, browser caching will often interfere with repeated requests of this type, serving up only the cached data from previous requests. Therefore, the variable nocache is created and assigned a random string to ensure that no two GET calls will be the same and therefore will not be cached:

```
var nocache = '&nocache=' + Math.random() * 1000000
```

Next, the variable ajax is assigned the new Ajax object returned by calling CreateAjaxObject(), and if the result is not true (meaning the call was unsuccessful), a value of false is returned:

```
var ajax = new CreateAjaxObject(callback)

if (!ajax) return false
```

If execution reaches this point, the Ajax object was successfully created, so the open method of ajax is called, passing it the string 'GET' for the type of request. This is followed by a string comprising the URL to be called that was passed in url, the arguments supplied in args, the nocache string just created, and the value true to tell the browser to make an asynchronous call (a value of false would tell it to make a synchronous call):

```
ajax.open('GET', url + '?' + args + nocache, true)
```

Finally, the call is made and the value `true` is returned to indicate success:

```
ajax.send(null)
return true
```

How to Use It

To use this recipe, decide what data you wish to load and from where, then call the recipe, passing it a function to call back when the data has been retrieved, along with any arguments that require passing.

The following example is somewhat interesting in that it gets around the problem of being unable to access web sites other than the one the Ajax web page came from by calling a PHP script on the server, which then fetches the requested data without a hitch:

```
<div id='info'>The data returned by Ajax will replace this text</div>

<script>
OnDOMReady(function()
{
    GetAjaxRequest(todiv, 'ajaxget.php', 'url=http://m.facebook.com/')

    function todiv()
    {
        Html('info', this)
    }
})
</script>
```

The *ajaxget.php* program is a very simple one-liner that looks like this:

```
<?php if (isset($_GET['url'])) echo file_get_contents($_GET['url']); ?>
```

If your server supports PHP (and most do), you can use the same script on it to check whether the server has been sent a query string that looks something like *url=http://website .com?args=vals*. (In the case of the preceding example, the *args=vals* section is specified in the line that assigns the string *url=http://m.facebook.com/* to the `args` variable.)

The *ajaxget.php* script then uses the `file_get_contents()` PHP function to fetch the requested data (in this case, the Wikipedia home page), which is then returned using the PHP `echo` command, which outputs the data it just fetched.

The `todiv()` callback function, which was passed to `GetAjaxRequest()`, is then called back and passed the retrieved data, which it then promptly inserts into the `innerHTML` property of the div.

As with the previous Ajax example, the restrictions put in place by browsers require that the example and PHP files reside on the same server, so here's a link you can try it out with: *webdeveloperscookbook.com/PHP/ajaxget.html*.

This code is the same as JavaScript Recipe 85, and you will need to load in the file *WDC. js* to the <head> section of your web page as follows in order to use this function:

```
<script src='WDC.js'></script>
```

The Recipe

```
function GetAjaxRequest(callback, url, args)
{
    var nocache = '&nocache=' + Math.random() * 1000000
    var ajax    = new CreateAjaxObject(callback)
    if (!ajax) return false

    ajax.open('GET', url + '?' + args + nocache, true)
    ajax.send(null)
    return true
}
```

PostAjaxRequest()

This recipe is very similar to `GetAjaxRequest()` except that it uses a `POST` request to interact with the web server. In Figure 11-3, the Facebook mobile web page has been pulled in via Ajax.

This is the same code as JavaScript Recipe 87 and is loaded in from the *WDC.js* file, like this:

```
<script src='WDC.js'></script>
```

About the Recipe

This recipe fetches data from a web site in the background. It requires the following arguments:

- **callback**   The function to pass the returned data to once it has been retrieved.
- **url**   The URL with which to communicate.
- **args**   Any arguments to pass to the URL.

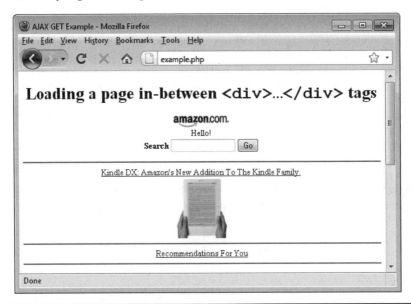

FIGURE 11-3   Ajax works equally well with either GET or POST requests, as shown here.

Variables, Arrays, and Functions

`contenttype`	Local variable containing the content type used for URL-encoded forms
`ajax`	Local variable assigned an Ajax object
`CreateAjaxObject()`	Function to return a new Ajax object
`open()`	Method of `ajax` for opening a request
`setRequestHeader()`	Method of `ajax` for setting various headers
`send()`	Method of `ajax` for sending a request
`Math.random()`	Function to return a random number

How It Works

This is the last of the JavaScript-only recipes in this part of the book. It's fairly similar to the previous one, *Get Ajax Request*, except that it handles the passing of arguments back to the server in a slightly different manner, using a POST request.

It starts by setting the content type of the data in the request being sent to that of a URL-encoded form. It then creates the Ajax object with a call to `CreateAjaxObject()`, and if the result is not `true`, returns the value `false` since it cannot proceed any further:

```
var contenttype = 'application/x-www-form-urlencoded'
var ajax        = new CreateAjaxObject(callback)
if (!ajax) return false
```

If the object creation was successful, it goes on to open up the request, passing a type of `'POST'`, the URL, and the value `true`, for an asynchronous request:

```
ajax.open('POST', url, true)
```

Next, the content type, content length, and connection headers are sent:

```
ajax.setRequestHeader('Content-type',   contenttype)
ajax.setRequestHeader('Content-length', args.length)
ajax.setRequestHeader('Connection',     'close')
```

Finally, the request is sent and the value `true` is returned to indicate success:

```
ajax.send(args)
return true
```

How to Use It

To use this recipe, you must first include the *WDC.js* file into the `<head>` section of your web page, like this:

```
<script src='WDC.php'></script>
```

You call this recipe in exactly the same way as `GetAjaxRequest()`—it's just that the process used by the recipe to perform the Ajax is a POST, not a GET request. Therefore, the target of the request also needs to respond to the POST request, as is the case with the following example, which fetches the Amazon mobile web site:

```
<div id='info'>The data returned by Ajax will replace this text</div>

<script>
OnDOMReady(function()
{
    PostAjaxRequest(todiv, 'ajaxpost.php', 'url=http://amazon.com/mobile')

    function todiv()
    {
        Html('info', this)
    }
})
</script>
```

The URL supplied to the recipe is the PHP script *ajaxpost.php*, which is in the same folder as the example file. It's another simple one-line PHP script, which looks like this:

```
<?php if (isset($_POST['url'])) echo file_get_contents($_POST['url']); ?>
```

This is almost the same as the *ajaxget.php* script, except that it processes POST requests. You can copy it to your own server, where it should work fine if it supports PHP.

As with the previous Ajax example, the restrictions put in place by browsers require that the example and PHP files reside on the same server, so here's a link you can try it out with: *webdeveloperscookbook.com/PHP/ajaxpost.html*.

The Recipe
```
function GetAjaxRequest(url, params, target)
{
    var contenttype = 'application/x-www-form-urlencoded'
    var ajax        = new CreateAjaxObject(callback)
    if (!ajax) return false

    ajax.open('POST', url, true)
    ajax.setRequestHeader('Content-type',   contenttype)
    ajax.setRequestHeader('Content-length', args.length)
    ajax.setRequestHeader('Connection',     'close')
    ajax.send(args)
    return true
}
```

ProtectEmail()
You know the dilemma; you need to get your e-mail address out there so that people can contact you, but doing so leaves you open to being added to spam lists by automatic e-mail address harvesting programs. Well, this recipe has the solution by obfuscating your e-mail address using JavaScript code.

FIGURE 11-4   Using this recipe, you can display your e-mail address while preventing access to most "bots."

Figure 11-4 shows an e-mail address that has been displayed, making it both copyable and clickable, but as the inset source view shows, the e-mail address itself doesn't appear as a whole within the page, because it has been split into three JavaScript variables and then reassembled, meaning that only a sophisticated harvesting "bot," capable of parsing and running JavaScript, could make sense of it.

About the Recipe

This recipe takes an e-mail address and returns JavaScript code that will display it as a hyperlink without leaving the full e-mail address in the HTML. Upon success, it returns the JavaScript or, on failure (for example, if the e-mail address doesn't validate), it returns FALSE. It requires the following argument:

- **$email** The e-mail address to obfuscate.

Variables, Arrays, and Functions

$t1	PHP integer pointer to the @ in $email
$t2	PHP integer pointer to the first period after the @ in $email
$e1	PHP string containing the pre @ part of $email
$e2	PHP string containing part of $email between @ and the first period
$e3	PHP string containing the remainder of $email after the first period
e1	JavaScript string copy of PHP variable $e1
e2	JavaScript string copy of PHP variable $e2
e3	JavaScript string copy of PHP variable $e3

How It Works

This recipe only requires that e-mail addresses have at least one character before an @ sign, and at least one period somewhere after the @. The remaining characters can be anything, including more periods, and even disallowed characters, since no serious validation is made on the e-mail address.

The code uses the PHP `strpos()` function to locate the positions of the @ character in `$email`, followed by the first period after the @. The values returned are assigned to `$t1` and `$t2`, respectively. If either of these values is zero, then that character is missing and so FALSE is returned because the e-mail address is invalid. This is the only validation performed:

```
$t1 = strpos($email, '@');
$t2 = strpos($email, '.', $t1);
if (!$t1 || !$t2) return FALSE;
```

Then, three variables representing the start, middle, and end portions of `$email` are assigned to `$e1`, `$e2`, and `$e3` using the `substr()` function to extract the parts, like this:

```
$e1 = substr($email, 0, $t1);
$e2 = substr($email, $t1, $t2 - $t1);
$e3 = substr($email, $t2);
```

Finally, some JavaScript within `<script>` and `</script>` tags is returned, which makes use of `$e1`, `$e2`, and `$e3` by first assigning their values to the JavaScript variables `e1`, `e2`, and `e3`. Then, a `document.write()` command is added to the string (this is similar to a PHP echo command) in which an HTML `mailto:` link is displayed by recombining the parts:

```
return "<script>e1='$e1';e2='$e2';e3='$e3';document.write" .
       "('<a href=\'mailto:' + e1 + e2 + e3 + '\'>' + e1 " .
       "+ e2 + e3 + '</a>');</script>";
```

How to Use It

To use this function, pass it a valid e-mail address and the returned value can then be output to a browser, like this:

```
$email  = 'billgates@microsoft.com';
$pemail = ProtectEmail($email);
echo "My email address is $pemail";
```

Or more concisely:

```
echo "My email address is " .
     ProtectEmail('billgates@microsoft.com');
```

So, assuming the e-mail address used is me@myserver.com, the recipe will create the JavaScript required to turn the e-mail address into the following format when viewed in a browser with JavaScript enabled:

```
<a href='mailto:me@myserver.com'>me@myserver.com</a>
```

But all an e-mail harvesting program will see is the following:

```
<script>e1='me'; e2='@myserver'; e3='.com'; document.write('<a
href=\'mailto:' + e1 + e2 + e3 + '\'>' + e1 + e2 + e3 + '</a>');
</script>
```

Of course, there is a downside, and that is that people without JavaScript or who have it disabled will not see anything, although that's likely to be very few people—nevertheless it's something you should bear in mind when using this recipe.

The Recipe

```
function ProtectEmail($email)
{
    $t1 = strpos($email, '@');
    $t2 = strpos($email, '.', $t1);
    if (!$t1 || !$t2) return FALSE;

    $e1 = substr($email, 0, $t1);
    $e2 = substr($email, $t1, $t2 - $t1);
    $e3 = substr($email, $t2);

    return "<script>e1='$e1';e2='$e2';e3='$e3';document.write" .
        "('<a href=\'mailto:' + e1 + e2 + e3 + '\'>' + e1 " .
        "+ e2 + e3 + '</a>');</script>";
}
```

ToggleText( )

A great use for JavaScript is to manipulate the contents of a web page without having to reload it. An effect I always feel is quite professional is the use of toggling to switch elements in and out. For example, Figure 11-5 shows this recipe being used to display a short explanation of photosynthesis, along with a link to a longer definition.

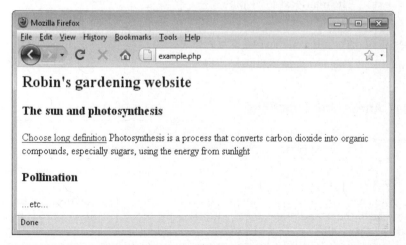

Figure 11-5   Using this recipe, you can toggle between two sets of text or HTML.

FIGURE 11-6   After clicking the toggle link, an alternative text and link are displayed.

When the link is clicked, instead of a new request being made to the server, JavaScript steps in and hides the current text and link, replacing it with an alternative pair, as you can see in Figure 11-6, where the new text has pushed down the heading on Pollination. If the new link is clicked, the previous text and link will be restored.

About the Recipe

This recipe toggles between two sets of text (or HTML) with accompanying links to cause the toggling when they are clicked. It requires the following arguments:

- **$text1**   The main text to display.
- **$link1**   The main link text to display.
- **$text2**   The alternate text.
- **$link2**   The alternate link text.

Variables, Arrays, and Functions

$token	Random integer between 0 and 1,000,000
$out	String containing the JavaScript to be returned

How It Works

This program creates two <div> elements and then displays the contents of $text1 and $link1 in one of them, and $text2 and $link2 in the other. The first <div> is made visible and the second invisible.

Using JavaScript and the `display` property, the links in each `<div>` are then set to make the other `<div>` visible and their own one invisible, having the effect of toggling between the two.

The links are created by setting the `<a href=` targets to `javascript://` and their `onClick` methods to change the display properties of the `<div>` contents. In order to allow you to use this recipe multiple times within a document, the values assigned to the `id` property of each `<div>` also incorporate a random number between 0 and a million, created in `$tok` using the `rand()` function, which is appended to the `id` strings `TT1_` and `TT2_`, as follows:

```
$tok   = rand(0, 1000000);
$out   = "<div id='TT1_$tok' style='display:block;'>" .
         "<a href=\"javascript://\" onClick=\"document." .
         "getElementById('TT1_$tok').style.display=" .
         "'none'; document.getElementById('TT2_$tok')" .
         ".style.display='block';\">$link1</a>$text1</div>\n";

$out  .= "<div id='TT2_$tok' style='display:none;'>" .
         "<a href=\"javascript://\" onClick=\"document." .
         "getElementById('TT1_$tok').style.display=" .
         "'block'; document.getElementById('TT2_$tok')" .
         ".style.display='none';\">$link2</a>$text2</div>\n";
```

All of this JavaScript is assembled into the string $out, which is then returned by the recipe:

```
return  $out;
```

How to Use It

To use this recipe, pass the two sets of texts and links to it, and the string returned will be JavaScript that you can output to your document at the current location. For example, if you are writing about photosynthesis, you might like to create the following strings:

```
$text1 = " Photosynthesis is a process that converts carbon " .
         "dioxide into organic compounds, especially sugars, " .
         "using the energy from sunlight.";
$link1 = "Choose long definition";

$text2 = $text1 .
         " Photosynthesis occurs in plants, algae, and many " .
         "species of Bacteria, but not in Archaea. " .
         "Photosynthetic organisms are called photoautotrophs, " .
         "since it allows them to create their own food.";
$link2 = "Choose short definition";
```

You can then allow for the toggling between each of them by calling up the recipe like this:

```
echo ToggleText($text1, $link1, $text2, $link2);
```

I have deliberately kept this all very simple so that you can replace the link text with any other text you like, or even a button or other image if you prefer, as you are also not restricted to only text in the $text1 and $text2 variables, and can include any HTML you like, including graphics and other tags.

If you would like to have your toggle link appear after (rather than before) the text, you'll have to modify the recipe, moving the variables $text1 and $text2 to before the <a href= sections. In fact, now that you see how this works, you should be able to come up with a range of recipes for your own purposes to handle multiple <div> sections, not just two.

The Recipe

```
function ToggleText($text1, $link1, $text2, $link2)
{
    $tok = rand(0, 1000000);
    $out  = "<div id='TT1_$tok' style='display:block;'>" .
            "<a href=\"javascript://\" onClick=\"document." .
            "getElementById('TT1_$tok').style.display=" .
            "'none'; document.getElementById('TT2_$tok')" .
            ".style.display='block';\">$link1</a>$text1</div>\n";

    $out .= "<div id='TT2_$tok' style='display:none;'>" .
            "<a href=\"javascript://\" onClick=\"document." .
            "getElementById('TT1_$tok').style.display=" .
            "'block'; document.getElementById('TT2_$tok')" .
            ".style.display='none';\">$link2</a>$text2</div>\n";
    return $out;
}
```

StatusMessage()

Sometimes it's useful to be able to change one element in an HTML page when the mouse passes over another one. A typical use for such a facility is offering a status message, or some additional information text. This technique can also be used to good effect by replacing an image or some HTML as the mouse passes over different items. Figure 11-7 shows this recipe used to provide a simple status message feature.

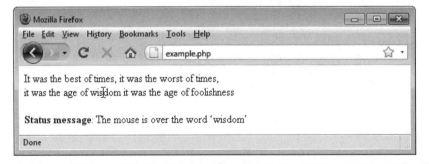

FIGURE 11-7   The opening words of Dickens' *A Tale of Two Cities*, with the mouse over the hotspot word "wisdom"

About the Recipe

This recipe takes some text to display, for which an `onMouseOver` event will be created, the ID of an HTML element into which a status is to be inserted, and the status message itself. Both the `$text` and `$status` can include text and HTML. It requires the following arguments:

- **`$text`** The main text and/or HTML to display.
- **`$id`** The ID of an element such as a `<span>` or `<div>`.
- **`$status`** The message text and/or HTML.

Variables, Arrays, and Functions

- None

How It Works

Although short and sweet, this is a powerful piece of code. What it does is create the JavaScript necessary to provide `onMouseOver` and `onMouseOut` events to *any* HTML element provided in `$text` by getting the contents of the element ID of `$id` (its `innerHTML` property) and then saving it in the JavaScript variable `temp`, before replacing it with the contents of `$status`, as follows:

```
$target = "getElementById('$id').innerHTML";
return    "<span onMouseOver=\"temp=$target; " .
          "$target='$status';\" onMouseOut=\"$target=" .
          "temp;\">$text</span>";
```

When the mouse then leaves the area, the contents of `temp` are replaced back into the `innerHTML` property of `$id`.

How to Use It

To use this recipe, decide on a part of your web page that will contain the status message. In the following example, a `<span>` with the ID of `status` is used. Then call the recipe, passing it some text or HTML to display, and which, when the mouse passes over it, will trigger the status change (in other words, it will be a *hotspot*), the ID of the target element (in this case, `status`), and the status message, like this:

```
echo "The ";
echo StatusMessage('JavaScript', 'status',
  'The mouse is over the word &lsquo;JavaScript&rsquo;');
echo " language is unconnected with the Java language.";
echo "<br /><br /><b>Status message</b>: <span id='status'>" .
  "Nothing to report</span>";
```

This will then display the following:

```
The JavaScript language is unconnected with the Java language.
Status message: Nothing to report
```

But when the mouse passes over the word JavaScript (the hotspot), this changes to the following:

```
The JavaScript language is unconnected with the Java language.
Status message: The mouse is over the word 'JavaScript'
```

However, because you can pass HTML as well as text to it, you can do much more with this recipe than simply displaying a status message. For example, you could create a photo gallery in which each of the image names is passed to the recipe, along with the associated HTML to display the photo, like the following example, which will work if you have the files *camping.jpg*, *fishing.jpg*, *hiking.jpg*, and *swimming.jpg* in the current directory:

```
echo "View some recent photos: ";
echo StatusMessage('Camping ', 'photos',
    '<img src=camping.jpg width=640 height=320 />');
echo StatusMessage('Fishing ', 'photos',
    '<img src=fishing.jpg width=640 height=320 />');
echo StatusMessage('Hiking ',  'photos',
    '<img src=hiking.jpg width=640 height=320 />');
echo StatusMessage('Swimming', 'photos',
    '<img src=swimming.jpg width=640 height=320 />');
echo "<br /><span id='photos'>(Photo will appear here)</span>";
```

You can also use HTML in the $text argument, too, so you could place images or other elements there instead of text. You can even take this effect to the extreme and display different subsections of HTML, including images and other content, when the mouse passes over the various hotspots.

There's only one slight drawback to this recipe, which is that, due to combining the two languages of PHP and JavaScript, it doesn't like any quotation marks, because each language has used up one of the two types. Therefore, you should replace any you need to display with HTML entities such as " for a double quotation mark, or ‘ and ’ for left and right single quotation marks, and “ and ” for left and right double quotation marks, and so forth. This means that where you would normally enclose HTML elements within quotes, such as <img src='image.jpg' />, you should ignore them like this: <img src=image.jpg />. But don't worry. Your HTML will still work without them.

The Recipe

```
function StatusMessage($text, $id, $status)
{
   $target = "getElementById('$id').innerHTML";
   return    "<span onMouseOver=\"temp=$target; " .
             "$target='$status';\" onMouseOut=\"$target=" .
             "temp;\">$text</span>";
}
```

SlideShow( )

If you have a collection of photos that you'd like to display in a smooth fading slide show, then this recipe is just what you need. With it, you simply pass an array of image URLs to it, and the JavaScript code you need to create a slide show is returned by it. Figure 11-8 shows it being used to display a series of photographs from a Flickr image stream.

About the Recipe

This recipe takes an array of image URLs and returns the JavaScript required to display them in a slide show. It requires the following argument:

- **$images**   An array of image URLs.

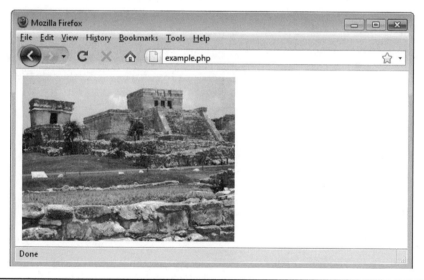

FIGURE 11-8   This recipe can display slide shows of images such as those in a Flickr stream.

Variables, Arrays, and Functions

$count	PHP integer containing the number of URLs in $images
$out	PHP string containing the JavaScript to return
$j	PHP integer counter for iterating through $images
images	JavaScript array containing the image URLs from $images
counter	JavaScript integer for stepping through the images in $images
step	JavaScript integer containing the amount to step through opacity values
fade	JavaScript integer containing the opacity amount
delay	JavaScript integer counter that counts up to a pause
pause	JavaScript integer containing the delay between changing images
startup	JavaScript integer containing the initial startup delay
opacity()	JavaScript function to set the degree of opacity of an image
load()	JavaScript function to load an image from a URL
$()	JavaScript function shorthand for document.getElementById()

How It Works

This recipe starts by counting the number of images passed in the array $images and assigning the value to $count. Then, $out is assigned the string <script> to indicate the start of JavaScript code, followed by a JavaScript statement to create a new array called images, like this:

```
$count = count($images);
$out   = "<script>images = new Array($count);\n";
```

Then, more JavaScript code is appended to $out by means of a for loop, which is used to assign each image URL from the PHP $images array into the src property of each element of the JavaScript images array:

```
for ($j=0 ; $j < $count ; ++$j)
{
   $out .= "images[$j] = new Image();";
   $out .= "images[$j].src = '$images[$j]'\n";
}
```

Afterward, the remaining JavaScript code is added to $out, beginning at this line:

```
$out .= <<<_END
```

Although this is a book on PHP, I'll very briefly explain what the JavaScript code does so you can modify it if you choose. At the start, a few variables are initialized that control the code's behavior. They mainly affect timing of the slide show and therefore you can increase the initial value of fade to have fewer steps during a fade and so speed it up, or you can decrease the value assigned to pause, which represents the number of loops through which the code should cycle before moving onto the next image, like this (remember that this is JavaScript, not PHP):

```
counter = 0
step    = 4
```

```
fade    = 100
delay   = 0
pause   = 250
startup = pause
```

The next three lines of code prepare the slide show by loading the first image in the images array into the HTML elements with the IDs of SS1 and SS2, which must exist in your web page for this recipe to work. Then, an event is set to trigger every 20 milliseconds (thousandths of a second), which will call the function below it, called process():

```
load('SS1', images[0]);

load('SS2', images[0]);

setInterval('process()', 20);
```

The process() function is the core of the program and it controls the fading of images by incrementing the variable fade by the amount in step until it reaches 100, during which time it sets the transparencies of the two images so that one starts to become more transparent, while the other becomes more opaque than the other, and so replaces it.

Then, the delay counter begins to increment in a loop, which first sets the invisible image to the same as the currently visible one and then makes the previously invisible one visible (and the currently visible one invisible). This happens without the user seeing any change, but means that a new image can now be loaded into the previously visible (but now invisible) image, ready to be faded in the next time around. Here is the process() function:

```
function process()
{
    if (startup-- > 0) return;

    if (fade == 100)
    {
        if (delay < pause)
        {
            if (delay == 0)
            {
                fade = 0;
                load('SS1', images[counter]);
                opacity('SS1', 100);
                ++counter;

                if (counter == $count) counter = 0;

                load('SS2', images[counter]);
                opacity('SS2', 0);
            }
            ++delay;
        }
        else delay = 0;
    }
    else
    {
        fade += step;
```

```
        opacity('SS1', 100 - fade);
        opacity('SS2', fade);
    }
}
```

Now we come to the other functions. The function `opacity()` has the commands necessary to change an object's opacity in Internet Explorer and most other browsers:

```
function opacity(id, deg)
{
    var object           = $(id).style;
    object.opacity       = (deg/100);
    object.MozOpacity    = (deg/100);
    object.KhtmlOpacity  = (deg/100);
    object.filter        = "alpha(opacity = " + deg + ")";
}
```

The function `load()` loads an image into an HTML element, and the function `$()` is simply a shorthand that many JavaScript programmers use to save on typing `document .getElementById()` since that is one of the most common statements you are likely to use in dynamic HTML processing, as follows:

```
function load(id, img)
{
    $(id).src = img.src;
}

function $(id)
{
    return document.getElementById(id)
}
```

How to Use It

To use this recipe, you need to prepare some HTML such that two elements with the IDs of SS1 and SS2 exactly overlap each other. The recipe will then place a different image in each of these elements and change the opacities of each to fade between them.

For example, I uploaded a few sample images to my *robinfnixon* Flickr account, which the following code will use:

```
$result = FetchFlickrStream('robinfnixon');
if (!$result[0]) echo "No images returned";
else
{
    $style = "'position:absolute; top:10px; left:10px'";
    echo "<img id='SS1' style=$style>";
    echo "<img id='SS2' style=$style>";
    echo SlideShow($result[1]);
}
```

By calling `FetchFlickrStream()` (Recipe 74), it saves you having to rummage about and assemble a few photos to try the recipe with, but you will need to copy the *Fetch Flickr Stream* recipe into your program, or otherwise include it, to use this example.

If you want to use your own images, then copy some into the same folder as the program and ignore the preceding example. Instead, use code such as the following, replacing photo1.jpg with the name of your first image, and so on:

```
$style = "'position:absolute; top:10px; left:10px'";
echo "<img id='SS1' style=$style>";
echo "<img id='SS2' style=$style>";
$images = array('photo1.jpg', 'photo2.jpg', 'photo3.jpg');
echo SlideShow($images);
```

To make this work, the style= attribute of the <img> tag is used to tell the web browser to place each image exactly 10 pixels in from the left and 10 pixels down from the top of the browser, which makes them overlap each other. The id= attributes then uniquely identify each image so it can be manipulated by the JavaScript code. Just replace the style details with coordinates of your choosing for the part of the web page in which you want the slide show to appear. You can even add borders to the images or any other elements you think would present them effectively.

The important thing about this recipe is that all the images displayed should preferably have the same width and height so that they will all fade into each other neatly. At the very least you can get away with having them all with the same relative dimensions and then force a run-time resize in the image tags, like this:

```
echo "<img id='SS1' style=$style width='320' height='240'>";
echo "<img id='SS2' style=$style width='320' height='240'>";
```

The images will then fade neatly between each other, but any that are enlarged or reduced by these forced widths and heights will not look as good as if they had been properly resized in a graphics program.

The Recipe

```
function SlideShow($images)
{
    $count = count($images);
    echo "<script>images = new Array($count);\n";

    for ($j=0 ; $j < $count ; ++$j)
    {
        echo "images[$j] = new Image();";
        echo "images[$j].src = '$images[$j]'\n";
    }

    return <<<_END
counter = 0
step    = 4
fade    = 100
delay   = 0
pause   = 250
startup = pause

load('SS1', images[0]);
load('SS2', images[0]);
setInterval('process()', 20);
```

```
function process()
{
   if (startup-- > 0) return;

   if (fade == 100)
   {
      if (delay < pause)
      {
         if (delay == 0)
         {
            fade = 0;
            load('SS1', images[counter]);
            opacity('SS1', 100);
            ++counter;

            if (counter == $count) counter = 0;

            load('SS2', images[counter]);
            opacity('SS2', 0);
         }
         ++delay;
      }
      else delay = 0;
   }
   else
   {
      fade += step;
      opacity('SS1', 100 - fade);
      opacity('SS2', fade);
   }
}

function opacity(id, deg)
{
   var object           = $(id).style;
   object.opacity       = (deg/100);
   object.MozOpacity    = (deg/100);
   object.KhtmlOpacity  = (deg/100);
   object.filter        = "alpha(opacity = " + deg + ")";
}

function load(id, img)
{
   $(id).src = img.src;
}

function $(id)
{
   return document.getElementById(id)
}

</script>
_END;
}
```

InputPrompt( )

Sometimes you can make the life of your users easier when filling web forms by placing a prompt for what is required in the form field itself. Obviously, you only want to do that when the field is blank; otherwise, if a field has a value, then that's likely to be what the user wanted to enter.

Using this recipe, whenever you create a form `<input>` element you can specify such a prompt, and it will only appear when the field contains no input. Figure 11-9 shows the recipe being used to display the string *Required Field: Please enter your Username here* in a field where a username is being requested.

The recipe is smart enough to note when a field has either been pre-supplied with a value or if a user has started entering input, in which case it will not replace it with the prompt text. Figure 11-10 shows how it leaves the input well alone in such cases.

About the Recipe

This recipe creates the HTML and JavaScript required to enable the automatic displaying of a prompt within an input field whenever the field is left blank. It requires the following arguments:

- **$params**   Any additional parameters needed by the tag, including name, type, rows, cols, name, size, value, and so on.

- **$prompt**   The prompt to display.

FIGURE 11-9   No text has been entered into the field, so the prompt text is displayed.

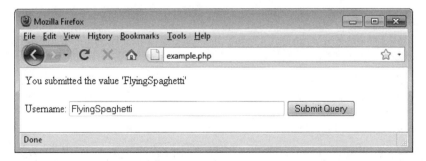

FIGURE 11-10   If a field already has some text, the recipe knows to not interfere.

Variables, Arrays, and Functions

$id	PHP string comprising IP_ and a random number
id	JavaScript string containing an input element ID
IP1()	JavaScript function called when an element is given focus
IP2()	JavaScript function called when an element loses focus
$()	JavaScript function shorthand for document.getElementById()

How It Works

So that this recipe can be used multiple times in a page, it first creates a unique ID in $id, comprising the string IP_ and a random number between 0 and a million. This ID is then used for all the form input elements wherever they are referenced by the HTML and JavaScript that the recipe assembles:

```
$id = 'IP_' . rand(0, 1000000);
```

Next, a string of HTML and JavaScript is returned, starting with an HTML <input> tag. The ID in $id is then assigned to the tag, as well as the parameters in $params. Additionally, two events are added to trigger calls to a pair of functions whenever the user selects or deselects the input field. When the user gives the field focus by clicking in it, the onFocus event handler calls IP1(), and when the field loses focus because the user has removed focus (generally by clicking elsewhere), then the onBlur event handler calls IP2(). In either case, the ID of the input field is passed as the only parameter:

```
$out = <<<_END
<input id='$id' $params
    onFocus="IP1('$id', '$prompt')"
    onBlur="IP2('$id', '$prompt')" />
_END;
```

Next, the JavaScript is created by opening a <script> tag, and the first statement there calls up IP2() to ensure that the prompt text is displayed if the input field has nothing in it:

```
static $IP_NUM;
if ($IP_NUM++ == 0) $out .= <<<_END
<script>
IP2('$id', '$prompt')
```

Next come the two functions just mentioned. The first one, IP1(), checks the value of the element referred to by the variable id, and if it is the same as the contents of the variable prompt, then the prompt is currently being displayed and so it is removed, ready for the user to enter their own data:

```
function IP1(id, prompt)
{
    if ($(id).value == prompt) $(id).value = ""
}
```

The second function, IP2(), does the inverse of that just mentioned. If the input field identified by id is empty, it inserts the value in the variable prompt into the field:

```
function IP2(id, prompt)
{
    if ($(id).value == "") $(id).value = prompt
}
```

Finally, the script is closed with a `</script>` tag, and the `_END;` indicates the end of the multiline string, which is then returned:

```
function $(id)
{
    return document.getElementById(id)
}

</script>
_END;
```

How to Use It

Use this recipe as a replacement for creating an `<input>` tag, like this:

```
$prompt = 'Please enter your Username here';
echo "<form method='post' action='program.php'>";
echo "Username: " . InputPrompt("name='uname' type='text'
        size='50'", $prompt);
echo "<input type=submit></form>";
```

In this example, an HTML form is created, within which the word `Username:` is displayed, followed by a call to `InputPrompt()`. Afterward, a submit button is added and the form is closed.

Two arguments are passed to the recipe. First, there are the parameters an `<input>` tag would generally need—in this case, they are a name, the type, and the size, in the string `name='uname' type='text' size='50'`. If required, an initial value could have been defined here by adding `value='a value'` to the string. This would be useful, for example, where a form has already been submitted but is being returned to the user for amending, and where you do have a submitted value for this field. If the user then removes such a predefined value, this recipe will kick in again and start placing the prompt in the field if it is left empty.

The second argument is the prompt to display, which might be something like *enter your e-mail address,* or *type your name here,* and so on. Just make sure it's not longer than the size of the input window or some of it won't display.

One thing to remember when you use this plug-in is that if a user submits the form with the prompt text still visible, that value that will be passed to your program. But this should be easy to catch because you already know the value of your prompt text, likely having it stored in a string such as `$prompt`, so you can easily check the input received against that value and act accordingly.

Once you start using this recipe, you should find that the number of successfully submitted forms you receive rises, because you will have added extra assistance for your users that is informational but doesn't distract them from completing your form. But remember that this recipe only provides an additional prompt to your users and doesn't ensure they actually follow it—for that, you need to validate the data received when it arrives at the server.

The recipe has also been designed to be smart enough to know when it has been called more than once, and will only return the necessary JavaScript functions a single time. This means you can safely use it multiple times within the same document, or even the same form. It manages this by using the `static` PHP variable `$IP_NUM` as a usage counter; a static variable being one that resumes its value when a function is reentered.

The Recipe

```
function InputPrompt($params, $prompt)
{
    $id = 'IP_' . rand(0, 1000000);

    $out = <<<_END
<input id='$id' $params
    onFocus="IP1('$id', '$prompt')"
    onBlur="IP2('$id', '$prompt')" />
_END;

    static $IP_NUM;
    if ($IP_NUM++ == 0) $out .= <<<_END
<script>
IP2('$id', '$prompt')

function IP1(id, prompt)
{
    if ($(id).value == prompt) $(id).value = ""
}

function IP2(id, prompt)
{
    if ($(id).value == "") $(id).value = prompt
}

function $(id)
{
    return document.getElementById(id)
}

</script>
_END;
    return $out;
}
```

WordsFromRoot()

Whenever you can save your users a little typing, you give them yet another reason to use your web site in preference to others. One neat trick is to provide a clickable list of words the user is likely to be entering. For example, Figure 11-11 shows the word part appl entered as part of the GET variable word, and underneath it the first 20 words found in a local dictionary beginning with those letters can be seen.

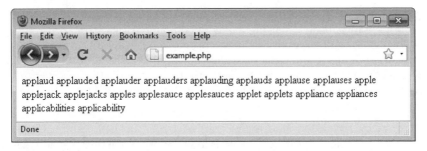

Figure 11-11   The recipe has returned 20 words beginning with the letters *appl*.

Of course, just displaying a list of words isn't too helpful, and the following recipe, *Predict Word*, will use some JavaScript to finish off the feature. However, I have still listed this recipe in its own right because it can often be handy to look up lists of words or phrases based on their first few letters, such as in crossword helper programs, contact directories, and so on, and this routine is flexible enough to deal with both words and phrases.

About the Recipe

This recipe takes the first few letters of a word and returns all the words or phrases in the dictionary that begin with those letters, up to a maximum number. It requires the following arguments:

- **$word**   A word root.
- **$filename**   The path to a dictionary file.
- **$max**   The maximum number of words/phrases to return.

Variables, Arrays, and Functions

$dict	String containing a collection of words or phrases separated by \n characters or \r\n pairs
$matches	Array containing all matching words found in $dict
$c	Integer containing either $max or the number of words found, if less
$out	Array of words to return

How It Works

This recipe loads a file of words or phrases into the string variable $dict, like this:

```
$dict = file_get_contents($filename);
```

The words or phrases must be separated by a character that isn't a letter or number, or the hyphen or underline character. Typically, the \n character or \r\n pair of characters will do the job, and also make the file easy to load into and edit in a text editor.

The `preg_match_all()` function is then called with a search regular expression of `\b$word[\w ]+`, which means "starting at any word boundary, look for occurrences of the string in `$word`, followed by any word characters or spaces,"—in other words, all letters, digits, hyphens, underlines, and spaces are allowed; anything else indicates a non-word/phrase. This will match any words or phrases in the dictionary file that begin with `$word`. All the matches found are then placed into the array `$matches[0]`:

```
preg_match_all('/' . $word . '[\w ]+/', $dict, $matches);
```

The variable `$c` is then set to either `$max` or to the number of matches made, whichever is the lower number, using the `min()` function. Then, the array `$out` is populated with exactly `$c` words from the `$matches[0]` array, and that array is returned, like this:

```
$c   = min(count($matches[0]), $max);
$out = array();
for ($j = 0 ; $j < $c ; ++$j) $out[$j] = $matches[0][$j];
return $out;
```

How to Use It

To use this recipe, pass it the three arguments it requires—a root word, the filename of a dictionary file, and the maximum number of words to return, like this:

```
$list = WordsFromRoot('appl', 'dictionary.txt', 20);
```

The array `$list` will then contain up to `$max` words. Or, for the purposes of the next recipe, *Predict Word,* you would use the following code to read up to two GET arguments from the command line and then return a string, with the words separated by | characters, like this:

```
$out = "";
$max = 5;
if (!isset($_GET['word'])) exit;
if (isset($_GET['max'])) $max = $_GET['max'];
$result = WordsFromRoot($_GET['word'],
   'dictionary.txt', $max);
if ($result != FALSE)
   foreach ($result as $word) $out .= "$word|";
echo substr($out, 0, -1);
```

On a server with the domain `myserver.com`, running the program `program.php`, the preceding example code could be called up using a URL such as this:

```
http://myserver.com/program.php?word=appr&max=20
```

By default, five words will be returned, but if a GET argument is passed in the variable `max`, as in `&max=20`, then `$max` will be changed to the supplied value. When output, each word has a | sign after it as a separator, so when the final word has been sent, a call is made to the `substr()` function to strip the last unwanted | from `$out` before echoing its contents.

If you download *recipes.zip* from the companion web site at *pluginphp.com* and extract it, you will find this program in the folder *11,* saved under the filename *wordsfromroot.php.* In that folder, there's also a dictionary file of over 80,000 words called *dictionary.txt.*

The Recipe

```
function WordsFromRoot($word, $filename, $max)
{
   $dict = file_get_contents($filename);
   preg_match_all('/\b' . $word . '[\w ]+/', $dict, $matches);
   $c    = min(count($matches[0]), $max);
   $out  = array();

   for ($j = 0 ; $j < $c ; ++$j) $out[$j] = $matches[0][$j];
   return $out;
}
```

RECIPE 90 · PredictWord()

Many more recent applications, such as web browsers, let the user select input from a dropdown list of words or phrases similar to what the user is typing. This predictive technology is also often used for texting in mobile phones. Using this recipe, you can add the same facility to your web forms, as shown by Figure 11-12.

About the Recipe

This recipe creates the HTML and JavaScript required to provide a selection of words or phrases beginning with the letters input so far, from which the user can choose to make a selection. It requires the following arguments:

- **$params** Any additional parameters needed by the tag, including name, type, rows, cols, name, size, value, and so on.

- **$view** The maximum number of items to display in the selection box (if there are any more than this, the list becomes scrollable).

- **$max** The maximum number of items to suggest.

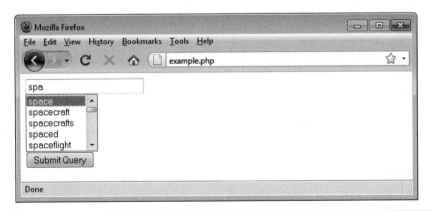

FIGURE 11-12 The recipe displays a selection of possible words the user may be intending to type.

Variables, Arrays, and Functions

`$id`	PHP random number between 0 and a million
`$out`	PHP string to be returned by the recipe
`$j`	PHP integer loop counter for creating the `<option>` list
`CopyWord()`	JavaScript function to copy a word to the input
`PredictWord()`	JavaScript function to display suggested words
`GetAjaxRequest2()`	JavaScript function to prepare an Ajax request
`AjaxRequest()`	JavaScript function to perform an Ajax request
`$()`	JavaScript function shorthand for `document.getElementById()`

How It Works

Some of the JavaScript functions in this recipe are modified versions of those used in Recipe 83, *Get Ajax Request*. As a whole, though, this JavaScript code is too complex to fully explain in a book on PHP, and I don't recommend you try to modify it unless you are very experienced with JavaScript. However, here's a general outline of what it does.

Whenever the user types a letter into the input field, an Ajax request is issued to the program *wordsfromroot.php*, which then returns a list of words that begin with the letters so far entered. Each of these words is then placed in the `<option>` fields of a `<select>` statement in order to display them in a dropdown list.

If the user then clicks any of these offered words, a function is called to copy the word into the input field, and the list of suggested words is then cleared. In the process, a lot of use is made of hiding and revealing elements using their `style.display` properties, and the size of the displayed list is also manipulated according to the number of words to show.

Due to appending a random number in `$id` to all ID names, this function can be successfully reused within a web page, or even the same form, since the code is smart enough to realize it has been called one or more additional times and only creates the form elements required, without re-creating the JavaScript functions. It manages this by implementing the `static` variable counter `$PW_NUM`, which retains its value between calls to the function.

How to Use It

Use this recipe as a replacement for a standard `<input>` tag inside an HTML form. As well as including the *WDC.php* file, you must also include *WDC.js*, like this:

```
echo "<script src='WDC.js'></script>";
```

You can then use code such as the following:

```
echo "<form method='post'>";
echo PredictWord("name='word' type='text'", 5, 20);
echo "<input type='submit'></form>\n";
```

Here, some standard parameters used in an `<input>` tag have been passed, along with two additional arguments: the maximum number of suggested words to show at a time in the dropdown box (the number of lines on view), and the maximum number of words to suggest in total. If the second parameter is larger, then the dropdown list will become scrollable. In the preceding case, the list will often be scrollable, since up to 20 words can be offered, with only 5 displayed at any time.

The supplied *dictionary.txt* file on the companion web site at *pluginphp.com* only includes single words, but you can also replace the contents of the file (or use a different one) with a list of useful phrases (perhaps gleaned from extracting common search terms from your log files). Just ensure you don't add any punctuation or you may get unpredicted results.

If you use a different PHP program to supply the suggested words or phrases, remember to change the reference in the code to *wordsfromroot.php* to that of the new program.

The Recipe

```
function PredictWord($params, $view, $max)
{
   $id  = rand(0, 1000000);
   $out = "<input id='PWI_$id' $params" .
          "onKeyUp='PredictWord($view, $max, $id)'><br />" .
          "<select id='PWS_$id' style='display:none' />\n";

   for ($j = 0 ; $j < $max ; ++$j)
     $out .= "<option id='PWO_$j" . "_$id' " .
             "onClick='CopyWord(this.id, $id)'>";

   $out .= '</select>';
   static $PW_NUM;
   if ($PW_NUM++ == 0) $out .= <<<_END
<script>

function CopyWord(id1, id2)
{
   $('PWI_' + id2).value = $(id1).innerHTML
   $('PWS_' + id2).style.display = 'none';
}

function PredictWord(view, max, id)
{
   if ($('PWI_' + id).value.length > 0)
   {
     GetAjaxRequest2('wordsfromroot.php',
         'word=' + $('PWI_' + id).value +
         '&max=' + max, view, max, id)
     $('PWS_' + id).scrollTop = 0
     $('PWO_0_' + id).selected = true
   }
   else $('PWS_' + id).style.display = 'none'
}
```

```
function GetAjaxRequest2(url, params, view, max, id)
{
   nocache = "&nocache=" + Math.random() * 1000000
   request = new AjaxRequest()

   request.onreadystatechange = function()
   {
      if (this.readyState == 4)
         if (this.status == 200)
            if (this.responseText != null)
            {
               a = this.responseText.split('|')
               c = 0

               for (j in a)
               {
                  $('PWO_' + c + '_' + id).innerHTML = a[j]
                  $('PWO_' + c++ + '_' + id). style.display = 'block'
               }

               n = c > view ? view : c
               while (c < max)
               {
                  $('PWO_' + c++ + '_' + id).
                     style.display = 'none'
               }
               $('PWS_' + id).size = n;
               $('PWS_' + id).style.display = 'block'
            }

   // You can remove these two alerts after debugging
            else alert("Ajax error: No data received")
         else alert( "Ajax error: " + this.statusText)
   }

   request.open("GET", url + "?" + params + nocache, true)
   request.send(null)
}

function $(id)
{
   return document.getElementById(id)
}

</script>
_END;
   return $out;
}
```

CHAPTER 12

Diverse Solutions

A number of recipes didn't quite fit into any of the categories of the other chapters. So here are the final 10 PHP recipes, which, as the chapter title suggests, offer diverse solutions to a variety of programming problems, including geo-location, "bot" detection, data about books, word and spelling functions, language translation, rounded table borders, and Bing Maps.

GetCountryFromIP( )

Knowing which country a web visitor is from can be extremely useful to a webmaster. For example, a personal ads site could use this information to match people up from the same country, as could an auction or classifieds web site. Or perhaps you have servers in different countries and want to refer visitors to the one nearest to them, or maybe you simply want to show different advertising or other content to different territories.

Whatever the reason, this recipe, which comes with its own data file, will tell you where a surfer is located, as can be seen from Figure 12-1, in which Google's IP number has been correctly identified as being located in the U.S.

About the Recipe

This recipe takes an IP address and then returns the name of the country to which the IP has been allocated. Upon failure, it returns FALSE. It requires the following argument:

- **$ip**   An IP address.

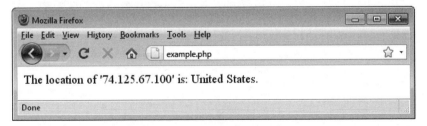

FIGURE 12-1   Provided with an IP number, this recipe correctly identifies its country.

Variables, Arrays, and Functions

$iptemp	Array containing the four parts of $ip
$ipdec	Integer containing the IP address after conversion to decimal
$file	String containing contents of the file *ips.txt*
$lines	Array of all data lines extracted from $file
$line	String containing a single line from $lines
$parts	Array containing all the parts of $line

How it Works

This recipe takes the four parts of an IP address and converts them into a decimal number. This can be done because all IP addresses actually refer to decimal numbers but are separated out into four parts for reasons of convenience and readability. Therefore, the *google.com* IP address of 173.194.41.101 can be turned into its decimal equivalent using the following process:

```
DecimalIP =
   173 * 256 * 256 * 256 +
   194 * 256 * 256 +
    41 * 256 +
   101
```

This results in the values 2902458368, 12713984, 10496, and 101, which add up to 2915182949. And you can prove to yourself that this works by using that number in a URL, like this (go ahead, try it!):

```
http://2915182949
```

Anyhow, what this means is that decimal numbers are a good way to store ranges of IP numbers, which is exactly what has been done in the file *ips.txt*, supplied on the accompanying *webdeveloperscookbook.com* web site. The file has over 80,000 lines in it, each one representing the allocation of a range of IP addresses. Each line has three items separated by commas: the start IP address, the end IP address, and the name of the country to which that range is allocated.

So, what the recipe does is convert $ip to its decimal equivalent in $ipdec by first extracting the four parts into the array $iptemp using the explode() function. Then, it loads *ips.txt* into the string $file, from where all the data lines are extracted into the array $lines, as follows:

```
$iptemp = explode('.', $ip);
$ipdec  = $iptemp[0] * 256 * 256 * 256 +
          $iptemp[1] * 256 * 256 +
          $iptemp[2] * 256 +
          $iptemp[3];
$file   = file_get_contents('ips.txt');
if (!strlen($file)) return FALSE;

$lines = explode("\n", $file);
```

A `foreach` loop is then used to iterate through the array, placing each line of data into the variable `$line`. Then, as long as `$line` contains a string value, it separates out the three items of data in `$line` into the `$parts` array. If `$ipdec` is then found to be equal to or within the two IP addresses in `$parts[1]` and `$parts[2]`, a match has been made and so the associated country name in `$parts[2]` is returned:

```
foreach($lines as $line)
{
   if (strlen($line))
   {
      $parts = explode(',', trim($line));

      if ($ipdec >= $parts[0] && $ipdec <= $parts[1])
         return $parts[2];
   }
}
```

If no match is found in the database, then `FALSE` is returned. This will most likely happen if you look up the country for a non-geographic IP address such as 127.0.0.1, for instance, which always refers to the local computer:

```
return FALSE;
```

How to Use It

To use this recipe, just pass it an IP address, like this:

```
$ip = '74.125.67.100';
$result = GetCountryFromIP($ip);
if (!$result) echo "Could not identify location for '$ip'.";
else echo "The location of '$ip' is: $result.";
```

Or, to look up the country of the current user, you could use this code to call the recipe:

```
$result = GetCountryFromIP($_SERVER['REMOTE_ADDR']);
```

Make sure the *ips.txt* file is in the same folder as your program, or modify the recipe to point to its location.

When using this recipe, remember that your users may be accessing your web site through a proxy server in a different locality, so you cannot guarantee that a user is actually from the country indicated. The best you can identify is the country in which the final IP at the end of any proxy chain resides. Therefore, you may wish to allow users to manually select their own country if the one you offer is incorrect.

The Recipe

```
function GetCountryFromIP($ip)
{
   $iptemp = explode('.', $ip);
   $ipdec  = $iptemp[0] * 256 * 256 * 256 +
             $iptemp[1] * 256 * 256 +
```

```
            $iptemp[2] * 256 +
            $iptemp[3];
    $file  = file_get_contents('ips.txt');
    if (!strlen($file)) return FALSE;

    $lines = explode("\n", $file);

    foreach($lines as $line)
    {
        $data  = trim($line);
        $parts = explode(',', $data);

        if (strlen($line))
        {
            $parts = explode(',', trim($line));

            if ($ipdec >= $parts[0] && $ipdec <= $parts[1])
                return $parts[2];
        }
    }

    return FALSE;
}
```

BypassCaptcha()

RECIPE 92

The reason you might use a Captcha system, such as PHP Recipe 33, is to prevent your web site from being overwhelmed with posts made by automated "bots." The trouble is, many people find it annoying to fill in a Captcha, so this recipe is there to help. Using it, your program can make a quick guess at whether the current user is human or not, and if it thinks they *are* human, bypass the use of a Captcha. Figure 12-2 shows a web page that has been typed in directly and which therefore has no referring page, so it has returned a value of FALSE.

However, the web page shown includes a link which, if it is clicked, will result in creating a referring page that will be sent to the browser. Most "bots" don't send one of these. Also, the page is being viewed in a web browser, so its User Agent string is also being sent to the recipe. In light of receiving these two items of data, the recipe returns a value of TRUE and, as Figure 12-3 suggests, it's probably safe to not use a Captcha.

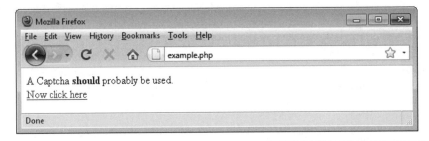

FIGURE 12-2 It appears that the page may have been called up by a "bot," so adding a Captcha is a good idea.

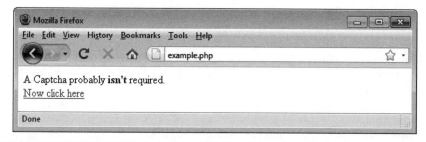

FIGURE 12-3   It looks like a person is using the web site, so there's probably no need for a Captcha.

About the Recipe

This recipe doesn't take any arguments, but if it thinks the current user is human, it returns TRUE; otherwise, it returns FALSE.

Variables, Arrays, and Functions

$_SERVER['HTTP_REFERER']	Array element containing any referring page
$_SERVER['HTTP_USER_AGENT']	Array element containing any User Agent string

How It Works

This is another of those short and sweet, yet highly useful recipes. All it does is check the values of both $_SERVER['HTTP_REFERER'] and $_SERVER['HTTP_USER_AGENT']. If they both have a value, then it returns FALSE; otherwise, it returns TRUE.

How to Use It

To use this recipe, just call it and decide what to do based on the result returned, like this:

```
if (!BypassCaptcha ())
{
   // Captcha code goes here
}
```

Just place this code surrounding your call to your Captcha routine, and again around the code where you verify the Captcha once it has been submitted. The code will then only run if the returned value is FALSE, indicating the possibility that the user may be a "bot."

The Recipe

```
function BypassCaptcha()
{
   if (isset($_SERVER['HTTP_REFERER']) &&
       isset($_SERVER['HTTP_USER_AGENT']))
         return TRUE;
   return FALSE;
}
```

GetBookFromISBN()

If you have a web site that has anything to do with books, you should find this recipe very useful. With it you can take an ISBN-10 number and it will return both the associated book's title and a thumbnail of its cover. Figure 12-4 shows details being returned for the ISBN-10 of 007149216X, another excellent McGraw-Hill publication.

All books also have an alternate ISBN-13 number, which starts with the digits 978. However, the Amazon web site uses ISBN-10 numbers in its web page URLs, and so only ISBN-10 numbers are supported by this recipe, although Amazon web services are also available to handle these and ISBN-13 lookups, but they require more code and that you have an Amazon Web Services account—hence, my settling on using this technique to keep the code short and simple.

About the Recipe

This recipe searches the *amazon.com* web site for details on a supplied ISBN-10 number. If it finds them, it returns a two-element array, the first of which is the book's title, while the second is the URL to a thumbnail image of the book's cover. It requires the following argument:

- **$isbn** An ISBN-10 number.

Variables, Arrays, and Functions

$find	String containing HTML text to find
$url	String containing the URL to load
$page	String containing the contents of $url
$ptr1	Integer pointer to the first occurrence of $find
$ptr2	Integer pointer to subsequent occurrence of " />
$title	String containing the book's title
$image	String containing the URL of a thumbnail image of the book's cover

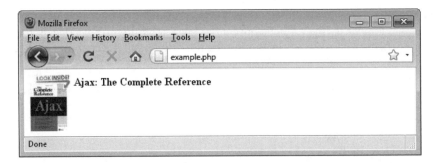

FIGURE 12-4   This recipe quickly looks up a book's title and also returns its cover.

How It Works

This recipe creates a number of string variables before getting into the main code:

```
$find  = '<meta name="description" content="Amazon:';
$url   = "http://www.amazon.com/gp/aw/d.html?a=$isbn";
$img   = 'http://ecx.images-amazon.com/images/I';
$nf    = '<i>Title not found on the Amazon US website</i>';
$none  = 'http://g-ecx.images-amazon.com/images/G/01/x-site/' .
         'icons/no-img-sm._AA75_.gif';
```

These include setting $find to a string for which to search, $url to the relevant URL, and $img to the location of Amazon's book images. In the case of a book not being found, $nf and $none are also pre-set.

The next line loads the contents of $url into the variable $page, using the CurlGetContents() function because Amazon doesn't return pages without also being passed a User Agent string (which this function creates for you automatically if you pass an empty string as the second argument). The URL comprises the main Amazon web address plus the details required to access details on the book referred to by $isbn:

```
$page = CurlGetContents($url, "");
```

If no matching book is found, then error values are returned:

```
if (!strlen($page)) return array($nf, $none);
```

Otherwise, the string in $find is searched for using the strpos() function. If it is located, then a book associated with $isbn has been found and the HTML following will be its title. Therefore, the end of the title is searched for, which is the string " />. Once both strings have been found, their start locations will be in $ptr1 and $ptr2, so using these values, the title is extracted with a call to substr(), like this:

```
$ptr1 = strpos($page, $find);
if (!$ptr1) return array($nf, $none);

$ptr1 += strlen($find);
$ptr2  = strpos($page, '" />', $ptr1);
$title = substr($page, $ptr1, $ptr2 - $ptr1);
$find  = $img;
```

The image thumbnail URL is extracted in a similar manner:

```
$ptr1  = strpos($page, $find) + strlen($find);
$ptr2  = strpos($page, '"', $ptr1);
$image = substr($page, $ptr1, $ptr2 - $ptr1);
```

The two strings are then returned in a two-element array:

```
return array($title, $img . $image);
```

How to Use It

To use this recipe, pass it a 10-digit ISBN number, like this:

```
$isbn = '007149216X';
$result = GetBookFromISBN($isbn);
if (!$result) echo "Could not find title for ISBN '$isbn'.";
else echo "<img src='$result[1]' align='left'><b>$result[0]";
```

The array element $result[0] will be FALSE if no book was found; otherwise, it contains the book's title, and $result[1] contains the URL of a thumbnail image of the book's cover.

If you have an Amazon Associates account, this is the perfect place to add a link to it in order to be paid a commission if the book is subsequently purchased.

The Recipe

```
function GetBookFromISBN($isbn)
{
    $find = '<meta name="description" content="Amazon:';
    $url  = "http://www.amazon.com/gp/aw/d.html?a=$isbn";
    $img  = 'http://ecx.images-amazon.com/images/I';
    $nf   = '<i>Title not found on the Amazon US website</i>';
    $none = 'http://g-ecx.images-amazon.com/images/G/01/x-site/' .
            'icons/no-img-sm._AA75_.gif';

    $page = CurlGetContents($url, "");
    if (!strlen($page)) return array($nf, $none);

    $ptr1 = strpos($page, $find);
    if (!$ptr1) return array($nf, $none);

    $ptr1 += strlen($find);
    $ptr2 = strpos($page, '" />', $ptr1);
    $title = substr($page, $ptr1, $ptr2 - $ptr1);
    $find = $img;
    $ptr1 = strpos($page, $find) + strlen($find);
    $ptr2 = strpos($page, '"', $ptr1);
    $image = substr($page, $ptr1, $ptr2 - $ptr1);


    return array($title, $img . $image);}
}
```

RECIPE 94 GetAmazonSalesRank()

Sometimes it can be interesting to know how well a book is doing at Amazon. With this utility, you can find that information from all the major worldwide Amazon web sites (except for China). Figure 12-5 shows the recipe being used to look up the sales rank information for the book used in the previous recipe.

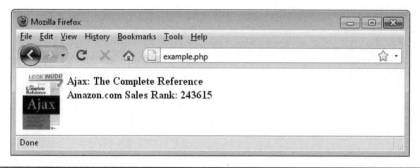

FIGURE 12-5   Using this recipe, sales rank information has also been returned from Amazon.

About the Recipe

This recipe takes an ISBN number and the domain of an Amazon web site and then returns the sales rank for that title on that site. Upon success, it returns a number representing the book's popularity, with 1 being the most popular. Upon failure (for example, if the book is not found, or if it doesn't have a rank) it returns FALSE. It requires the following arguments:

- **$isbn**   An ISBN-10 number.

- **$site**   An Amazon web domain, out of: amazon.com, amazon.ca, amazon.co.uk, amazon.fr, amazon.it, amazon.es, amazon.de, and amazon.co.jp.

Variables, Arrays, and Functions

$url	String containing the URL of the Amazon mobile web site (for speed)
$find	String containing the text to find immediately preceding a Sales Rank
$end	String containing the text to find immediately following a Sales Rank
$page	String containing the contents of $url
$ptr1	Integer pointer to start of $find
$ptr2	Integer pointer to start of $end
$temp	String containing Sales Rank before removing non-digit characters

How It Works

This recipe extracts sales rank information from five of the six Amazon mobile web sites. The final site used, however—*amazon.co.jp*—is the main web URL, since its mobile site appears not to provide sales rank information. This is achieved by loading the default URL, comprising the value in $site into $url, and the HTML immediately following the sales rank details into $end:

```
$url = "http://www.$site/gp/aw/d.html?pd=1" .
    "&l=Product%20Details&a=$isbn";
$end = '<br />';
```

Then, a `switch` statement is used for the different values of `$site`. In the case of the three English-speaking countries (the sites *amazon.com, amazon.ca,* and *amazon.co.uk*) the variable `$find` is set to the string `Sales Rank:`, which is what will be searched for in the web page.

The European web sites (*amazon.fr, amazon.it, amazon.es,* and *amazon.de*) replace the string with French, Italian, Spanish, and German translations of the phrase Sales Rank, while the Japanese web site at *amazon.co.jp* has a different pre– and post–sales rank data string to search for. It also uses a different value for `$url` because the mobile version of their site appears to not provide sales rank information:

```
switch(strtolower($site))
{
    case 'amazon.com':
    case 'amazon.ca':
    case 'amazon.co.uk':
        $find = 'Sales Rank: ';
        break;
    case 'amazon.fr':
        $find = 'ventes Amazon.fr: ';
        break;
    case 'amazon.de':
        $find = 'Verkaufsrang: ';
        break;
    case 'amazon.es':
        $find = 'ventas de Amazon.es: ';
        break;
    case 'amazon.it':
        $find = "vendite Amazon.it: ";
        break;
    case 'amazon.co.jp':
        $find = '<li id="SalesRank">';
        $url  = "http://$site/gp/product/$isbn";
        $end  = '(<a';
        break;
}
```

With these details prepared, the contents of `$url` are loaded into `$page`. If this is unsuccessful, then FALSE is returned. Otherwise, the `strpos()` function is used to find the first occurrence of `$find`, the location of which is placed in `$ptr1`. Again, if it is not found, FALSE is returned, like this:

```
$page = CurlGetContents($url, "");
if (!strlen($page)) return FALSE;

$ptr1 = strpos($page, $find);
if (!$ptr1) return FALSE;
```

Next, `$ptr2` is given the location of the subsequent occurrence of `$end`, and the string in between the two is extracted into `$temp`, from where any non-digit characters are removed before returning its value:

```
$ptr2 = strpos($page, $end, $ptr1);
$temp = substr($page, $ptr1, $ptr2 - $ptr1);
return trim(preg_replace('/[^\d]/', '', $temp));
```

How to Use It

To obtain a book's sales rank at a particular Amazon site, just pass the ISBN and domain to
the recipe like this (which should achieve a similar result to that shown in Figure 12-5):

```
echo GetAmazonSalesRank('007149216X', 'amazon.com');
```

Or you could combine this recipe with the previous one, as follows:

```
$isbn = '007149216X';
$result = GetBookFromISBN($isbn);
if (!$result) echo "Could not find title for ISBN '$isbn'.";
else
{
    echo "<img src='$result[1]' align='left'><b>$result[0]<br>" .
        "Amazon.com Sales Rank: ";
    echo GetAmazonSalesRank($isbn, 'amazon.com');
}
```

The Recipe

```
function GetAmazonSalesRank($isbn, $site)
{
    $url = "http://www.$site/gp/aw/d.html?pd=1" .
        "&l=Product%20Details&a=$isbn";
    $end = '<br />';

    switch(strtolower($site))
    {
        case 'amazon.com':
        case 'amazon.ca':
        case 'amazon.co.uk':
            $find = 'Sales Rank: ';
            break;
        case 'amazon.fr':
            $find = 'ventes Amazon.fr: ';
            break;
        case 'amazon.de':
            $find = 'Verkaufsrang: ';
            break;
        case 'amazon.es':
            $find = 'ventas de Amazon.es: ';
            break;
        case 'amazon.it':
            $find = "vendite Amazon.it: ";
            break;
        case 'amazon.co.jp':
            $find = '<li id="SalesRank">';
            $url  = "http://$site/gp/product/$isbn";
            $end  = '(<a';
            break;
    }
```

```
$page = CurlGetContents($url, "");
if (!strlen($page)) return FALSE;

$ptr1 = strpos($page, $find);
if (!$ptr1) return FALSE;

$ptr2 = strpos($page, $end, $ptr1);
$temp = substr($page, $ptr1, $ptr2 - $ptr1);
return trim(preg_replace('/[^\d]/', '', $temp));
}
```

PatternMatchWord()

Having a dictionary of 80,000 words at hand, it's a shame not to do more with it, so this and the next recipe provide more word-related features.

This recipe will be of use in crossword- or Scrabble game–like scenarios, where you know the number of letters in a word and even have a few letters in place. Given such details, as Figure 12-6 shows, this recipe will return all possible words in the dictionary that could fit.

About the Recipe

This recipe takes a word pattern and then returns a two-element array in which the first is the number of matching words found and the second is an array of the words themselves. On failure, it returns a single-element array with the value FALSE. It requires the following arguments:

- **$word**   A word pattern comprising letters and periods (for unknowns).
- **$dictionary**   The path to a file of words.

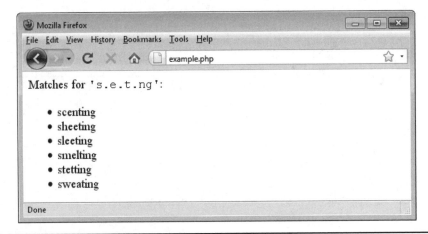

FIGURE 12-6   The recipe has found six matches for the pattern 's.e.t.ng'.

Variables, Arrays, and Functions

`$dict`	String containing the contents of `$dictionary`
`$matches[0]`	Array containing all the matching words

How It Works

This recipe takes advantage of PHP's built-in regular expression handling by loading the dictionary file in `$dictionary` into `$dict` and then matching its contents against the pattern supplied in $word.

If $dict has no value, the dictionary wasn't found and so a single-element array with the value FALSE is returned:

```
$dict = @file_get_contents($dictionary);
if (!strlen($dict)) return array(FALSE);
```

Otherwise, the dictionary contents are loaded into $dict. The dictionary file should contain words separated by non-word characters or sequences of characters. If you use \n or \r\n pairs as separators (as in the supplied *dictionary.txt* file on the companion web site), then the file can be loaded into and edited by most program and text editors.

Before performing the matching, the contents of $word are processed with the preg_replace() function to remove any non-alphabetic or period characters and to convert the entire string to lowercase using the strtolower() function:

```
$word = preg_replace('/[^a-z\.]/', '', strtolower($word));
```

A call to the preg_match_all() function is then made, passing the value in $match, surrounded by \b metacharacters to indicate word boundaries. Any and all matches made are then placed into the array in $matches[0]. A two-element array is then returned containing the number of matches found and the matches themselves:

```
preg_match_all('/\b' . $word . '\b/', $dict, $matches);
return array(count($matches[0]), $matches[0]);
```

How to Use It

To use this recipe, pass it a pattern to match and the path to a file of words, like this:

```
$result = PatternMatchWord('s.e.t.ng', 'dictionary.txt');

if ($result[0] != FALSE)
{
    echo "Matches for <font face='Courier New'>" .
        "'$word'</font>:<br><ul>";
    foreach ($result[1] as $match) echo "<li>$match</li>";
}
```

In this example, as long as $result[0] isn't FALSE, then some matches were made, so a foreach loop iterates through them all in $result[1], displaying them as list elements within an unsorted list, but you could use these words in dropdown lists, with checkboxes, or in a variety of other ways.

You will find a copy of the *dictionary.txt* file in the download available at *webdeveloperscookbook.com*.

The Recipe

```
function PatternMatchWord($word, $dictionary)
{
    $dict = @file_get_contents($dictionary);
    if (!strlen($dict)) return array(FALSE);

    $word = preg_replace('/[^a-z\.]/', '', strtolower($word));
    preg_match_all('/\b' . $word . '\b/', $dict, $matches);
    return array(count($matches[0]), $matches[0]);
}
```

 SuggestSpelling()

In Chapter 3, Recipe 8, I introduced a simple spelling checker. Well, here's a companion recipe you could use with it to actually offer suggested replacements for misspelled words. As Figure 12-7 shows, using the same dictionary of words, this recipe attempts to find the closest matches to a word it is passed, and returns them in the order of likelihood.

About the Recipe

This recipe takes a word that has been unrecognized and finds the closest matches to it from a dictionary of words. Upon success, it returns a two-element array, the first of which contains the number of words returned, while the second contains an array of words. On failure, it returns a single-element array with the value FALSE. It requires the following arguments:

- **$word** A word.
- **$dictionary** The path to a file of words.

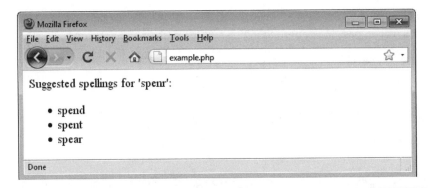

FIGURE 12-7 The recipe has chosen three possible spelling corrections for the word *spenr*.

Variables, Arrays, and Functions

`$count`	Static integer containing number of calls to the recipe
`$words`	Static array containing words extracted from `$dict`
`$dict`	String containing the contents of `$dictionary`
`$possibles`	Array containing possible similar words
`$known`	Array containing all words both on `$possibles` and `$words`
`$suggested`	Array containing all the suggested words
`$wordlen`	Integer containing the length of `$word`
`$chars`	Array containing all the letters of the alphabet
`$temp`	String containing key extracted from element of `$known`
`$val`	String containing value extracted from element of `$known`

How It Works

The first thing this recipe does is check whether `$word` has a value, and if not, it returns a single-element array with the value FALSE:

```
if (!strlen($word)) return array(FALSE);
```

After that, two variables are declared as *static*. The reason is that this recipe is built in such a way that it can be called more than once, something that's likely if a section of text has more than one unknown word. Therefore, for optimum speed it uses static variables, which retain their value between calls to the function (but outside the function, they have no value or a different value). This avoids re-creating large arrays each time the function is called:

```
static $count, $words;
```

The two static variables used are `$count`, which counts the number of times the function has been called, and `$words`, which contains an array of words. If `$count` has a value of zero, then this is the first time the function has been called and so the contents of `$dictionary` are loaded into `$dict`. As long as the load was successful, the words are split out into the array `$words` using the `explode()` function, like this:

```
if ($count++ == 0)
{
    $dict = @file_get_contents($dictionary);
    if (!strlen($dict)) return array(FALSE);
    $words = explode("\r\n", $dict);
}
```

On future calls to the function, `$count` will have a value greater than zero. Therefore, populating the `$words` array is unnecessary since `$words` is a static variable that will remember its contents from the last call. Note that this static value is accessible each time the function is recalled, but only persists during the response to a single web request. Subsequent web requests always start with PHP variables not existing until they are defined.

Next, three arrays are prepared. These are $possibles, which will contain a large number of words the program will make up that are similar to $word. Then there is $known, which will contain all the words in $possibles that also exist in the dictionary of words in $words (so they are proper words, even though they were created by an algorithm). Lastly, there's $suggested, which will be populated with all the words the recipe chooses to return as suggested replacements for $word:

```
$possibles = array();
$known     = array();
$suggested = array();
```

The variable $wordlen is then set to the length of $word, and the array $chars is created out of the 26 letters of the alphabet by using str_split() to split up the provided string:

```
$wordlen = strlen($word);
$chars   = str_split('abcdefghijklmnopqrstuvwxyz');
```

Next, a whole collection of made-up words similar to $word have to be placed in $possibles. Four types of new words are created:

- The set of words similar to $word, but with each letter missing in turn
- The set of words similar to $word, but with each letter in turn substituted with another
- The set of words similar to $word, but with consecutive letter pairs swapped
- The set of words similar to $word, but with new letters inserted between each existing pair of letters

This is all achieved within separate for and foreach loops, as follows:

```
for($j = 0 ; $j < $wordlen ; ++$j)
{
    $possibles[] = substr($word, 0, $j) .
                   substr($word, $j + 1);

    foreach($chars as $letter)
       $possibles[] = substr($word, 0, $j) .
                  $letter .
                  substr($word, $j + 1);
}

for($j = 0; $j < $wordlen - 1 ; ++$j)
    $possibles[] = substr($word, 0, $j) .
                   $word[$j + 1] .
                   $word[$j] .
                   substr($word, $j +2 );

for($j = 0; $j < $wordlen + 1 ; ++$j)
    foreach($chars as $letter)
        $possibles[] = substr($word, 0, $j).
                   $letter.
                   substr($word, $j);
```

For a word length of five characters, 295 variations will be created; for six, it's 349, and so on. Most of these will be meaningless gibberish, but because (we assume) the user meant to type something meaningful but probably just made a typo, some of them stand a chance of being real words, and could be what the user intended to type.

To extract the good words, the `array_intersect()` function is called to return all words that exist in both the arrays `$possibles` and `$words`, the result of which is placed in `$known`, which becomes our set of known real words that could be what the user intended:

```
$known = array_intersect($possibles, $words);
```

Next, all the duplicate occurrences of words in `$known` are counted up using the `array_count_values()` function, which returns an array of keys and values in which the key is the word and the value is the number of times it appears in the array. This array is then sorted into reverse order using the `arsort()` function so that those words that appeared the most frequently come first. That means the most likely candidates will always be at the start of the array, with less and less likely ones further down the array:

```
$known = array_count_values($known);
arsort($known, SORT_NUMERIC);
```

A `foreach` statement then steps through each of the elements to extract just the key into the variable `$temp` (discarding the value in `$val`), which is then used to populate the next available element of the array `$suggested`, like this:

```
foreach ($known as $temp => $val)
   $suggested[] = $temp;
```

When the loop completes, `$suggested` contains the list of words the recipe thinks the user may have meant, in order of likelihood. So a two-element array is returned, the first of which is the number of words returned, while the second is an array containing the words:

```
return array(count($suggested), $suggested);
```

How to Use It

When you want to offer alternate spelling suggestions to a user, just call this recipe with the misspelled word and the path to a file of words, like this:

```
$word = 'spenr';
echo "Suggested spellings for '$word':<br /><ul>";
$results = SuggestSpelling($word, 'dictionary.txt');
if (!$results[0]) echo "No suggested spellings.";
else foreach ($results[1] as $spelling) echo "<li>$spelling</li>";
```

You can call the recipe multiple times and could therefore use dropdown lists inserted within the text at the occurrence of each unrecognized word, or one of many other methods to offer suggestions for all misspelled words found in a section of text.

Of course, to be truly interactive, you ought to rewrite the function in JavaScript and offer interactive spelling management directly within a web page—perhaps an interesting project for you to consider undertaking based on this recipe.

The Recipe

```
function SuggestSpelling($word, $dictionary)
{
   if (!strlen($word)) return array(FALSE);

   static $count, $words;

   if ($count++ == 0)
   {
      $dict = @file_get_contents($dictionary);
      if (!strlen($dict)) return array(FALSE);
      $words = explode("\r\n", $dict);
   }

   $possibles = array();
   $known     = array();
   $suggested = array();
   $wordlen   = strlen($word);
   $chars     = str_split('abcdefghijklmnopqrstuvwxyz');

   for($j = 0 ; $j < $wordlen ; ++$j)
   {
      $possibles[] =    substr($word, 0, $j) .
                        substr($word, $j + 1);

      foreach($chars as $letter)
         $possibles[] = substr($word, 0, $j) .
                        $letter .
                        substr($word, $j + 1);
   }

   for($j = 0; $j < $wordlen - 1 ; ++$j)
      $possibles[] =    substr($word, 0, $j) .
                        $word[$j + 1] .
                        $word[$j] .
                        substr($word, $j +2 );

   for($j = 0; $j < $wordlen + 1 ; ++$j)
      foreach($chars as $letter)
         $possibles[] = substr($word, 0, $j).
                        $letter.
                        substr($word, $j);

   $known = array_intersect($possibles, $words);
   $known = array_count_values($known);
   arsort($known, SORT_NUMERIC);

   foreach ($known as $temp => $val)
      $suggested[] = $temp;

   return array(count($suggested), $suggested);
}
```

AnagramFinder()

This handy recipe is useful when you are working with word puzzles, for example, because it will find all full-word anagrams of any word you give it from a dictionary of words you supply (see Figure 12-8).

About the Recipe

This recipe takes a string of text and then looks up all possible anagrams of it in a dictionary of words. It returns only single-word anagrams, rather than multiword phrases.

- **$word** Word to be anagramized.
- **$dict** Location of a file containing a list of words.

Variables, Arrays, and Functions

$dict	String variable containing all the words loaded in from the dictionary file
$check	A string created using the source word with which a regular expression is crafted for searching $dict
$w	The length of the supplied word
$j and $k	Loop counters
$out	The array of found anagrams
$maybe	On finding a candidate anagram, it is stored in this variable
$found	Set to TRUE if an anagram is found; otherwise, FALSE
$matches	Array containing all the matches found in the dictionary before checking whether they are anagrams

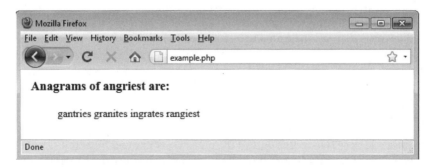

FIGURE 12-8   Looking up anagrams for the word "angriest" using this recipe.

How It Works

This recipe loads in a dictionary of words separated by \r\n (return and linefeed) pairs of characters into the string variable $dict. Then, the variable $check (which will be used later) is initialized to the empty string, the variable $w is set to the length of the supplied word, and the array $out is prepared for later use:

```
$dict   = file_get_contents($filename);
$check  = '';
$w      = strlen($word);
$out    = array();
```

Next, a string is crafted for using in a regular expression that will quickly search the dictionary of words. For example, if the input word is cat, then this word will be turned into the string [cat][cat][cat]. When used as part of a regular expression, this tells the program to find any word that begins with any of the letters c, a, or t, has any of c, a, or t in the middle, and ends with c, a, or t. This will result in the anagram act being found. However, it means that the word tat will also be returned by this expression (which is not an anagram of cat). This is all right since the expression gets close enough to weed out 99 percent of the wrong words from the dictionary. Afterward, a simple check on the remaining ones will weed out the few non-anagrams.

The code to create the string of repeated start words is as follows:

```
for ($j = 0 ; $j < $w ; ++$j)
   $check .= "[$word]";
```

Now this string expression (in $check) is inserted into a larger regular expression that searches only for complete words by ensuring that there is a line feed or carriage return both before and after each word, like this:

```
preg_match_all('/[\n\r](' . $check . ')[\n\r]/', $dict, $matches);
```

This code returns all words that match the expression in the $matches array. So the code next needs to go through all the matches and weed out those that are not anagrams, allowing the words that are anagrams to be inserted into the $out array for returning:

```
for ($j = 0 ; $j < count($matches[0]); ++$j)
{
   $maybe = trim($matches[0][$j]);
   $t     = " $maybe";
   $found = TRUE;
```

What this code does is loop through all the matches as counted by count($matches[0]), then any newlines or returns are removed from each match using the trim() function, after which the word is stored in $maybe. Then, a copy of $maybe is placed into $t, which is a temporary variable that will be used inside a second loop, and which has a space character added at the front so that when searching it for characters, it won't return 0 as an offset, which could be misinterpreted as not finding a match. At the same time, the flag $found is set to TRUE. If the word is indeed an anagram, it will remain set to that value; otherwise, it will be set to FALSE.

Next, a for() loop steps through each letter of the source word and checks that there is a matching same letter in the variable $t for each one in $word, like this:

```
for ($k = 0 ; $k < $w ; ++$k)
{
    $p = strpos($t, $word[$k]);

    if ($p) $t[$p] = ' ';
    else    $found = FALSE;
}
```

Here $p is set to the offset of any match. Then, as long as $p is not zero, a match was found and the letter in the word held in $t has the matched letter replaced with a space character, preventing it from being matched again. But if the test returns a value of 0, there was no match, and so $found is set to FALSE to indicate this.

Finally, in this loop, if $found is still TRUE, then $maybe contains an anagram. As long as the anagram is not the same word as the source word in $word, it is added to the $out array using the array_push() function:

```
    if ($found && $word != $maybe)
        array_push($out, $maybe);
```

The contents of $out are then returned:

```
return $out;
```

How to Use It

To search for anagrams of a word in a dictionary of words, use code such as this:

```
$result = AnagramFinder('angriest', 'dictionary.txt');

for ($j = 0 ; $j < count($result) ; ++$j)
    echo "$result[$j] ";
```

The first line calls the recipe, passing it (in this case) the word angriest, and also the name dictionary.txt as the file in which to do the lookup.

Upon return, the recipe returns an array. If the array has a length of 0, no anagrams were found. Otherwise, the simple for() loop steps through and displays all the anagrams that were found.

The Recipe

```
function AnagramFinder($word, $filename)
{
    $dict  = file_get_contents($filename);
    $check = '';
    $w     = strlen($word);
    $out   = array();
```

```
for ($j = 0 ; $j < $w ; ++$j)
    $check .= "[$word]";

preg_match_all('/[\n\r](' . $check . ')[\n\r]/', $dict, $matches);

for ($j = 0 ; $j < count($matches[0]); ++$j)
{
    $maybe = trim($matches[0][$j]);
    $t     = " $maybe";
    $found = TRUE;

    for ($k = 0 ; $k < $w ; ++$k)
    {
        $p = strpos($t, $word[$k]);

        if ($p) $t[$p] = ' ';
        else    $found = FALSE;
    }

    if ($found && $word != $maybe)
        array_push($out, $maybe);
}

return $out;
}
```

98   CornerGif()

Displaying content in a table with rounded borders can make it look more professional, but usually you need to create a different set of images to achieve this for each color palette used. This recipe solves the problem by generating the GIF images needed on the fly, as you can see in Figure 12-9, which shows the top-left corner of a table (enlarged) as returned by the recipe.

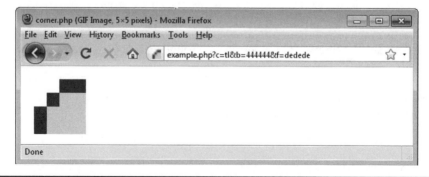

FIGURE 12-9   A top-left corner GIF for a table (shown enlarged) as created by this recipe.

About the Recipe

This recipe creates corner and edge GIFs for building a table with rounded borders. Upon success, it returns a GD image containing the constructed GIF. On failure, it returns an unknown value or an unknown image. It requires the following arguments:

- **$corner**   An identifier for the image to create, out of: tl, t, tr, l, r, bl, b, and br, representing top-left, top, top-right, left, right, bottom-left, bottom, and bottom-right.
- **$border**   The color of the border as a six-digit hexadecimal number.
- **$bground**   The color of the background as a six-digit hexadecimal number.

Variables, Arrays, and Functions

$data	Array containing a pixel map for the image
$image	GD image to be returned
$bcol	GD background color
$fcol	GD foreground color
$tcol	GD transparent color
GD_FN1()	PHP function to convert a six-digit hex number to a GD color

How It Works

When a corner GIF is required, this recipe uses the pre-populated array in $data to create the top left-hand GIF, and then rotates it if necessary. It does this by creating a new GD image in $image using the imagecreatetruecolor() function and then creating three colors to use—$bcol, $fcol, and $tcol for the background, foreground, and transparent colors, as passed in the arguments $border and $bground. The image is then filled with the transparent color, and is ready for the main colors, like this:

```
$data  = array(array(0, 0, 0, 0, 0),
               array(0, 0, 0, 1, 1),
               array(0, 0, 1, 2, 2),
               array(0, 1, 2, 2, 2),
               array(0, 1, 2, 2, 2));

$image = imagecreatetruecolor(5, 5);
$bcol  = GD_FN1($image, $border);
$fcol  = GD_FN1($image, $bground);
$tcol  = GD_FN1($image, 'ffffff');

imagecolortransparent($image, $tcol);
imagefill($image, 0 , 0, $tcol);
```

In the following code, the if (strlen($corner) == 2) statement simply checks whether a corner piece has been requested by seeing whether $corner has one or two letters. If it's two, then a corner is wanted because $corner must contain one of the strings tl, tr, bl, or br, and so each of the pixels in the image that match those in the $data array is populated with either $bcol or $fcol, depending on whether the array has a value of 1 or 2, with a 0 indicating that a pixel should be left alone since it will be transparent:

```
if (strlen($corner) == 2)
{
   for ($j = 0 ; $j < 5 ; ++$j)
   {
      for ($k = 0 ; $k < 5 ; ++ $k)
      {
         switch($data[$j][$k])
         {
            case 1: imagesetpixel($image, $j, $k, $bcol); break;
            case 2: imagesetpixel($image, $j, $k, $fcol); break;
         }
      }
   }
}
else
{
   imagefilledrectangle($image, 0, 0, 4, 0, $bcol);
   imagefilledrectangle($image, 0, 1, 4, 4, $fcol);
}
```

If $corner has only one letter, it must contain one of the strings t, l, r, or b, so an edge piece was requested and therefore two rectangles are created in the background and foreground colors. Actually, the first rectangle is a line and represents the border, while the other fills in the rest of the area with the background color.

Next, a switch statement looks at the type of image requested in $corner, and if necessary, rotates the image before it is returned, with returned images being typically no more than about 50 bytes:

```
switch($corner)
{
   case 'tr': case 'r':
      $image = imagerotate($image, 270, $tcol); break;
   case 'br': case 'b':
      $image = imagerotate($image, 180, $tcol); break;
   case 'bl': case 'l':
      $image = imagerotate($image,  90, $tcol); break;
}

return $image;
```

How to Use It

This recipe is best used to create a self-contained program to return a GIF image, which is what the following code does:

```
$corner  = $_GET['c'];
$border  = $_GET['b'];
$bground = $_GET['f'];
$result  = CornerGif($corner, $border, $bground);
```

```
if ($result)
{
    header('Content-type: image/gif');
    imagegif($result);
}
```

This code accepts three GET arguments: c, b, and f for *corner, border,* and *fill.* It then passes these to the recipe, and if an image is successfully returned, the correct header to preface sending a GIF image is output, followed by sending the image in GIF format by calling the imagegif() function.

The preceding example code will be used by the following recipe, RoundedTable(), so type it into a new program file, and then also add the following recipe code to it, and save the result as *corner.php,* ensuring you also include the opening <?php and closing ?> tags. Alternatively, you can download *examples.zip* from the companion web site and will find *corner.php* in the *PHP* folder.

A typical call to the program will then look like the following, which will result in the image displayed in Figure 12-9 (if you enlarge it):

```
corner.php?c=tl&b=444444&f=dedede
```

Here, a top-left corner has been requested by the parameter c=tl, the background color has been set to 444444 by the parameter b=444444, and the foreground color has been set to dedede by the parameter f=dedede.

The Recipe

```
function CornerGif($corner, $border, $bground)
{
    $data   = array(array(0, 0, 0, 0, 0),
                    array(0, 0, 0, 1, 1),
                    array(0, 0, 1, 2, 2),
                    array(0, 1, 2, 2, 2),
                    array(0, 1, 2, 2, 2));

    $image = imagecreatetruecolor(5, 5);
    $bcol  = GD_FN1($image, $border);
    $fcol  = GD_FN1($image, $bground);
    $tcol  = GD_FN1($image, 'ffffff');

    imagecolortransparent($image, $tcol);
    imagefill($image, 0 , 0, $tcol);


    if (strlen($corner) == 2)
    {
        for ($j = 0 ; $j < 5 ; ++$j)
        {
            for ($k = 0 ; $k < 5 ; ++ $k)
            {
                switch($data[$j][$k])
                {
```

```
                    case 1: imagesetpixel($image, $j, $k, $bcol); break;
                    case 2: imagesetpixel($image, $j, $k, $fcol); break;
                }
            }
        }
    }
    else
    {
        imagefilledrectangle($image, 0, 0, 4, 0, $bcol);
        imagefilledrectangle($image, 0, 1, 4, 4, $fcol);
    }

    switch($corner)
    {
        case 'tr': case 'r':
            $image = imagerotate($image, 270, $tcol); break;
        case 'br': case 'b':
            $image = imagerotate($image, 180, $tcol); break;
        case 'bl': case 'l':
            $image = imagerotate($image,  90, $tcol); break;
    }

    return $image;
}

function GD_FN1($image, $color)
{
    return imagecolorallocate($image,
        hexdec(substr($color, 0, 2)),
        hexdec(substr($color, 2, 2)),
        hexdec(substr($color, 4, 2)));
}
```

RoundedTable()

With this recipe, not only do you get the GIFs needed to create rounded table corners in any colors, you also get the HTML code. Figure 12-10 shows it being used to display some monologue from a Shakespeare play to good effect.

About the Recipe

This recipe returns the HTML to use, as well as the corner and edge GIFs, for building a table with rounded borders. It requires the following arguments:

- **$width**   The width of the table—use a pair of quotes for the default.
- **$height**   The height of the table—use a pair of quotes for the default.
- **$bground**   The table's background color.
- **$border**   The table's border color.
- **$contents**   The table's text and/or HTML contents.
- **$program**   The path to the program to create the GIF images.

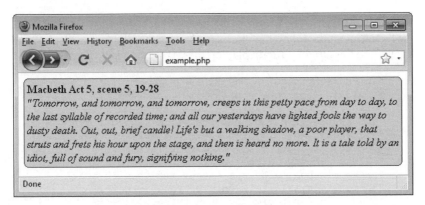

Figure 12-10   All the corners of this table have been neatly rounded.

Variables, Arrays, and Functions

$t1 - $t5	Temporary string variables to avoid string duplication

How It Works

This recipe returns the HTML required to display the supplied contents of $contents within a table that has rounded borders. If a width and/or height are specified, then the table dimensions are set to those values; otherwise, the browser is left to determine how to size it:

```
if ($width)  $width  = "width='$width'";
if ($height) $height = "height='$height'";
```

The table is created in nine segments, with the eight outer ones containing either a corner or edge GIF, each of which is created and displayed by the program contained in $program. The inner segment is populated with the string value in $contents. To do this, the various variables $t1 through $t5 are used as shortcuts for repeated sequences to reduce the recipe in size:

```
$t1 = "<td width='5'><img src='$program?c";
$t2 = "<td background='$program?c";
$t3 = "<td width='5' background='$program?c";
$t4 = "$border&f=$bground' /></td>";
$t5 = "<td bgcolor='#$bground'>$contents</td>";
```

The resulting HTML is then assembled and returned:

```
return <<<_END
<table border='0' cellpadding='0' cellspacing='0'
   $width $height>
<tr>$t1=tl&b=$t4 $t2=t&b=$t4 $t1=tr&b=$t4</tr>
<tr>$t3=l&b=$t4 $t5 $t3=r&b=$t4</tr>
<tr>$t1=bl&b=$t4 $t2=b&b=$t4 $t1=br&b=$t4</tr></table>
_END;
```

How to Use It

You can use the recipe in the following manner, which passes the text to display, colors to use, and the path to the program for displaying the GIFs, like this:

```
$contents = "<b>Macbeth Act 5, scene 5, 19-28</b><br />" .
            "<i>&quot;Tomorrow, and tomorrow, and tomorrow, " .
            "creeps in this petty pace from day to day, to " .
            "the last syllable of recorded time; and all our " .
            "yesterdays have lighted fools the way to dusty " .
            "death. Out, out, brief candle! Life's but a " .
            "walking shadow, a poor player, that struts and " .
            "frets his hour upon the stage, and then is heard " .
            "no more. It is a tale told by an idiot, full of " .
            "sound and fury, signifying nothing.&quot</i>";
echo RoundedTable('', '', 'dedede', '444444', $contents,
    'corner.php');
```

In this code segment, the width and height of the table to create are set to the empty string using pairs of single quotes to let the browser choose suitable dimensions. Then, a background color of dedede and a foreground color of 444444 are passed, followed by the string value in $contents, and the program for displaying the GIFs: corner.php.

As you can see, HTML can also be passed to the recipe, so you can place an unlimited variety of contents within these rounded border tables.

The Recipe

```
function RoundedTable($width, $height, $bground,
    $border, $contents, $program)
{
    if ($width)  $width  = "width='$width'";
    if ($height) $height = "height='$height'";

    $t1 = "<td width='5'><img src='$program?c";
    $t2 = "<td background='$program?c";
    $t3 = "<td width='5' background='$program?c";
    $t4 = "$border&f=$bground' /></td>";
    $t5 = "<td bgcolor='#$bground'>$contents</td>";

    return <<<_END
    <table border='0' cellpadding='0' cellspacing='0'
        $width $height>
    <tr>$t1=tl&b=$t4 $t2=t&b=$t4 $t1=tr&b=$t4</tr>
    <tr>$t3=l&b=$t4 $t5 $t3=r&b=$t4</tr>
    <tr>$t1=bl&b=$t4 $t2=b&b=$t4 $t1=br&b=$t4</tr></table>
_END;
}
```

DisplayBingMap()

Maps are as popular as ever, and in a bid to compete with Google, Microsoft's Virtual Earth project is now used for Bing Maps, which has an API that this recipe makes very easy for you to use. Figure 12-11 shows a scrollable Bing Map, which has been dropped into a web page, with the Bird's Eye view selected.

About the Recipe

This recipe creates the JavaScript and HTML required to embed a scrollable Bing Map into a web page. It requires the following arguments:

- **$lat**   The latitude of a location.
- **$long**   The longitude of a location.
- **$zoom**   The amount to zoom in by (0 for none, 19 for maximum).
- **$style**   The type of map out of Road or Aerial (exact spelling required).
- **$width**   The width of the map.
- **$height**   The height of the map.

Variables, Arrays, and Functions

$root	The base part of the API URL

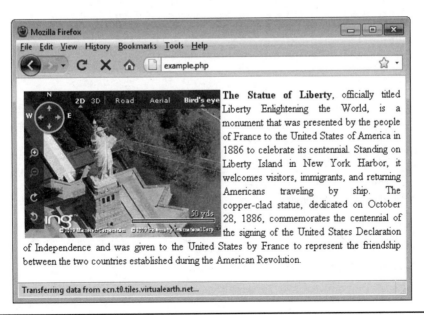

FIGURE 12-11   With this recipe, you can incorporate Bing Maps in your web pages.

How It Works

Normally, when you wish to include a Bing Map into a web page, you have to call it up from the <body> tag and separately include the JavaScript and a <div> in which to display the map.

But this recipe removes the need for all that by using PHP to create the JavaScript code to load a map of the correct dimensions exactly where you want it. It does this by attaching automatically to the events required so that only a single call is needed.

The JavaScript is based on the Virtual Earth API and is beyond the scope of this book to explain, other than to say that all the code required is ready made for you, along with a <div> tag in which to display the map.

How to Use It

To insert a Bing Map into a page, just pass this recipe the location details, zoom level, type of map, and dimensions, like this:

```
$result = DisplayBingMap(40.68913, -74.0446, 18, 'Aerial',
    300, 214);
$text = "<b>The Statue of Liberty</b>, officially titled " .
        "Liberty Enlightening the World, is a monument that " .
        "was presented by the people of France to the United " .
        "States of America in 1886 to celebrate its " .
        "centennial. Standing on Liberty Island in New York " .
        "Harbor, it welcomes visitors, immigrants, and " .
        "returning Americans traveling by ship. The copper-" .
        "clad statue, dedicated on October 28, 1886, " .
        "commemorates the centennial of the signing of the " .
        "United States Declaration of Independence and was " .
        "given to the United States by France to represent " .
        "the friendship between the two countries " .
        "established during the American Revolution.";
echo "<table width='300' height='214' align=left><tr><td>" .
        $result . "</td></tr></table><p align='justify'>$text";
```

The preceding code places the map into a table, which is aligned to the left with text flowing around it. You can equally use a <div> or <span> to include it, or just drop a map in without placing it within an element.

The map style should be one of Aerial or Road and the zoom level should be between 0 (for none) and 19 (for maximum). When you need to know the latitude and longitude of a location, you can look it up in a search engine, or there are useful web sites such as the one for UK maps at *tinyurl.com/longandlat*.

The Recipe

```
function DisplayBingMap($lat, $long, $zoom, $style,
    $width, $height)
{
    if ($style != 'Aerial' && $style != 'Road') $style = 'Road';

    $width  .= 'px';
    $height .= 'px';
```

```
    $root = 'http://ecn.dev.virtualearth.net/mapcontrol';
    return <<<_END
<script src = "$root/mapcontrol.ashx?v=6.2"></script>
<script>
if (window.attachEvent)
{
    window.attachEvent('onload',   Page_Load)
    window.attachEvent('onunload', Page_Unload)
}
else
{
    window.addEventListener('DOMContentLoaded', Page_Load, false)
    window.addEventListener('unload', Page_Unload, false)
}

function Page_Load()
{
    GetMap()
}

function Page_Unload()
{
    if (map != null)
    {
        map.Dispose()
        map = null
    }
}

function GetMap()
{
    map = new VEMap('DBM')
    map.LoadMap(new VELatLong($lat, $long),
        $zoom, VEMapStyle.$style, false)
}
</script>
<div id='DBM' style="position:relative;
    width:$width; height:$height;"></div>
_END;
}

?>
```

PART III
JavaScript Recipes

CHAPTER 13

The Core Recipes

In Part II of this book I was able to draw upon the wealth of ready-made functions supplied with the PHP language. However, this hasn't turned out to be the case with JavaScript, so this chapter concentrates on providing a selection of basic functions needed to develop JavaScript programs as quickly and efficiently as possible.

This chapter contains 18 recipes and a collection of handy global variables to make your life much simpler. It will also make the remaining recipes in this section easier to understand and modify.

Since these core recipes and global variables are used throughout this part of the book, I recommend you take the time to digest the contents of this chapter as fully as possible before starting to use the remaining functions. I apologize in advance for the amount of documentation on these first few recipes, but they are important ones, and it's essential you be completely familiar with their use.

Loading the Recipes

In order to use the recipes from this part of the book, you should include them at the start of your web page, preferably within the <head> section, but if not, right at the start of the <body>. To do this, load them in using the following command:

```
<script src='WDC.js'></script>
```

If you have the *WDC.js* file in a location other than the current folder, make sure you precede the filename with the correct path. If you prefer, you may choose to use the compressed version of this file instead (called *WDCsmall.js*), to save on bandwidth. The file is identical in action, except that being highly compressed you cannot edit it. You load it in like this:

```
<script src='WDCsmall.js'></script>
```

Once you have the recipes loaded, you can access them from within other sets of <script> and </script> tags, or even directly within HTML using the javascript: prefix, attaching them to events and so forth.

O()

The O() function is the most fundamental of the recipes provided in this part of the book and is used by almost all the others. In its simplest form, it replaces the long-winded JavaScript function name document.getElementById(), which takes the string argument supplied to it and then returns the HTML DOM (Document Object Model) object that has been assigned that ID. The letter O is short for the word *Object* since the main purpose of this function is to retrieve an object or modify its properties.

About the Recipe

This recipe takes one required and two optional arguments as follows:

- **id**   This can be a string containing the ID of an object, an object, or even an array containing several objects and/or object IDs. If none of the optional arguments are also provided, then the function returns the object or objects represented by id. If there *are* optional arguments, then the purpose of the function changes to assign the value in value to the property in property of the object (or objects) in id.

- **property**   This optional string argument can contain the name of a property belonging to the object (or objects) in id that requires modifying.

- **value**   If this optional argument is set, it represents the value to be assigned to the property in property of the object (or objects) in id. Both the property and value arguments must have values; otherwise, O() will simply return the object (or objects) in id.

Variables, Arrays, and Functions

tmp[]	Array holding the result of processing the id array
j	Integer loop variable for indexing into id
UNDEF	Global string variable with the value 'undefined'
InsVars()	Function to insert values into a string
push()	Function to push a value onto an array
substr()	Function to return a substring from a string
eval()	Function to evaluate a string as JavaScript code
try()	Function to run a function passing any error to a matching catch() statement
catch()	Function called when a try() statement fails
getElementById	Function to return an object by its name

How It Works

This recipe does a lot more than simply provide a shortened name for an existing function, because you can pass it either the string ID name of an object or the object itself. For example, consider the following HTML div:

```
<div id='outerdiv'> … </div>
```

Using the O() recipe, you can access the div object directly with the following command:

```
mydiv = O('outerdiv')
```

This command is equivalent to the following, which sets the variable mydiv to represent the div object that has the ID 'outerdiv':

```
mydiv = document.getElementById('outerdiv')
```

This means you can, for example, use the value returned by this recipe to change the HTML contents of the div (the text between its opening and closing tags) as follows, by modifying its innerHTML property:

```
mydiv.innerHTML = "<h1>A Heading</h1>"
```

Or, you can bypass assigning the object to a variable and access the object directly from the O() recipe, like this:

```
O('outerdiv').innerHTML = '<h1>A Heading</h1>'
```

Passing Either Strings or Objects

The O() function is also very versatile in that sometimes you may have a variable containing a string name, like this:

```
myvariable = 'outerdiv'
```

On the other hand, it can represent the actual object itself, like this:

```
myvariable = O('outerdiv')
```

The former contains simply the string of characters comprising 'outerdiv', while the latter is an object. Because the job of O() is to return the object referred to by the argument it is passed, if you happen to pass it an object instead of a string, it will simply return that object to you. Therefore, whether myvariable contains a string that refers to an object or the object itself, you can use just the one statement to access it, like this:

```
othervariable = O(myvariable)
```

Or like this:

```
O(myvariable).innerHTML = '<h2>A Subheading</h2>'
```

Note that there are no quotation marks around myvariable in this instance because a variable (or, more precisely, an object), not a string, is being passed.

NOTE *I have used single quotation marks in these examples, but JavaScript allows you to use either single or double quotation marks. However, for the sake of standardization, I usually use single quotes for strings, unless a string includes single quotes within it. In which case I use double quotation marks to enclose the string.*

PART III

Additional Arguments

As well as accepting both strings and objects, the O() recipe allows you to pass it an optional pair of arguments that are then used to modify object properties. For example, the previous examples can also be rewritten like this:

```
O('outerdiv', 'innerHTML', '<h1>A Heading</h1>')
O(myvariable, 'innerHTML', '<h2>A Subheading</h2>')
```

Both of the preceding are acceptable alternative syntax for assigning a value to an object's property.

Passing Arrays

You may be wondering about the point of this alternative syntax. Well, it comes into its own when you want to access many different objects at a time. This is something you can't do with standard JavaScript, but you can achieve it with the O() recipe, which allows you to pass an array of objects, object ID names, or a combination of both.

For example, let's say you would like to clear the HTML contents of three objects that have the names 'Fred', 'Mary', and 'Bill'. Regular JavaScript would require three separate commands, but you can easily achieve the same result with the following code:

```
ids = Array('Fred', 'Mary', 'Bill')
O(ids, 'innerHTML', '')
```

You can even mix objects and object ID names within an array, as follows:

```
ids = Array('Fred', 'Mary', 'Bill', myobject)
```

Or, you can combine everything into one line of code, as in the following example, which will clear out the innerHTML contents of all the objects:

```
O(Array('Fred', 'Mary', 'Bill', myobject), 'innerHTML', '')
```

Figure 13-1 shows a group of three divs that have all had their innerHTML properties set to the same value, using the code in the following example web page:

```
<!DOCTYPE html>
<html><head><title>Example Web Page</title>
<script src="WDC.js"></script>
</head><body>
  Fred: <span id='Fred'></span><br />
  Mary: <span id='Mary'></span><br />
  Bill: <span id='Bill'></span>

  <script>
    ids = Array('Fred', 'Mary', 'Bill')
    O(ids, 'innerHTML', 'New contents...')
  </script>
</body></html>
```

This web page begins with the <!DOCTYPE html> setting, then adds both the page's <title> and the two <script> lines required to include and set up the recipes. After that,

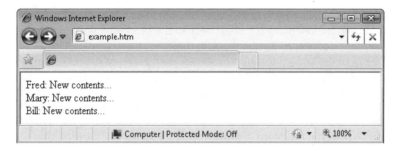

Figure 13-1 Changing the HTML contents of objects using O()

the <head> is closed and the <body> of the page is opened. Then, three lines of HTML create simple <span> sections that don't contain any content.

Finally, there is another <script> section in which the contents of these spans is changed so that each displays the string 'New contents...'. This is the format that most standard web pages will follow when using the recipes. The result of loading this page into a browser is shown in Figure 13-1.

Now that you've seen how easy it is to use the recipes and where the different parts fit within a web page, throughout the rest of these examples I will omit everything before (and including) the <body> tag (except where a recipe affects that particular section) and concentrate only on the relevant HTML and JavaScript required to explain the use of a recipe.

When an Array Is Passed

The O() recipe comprises three parts. The first one tests the argument id to see if it is an array, which it does by using the instanceof operator, like this:

```
if (id instanceof Array) …
```

If it *is* an array, then more than one object has been passed to the function, so the array tmp is declared as a local array (that can only be accessed by this instance of the function) using the var keyword, like this:

```
var tmp = []
```

Then, a for() loop iterates through the array, using the integer variable j as an index pointer to each individual array element.

Making Recursive Calls

Interestingly, the O() function is called again within each iteration, but just with the single element located at the current array index pointed to by j. This is known as a *recursive* function call, meaning that the function calls itself. It's a very neat way to reuse code to get a job done once you have broken it down into a more manageable chunk. The loop code looks like this:

```
for (var j = 0 ; j < id.length ; ++j)
    tmp.push(O(id[j], property, value))
```

To explain how it works in this instance, one element has been extracted from an array of elements and then that element is passed back to the same function, which will then process that element and return a value back to itself. So, for example, if an array of items is passed to O(), it will be iterated through in stages, each time passing one element from the array in turn to the same function, until all elements have been processed.

Looked at from the function's receiving end, when it sees that it has received a single item (and not an array), control flow drops through to the remaining code, where that item is processed and whatever value or object is calculated is returned. Upon return from the function (back to the same function), the result of the function call is placed in the next free location in the tmp array by using the JavaScript push() function and is promptly forgotten about (since it has been dealt with), and the next element of the array is then processed.

Once all elements are done with (in other words, the value of j equals the number of items in the array, as indicated by id.length), the array tmp is returned to the calling code.

You will notice that the variables property and value are not treated as arrays, because they aren't. If the variable property has a value it should be the name of an object's property, and value will contain the value to assign to that property. These arguments are optional but can be used to give the same value to the same properties of all objects in an array. Because the function calls itself recursively, it also has to pass property and value (whether or not they have values) along with the object to be processed; otherwise, if they have values, they will be lost.

TIP *If you're new to recursion and it seems somewhat complicated to you, try reading through this section a couple more times and you should soon get the hang of it. Wikipedia also has quite a good explanation of the concept at* wikipedia.org/wiki/Recursion, *and no, it doesn't just say "see Recursion"!*

Processing the Additional Arguments

In the previous section I talked about property and value, the optional arguments for modifying an object's properties. The second main section of this function is where that modification happens. The code starts by testing whether or not both property and value have a value by using the typeof operator, like this:

```
if (typeof property != UNDEF && (typeof value != UNDEF)
```

The variable UNDEF is a global variable that has been assigned the value 'undefined' by the Initialize() function, which is detailed a little later.

Both arguments must have a value for this if() statement to execute. If they *do*, it's time to make another recursive call, passing the value of id back to the same function. This illustrates the power of the O() recipe in that you never have to worry whether the main argument you pass it is an object or the ID name of an object; either is acceptable, and so this part of the function simply passes on the value of id, whatever type of variable it is.

Inside this if() statement, the eval() function is used to assign the value to the property, first surrounding the value with single quotation marks if it is a string (otherwise, eval() would try to evaluate it, rather than treat it as a string):

```
if (typeof value == 'string') value = "'" + value + "'"
if (typeof id == 'object') return eval(id.property = value)
return eval("O('" + id + "').") + property + " = " + value)
```

The value returned by eval() is then returned by the function in one of two different ways, according to whether or not id is an object. This code gets around odd anomalies in the JavaScript language and is obscure enough that explaining it might be confusing. Suffice it to say that the code, as written, can evaluate value, whatever type it is.

At the Deepest Level

The remaining lines of the recipe execute only when id is not an array and when no optional parameters have been passed. Since they come after both of the sections that can make recursive calls, they are the place where the function ultimately returns from these recursive calls.

These lines also represent the heart of the O() function in that they will return an object by providing its ID name. The code looks like this:

```
if (typeof id == 'object') return id
else
{
   try { return document.getElementById(id) }
   catch(e) { alert('Unknown ID: ' + id) }
}
```

The first line ends function execution if id is an object by simply returning it. Otherwise, an attempt is made to return the object whose ID is id. Sometimes, though, you will accidentally pass an ID to the O() function that hasn't yet been assigned. If this happens, rather than having JavaScript come to a halt (which it would do if the object doesn't exist), an error message alert is displayed to let you know this has happened.

This is achieved by using a pair of try ... catch() statements. The first tries the code and passes execution to the second if there is an error.

You may wish to remove the alert() call in a production web site so that your users won't see any errors you might leave in your code. However, remember that trying to access a nonexistent object is a critical error that stops all program flow, and you really don't want to leave any such errors in your production code.

How to Use It

This recipe has two distinct modes. In the first, it returns an object referred to by an ID string, while in the second it updates an object's property with a new value. In either case, if the object itself is passed to the recipe (instead of its ID name) then the object is accessed directly, since there's no need to look it up.

Furthermore, in both the lookup and property setting modes, you can pass an array of objects and/or ID names. If you are looking up objects, the recipe returns an array. If you are setting properties, all the objects have the specified property set to the given value, and those values are returned.

However, the value returned by the recipe is really only of use when looking up an object, such as in the following, which are just four of the countless ways of using the recipe:

```
objectname = O('mydiv')
O('copyrightspan').innerHTML = '&copy; 2014'
background = O('menu').style.backgroundColor
O('menu').style.color = 'yellow'
```

When you are assigning a value to one or more properties, as in the following examples, the returned value will simply be that of the assigned value, which is not particularly useful to you, except perhaps when you are debugging code:

```
O(objectname, 'innerHTML', '<h1>Heading Text</h1>')
O(Array('first', 'second'), 'mouseover', 'mousehandler')
```

As you will see throughout this part of the book, the O() recipe is used in a variety of different ways, and you will soon get used to thinking of it as the main way to access individual elements in a web page.

NOTE *Well-known JavaScript frameworks, such as jQuery, Script.aculo.us Prototype, and many others, make use of a similar function to O(), but they usually call it $(). Some add even more functionality to it than there is in the O() recipe, which makes it even more powerful, but also more complicated. The $ is a sensible choice of character for naming such functions because it's short and instantly recognizable. However, I have deliberately not used the same convention precisely because other frameworks do use it. That way, the recipes in this book should be less likely to conflict with third-party frameworks if you use them both on the same web pages.*

The Recipe

```
function O(id, property, value)
{
    if (id instanceof Array)
    {
        var tmp = []
        for (var j = 0 ; j < id.length ; ++j)
            tmp.push(O(id[j], property, value))
        return tmp
    }

    if (typeof property !=  UNDEF && typeof value != UNDEF)
    {
        if (typeof value == 'string') value = "'" + value + "'"
        if (typeof id == 'object') return eval(id.property = value)
        else return eval("O('" + id + "')." + property + " = " + value)
    }

    if (typeof id == 'object') return id
    else
    {
        try { return document.getElementById(id) }
        catch(e) { alert('Unknown ID: ' + id) }
    }
}
```

S()

Probably the most common use to which JavaScript is put is modifying CSS properties in HTML documents. These include colors, dimensions, location, opacity, and much more. Generally, this is done using code such as the following, which changes the foreground text color of a div:

```
document.getElement.ById('element').style.color = 'red'
```

Or, using the previous recipe, this can be shortened to:

```
O('element').style.color = 'red'
```

This is such a common action that I have created a companion recipe to O() called S() (for Style), which deals with handling an object's `style` property (or, more precisely, subobject). Using it, the preceding commands can be reduced to the following:

```
S('element').color = 'red'
```

Figure 13-2 shows the recipe being used to change the background colors of the three divs.

About the Recipe

The S() recipe is similar to O(), with the exception that instead of referencing an object, that object's `style` subobject is accessed. Also, since events are not used by it, there is no need to check for them in this function. It accepts the following arguments:

- **id** This can be a string containing the ID of an object, an object, or even an array containing several objects and/or object IDs. If none of the optional arguments are also provided, then the function returns the `style` subobject of the object (or objects) represented by `id`. If there *are* optional arguments, then the purpose of the function changes to assign the value in `value` to the property in `property` of the `style` subobject of the object (or objects) in `id`.

- **property** This optional string argument can contain the name of a property belonging to the `style` subobject of the object (or objects) in `id` that requires modifying.

- **value** If this optional argument is set, it represents the value to be assigned to the property in `property` of the `style` subobject of the object (or objects) in `id`. Both the `property` and `value` arguments must have values; otherwise, S() will simply return the `style` subobject of the object (or objects) in `id`.

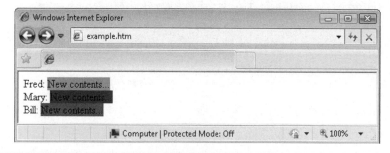

FIGURE 13-2 Using S() to change the background colors of some divs

Variables, Arrays, and Functions

`tmp[]`	Array holding the result of processing the `id` array.
`j`	Integer loop variable for indexing into `id`.
`style`	Style subobject.
`push()`	Function to push a value onto an array.
`try`	Construct used to run code, passing any error to a matching `catch()` statement.
`catch()`	Function called when a `try` keyword fails.
`O()`	The main "object" function. Since `O()` and `S()` are both used by almost all recipes, this is the last time either will be listed in a "Variables, Arrays, and Functions" section.

How It Works

Now that you understand how the `O()` recipe works, you will also have an idea how this one functions. Because it is so similar, I'll just outline the basics.

As with `O()`, this function has three main parts. The first processes `id` if it happens to be an array. It does this by recursively calling itself with each element within the array so as to deal with each one separately. The code that does this is as follows, with the final line returning an array of all the values returned during the process:

```
if (id instanceof Array)
{
   var tmp = []
   for (var j = 0 ; j < id.length ; ++j)
      tmp.push(S(id[j], property, value))
   return tmp
}
```

The second section handles the case when you are using the recipe in its property assigning mode. It determines this by checking whether both the arguments `property` and `value` have values. If they do, then the property in `property` of the `style` subobject of the object represented by `id` is assigned the value in `value`.

Otherwise, the object fetching mode is entered, and so the style subobject of `id` is returned.

However, for the reasons given in the previous section, accessing the object is embedded within `try` and `catch()` statements so that any errors can be caught and displayed via a call to `alert()`, using the matching `catch()` function:

```
if (typeof property != UNDEF && typeof value != UNDEF)
{
   try { return O(id).style[property] = value }
   catch(e) { alert('Unknown ID: ' + id) }
}
else if (typeof id == 'object') return id.style
else
{
   try { return O(id).style }
   catch(e) { alert('Unknown ID: ' + id) }
}
```

During development, you will find this error catching very useful, as mistyping ID names or accessing them before they have been declared are common errors.

NOTE *I refer to the `style` subobject, but I could also call it the `style` property, because it is both: It's a property called `style`, which is itself an object that has properties. Therefore, I tend to refer to properties that are also objects as subobjects.*

How to Use It

You use this recipe in much the same way you use the O() function. With it, you can either fetch the style subobject of an object, or you can modify one of the style properties of that object. Here's one way you could use the recipe to first fetch and then use an object's style subobject:

```
var styleobject = S('mydiv')
styleobject.backgroundColor = 'cyan'
```

Or, you can access the style subobject directly, like this:

```
S('mydiv').backgroundColor = 'cyan'
```

If you wish, you can also set the value of a property from within the recipe like this:

```
S('mydiv', 'backgroundColor', 'cyan')
```

This latter form also allows you to set style properties for several objects at once, like this:

```
ids = Array('one', 'two', 'three')
S(ids, 'backgroundColor', 'cyan')
```

In this case, all the objects in the ids array will have their backgroundColor style property set to 'cyan'. Omitting the head section and any other parts of the web page, the code used to create the output in Figure 13-2 is as follows:

```
Fred: <span id='Fred'></span><br />
Mary: <span id='Mary'></span><br />
Bill: <span id='Bill'></span>

<script>
  ids = Array('Fred', 'Mary', 'Bill')
  O(ids, 'innerHTML', 'New contents...')
  S('Fred').backgroundColor = 'red'
  S('Mary').backgroundColor = 'blue'
  S('Bill').backgroundColor = 'green'
</script>
```

First, the divs are created within HTML, then a section of JavaScript follows in which the ids array is populated with the three ID names of the divs. After that, the O() recipe is used to assign vales to the innerHTML properties of these divs as a group, and then each div's backgroundColor property is individually set using three separate calls to S().

Over the coming chapters, you will see the S() recipe used in many different contexts, and I think you'll find that in the future you'll never want to access style properties in any other way.

The Recipe

```
function S(id, property, value)
{
    if (id instanceof Array)
    {
        var tmp = []
        for (var j = 0 ; j < id.length ; ++j)
            tmp.push(S(id[j], property, value))
        return tmp
    }

    if (typeof property != UNDEF && typeof value != UNDEF)
    {
        try { return O(id).style[property] = value }
        catch(e) { alert('Unknown ID: ' + id) }
    }
    else if (typeof id == 'object') return id.style
    else
    {
        try { return O(id).style }
        catch(e) { alert('Unknown ID: ' + id) }
    }
}
```

RECIPE 3 Initialize()

In order to set up the recipes so they are ready to use, it is necessary to call up a small initialization recipe. As previously mentioned, I recommend you always include the following line of code at the start of each web page that uses these recipes:

```
<script src="WDC.js"></script>
```

Or if you are using the compressed version of the recipes, *WDCsmall.js,* then you would use that file in place of *WDC.js.*

This recipe is the Initialize() function that is called up as soon as *WDC.js* is loaded in, and it prepares a wide range of functionality you can draw on, as shown in Figure 13-3, for example, in which the browser type is detected.

About the Recipe

This recipe requires no arguments and doesn't return any. However, please refer to the table of variables, arrays, and functions in the next section, as some very important global variables are set up by it.

FIGURE 13-3 Displaying the variable BROWSER after calling this recipe

Variables, Arrays, and Functions

MOUSE_DOWN	Global integer set to true if a mouse button is currently held down; otherwise, false
MOUSE_IN	Global integer set to true if the mouse pointer is currently within the browser window; otherwise, false
MOUSE_X	Global integer containing the current horizontal coordinate of the mouse pointer
MOUSE_Y	Global integer containing the current vertical coordinate of the mouse pointer
SCROLL_X	Global integer containing the amount the browser has been scrolled vertically, in pixels
SCROLL_Y	Global integer containing the amount the browser has been scrolled horizontally, in pixels
KEY_PRESS	Global integer containing the value of the last key pressed
ZINDEX	Global integer containing the maximum Z Index of any object accessed via the recipes
CHAIN_CALLS	Global array containing recipes that have been chained together and that are yet to be executed
INTERVAL	Global integer containing the time in milliseconds between calls to a repeated event
UNDEF	Global string containing the value 'undefined'
HID	Global string containing the value 'hidden'
VIS	Global string containing the value 'visible'
ABS	Global string containing the value 'absolute'
FIX	Global string containing the value 'fixed'
REL	Global string containing the value 'relative'
TP	Global string containing the value 'top'
BM	Global string containing the value 'bottom'

PART III

LT	Global string containing the value 'left'
RT	Global string containing the value 'right'
BROWSER	Global string containing the name of the current browser
NavCheck()	Subfunction to check for the existence of a string in the browser User Agent string

How It Works

Let's look first at each of this recipe's global variable definitions:

- **MOUSE_DOWN**   This integer variable is updated by the two inline, anonymous functions (later in the recipe) that are attached to the document.onmouseup and document.onmousedown events. With it, you can quickly make a check to see whether or not a mouse button is being pressed anywhere in the browser window by simply looking at this variable, which has a value of true if down; otherwise, it is set to false.

- **MOUSE_IN**   In a similar fashion, the document.onmouseout and document .onmouseover events are captured, and this global variable is set to true when the mouse pointer is within the bounds of the browser window; otherwise, it is set to false.

- **MOUSE_X** and **MOUSE_Y**   This pair of global variables is constantly updated by the CaptureMouse() recipe (the recipe following this one), which is attached to the document.onmousemove event. Therefore, you can reference these variables at any time to determine the position of the mouse pointer.

- **SCROLL_X** and **SCROLL_Y**   These global variables are also kept updated by the CaptureMouse() recipe. They are continuously updated with values representing the amount by which the browser has scrolled in both vertical and horizontal directions.

- **KEY_PRESS**   This global variable is updated by the CaptureKeyboard() recipe, which captures the document.onkeydown and document.onkeypress events and sets the variable depending on the key that was pressed.

- **ZINDEX**   This global variable starts off with a default value of 1,000. It is used by the recipes to determine the zIndex property of objects it uses. This is the depth at which it will be displayed on the screen, with lower or negative numbers being behind higher and positive numbers. For example, the ContextMenu() recipe in Chapter 8, which opens a drop-down element when you right-click, uses this value to ensure that the element it displays appears in front of all other windows. Also, the BrowserWindow() recipe (also in Chapter 8), which creates in-browser, moveable pop-up windows, sets windows that are clicked to the value of ZINDEX + 1 to ensure that they come to the front.

- **CHAIN_CALLS**   Some of the recipes have the ability to be chained together so that they run consecutively, each one starting after the previous recipe has finished. Normally, JavaScript doesn't allow such behavior and, if you call up a function that, for example, sets up an interrupt to perform an animation, that function will return immediately to the calling code without waiting for the sequence of interrupts to complete. This is exactly the behavior normally required, because it allows other things to happen at the same time. But some of these recipes work better when they are chained, which is achieved by placing a sequence of functions in the CHAIN_ CALLS array so that as each function completes, the next in the chain can be called. The only reasons you might want to access this array are either to determine if (and how many) functions are queued up, or possibly to empty the array to cancel all queued up functions.

- **INTERVAL**   After many hours of experimentation on all the major browsers across a range of computers and operating systems, I have derived a value of 30 milliseconds as being the optimal time to allow between interrupt calls, because some shorter functions complete in under 10 milliseconds, while others may take 20 or more, but none should take any longer than 30 milliseconds. Therefore, I have set the global variable INTERVAL to 30. This fixed value is required for timing purposes, so that all the interrupt functions in these recipes can therefore ensure that they take exactly the number of milliseconds passed to them. As JavaScript speeds creep up over the next few years, this allows you to optimize the recipe and drop the value of this variable to 25, 20, 15, or even fewer milliseconds. This will not speed up the recipes, but it will allow animations to have extra steps between the first and last frame, making the transitions smoother.

Global String Variables

After these first 10 global variables, a further 10 global string variables are defined. These are UNDEF, HID, VIS, ABS, FIX, REL, TP, BM, LT, and RT. In order, they stand for the strings 'undefined', 'hidden', 'visible', 'absolute', 'fixed', 'relative', 'static', 'inherit', 'top', 'bottom', 'left', and 'right'.

Although they are not essential, I have created these variables because the strings to which they refer are used frequently by the recipes, and this helps to keep the code more compact. It also serves to make the listings in this book narrower, so that lines that might previously have wrapped around now display on a single line. Additionally, they help make the code more readable, as long as you refer back to this section if you forget the values of any of them.

Determining the Current Browser

Because JavaScript varies in its implementation between different developers, you sometimes need to know which browser you are dealing with. So, in conjunction with the subfunction NavCheck(), the next six lines of code will set the global variable BROWSER to one of the following strings, depending on the browser used: 'IE', 'Opera', 'Chrome', 'iPod', 'iPhone', 'iPad', 'Android', 'Safari', 'Firefox', and 'UNKNOWN'. You can then refer to this variable in the same way that some of the recipes do in order to offer different code to different browsers. When 'Firefox' is returned, it means that a browser running on the Gecko rendering engine is in use, which includes browsers other than Firefox.

Attaching Functions to Events

Much of the functionality of these recipes rests on the capturing of various built-in browser events, as is done by the remaining seven lines of code. The first three attach the CaptureMouse() function to the document.ommousemove event, and the CaptureKeyboard() function to the document.onkeydown and document.onkeypress events. What these recipes do is documented in their own sections, but suffice it to say that they are called each time one of those events occurs and they keep the global variable KEY_ PRESS updated.

The final four lines attach functions that are so small I have created them as anonymous inline functions. All they do is capture the document.onmouseout, document.onmouseover, document.onmouseup, and document.onmousedown events, keeping the global variables MOUSE_IN and MOUSE_DOWN updated.

How to Use It

This recipe is called automatically as soon as you include the *WDC.js* (or *WDCsmall.js*) JavaScript file. If you wish to check that it has been successfully called, you can try issuing the following statement from within <script> tags, which will display the name of the browser being used, as shown in Figure 13-3:

```
alert('Your browser is ' + BROWSER)
```

However, you will normally wish to use this and the other recipes only once a page has fully loaded and all its elements' locations and dimensions are known and can be manipulated. Therefore, the command (and the rest of your code) is best placed within the body of an OnDOMReady() function, like this:

```
OnDOMReady(function()
{
    alert("Your browser is " + BROWSER)
})
```

The OnDOMReady() function is supplied in the *WDC.js* (and *WDCsmall.js*) file and is based on a function by Ryan Morr at *tinyurl.com/ryanmorr*.

It is a replacement for the more typical window.onload = function() you may have used (or seen). It will start your code much more quickly than waiting for window.onload, which only triggers after all contents such as images are also loaded—whereas the contents of the OnDOMReady() function are called as soon as the DOM is complete and in a useable state, and so your JavaScript will begin running that much sooner.

When you use this function, remember to place a final bracket after the code you place within it, so that you close off the function properly. Otherwise, you will get a syntax error. Basically, just remember to place this before your code:

```
OnDOMReady(function()
{
```

And this afterwards:

```
})
```

TIP *I recommend enclosing all your JavaScript inside an OnDOMReady() function so you can be sure that all the elements of a web page are available when you try to access them.*

The Recipe

```
function Initialize()
{
    MOUSE_DOWN   = false
    MOUSE_IN     = true
    MOUSE_X      = 0
    MOUSE_Y      = 0
    SCROLL_X     = 0
    SCROLL_Y     = 0
    KEY_PRESS    = ''
    ZINDEX       = 1000
    CHAIN_CALLS  = []
    INTERVAL     = 30

    UNDEF = 'undefined'
    HID   = 'hidden'
    VIS   = 'visible'
    ABS   = 'absolute'
    FIX   = 'fixed'
    REL   = 'relative'
    STA   = 'static'
    INH   = 'inherit'
    TP    = 'top'
    BM    = 'bottom'
    LT    = 'left'
    RT    = 'right'

    if      (document.all)           BROWSER = 'IE'
    else if (window.opera)           BROWSER = 'Opera'
    else if (NavCheck('Chrome'))     BROWSER = 'Chrome'
    else if (NavCheck('iPod'))       BROWSER = 'iPod'
    else if (NavCheck('iPhone')      BROWSER = 'iPhone'
    else if (NavCheck('iPad'))       BROWSER = 'iPad'
    else if (NavCheck('Android'))    BROWSER = 'Android'
    else if (NavCheck('Safari'))     BROWSER = 'Safari'
    else if (NavCheck('Gecko'))      BROWSER = 'Firefox'
    else                             BROWSER = 'UNKNOWN'

    document.onmousemove  = CaptureMouse
    document.onscroll     = CaptureMouse
    document.onmousewheel = CaptureMouse
    document.onkeydown    = CaptureKeyboard
    document.onkeypress   = CaptureKeyboard

    document.onmouseout  = function() { MOUSE_IN   = false }
    document.onmouseover = function() { MOUSE_IN   = true  }
    document.onmouseup   = function() { MOUSE_DOWN = false }
    document.onmousedown = function() { MOUSE_DOWN = true  }

    function NavCheck(check)
    {
        return navigator.userAgent.indexOf(check)  != -1
    }
}
```

PART III

4 CaptureMouse()

This recipe is called only by the `Initialize()` function, and you should not need to call it yourself. What it does is attach to the mouse movement event, updating various global variables with details about the mouse position, as shown in Figure 13-4.

About the Recipe

This recipe attaches to the `document.onmousemove` event, updating the global variables `MOUSE_X`, `MOUSE_Y`, `SCROLL_X`, and `SCROLL_Y`. The event passes the value e to it, which is only used by browsers other than Internet Explorer. It does not require you to pass it any arguments, nor does it return any values.

Variables, Arrays, and Functions

E	The event as passed to the function by browsers other than Internet Explorer. `e.pageX` and `e.pageY` contain the X and Y locations of the mouse pointer.
Window.event	Internet Explorer uses the `window.event` property instead of an event passed as an argument. The `clientX` and `clientY` subproperties contain the X and Y locations of the mouse pointer.
document.documentElement	If the browser is Internet Explorer, then the `scrollLeft` and `scrollTop` properties of this property are accessed to determine the amount of horizontal and vertical scroll.
Window	On browsers other than Internet Explorer, the `pageXOffsett` and `pageYOffset` properties of `window` are accessed to determine the amount of horizontal and vertical scroll.
MOUSE_X	Global integer containing the current horizontal coordinate of the mouse pointer.
MOUSE_Y	Global integer containing the current vertical coordinate of the mouse pointer.
SCROLL_X	Global integer containing the amount the browser has been scrolled vertically, in pixels.
SCROLL_X	Global integer containing the amount the browser has been scrolled vertically, in pixels.

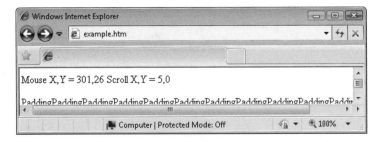

Figure 13-4   This recipe lets you know where the mouse pointer is.

How It Works

This function traps the document.onmousemove event and accesses either the e value passed to it in browsers other than Internet Explorer or, in Internet Explorer, it accesses the global window.event property. Using these values, it sets the values of the global variables MOUSE_X and MOUSE_Y to the current X and Y coordinates of the mouse pointer.

The scrollLeft and scrollTop properties of document.documentElement are also accessed in Internet Explorer to determine the amount of any horizontal and vertical scrolling. These values are placed in the global variables SCROLL_X and SCROLL_Y. In browsers other than Internet Explorer, SCROLL_X and SCROLL_Y are given their values based on the pageXOffset and pageYOffset properties of window.

The value true is then returned to allow the event to be acted on by the browser.

How to Use It

You will not access this function directly. Instead, by calling the Initialize() recipe as recommended, the values needed to determine the X and Y locations of the mouse pointer and any horizontal or scrolling values are placed in the global variables MOUSE_X, MOUSE_Y, SCROLL_X, and SCROLL_Y and are kept constantly updated.

To illustrate how you can use these, the following code will display these values in real time:

```
<div id='output'></div><p>
PaddingPaddingPaddingPaddingPaddingPaddingPaddingPaddingPaddingPadding

<script>
OnDOMReady(function()
{
    setInterval(simpleInterrupt, INTERVAL)

    function simpleInterrupt()
    {
        O('output').innerHTML =
            ' Mouse X,Y = ' + MOUSE_X  + ',' + MOUSE_Y +
            ' Scroll X,Y = ' + SCROLL_X + ',' + SCROLL_Y
    }
})
</script>
```

The first section is within the HTML body of a web page and is used to create a div into which the output will be inserted. Underneath the div, there's a line of text made up from repeating the word Padding. This is used to make the text overflow (since there are no spaces in it), causing the bottom scroll bar to appear so you can move the scroll bar and see the offset value change in real time. If your browser is set very wide, you should resize it until the scroll bar appears.

In the <script> section, there's a single main line of code that sets up a regular interrupt using the setInterval() function, passing it the name of the function to call (which is simpleInterrupt) and the frequency at which it should be called in INTERVAL (which is 30 by default). This means the function simpleInterrupt() will be called up every 30 milliseconds.

TIP *In JavaScript, whenever you wish to reference a function by its name without actually calling the function, you omit the final brackets. In this instance, the setInterval() function knows that you are passing only the name of the function. If you used brackets, the function would first be called and the value it returned would be passed to the setInterval() function, which is probably not what you want.*

The simpleInterrupt() function uses the O() recipe you have already seen to select the div 'output' object by name. It then assigns the following string to that object's innerHTML property. This has the effect of inserting the string as if it were entered between the opening and closing div tags. The value assigned is some text and the values in the four global variables.

To try this for yourself, enter the example code (as well as the required <script> commands to load in the *WDC.js* file), or select *example4.htm* from the *JS* folder in the download available from the companion web site at *webdeveloperscookbook.com*.

Then, resize your browser so it is fairly small and the bottom scroll bar is visible. Move the mouse about within the browser and move the scroll bar to see the values displayed change in real time. Because of the way the scrolling event works, you will only see its values change when you release the mouse button after moving one of the scroll bars.

As you can see, with very little work you can look up important values associated with the mouse whenever you need them. You also just saw the O() recipe being used in a real situation.

The Recipe

```
function CaptureMouse(e)
{
    if (BROWSER == 'IE')
    {
        SCROLL_X = document.documentElement.scrollLeft
        SCROLL_Y = document.documentElement.scrollTop
        MOUSE_X  = window.event.clientX + SCROLL_X
        MOUSE_Y  = window.event.clientY + SCROLL_Y
    }
    else
    {
        SCROLL_X = window.pageXOffset
        SCROLL_Y = window.pageYOffset
        MOUSE_X  = e.pageX
        MOUSE_Y  = e.pageY
    }

    return true
}
```

CaptureKeyboard()

This recipe makes a note of any keypresses made and stores the result in the global variable KEY_PRESS, as demonstrated by the example in Figure 13-5, which has detected the ALT key being pressed.

FIGURE 13-5   Determining which keys have been pressed is easy with this recipe.

About the Recipe

You will not need to call this recipe yourself because it should already have been called by the `Initialize()` recipe. It doesn't require any arguments and doesn't return any that you can use.

Variables, Arrays, and Functions

`e`	The event as passed to the function by browsers other than Internet Explorer. Either `e.charCode` or `e.keyCode` contains the value of the key pressed.
`window.event`	Internet Explorer uses the `window.event` property instead of an event passed as an argument. The `keyCode` contains the value of the key pressed.
`BROWSER`	Global variable used to determine the browser.
`KEY_PRESS`	Global variable to be assigned the value of the keypress.
`fromCharCode()`	JavaScript function to convert Unicode values to characters.
`FromKeyCode()`	Function to return the value of a keypress or its name if it is one of many special characters such as 'Esc', 'Home', and so on.

How It Works

This function works differently depending on whether you are using Internet Explorer or not. If you are, it looks up the keypress in `window.event.keyCode` and passes it through the `FromKeyCode()` recipe, which will assign a string if the keypress was a special one such as 'PgUp', 'Backspace', and so on. Then, if the value is still a number (that is, it hasn't been substituted for a special key name), the JavaScript `fromCharCode()` function converts it from its Unicode value to an actual key value, so that if, for example, the key e is pressed, then the value 'e' is returned.

On non–Internet Explorer browsers, both `e.charCode` and `e.keyCode` are checked for a value because both the events `document.onkeydown` and `document.onkeypress` are captured by this function. One function captures regular keys, while the other handles the special keys already referred to, so combining both into the same function makes sense. So, if `e.charCode` has a value, it is passed through the JavaScript `fromCharCode()` function to convert it from its Unicode value. Or, if `e.keycode` has a value, a special key was pressed, so its value is passed through the `FromKeyCode()` recipe to look up the key name.

In either case, the result is that KEY_PRESS will contain a letter, number, punctuation symbol, the name of a special key, or simply a key number if it is none of the others. There is no keyboard buffering to, for example, create strings of input, since only the last key pressed is saved. However, it is quite possible to create an input function using this if you need one.

Finally, a value of true is returned to allow further processing of the event by the browser.

How to Use It

Using this recipe is as simple as referencing the global variable, KEY_PRESS, that it maintains. The following is a simple example that continuously updates the contents of a div with the value of the last key pressed:

```
<div id='output'></div>

<script>
OnDOMReady(function()
{
    setInterval(simpleInterrupt, INTERVAL)

    function simpleInterrupt()
    {
        O('output').innerHTML = ' You pressed: ' + KEY_PRESS
    }
})
</script>
```

Again (and I won't mention this anymore), this assumes you have already included the *WDC.js* (or *WDCsmall.js*) file.

The interrupt is set up so that the value of the last keypress can be continuously displayed. If you prefer, you can always use a command such as the following in the loop instead:

```
alert('You pressed: ' + KEY_PRESS)
```

However, it is intrusive, and you have to click the OK button to close the alert each time it is called. What's more, it locks up the browser because the alert() function prevents you from doing anything else (even closing the browser) until you have clicked OK, and even then the alert will pop up again, and again, forever.

Tip *Because of the problem of* alert() *potentially taking over a browser if placed within a loop, this section includes an alternate function called* Alert() *(with an uppercase A), which you may prefer to use. It does not lock the browser and has other benefits, too. For further details, please refer to Chapter 23.*

The Recipe

```
function CaptureKeyboard(e)
{
    if (BROWSER == 'IE')
    {
        KEY_PRESS = FromKeyCode(window.event.keyCode)
```

```
      if (KEY_PRESS > 0)
         KEY_PRESS = String.fromCharCode(KEY_PRESS)
   }
   else
   {
      if (e.charCode)      KEY_PRESS = String.fromCharCode(e.charCode)
      else if (e.keyCode)  KEY_PRESS = FromKeyCode(e.keyCode)
   }

   return true
}
```

FromKeyCode()

This recipe returns the name of the key pressed if it is a special one such as CTRL or ALT; otherwise, the value passed to it is returned, as shown in Figure 13-6, in which the translations for key codes 1 through 144 are displayed.

About the Recipe

This plug-in takes a key code as an argument and returns either a string representing the special key that was pressed, or the code if no such key was pressed.

Variables, Arrays, and Functions

c	Key code passed to the function and returned by it if it does not represent a special key

How It Works

This function uses a switch() statement to test the value of c and return various strings if it matches set values. If none of the values match, then c is returned.

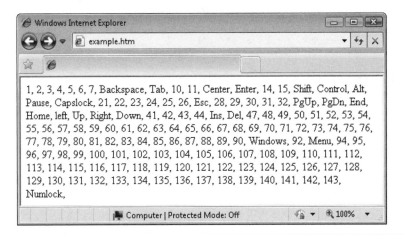

FIGURE 13-6   This recipe returns meaningful names for key codes.

How to Use It

Generally, this recipe will be called for you by the `CaptureKeyboard()` recipe. However, you may have an application for which you'd rather not return the strings given, or you'd rather return different names. In these cases, feel free to modify the recipe to your requirements.

For example, if you don't want the keypresses created by pressing the SHIFT key, you might prefer to return a value of the empty string for that value instead of the string 'Shift'. That way, when the user presses the SHIFT key followed by the M key, for example, you will only see the value 'M' and not 'Shift' followed by 'M'.

The reason I've gone to the bother of trapping these special keys is that, although there are already useful input features built into JavaScript, these recipes allow you to, for example, set up various special keys to move objects around the screen or perform particular functions the moment a key is pressed.

Here's a combined HTML and JavaScript example to return the translations for codes 1 through 144:

```
<div id='output'></div>

<script>
OnDOMReady(function()
{
  for (j = 1 ; j < 145 ; ++j)
    O('output').innerHTML += FromKeyCode(j) + ', '
})
</script>
```

An interesting point to note here is the use of the `+=` operator to keep appending to the contents of the `innerHTML` property of the 'output' div.

The Recipe

```
function FromKeyCode(c)
{
    switch (c)
    {
        case   8: return 'Backspace'
        case   9: return 'Tab'
        case  12: return 'Center'
        case  13: return 'Enter'
        case  16: return 'Shift'
        case  17: return 'Control'
        case  18: return 'Alt'
        case  19: return 'Pause'
        case  20: return 'Capslock'
        case  27: return 'Esc'
        case  33: return 'PgUp'
        case  34: return 'PgDn'
        case  35: return 'End'
        case  36: return 'Home'
        case  37: return 'left'
        case  38: return 'Up'
```

```
    case  39: return 'Right'
    case  40: return 'Down'
    case  45: return 'Ins'
    case  46: return 'Del'
    case  91: return 'Windows'
    case  93: return 'Menu'
    case 144: return 'Numlock'
  }

  return c
}
```

RECIPE 7

GetLastKey( )

This recipe returns the value of whatever the last keypress was and then resets the stored value to the empty string to show that the key value has been retrieved. Figure 13-7 shows a simple input function created using this recipe.

About the Recipe

This recipe doesn't take any arguments and returns the value of the most recently pressed key (if any).

Variables, Arrays, and Functions

k	Local string variable that holds the value of KEY_PRESS before resetting it and returning k

How It Works

This recipe assigns the value in KEY_PRESS, the global variable that contains the last key pressed, to the local variable k. Then, it resets KEY_PRESS to the empty string to show that the value has been read. Finally, the contents of k are returned. If there was no keypress, the empty string is returned.

How to Use It

To use this recipe, call it with no arguments and it will return either a letter, number, punctuation symbol, or a special key name. If the key was none of these, then its code is returned.

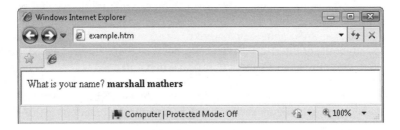

FIGURE 13-7   This recipe can build an input function.

You can use this recipe to create a very simple input function, like this:

```
What is your name? <b><span id='name'></span></b>

<script>
OnDOMReady(function()
{
   input('name')

   function input(id)
   {
      var interrupt = setInterval(simpleInterrupt, INTERVAL)

      function simpleInterrupt()
      {
         var k = GetLastKey()

         if (k == 'Enter')
         {
            k = '.'
            clearInterval(interrupt)
         }
         O(id).innerHTML += k
      }
   }
})
</script>
```

To make this work, a span is created in which the input will be placed. Then, the JavaScript code makes a call to a new function called `input()`, passing the ID of the span. The `input()` function then sets up a repeating interrupt using `setInterval()` to the subfunction `simpleInterrupt()`.

The `simpleInterrupt()` function then calls `GetLastKey()` each time it is called. If the value is ever 'Enter', it means the user has pressed the ENTER key and `k` is assigned the value '.' (a period), and the interrupt is disabled using `clearInterval()`, with the interrupt ID previously assigned to `interrupt`.

Finally, the `innerHTML` property of the object indicated by `id` has the latest key value returned appended to it. If the value is the empty string, then nothing is appended.

All your code has to do then is look at the end of the string to see if it is the period character to indicate that the user has pressed ENTER. Your code then removes that character and uses the remainder of the string. Alternatively, you can use a different end of input marker. Whatever you do, if you want to create your own input routine rather than use a ready-made one such as an `<input type='text'>` tag, you have to go through all these swings and roundabouts of interrupt driven calls, because that's the way JavaScript works. However, at least you now have a way of doing so when you need it.

For a bit of fun, if you store the input somewhere hidden rather than in a span, you can check for a sequence of characters to be entered—much like entering cheat codes into a game—and if a recognizable sequence is entered, you can trigger a bonus feature.

The Recipe

```
function GetLastKey()
{
   var k = KEY_PRESS
   KEY_PRESS = ''
   return k
}
```

PreventAction()

This recipe is for preventing an object's drag or select event (or both) from occurring. For example, sometimes you may wish to prevent a section of text from being copied, or at least from being highlighted, and you can easily do that with this recipe. Figure 13-8 shows one section of text that is being selected, while the second sentence is not selectable. The GIF image is also undraggable.

About the Recipe

This recipe takes three arguments and, depending on their values, either prevents or enables certain events to occur. The arguments are as follows:

- **id**   The ID of an object, such as a div or span section of HTML, a GIF image, or any other object.

- **type**   This argument can have one of three string values: 'drag', 'select', or 'both'. If the value is 'drag', then the object referred to by id will either be prevented from being dragged or allowed to be dragged, depending on the value of onoff. If it is 'select', then the selection of text will be either prevented or allowed, depending on the value of onoff. If it is 'both', then both these events will be either prevented or allowed.

- **onoff**   This argument should be either true or false; alternatively, the values 1 or 0 are acceptable. The values true or 1 mean the event (or events) in the variable type are prevented. If onoff is false or 0, then the event (or events) are allowed.

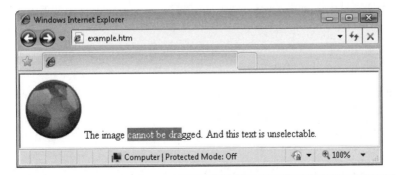

FIGURE 13-8   The image and the second sentence cannot be dragged or selected.

Variables, Arrays, and Functions

ondragstart	Event of the object passed in id
onselectstart	Event of the object passed in id
onmousedown	Event of the object passed in id
MozUserSelect	Property of the object passed in id (only used by Mozilla-based browsers such as Firefox)

How It Works

The recipe code is divided into two main sections. In the first, the drag event of the object referenced by id is managed, while the second half is for handling the id object's select event. Each of these halves is again split into two parts. In the first half of each, the events it handles are prevented, while the second half is for re-enabling an event after it has been disabled.

To provide these features, if the browser supports it, either the ondragstart or onselectstart event of the object in id (or both events if the value in type is 'both') is assigned an inline anonymous function that returns the value false, which has the effect of canceling any further action.

If the event is not recognized, then the onmousedown event for the object in id is caught and set to return false. This is not that great a solution because it prevents other onmousedown events from being attached, but it does have the effect of preventing the event from occurring.

In the case of Mozilla-based browsers such as Firefox, the special property MozUserSelect is set to either 'none' to prevent text from being selected, or 'text' to re-enable it. This is necessary because these browsers will not use the onselectstart event, and using this property is less intrusive than capturing the onmousedown event.

How to Use It

To prevent the copying and pasting of the contents of a div, for example, you can attach this function to its onselectstart event, like this:

```
PreventAction('mydiv', 'select', true)
```

If a user tries to select any text, this recipe stops the event before it can get going. This is not merely a relatively easy way to prevent people from copying text from your web pages; it also helps prevent text from being inadvertently highlighted when you are using the mouse to drag items about.

You can also use it to prevent an object from being dragged in the browser or dragged and dropped elsewhere, like this:

```
PreventAction('mygif', 'drag', true)
```

Here's some code that illustrates both of these uses:

```
<img id='gif' src='i1.gif' />
The image cannot be dragged.
<span id='text'>And this text is unselectable</span>
```

```
<script>
OnDOMReady(function()
{
   PreventAction('gif',  'drag',   true)
   PreventAction('text', 'select', true)
})
</script>
```

In the HTML section of the example, a GIF image with the name *i1.gif* is displayed and given the ID of 'gif'. This is followed by some regular text and a span with the ID of 'text'.

Below that, in the <script> section, the GIF image has its drag property disabled, and the span text is made unselectable. If you try either of these actions, they will fail. However, Internet Explorer will allow you to continue the selection within the span if you commence a select action from outside the span. You can work around this bug by setting the whole document as unselectable, like this:

```
PreventAction(document.body, 'select', true)
```

However, this means that nothing at all on your web page can be selected. Other browsers do not have this bug.

The Recipe

```
function PreventAction(id, type, onoff)
{
   if (type == 'drag' || type == 'both')
   {
      if (onoff == true)
      {
         if (typeof O(id).ondragstart != UNDEF)
            O(id).ondragstart   = function() { return false }
         else O(id).onmousedown = function() { return false }
      }
      else
      {
         if (typeof O(id).ondragstart != UNDEF)
             O(id).ondragstart = ''
         else O(id).onmousedown = ''
      }
   }

   if (type == 'select' || type == 'both')
   {
      if (onoff == true)
      {
         if (typeof O(id).onselectstart != UNDEF)
            O(id).onselectstart = function() { return false }
         else if (typeof S(id).MozUserSelect != UNDEF)
            S(id).MozUserSelect = 'none'
         else O(id).onmousedown = function() { return false }
      }
      else
      {
         if (typeof O(id).onselectstart != UNDEF)
```

```
            O(id).onselectstart = ''
        else if (typeof S(id).MozUserSelect != UNDEF)
            S(id).MozUserSelect = 'text'
        else O(id).onmousedown = ''
    }
  }
}
```

NoPx() and Px()

These recipes are short but powerful functions that provide inverse functionality to each other. NoPx() removes the 'px' suffix attached to some CSS properties, while Px() attaches the 'px' suffix to a property. Figure 13-9 shows the recipes in use.

About the Recipes

These recipes require an object's property to be passed to them. If NoPx() is passed a value, then the value returned will be that of the value less any 'px' suffix. If Px() is called, then the value returned is that of the value passed to the recipe, combined with the suffix 'px'. In no case is any property actually changed by these recipes, as values are merely derived based on the properties, and it is up to you to use them as required. The recipes require the following argument:

- **value**   The property to be modified.

Variables, Arrays, and Functions

replace()	JavaScript function for replacing a subsection of a string

How They Work

The NoPx() function uses the JavaScript replace() function to replace any occurrences of 'px' in the string it is passed, and then returns the result, multiplied by 1 to ensure it is turned from a string into a number.

The Px() function adds the suffix 'px' to any value it is passed and then returns the result.

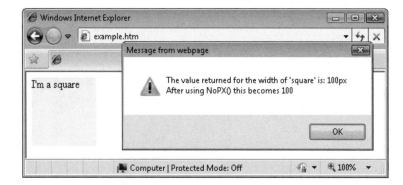

FIGURE 13-9   These recipes make it easier to work in values of pixels.

How to Use Them

The NoPx() function is very simple in that all it does is replace the substring 'px' (if found) with the empty string in any string it is passed. Thus, it can strip away the trailing 'px' suffix that many object properties have. For example, the style.marginLeft property is just one of many that may end in 'px', so the following call will strip it out:

```
value = NoPx(S(id).marginLeft)
```

In this example, the object referred to by id is passed to the S() function, which returns the style subobject. The marginLeft property is then appended to this and the resulting string value. This could be '10px', for example, which is then passed to the NoPx() function. In this case, it would return the number 10, which is then assigned to the variable value.

The Px() function performs the inverse, adding the 'px' suffix to a value. This is useful when you need to assign 'px' to an object's property that needs to know you are working in pixels. For example, the style.width property can be used to set the width of an object, but it needs to have 'px' added to it if working in pixels. To save you having to do this, you can make the following call instead:

```
S(id).left = Px(135)
```

This command uses the S() function to set the width of the object referred to by id to 135 pixels, since Px(135) evaluates to the string '135px'.

Here's an example of how you might use these recipes:

```
<div id='square'>I'm a square</div>

<script>
OnDOMReady(function()
{
    S('square').width           = Px(100)
    S('square').height          = Px(100)
    S('square').backgroundColor = 'yellow'

    alert("The value returned for the width of 'square' is: "   +
        S('square').width + '\nAfter using NoPX() this becomes ' +
        NoPx(S('square').width))
})
</script>
```

The HTML section contains a single div element with some text. In the <script> section, the div is resized to become 100 pixels wide by 100 high, using the Px() function to create the values. The background is also set to yellow so you can see the square.

After this, there's a call to the JavaScript alert() function in which the value of the object's width style property is displayed ('100px'), and that value is passed through the NoPx() function and redisplayed. This time it's the number 100.

The Recipes

```
function NoPx(value)
{
    return value.replace(/px/, '') * 1
}
```

```
function Px(value)
{
    return value + 'px'
}
```

X() and Y()

This pair of similar functions returns an object's exact horizontal or vertical offset from the left or top of the browser. The recipe names are so short because they are used very frequently and it saves on typing. This also makes your source code easier to follow. In Figure 13-10, you can see that the left and top edges of the div are inset from the browser edge by 8 pixels.

About the Recipes

These recipes return the absolute horizontal or vertical offsets of an object from the left or top of the browser window. They take this argument:

- **id**   The object whose offset is to be returned.

Variables, Arrays, and Functions

obj	Local object copy of the id object
offset	Local integer used to hold the horizontal or vertical offset
offsetParent	The parent offset object
offsetLeft	The object's left offset
offsetTop	The object's top offset

How They Work

These recipes first make a copy of the object represented by id in obj and set the local variable offset to either the offsetLeft or offsetTop property of the object. This is the amount by which the object is offset from its parent.

FIGURE 13-10   Looking up the absolute horizontal and vertical offsets of an object

Then, in case the parent object is also a subobject, the `if()` and `while()` statements recurse back through all parent objects, adding their offsets in turn to `offset`, until there are no more parent objects. At this point, `offset` contains the absolute distance in pixels from the left side or top edge of the browser window to the left or top of the object. This value is then returned.

How to Use Them

To use these recipes, pass the ID of an object to them and they will return either the absolute horizontal or absolute vertical position of its left side or top edge in pixels. Here's some code to illustrate their use:

```
<div id='square'>I'm a square</div>

<script>
OnDOMReady(function()
{
    S('square').width          = Px(100)
    S('square').height         = Px(100)
    S('square').backgroundColor = 'yellow'
    alert("The object 'square' is at position " +
        X('square') + ',' + Y('square'))
})
</script>
```

This example is similar to the previous one in that it creates a square div with the ID of square, but in this example the object's absolute left and top offsets are returned by the `alert()` statement, with calls to `X()` and `Y()`.

The Recipes

```
function X(id)
{
    var obj    = O(id)
    var offset = obj.offsetLeft

    if (obj.offsetParent)
        while(obj = obj.offsetParent)
            offset += obj.offsetLeft

    return offset
}


function Y(id)
{
    var obj    = O(id)
    var offset = obj.offsetTop

    if (obj.offsetParent)
        while(obj = obj.offsetParent)
            offset += obj.offsetTop

    return offset
}
```

W() and H()

In addition to needing to know the location of an object, as in the previous pair of recipes, you often need to know their width and height, which you can determine with these functions. Figure 13-11 shows the recipes being used to discover an object's width and height.

About the Recipes

These recipes return an object's exact width or height, including any margins and borders. They require the following argument:

- **id** The object whose dimensions are to be returned.

Variables, Arrays, and Functions

offsetWidth	The object's width
offsetHeight	The object's height
marginLeft	The object's left margin width
marginRight	The objects' right margin width
marginTop	The object's top margin width
marginBottom	The object's bottom margin width
borderLeft	The object's left border width
borderRight	The object's right border width
borderTopWidth	The object's top border width
borderBottomWidth	The object's bottom border width
border	The image object's border property
NoPx()	Function to remove 'px' suffixes

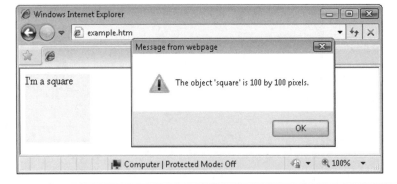

FIGURE 13-11   Determining the width and height of an object

How They Work

Each function adds together all the properties that affect either an object's width or its height. To return the width of an object, its `offsetWidth` is added to its `marginLeft` and `marginRight` properties, like this:

```
var width = O(id).offsetWidth +
            NoPx(S(id).marginLeft) +
            NoPx(S(id).marginRight)
```

Next, a check is made of its `borderLeftWidth` and `borderRightWidth` properties by adding the two values together to obtain their sum. If the result is greater than 0, then that amount is placed in the variable `bord`. Here is that code section:

```
var bord = NoPx(S(id).borderLeftWidth) +
           NoPx(S(id).borderRightWidth)
```

Next, because an object's border style property overrides an image's border property (even though the border image property retains its value), if `bord` has a value it is subtracted from the value to be returned. If it doesn't have a value, then the object's image border property value, multiplied by two (once for the left and once for the right border), is subtracted from the value to be returned. This is because the `offsetWidth` property already includes the widths of any borders, so they are taken off so as to return only the object and its margin's width. Here is the code for this section:

```
if (bord > 0)            width -= bord
else  if (O(id).border) width -= O(id).border * 2
return width
```

An object's padding width is not returned because none of the recipes need to know this value.

To return the height of an object, the same process is used in the `H()` recipe, with the properties `offsetHeight`, `marginTop`, `marginBottom`, `borderTopWidth`, `borderBottomWidth`, and `border`.

In either case, the calculated value is returned.

CAUTION *If you add together the H() heights of two vertically adjacent boxes (perhaps in order to specify the height of a containing div), and if there are margins, the calculated height will be greater than the height the browser actually uses to render both boxes on top of each other, due to vertical margin collapsing where only the largest of the two margins is used.*

How to Use Them

To use these recipes, pass them the ID of an object whose dimensions you need. Here's some code showing how you might use them:

```
<div id='square'>I'm a square</div>

<script>
OnDOMReady(function()
{
```

```
    S('square').width      = Px(100)
    S('square').height     = Px(100)
    S('square').background = 'yellow'

    alert("The object 'square' is " +
        W('square') + ' by ' + H('square') + ' pixels.')
})
</script>
```

This example is quite similar to previous ones in that the div called 'square' is created in the HTML section. The difference here is that the `alert()` function displays the width and height of the object using the `W()` and `H()` recipes.

NOTE *You may find it interesting to note the use of all the S(), W(), H(), and NoPx() recipes here. Already you can see how these recipes are coming together to make your programming much easier. Without the earlier functions to build on, these recipes might be two or three times the size, but this way they only use a handful of characters, such as W('obj'). Once you get a little further into this section, even more powerful functions will become available to you that would take dozens, if not hundreds, of lines of code to write from scratch.*

The Recipes

```
function W(id)
{
    var width   = O(id).offsetWidth +
                  NoPx(S(id).marginLeft) +
                  NoPx(S(id).marginRight)

    var bord    = NoPx(S(id).borderLeftWidth) +
                  NoPx(S(id).borderRightWidth)

    if (bord > 0)          width -= bord
    else if (O(id).border) width -= O(id).border * 2

    return width
}


function H(id)
{
    var height  = O(id).offsetHeight +
                  NoPx(S(id).marginTop) +
                  NoPx(S(id).marginBottom)

    var bord    = NoPx(S(id).borderTopWidth) +
                  NoPx(S(id).borderBottomWidth)

    if (bord > 0)           height -= bord
    else if(O(id).border)  height -= O(id).border * 2

    return height
}
```

Html()

Because you will frequently find yourself needing to write to the innerHTML property of objects, I wrote this simple recipe to keep the code short and improve its readability, as shown in Figure 13-12.

About the Recipe

This recipe returns the innerHTML property of the object it is passed. You can use it to either read or write this property. Only the first argument is required to read a value, but both are required to write one:

- **id** The ID of the object with the innerHTML property to access.
- **value** The value to assign to the innerHTML property.

Variables, Arrays, and Functions

innerHTML	The property containing the HTML text of an object

How It Works

To read a value, the recipe uses the O() recipe to reference the object in id and return its innerHTML property. To write a value, you pass a second argument, value, to the recipe. If the code notices that this argument has been passed, the innerHTML property of id is changed to value. In either case, the value of the innerHTML property is returned.

How to Use It

You can either read or write to the innerHTML property of an object that supports it using this function. To write to it, use a statement such as this:

```
Html('mydiv', 'This is some new text')
```

To read from the property, use a statement like this:

```
var contents = Html('mydiv')
```

Figure 13-12 This recipe makes it easy to read and write the HTML contents of an object.

Here's some code that uses a couple of `alert()` calls so you can see the before and after effects of using the recipe:

```
<div id='heading'><h1>This is a heading</h1></div>

<script>
OnDOMReady(function()
{
   alert(Html('heading'))
   Html('heading', '<h2>This is a subheading</h2>')
   alert(Html('heading'))
})
</script>
```

The first section of HTML creates a div with an `<h1>` heading. Then, the `<script>` section immediately pops up an alert showing this value by using a call to `Html()`. After that, the value of the object's `innerHTML` property is changed to a subheading, again using `Html()`, and then a second call to the JavaScript `alert()` function redisplays the property, using the `Html()` function—at which time you will see that the contents have changed.

The Recipe

```
function Html(id, value)
{
   if (typeof value != UNDEF)
      O(id).innerHTML = value
   return O(id).innerHTML
}
```

SaveState()

After you change the properties for an object, there are times when you might want to restore it to its original state. This recipe allows you to back up all the most important style properties of an object. Figure 13-13 shows a div being prepared with a few values prior to testing the `SaveState()` recipe.

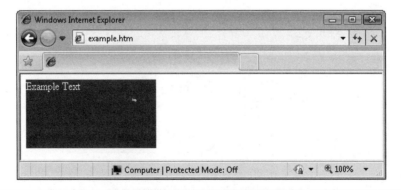

FIGURE 13-13 Creating a div with which to test saving and restoring states

About the Recipe

This recipe backs up several of the most important style properties of an object, where they can be later retrieved should you need them. It takes the following argument:

- **id** The object whose properties are to be backed up.

Variables, Arrays, and Functions

`left`	The object's `style.left` property
`top`	The object's `style.top` property
`visibility`	The object's `style.visibility` property
`color`	The object's `style.color` property
`background`	The object's `style.background` property
`display`	The object's `style.display` property
`opacity`	The object's `style.opacity` property
`MozOpacity`	The object's `style.MozOpacity` property
`KhtmlOpacity`	The object's `style.KhtmlOpacity` property
`filter`	The object's `style.filter` property
`zIndex`	The object's `style.zIndex` property

How It Works

This is a very simple recipe that creates backup properties for each of the properties. Each new backup property name begins with the string "Save_" and ends with the original property name. The ones you may not know are `MozOpacity`, which is the opacity property used by Mozilla-based browsers such as Firefox, and `KhtmlOpacity`, which is used by older versions of the Apple Safari browser.

How to Use It

To create a set of backup properties for an object, pass its ID to the `SaveState()` recipe, like this:

```
SaveState('myobject')
```

The following code shows a few style settings being made to an object and then its state being saved:

```
<div id='mydiv'>Example Text</div>

<script>
OnDOMReady(function()
{
    S('mydiv').width      = Px(200)
    S('mydiv').height     = Px(100)
    S('mydiv').background = 'green'
```

```
    S('mydiv').color      = 'white'
    S('mydiv').position   = 'absolute'

    SaveState('mydiv')
})
</script>
```

This creates a green, 200 × 100–pixel rectangle with white text whose position is absolute (and the object is therefore movable). In the next recipe, you'll see what happens if these values are changed and the saved state is restored.

The Recipe

```
function SaveState(id)
{
    O(id).Save_left        = S(id).left
    O(id).Save_top         = S(id).top
    O(id).Save_visibility  = S(id).visibility
    O(id).Save_color       = S(id).color
    O(id).Save_background   = S(id).background
    O(id).Save_display     = S(id).display
    O(id).Save_opacity     = S(id).opacity
    O(id).Save_MozOpacity  = S(id).MozOpacity
    O(id).Save_KhtmlOpacity = S(id).KhtmlOpacity
    O(id).Save_filter      = S(id).filter
    O(id).Save_zIndex      = S(id).zIndex
}
```

RECIPE 14 RestoreState()

This is the partner recipe for `SaveState()`. It will restore an object's major style settings to the way they were when they were saved. Figure 13-14 shows that the div created in the previous recipe has been modified; its colors are different and it has been moved to the right. An alert box has popped up to let you see this before the `RestoreState()` recipe is called to restore the div to its original state.

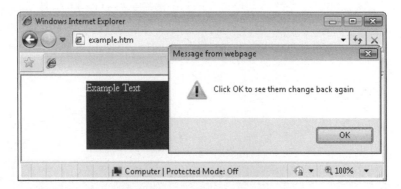

FIGURE 13-14   The SaveState() and RestoreState() recipes in action

About the Recipe

This recipe restores the style properties that have been saved using the `SaveState()` recipe. It takes this argument:

- **id**   The object whose style properties are to be restored.

Variables, Arrays, and Functions

left	The object's `style.left` property
top	The object's `style.top` property
visibility	The object's `style.visibility` property
color	The object's `style.color` property
backgroundColor	The object's `style.backgroundColor` property
display	The object's `style.display` property
opacity	The object's `style.opacity` property
MozOpacity	The object's `style.MozOpacity` property
KhtmlOpacity	The object's `style.KhtmlOpacity` property
filter	The object's `style.filter` property
zIndex	The object's `style.zIndex` property

How It Works

This recipe reverses the action of the `SaveState()` recipe by retrieving the values saved in the properties, beginning with the string 'Save_', and restoring them. If there are any additional properties you need to save and restore, they are very easy to add to these functions.

How to Use It

To use it, just pass this recipe the ID of an object whose state has already been saved, like this:

```
RestoreState('myobject')
```

The following example extends the previous recipe to both create a div and then change it twice, the first time by modifying a few of its style properties, and the second by changing it back by calling `RestoreState()`. In between, the JavaScript `alert()` function is called to give you a chance to view the screen before moving on:

```
<div id='mydiv'>Example Text</div>

<script>
OnDOMReady(function()
{
    S('mydiv').width      = Px(200)
    S('mydiv').height     = Px(100)
    S('mydiv').background = 'green'
    S('mydiv').color      = 'white'
    S('mydiv').position   = 'absolute'
```

```
    SaveState('mydiv')

    alert('Click OK to see some changes')

    S('mydiv').background = 'blue'
    S('mydiv').color      = 'yellow'
    S('mydiv').left       = Px(100)

    alert('Click OK to see them change back again')

    RestoreState('mydiv')
})
</script>
```

If you enter this example into your browser, the div will start off as white text on green, then it will change to yellow on blue and move to the right, and finally it will return to its original colors and position, all with a single call to RestoreState().

The Recipe

```
function RestoreState(id)
{
    S(id).left        = O(id).Save_left
    S(id).top         = O(id).Save_top
    S(id).visibility  = O(id).Save_visibility
    S(id).color       = O(id).Save_color
    S(id).background  = O(id).Save_background
    S(id).display     = O(id).Save_display
    S(id).opacity     = O(id).Save_opacity
    S(id).MozOpacity  = O(id).Save_MozOpacity
    S(id).KhtmlOpacity = O(id).Save_KhtmlOpacity
    S(id).filter      = O(id).Save_filter
    S(id).zIndex      = O(id).Save_zIndex
}
```

InsVars()

In JavaScript, when you want to create a string of text that also includes the values of different variables, you have to keep closing the string, then use a + sign followed by the variable name, follow it with another +, and then re-open the string—and you have to do this for every single variable. However, this recipe lets you easily drop the values of variables into any string. Figure 13-15 shows three values being inserted in this manner.

About the Recipe

This recipe requires at least two arguments. The first is the string in which to insert various values, and the second, third, and so on are the values to be inserted, as follows:

- **string**   The string in which to insert values.
- **value1**   A value to insert in string.
- **value2**   As value1 (etc...).

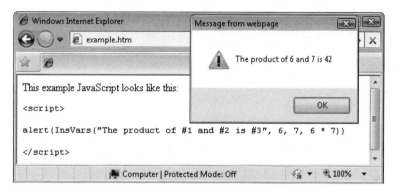

FIGURE 13-15 This recipe makes it easy to insert values into strings.

Variables, Arrays, and Functions

tmp	Local variable containing the string to process
arguments	Array of arguments passed to the recipe
replace()	JavaScript function to replace substrings in a string
regExp()	JavaScript function to create a regular expression

How It Works

This recipe makes use of the handy fact that JavaScript passes an array to every function that is called. This array is called arguments, and each element of it is one of the values that has been passed to the function.

Therefore, the first element is extracted and placed in tmp, a local variable. This is the string in which to make the variable substitutions, like this:

```
var tmp = arguments[0]
```

Then, a for() loop is used to iterate through each remaining element. If there is a substring with the value '#1' within the string tmp, the first value is inserted in its place. The same happens for '#2', '#3', and any number of similar substrings, with each being replaced by the next in line of the values passed to the recipe, like this:

```
tmp = tmp.replace(new RegExp('#' + j, 'g'), arguments[j])
```

To allow one value to be inserted in many places in a string, a global replace is enabled by using the RegExp() object to create a new regular expression, with the value 'g' supplied to indicate a global search and/or replace.

Finally, the modified tmp string is returned.

How to Use It

To insert values into a string using InsVars(), call it up in the following manner:

```
string = InsVars('The product of #1 and #2 is #3', 6, 7, 6 * 7)
```

This statement will assign the value "The product of 6 and 7 is 42" to string. All you have to remember is to use the same number of '#?' tokens as there are values to be inserted.

The Recipe

```
function InsVars()
{
   var tmp = arguments[0]

   for (var j = 1 ; j < arguments.length ; ++j)
      tmp = tmp.replace(new RegExp('#' + j, 'g'), arguments[j])
   return tmp
}
```

 ## StrRepeat()

Unlike many other languages, JavaScript doesn't come with a function to create a new string from a repeated substring. So here's a recipe to do the job, as shown in Figure 13-16, in which a cheer is repeated three times.

About the Recipe

This recipe creates a repeated string based on a string and a number. It takes these arguments:

- **str**   A string to repeat.
- **num**   The number of times to repeat the string.

Variables, Arrays, and Functions

tmp	Local string variable used to store the string as it is assembled
j	Local integer variable used for looping

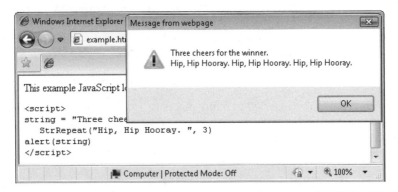

FIGURE 13-16   Using this recipe to create a cheer

How It Works

The recipe uses a `for()` loop to assemble a final string created from num copies of `str`. It then returns the new string.

How to Use It

To use this function, pass it a string and a number, like this:

```
string = 'Three cheers for the winner. ' +
   StrRepeat('Hip, Hip Hooray', 3)
alert(string)
```

This code places the repeated cheer into string and then displays it using a call to the JavaScript `alert()` function.

The Recipe

```
function StrRepeat(str, num)
{
   var tmp = ''

   for (var j = 0 ; j < num ; ++j)
      tmp += str

   return tmp
}
```

RECIPE 17 HexDec()

The final two recipes in this chapter concern handling hexadecimal numbers, something you have to do quite often in JavaScript, particularly when managing colors. This one converts a hexadecimal number into decimal, as shown in Figure 13-17.

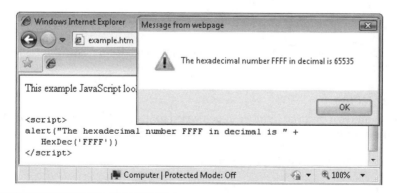

FIGURE 13-17   Converting a number from hexadecimal to decimal

About the Recipe

This recipe requires a hexadecimal string to be passed to it. It then returns that number in decimal. It requires this argument:

- **n** A string containing a hexadecimal number.

Variables, Arrays, and Functions

parseInt()	JavaScript function to convert a string to a number

How It Works

This recipe uses the JavaScript function parseInt() to convert a hexadecimal string to a decimal number. It does this because the second parameter passed to it is 16. If the second number was 8, for example, it would try to convert it from an octal number, and so on.

How to Use It

Pass the HexDec() function any string containing a hexadecimal number and it will return a decimal number, like this:

```
alert('The hexadecimal number FFFF in decimal is ' +
    HexDec('FFFF'))
```

In this instance the hexadecimal number FFFF is converted to 65,535 in decimal, and the result is displayed using a call to the JavaScript alert() function.

The Recipe

```
function HexDec(n)
{
    return(parseInt(n, 16))
}
```

DecHex()

This recipe takes a decimal number and turns it into a hexadecimal string, as shown in Figure 13-18.

About the Recipe

This recipe requires a decimal number to be passed to it, and then returns that number in the form of a hexadecimal string. It requires this argument:

- **n** A decimal number to be converted into hexadecimal.

Variables, Arrays, and Functions

to.String()	JavaScript function for converting a number to a string

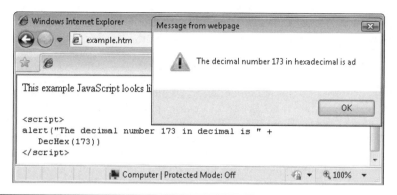

FIGURE 13-18   Converting a number from decimal to hexadecimal

How It Works

This recipe uses two code segments combined into a single statement. The first segment looks like this:

```
n < 16 ? '0' : ''
```

This is known as a ternary expression, in which n < 16 is an initial test. The ? symbol indicates that if the result of the test is true, the value immediately following the ? should be returned. Otherwise, the value following the : should be returned. In this example, that means that values of n that are lower than 16 will result in the string '0' being returned, while values of n that are 16 and above result in ' ' being returned.

The reason for this is that this recipe will mostly be used by code that wants to create color triplets for setting a color. These triplets are made up of three groups of two hexadecimal characters, like these: FF0088, 112233, CCCCCC, and so on.

Each of these stands for hexadecimal FF (256 decimal) shades of the colors red, green, and blue. For example, FF0088 means the intensity values for the given color should be FF red, 00 green, and 88 blue in hexadecimal. Therefore, going back to the code segment, if n is less than 16, it becomes a single digit in hexadecimal (a number between 0 and F), and in such cases a leading 0 is added to pad the number up to the required two digits.

Having padded the number with a 0 (if necessary), the number n is then passed to the JavaScript `toString()` function with an argument of 16, like this code segment:

```
n.toString(16)
```

This tells it to convert the number to base 16, which is hexadecimal. The results of the two segments are then concatenated and returned. When you put both pieces of code together, they look like this:

```
return (n < 16 ? '0' : '') + n.toString(16)
```

How to Use It

To convert a decimal number to hexadecimal, pass it to the DecHex() recipe, like this:

```
alert('The decimal number 173 in hexadecimal is ' + DecHex(173))
```

The value displayed by this statement is 'ad', which is an acceptable hexadecimal number for JavaScript when used as part of a color, so there's usually no need to convert it to uppercase or add any prefix to it.

This now completes the fundamentals of your basic JavaScript toolkit and, by necessity, it's one of the longest chapters in the book. In the next chapter, we'll start adding recipes to provide location and positioning features, and then the fun will really start.

The Recipe

```
function DecHex(n)
{
    return (n < 16 ? '0' : '') + n.toString(16)
}
```

CHAPTER 14

Location and Dimensions

The previous chapter concentrated on providing a basic subset of core JavaScript functionality. This one does the same, but there are enough recipes in the collection now that we can also start to create some interesting effects, including resizing and repositioning objects.

ResizeWidth()

When creating dynamic web pages, you will often need to change the dimensions of objects. You might do this to emphasize a section by enlarging it, you may allow the contents of a page to be rearranged by the user, or you might wish to open up elements such as forms or light boxes, and so forth.

With this recipe, you can resize the width of any object that has a `width` property, such as the example div shown in Figure 14-1, which has had its width resized to 300 pixels.

About the Recipe

This recipe changes the width of an object. It requires the following arguments:

- **id**   The ID of an object or the object itself. You can also pass an array of objects and/or object IDs.

- **width**   The new width for the object. If `id` is an array, all the objects referred to are set to this width.

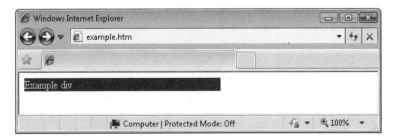

FIGURE 14-1   Resizing the width of an object

Variables, Arrays, and Functions

j	Local integer loop variable
overflow	The object's `style.overflow` property
width	The object's `style.width` property
HID	Global string variable with the value 'hidden'
Px()	Function to add the suffix 'px'

How It Works

This recipe also offers the multifunctionality of the `O()` and `S()` recipes, in which you can pass either the ID of an object or the object itself, and you can even pass an array of IDs and/or objects to change them all at the same time.

It achieves this by taking advantage of the fact that the `S()` recipe is already set up to deal with an object ID, an object, or an array of objects and/or object IDs. Therefore, all that is necessary is to call `S()` twice; once to set the object's or array of objects' `style.overflow` properties to 'hidden', and then to set the `style.width` properties to the value in `width`.

The variable `Hid` is a global variable created by the `Initialize()` recipe, and it has the value 'hidden'. The `style.overflow` property of the object is set to this value to allow objects to be reduced as well as enlarged, and when reduced, text that would have overflowed is simply ignored.

How to Use It

To use this recipe, pass it an object and a width, like this:

```
ResizeWidth('mydiv', 200)
```

Or you can pass an array of objects, like this:

```
ids = Array('objone', 'objtwo', 'objthree')
ResizeWidth(ids, 480)
```

Here's an example you can try that resets the width of the div to 300 pixels. It also changes the text and background colors so you can see the change:

```
<div id='example'>Example div</div>

<script>
OnDOMReady(function()
{
   S('example').background = 'blue'
   S('example').color      = 'yellow'
   ResizeWidth('example', 300)
})
</script>
```

The Recipe

```
function ResizeWidth(id, width)
{
   S(id, 'overflow', HID)
   S(id, 'width',    Px(width))
}
```

ResizeHeight()

In the same way that you may need to resize the width of an object, there's a recipe to resize its height. Figure 14-2 shows the div created in the previous recipe, now increased in height to 100 pixels.

About the Recipe

This recipe changes the height of an object. It requires the following arguments:

- **id**   The ID of an object or the object itself. You can also pass an array of objects and/or object IDs.
- **height**   The new height for the object. If id is an array, all the objects referred to are set to this height.

Variables, Arrays, and Functions

j	Local integer loop variable
overflow	The object's style.overflow property
height	The object's style.height property
HID	Global string variable with the value 'hidden'
Px()	Function to add the suffix 'px'

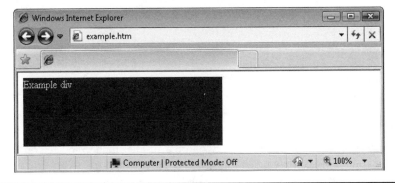

FIGURE 14-2   Resizing the height of an object

How It Works

This is the companion recipe to ResizeWidth(), and it works in exactly the same manner as the previous one, with the only difference being that the object's style.height property is modified instead of style.width.

As with ResizeWidth(), you can pass either object IDs or objects, and you can also pass an array of IDs and/or objects. For further details on how this recipe works, please refer to the ResizeWidth() recipe.

How to Use It

To use this recipe, pass it an object and a height, like this:

```
ResizeHeight('mydiv', 100)
```

Or you can pass an array of objects, like this:

```
ids = Array('objone', 'objtwo', 'objthree')
ResizeHeight(ids, 240)
```

Here's an example you can try that modifies the example in the previous recipe by resizing the div to 100 pixels in height:

```
<div id='example'>Example div</div>

<script>
OnDOMReady(function()
{
    S('example').background = 'blue'
    S('example').color      = 'yellow'
    ResizeWidth('example',  300)
    ResizeHeight('example', 100)
}
</script>
```

The Recipe

```
function ResizeHeight(id, height)
{
    S(id, 'overflow', HID)
    S(id, 'height',   Px(height))
}
```

Resize()

This simple recipe combines the previous two into a single function to save on typing and to make your code more compact. With it, you can change both the width and height of an object or array of objects, as shown in Figure 14-3.

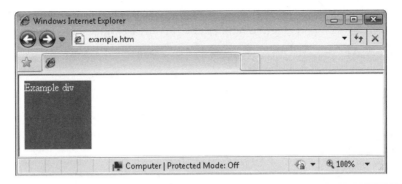

FIGURE 14-3   Resizing both the width and the height of an object

About the Recipe

This recipe changes the width and height of an object. It requires the following arguments:

- **id**   The ID of an object or the object itself. You can also pass an array of objects and/or object IDs.
- **width**   The new width for the object. If id is an array, all the objects referred to are set to this width.
- **height**   The new height for the object. If id is an array, all the objects referred to are set to this height.

Variables, Arrays, and Functions

ResizeWidth()	Function to change an object's width
ResizeHeight()	Function to change an object's height

How It Works

This recipe simply makes a call to ResizeWidth() followed by one to ResizeHeight().

How to Use It

To use this recipe, pass it an object along with a width and height, like this:

```
Resize('mydiv', 100, 100)
```

Or you can pass an array of objects, like this:

```
ids = Array('obj1', 'obj2', 'obj3')
Resize (ids, 128, 128)
```

Here's an example you can try that further improves the example in the previous recipe to resize both the width and height of an object with only a single call:

```
<div id='example'>Example div</div>

<script>
OnDOMReady(function()
{
    S('example').background = 'red'
    S('example').color      = 'white'
    Resize('example', 100, 100)
})
</script>
```

The Recipe

```
function Resize(id, width, height)
{
    ResizeWidth(id,  width)
    ResizeHeight(id, height)
}
```

Position()

This recipe sets the CSS `style.position` property of an object. This is useful when you wish to control an object's offset from its parent's location, or even completely move it to any absolute position. Figure 14-4 shows a div that has been offset horizontally from its previous position by 100 pixels.

About the Recipe

This plug-in sets the CSS `style.position` property of an object. It requires the following arguments:

- **id**   An object, an object ID, or an array of objects and/or object IDs.
- **type**   The type of `style.position` property to assign, out of 'absolute', 'fixed', 'relative', 'static', or 'inherit'. You can also use the shorter, global variables (created by the `Initialize()` recipe) of ABS, FIX, REL, STA, and INH.

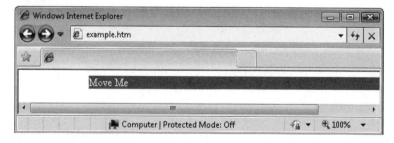

Figure 14-4   This recipe enables objects to be moved.

Variables, Arrays, and Functions

position	The object's `style.position` property

How It Works

This function uses the capability of the `S()` function that accepts an object, an object ID, or even an array of objects and/or object IDs. Therefore, it simply passes the values in `id` and `type` directly to the `S()` recipe.

How to Use It

To set an object's `style.position` property using this recipe, make a call such as:

```
Position('myobject', ABS)
```

For example, to change an object to have an 'absolute' position (using the shorter, global variable ABS created by the `Initialize()` recipe) and then move it, you could use code such as the following:

```
<div id='moveme'>Move Me</div>

<script>
OnDOMReady(function()
{
   S('moveme').background = 'red'
   S('moveme').color      = 'white'
   Position('moveme', REL)
   S('moveme').left        = Px(100)
})
</script>
```

This example creates a div called 'moveme', which is then set to white text on a red background, and then the `Position()` recipe is called to give it a 'relative' position. Finally, its `style.left` property is set to 100 using the `Px()` recipe, which offsets it horizontally from its parent object by 100 pixels.

CAUTION As well as the difference in location change between divs that use 'absolute' and 'relative' style positions, you also need to take into account the fact that a div with an 'absolute' style position is automatically shrunk to fit its contents, whereas one with a 'relative' style position will retain its previous width, which, by default, extends to the right-hand edge of its containing object. If you use a span instead, it will always shrink to fit its contents, regardless of where or how it is positioned.

The Recipe

```
function Position(id, type)
{
   S(id, 'position', type)
}
```

GoTo()

If an object has been set free from the page, for example, by using the previous recipe, Position(), you can move it to another location by changing its style.left and style.top properties. This recipe makes it quicker and easier by providing a single function to do so. In Figure 14-5, a div has been moved 200 pixels to the right and 25 pixels down.

About the Recipe

This recipe moves an object (if it is movable) to a new location. It takes the following arguments:

- **id**   An object, an object ID, or an array of objects and/or object IDs.
- **x**   The horizontal offset, from the left edge of the parent object, to which the object should be moved (or from the browser edge if the object has a style.position property of 'fixed' or 'absolute').
- **y**   The vertical offset, from the top edge of the parent object, to which the object should be moved (or from the browser top if the object has a style.position property of 'fixed' or 'absolute').

Variables, Arrays, and Functions

left	The object's style.left property
top	The object's style.top property
Px()	Function to add the suffix 'px'

How It Works

This recipe also takes advantage of the S() recipe's capability to manage arrays of objects and/or object IDs, single objects, or object IDs. It makes just two calls: one to set the object's style.left property to the value in x with the suffix 'px' appended, as is required by the rules of CSS, and the other to do the same but with the style.top property using the value in y.

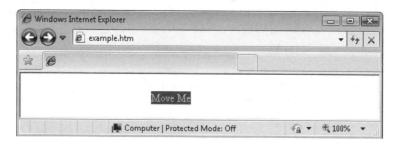

FIGURE 14-5   The GoTo() recipe moves an object.

How to Use It

To use this recipe, make sure that an object is movable by first issuing a command such as this (using the global variable REL, which contains the string 'relative'):

```
Position('advertdiv', REL)
```

The following example gives the div an 'absolute' position (using the global variable ABS) and then moves it:

```
<div id='moveme'>Move Me</div>

<script>
OnDOMReady(function()
{
    S('moveme').background = 'green'
    S('moveme').color      = 'cyan'
    Position('moveme', ABS)
    GoTo('moveme', 200, 25)
})
</script>
```

The Recipe

```
function GoTo(id, x, y)
{
    S(id, 'left', Px(x))
    S(id, 'top',  Px(y))
}
```

Locate()

This recipe combines the Position() and GoTo() recipes into a very handy single recipe that is especially useful when first setting up objects on a web page. With it, you can set an object's style.position property at the same time as its horizontal and vertical offsets. Figure 14-6 shows this recipe moving an object with an 'absolute' position to the location 100,40.

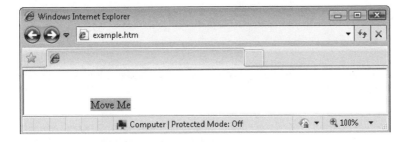

Figure 14-6   Setting an object's position and location at the same time

About the Recipe

This recipe sets an object's `style.position` property as well as its horizontal and vertical offsets. It requires the following arguments:

- **id**   An object, an object ID, or an array of objects and/or object IDs.
- **type**   The type of `style.position` property to assign, out of 'absolute', 'fixed', 'relative', 'static', or 'inherit' (or the global variables ABS, FIX, REL, STA, and INH).
- **x**   The horizontal offset, from the left edge of the parent object (or browser for 'fixed' objects), to which the object should be moved (or from the browser edge if the object has a `style.position` property of 'fixed' or 'absolute').
- **y**   The vertical offset, from the top edge of the parent object (or browser for 'fixed' objects), to which the object should be moved (or from the browser top if the object has a `style.position` property of 'fixed' or 'absolute').

Variables, Arrays, and Functions

Position()	Function to set an object's `style.position` property
GoTo()	Function to move an object to a new location

How It Works

This recipe draws on the functionality of the recipes `Position()` and `GoTo()`, which both allow an object, an object ID, or an array of objects and/or object IDs to be accessed. Therefore, it simply calls each in turn, passing the arguments id, style, x, and y, as necessary.

How to Use It

To set an object's `style.position` property and move it to its correct location using this recipe, you might use code such as the following:

```
<div id='moveme'>Move Me</div>

<script>
OnDOMReady(function()
{
   S('moveme').background = 'orange'
   S('moveme').color      = 'black'
   Locate('moveme', ABS, 100, 40)
})
</script>
```

In the preceding, you can see the `Locate()` recipe provides a wide range of functionality with a single call.

NOTE *The absolute position property is always made relative to the first parent element that has a position other than static. A relative position is relative to its containing object, and a fixed property is relative to the browser borders.*

The Recipe

```
function Locate(id, type, x, y)
{
    Position(id, type)
    GoTo(id, x, y)
}
```

 ## GetWindowWidth()

There are many reasons to need to know the width of the browser window, the most obvious of which is so you can determine which objects you can display (and where) in a dynamically generated web site. This recipe gives you that exact information, as shown by the alert box in Figure 14-7. It also takes into account any scroll bars that might reduce the available width.

About the Recipe

This function will tell you the width of the browser window to the nearest pixel. It doesn't require any arguments and returns the width as an integer.

Variables, Arrays, and Functions

de	Local object copy of `document.documentElement`
BROWSER	Global variable containing the browser name
barwidth	Local integer variable set if a vertical scroll bar exists
scrollHeight	The `de.scrollHeight` property
clientHeight	The `de.clientHeight` property
innerWidth	The `window.innerWidth` property
clientWidth	The `de.clientWidth` and `document.body.clientWidth` properties

FIGURE 14-7 Determining the available width of the browser window

How It Works

This recipe first copies the `document.documentElement` object into `de` to provide a much shorter name, reducing the amount of code to enter. Next, if the browser is not Internet Explorer (as determined by the value in the global variable `BROWSER`), then the local integer variable `barwidth` is set to a value of 17 if the value in `de.scrollHeight` is greater than that in `de.clientHeight`.

The `de.scrollHeight` value is bigger when there is more web page below the bottom that can be scrolled to. In that case, there will be a scroll bar, so `barwidth` is given the value of 17, which is the default width of scroll bars in all browsers. This value is then subtracted from the full window width and the result is returned.

Otherwise, as is often the case if the browser is Internet Explorer, the code simply returns the value of whichever has a value, either `de.clientWidth` or `document.body` `.clientWidth` (allowing for either strict or quirks mode). This value already takes into account any scroll bar, so no further code is required.

How to Use It

To use this recipe, simply call it and use the value returned, as in the following example, which passes the returned value to an `alert()` statement, where it is displayed:

```
<script>
OnDOMReady(function()
{
    alert('This browser has a window width of: ' + GetWindowWidth())
})
</script>
```

The Recipe

```
function GetWindowWidth()
{
    var de = document.documentElement

    if (BROWSER != 'IE')
    {
        var barwidth = de.scrollHeight > de.clientHeight ? 17 : 0
        return window.innerWidth - barwidth
    }

    return de.clientWidth || document.body.clientWidth
}
```

GetWindowHeight()

This is the companion recipe to `GetWindowWidth()`. It returns the height of the browser window, bearing in mind any scroll bars. In Figure 14-8, the height of the usable area of this browser has been determined by this recipe to be 124 pixels.

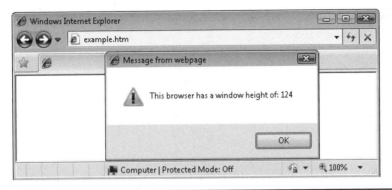

FIGURE 14-8   Determining the usable height of the current browser window

About the Recipe

This recipe takes no arguments and returns the available height of the current window, taking any scroll bars into account.

Variables, Arrays, and Functions

de	Local object copy of document.documentElement
BROWSER	Global variable containing the browser name
barwidth	Local integer variable set if a vertical scroll bar exists
scrollWidth	The de.scrollWidth property
clientWidth	The de.clientWidth property
innerHeight	The window.innerHeight property
clientHeight	The de.clientHeight and document.body.clientHeight properties

How It Works

This recipe works in almost the same way as GetWindowWidth() except that it returns the available height in the current browser window, taking any scroll bars into account. Please refer to GetWindowWidth() for further details.

How to Use It

To use this recipe, simply call it and use the value returned, as in the following example, which passes the returned value to an alert() statement, where it is displayed:

```
<script>
OnDOMReady(function()
{
   alert('This browser has a window height of: ' + GetWindowHeight())
})
</script>
```

Recipe 27 (following) is a good example of how this and the previous recipe, GetWindowWidth(), come in very handy.

The Recipe

```
function GetWindowHeight()
{
   var de = document.documentElement

   if (BROWSER != 'IE')
   {
      var barwidth = de.scrollWidth > de.clientWidth ? 17 : 0
      return window.innerHeight - barwidth
   }

   return de.clientHeight || document.body.clientHeight
}
```

GoToEdge()

These recipes are starting to come together in such a way that it's now easy to build a recipe that will move one or more objects to one of the edges of the browser, which is what this one does: It allows you to move objects to the top, left, right, or bottom edges of the browser, as shown in Figure 14-9.

About the Recipe

This recipe locates one or more objects at one of the four edges of the browser window. It requires the following arguments:

- **id**   An object, an object ID, or an array of objects or object IDs.
- **where**   The edge to which the object or objects should be moved, out of 'top', 'bottom', 'left', or 'right'.
- **percent**   The distance from the left or top of the browser, depending on the value in where.

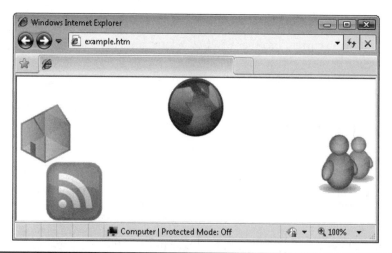

FIGURE 14-9   Attaching GIF images to different edges of the browser

Variables, Arrays, and Functions

`j`	Local integer for indexing into `id` if it's an array
`width`	Local variable containing the width of the browser, less that of `id`
`height`	Local variable containing the height of the browser, less that of `id`
`amount`	Local variable containing `percent` as a percent
`TP, BM, LT and RT`	Global variables with the values 'top', 'bottom', 'left', and 'right'
`GetWindowWidth()`	Function to return the browser width
`GetWindowHeight()`	Function to return the browser height
`W()`	Function to return the width of an object
`H()`	Function to return the height of an object
`GoTo()`	Function to move an object to a new location

How It Works

Like many others, this recipe supports the passing of an object, an object ID, or an array of objects and/or object IDs. This is managed by the initial `if()` section, which determines whether `id` is an array using the `instanceof` operator. If it is, then each element of the array is recursively passed to the same function, along with the values of `where` and `percent`. Once all have been processed, the function then returns.

After this, the three local variables `width`, `height`, and `amount` are assigned values representing the amount of width and height remaining in the browser window (after the width and height of the object are taken into account). This is done by fetching the width and height of the browser window using the `GetWindowWidth()` and `GetWindowHeight()` recipes, and then subtracting the object's width from one and its height from the other, as determined by calls to `W()` and `H()`.

The variable `amount` is set to `percent/100` so that it can be used as a multiplier. For example, if `percent` has a value of 40, then dividing it by 100 assigns it the value of 0.40, which can then be multiplied by any number to reduce it to 40 percent of its original value. In this case, the multiplier determines how far along an edge the object should appear.

Next, a `switch()` statement tests for the four allowed argument values for `where`, which are 'top', 'bottom', 'left', or 'right'. The shorthand global variable equivalents of `TP`, `BM`, `LT`, and `RT` are used in place of these values to make the code shorter and clearer. A `break` command ends each subsection of the `switch()` statement except for the final one, where it is not required because program flow will continue on the next line down anyway.

Depending on which of the four values has been passed in `where`, the local variables `x` and `y` are set to align the object in `id` right up against the edge specified. The object is also displayed at a position between 0 and 100 percent along (or down), according to the value in `percent`. Finally, a call to `GoTo()` is made to move the object to the new location.

There are many uses for this recipe; one in particular is a dock bar, similar to the one used at the bottom of the screen on the Apple OS X operating system, with a row or column of expanding and collapsing icons. JavaScript Recipe 66, `DockBar()`, provides exactly this functionality, for any web page.

How to Use It

To use this recipe, pass an object to it along with details on where to display it, as in the following example, which displays four different icons, one per edge:

```
<img id='i1' src='i1.gif' />
<img id='i2' src='i2.gif' />
<img id='i3' src='i3.gif' />
<img id='i4' src='i4.gif' />

<script>
OnDOMReady(function()
{
   ids = Array('i1', 'i2', 'i3', 'i4')
   Position(ids, FIX)
   GoToEdge('i1', TP, 50)
   GoToEdge('i2', BM, 10)
   GoToEdge('i3', LT, 33)
   GoToEdge('i4', RT, 66)
})
</script>
```

In the first section of HTML, four GIF images are loaded in, with each given a different ID. Then, in the `<script>` section, the array `ids` is populated with these IDs so that the following `Position()` command can set all of them to have a `style.position` of 'fixed'. This means they will stay where they are put, even if the browser page scrolls.

Finally, each image is attached to a different edge using four different calls to `GoToEdge()`. The top one is 50 percent in, the bottom 10 percent in, the left 33 percent down, and the right 66 percent down.

NOTE *As with all of this book's examples, you can download this example and all associated content (such as the images used) from the companion web site at* webdeveloperscookbook.com.

The Recipe

```
function GoToEdge(id, where, percent)
{
   if (id instanceof Array)
   {
      for (var j = 0 ; j < id.length ; ++j)
         GoToEdge(id[j], where, percent)
      return
   }

   var width  = GetWindowWidth()  - W(id)
   var height = GetWindowHeight() - H(id)
   var amount = percent / 100
```

```
switch(where)
{
   case TP: var x = width * amount
            var y = 0
            break
   case BM: var x = width * amount
            var y = height
            break
   case LT: var x = 0
            var y = height * amount
            break
   case RT: var x = width
            var y = height * amount
}

   GoTo(id, x, y)
}
```

CenterX( )

RECIPE 28

Another very useful function is to center an object, which is what this recipe does. By using the browser width and object width, it moves an object horizontally to exactly the center of the browser. Figure 14-10 shows a div that has been centered horizontally using this recipe.

About the Recipe

This recipe centers an object (or objects) on a horizontal axis. It requires the following argument:

- **id**   An object, an object ID, or an array of objects or object IDs.

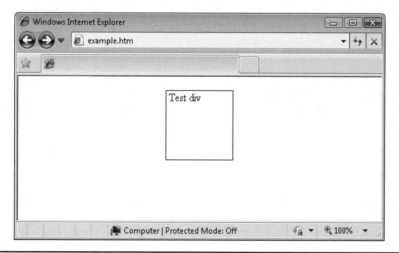

FIGURE 14-10   Centering a div horizontally

Variables, Arrays, and Functions

`j`	Local integer variable for indexing into `id` if it is an array
`Left`	The `style.left` property of an object
`SCROLL_X`	Global variable containing the number of pixels by which the browser has scrolled horizontally
`GetWindowWidth()`	The available width of the browser window, taking into account any scroll bars
`W()`	Function to fetch an object's width
`Px()`	Function to append the suffix 'px'

How It Works

This recipe allows arrays of objects and/or object IDs, as well as single objects or object IDs. It does this by using the `instanceof` operator to tell whether `id` is an array, and if it is, it iterates through the array using the local variable `j` as an index, recursively calling itself with the single-element values. Upon completion, the `if()` section of code returns.

In the second part of the recipe, the `S()` recipe sets the object's `style.left` property to the correct value (using a call to `Px()` to add the 'px' suffix) to center the object horizontally.

The correct value is determined by looking up the width of the window (less 17 if there's a scroll bar), minus the width of `id`. This value is then divided by 2. For example, if the window is 600 pixels wide and the object is 100 (and there is no scroll bar), the value is determined by subtracting 100 from 600, which equals 500. This number is divided by 2 to get a final result of 250. Therefore, an offset of 250 pixels from the left will exactly center an object of 100 pixels width in a 600-pixel-wide browser. If there is a scroll bar, the values become 583 – 100 / 2, which equals 241.5. The `Math.round()` call deals with a fractional result, which in this case is rounded up to 242.

If the browser has not scrolled, this is all the calculation that is needed. However, because the horizontal offset is from the left edge of the document (not the window), if there has been a horizontal scroll, the object will be displayed left of center by the amount of the scrolling. Therefore, the global variable `SCROLL_X` is added to the calculated value in order to place the object exactly between the left- and right-hand edges of the window.

How to Use It

To center an object, as long as it is capable of being moved, just call `CenterX()` in the following manner, which creates a simple div and then centers it:

```
<div id='test'> Test div</div>

<script>
OnDOMReady(function()
{
   Locate('test', ABS, 20, 20)
   Resize('test', 100, 100)
   S('test').border = 'solid ' + Px(1)
   CenterX('test')
})
</script>
```

The   entity is there to separate the text from the border, which it otherwise runs into. The Locate() call sets the 'test' div to an 'absolute' position using the global variable ABS for shorthand. It also locates the div at the position 20,20. The Resize() call then turns the div into a 100 by 100–pixel square. Then, in this example, rather than using colors to make the div easy to see, the div has been given a solid border with a call to S().

Finally, a call is made to CenterX() and the div is centered horizontally.

The Recipe

```
function CenterX(id)
{
   if (id instanceof Array)
   {
      for (var j = 0 ; j < id.length ; ++j)
         CenterX(id[j])
      return
   }

   S(id).left = Px(Math.round((GetWindowWidth() - W(id))) / 2 + SCROLL_X)
}
```

CenterY()

This is the partner recipe to CenterX(), which enables you to center an object vertically. Figure 14-11 shows a div that has been centered using this recipe.

About the Recipe

This recipe centers an object (or objects) on a vertical axis. It requires the following argument:

- **id**   An object, an object ID, or an array of objects or object IDs.

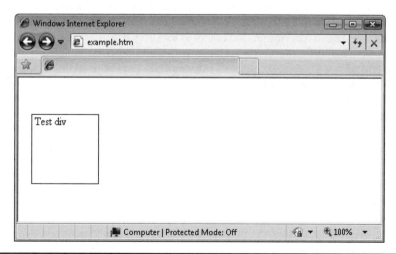

FIGURE 14-11   Centering a div vertically

Variables, Arrays, and Functions

j	Local integer variable for indexing into `id` if it is an array
top	The `style.top` property of an object
SCROLL_Y	Global variable containing the number of pixels by which the browser has scrolled vertically
GetWindowHeight()	The available height of the browser window, taking into account any scroll bars
H()	Function to fetch an object's height
Px()	Function to append the suffix 'px'

How It Works

This recipe is almost identical to `CenterX()`, except that an object is centered along its vertical axis. See the section on `CenterX()` for more details.

How to Use It

To center an object vertically using this recipe, you might use code such as the following:

```
<div id='test'> Test div</div>

<script>
OnDOMReady(function()
{
   Locate('test', ABS, 20, 20)
   Resize('test', 100, 100)
   S('test').border = 'solid ' + Px(1)
   CenterY('test')
})
</script>
```

This example creates a div in the HTML section and then, in the `<script>` section, it sets the object's `style.position` property to 'absolute' using the `Locate()` command and the global variable `ABS`. It also moves the object to location 20,20.

The div is then resized using `Resize()` to a width and height of 100. After that, it is given a single-pixel border to make it stand out and then, on the final line, the `CenterY()` recipe is called to center it vertically.

The Recipe

```
function CenterY(id)
{
   if (id instanceof Array)
   {
      for (var j = 0 ; j < id.length ; ++j)
         CenterY(id[j])
      return
   }

   S(id).top = Px(Math.round(((GetWindowHeight() - H(id))) / 2 + SCROLL_Y) }
```

Center()

More often than not, when you center an object you usually want to do so in both horizontal and vertical directions, so this recipe brings both the previous ones together into a single function, as shown in Figure 14-12.

About the Recipe

This recipe centers an object (or objects) on both its vertical and horizontal axes. It requires the following argument:

- **id**   An object, an object ID, or an array of objects or object IDs.

Variables, Arrays, and Functions

CenterX()	Function to center an object horizontally
CenterY()	Function to center an object vertically

How It Works

Since both the CenterX() and CenterY() recipes have been written to take arguments that can be an array of objects and/or object IDs, an object, or an object ID, there is little work for this recipe to do, so it simply calls each one in turn, passing id (whether or not it's an array) to each.

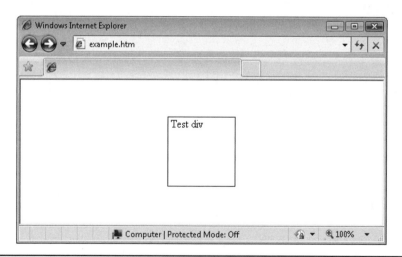

FIGURE 14-12   Centering a div both horizontally and vertically

How to Use It

To fully center an object in both the horizontal and vertical directions, you could use code such as the following:

```
<div id='test'>Test div</div>

<script>
OnDOMReady(function()
{
   Locate('test', ABS, 20, 20)
   Resize('test', 100, 100)
   S('test').border = 'solid ' + Px(1)
   Center('test')
})
</script>
```

This example is very similar to the previous two, except that it calls the Center() recipe at the end to fully center the div.

That covers this chapter's recipes. Now we're about to start really cooking, because in the following chapter we'll begin making objects invisible, make them reappear, smoothly fade them in and out, and even more. Along the way, I'll show you how to put these effects to good use.

The Recipe

```
function Center(id)
{
   CenterX(id)
   CenterY(id)
}
```

CHAPTER 15

Visibility

Many of the most impressive effects you'll see on web sites are also the simplest. For example, a smooth fade from one image to another is often far more beautiful than other wipe or dissolve transformations. Likewise, instantly revealing or hiding an object, when done well, is clean and easy on the eye.

This chapter focuses on these types of effects, ranging from setting the visibility (or invisibility) of an object to fading objects in and out, fading between objects, and so on. The recipes in this chapter also provide the basic functionality required by many later recipes—most particularly, the menu and navigation recipes in Chapter 18.

Invisible()

To ease into this chapter, we'll begin with a few short and sweet recipes that every JavaScript programmer needs in their toolkit. The first one is `Invisible()`, which makes an object disappear from a web page while the space it occupies remains, as opposed to hiding an object that collapses and causes elements around it to assume its space (see JavaScript Recipe 40, `Hide()`, for that effect).

Figure 15-1 shows a span with the text "Now you see me…" followed by some plain text not in a div that reads "and soon you won't". An alert window has been raised to let you see these elements before the call to `Invisible()` is made. Figure 15-2 shows what happens after clicking the alert: The shaded text in the span is invisible, but the other text snippet remains in place, demonstrating that the span is still there, just not visible.

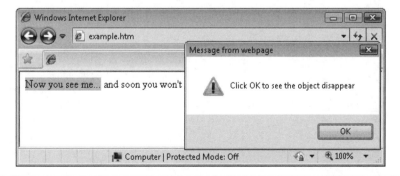

FIGURE 15-1   The shaded area is a span set to disappear when the alert is clicked.

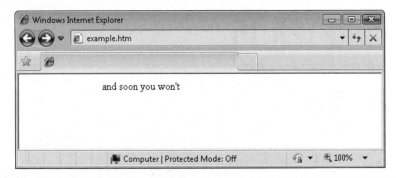

About the Recipe

This recipe makes an object invisible while retaining the object's position and dimensions. It requires the following argument:

- **id**   An object, an object ID, or an array of objects and/or object IDs.

Variables, Arrays, and Functions

visibility	The style.visibility property of the object(s)
HID	Global variable with the value 'hidden'

How It Works

This recipe makes a call to the S() recipe in such a way that you can pass it an array of objects and/or object IDs, a single object, or an object ID. The style.visibility property of the object (or objects) is then set to the value in the global variable HID, which is 'hidden'.

How to Use It

To use this recipe, pass it the object or objects to make invisible. The following example shows one way you might incorporate it:

```
<span id='ghost'>Now you see me...</span> and soon you won't

<script>
OnDOMReady(function()
{
   S('ghost').backgroundColor = 'lightblue'
   Resize('ghost', 128, 32)
   alert('Click OK to see the object disappear')
   Invisible('ghost')
})
</script>
```

This example first creates a span in the HTML section and gives it some text. Following this is more text that isn't included within the span. Then, in the `<script>` section, the span's background color is set to light blue and resized to make it stand out.

Next, an alert is raised to give you the chance to see the initial display before the call to the `Invisible()` recipe is made. After clicking the alert OK button, the call is made, and the contents of the span become invisible.

TIP *When you want to keep your layout unchanged when hiding an object, use this recipe in preference to JavaScript Recipe 40,* `Hide()`*. This recipe preserves an object's dimensions, while Recipe 40 fully collapses an object, causing elements surrounding it to move in and occupy the newly vacant space.*

The Recipe

```
function Invisible(id)
{
    S(id, 'visibility', HID)
}
```

Visible()

This is the partner recipe to `Invisible()`. It makes a previously invisible object visible. Figure 15-3 expands the example in the previous recipe. Now, when the alert message's OK button is clicked, the invisible text will reappear and the browser will look like Figure 15-1 again (but without the alert window).

About the Recipe

This recipe makes an object visible after it has been made invisible. It requires the following argument:

- **id** An object, an object ID, or an array of objects and/or object IDs.

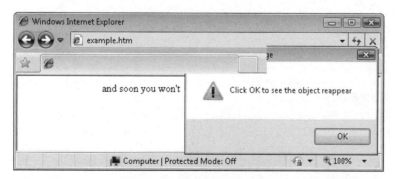

FIGURE 15-3 After clicking OK, the hidden text reappears.

Variables, Arrays, and Functions

visibility	The style.visibility property of the object(s)
VIS	Global variable with the value 'visible'

How It Works

This recipe makes a call to the S() function in such a way that you can pass it an array of objects and/or object IDs, a single object, or an object ID. Then, the style.visibility property of the object (or objects) is set to the value in the global variable VIS, which is 'visible'.

How to Use It

To make invisible objects reappear, just pass them to this recipe. The following example extends the previous recipe example to make the hidden span reappear:

```
<span id='ghost'>Now you see me...</span> and soon you won't

<script>
OnDOMReady(function()
{
   S('ghost').backgroundColor = 'lightblue'
   Resize('ghost', 128, 32)
   alert('Click OK to see the object disappear')
   Invisible('ghost')
   alert('Click OK to see the object reappear')
   Visible('ghost')
})
</script>
```

Just the final two lines of code in this example are new: an alert, so that you can verify that the span was made invisible; and a call to Visible() that is executed after clicking OK, which makes the object reappear.

The Recipe

```
function Visible(id)
{
   S(id, 'visibility', VIS)
}
```

VisibilityToggle()

This recipe inverses the visibility of an object. If it is visible, it becomes invisible, or if it is invisible, it becomes visible. In Figure 15-4, each time the button is clicked, the text to the right toggles between being visible and invisible.

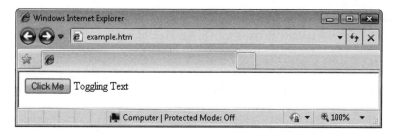

Figure 15-4 Attaching a recipe to a button's click event

About the Recipe

Each time this recipe is called, the object or objects passed to it change their visibility to the opposite state. It requires the following argument:

- **id** An object, an object ID, or an array of objects and/or object IDs.

Variables, Arrays, and Functions

j	Local integer for indexing into id if it is an array
visibility	The object's style.visibility property
HID	Global variable with the value 'hidden'
VIS	Global variable with the value 'visible'

How It Works

This recipe uses the recursive trick that many others employ to handle arrays of objects and/or object IDs, as well as single objects and object IDs. It does this using the instanceof operator to test whether id is an array. If it is, the array is iterated through using the local variable j in a for() loop, individually calling the function itself recursively for each element of the array. Once it's done, the function returns.

If id is not an array, the S() function is called, along with the inverse value of the object's style.visibility property. This is achieved using the following ternary expression, along with the two variables HID and VIS, which stand for the strings 'hidden' and 'visible':

```
S(id).visibility = (S(id).visibility == HID) ? VIS : HID
```

In plain English, this statement equates to "If the current value of the object's style .visibility property is 'hidden', then return the value 'visible'; otherwise, return the value 'hidden'." Everything after the first equal sign and before the question mark is the test. The value immediately following it is the one to return if the test result is true, and the final value is to be returned if the test result is false.

All this has the effect of applying the opposite state of the visibility property to the object.

How to Use It

You can call this recipe directly from within JavaScript, like this:

```
VisibilityToggle('myobject')
```

Or you can pass an array of objects, like this:

```
ids = Array('firstobj', 'secondobj', 'thirdobj')
VisibilityToggle(ids)
```

Alternatively, you can incorporate the call within an HTML statement, as in the following two lines of HTML that cause the text in the span called 'toggle' to switch between being invisible or invisible each time the button is clicked (you could equally attach it to an onmouseover or other event, too):

```
<input type='submit' value='Click Me'
    onclick="VisibilityToggle('toggle')" />
<span id='toggle'>Toggling Text</span>
```

You will see this recipe used in a number of the other recipes in various ways.

NOTE *Calling this recipe from HTML illustrates the main reason why nearly all these recipes allow you to pass either an object or an object ID. In the preceding example, the object ID of 'toggle' is passed to the recipe, but the object* this *(which is an object, not the ID of an object) can also be passed, thus telling the recipe that the HTML object in which the call is embedded is the one to manipulate. This is how rollover and other similar effects are achieved—you'll see more on this in the next recipe and in Chapter 18.*

The Recipe

```
function VisibilityToggle(id)
{
    if (id instanceof Array)
    {
        for (var j = 0 ; j < id.length ; ++j)
            VisibilityToggle(id[j])
        return
    }

    S(id).visibility = S(id).visibility == HID ? VIS : HID
}
```

Opacity()

Being able to switch an object from visible to invisible is great, but sometimes you need finer control over an object's visibility. This is referred to in JavaScript by the inverse term: its *opacity*. With this recipe, you can set the opacity of any object to a value between 0 percent (totally transparent, or invisible) and 100 percent (fully opaque, nothing behind shows through).

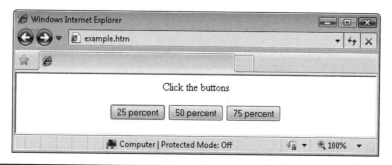

FIGURE 15-5 Three button objects at the default opacity of 100 percent

Figure 15-5 shows three buttons displayed using the default opacity of 100 percent. In Figure 15-6, each button has been clicked to change its value to 25 percent, 50 percent, or 75 percent, respectively.

About the Recipe

This recipe applies the opacity setting supplied to the object or objects it is passed. It requires the following arguments:

- **id** An object, an object ID, or an array of objects and/or object IDs.
- **percent** The amount of opacity to apply to the object or objects, from 0 percent, which is fully transparent, to 100 percent, which is fully opaque.

Variables, Arrays, and Functions

opacity	The `style.opacity` property as used by most browsers
MozOpacity	The version of the `opacity` property used by Mozilla-based browsers such as Firefox
KhtmlOpacity	The version of the `opacity` property used on older versions of the Apple Safari browser
filter	Used to implement Microsoft's version of the `opacity` property (and many other properties, too)

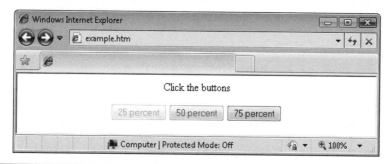

FIGURE 15-6 After being clicked, the buttons are at 25 percent, 50 percent, and 75 percent opacity.

How It Works

This recipe makes four different calls in turn because various browsers approach the subject of opacity in different ways. Fortunately, none of the methods clash with each other, so a lot of `if...then...else` code is not necessary.

The first line for most browsers (such as Opera, Google Chrome, and recent versions of Apple Safari) looks like this:

```
S(id, 'opacity', percent / 100)
```

This simply takes the value in `percent`, divides it by 100, and applies it to the `style.opacity` property of `id`. Of course, if `id` is an array, all its elements will have that property updated.

However, Mozilla-based browsers such as Firefox have their own property for this function, so the following line of code performs the equivalent for them by changing the `style.MozOpacity` property. Likewise, the third line is for Safari browsers that use the old rendering engine (before Webkit was introduced) and therefore require the `style.KhtmlOpacity` property be changed.

Finally, Microsoft chose a more complicated approach and includes opacity as part of their nonstandard filters and transitions group of features. The object's filter property is set in the following manner (for a setting of 25 percent, for example):

```
S(id).filter = 'alpha(opacity = 25)'
```

However, because you need to take into account the fact that `id` could be an array, the following version of the call is made, with both the property and setting values also passed to the `S()` recipe:

```
S(id, 'filter', 'alpha(opacity = 25)')
```

Also, rather than a numeric value, a string has to be assigned to the `filter` property, which requires construction. So, in order to place the value in `percent` into the string, the following code is used (employing the `InsVars()` recipe from Chapter 13):

```
S(id, 'filter', InsVars("alpha(opacity = '#1')", percent))
```

How to Use It

To change an object's opacity, just pass it along with the object or its ID (or an array of objects and/or object IDs). You can use a JavaScript command like this:

```
Opacity('fadeddiv', 64)
```

Or, you can embed the call within HTML, as in the following example, which creates three clickable buttons:

```
<center>Click the buttons<p>
<input type='submit' value='25%' onclick='Opacity(this, 25)' />
<input type='submit' value='50%' onclick='Opacity(this, 50)' />
<input type='submit' value='75%' onclick='Opacity(this, 75)' />
```

When clicked, the different buttons will change their opacity by the assigned amount (25 percent, 50 percent, or 75 percent, respectively). Notice that none of these HTML elements have been assigned IDs because the keyword `this` has been passed to the `Opacity()` recipe, thus taking advantage of the fact that this recipe (like most of them) will accept either an object ID or an object. The `this` keyword directly passes the calling object to the function, which is why no ID name is required.

The Recipe

```
function Opacity(id, percent)
{
    S(id, 'opacity',      percent / 100)
    S(id, 'MozOpacity',   percent / 100)
    S(id, 'KhtmlOpacity', percent / 100)
    S(id, 'filter',       InsVars("alpha(opacity = '#1')", percent))
}
```

Fade()

This recipe makes great use of the previous one, `Opacity()`, by making it possible to smoothly change an object's opacity over time. In Figure 15-7, two images have had their IDs attached to mouse events so they will fade in and out.

About the Recipe

This recipe fades an object from one opacity value to another (either increasing or decreasing it) over a set number of milliseconds. It requires the following arguments:

- **id**   An object, an object ID, or an array of objects and/or object IDs.
- **start**   The beginning level of opacity.
- **end**   The final level of opacity.
- **msecs**   The number of milliseconds the fade should take.
- **interruptible**   If this option is set, an object's fade can be interrupted and replaced with a new fade on the same object; otherwise, the fade will continue until it has finished.

FIGURE 15-7   The left image is slowly fading into the background.

- **CC** Generally, this argument should not be passed, as it is a special variable for notifying a recipe that it is being called as part of a chain (the CC stands for "Chained Call"). Because of this, I will no longer mention CC in the list of arguments, unless it is being used in a different manner.

Variables, Arrays, and Functions

j	Local variable for indexing into id if it is an array
Stepval	Local variable used in the calculation of the amount of opacity to change in each frame of animation
INTERVAL	Global variable with a default value of 30—the number of milliseconds between each call to the interrupt
FA_Flag	Property of id that is set to true if a fade is in progress; otherwise, it is false
FA_Start	Property of id assigned the value of start
FA_End	Property of id assigned the value of end
FA_Level	Property of id containing the current opacity level
FA_Step	Property of id containing the amount by which to change the opacity in each step
FA_Int	Property of id containing the value passed in the interruptible argument
Fadeout	Property of id used by the FadeToggle() recipe: true if it has been faded out, or false if it has been faded in
FA_Iid	Property of id containing the value returned by setInterval()—this value is used by clearInterval() to turn off the DoFade() interrupt attached to id
DoFade()	Subfunction called every INTERVAL milliseconds until the fade is completed or interrupted—this function updates the opacity of id each time it is called
Opacity()	Function to change the opacity of an object or array of objects
Math.abs()	Function to return an absolute positive value from a number that may be positive or negative
Math.max()	Function to return the largest of two values
Math.min()	Function to return the smallest of two values
setInterval()	Function to start periodic interrupt calls to another function
clearInterval()	Function to stop the interrupts started by SetInterval()

How It Works

This is the first of the really substantial recipes. At almost 50 lines of code it isn't short, but don't be put off by it; the coding is straightforward, and you've seen many of its parts before. If you can work through this recipe, you'll be able to follow them all.

This function works by using interrupts to call a function at regular intervals to change the opacity of an object by a small amount each time (which is how all the transition and animation recipes in this book work). To do this, the recipe comes in two parts. The first part prepares all the variables and initiates the interrupts, and the second part receives the interrupt calls and performs the incremental opacity changes.

Let's start with the first `if()` section of code. There's nothing unusual here; it simply passes `id` back to the same function recursively to be dealt with an element at a time if it's an array:

```
if (id instanceof Array)
{
    for (var j = 0 ; j < id.length ; ++j)
        Fade(id[j], start, end, msecs, interruptible, CB)
    return
}
```

After that, the local variable `stepval` is created, like this:

```
var stepval = Math.abs(start - end) / (msecs / INTERVAL)
```

Its value is calculated by finding the difference between the `start` and `end` opacity values; that is, it subtracts one from the other and then passes the result through the `Math.abs()` function. This gives a positive integer representing the difference, like this:

```
Math.abs(start - end)
```

Then, the length of time the fade should take, which has been passed as a value in milliseconds in the variable `msecs`, is divided by `INTERVAL`, which is the number of milliseconds between each frame of the transition (30 by default). The code for that is simple division:

```
(msecs / INTERVAL)
```

The first value (the `start` and `end` difference) is then divided by the second (the timing), and then assigned to the variable `stepval`.

A Specific Case

Let's see what value this calculation comes out as by assuming that `start` has a value of 0, `end` has a value of 100, and `msecs` has a value of 1000. This gives us the following formula:

```
Math.abs(0 - 100) / (1000 / 30)
```

The calculation comes to 100 / (1000 / 30), and the answer is the value 3. In terms of this code, this means that if the following three things are `true`:

- The interrupt is going to take place once every 30 milliseconds.
- You want the animation to take 1000 milliseconds.
- There are 100 steps of opacity.

Then the distance between each level of opacity should be 3. In other words, to smoothly fade from a value of 0 to 100 over the course of 1 second, there will be 33.33 steps, separated by 3 levels of opacity.

A Standard Formula

The preceding formula is how almost all the animations and transitions in this book work. They take the value in milliseconds that you supply for their duration, they then divide that by the interval (usually 30 milliseconds), and finally they divide the distance between the start and end points of the animation by the timing value in order to find out the amount the animation needs to move in each step, as shown in the following statement:

```
var stepval = Math.abs(start - end) / (msecs / INTERVAL)
```

If a Fade Is Already in Progress

This recipe has been designed so you can force it to proceed until it has finished, or you can allow it to be interrupted (but only by another Fade() call on the same object). This is so that you can offer onmouseover and onmouseout routines that will interrupt if you move your mouse again before the transition completes. That way, a partially faded object can be made to fade back to its start point again if you take the mouse away.

Alternatively, sometimes you may need to display an uninterrupted animation on the screen and maybe even chain a few together. You have the option to choose either by setting the interruptible argument to true if a fade can be interrupted, or false if it cannot. You can also use 1 and 0 for these values if you prefer.

The next section of code deals with this by looking at the FA_Flag property of id. This is a new property given to id, which has the value true only when a fade is in progress.

NOTE *Assigning new properties directly to objects is a technique used throughout this book. It's a very convenient way of using some object-oriented aspects of JavaScript.*

The next section of code checks whether a fade is already in progress. If it is, the code checks whether the FA_Int property of id is set (to see whether an interrupt is allowed). If it isn't, the function immediately exits because it cannot be interrupted. Otherwise, the clearInterval() function is called to end the currently repeating interrupts, and the object's new FA_Start property is set to the current value in FA_Fade.

This primes the new fade to start only where the previous one (that was just canceled) left off, which means that the new fade will ignore the start value that was passed. This override ensures a very smooth and natural flow between the two transitions. The following code performs this process:

```
if (O(id).FA_Flag)
{
   if (!O(id).FA_Int) return

   clearInterval(O(id).FA_Iid)
   O(id).FA_Start = O(id).FA_Level
}
```

If a Fade Is Not in Progress

If a fade isn't already in progress, the new id property FA_Start is assigned the value in start so that the remaining code can use this value to know where the fade started from. The id property FA_Level is also set to start because that is the property that will be manipulated to track the opacity level on each interrupt. These statements are placed within an else segment, like this:

```
else
{
   O(id).FA_Start = start
   O(id).FA_Level = start
}
```

The Remaining Assignments

In the final few lines of the setup portion of this recipe, a few other new properties of id have to be assigned, as follows:

```
O(id).FA_Flag = true
O(id).FA_End  = end
O(id).FA_Int  = interruptible
```

The first line sets the object's FA_Flag to true, and this is used in other parts of the code to decide whether or not the recipe can be entered (or reentered). The second line makes a copy of the end value in the new property FA_End, and the last assigns the value in interruptible to the property FA_Int.

Next, the amount by which to change the opacity has to be stored in FA_Step. This is either stepval if the opacity is going to increase, or -stepval if it will be decreasing, as determined by this line:

```
O(id).FA_Step = end > O(id).FA_Start ? stepval : -stepval
```

Assisting the FadeToggle() Recipe

The FadeToggle() recipe, which is covered a little later in this chapter, needs a way to know whether an object has been faded in or out. To give it this information, the next new property of id, Fadeout, is set to either true if the object is being faded out, or false if it is being faded in, like this:

```
O(id).Fadeout = end < O(id).FA_Start ? true : false
```

Initiating the Interrupts

The last line of the setup section of the recipe sets up the repeating interrupts in the following way:

```
O(id).FA_Iid  = setInterval(DoFade, INTERVAL)
```

This statement starts off a repeating interrupt that will call the DoFade() subfunction every INTERVAL milliseconds. The value returned by calling setInterval() is saved in the new id property FA_Iid since it is needed later when it's time to cancel the interrupts.

The DoFade() Subfunction

This function is a subfunction of Fade() and is known as a private method or private function. Such functions share all the local variables of the parent function, so there's no need to pass them as arguments, and because they can only be used by the parent function, they don't clutter up the namespace.

This makes them ideal to use as interrupt or event-driven functions, which is exactly what I have done in this recipe. Every INTERVAL milliseconds (30 by default), DoFade() is called up by JavaScript. It has one main job, which is to change the opacity of id by just a little. The following line is the one that changes the value for this:

```
O(id).FA_Level += O(id).FA_Step
```

This simply adds the value of the FA_Step property of id to its FA_Level property. If FA_Step is positive, the value is therefore added, but if it is negative, it is subtracted (for example, 100 + –3 is 97, because the first + gets ignored).

If the Final Opacity Has Been Reached

Having derived this new value, it's time to check whether it is the final value wanted, and if so, whether the animation has completed. The code to do that is slightly verbose:

```
if (O(id).FA_Level >= Math.max(O(id).FA_Start, O(id).FA_End) ||
    O(id).FA_Level <= Math.min(O(id).FA_Start, O(id).FA_End))
```

Essentially, it checks whether the current opacity value (in FA_Level) has reached the final required value (in FA_End). If it is the same as or greater than (or less than, in the case of decreasing) the final value, then the following code segment is executed:

```
O(id).FA_Level = O(id).FA_End
O(id).FA_Flag  = false
clearInterval(O(id).FA_Iid)
```

In this section, the value of FA_Level is set to the exact value in FA_End. This must be done because FA_Level will often have a fractional value, and one final frame of animation is almost always required to ensure that the correct final opacity level is reached.

After this, the FA_Flag property of id is set to false to indicate that the fade has finished. This is immediately followed by a call to clearInterval() with the value that was saved in the FA_Iid property. This cancels any further interrupts.

The CB Argument

The final statement in this if() section is as follows:

```
if (typeof CB != UNDEF) eval(CB)
```

It checks the argument passed in CB (if any) and uses the eval() function to evaluate it. This type of procedure is called a *callback* and is used by the chaining recipes. In a nutshell, now that this recipe has completed running, this call allows any recipes that may be chained to follow this one to begin their execution. However, this happens only if the argument CB has a value.

This argument is generally passed when you wish to have a second function run when the recipe has finished executing. You simply pass the function to call in a string as the final parameter to recipes that support callbacks natively.

NOTE *Chapter 17 covers callbacks and chaining in much more detail, but I have placed this brief description here due to this being the first recipe that supports callbacks.*

Changing the Opacity

The last thing this subfunction does is call the `Opacity()` recipe to set the current opacity value, with this line of code:

```
Opacity(id, O(id).FA_Level)
```

If `clearInterval()` has been called, that's the end of it; otherwise, INTERVAL milliseconds later `DoFade()` will get called again, and a slightly different value for FA_Level will be computed and passed to the `Opacity()` recipe, until the transition has finished.

NOTE   *We spent a lot of time going over this particular recipe because most of the other animation and transition recipes work in a similar fashion. So, once you understand this one, you will more easily see how the others work.*

How to Use It

To make an object fade, you would use a command such as this:

```
Fade('object', 100, 0, 1000, 0)
```

This will fade the object out, starting with full opacity down to being totally transparent, over the course of one second. The final argument of 0 prevents the fade from being interrupted.

You can also embed calls to this recipe within HTML, like this:

```
<a href='http://abc.com'
   onmouseover="Fade('object', 75, 100, 500, 1)"
   onmouseout="Fade('object', 100, 75, 500, 1)">My Link</a>
```

If the link was previously given an opacity of 75, then each time the mouse passes over it the link will gradually increase opacity over half a second, darkening it. When the mouse leaves, it will fade back to a 75 percent opacity level.

Here's some example code you can try for yourself (or download from the companion web site at *webdeveloperscookbook.com* to ensure you have the images):

```
<center><br />
<img id='i1' src='i1.gif' />
<img id='i2' src='i2.gif' />

<script>
OnDOMReady(function()
{
   O('i1').onmouseover = function() { Fade('i1', 100, 0, 1000, 0) }
   O('i1').onmouseout  = function() { Fade('i1', 0, 100, 1000, 0) }
   O('i2').onmouseover = function() { Fade('i2', 100, 0, 1000, 1) }
   O('i2').onmouseout  = function() { Fade('i2', 0, 100, 1000, 1) }
})
</script>
```

The HTML section sets up two images with the IDs of 'i1' and 'i2'. In the `<script>` section, the onmouseover and onmouseout events of each are attached so the objects will fade out when the mouse passes over them and fade back in again when the mouse leaves. For the sake of brevity, I used inline anonymous functions here instead of named functions.

The calls made to Fade() for the first image, 'i1', have the interruptible argument set to 0, which means they cannot be interrupted and will always continue to completion. The second image has the interruptible argument set to 1, which allows interruptions.

The Difference Between Interruptible and Noninterruptible Calls

Try passing your mouse over the pair of images and note what happens. You will see that the second image smoothly fades in and out as soon as the mouse enters or leaves it, always picking up from the opacity level of the fade that was interrupted.

On the other hand, the first image is harder to control because you can only make it fade out or in from either a fully opaque or a fully transparent state; you cannot interrupt it part way. This also means that if you move the mouse away from the first image before the transition has completed, the mouse will already be out, so there will be no onmouseout event to trigger until you move it back in again and wait for the transition to complete, and *then* move the mouse out.

You'll see what I mean as you experiment with the example, and it will become clear how the noninterruptible method is ideal for animations and transitions that you want to always complete, while interruptible ones are best used where user interaction with the mouse is required.

The Recipe

```
function Fade(id, start, end, msecs, interruptible, CB)
{
   if (id instanceof Array)
   {
      for (var j = 0 ; j < id.length ; ++j)
         Fade(id[j], start, end, msecs, interruptible, CB)
      return
   }

   var stepval = Math.abs(start - end) / (msecs / INTERVAL)

   if (O(id).FA_Flag)
   {
      if (!O(id).FA_Int) return

      clearInterval(O(id).FA_IID)
      O(id).FA_Start = O(id).FA_Level
   }
   else


   {
      O(id).FA_Start = start
      O(id).FA_Level = start
   }

   O(id).FA_Flag = true
   O(id).FA_End  = end
   O(id).FA_Int  = interruptible
   O(id).FA_Step = end > O(id).FA_Start ? stepval : -stepval
```

```
O(id).Fadeout = end < O(id).FA_Start ? true : false
O(id).FA_IID  = setInterval(DoFade, INTERVAL)

function DoFade()
{
   O(id).FA_Level += O(id).FA_Step

   if (O(id).FA_Level >= Math.max(O(id).FA_Start, O(id).FA_End) ||
       O(id).FA_Level <= Math.min(O(id).FA_Start, O(id).FA_End))
   {
      O(id).FA_Level = O(id).FA_End
      O(id).FA_Flag  = false
      clearInterval(O(id).FA_IID)
      if (typeof CB != UNDEF) eval(CB)
   }

   Opacity(id, O(id).FA_Level)
}
}
```

FadeOut()

This recipe will fade out any object or objects passed to it. In Figure 15-8, each of the images has some text above it that will fade out the image below when the mouse passes over it.

About the Recipe

This recipe will fade out an object over a period of time specified. It takes the following arguments:

- **id**   An object, an object ID, or an array of objects and/or object IDs.
- **msecs**   The number of milliseconds the transition should take.
- **interruptible**   If set, the fade out can be interrupted; otherwise, it cannot.

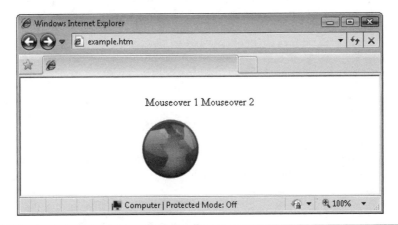

FIGURE 15-8   The right-hand image has been faded out.

Variables, Arrays, and Functions

Fade()	Function to fade an object between two levels of opacity

How It Works

This recipe calls the Fade() recipe, but it requires fewer arguments. Because of the way Fade() works, this recipe also accepts an object, an object ID, or an array of objects and/or object IDs.

How to Use It

Place a call to FadeOut() wherever you would like an object to be faded out. This can be from within HTML in the form of an onmouseover or onclick event, for example, or you can place the calls within a section of JavaScript code, as in the following example:

```
<center><br />
<span id='sp1'>Mouseover 1</span>
<span id='sp2'>Mouseover 2</span><p>
<img id='i1' src='i1.gif' />
<img id='i2' src='i2.gif' />

<script>
OnDOMReady(function()
{
    O('sp1').onmouseover = function() { FadeOut('i1', 500, 1) }
    O('sp2').onmouseover = function() { FadeOut('i2', 500, 1) }
})
</script>
```

The HTML portion of this example creates two spans to accompany two images. The <script> section then attaches to the onmouseover events of each span so that the image below each one will fade out if the mouse is passed over the span text.

Once an image has been faded out, you can still pass the mouse over each span and the image will then fade out again. This doesn't look very good, as the images suddenly appear before fading, but it can be corrected with the following recipe.

The Recipe

```
function FadeOut(id, msecs, interruptible, CB)
{
    Fade(id, 100, 0, msecs, interruptible, CB)
}
```

FadeIn()

This recipe is a simple front-end to the Fade() recipe. It fades in an object that has been previously faded out, as can be seen in Figure 15-9.

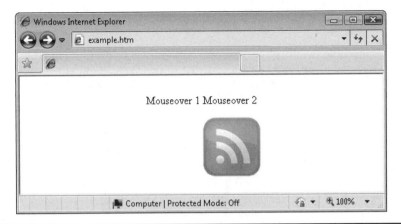

FIGURE 15-9 The right-hand image has been faded in and the left one has been faded back out.

About the Recipe

This recipe will fade in an object over a period of time specified. It takes the following arguments:

- **id** An object, an object ID, or an array of objects and/or object IDs.
- **msecs** The number of milliseconds the transition should take.
- **interruptible** If set, the fade in can be interrupted; otherwise, it cannot.

Variables, Arrays, and Functions

Fade ()	Function to fade an object between two levels of opacity

How It Works

This recipe calls the Fade () recipe, but it requires fewer arguments. Because of the way Fade () works, this recipe also accepts an object, an object ID, or an array of objects and/or object IDs.

How to Use It

You can use this recipe in much the same way as the previous one: from within HTML or from a JavaScript section of code. The following example is a modified version of the previous example. This example will fade the images in and out as you pass the mouse over the Mouseover 1 and Mouseover 2 spans:

```
<center><br />
<span id='sp1'>Mouseover 1</span>
<span id='sp2'>Mouseover 2</span><p>
<img id='i1' src='i1.gif' />
<img id='i2' src='i2.gif' />
```

```
<script>
OnDOMReady(function()
{
   O('sp1').onmouseover = function() { FadeOut('i1', 500, 1) }
   O('sp2').onmouseover = function() { FadeOut('i2', 500, 1) }
   O('sp1').onmouseout  = function() { FadeIn('i1',  500, 1) }
   O('sp2').onmouseout  = function() { FadeIn('i2',  500, 1) }
})
</script>
```

The main benefit from using this recipe with `FadeOut()` is that together they require fewer arguments than the `Fade()` recipe, are easier to remember, and are shorter. They are also used by the next two recipes, which toggle an object between being faded out and in, and which create a smooth fade between two objects, respectively.

The Recipe

```
function FadeIn(id, msecs, interruptible, CB)
{
  Fade(id, 0, 100, msecs, interruptible, CB)
}
```

 ## FadeToggle()

If you use this recipe, you don't need to know the current faded out or in state of an object. It tracks the state for you and inverts whatever that state is. Figure 15-10 shows an icon of a house that is being refaded into view with this recipe.

About the Recipe

This recipe either fades an object in or out, depending on its previous state. It requires the following arguments:

- **id**   An object, an object ID, or an array of objects and/or object IDs.
- **msecs**   The number of milliseconds the transition should take.
- **interruptible**   If set, the fade can be interrupted; otherwise, it cannot.

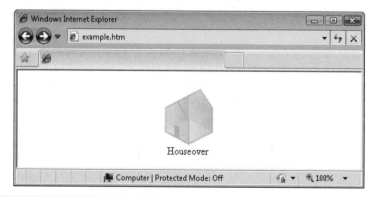

FIGURE 15-10   The house is starting to fade into view.

Variables, Arrays, and Functions

j	Local variable that iterates through the elements in id if it is an array
Fadeout	New property given to id and set to true if it has been faded out
FadeIn()	Function to fade an object in
FadeOut()	Function to fade an object out

How It Works

This recipe must make use of its own code to iterate through id if it is an array because of the need to individually check the Fadeout property of id for each object. It uses the standard form of many prior recipes to call the same function recursively with single-array elements.

The second half of the recipe is where the Fadeout property is checked. If it is set to true, then that value will have been assigned from within the Fade() recipe, discussed earlier in this chapter. When set to true, it means that the object has been faded out. If the Fadeout property doesn't exist or is set to false, then the object has not been faded out.

Therefore, based on the value of Fadeout, a decision is made by the FadeToggle() recipe to call either the FadeIn() recipe to fade the object in or the FadeOut() recipe to fade it out.

How to Use It

You can attach this recipe to an event from within HTML, or you can call it up from a section of JavaScript code. In the following example, the same call to FadeToggle() is attached to both the onmouseover and the onmouseout events of the span:

```
<center><br />
<img id='i1' src='i3.gif' /><br />
<span id='sp1'>Houseover</span>

<script>
OnDOMReady(function()
{
    FadeToggle('i1', 1, 1)
    O('sp1').onmouseover = function() { FadeToggle('i1', 500, 1) }
    O('sp1').onmouseout  = function() { FadeToggle('i1', 500, 1) }
})
</script>
```

Make sure to look at the first call in the OnDOMReady(...) section. Notice how it sets a transition time of just 1 millisecond for the fade. This is the recommended way to set up toggleable elements to start up in their inverse state because it causes the transition to occur, but over only a single frame of animation.

This technique is useful if you want the house image to start faded out: the call to FadeToggle() accomplishes the first fade out as quickly as possible—faster than the eye can see. When you run the example, you should hardly even see the image until you pass the mouse over the text.

With the image faded out, the remaining two lines of code attach to the two mouse events. The house will smoothly fade in and out as you pass your mouse over the text because the interruptible argument is set to 1 and allows smooth interrupts to the transitions.

The Recipe

```
function FadeToggle(id, msecs, interruptible, CB)
{
    if (id instanceof Array)
    {
        for (var j = 0 ; j < id.length ; ++j)
            FadeToggle(id[j], msecs, interruptible, CB)
        return
    }

    if (O(id).Fadeout) FadeIn( id, msecs, interruptible, CB)
    else               FadeOut(id, msecs, interruptible, CB)
}
```

FadeBetween()

This recipe fades smoothly between two images in a similar manner to a fade transition in a slide show program. Figure 15-11 shows two overlaid images in the process of fading between each other.

About the Recipe

This recipe fades smoothly between two images. It requires the following arguments:

- **id1**   An object, an object ID, or an array of objects and/or object IDs.
- **id2**   An object, an object ID, or an array of objects and/or object IDs.
- **msecs**   The number of milliseconds the transition should take.
- **interruptible**   If set, the fade can be interrupted; otherwise, it cannot.

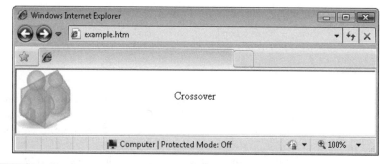

FIGURE 15-11   The house and people icons are fading between each other.

Variables, Arrays, and Functions

FadeOut()	Function to fade an object out
FadeIn()	Function to fade an object in

How It Works

This recipe calls the `FadeOut()` recipe for id1 and the `FadeIn()` recipe for id2. It is also possible to supply an object, an object ID, or an array of objects and/or object IDs to both recipes.

How to Use It

To use this recipe, pass it two IDs, objects, or arrays of objects and/or object IDs, and they will fade from the first object to the second. For the best results, you will probably want to overlay the objects on top of each other so you can get smooth transitions. However, the recipe still works fine if you wish to fade between objects in different locations.

The following example illustrates the setting up of your objects and then fading between them:

```
<center><br />
<span id='sp1'>Crossover</span>
<img id='i1' src='i3.gif' />
<img id='i2' src='i4.gif' />

<script>
OnDOMReady(function()
{
   Locate(Array('i1', 'i2'), ABS, 0, 0)
   FadeToggle('i2', 1, 1)
   O('sp1').onmouseover = function() { FadeBetween('i1', 'i2', 500, 1) }
   O('sp1').onmouseout  = function() { FadeBetween('i2', 'i1', 500, 1) }
})
</script>
```

In the HTML section, a span is created to which mouse events will be attached and then two GIF images are loaded.

In the `<script>` section, the two images are lifted out of the layout by making their position setting 'absolute'. Then, the second image is speedily faded out (over a period of 1 millisecond) so that only the first image is visible.

The mouse events are attached to the `FadeBetween()` recipe so that passing your mouse over the span text smoothly fades between the images over a period of half a second. The first `FadeBetween()` call fades from the first image to the second, while the second call fades back again.

The Recipe

```
function FadeBetween(id1, id2, msecs, interruptible, CB)
{
   FadeOut(id1, msecs, interruptible, CB)
   FadeIn( id2, msecs, interruptible, CB)
}
```

Hide()

This recipe is different from JavaScript Recipe 31, Invisible(), in that when called it completely collapses the object down to a 0 by 0–pixel space. The object is still there so that it can be unhidden, but it is not visible. Because it occupies no space, other elements will often move in to occupy the freed-up space. This makes it perfect for menuing and similar features.

In Figure 15-12, a row of three buttons has been created, each of which is attached by its onclick event to a call to the Hide() recipe. In Figure 15-13, the middle button is hidden after being clicked, and the other buttons have moved in to take up the vacant space.

About the Recipe

This recipe will hide an object, effectively removing it from a web page. It requires the following argument:

- **id**   An object, an object ID, or an array of objects and/or object IDs.

Variables, Arrays, and Functions

HI_Flag	New property assigned to id and set to true when id is hidden
display	The style.display property of id
NextInChain()	Function to start up the next function in a chain (if any)

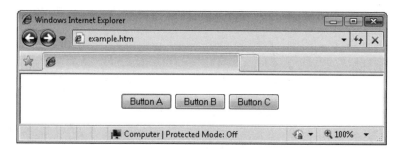

FIGURE 15-12   Three buttons created with click events to hide them

FIGURE 15-13   The middle button has been clicked and is now hidden.

How It Works

This recipe makes a call to the `S()` recipe using the assignment version of the call so that `id` can be an object, an object ID, or an array of objects and/or object IDs. Each object has its `style.display` property set to 'none', which hides it. Additionally, a call to `O()` is made with the arguments `HI_Flag` and `true`, which sets the new object property `Hi_Flag` to `true` so that other recipes can tell that the object has been hidden. This call also supports arrays.

Finally, any callback function contained in `CB` is evaluated with the `eval()` function but only if the argument `CB` (explained in Chapter 17) has a value.

How to Use It

To hide an object, pass it to the `Hide()` recipe, either from inside a section of JavaScript code or from within HTML. The following example creates three buttons, each of which can be clicked to make it hide:

```
<br /><center>
<input id='a' type='submit' value=' Button A ' />
<input id='b' type='submit' value=' Button B ' />
<input id='c' type='submit' value=' Button C ' />

<script>
OnDOMReady(function()
{
   O('a').onclick = function() { Hide('a') }
   O('b').onclick = function() { Hide('b') }
   O('c').onclick = function() { Hide('c') }
})
</script>
```

Alternatively, the input tags could be written as follows, and then no `<script>` section is necessary:

```
<input type='submit' value=' Button A ' onclick='Hide(this)' />
<input type='submit' value=' Button B ' onclick='Hide(this)' />
<input type='submit' value=' Button C ' onclick='Hide(this)' />
```

Or, one button can hide another, like this:

```
<input id='a' type='submit' value=' A ' onclick="Hide('b')" />
<input id='b' type='submit' value=' B ' onclick="Hide('a')" />
```

The previous two lines each hide the other button, so whichever is clicked first will stay displayed, since the other button will now be hidden and therefore can't be clicked.

In the following recipe you'll see how `Hide()` can be combined with `Show()` for creating dynamic web page interaction.

The Recipe

```
function Hide(id, CB)
{
   S(id, 'display', 'none')
   O(id, 'HI_Flag', true)
   if (typeof CB != UNDEF) eval(CB)
}
```

Show()

This is the partner recipe for Hide(). With it you can reveal an object that has previously been hidden. In Figure 15-14, the two recipes have been combined to create a mouseover menu of limericks.

About the Recipe

This recipe will show an object, restoring its dimensions and location and moving back any elements that have moved in to take its space. It requires the following argument:

- **id** An object, an object ID, or an array of objects and/or object IDs.

Variables, Arrays, and Functions

HI_Flag	New property assigned to id and set to true when id is hidden or false when it is not
Display	The style.display property of id
NextInChain()	Function to start up the next function in a chain (if any)

How It Works

This recipe makes a call to the S() recipe using the assignment version of the call so that id can be an object, an object ID, or an array of objects and/or object IDs. Each object has its style.display property set to 'block', which restores its full width and height. Additionally, a call to O() is made with the arguments HI_Flag and false, which sets the new object property Hi_Flag to false, so that other recipes can tell that the object is not hidden. This call also supports arrays.

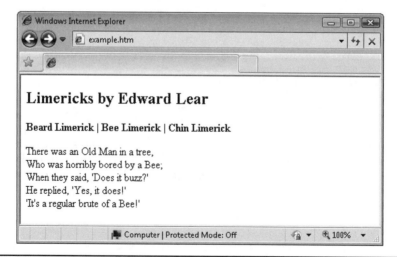

FIGURE 15-14   Different limericks appear as the mouse passes each heading.

Finally, any callback function contained in CB is evaluated with the eval() function, but only if the argument CB (explained in Chapter 17) has a value.

How to Use It

Now that you have both Hide() and Show() in your toolkit, you can start to create some professional results, as in the following example, which features a simple mouseover menu of headings that call up different sections of HTML when the mouse passes over them:

```
<h2>Limericks by Edward Lear</h2><b>

<span id='h1'>Beard Limerick</span> |
<span id='h2'>Bee Limerick</span> |
<span id='h3'>Chin Limerick</span></b><p>

<div id='l1'>There was an Old Man with a beard,<br />
Who said, 'It is just as I feared!<br />
Two Owls and a Hen,<br />
Four Larks and a Wren,<br />
Have all built their nests in my beard!'</div>

<div id='l2'>There was an Old Man in a tree,<br />
Who was horribly bored by a Bee;<br />
When they said, 'Does it buzz?'<br />
He replied, 'Yes, it does!'<br />
'It's a regular brute of a Bee!'</div>

<div id='l3'>There was a Young Lady whose chin,<br />
Resembled the point of a pin;<br />
So she had it made sharp,<br />
And purchased a harp,<br />
And played several tunes with her chin.</div>

<script>
OnDOMReady(function()
{
   Hide(Array('l1', 'l2', 'l3'))
   O('h1').onmouseover = function() { Show('l1') }
   O('h1').onmouseout  = function() { Hide('l1') }
   O('h2').onmouseover = function() { Show('l2') }
   O('h2').onmouseout  = function() { Hide('l2') }
   O('h3').onmouseover = function() { Show('l3') }
   O('h3').onmouseout  = function() { Hide('l3') }
})
</script>
```

This is all pretty straightforward. The HTML section is in two parts. The first displays a header along with the three spans containing subheadings, and the second displays three divs, each containing a different limerick.

The <script> section then hides all three of the divs with a single call to Hide() in which an array of object IDs is passed. Then follow six statements that attach either the

Hide() or Show() recipe to the onmouseover or onmouseout events of the subheadings via the use of anonymous inline functions.

Whenever the mouse is passed over any subheading, the matching div will be displayed using a call to Show(). As soon as the mouse passes out of the subheading, a matching call to Hide() is made to remove it again.

Placing the JavaScript Within HTML

As you will have noticed, my preference when creating such interactive sections of a web page is to proceed using a strong separation between HTML and JavaScript. I find that it makes the HTML much more readable and far easier to update. However, if you prefer to embed JavaScript calls within HTML, you could replace the three span lines with the following:

```
<span id='h1' onmouseover="Show('l1')" onmouseout="Hide('l1')">Beard
    Limerick</span> |
<span id='h2' onmouseover="Show('l2')" onmouseout="Hide('l2')">Bee
    Limerick</span> |
<span id='h3' onmouseover="Show('l3')" onmouseout="Hide('l3')">Chin
    Limerick</span></b><p>
```

If you *do* choose this method of attaching to the mouse events, you can remove the final six statements from the <script> section, but you will still need to keep the initial Hide() statement in order to hide all the divs away on page load.

The Recipe

```
function Show(id, CB)
{
    S(id, 'display', 'block')
    O(id, 'HI_Flag', false)
    if (typeof CB != UNDEF) eval(CB)
}
```

HideToggle()

This chapter's final recipe combines the Hide() and Show() recipes into a single recipe that will toggle the value of an object from one state to the other, without you having to know which state it was in to begin with. Figure 15-15 shows an informational paragraph that, when clicked, will replace itself with another, simply by issuing a single call to this recipe.

About the Recipe

This recipe will make an object hidden if it is shown, or show it if it is hidden. It requires the following argument:

- **id** An object, an object ID, or an array of objects and/or object IDs.

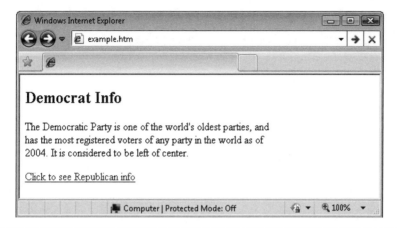

PART III

FIGURE 15-15   Toggling between sets of info

Variables, Arrays, and Functions

j	Local variable to iterate through id if it is an array.
HI_Flag	Flag set by the Hide() and Show() recipes. If true, an object is hidden; if false or unset, it is shown.
display	The style.display property of id.
Show()	Function to show an object that has been hidden.
Hide()	Function to hide an object.

How It Works

This recipe uses the usual code you have seen a few times to iterate through id if it happens to be an array. It determines this with the instanceof operator, and if it *is* an array, the local variable j iterates through id using a for() loop, passing each individual element of the array back to the same function recursively. Once the array has been processed, the function returns.

If id is not an array, the display property of id is inspected. If its value is not 'none', the object is visible, so the Hide() recipe is called. Otherwise, the object is visible, so the Show() recipe is called.

How to Use It

To use this recipe, pass it an object to be hidden or shown. As in most cases, you can also pass an object ID or an array of objects and/or object IDs. The following example illustrates creating a couple of different elements and toggling between them:

```
<div id='democrat'><h2>Democrat Info</h2>
The Democratic Party is one of the world's oldest parties, and<br />
has the most registered voters of any party in the world as of<br />
2004. It is considered to be left of center.<p>
<a id='democrat' href='#'>Click to see Republican info</a></div>
```

```
<div id='republican'><h2>Republican Info</h2>
The Republican Party is often called the Grand Old Party or<br />
the GOP, despite being the younger of the two major parties.<br />
It is considered to be right of center.<p>
<a id='republican' href='#'>Click to see Democrat info</a></div>

<script>
OnDOMReady(function()
{
   Hide('republican')
   O('democrat').onclick   = toggle
   O('republican').onclick = toggle

   function toggle()
   {
      HideToggle(Array('democrat', 'republican'))
   }
})
</script>
```

In the HTML section, two divs are created, one for info on the U.S. Democratic Party, and the other for the U.S. Republican Party. After the informational text (taken from Wikipedia), each div also includes a link with which the alternate information can be displayed.

In the <script> section, the second div (with the ID of 'republican') is hidden so that only one div is shown. The other div could be hidden instead, but *one* of them must be hidden to start with in order for the toggling to work.

Then, two attachments are made, one to each onclick event of the divs. They simply attach the function toggle() to the events, remembering that by leaving out the brackets the *function* is attached to the event, rather than the *value returned* by the function being attached.

Finally, the toggle() function calls the HideToggle() recipe, passing it both of the div IDs. Since one is shown and one is hidden, toggling them both replaces one with the other.

The Recipe

```
function HideToggle(id, CB)
{
   if (id instanceof Array)
   {
      for (var j = 0 ; j < id.length ; ++j)
         HideToggle(id[j], CB)
      return
   }

   if (S(id).display != 'none') Hide(id, CB)
   else Show(id, CB)
}
```

CHAPTER 16

Movement and Animation

From this point on, the JavaScript recipes really start to get interesting, as most of the core recipes have now been covered. Using the tools already outlined, the recipes in this chapter enable you to slide objects around the screen, deflate and inflate objects over time, and zoom objects in a variety of ways. With all of this, you can create some very impressive effects with only a few lines of code.

Slide()

This recipe allows you to slide an object from one place to another over time, making it useful for sliding elements in on demand, hiding and revealing objects, or creating animation effects. Figure 16-1 shows an image in the process of sliding from the bottom left to the top right of the browser.

About the Recipe

This recipe moves an object from one location to another over a period of time. It supports single objects only (not arrays), because if there were more than one object, only the topmost

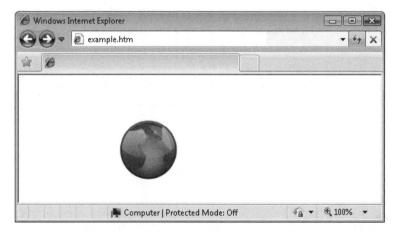

FIGURE 16-1 This recipe smoothly slides objects over time.

one would be seen. Therefore, you can pass only an object or an object ID to this recipe. It requires the following arguments:

- **id** Either an object or an object ID—it cannot be an array of objects.
- **frx**, **fry** The top-left corner of the initial position for **id**.
- **tox**, **toy** The top-left corner of the final position for **id**.
- **msecs** The number of milliseconds the animation should take.
- **interruptible** If **true** (or 1), this recipe can be interrupted by a new call on the same object; if **false** (or 0), the call is uninterruptible.

Variables, Arrays, and Functions

stepx	Local variable containing the amount by which to move horizontally in each step
stepy	Local variable containing the amount by which to move vertically in each step
count	Local variable to count the steps
len1	Local variable containing the start-to-end distance
len2	Local variable containing the new start-to-end distance after an animation is interrupted and given new coordinates
SL_Flag	New property assigned to id: true when a slide is in progress; otherwise, false or unset
SL_Int	New property assigned to id: true if the previous call to this recipe set the slide to uninterruptible
SL_Iid	New property assigned to id with which the repeating interrupts can be stopped
INTERVAL	Global variable with the value 30
Distance()	Subfunction to calculate the distance between two locations
DoSlide()	Subfunction to perform the sliding animation
GoTo()	Function to move an object to a new location
NextInChain()	Function to execute the next function in a chain (if there is one)
setInterval()	Function to set another function to be called repeatedly
clearInterval()	Function to stop the interrupts created by setInterval()

How It Works

The first section of code tests for the existence of the SL_Flag property of id. If it has a value of true (or 1), then a slide on id is already in progress. This is the statement used:

```
if (O(id).SL_Flag)
```

Next, the property of id, SL_Int is tested. If it is false, then the previous call to Slide() for this id set this variable to indicate that the function could not be interrupted, so the function returns.

Otherwise, interrupting the recipe is allowed, so the current slide is stopped by calling `clearInterval()`, passing it the `SL_IID` property of `id`, as returned by `SetInterval()`. The code to do this is as follows:

```
if (!O(id).FL_Int) return
else clearInterval(O(id).SL_IID)
```

Next, because the recipe has been interrupted, it's necessary to allow the interrupting slide to commence from wherever the previous one was halted. What's more, because the coordinates of the halted object will not be the start coordinates passed to the interrupting call, it's necessary to ensure that the interrupting call moves at the same speed as the one specified in the call.

For example, if the call to `Slide()` specifies an animation time of 1000 milliseconds, but it interrupts another slide and discovers that the object is now only one-third of the distance from the destination (instead of the 100 percent it would have been if this was the first `Slide()` call on the object), then the new slide should only take one-third of 1000 milliseconds to move, or 333 milliseconds.

Using the Pythagorean Theorem

To calculate the new distance to travel, and therefore determine the speed of the new slide, the recipe uses the Pythagorean theorem, which states that on a right-angled triangle, the volume of the square on the hypotenuse is equal to the sum of the volumes of the squares on the other two sides.

This works because if you draw a line between any two points on a two-dimensional surface such as a browser, you can draw a horizontal line from one point and a vertical line from the other so they meet each other at a single coordinate to create a right-angled triangle, with the longest edge being the line connecting the two locations.

Therefore, using the Pythagorean theorem, the distance between the requested start and end locations is determined by passing the results of `tox - frx` and `toy - fry` to the subfunction `Distance()`, like this:

```
var len1 = Distance(tox - frx, toy - fry)
```

The `Distance()` subfunction looks like this:

```
function Distance(x, y)
{
   x = Math.max(1, x)
   y = Math.max(1, y)
   return Math.round(Math.sqrt(Math.abs(x * x) + Math.abs(y * y)))
}
```

The variable `x` is the length of one short side of the triangle, while `y` is the length of the other short side. If either value is 0, then it is changed to 1; otherwise, division-by-zero errors may occur.

Each value is then multiplied by itself to determine the volumes of the squares, and they are then converted to absolute values since they could be negative numbers. These figures are then added together to give their combined volume, which is also the volume of the square on the long side of the triangle.

Finally, to discover the length of the triangle's longest side, the square root of this new volume is returned—the distance in pixels between the locations `frx,fry` and `tox,toy`.

With the distance now stored in `len1`, the values of `frx` and `fry` are overridden with those of the actual coordinates of the object by looking them up with the `X()` and `Y()` recipes using the following code. The recipe will use this new start location, overriding the one passed to it by the calling code:

```
frx = X(id)
fry = Y(id)
```

The preceding process is then repeated to discover the distance between the new start location of `frx,fry` and the final location of `tox,toy`, and this distance is then placed in the variable `len2`, like this:

```
var len2 = Distance(tox - frx, toy - fry)
```

It is now possible to adjust the value of `msecs` (the length of time the animation should take in milliseconds) by multiplying it by the result of dividing `len2` by `len1`, like this:

```
msecs *= len2 / len1
```

For example, if the original length is 240 pixels and the new length is 200 pixels, then the preceding statement is the equivalent of:

```
msecs *= 200 / 240
```

Or:

```
msecs *= 0.833
```

Therefore, the length of time the animation should take will become 833 milliseconds. This formula also works when the interrupting call discovers that the actual location of the object is further away than the start position it has specified. If that is the case, `msecs` will end up being multiplied by a value larger than 1, which will extend the time that should be taken.

Determining the Movement Distance for Each Step

Next, the recipe computes the distance between the start and end positions (whether as originally requested by the calling code, or modified due to interrupting a previous slide) and divides the horizontal and vertical differences into the number of steps required to make the animation last for the number of milliseconds specified in `msecs` (which again could be the original value, or a new value computed from interrupting a previous slide). The following code calculates these step values:

```
var stepx = (tox - frx) / (msecs / INTERVAL)
var stepy = (toy - fry) / (msecs / INTERVAL)
```

To explain how these two lines of code work, I have determined that the value in INTERVAL (which is 30 by default) is the optimal time in milliseconds between animation frames.

Therefore, the following calculation calculates the number of steps required to make an animation last msecs milliseconds (if each step happens every INTERVAL milliseconds):

```
(msecs / INTERVAL)
```

TIP *Always ensure you pass the* msecs *argument a value greater than zero, because this recipe (as with all of the animation and transition recipes) does not check for it having a value of zero, which will cause errors and halt the animation.*

The distance between the start and end locations is determined by subtracting the end from the start, as in these two calculations:

```
(tox - frx)
(toy - fry)
```

If the start is before the end, then the result of a calculation is a negative number; otherwise, it is positive. The results are then divided by the result of the previous calculation to divide the distance by the steps required to determine the amount of movement for each axis, for each step of animation.

Setting Up the Repeating Interrupts

The last four lines of the setup portion of the recipe set the local variable count to zero; it will count each step and inform the recipe when it's time to stop. Then, the new SL_Int property of id is set to the value in interruptible. This causes any call that attempts to interrupt the slide to be prevented unless it has the value true or 1. Next, the new SL_Flag property of id is given the value true to tell this and any other recipes that a slide is currently in progress on the object id.

Finally, setInterval() is called, passing it the DoSlide function name and the value in INTERVAL. Because the brackets are left off the end of the function name, the function itself is passed to setInterval(). If brackets were placed after the name, then the *result* of calling the DoSlide() function would be passed to setInterval(), which is another value altogether.

This statement has the effect of initiating an interrupt call to the DoSlide() function every INTERVAL (30 by default) milliseconds. The value returned by the function is stored in SL_IID (IID stands for Interrupt ID), so it can be used as an argument to clearInterval() when the slide has completed (or if it is interrupted). The code to do all this is as follows:

```
var count    = 0
O(id).SL_Int  = interruptible
O(id).SL_Flag = true
O(id).SL_IID  = setInterval(DoSlide, INTERVAL)
```

Performing the Slide

The portion of code that performs the animation is the DoSlide() subfunction. Subfunctions retain access to the main function's local variables and are therefore a neat way to create a repeating interrupt without having to keep passing the arguments required.

The first thing the subfunction does is call the `GoTo()` recipe to move the object to its next location, as follows:

```
GoTo(id, frx + stepx * count, fry + stepy * count)
```

The two values `stepx` and `stepy` were calculated earlier in the recipe, so this simply takes the value in `frx` and adds to it the result of multiplying `stepx` by `count` (the current step number). The same is also calculated for the vertical location.

Next, an `if()` section of code is entered, in which the value of `count` is tested against the result of the calculation `msecs / INTERVAL`. The current value of `count` is tested, but the suffix of `++` then increments `count` after making the test so that it has its new value ready for the next time the subfunction is called. The statement looks like this:

```
if (count++ >= (msecs / INTERVAL))
{
    ...
}
```

If `count` is greater than or equal to `msecs / INTERVAL`, the object has reached its final destination and the animation is complete, so the following four lines of code (shown as ... in the previous `if()` segment) are executed:

```
O(id).SL_Flag = false
GoTo(id, tox, toy)
clearInterval(O(id).SL_Iid)
if (typeof CB != UNDEF) eval(CB)
```

The first line sets the `SL_Flag` property of `id` to `false` to indicate no slide is running on `id`. Then, a `GoTo()` call ensures that the object has ended in exactly the correct position, by passing it the values of `tox` and `toy`. This is necessary because the values of `stepx` and `stepy` will usually be floating point numbers and therefore the final location as calculated using them could be a tiny bit off. The `tox` and `toy` arguments for this call ensure that any imprecision is not an issue.

After this, the `clearInterval()` function is called with an argument of `SL_Iid`, the property of `id` that was created from the result of calling `setInterval()`. This turns off the repeated interrupts.

Finally, any callback function contained in `CB` is evaluated with the `eval()` function, but only if the argument `CB` (explained in Chapter 17) has a value.

How to Use It

To slide an object from one place to another, it must first be released from its default location by giving its `style.position` property a value such as 'absolute'. The following example moves an object from the coordinates 0,100 to 450,0 over the course of 1500 milliseconds (1.5 seconds):

```
<img id='globe' src='i1.gif'>

<script>
OnDOMReady(function()
{
    Position('globe', ABS)
```

```
    Slide('globe', 0, 100, 450, 0, 1500, 0)
})
</script>
```

The HTML section displays an image and gives it the ID 'globe'. Then, in the `<script>` section, the image is given an 'absolute' position using the `Position()` recipe and is then animated with a single call to `Slide()`. The final argument passed is for whether the animation is interruptible. In this case, it is not.

Let's look at another example that responds to mouse events and allows interruption by adding a couple of commands to the `<script>` section of the previous example:

```
O('globe').onmouseover = function()
    { Slide(this, 450, 0,  450, 50, 500, 1) }
O('globe').onmouseout = function()
    { Slide(this, 450, 50, 450, 0,  500, 1) }
```

Now when you pass the mouse over the globe, it will move from the position 450,0 to 450,50. When you move the mouse away, it will slide back to 450,0. As you'll see, it doesn't matter where you interrupt the slide, it always maintains the correct speed. Notice that the keyword `this` tells `Slide()` which object to slide.

However, if you interrupt one slide with another that has a different distance to go or a different length of time specified, then the interrupted and interrupting speeds will not match. I recommend you generally disallow interrupting a slide with a dissimilar one, just as in the first `Slide()` call in the example, which you cannot interrupt.

The Recipe

```
function Slide(id, frx, fry, tox, toy, msecs, interruptible, CB)
{
    if (O(id).SL_Flag)
    {
        if (!O(id).SL_Int) return
        else clearInterval(O(id).SL_IID)

        var len1  = Distance(tox - frx, toy - fry)
        frx       = X(id)
        fry       = Y(id)
        var len2  = Distance(tox - frx, toy - fry)
        msecs    *= len2 / len1
    }

    var stepx = (tox - frx) / (msecs / INTERVAL)
    var stepy = (toy - fry) / (msecs / INTERVAL)

    var count     = 0
    O(id).SL_Int  = interruptible
    O(id).SL_Flag = true
    O(id).SL_IID  = setInterval(DoSlide, INTERVAL)

    function Distance(x, y)
    {
        x = Math.max(1, x)
        y = Math.max(1, y)
```

```
        return Math.round(Math.sqrt(Math.abs(x * x) + Math.abs(y * y)))
    }

function DoSlide()
{
    GoTo(id, frx + stepx * count, fry + stepy * count)

    if (count++ >= (msecs / INTERVAL))
    {
        O(id).SL_Flag = false
        GoTo(id, tox, toy)
        clearInterval(O(id).SL_IID)
        if (typeof CB != UNDEF) eval(CB)
    }
}
}
```

RECIPE 44 SlideBetween()

This recipe swaps the positions of two objects by sliding them past each other. This is a great effect for swapping requested objects into a chosen location. For example, Figure 16-2 shows a collection of photos that can be individually displayed by passing the mouse over the associated title. When you do this, the previous photograph is swapped with the new one and they slide past each other. The old one returns to the stack of pictures, and the new one moves to the main viewing area.

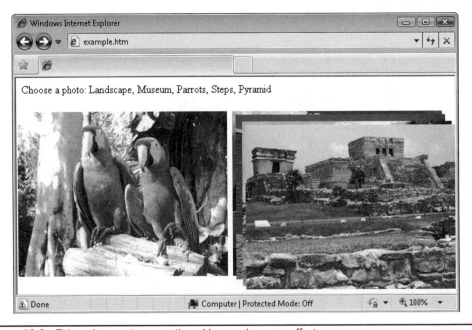

Figure 16-2 This recipe creates smooth and impressive swap effects.

About the Recipe

This recipe takes the positions of two objects and then swaps the two by sliding the objects past each other. It takes the following arguments:

- **id** Either an object or an object ID. It cannot be an array of objects.
- **msecs** The number of milliseconds the animation should take.
- **interruptible** If true (or 1), this recipe can be interrupted by a new call on the same objects; otherwise, if false (or 0), the call is uninterruptible.

Variables, Arrays, and Functions

SL_Flag	Property of both id1 and id2—true if a slide is in progress
SL_Int	Property of both id1 and id2—true if a slide can be interrupted
t1	Local temporary variable to store a copy of id1's SB_X property
t2	Local temporary variable to store a copy of id1's SB_Y property
x1	Local temporary variable to store a copy of id1's SB_X property
y1	Local temporary variable to store a copy of id1's SB_Y property
x2	Local temporary variable to store a copy of id2's SB_X property
y2	Local temporary variable to store a copy of id2's SB_Y property
SB_X	Property of both id1 and id2 containing their horizontal locations
SB_Y	Property of both id1 and id2 containing their vertical locations

How It Works

This recipe first checks whether either of the objects passed to it is currently being used in a slide animation by testing their SL_Flag properties. If so, both objects then have their SL_Int properties tested. If neither has a value of true or 1, then the slide may not be interrupted and the function returns. The code to do this is as follows:

```
if (O(id1).SL_Flag || O(id2).SL_Flag)
{
    if (!O(id1).SL_Int || !O(id2).SL_Int)
        return
```

If the function is interruptible, then the locations of each object require swapping so they can return to their start locations. This behavior has been chosen because the only details passed to the recipe are the object IDs. Therefore, if an interrupting call to SlideBetween() is requested on an object, the only different action it can take is to reverse the current slide.

To do this, the temporary variables t1 and t2 are given the current horizontal and vertical locations of id1. Then, id1 is given the position of id2. Finally, id2 is given the position stored in t1 and t2, using the following statements:

```
var t1       = O(id1).SB_X
var t2       = O(id1).SB_Y
O(id1).SB_X = O(id2).SB_X
O(id1).SB_Y = O(id2).SB_Y
O(id2).SB_X = t1
O(id2).SB_Y = t2
```

If a slide is not currently in progress on either object, copies are made of the current horizontal and vertical locations of each object. These are created as new properties of each object (rather than local variables) so that interrupting calls (if allowed) can have access to them, as follows:

```
else
{
    O(id1).SB_X = X(id1)
    O(id1).SB_Y = Y(id1)
    O(id2).SB_X = X(id2)
    O(id2).SB_Y = Y(id2)
}
```

Next, although not necessary, temporary copies are made of the locations of each object in the short named variables x1, x2, y1, and y2. This is so that the final two statements are easier to read and can fit on single lines. The four lines that do it look like this:

```
var x1 = O(id1).SB_X
var y1 = O(id1).SB_Y
var x2 = O(id2).SB_X
var y2 = O(id2).SB_Y
```

The final statements that start the animations going with calls to the Slide() recipe are as follows:

```
Slide(id1, x1, y1, x2, y2, msecs, interruptible, CB)
Slide(id2, x2, y2, x1, y1, msecs, interruptible, CB)
```

The first statement sets up id1 to move from its location to that of id2, and the second sets id2 up to move from its location to that of id1.

How to Use It

There are many ways you can use this recipe. All you need is a single line of code to smoothly swap two objects, like the following, which swaps object1 and object2 by sliding them past each other over the course of 1000 milliseconds (1 second):

```
SlideBetween(object1, object2, 1000, 0)
```

The final argument of 0 specifies that the animation may not be interrupted and must proceed until it completes.

Here's an example of how you could use this recipe to create a simple but effective way to display photographs:

```
Choose a photo:
<span id='m1'>Landscape</span>,
<span id='m2'>Museum</span>,
<span id='m3'>Parrots</span>,
<span id='m4'>Steps</span>,
<span id='m5'>Pyramid</span>
<div id='b1'></div>
<div id='b2'></div>
<div id='b3'></div>
```

```
<div id='b4'></div>
<div id='b5'></div>
<img id='p1' src='photo1.jpg' />
<img id='p2' src='photo2.jpg' />
<img id='p3' src='photo3.jpg' />
<img id='p4' src='photo4.jpg' />
<img id='p5' src='photo5.jpg' />

<script>
OnDOMReady(function()
{
   Locate(Array('b1', 'b2', 'b3', 'b4', 'b5'), 'absolute',  2, 50)
   Locate('p1', ABS, 330, 50)
   Locate('p2', ABS, 335, 55)
   Locate('p3', ABS, 340, 60)
   Locate('p4', ABS, 345, 65)
   Locate('p5', ABS, 350, 70)

   swap('m1', 'p1', 'b1')
   swap('m2', 'p2', 'b2')
   swap('m3', 'p3', 'b3')
   swap('m4', 'p4', 'b4')
   swap('m5', 'p5', 'b5')

   function swap(o1, o2, o3)
   {
      O(o1).onmouseover = function() {SlideBetween(o2, o3, 200, 1)}
      O(o1).onmouseout  = function() {SlideBetween(o2, o3, 200, 1)}
   }
})
</script>
```

PART III

The HTML section of this example displays some text and five headings that describe five photographs. Each heading is given an ID and placed in its own span tag. Underneath this, five empty divs are created with unique IDs. These will be used as objects with which to swap the photographs. Finally, the photographs are displayed, with each one having a unique ID assigned to it.

In the <script> section, the first statement sets all the blank divs to have a position property of 'absolute' and places them all at the location 2,50. Then the photos are also made 'absolute' and placed in their locations. I chose to give them slightly different coordinates to show them as a stack of images.

After this, five calls to a new function called swap() are made to attach to the image's mouse events. The swap() function takes three arguments, o1, o2, and o3, for the three objects passed to it. The o1 object is one of the heading divs, which then has its onmouseover and onmouseout events attached to by inline anonymous functions that call the SlideBetween() recipe, passing o2 and o3 (the two objects to swap) to it, and a time period of 200 milliseconds that the swap should take.

All this has the effect of swapping a photo with its blank companion div when the mouse passes over its heading. It swaps them back when the mouse passes out of the heading. Because the final argument passed to SlideBetween() is a 1, the animations are interruptible, so if you move the mouse away before a picture has finished sliding, it will simply slide back to its position in the stack of images.

I have deliberately only given you the guts of how this works so you can see how to easily create your own functions. With suitable CSS and graphics, you can use these techniques to create very impressive dynamic effects.

The Recipe

```
function SlideBetween(id1, id2, msecs, interruptible, CB)
{
    if (O(id1).SL_Flag || O(id2).SL_Flag)
    {
        if (!O(id1).SL_Int || !O(id2).SL_Int)
            return

        var t1       = O(id1).SB_X
        var t2       = O(id1).SB_Y
        O(id1).SB_X = O(id2).SB_X
        O(id1).SB_Y = O(id2).SB_Y
        O(id2).SB_X = t1
        O(id2).SB_Y = t2
    }
    else
    {
        O(id1).SB_X = X(id1)
        O(id1).SB_Y = Y(id1)
        O(id2).SB_X = X(id2)
        O(id2).SB_Y = Y(id2)
    }

    var x1 = O(id1).SB_X
    var y1 = O(id1).SB_Y
    var x2 = O(id2).SB_X
    var y2 = O(id2).SB_Y

    Slide(id1, x1, y1, x2, y2, msecs, interruptible, CB)
    Slide(id2, x2, y2, x1, y1, msecs, interruptible, CB)
}
```

Deflate()

With this recipe, you can make an object shrink down over time until it is no longer visible. You can also specify whether to deflate (or shrink) the width, height, or both. Figure 16-3 shows three images, each of which is in the process of being deflated with this recipe. The first is shrinking horizontally, the last vertically, and the middle one is deflating in both dimensions.

About the Recipe

This recipe takes an object and, over a specified time period, shrinks it down until it is no longer visible. The following are the required arguments:

- **id** An object, an object ID, or an array of objects and/or object IDs.
- **w** If true or 1, the object's width will shrink.

FIGURE 16-3 Three different types of deflation are supported by this recipe.

- **h** If true or 1, the object's height will shrink.
- **msecs** The number of milliseconds the animation should take.
- **interruptible** If true (or 1), this recipe can be interrupted by a new call on the same object; otherwise, if false (or 0), the call is uninterruptible.

Variables, Arrays, and Functions

j	Local variable to index into id if it is an array
stepw	Local variable containing the amount of horizontal change per frame
steph	Local variable containing the amount of vertical change per frame
width	Local variable containing the width to which id should be changed at each step
height	Local variable containing the height to which id should be changed at each step
overflow	The object's style.overflow object, which is set to Hid ('hidden') to prevent an object's contents overflowing as it shrinks
DF_Flag	Property of id that is true if a Deflate() call is in progress
DF_Int	Property of id containing true if the deflation is interruptible
DF_Iid	Property of id used to clear an interrupt with clearInterval()
DF_OldW	Property of id containing the unshrunk width of id
DF_OldH	Property of id containing the unshrunk height of id
DF_Count	Property of id that counts the number of frames in the animation

Deflated	Property of id set to true if it has been deflated—used by the DeflateToggle() recipe
INTERVAL	Global variable with the value 30
HID	Global variable with the value 'hidden'
setInterval()	Function to set up repeating interrupts
clearInterval()	Function to stop repeating interrupts
DoDeflate()	Subfunction to perform the animation
W()	Function to fetch an object's width
H()	Function to fetch an object's height
Resize()	Function to resize an object
NextInChain()	Function to call the next function in a chain of functions (if there is one)

How It Works

This recipe has a few different parts. The first part tests whether id is an array; if it is, it calls itself recursively with each element of id using the following code:

```
if (id instanceof Array)
{
   for (var j = 0 ; j < id.length ; ++j)
      Deflate(id[j], w, h, msecs, interruptible, CB)
   return
}
```

This allows many objects to be deflated at once, as long as they are passed to Deflate() in an array.

Next, the code has to take into account the fact that when only one dimension of an image is changed, most browsers will automatically modify the other one to keep the image at the same aspect ratio. However, in this case, that feature is not wanted, so if either the horizontal or vertical width is not to be changed (as decided by the values in the w and h arguments), that dimension is given a fixed value representing its current length to replace its default value of 'auto'. This allows one dimension to be altered, while the other will not change:

```
if (!w) ResizeWidth( id, W(id))
if (!h) ResizeHeight(id, H(id))
```

Next, if a deflate animation is already in progress on id (as determined by its DF_Flag property having a value of true or 1, its DF_Int property is checked. This contains true or 1 if the animation may be interrupted; if it is not true or 1, the function returns. Otherwise, if any deflate interrupt is currently running, it is stopped with a call to clearInterval(). The code for these two actions is as follows:

```
if (O(id).DF_Flag)
{
   if (!O(id).DF_Int) return
   else clearInterval(O(id).DF_IID)
}
```

Otherwise, if this is the first time the id object has been used by the Deflate() recipe, there are some properties that need assigning, as follows:

```
else
{
   if (w) O(id).DF_OldW  = W(id)
   if (h) O(id).DF_OldH  = H(id)
   O(id).DF_Count = msecs / INTERVAL
}
```

In this section, the properties DF_OldW and DF_OldH are assigned the current width and height of the object so they can be restored later—but only those dimensions that are to be resized have this value saved.

Also, the DF_Count property is assigned the result of msecs / INTERVAL, which is the number of steps in the animation. This variable will later count down one step at a time to zero (in the DoDeflate() subfunction), and each time its value will be multiplied by the values in stepw and/or steph to calculate the correct width and/or height of id for each step of the animation.

Next, some properties have to be assigned a certain value (whether or not this is the first time id has been used with this recipe) using the following statements:

```
var stepw = O(id).DF_OldW / (msecs / INTERVAL)
var steph = O(id).DF_OldH / (msecs / INTERVAL)

S(id).overflow = HID
O(id).Deflated = true
O(id).DF_Flag  = true
O(id).DF_Int   = interruptible
O(id).DF_IID   = setInterval(DoDeflate, INTERVAL)
```

First, the horizontal and vertical distances for each step of the animation are assigned to stepw and steph. This determines the amount of horizontal and vertical shrinkage required in each step to ensure the animation lasts msecs milliseconds.

The next statement ensures that the contents of the id object will not overflow its boundaries during resizing by setting the style.overflow property of id to HID (which stands for 'hidden'). This is not an issue when resizing images, but it certainly is when the object is a div or span that contains multiple items such as text and images.

The Deflated property is then set to true to indicate the object's current deflated/inflated state to this and other recipes, such as DeflateToggle().The DF_Flag is also set to true to tell this and any other recipes that a Deflate() call is now in progress on id.

Next, DF_Int is given the value in interruptible so that if the recipe is called again on id while the animation is still running, this value can be tested and, if not true or 1, the recipe will not be interrupted.

The final statement in this part of the code uses setInterval() to set up an interrupt call to DoDeflate() every INTERVAL milliseconds. The result of making this call is a value that can later be passed to clearInterval() to cancel the interrupts. It is saved in the DF_IID property of id.

PART III

The DoDeflate( ) Subfunction

Once initialized by the main part of the recipe, the `DoDeflate()` subfunction is called every `INTERVAL` milliseconds, and each time it shrinks the object a little more, like this:

```
if (w) ResizeWidth( id, stepw * O(id).DF_Count)
if (h) ResizeHeight(id, steph * O(id).DF_Count)
```

These two lines calculate the new width and/or height of `id` and then resize either or both.

Next, a check is made to see if this was the final resize and whether the animation can now stop. This is done by checking the value of `DF_Count`, which is decremented after each frame of animation.

When the Animation Is Finished

If the `DF_Count` property is less than 1, the animation has completed and the `DF_Flag` property of `id` is set to `false` to indicate there is now no deflate operation running on `id`.

Finally, the width and/or height of the dimension(s) being resized are set to zero to complete the transition.

In the final two lines of the recipe, the `clearInterval()` function is called to prevent any further interrupts. Any callback function contained in `CB` is evaluated with the `eval()` function, but only if the argument `CB` (explained in Chapter 17) has a value. The code for these actions is as follows:

```
if (O(id).DF_Count-- < 1)
{
   O(id).DF_Flag = false

   if (w) ResizeWidth(id, 0)
   if (h) ResizeHeight(id, 0)

   clearInterval(O(id).DF_IID)
   if (typeof CB != UNDEF) eval(CB)
}
```

TIP *The double-hyphen (--) operator following* DF_Count *is a handy way of telling JavaScript to decrement the variable, but only after its current value has been used in the* if() *statement, thus saving an extra line of code.*

How to Use It

Using `deflate()` is a great way to make an object disappear smoothly and is much more fun than just fading it out or hiding it. Here's some example code illustrating the three different types of effects supported by this recipe:

```
<span id='d'>Mouseover Me</span>

<img id='p1' src='photo1.jpg' />
<img id='p2' src='photo2.jpg' />
<img id='p3' src='photo3.jpg' />
```

```
<script>
OnDOMReady(function()
{
   Locate('p1', ABS, 0,   0)
   Locate('p2', ABS, 160, 0)
   Locate('p3', ABS, 320, 0)
   Deflate('p1', 1, 0, 2000, 0)
   Deflate('p2', 1, 1, 2000, 0)
   Deflate('p3', 0, 1, 2000, 0)
})
</script>
```

The HTML section of this example places three images on the screen and assigns them unique IDs. The `<script>` section then uses the `Locate()` recipe to give them all a position of 'absolute' and places them along the top of the browser, overlapping each other.

The final three lines call up a different `Deflate()` effect on each, which is achieved by passing different values of the second and third parameters. The first image shrinks only in a horizontal direction because the two width and height parameters are 1 and 0. The middle image has width and height parameters of 1 and 1, so it shrinks in both directions. The last image has width and height parameters of 0 and 1 and shrinks only in a vertical direction.

The final two parameters of 2000 and 0 cause the animations to take 2000 milliseconds each (although they run concurrently), and the 0 specifies that they are not interruptible.

The Recipe

```
function Deflate(id, w, h, msecs, interruptible, CB)
{
   if (id instanceof Array)
   {
      for (var j = 0 ; j < id.length ; ++j)
         Deflate(id[j], w, h, msecs, interruptible, CB)
      return
   }

   if (!w) ResizeWidth( id, W(id))
   if (!h) ResizeHeight(id, H(id))

   if (O(id).DF_Flag)
   {
      if (!O(id).DF_Int) return
      else clearInterval(O(id).DF_IID)
   }
   else
   {
      if (w) O(id).DF_OldW  = W(id)
      if (h) O(id).DF_OldH  = H(id)
      O(id).DF_Count = msecs / INTERVAL
   }

   var stepw = O(id).DF_OldW / (msecs / INTERVAL)
   var steph = O(id).DF_OldH / (msecs / INTERVAL)
```

```
   S(id).overflow = HID
   O(id).Deflated = true
   O(id).DF_Flag   = true
   O(id).DF_Int    = interruptible
   O(id).DF_IID    = setInterval(DoDeflate, INTERVAL)

   function DoDeflate()
   {
      if (w) ResizeWidth( id, stepw * O(id).DF_Count)
      if (h) ResizeHeight(id, steph * O(id).DF_Count)

      if (O(id).DF_Count-- < 1)
      {
         O(id).DF_Flag = false
         if (w) ResizeWidth( id, 0)
         if (h) ResizeHeight(id, 0)
         clearInterval(O(id).DF_IID)
         if (typeof CB != UNDEF) eval(CB)
      }
   }
}
```

Reflate()

This is the companion recipe to Deflate(). With it, you can expand a deflated object back to its original dimensions over a specified period of time, with a choice of three different animation types. In Figure 16-4, a div has been added to the example in the Deflate() recipe with which you can deflate or reflate the objects.

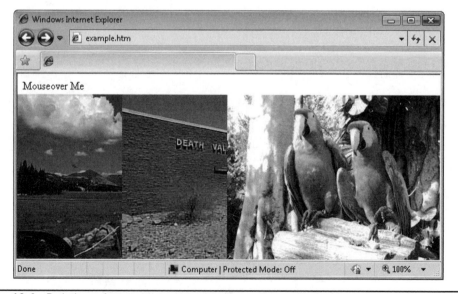

FIGURE 16-4 Both the recipes Deflate() and Reflate() are attached to mouse events.

About the Recipe

This recipe takes an object (or an array of objects) and reinflates it to its original dimensions after it was deflated using the Deflate() recipe. You can call this recipe only on objects that have been previously deflated; otherwise, the call will be ignored. It takes the following arguments:

- **id**   An object, an object ID, or an array of objects and/or object IDs.
- **w**   If true or 1, the object's width will expand to its original value.
- **h**   If true or 1, the object's height will expand to its original value.
- **msecs**   The number of milliseconds the animation should take.
- **interruptible**   If true (or 1), this recipe can be interrupted by a new call on the same object; otherwise, if false (or 0), the call is uninterruptible.

Variables, Arrays, and Functions

j	Local variable to index into id if it is an array
stepw	Local variable containing the amount of horizontal change per frame
steph	Local variable containing the amount of vertical change per frame
width	Local variable containing the width to which id should be changed at each step
height	Local variable containing the height to which id should be changed at each step
DF_Flag	Property of id that is true if a Deflate() call is in progress
DF_Int	Property of id containing true if the deflation is interruptible
DF_IID	Property of id that clears an interrupt with clearInterval()
DF_OldW	Property of id containing the unshrunk width of id
DF_OldH	Property of id containing the unshrunk height of id
DF_Count	Property of id that counts the number of frames in the animation
Deflated	Property of id set to true if it has been deflated—used by the DeflateToggle() recipe
INTERVAL	Global variable with the value 30
setInterval()	Function to set up repeating interrupts
clearInterval()	Function to stop repeating interrupts
DoReflate()	Subfunction to perform the animation
Resize()	Function to resize an object
NextInChain()	Function to call the next function in a chain of functions (if there is one)

How It Works

This recipe works in a very similar way to the Deflate() recipe, but with two main differences. First, if the Deflated property of id is not true, the recipe returns because the object cannot be reinflated. Here is the piece of code that does this:

```
if (!O(id).Deflated) return
```

Second, instead of DF_Count counting down from the maximum step count to zero, it counts upward from 0 and so is initialized to a value of zero in this recipe (as opposed to the value it is assigned with msecs / INTERVAL in the Deflate() recipe). The DoReflate() subfunction uses the following statement to increment the DF_Count property in each frame of the animation (instead of decrementing, as in the DoDeflate() subfunction of Deflate()):

```
if (O(id).DF_Count++ >= msecs / INTERVAL)
```

The Deflated property of id that indicates whether an object is deflated or inflated is set to false by this recipe (rather than true, as with Deflate()), but the rest of the code is virtually the same, so please read the details on Deflate() for further details.

How to Use It

You should call this recipe on an object only after the object has been deflated using the Deflate() recipe. If you try to use it on an object that hasn't yet been deflated, the recipe will simply return.

The following example is expanded from the one in the Deflate() recipe section. It has a div inserted before the images that you can pass the mouse over to either deflate or reflate the images:

```
<span id='d'>Mouseover Me</span>

<img id='p1' src='photo1.jpg' />
<img id='p2' src='photo2.jpg' />
<img id='p3' src='photo3.jpg' />

<script>
OnDOMReady(function()
{
   Locate('p1', ABS, 0,    30)
   Locate('p2', ABS, 160, 30)
   Locate('p3', ABS, 320, 30)

   O('d').onmouseover = down
   O('d').onmouseout  = up

   function down()
   {
      Deflate('p1', 1, 0, 2000, 1)
      Deflate('p2', 1, 1, 2000, 1)
      Deflate('p3', 0, 1, 2000, 1)
   }

   function up()
   {
      Reflate('p1', 1, 0, 2000, 1)
      Reflate('p2', 1, 1, 2000, 1)
      Reflate('p3', 0, 1, 2000, 1)
   }
}
</script>
```

This example replaces the direct calls to the Deflate() recipe with a pair of new functions, down() and up(). These are attached to the onmouseover and onmouseout events of the span displaying the text "Mouseover Me," so that when you move the mouse over the text, the objects deflate, and when you move it away, they inflate.

The calls to the two recipes have their final parameter set to 1. This is the interruptible argument, and therefore interrupting of the recipes has been enabled. This means that the example is very responsive and the animations occur immediately upon moving the mouse in or out of the span, taking into account the current amount of deflation or reflation to smoothly inverse the previous animation.

The Recipe

```
function Reflate(id, w, h, msecs, interruptible, CB)
{
    if (id instanceof Array)
    {
        for (var j = 0 ; j < id.length ; ++j)
            Reflate(id[j], w, h, msecs, interruptible, CB)
        return
    }

    if (!O(id).Deflated) return
    else if (O(id).DF_Flag)
    {
        if (!O(id).DF_Int) return
        else clearInterval(O(id).DF_IID)
    }
    else O(id).DF_Count = 0

    var stepw  = O(id).DF_OldW / (msecs / INTERVAL)
    var steph  = O(id).DF_OldH / (msecs / INTERVAL)

    O(id).DF_Flag  = true
    O(id).Deflated = false
    O(id).DF_Int   = interruptible
    O(id).DF_IID   = setInterval(DoReflate, INTERVAL)

    function DoReflate()
    {
        if (w) ResizeWidth( id, stepw * O(id).DF_Count)
        if (h) ResizeHeight(id, steph * O(id).DF_Count)

        if (O(id).DF_Count++ >= msecs / INTERVAL)
        {
            O(id).DF_Flag = false
            if (w) ResizeWidth( id, O(id).DF_OldW)
            if (h) ResizeHeight(id, O(id).DF_OldH)
            clearInterval(O(id).DF_IID)
            if (typeof CB != UNDEF) eval(CB)
        }
    }
}
```

DeflateToggle()

If you use this recipe, you don't need to keep track of which objects have or haven't been deflated, and it saves on extra code, too. In Figure 16-5, the example in the `Reflate()` recipe section has been updated to use this recipe.

About the Recipe

This recipe toggles an object between being deflated or inflated. It takes the following arguments:

- **id**   An object, an object ID, or an array of objects and/or object IDs.
- **w**   If `true` or 1, the object's width will deflate or reflate.
- **h**   If `true` or 1, the object's height will deflate or reflate.
- **msecs**   The number of milliseconds the animation should take.
- **interruptible**   If `true` (or 1), this recipe can be interrupted by a new call on the same object; otherwise, if `false` (or 0), the call is uninterruptible.

Variables, Arrays, and Functions

j	Local variable for indexing into id if it is an array
Deflated	Property of id that is true if id is deflated
Deflate()	Function to deflate an object to 0 width by 0 height
Reflate()	Function to reflate an object to its original dimensions

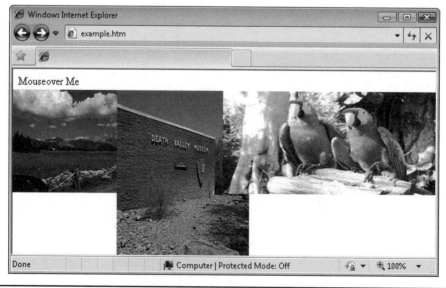

FIGURE 16-5   The images automatically toggle between being inflated and deflated.

How It Works

This recipe uses the standard recursive techniques of many of the others to determine whether id is an array, and if it is, to pass each element of the array recursively back to the same function to be dealt with individually, as follows:

```
if (id instanceof Array)
{
    for (var j = 0 ; j < id.length ; ++j)
        DeflateToggle(id[j], w, h, msecs, interruptible, CB)
    return
}
```

After that, there are just two statements, the first of which tests the Deflated property of id. If it is true, the object has been (or is in the process of being) deflated, so the Reflate() recipe is called. Otherwise, the object is inflated (or is in the process of being reinflated), so the Deflate() recipe is called, like this:

```
if (O(id).Deflated) Reflate(id, w, h, msecs, interruptible, CB)
else                Deflate(id, w, h, msecs, interruptible, CB)
```

How to Use It

You can use this recipe to replace having to call both of the Deflate() and Reflate() recipes and to save having to track their deflated/inflated states. The following code is similar to the previous example in the Reflate() section, except that it is shorter because it uses DeflateToggle() instead of both the Deflate() and Reflate() recipes:

```
<span id='d'>Mouseover Me</span>

<img id='p1' src='photo1.jpg' />
<img id='p2' src='photo2.jpg' />
<img id='p3' src='photo3.jpg' />

<script>
OnDOMReady(function()
{
    Locate('p1', ABS, 0,   30)
    Locate('p2', ABS, 160, 30)
    Locate('p3', ABS, 320, 30)
    Deflate('p2', 1, 0, 1, 1)

    O('d').onmouseover = toggle
    O('d').onmouseout  = toggle

    function toggle()
    {
        DeflateToggle('p1', 1, 1, 2000, 1)
        DeflateToggle('p2', 1, 0, 2000, 1)
        DeflateToggle('p3', 0, 1, 2000, 1)
    }
})
</script>
```

PART III

For variety, I added a call to `Deflate()` just after those to the `Locate()` recipe so that the second picture will start off deflated. Notice that I passed a value of 1 millisecond for the call (the fastest allowed) so that, for all intents and purposes, it is instant.

Try passing your mouse in and out of the Mouseover Me text and watch how the pictures toggle their deflated/inflated states as you do so, smoothly changing between each animation type as soon as you move the cursor in and out.

To become fully acquainted with what this recipe can do for you, you might want to change the animation length from 2000 milliseconds to other values, change the `interruptible` argument to 0, change the animation types by varying the w and h parameters, or use different images in varying locations.

TIP *Remember that the second and third arguments (w and h, which specify whether the width and/ or height is to be modified) must be the same for all deflates, inflates, and toggles on an object for it to correctly deflate and inflate. For example, if you deflate just the width of an object and then try to inflate just its height, nothing will happen since the height has not been deflated. In this case, only the object's width can be inflated.*

The Recipe

```
function DeflateToggle(id, w, h, msecs, interruptible, CB)
{
    if (id instanceof Array)
    {
        for (var j = 0 ; j < id.length ; ++j)
            DeflateToggle(id[j], w, h, msecs, interruptible, CB)
        return
    }

    if (O(id).Deflated) Reflate(id, w, h, msecs, interruptible, CB)
    else                Deflate(id, w, h, msecs, interruptible, CB)
}
```

 ## 48 DeflateBetween()

This recipe provides similar functionality to the `FadeBetween()` recipe, except that it resizes a pair of objects in a choice of three different ways (height, width, or width and height), rather than simply fading from one to the other. This recipe is good for creating professional slideshow effects, or for swapping content. In Figure 16-6, two images have been overlaid on each other, and while the larger one deflates, the smaller picture inflates and will soon be as large as the original image, which will have disappeared by the time the original smaller picture reaches that size.

About the Recipe

This recipe swaps two objects by deflating one and inflating the other at the same time. It requires these arguments:

- **id1**   An object, an object ID, or an array of objects and/or object IDs.
- **id2**   An object, an object ID, or an array of objects and/or object IDs.

FIGURE 16-6   Swapping two objects by deflating one and inflating the other

- **w**   If `true` or 1, the object's width will deflate or reflate.
- **h**   If `true` or 1, the object's height will deflate or reflate.
- **msecs**   The number of milliseconds the animation should take.
- **interruptible**   If `true` (or 1), this recipe can be interrupted by a new call on the same object; otherwise, if `false` (or 0), the call is uninterruptible.

Variables, Arrays, and Functions

`Deflate()`	Function to deflate an object to zero width and height
`Reflate()`	Function to reinflate an object to its previous dimensions

How It Works

This recipe simply makes one call to `Deflate()` for the first object, and another to `Reflate()` for the second.

How to Use It

To use this recipe, you need to ensure that the second object has already been deflated. Ideally, you will have also released each object from its position in the HTML by giving it a position style of 'absolute' or 'relative'. You will probably also have overlaid the objects on each other.

The following example does all of this and features a span you can pass your mouse over to initiate the swaps:

```
<span id='d'>Mouseover Me</span>

<img id='p1' src='photo1.jpg' />
<img id='p2' src='photo2.jpg' />
```

```
<script>
OnDOMReady(function()
{
   Locate(Array('p1', 'p2'), ABS, 0, 30)
   Deflate('p2', 1, 1, 1, 0)

   O('d').onmouseover = swap1
   O('d').onmouseout  = swap2

   function swap1()
   {
      DeflateBetween('p1', 'p2', 1, 1, 1000, 1)
   }

   function swap2()
   {
      DeflateBetween('p2', 'p1', 1, 1, 1000, 1)
   }
})
</script>
```

The HTML section creates a span with the text "Mouseover Me" and also displays two images. All three items are given unique IDs.

In the <script> section, both of the images are given a position style setting of 'absolute', and are located at 0 pixels across and 30 down using calls to the Locate() recipe. The second image is then deflated using the Deflate() recipe over the shortest time possible (1 millisecond), which is virtually instantaneous.

Finally, the onmouseover and onmouseout events of the div are attached, in order, to the swap1() and swap2() functions, which call the DeflateBetween() recipe to either swap from image 1 to image 2 or from image 2 to image 1.

The transitions are given 1000 milliseconds (or 1 second) to complete. Because the interruptible parameter is set to 1, you can pass your mouse in and out of the Mouseover Me text to instantly change between displaying one image or the other.

You may want to try changing the w and h arguments to see the various different effects you can achieve.

The Recipe

```
function DeflateBetween(id1, id2, w, h, msecs, interruptible, CB)
{
   Deflate(id1, w, h, msecs, interruptible, CB)
   Reflate(id2, w, h, msecs, interruptible, CB)
}
```

49 Zoom()

This recipe is similar in some ways to the `Deflate()` and `Reflate()` recipes, but it can do much more, including zooming in and out using the center of an object as the focus, padding margins during zooms to retain the same width and height (ensuring other objects don't get disturbed by the resizing), and specifying end widths and heights.

In Figure 16-7, four icons are displayed, each of which is attached by its mouse events to the `Zoom()` recipe so that when the mouse passes over them they enlarge, and when it moves away they shrink back down. In the figure, the second icon is currently zoomed up.

About the Recipe

This recipe will zoom an object over a period of time between two supplied sets of width and height. It can also pad the object to retain its overall dimensions and supports three different styles of zoom. It requires the following arguments:

- **id** An object, an object ID, or an array of objects and/or object IDs.
- **w** If `true` or 1, the object's width will be zoomed.
- **h** If `true` or 1, the object's height will be zoomed.
- **fromw** The width from which the object should be zoomed.
- **fromh** The height from which the object should be zoomed.
- **tow** The width to which the object should be zoomed.
- **toh** The height to which the object should be zoomed.
- **msecs** The number of milliseconds the animation should take.
- **pad** If greater than 0, the object will be padded with CSS padding (so that it always keeps the same dimensions); otherwise, if it is –1, no padding is required and `id` may not be moved during a zoom. If pad is 0 or `null`, then in addition to not applying padding, the object will be moved during resizing so it remains centered.
- **interruptible** If `true` (or 1), this recipe can be interrupted by a new call on the same object; otherwise, if `false` (or 0), the call is uninterruptible.

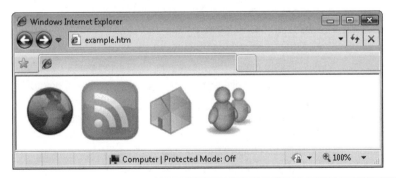

FIGURE 16-7 Zooming icons when the mouse passes over them

Variables, Arrays, and Functions

j	Local variable for indexing into id if it is an array
tox	Local variable containing the final horizontal offset
toy	Local variable containing the final vertical offset
midx	Local variable containing the horizontal center offset
midy	Local variable containing the vertical center offset
width1	Local variable containing the amount of padding for the left of the object
width2	Copy of width1 containing the amount of padding for the right of the object
height1	Local variable containing the amount of padding for the top of the object
height2	Copy of height1 containing the amount of padding for the bottom of the object
stepw	Local variable containing the amount of change in width for each step
steph	Local variable containing the amount of change in height for each step
INTERVAL	Global variable containing the value 30
HID	Global variable containing the value 'hidden'
ZO_W	Property of id containing its current width
ZO_H	Property of id containing its current height
ZO_Flag	Property of id set to true if a zoom is in progress
ZO_Int	Property of id set to true if a zoom may be interrupted
ZO_Count	Property of id containing the current frame number of the animation
ZO_IID	Property of id containing the value required to cancel the interrupts with clearInterval()
paddingLeft	The style.paddingLeft property of id
paddingTop	The style.paddingTop property of id
paddingRight	The style.paddingRight property of id
paddingBottom	The style.paddingBottom property of id
overflow	The style.overflow property of id
setInterval()	Function to start repeated interrupts to another function
clearInterval()	Function to stop repeated interrupts
Math.max()	Function to return the maximum out of two values
Math.floor()	Function to remove any numbers after the decimal point in a floating point number and return an integer
Math.round()	Function to round a floating point number either up or down to the nearest integer
DoZoom()	Subfunction to perform the zoom animation
ZoomPad()	Subfunction to pad an object while zooming so that it retains the same dimensions
NoPx()	Function to remove the 'px' suffix of a property

Px()	Function to add the 'px' suffix to a value
W()	Function to return an object's width
H()	Function to return an object's height
X()	Function to return an object's horizontal offset
Y()	Function to return an object's vertical offset
GoTo()	Function to move an object to a new location
Resize()	Function to resize the dimensions of an object
NextInChain()	Function to initiate the next function in a chain (if there is one)

How It Works

This recipe is quite long because it has to achieve a number of different objectives, but if you follow this explanation you'll see how it breaks down into easily digestible chunks. However, you don't need to understand how this function works if you just want to use it, so please don't be put off by this extended commentary.

You should be fully familiar with the first section of code by now, because it checks whether id is an array, and if it is, it passes each element recursively to the same function to be dealt with individually, as follows:

```
if (id instanceof Array)
{
    for (var j = 0 ; j < id.length ; ++j)
        Zoom(id[j], w, h, fromw, fromh, tow, toh,
            msecs, pad, interruptible, CB)
    return
}
```

After this, copies of the object's current x and y coordinates need saving (if they haven't already been saved), like this:

```
if (typeof O(id).ZO_X == UNDEF)
{
    O(id).ZO_X = X(id)
    O(id).ZO_Y = Y(id)
}
```

The typeof operator checks whether the property ZO_X is already defined. If it isn't, it assigns values to both it and the property ZO_Y, taken from the recipes X() and Y().

If a Zoom Is Not Currently in Progress

Next, the recipe checks whether a zoom is currently in progress on id by looking at its ZO_Flag property. If a zoom is not in progress, then three variables require initializing prior to starting the zoom, as follows:

```
if (!O(id).ZO_Flag)
{
    O(id).ZO_W     = Math.max(fromw, tow)
    O(id).ZO_H     = Math.max(fromh, toh)
    O(id).ZO_Count = 0
}
```

The first two statements assign whichever value is larger out of the start and destination widths and heights in `fromw`, `tow`, `fromh`, and `toh` to the `ZO_W` and `ZO_H` properties of `id`. This sets default values for the width and height of a zoom should only one of the dimensions be set to change (therefore, the nonchanging dimension will retain this value). The `ZO_Count` property is also initialized to zero.

If a Zoom Is in Progress

If a zoom is in progress, the `ZO_Int` property is inspected. If it is not `true`, the recipe may not be interrupted, so it returns. Next, the repeating interrupts are stopped by calling the `clearInterval()` function. Also, because the only useful action an interrupt can do to a zoom in progress is to reverse the direction of zooming, the `ZO_Count` property of `id` is set to its inverse. Here is the section of code that does this:

```
else
{
    if (!O(id).ZO_Int) return
    else clearInterval(O(id).ZO_IID)

    O(id).ZO_Count = (msecs / INTERVAL) - O(id).ZO_Count
}
```

If the zoom can't be interrupted, then the recipe returns. Otherwise, the current repeating interrupts are canceled.

The final statement is based on the result of `msecs / INTERVAL` being the number of steps required to make the zoom last for `msecs` milliseconds. Therefore, if the `ZO_Count` property has a value of 10 out of 34 (for example), then for the zoom to reverse, there will be only 10 steps remaining to return to the starting zoom level.

Setting Up the Variables

After this, a few local variables require setting up (whether or not a zoom is currently running), using this code:

```
var maxw  = Math.max(fromw, tow)
var maxh  = Math.max(fromh, toh)
var stepw = (tow - fromw) / (msecs / INTERVAL)
var steph = (toh - fromh) / (msecs / INTERVAL)
```

The first two statements use the `Math.max()` function to determine the maximum width and height an object will be at either the start or end of the zoom, and places these values in `maxw` and `maxh`. Then, the horizontal and vertical distance between each frame of the zoom is calculated and placed in `stepw` and `steph`.

The last four statements of the initial setup process are these:

```
S(id).overflow = HID
O(id).ZO_Flag  = true
O(id).ZO_Int   = interruptible
O(id).ZO_IID   = setInterval(DoZoom, INTERVAL)
```

The first one ensures that the object will not overflow outside its boundaries if it is made smaller than the contents. This isn't applicable to images but must be done for objects such as divs and spans that can contain many different elements. The overflowing is prevented by setting id's style.overflow property to the value in HID, which is 'hidden'.

Next, the ZO_Flag property is set to true to indicate to this and other recipes that a zoom is in progress on id. The ZO_Int property is also assigned the value in interruptible, which will be true if this zoom can be interrupted.

Finally, the setInterval() function is called in such a way that the DoZoom() subfunction will be called every INTERVAL milliseconds. The result returned by the function is placed in ZO_IID so it can later be used to cancel the interrupts using a call to clearInterval().

The DoZoom() Subfunction

The job of the DoZoom() subfunction is to perform the resizing required by changing the object's dimensions just a little each time it is called. The first three lines calculate the new width and height and perform the resizing as follows:

```
if (w) O(id).ZO_W = Math.round(fromw + stepw * O(id).ZO_Count)
if (h) O(id).ZO_H = Math.round(fromh + steph * O(id).ZO_Count)
Resize(id, O(id).ZO_W, O(id).ZO_H)
```

In the first line, if the argument w is true, then horizontal resizing is allowed so the ZO_W property of id is assigned the new value required for the object's width. This value is calculated by multiplying stepw (the amount of change for each step of the animation) by ZO_Count (the number of this animation step) and adding it to the value of the fromw argument (the original width of the object). If the zoom is reducing id, then a negative value is added to fromw; otherwise, a positive value is added.

The second line does exactly the same but for the object's height, and then places the result in id's ZO_H property. If either w or h is not true, that dimension is not to be resized during the zoom, and the value previously assigned to either the ZO_W or ZO_H property earlier in the recipe will be the default used. The third line performs the resizing by calling the Resize() recipe.

After this, the values required to center the object are placed in midx and midy, like this:

```
var midx = O(id).ZO_X + Math.round((maxw - O(id).ZO_W) / 2)
var midy = O(id).ZO_Y + Math.round((maxh - O(id).ZO_H) / 2)
```

These are calculated by taking the maximum width and height of the object and then subtracting its current width and height from them. These values are then divided by 2 to obtain the offset from the top left of the object, which has been stored in the ZO_X and ZO_T properties of id.

When the Pad Argument Is True

If the pad argument is greater than zero, the calling code of this recipe will pad out id as it changes dimensions so it will retain the same overall size, and therefore elements resting against it will also stay aligned where they are. Without this setting, as the width and height of id changes, any objects surrounding it might move about to take the new dimensions into account. The following line of code calls the ZoomPad() subfunction to create the padding required:

```
if (pad > 0) ZoomPad(Math.max(fromw, tow),
  Math.max(fromh, toh), O(id).ZO_W, O(id).ZO_H)
```

This finds the maximum width and height that the object will be out of its start and end values of fromw, tow, fromh, and toh, by using the Math.max() function. The object will then have its padding adjusted so that if it is going to zoom larger, padding is placed around it in advance, into which the resizing can grow. Or, if it will be reducing, then no padding is added, but as the object reduces, more and more padding is added to make up for the reduction in size. The overall result is that when pad is greater than zero, id will always have the same overall dimensions (when you add its width and height to its padding).

Otherwise, if pad doesn't have a value of –1, id is moved to keep it centered (if pad is –1, no padding is required and no moving of id is wanted).

If This Recipe Has Been Called by the DockBar() Recipe

Next, there's an interesting piece of code used only by the DockBar() recipe, covered in Chapter 18. It looks like this:

```
else if (O(id).DB_Parent)
   GoToEdge(O(id).DB_Parent, O(id).DB_Where, 50)
```

This code examines the DB_Parent property of id. If it is true, the recipe has been called from DockBar(), in which case the GoToEdge() recipe from Chapter 14 is called to keep id up against the edge to which it has been assigned by the value in the DB_Where property.

If this recipe isn't being used as part of the DockBar() recipe, then it's necessary to keep id centered (unless the pad argument is –1, in which case centering is disabled). Of course, if id has not been lifted up from the page by making it have an 'absolute', 'relative', or other position style property, then any attempt to change its location will be ignored (in which case the best way to keep the object centered is to set pad to true).

However, if the object does have a set x and y coordinate, then each time it reduces or enlarges, its top-left corner will require moving slightly to keep its center in the middle, although an object that is using padding will not change position as it will always have the same overall dimensions.

When the Animation Has Completed

To check whether the zoom has completed, the following if() statement is used:

```
if (++O(id).ZO_Count >= (msecs / INTERVAL))
```

This statement increments the ZO_Count property of id and then checks whether it is greater than or equal to the result of msecs / INTERVAL (which gives the number of steps in the animation). If it isn't, then the contents of the if() statement are ignored and the subfunction returns and will be called up again in INTERVAL milliseconds time.

Otherwise, the zoom has finished and the following statements are executed:

```
var endx      = O(id).ZO_X + Math.round((maxw - tow) / 2)
var endy      = O(id).ZO_Y + Math.round((maxh - toh) / 2)
O(id).ZO_Flag = false
Resize(id, tow, toh)
clearInterval(O(id).ZO_IID)
```

The first two lines calculate the final top x and y locations for the object and place them in endx and endy. The next line sets the ZO_Flag property of id to false to indicate that no zoom is running on id. Next, the object is resized to its final width and height in tow and toh, and the repeating interrupts are stopped by calling clearInterval(), passing it the property ZO_IID that was stored when setInterval() was called.

After this, if padding is being used, ZoomPad() is called to update the padding; otherwise, if pad is not –1, the GoTo() recipe is called to ensure that id is located exactly at its final position in endx and endy:

```
if (pad > 0) ZoomPad(fromw, fromh, tow, toh)
else if (pad != -1) GoTo(id, endx, endy)
```

Then, if this recipe is being called by the DockBar() recipe, id is moved to its final place at the required edge:

```
if (O(id).DB_Parent) GoToEdge(O(id).DB_Parent, O(id).DB_Where, 50)
```

The final statement checks whether the CB argument has been passed, and if so it calls eval() to execute it, as explained in Chapter 17:

```
if (typeof CB != UNDEF) eval(CB)
```

The ZoomPad() Subfunction

The ZoomPad() subfunction applies sufficient CSS padding to id in order to ensure that the object always has the same overall dimensions. It takes four arguments, frw, frh, padw, and padh. The variables frw and frh contain the initial width and height of id, and padw and padh contain the overall required width and height for id.

Therefore, if frw is less than padw or frh is less than padh, some padding must be applied. This is calculated by subtracting padw from frw and padh from frh. Along the way, padw and padh are passed through the Math.round() function to return integer values.

Then, left and top are given the new padding width and height to be given to the left and top of id. The variables right and bottom are also assigned these values, which will apply the padding width and height to the right and bottom of id. This is the code used, which simply divides each padding value by 2:

```
var left   = Math.max(0, frw - Math.round(padw)) / 2
var right  = left
var top    = Math.max(0, frh - Math.round(padh)) / 2
var bottom = top
```

If the amount of padding to add to either the width or height of id is an odd number, then left and/or top (being half that number) will have a fractional part of .5.

For example, if 5 pixels width padding is required, then left will have a value of 2.5, as will right. This is because left contains the padding to add to one side of id, right contains the amount to add to the other, top contains the amount of padding to add to the top, and bottom contains the amount to add to the bottom of id.

However, because most browsers don't allow floating point values for these properties (although, strangely, some do), left is compared with the value of Math.floor(left), which returns the value passed to it, less any fractional part. So if left has a value of 2.5, Math.floor(left) returns 2.

Therefore, if the following code finds that `left` does have a fractional part, it removes it and gives that value plus 1 to `right` so that, in the current example, if `left` was 2.5, it will now have a value of 2, and `right` will be 3:

```
if (left != Math.floor(left))
{
   left  = Math.floor(left)
   right = left + 1
}
```

The next five lines of code are the same, except they set up `top` and `bottom` padding amounts, like this:

```
if (top != Math.floor(top))
{
   top    = Math.floor(top)
   bottom = top + 1
}
```

The final four statements actually set all the object's padding values, like this:

```
S(id).paddingLeft   = Px(left)
S(id).paddingRight  = Px(right)
S(id).paddingTop    = Px(top)
S(id).paddingBottom = Px(bottom)
```

How to Use It

Thankfully, using this recipe is a great deal simpler than describing it. To zoom an object either up or down, all you need to do is pass the object to `Zoom()`, along with start and end dimensions, like this:

```
Zoom(myobject, 1, 1, 100, 100, 20, 20, 1000, 0, 0)
```

This statement will zoom `myobject` from a width and height of 100 pixels each to just 20 each. You can also get fancy and turn a horizontal rectangle into a vertical one, like this:

```
Zoom(myobject, 1, 1, 100, 10, 10, 100, 1000, 0, 0)
```

This will change `myobject` from being 100 by 10 pixels to 10 by 100 pixels over the course of 1000 milliseconds.

The following example displays four 86 by 86–pixel icons at a width and height of 70 by 70 pixels. You can then pass your mouse over them to zoom them up to their original size and back down again:

```
<img id='i1' src='i1.gif' />
<img id='i2' src='i2.gif' />
<img id='i3' src='i3.gif' />
<img id='i4' src='i4.gif' />

<script>
OnDOMReady(function()
{
   ids = Array('i1', 'i2', 'i3', 'i4')
```

```
Zoom(ids, 1, 1, 86,86, 70,70, 1, 1, 0)
O(ids, 'onmouseover', 'up')
O(ids, 'onmouseout',  'down')

function up()
{
    Zoom(this, 1, 1, 70, 70, 86, 86, 200, 1, 1)
}

function down()
{
    Zoom(this, 1, 1, 86, 86, 70, 70, 200, 1, 1)
}
})
</script>
```

The first four lines of HTML display the icons and give them unique IDs. The <script> section then creates the array ids out of these IDs, which is used in the following line to zoom down all the icons from 86 by 86 pixels to 70 by 70. It passes a value of 1 millisecond so that the change is virtually instantaneous.

Then, the O() recipe attaches the up() and down() functions to all these icons' onmouseover and onmouseout events en masse. In these functions, the calls to Zoom() set the pad argument to true so that all the icons are padded as they zoom and therefore retain the same overall dimensions (thus keeping the surrounding icons from moving about during the zooms).

The interruptible argument is set to true so that each zoom can be smoothly interrupted and reversed as you pass your mouse over and away from each icon.

If you wish to experiment, try changing the values of the pad and interruptible arguments to false or zero and see what happens when you toggle the values of the w and h arguments (as long as at least one remains true or 1) to change the types of zooms.

The Recipe

```
function Zoom(id, w, h, fromw, fromh, tow, toh,
   msecs, pad, interruptible, CB)
{
    if (id instanceof Array)
    {
      for (var j = 0 ; j < id.length ; ++j)
        Zoom(id[j], w, h, fromw, fromh, tow, toh,
           msecs, pad, interruptible, CB)
      return
    }

    if (typeof O(id).ZO_X == UNDEF)
    {
      O(id).ZO_X = X(id)
      O(id).ZO_Y = Y(id)
    }

    if (!O(id).ZO_Flag)
    {
      O(id).ZO_W      = Math.max(fromw, tow)
```

```
      O(id).ZO_H     = Math.max(fromh, toh)
      O(id).ZO_Count = 0
}
else
{
   if (!O(id).ZO_Int) return
   else clearInterval(O(id).ZO_IID)


   O(id).ZO_Count = (msecs / INTERVAL) - O(id).ZO_Count
}

var maxw  = Math.max(fromw, tow)
var maxh  = Math.max(fromh, toh)
var stepw = (tow - fromw) / (msecs / INTERVAL)
var steph = (toh - fromh) / (msecs / INTERVAL)

S(id).overflow = HID
O(id).ZO_Flag  = true
O(id).ZO_Int   = interruptible
O(id).ZO_IID   = setInterval(DoZoom, INTERVAL)

function DoZoom()
{
   if (w) O(id).ZO_W = Math.round(fromw + stepw * O(id).ZO_Count)
   if (h) O(id).ZO_H = Math.round(fromh + steph * O(id).ZO_Count)

   Resize(id, O(id).ZO_W, O(id).ZO_H)

   var midx = O(id).ZO_X + Math.round((maxw - O(id).ZO_W) / 2)
   var midy = O(id).ZO_Y + Math.round((maxh - O(id).ZO_H) / 2)

   if (pad > 0) ZoomPad(Math.max(fromw, tow),
      Math.max(fromh, toh), O(id).ZO_W, O(id).ZO_H)
   else if (pad != -1) GoTo(id, midx, midy)

   if (O(id).DB_Parent)
      GoToEdge(O(id).DB_Parent, O(id).DB_Where, 50)

   if (++O(id).ZO_Count >= (msecs / INTERVAL))
   {
      var endx      = O(id).ZO_X + Math.round((maxw - tow) / 2)
      var endy      = O(id).ZO_Y + Math.round((maxh - toh) / 2)
      O(id).ZO_Flag = false

      Resize(id, tow, toh)
      clearInterval(O(id).ZO_IID)


      if (pad > 0) ZoomPad(fromw, fromh, tow, toh)
      else if (pad != -1) GoTo(id, endx, endy)

      if (O(id).DB_Parent)
         GoToEdge(O(id).DB_Parent, O(id).DB_Where, 50)
```

```
      if (typeof CB != UNDEF) eval(CB)
   }

   function ZoomPad(frw, frh, padw, padh)
   {
      var left   = Math.max(0, frw - Math.round(padw)) / 2
      var right  = left
      var top    = Math.max(0, frh - Math.round(padh)) / 2
      var bottom = top

      if (left != Math.floor(left))
      {
         left  = Math.floor(left)
         right = left + 1
      }

      if (top != Math.floor(top))
      {
         top    = Math.floor(top)
         bottom = top + 1
      }

      S(id).paddingLeft   = Px(left)
      S(id).paddingRight  = Px(right)
      S(id).paddingTop    = Px(top)
      S(id).paddingBottom = Px(bottom)
   }


   }
}
```

ZoomDown( )

This recipe zooms an object down over time from its current size to zero dimensions. It does this in such a way that the object can also be zoomed back up again with the following recipe, ZoomRestore(). Figure 16-8 shows four icons that have had their onmouseover events attached to this recipe and that are in varying states of zooming after the mouse has swept across them.

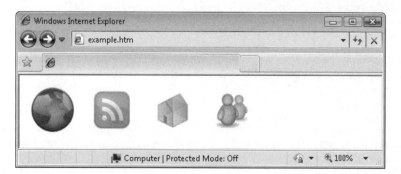

FIGURE 16-8   These icons are in varying states of zooming down.

About the Recipe

This recipe takes an object and zooms it down until it has zero dimensions. It requires the following arguments:

- **id**   An object, an object ID, or an array of objects and/or object IDs.
- **w**   If `true` or 1, the object's width will be zoomed down.
- **h**   If `true` or 1, the object's height will be zoomed down.
- **msecs**   The number of milliseconds the animation should take.
- **pad**   If 0, the object will be moved during resizing so as to remain centered. If greater than 0, the object will be padded with CSS padding to retain its original dimensions as it zooms down. If –1, no padding will be applied and the object will not be moved during resizing.
- **interruptible**   If `true` (or 1), this recipe can be interrupted by a new call on the same object; otherwise, if `false` (or 0), the call is uninterruptible.

Variables, Arrays, and Functions

j	Local variable for indexing into `id` if it is an array
ZO_Flag	Property of `id` that contains `true` if a zoom on `id` is in process
ZO_Int	Property of `id` that contains `true` if a zoom is interruptible
ZO_OldW	Property of `id` containing its previous width
ZO_OldH	Property of `id` containing its previous height
Zoomdown	Property of `id` that contains `true` if it has been zoomed down
Zoom()	Function to zoom an object from one size to another

How It Works

This recipe starts off with the familiar code to iterate through `id` if it is an array and recursively call itself with each element to process them individually, as follows:

```
if (id instanceof Array)
{
   for (var j = 0 ; j < id.length ; ++j)
     ZoomDown(id[j], w, h, msecs, pad, interruptible, CB)
   return
}
```

Next, the recipe checks whether a zoom is already in process on `id`, and if so, it checks whether that zoom is interruptible, like this:

```
if (O(id).ZO_Flag && !O(id).ZO_Int) return
```

If there is a zoom in action (as determined by the ZO_Flag property of `id`) and it cannot be interrupted (as determined by `id`'s ZO_Int property), then the recipe returns. Otherwise, the following code is executed:

```
else if (!O(id).ZO_OldW)
{
   O(id).ZO_OldW = W(id)
   O(id).ZO_OldH = H(id)
   O(id).ZO_X    = X(id)
   O(id).ZO_Y    = Y(id)
}
```

This checks whether the ZO_OldW property exists. If it doesn't, id has not been zoomed down before, so its current width and height are stored in its ZO_OldW and ZO_OldH properties. These values are obtained using the W() and H() recipes. Also, the coordinates of the object are read from X(id) and Y(id) and stored in the ZO_X and ZO_Y properties.

The first of the final three statements sets the Zoomdown property of id to true to indicate that the object is (or is in the process of being) zoomed down. Then, the object's location is reset to the stored values in ZO_X and ZO_Y (to handle the case where an object has an odd dimension length and sometimes gets disturbed by a pixel), and the Zoom() recipe is called, passing it the original width and height of id, the new zero width and height values, and the value of pad and interruptible, as follows:

```
O(id).Zoomdown = true
GoTo(id, O(id).ZO_X, O(id).ZO_Y)
Zoom(id, w, h, O(id).ZO_OldW, O(id).ZO_OldH, 0, 0,
   msecs, pad, interruptible, CB)
```

How to Use It

To use this function, you pass it an object (or array of objects) and specify the type of zoom down you want (whether to zoom down the horizontal or vertical axis, or both), along with the number of milliseconds it should take, whether to use padding, and whether the zoom should be interruptible, like this:

```
ZoomDown(myobject, 1, 1, 1000, 0, 0)
```

This zooms down myobject from whatever its current dimensions are in both the horizontal and vertical directions, over a period of 1000 milliseconds. The final two values specify that no padding should be used and that the zoom should not be interruptible.

Here's an example in which four icons are displayed, which have their onmouseover events attached to this recipe:

```
<img id='i1' src='i1.gif' />
<img id='i2' src='i2.gif' />
<img id='i3' src='i3.gif' />
<img id='i4' src='i4.gif' />

<script>
OnDOMReady(function()
{
   ids = Array('i1', 'i2', 'i3', 'i4')
   O(ids, 'onmouseover', 'down')
```

```
    function down()
    {
        ZoomDown(this, 1, 1, 500, 1, 1)
    }
})
</script>
```

The first section of HTML displays the images and assigns them unique IDs. The `<script>` section creates the array `ids` out of the ID names and then passes them to the `O()` recipe, which attaches the `down()` function to their `onmouseover` events.

The function `down()` simply calls `ZoomDown()` to zoom each icon down when the mouse passes over it. Notice that once an icon has been zoomed down, you can still pass the mouse over the empty space it leaves to activate another zoom. This is because the previous width and height values of each object are stored by the `ZoomDown()` recipe.

Rather than allowing this messy behavior, you can attach the following recipe, `ZoomRestore()`, to the icons so they will first zoom back up when the mouse moves away.

The Recipe

```
function ZoomDown(id, w, h, msecs, pad, interruptible, CB)
{
    if (id instanceof Array)
    {
        for (var j = 0 ; j < id.length ; ++j)
            ZoomDown(id[j], w, h, msecs, pad, interruptible, CB)
        return
    }

    if (O(id).ZO_Flag && !O(id).ZO_Int) return
    else if (!O(id).ZO_OldW)
    {
        O(id).ZO_OldW = W(id)
        O(id).ZO_OldH = H(id)
        O(id).ZO_X    = X(id)
        O(id).ZO_Y    = Y(id)
    }

    O(id).Zoomdown = true
    GoTo(id, O(id).ZO_X, O(id).ZO_Y)
    Zoom(id, w, h, O(id).ZO_OldW, O(id).ZO_OldH, 0, 0,
        msecs, pad, interruptible, CB)
}
```

ZoomRestore()

This is the partner recipe for `ZoomDown()`. With it you can restore a previously zoomed down object over time to its original dimensions. In Figure 16-9, four icons have been displayed with their `onmouseover` events attached to the `ZoomDown()` recipe and their `onmouseout` events attached to this recipe.

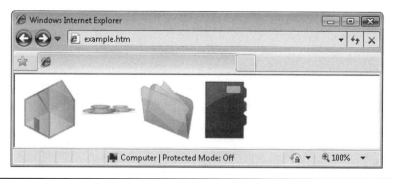

Figure 16-9   The icons can now be zoomed down and back up with the mouse.

About the Recipe

This recipe takes an object that has been zoomed down and over time zooms it back to its original dimensions. It takes the following arguments:

- **id**   An object, an object ID, or an array of objects and/or object IDs.
- **w**   If true or 1, the object's width will be zoomed up.
- **h**   If true or 1, the object's height will be zoomed up.
- **msecs**   The number of milliseconds the animation should take.
- **pad**   If 0, the object will be moved during resizing so it remains centered. If greater than 0, the object will be padded with CSS padding to retain its original dimensions as it zooms down. If –1, no padding will be applied and the object will not be moved during resizing.
- **interruptible**   If true (or 1), this recipe can be interrupted by a new call on the same object; otherwise, if false (or 0), the call is uninterruptible.

Variables, Arrays, and Functions

j	Local variable for indexing into id if it is an array
ZO_Flag	Property of id that contains true if a zoom on id is in process
ZO_Int	Property of id that contains true if a zoom is interruptible
ZO_OldW	Property of id containing its previous width
ZO_OldH	Property of id containing its previous height
Zoomdown	Property of id that contains true if it has been zoomed down
Zoom()	Function to zoom an object from one size to another

How It Works

This recipe begins with the familiar code to iterate through `id` if it is an array and recursively call itself with each element to process it individually, as follows:

```
if (id instanceof Array)
{
   for (var j = 0 ; j < id.length ; ++j)
      ZoomRestore(id[j], w, h, msecs, pad, interruptible, CB)
   return
}
```

Next, the recipe checks whether a zoom is already in process on `id`, and if so, it checks whether that zoom is interruptible, like this:

```
if ((O(id).ZO_Flag && !O(id).ZO_Int) || !O(id).Zoomdown)
   return
```

If there is a zoom in action (as determined by the `ZO_Flag` property of `id`) and it cannot be interrupted (as determined by `id`'s `ZO_Int` property), then the recipe returns. The `Zoomdown` property of `id` is also checked, because if it is not `true` then the object is not zoomed down, so the recipe also returns.

The final two statements set the `Zoomdown` property of `id` to `false` to indicate that the object is (or is in the process of being) zoomed up, and then the `Zoom()` recipe is called, passing it the current zero width and height of `id`, the object's previously saved original width and height values in the `ZO_OldW` and `ZO_OldH` properties, and the value of `pad` and `interruptible`, as follows:

```
O(id).Zoomdown = false
Zoom(id, w, h, 0, 0, O(id).ZO_OldW, O(id).ZO_OldH,
   msecs, pad, interruptible, CB)
```

How to Use It

To use this function, you pass it an object (or array of objects) that has already been zoomed down and specify the type of zoom up you want (whether to zoom the horizontal or vertical axis, or both), along with the number of milliseconds it should take, whether to use padding, and whether the zoom should be interruptible, like this:

```
ZoomRestore(myobject, 1, 1, 1000, 0, 0)
```

This restores the dimensions of `myobject` over a period of 1000 milliseconds from zero width and height back to its original values. The final two values specify that no padding should be used, and that the zoom should not be interruptible.

The following examples extend the previous recipe, `ZoomDown()`, to restore the icons back to their original sizes when the mouse moves away from them:

```
<img id='i1' src='i3.gif' />
<img id='i2' src='i4.gif' />
<img id='i3' src='i5.gif' />
<img id='i4' src='i6.gif' />
```

```
<script>
OnDOMReady(function()
{
   ids = Array('i1', 'i2', 'i3', 'i4')
   O(ids, 'onmouseover', 'down')
   O(ids, 'onmouseout',  'up')

   function down()
   {
      ZoomDown(this, 0, 1, 500, 1, 1)
   }

   function up()
   {
      ZoomRestore(this, 0, 1, 500, 1, 1)
   }
})
</script>
```

For this example, I set the horizontal w argument of the calls to 0 so that only the height of the objects is allowed to be resized. This has the effect of making the icons appear to spin around their horizontal axes if you let them zoom all the way down and back up again. You could alternatively set the vertical h argument to zero instead (but not both), and then the icons would appear to spin around their vertical axes.

The Recipe

```
function ZoomRestore(id, w, h, msecs, pad, interruptible, CB)
{
   if (id instanceof Array)
   {
      for (var j = 0 ; j < id.length ; ++j)
         ZoomRestore(id[j], w, h, msecs, pad, interruptible, CB)
      return
   }

   if ((O(id).ZO_Flag && !O(id).ZO_Int) || !O(id).Zoomdown)
       return

   O(id).Zoomdown = false
   Zoom(id, w, h, 0, 0, O(id).ZO_OldW, O(id).ZO_OldH,
      msecs, pad, interruptible, CB)
}
```

52 ZoomToggle()

The final recipe in this chapter brings the last few zooming recipes together into a single one that can zoom both down and up in three different ways. In Figure 16-10, four icons have been displayed, each of which is attached to this recipe and set to zoom around its vertical axis when the mouse passes in and out.

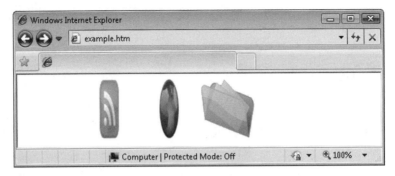

FIGURE 16-10 The `ZoomToggle()` recipe being used on various icons

About the Recipe

This recipe toggles the zoomed-down state of an object. If it is zoomed down, then the object is restored to its original dimensions; otherwise, the object is zoomed down to zero width and height. It requires the following arguments:

- **id** An object, an object ID, or an array of objects and/or object IDs.
- **w** If true or 1, the object's width will be zoomed.
- **h** If true or 1, the object's height will be zoomed.
- **msecs** The number of milliseconds the animation should take.
- **pad** If 0, the object will be moved during resizing so it remains centered. If greater than 0, the object will be padded with CSS padding to retain its original dimensions as it zooms down. If –1, no padding will be applied and the object will not be moved during resizing.
- **interruptible** If true (or 1), this recipe can be interrupted by a new call on the same object; otherwise, if false (or 0), the call is uninterruptible.

Variables, Arrays, and Functions

j	Local variable for indexing into id if it is an array
ZO_Flag	Property of id that contains true if a zoom on id is in process
ZO_Int	Property of id that contains true if a zoom is interruptible
Zoomdown	Property of id that contains true if it has been zoomed down
ZoomDown()	Function to zoom an object down to zero width and height
ZoomRestore()	Function to zoom an object back to its original dimensions

How It Works

This recipe begins with the familiar code to iterate through `id` if it is an array and recursively call itself with each element to process it individually, as follows:

```
if (id instanceof Array)
{
   for (var j = 0 ; j < id.length ; ++j)
      ZoomRestore(id[j], w, h, msecs, pad, interruptible, CB)
   return
}
```

Next, the `ZO_Flag` property of `id` is tested. If it is `true`, a zoom is currently in progress on `id` so the `ZO_Int` property is then tested. If it is not `true`, the current zoom may not be interrupted, so the recipe returns, using the following code:

```
if (O(id).ZO_Flag && !O(id).ZO_Int) return
```

The final two statements check the `Zoomdown` property of `id`. If it is not `true`, the object is not zoomed down, so the `ZoomDown()` recipe is called; otherwise, the object is zoomed down so the `ZoomRestore()` recipe is called, as follows:

```
if (!O(id).Zoomdown)
        ZoomDown(id, w, h, msecs, pad, interruptible, CB)
else ZoomRestore(id, w, h, msecs, pad, interruptible, CB)
```

How to Use It

To use this recipe, you don't need to keep track of an object's zoom-down state because you can just call it and the recipe will decide whether an object requires zooming down or up. All you need to do is specify whether the zoom can occur in the horizontal or vertical direction (or both), the speed of the zoom, whether to pad the object, and if the zoom should be interruptible, like this:

```
ZoomToggle(myobject, 1, 0, 750, 0, 0)
```

This statement will toggle the zoom-down state of the object `myobject` and allows the zoom to progress only on its width (so the object will appear to rotate about its vertical axis). The zoom will take 750 milliseconds, will not pad `myobject`, and is not interruptible.

The following example is similar to those in the last couple of recipes in that four icons are displayed and their zoom states can be controlled by passing the mouse in and out of them:

```
<img id='i1' src='i6.gif' />
<img id='i2' src='i2.gif' />
<img id='i3' src='i1.gif' />
<img id='i4' src='i5.gif' />
```

```
<script>
OnDOMReady(function()
{
   ids = Array('i1', 'i2', 'i3', 'i4')
   ZoomToggle(Array('i1', 'i3'), 1, 1, 1, 1, 0)
   O(ids, 'onmouseover', 'toggle')
   O(ids, 'onmouseout',  'toggle')

   function toggle()
   {
      ZoomToggle(this, 1, 0, 500, 1, 1)
   }
})
</script>
```

There is an extra call to ZoomToggle() just after the ids array is assigned, which toggles the zoom-down state of the first and third icons. This means that the ZoomToggle() effect can be easily seen as you pass your mouse over the icons, and some zoom into view while others zoom down. I have chosen to allow the zoom to occur only on an object's width so that the icons appear to be spinning around their vertical axes.

In Chapter 17, I'll show how you can connect or chain a set of recipes together, among other goodies, so that each one is called only when the previous one has finished. This allows for some very creative and professional-looking animation effects, and also further extends user interaction.

NOTE *Don't forget that while I have concentrated on images in this chapter, all the recipes will work on any type of object, so you can slide, deflate, and zoom chunks of HTML or anything that can be placed in them or that is a visible object.*

The Recipe

```
function ZoomToggle(id, w, h, msecs, pad, interruptible, CB)
{
   if (id instanceof Array)
   {
      for (var j = 0 ; j < id.length ; ++j)
         ZoomToggle(id[j], w, h, msecs, pad, interruptible, CB)
      return
   }

   if (O(id).ZO_Flag && !O(id).ZO_Int) return

   if (!O(id).Zoomdown)
           ZoomDown(id, w, h, msecs, pad, interruptible, CB)
   else ZoomRestore(id, w, h, msecs, pad, interruptible, CB)
}
```

CHAPTER 17

Chaining and Interaction

In this chapter, I'll show you how you can chain together many of the JavaScript recipes in this book to form sequences of actions or animations. These can be animations you write to create stunning opening effects, or they can be small chains to perform simple actions such as moving menu elements.

Chaining is also useful for ensuring that one action will follow another. This can be very hard to do in JavaScript because it is event-driven, and therefore recipes called at the same time will normally run in parallel with each other. However, by adding what is known as a *callback* function at the end of many of the recipes, one recipe can be set to call another when it completes—hence, the term chaining.

You'll also learn how you can use callbacks (like a mini two-part chain) on those functions that support chaining.

Chain(), NextInChain(), and CallBack()

These recipes are a suite of functions that enable you to line up a sequence of recipe calls to run in sequence, with each one calling the next when it has finished. This is a great way to create amazing animation effects in JavaScript that you might think can only be done in programs such as Java or Flash. Figure 17-1 shows a ball that has been set to bounce around the screen by chaining together four calls to the Slide() recipe.

About the Recipes

The Chain() recipe accepts an array of recipe calls and then pushes them onto a stack so that each call can be popped off one at a time and executed when the previous one finishes. It requires the following argument:

- **calls** An array of strings containing a sequence of recipes to call.

Table 17-1 lists the recipes that have the ability to call other recipes via a callback.

Table 17-2 lists the recipes that can be called by a recipe with a callback. You should not include any other recipe calls within a chain sequence (unless you use the ChainThis() recipe, discussed later), as they will not call up any remaining recipes in a chain, so a sequence may be interrupted. However, you can always include your own recipes in a chain if you place a call to NextInChain() after the final instruction has executed.

CAUTION *Never attempt to insert any of the* Chain(), Repeat(), *or* While() *recipes into a chain or you'll get an "out of memory" message, recursion, and possibly other errors. These functions can only be used for creating chains that* don't *contain calls to themselves.*

Chain()	DeflateToggle()	FadeToggle()	Repeat()	While()
CallBack()	Fade()	Hide()	Show()	Zoom()
ChainThis()	FadeBetween()	HideToggle()	Slide()	ZoomDown()
Deflate()	FadeIn()	Pause()	SlideBetween()	ZoomRestore()
DeflateBetween()	FadeOut()	Reflate()	WaitKey()	ZoomToggle()

TABLE 17-1 The Recipes that Support the Chaining of Other Recipes

ChainThis()	FadeIn()	Reflate()	ZoomDown()
Deflate()	FadeOut()	Show()	ZoomRestore()
DeflateBetween()	FadeToggle()	Slide()	ZoomToggle()
DeflateToggle()	Hide()	SlideBetween()	
Fade()	HideToggle()	WaitKey()	
FadeBetween()	Pause()	Zoom()	

TABLE 17-2 The Recipes that Support Being Chained or Using Callbacks

The NextInChain() and CallBack() recipes are generally not expected to be called directly, although you can do so using the information that follows.

Variables, Arrays, and Functions

J	Local variable to iterate through the calls array
CHAIN_CALLS	Global array in which chained recipes are stored prior to their execution.
push()	Function to push a value onto an array
pop()	Function to pop a value off an array
eval()	Function to evaluate a string as JavaScript code

How They Work

The Chain() recipe takes the recipes stored in the calls array and pushes them all onto the global CHAIN_CALLS array. Because the last item pushed onto an array is always the first one out when using the JavaScript push() and pop() functions, they would all come out in the reverse order if the elements were pushed onto the array in the order they were encountered. Therefore, the calls array is traversed from end to start, pushing each element in turn onto CHAIN_CALLS, like this:

```
function Chain(calls)
{
   for (var j = calls.length ; j >= 0 ; --j)
      if (calls[j])
         CHAIN_CALLS.push(calls[j])

   NextInChain()
}
```

The first line is the one that iterates backward through the calls array. The second checks that there is something stored in that element, and if there is, the third pushes it onto the CHAIN_CALLS global array.

Finally, the NextInChain() recipe (discussed next) is called to start executing the chain.

NOTE *The push() and pop() JavaScript functions create what is known as a LIFO stack, which stands for* Last In First Out. *With such a system, the most recently pushed element is popped off first, and the first element pushed onto the stack is the last one popped off it. But in the case of the Chain() recipe, a FIFO (First In First Out) stack is required, which is achieved by pushing the contents of the calls array onto the stack in reverse order, so that the sequence in which the stack of calls is executed is the same as in the array originally passed to the Chain() recipe.*

The NextInChain() Recipe

The NextInChain() recipe simply examines the global CHAIN_CALLS array, and if it has any chained calls left to run, pops the next one off and passes it to the CallBack() recipe to execute it, like this:

```
if (CHAIN_CALLS.length)
   CallBack(CHAIN_CALLS.pop())
```

The CallBack() Recipe

This recipe allows you to attach a recipe to be called after the current one finishes execution, like this:

```
var insert = expr.lastIndexOf(')')
var left   = expr.substr(0, insert)
var right  = expr.substr(insert)
var middle = "'NextInChain()'"

if (expr.substr(insert - 1, 1) != '(')
   middle = ', ' + middle

eval(left + middle + right)
```

This code works by passing the name of a recipe to be called in the CB argument for a function call that supports it. It does this by taking the expression passed to it and inserting the next call in the chain into this expression as its final argument.

To do this, the string variables `left`, `right`, and `middle` are first created, with `left` containing all of the expression up to the insertion point, `middle` being a string containing a reference to the `'NextInChain()'` recipe, and `right` containing the remainder of the expression after the insertion point. The reference to `'NextInChain()'` uses single quotes within double quotes to ensure that when the string is evaluated, the single quoted string will be processed as a string, and will not be the result of calling the function named in the string.

Then, if the character immediately preceding the final ')' is not a '(', this means that the expression passed to `CallBack()` includes arguments, so the variable `middle` has a comma and space prepended to it, to act as a variable separator. Otherwise, it keeps its assigned value of `'NextInChain()'`. Finally, the three values of `left`, `middle`, and `right` are concatenated and passed to the `eval()` function.

When a recipe is called up this way, it will notice that the CB argument is not empty and will therefore evaluate it. In this instance, the `NextInChain()` recipe will be called.

NOTE *The reason for passing the name of a function (or an expression) in CB this way, rather than simply having the recipe just call NextInChain(), is to let you pass expressions of your own to be executed as a callback. To do this, you place an expression (or function call) in a string and pass it in the CB argument to any recipe that accepts it (listed in Table 17-1). Your expression will then be evaluated when the called recipe completes.*

The ChainThis() Recipe

This recipe allows you to take a recipe or function that is not chainable (which you can determine by checking Table 17-2) and then use it within a chain. The code is quite simple and looks like this:

```
eval(expr)
NextInChain()
```

For example, suppose that for one of the instructions in a chain you want to move an object using the following statement:

```
GoTo('myobject', x / 2, y + 100)
```

You can make this call chainable by turning it into a string using the InsVars() recipe and ChainThis(), as follows:

```
string = InsVars("ChainThis('GoTo(\"myobject\", #1, #2)')",
    x / 2, y + 100)
```

The InsVars() recipe makes it easy to insert variables into a string by using tokens such as #1 and #2 as place holders for them and passing the variables or expressions after the main string.

If you then pass the string string to Chain() (or Repeat() or While()) as one of the elements in a chain, the GoTo() call will be executed when its turn comes up, and the program flow will pass onto the next item in the chain (if any).

This technique only works well with functions that work procedurally from start to end in a single process. If you use ChainThis() on a function that does its job using events or interrupts, you will usually get very unexpected results.

NOTE *You may find with the InsVars() recipe that you use up the main two levels of quotation marks, both double and single, and need a third level of quotation. This is easily accomplished by using the \ escape character before a quotation mark, like this: \" or this: \'. In fact, you will see that the previous example statement uses this technique when passing the "myobject" ID to GoTo(), because the double quote has already been used for the outside of the string and the single quote is used for the substring being passed to CallBack().*

How to Use Them

To use the Chain() recipe, you need to create an array of recipe calls to be chained together, and each call must be assembled into a string before it is placed into the array. For example, assume you wish to add the following call to a chain:

```
FadeOut(myobject, 1000, 0)
```

To do so, you must first convert it to a string, like this:

```
string1 = 'FadeOut(' + myobject + ', 1000, 0)'
```

Or, if you have a more complicated call, like this:

```
Slide('a', width / 2,      height / 2 - 50,
          width / 2 -20, height / 2, 500, 0)
```

then it would need to be turned into a string, like this:

```
string2 = "Slide('" + a + "', " + width / 2 + ", " + height / 2 - 50
    + ", " + width / 2 -29 + ", " + "height / 2, 500, 0)"
```

Obviously, this quickly gets very messy, so it's almost always much easier to make use of JavaScript Recipe 15, `InsVars()`, as in these two simpler versions of the preceding statements:

```
string1 = InsVars('FadeOut('#1', 1000, 0)', myobject)
string2 = InsVars("Slide('#1', #2, #3, #4, #5, 500, 0",
   ball, width / 2, height / 2 - 50, width / 2 -20, height / 2)
```

In these two lines, the argument list has simply been placed at the end of the main string, with each value position replaced with a #1, #2, and so on, for each value to be inserted.

The two strings can then be placed in a chain, and the first item in the chain started, using the following statement:

```
Chain(Array(string1, string2))
```

The first statement places the strings in an array, which it then passes to the `Chain()` recipe. Here's an example that uses these techniques to make a ball bounce around the browser:

```
<img id='ball' src='ball.png' />

<script>
OnDOMReady(function()
{
    Position('ball', ABS)
    width  = GetWindowWidth()
    height = GetWindowHeight()
    r      = width  - 100
    b      = height - 100
    x      = width  / 2 - 50
    y      = height / 2 - 50

    ch1 = InsVars("Slide('ball', #1, #2, #3, #4, 500,0)", 0,y, x,0)
    ch2 = InsVars("Slide('ball', #1, #2, #3, #4, 500,0)", x,0, r,y)
    ch3 = InsVars("Slide('ball', #1, #2, #3, #4, 500,0)", r,y, x,b)
    ch4 = InsVars("Slide('ball', #1, #2, #3, #4, 500,0)", x,b, 0,y)

    Chain(Array(ch1, ch2, ch3, ch4))
})
</script>
```

The HTML section displays a 100 by 100–pixel image of a ball; then the first line of the `<script>` section sets the ball's property style to 'absolute' so it can be moved about.

After this, the width and height of the browser are calculated and stored in `width` and `height`, then the right and bottom positions required to place the ball against these edges are placed in `r` and `b`. These values are simply the width and height of the browser less the ball's width and height of 100 pixels each.

The variables `x` and `y` are also calculated to set them to coordinates that place the ball exactly in the center of the browser (bearing in mind its width and height of 100 pixels).

Next, four `Slide()` recipe calls are assembled into strings using the `InsVars()` recipe. In turn, the calls slide the ball from the center left of the browser to the top middle, then to the center right, then to the bottom middle, and finally back to the center left of the browser.

These call strings are then placed in an array and passed to the `Chain()` recipe to get the ball rolling (so to speak).

NOTE *Because of the way chaining has been implemented with a single global array, you can have only one chain of recipes running at a time. You can sometimes carefully create a chain that interleaves two or more separate sets of recipes so that a number of different animations appear to be running concurrently. However, you will need to use trial and error to get the best results with this technique.*

Using the CallBack() Function Directly

The `CallBack()` recipe achieves its functionality by adding the name of a function to call back after the current one has finished execution. You can also do this if the recipe you call supports chaining, as detailed in Table 17-2.

For example, if you would like to have the `Hide()` recipe called immediately after a `Deflate()`, you can use code such as this:

```
Deflate(myobject, 1, 1, 500, 0, 'Hide(myobject)')
```

This calls up the `Deflate()` recipe, passing it `myobject`, with the required parameters to deflate it over 500 milliseconds and without the possibility of the recipe being interrupted. However, there is a final argument—a call to `Hide()`—which is placed within a string so that the string, not the result of executing the function, is passed.

You will need to tweak the syntax slightly if you are passing object IDs rather than objects within a callback, like this:

```
Deflate('myobject', 1, 1, 500, 0, "Hide('myobject')")
```

This way, after the double quotes are stripped off by the `eval()` function that will eventually execute this callback string, the single quotes will remain to indicate that `myobject` is a string that is an object ID, and not the name of an object.

This procedure is a quick and easy way to create a two-part chain without having to assemble a chain. Remember, however, that it works only on recipes that can be inserted into a chain.

The Recipes

```
function Chain(calls)
{
    for (var j = calls.length ; j >= 0 ; --j)
        if (calls[j])
            CHAIN_CALLS.push(calls[j])

    NextInChain()
}
```

```
function NextInChain()
{
   if (CHAIN_CALLS.length)
      CallBack(CHAIN_CALLS.pop())
}

function CallBack(expr)
{
   var insert = expr.lastIndexOf(')')
   var left   = expr.substr(0, insert)
   var right  = expr.substr(insert)
   var middle = "'NextInChain()'"

   if (expr.substr(insert - 1, 1) != '(')
      middle = ', ' + middle

   eval(left + middle + right)
}

function ChainThis(expr)
{
   eval(expr)
   NextInChain()
}
```

Repeat()

As well as chaining recipes together, you can make one or more recipes repeat a specified number of times using the Repeat() recipe. In a medium such as a book, it's not possible to capture the motion in these examples, so Figure 17-2 shows the ball (slightly grayed out) as it was captured on different repetitions of an animation created using this recipe.

About the Recipe

This recipe lets you repeat a chain of actions as many times as you like. It requires the following arguments:

- **number** The number of times the chain should be repeated.
- **calls** An array of strings containing a sequence of recipes to call.

Variables, Arrays, and Functions

j	Local variable used for counting the repeats
temp	Local copy of the `calls` array
concat()	Function to merge two or more arrays
Chain()	Function used to chain a group of recipes together

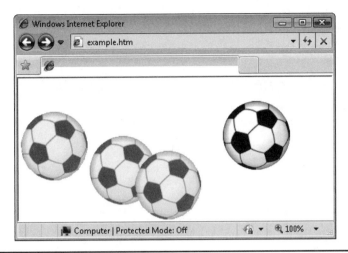

FIGURE 17-2   You can repeat a chain multiple times.

How It Works

This recipe takes the `calls` array and duplicates it enough times so that there are number copies of the calls, like this:

```
var temp = calls
for (var j = 1 ; j < number ; ++j)
   calls = calls.concat(temp)
Chain(calls)
```

First, the local array `temp` is assigned a copy of `calls`, then the `concat()` function merges the contents of `temp` with `calls` until there are number copies altogether. Finally, the `Chain()` recipe is called to start the first call running.

How to Use It

Using this recipe is the same as calling `Chain()` except that you also pass an additional parameter to specify the number of times the chain should repeat.

The following example slightly modifies the one in the `Chain()` and `NextInChain()` recipes section to make the ball bounce around the browser 10 times:

```
<img id='ball' src='ball.png' />

<script>
OnDOMReady(function()
{
   Position('ball', ABS)
   width  = GetWindowWidth()
   height = GetWindowHeight()
```

```
r       = width  - 100
b       = height - 100
x       = width  / 2 - 50
y       = height / 2 - 50

ch1 = InsVars("Slide('ball', #1, #2, #3, #4, 500,0)", 0,y, x,0)
ch2 = InsVars("Slide('ball', #1, #2, #3, #4, 500,0)", x,0, r,y)
ch3 = InsVars("Slide('ball', #1, #2, #3, #4, 500,0)", r,y, x,b)
ch4 = InsVars("Slide('ball', #1, #2, #3, #4, 500,0)", x,b, 0,y)

    Repeat(10, Array(ch1, ch2, ch3, ch4))
})
</script>
```

The Recipe

```
function Repeat(number, calls)
{
    var temp = calls

    for (var j = 1 ; j < number ; ++j)
       calls = calls.concat(temp)

    Chain(calls)
}
```

While()

Sometimes you may find it convenient for a chain of recipes to keep repeating while a certain condition is true—for example, if no key has been pressed or the mouse hasn't been clicked. With this recipe, you can supply a test condition along with a chain, and as long as the condition returns true, the chain will keep repeating.

Figure 17-3 shows an animation of a sailing ship that slowly fades into view and sails across the browser, then fades out again. Before each trip, the global variable KEY_PRESS is checked and the animation repeats until the SPACE BAR is pressed.

About the Recipe

This plug-in takes an expression and an array of statements to chain if the expression evaluates to true. It requires the following parameters:

- **expr**   A string containing an expression that can be evaluated to either true or false.

- **calls**   An array of strings containing a sequence of recipes to place in a chain.

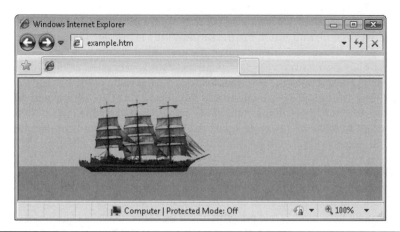

FIGURE 17-3   The ship keeps on sailing until the SPACE BAR is pressed.

Variables, Arrays, and Functions

`Temp`	Local string variable used for reconstructing a string from the array in `calls`
`j`	Local variable for iterating through the `calls` array
`eval()`	Function to evaluate a JavaScript expression
`replace()`	Function to replace parts of a string
`substr()`	Function to return part of a string
`push()`	Function to push a value onto an array
`InsVars()`	Function for inserting values into a string
`Chain()`	Function for chaining sequences of recipes together

How It Works

This recipe resides within an `if()` statement and completes only if the string value passed in expr evaluates to `true`, like this:

```
if (eval(expr))
```

If it does, the local string `temp` is created and the `calls` array is iterated through using the local variable j as an index into it. This is done because the way the chain keeps repeating is to continually pass an entire chain as a single statement of a new chain. To understand this, consider the following pseudo-code:

```
if expr is true then...
    Add this statement to a chain
    Also add this statement
    And then add this statement
    Now add all of the above including the if statement to the chain
```

What is happening here is the same as what the code in the While() recipe does. It first evaluates the expression, and if it is true it sends all the statements it has been passed to the Chain() recipe. Then, it also sends all of the preceding statements, so that when the first sequence has finished executing, the if() statement and associated calls will come up once again and will be passed once more to the While() recipe to deal with.

The next time around, if expr evaluates to false, the While() recipe will finish. But if it still evaluates to true, then all the statements are again sent to Chain(), followed by all the code required to make it start over again. And so the process continues, going round and round until expr evaluates to false, if it ever does.

How the Additional Call to While() Is Added to a Chain

In essence, what the preceding does is add a call to While() as one of the items in a chain. To do this, each element in calls is extracted from the array and appended to the string temp.

This is because the Chain() recipe, which will be called later, does not accept array elements that are themselves arrays. Instead, such elements must be a string value that will later be converted into an array by a call to eval() (by the NextInChain() recipe, which occurs when it is the statement's turn to be executed). The code that creates temp is as follows:

```
var temp = ''
for (var j = 0 ; j < calls.length ; ++j)
   temp += '"' + calls[j].replace(/"/g, '\\\"') + '",'
```

Each time around the loop, the value in calls[j] is extracted, the replace() function is used to escape any double quotes, changing them from " to \". Because a double quote is also added to the start and end of each string section (followed by a comma), any double quotes that appear inside the strings and are not escaped will clash with the outside quotes and create a syntax error. This happens in the following statement, which would fail:

```
string = "She said "Hello""
```

The correct version of this statement with escaped double quotes is:

```
string = "She said \"Hello\""
```

The Assembled String

Let's assume that calls contains the following two strings:

```
FadeOut('obj', 50, 0)
FadeIn("Obj", 50, 0)
```

After processing through the previous code, it will be turned into the following string:

```
"FadeOut('obj', 50, 0)","FadeIn(\"Obj\", 50, 0)",
```

Now we have a string that can be merged with another string containing the word Array() to look like the following (once the final comma is removed):

```
Array("FadeOut('obj', 50, 0)","FadeIn(\"Obj\", 50, 0)")
```

The eval() function can then evaluate this string back into an array. As I mentioned, the final comma needs removing, and this is done by the following line of code, which uses the substr() function to trim it off:

```
temp = temp.substr(0, temp.length -1)
```

The new string in temp is now ready to convert into the final string to be added to the calls array as part of the chain, which is done with the following statement:

```
calls.push(InsVars("While('#1', Array(#2))", expr, temp))
```

This uses the InsVars() recipe to insert the value in expr and the string just assembled in temp into the string that is passed to the push() call.

In the case of the previous calls.push() statement, if the contents of expr are simply the number 1 (an expression that will always be true), the entire new string would look like this:

```
while('1', Array("FadeOut('obj', 50, 0)","FadeIn(\"Obj\", 50, 0)"))
```

As you can see, this is a perfectly formatted call to the While() recipe itself. In fact, it will always be identical to the call that your code made to the recipe in the first case.

How to Use It

Using this recipe is much simpler than explaining its workings. All you have to do is make a call to While(), passing it an expression as a string and an array of calls to be chained if the expression evaluates to true, like this:

```
var c = 0
while("c++ < 3", Array("FadeIn('obj', 50, 0)", "FadeOut('obj', 50, 0)"))
```

Here, the variable c is assigned the value 0, then While() is called, passing it the expression c++ < 3. Each time the chain repeats, the value of c will be incremented until it is 3, at which point the expression will evaluate as false, so the While() will finish. In this instance, the object 'obj' will pulsate three times and then be invisible.

Here's a much more interesting example that animates a ship sailing on the sea, including effects such as fading in and out:

```
<div id='sea'></div>
<img id='ship' src='ship1.png' />

<script>
OnDOMReady(function()
{
    width  = GetWindowWidth()
    height = GetWindowHeight()
    x      = width  - 200
    y      = height - 150

    Locate('sea', ABS, 0, height - 50)
    Resize('sea', width, 50)
```

```
S(document.body).background = '#b7d4dc'
S('sea').background          = '#90a5a6'
Locate('ship', ABS, 0, y)

While("KEY_PRESS != ' '",
    Array(
        "FadeIn('ship', 500, 0)",
        InsVars("Slide('ship', #1, #2, #3, #4, 5000,0)", 0,y, x,y),
        "FadeOut('ship', 500, 0)",
        InsVars("CallBack('GoTo(\"ship\", #1, #2)')", 0,y)
    )
)
})
</script>
```

The two lines of HTML set up a div to represent the sea and display an image of a sailing ship. Next, the `<script>` section starts off by obtaining the width and height of the browser and setting x and y to values for the sailing ship to use in a call to the `Slide()` recipe.

After this, the sea is given the property style of 'absolute' so that it can be placed in an exact location, and is then resized so that it takes up the bottom 50 pixels of the browser. To represent the sky and sea colors, the `document.body` object has its background color changed, while the 'sea' object also has its background color changed. Finally, the ship is located at its start position of 0,y.

The final part of this example is the `While()` statement, which passes the following expression:

```
"KEY_PRESS != ' '"
```

KEY_PRESS is a global variable that is automatically set to whatever the value of the last key pressed happens to be, so this expression will return `true` until the SPACE BAR is pressed.

The first three statements in the chain of calls are pretty obvious; they fade the ship in, move it across the browser, and then fade it out. However, the final call is a little more interesting because it's an example of using the `CallBack()` recipe to turn a nonchainable recipe (in this case, `GoTo()`) into a chainable one, for just this single call.

It uses the `InsVars()` recipe to insert the variables and values into the string containing the `GoTo()` call. This string is then placed within a call to `CallBack()` and becomes chainable.

Therefore, the fourth statement moves the ship back to the start position ready for its next voyage—if the SPACE BAR still hasn't been pressed.

NOTE *Because the expression passed to the while() statement is tested only at the start of each chain of calls, an entire chain will always execute before it can be stopped. If you need more precise control than this, you can always empty the global array CHAIN_CALLS (which contains all the items in a chain). This will stop a chain after the current statement has finished and can be done by issuing the statement CHAIN_CALLS.length = 0. If you need an even speedier reaction to user input, a While() statement is not your best choice of recipe, and you should be looking at creating some event-driven code.*

The Recipe

```
function While(expr, calls)
{
   if (eval(expr))
   {
      var temp = ''

      for (var j = 0 ; j < calls.length ; ++j)
         temp += '"' + calls[j].replace(/"/g, '\\"') + '",'

      temp = temp.substr(0, temp.length -1)
      calls.push(InsVars("While('#1', Array(#2))", expr, temp))
      Chain(calls)
   }
}
```

Pause()

There are often times during an animation when you need it to stop for a while, and you can do this with the Pause() recipe. With it, you can specify a period of time in milliseconds until the next recipe in a chain is called. In Figure 17-4, the example from the previous recipe, While(), has a few extra commands inserted into the chain, which zoom the ship down when it reaches the center of the browser and then pause for 1 second before zooming it back again to resume its journey.

About the Recipe

This recipe pauses between commands in a chain for the length of time specified. It takes the following argument:

- **wait**   Length of time to pause in milliseconds.

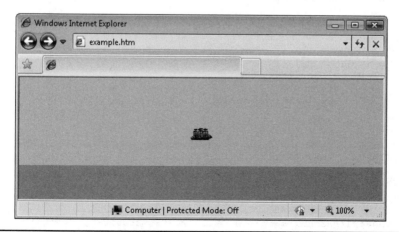

FIGURE 17-4   Inserting time delays into chains

Variables, Arrays, and Functions

`setTimeout()`	Function to create a single interrupt at some point in the future
`NextInChain()`	Function to run the next command in a chain (if there is one)

How It Works

This recipe is quite straightforward. It simply makes a call to the `SetTimeout()` function to make it call the `NextInChain()` recipe after `wait` milliseconds have expired.

Because commands within a chain are linked together via the `NextInChain()` recipe, this is the only means by which the next command in a chain can be run. By setting the timeout to occur at a future time, the chain will not continue execution until that timeout occurs and `NextInChain()` is called.

Unlike the `setInterval()` function, `setTimeout()` sets up a single interrupt and then forgets all about it once it has occurred, so there is no need to clear it.

How to Use It

To use this recipe, insert a string such as the following, which will create an event 1.5 seconds in the future to resume execution of the chain, into an array of chain commands:

```
"Pause(1500)"
```

The following is a fun example that illustrates the use of `Pause()` by zooming down the ship in the previous recipe, `While()`. Here, it reaches the center of the browser, and then pauses for a second before zooming it back in again, letting the ship continue on its course:

```
<div id='sea'></div>
<img id='ship' src='ship.png' />

<script>
OnDOMReady(function()
{
    width   = GetWindowWidth()


    height = GetWindowHeight()
    x      = width  - 200
    y      = height - 150
    mid    = width / 2 - 100

    Locate('sea', ABS, 0, height - 50)
    Resize('sea', width, 50)
    S(document.body).background = '#b7d4dc'
    S('sea').background         = '#90a5a6'
    Locate('ship', ABS, 0, y)

    While("KEY_PRESS != \" \"",
        Array(
            "FadeIn('ship', 500, 0)",
            InsVars("Slide('ship', 0, #1, #2, #1, 2500,0)", y, mid),
            "ZoomDown('ship', 1, 1, 250, 0, 0)",
```

```
            "Pause(1000)",
            "ZoomRestore('ship', 1, 1, 250, 0, 0)",
            InsVars("Slide('ship', #1, #2, #3, #2, 2500,0)", mid, y,x),
            "FadeOut('ship', 500, 0)",
            InsVars("CallBack('GoTo(\"ship\", 0, #1)')", y)
        )
    )
})
</script>
```

The changes from the previous example are highlighted in bold. As you can see, the main difference is the insertion of a call to Pause() between calls to ZoomDown() and ZoomRestore(). The Slide() command for moving the ship has also been split into two halves, and the variable mid is used for the midpoint of the ship's journey.

NOTE *Where you already know values and they do not require calculating with an expression (or taking them from a variable), there is no need to use the InsVars() recipe to insert them into a string because you can simply put the values in the string yourself, as I did with the FadeIn(), ZoomDown(), Pause(), ZoomRestore(), and FadeOut() calls.*

The Recipe

```
function Pause(wait)
{
    setTimeout("NextInChain()", wait)
}
```

WaitKey()

This recipe is useful for inserting a pause in a chain that waits until a key is pressed. In Figure 17-5, the chain has been paused and is using this recipe to wait for a keypress.

About the Recipe

This recipe halts execution of a chain until a key is pressed. It requires no arguments.

Variables, Arrays, and Functions

KEY_PRESS	Global variable containing the value of the last key pressed
INTERVAL	Global variable containing the value 30
GetLastKey()	Function to return the value of the last key pressed
NextInChain()	Function to run the next command in a chain
DoWaitKey()	Subfunction to wait for a keypress before allowing a chain to continue execution
SetTimeout()	Function to create a single call to another function at a future time

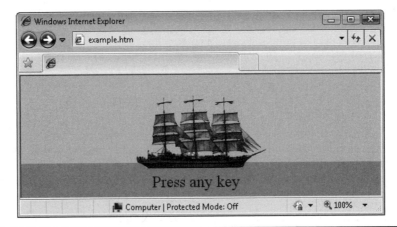

FIGURE 17-5 A chain waits for a keypress.

How It Works

This recipe first calls the GetLastKey() function, which removes any key that has been pressed and leaves the global variable KEY_PRESS containing the empty string. Next, the setTimeout() function is called to create an interrupt call to the DoWaitKey() subfunction in INTERVAL milliseconds. Here is the code for these two statements:

```
GetLastKey()
setTimeout(DoWaitKey, INTERVAL)
```

When the DoWaitKey() subfunction is called, it checks the value of KEY_PRESS and, if it is no longer the empty string, the NextInChain() recipe is called to allow the next command in a chain to run (if there is one).

Otherwise, if no key has been pressed, another call to setTimeout() is made, which calls DoWaitKey() after another INTERVAL milliseconds to see if a key has been pressed, using this code:

```
if (KEY_PRESS != '') NextInChain()
else setTimeout(DoWaitKey, INTERVAL)
```

Therefore, if there is a keypress, after calling NextInChain() the subfunction returns and will not be called again unless a new call is made to WaitKey(). Otherwise, DoWaitKey() will be repeatedly called every INTERVAL milliseconds until a key is pressed.

How to Use It

To use this recipe, you will need to insert it as a string within an array of chain commands, as follows:

```
"WaitKey()"
```

You can then choose to ignore the key that was pressed or have a later command in the chain use the GetLastKey() recipe to return the key and use it.

The following example replaces the somewhat zany zooming down and back up of the previous example in the Pause() recipe section, with a "Press any key" message that fades in, waits for a keypress, and then fades out again—allowing the ship to sail on its way:

```
<div id='sea'></div>
<img id='ship' src='ship.png' />
<span id='note'><font size='5'>Press any key</font></span>

<script>
OnDOMReady(function()
{
    width  = GetWindowWidth()
    height = GetWindowHeight()
    x      = width  - 200
    y      = height - 150
    mid    = width / 2 - 100

    Locate('sea', ABS, 0, height - 50)
    Resize('sea', width, 50)
    S(document.body).background = '#b7d4dc'
    S('sea').background         = '#90a5a6'
    Locate('ship', ABS, 0, y)
    Locate('note', ABS,0, y + 115)
    CenterX('note')
    Opacity('note', 0)

    While("KEY_PRESS != ' '",
        Array(
            "FadeIn('ship', 500, 0)",
            InsVars("Slide('ship', 0, #1, #2, #1, 2500,0)", y, mid),
            "FadeIn('note', 1000, 0)",
            "WaitKey()",
            "FadeOut('note', 1000, 0)",
            InsVars("Slide('ship', #1, #2, #3, #2, 2500,0)", mid, y,x),
            "FadeOut('ship', 500, 0)",
            InsVars("CallBack('GoTo(\"ship\", 0, #1)')", y)
        )
    )
})
</script>
```

The differences between this and the last example are highlighted in bold. In the HTML section, a new span has been added with the message text. In the <script> section, the span is moved to the location where it will later be displayed, and its opacity is set to zero to make it invisible.

Finally, within the chain of commands the previous zoom instructions have been replaced with calls to FadeIn(), WaitKey(), and FadeOut().

If you press any key except the SPACE BAR when the message is displayed, the ship will then proceed on its way and continue repeating in a loop. However, if the key you press *is* the SPACE BAR, then the expression at the start of the While() command will evaluate to true, and the chain will stop repeating.

The Recipe

```
function WaitKey()
{
   GetLastKey()
   setTimeout(DoWaitKey, INTERVAL)

   function DoWaitKey()
   {
      if (KEY_PRESS != '') NextInChain()
      else setTimeout(DoWaitKey, INTERVAL)
   }
}
```

Flip()

This recipe provides a professional flip effect that will appear to spin an object around to reveal its reverse side. Three different spin effects are provided, making this a great way to provide interesting visual effects and offer more information on your web pages.

In Figure 17-6, the photograph of Albert Einstein is attached to a mouse event so that when the mouse passes over the image, it flips to reveal more information. It's not possible to show you the effect in the medium of a book, but think of the image as a trading or similar type of card with a picture on the front and further information on the back. Figure 17-7 shows the "reverse" of the image as the mouse is held over it.

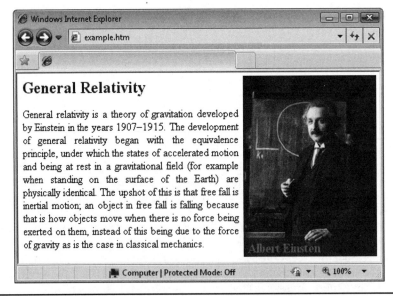

FIGURE 17-6   The image in this web page is reversible when moused over.

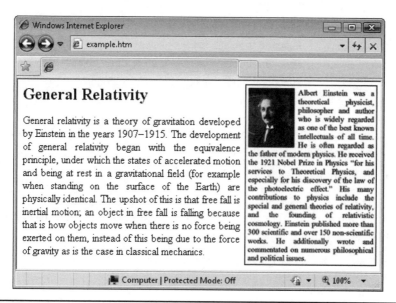

FIGURE 17-7 When the mouse is passed over the image, it smoothly flips over.

About the Recipe

This recipe takes two objects and then animates them so they appear to flip over as if they are attached back to back. It requires these arguments:

- **id1** An object or object ID—it may not be an array.
- **id2** An object or object ID—it may not be an array.
- **w** If true or 1, the width will be flipped.
- **h** If true or 1, the height will be flipped.
- **msecs** The number of milliseconds the flip should take.
- **pad** If set, the objects will be padded to retain their overall dimensions during the flip.

Variables, Arrays, and Functions

swap	Local string variable containing a command string suitable for InsVars() to add a call to VisibilityToggle() to a chain
fast	Local string variable containing a command string suitable for InsVars() to add a 1-millisecond call to ZoomToggle() to a chain
slow	Local string variable containing a command string suitable for InsVars() to add a call of length msecs / 2 to ZoomToggle() to a chain
ZO_Flag	Property of either or both id1 and id2, which is set if a zoom is already in operation on an object

CallBack()	Function to enable any command to be added to a chain
VisibilityToggle()	Function to toggle the visibility of an object
ZoomToggle()	Function to toggle the zoom state of an object
Chain()	Function to start a chain of calls executing

How It Works

This function first checks the state of both id1 and id2's ZO_Flag property. If either is true, a zoom is already in operation on an object, so the function returns, like this:

```
if (O(id1).ZO_Flag || O(id2).ZO_Flag) return
```

Next, three local string variables are created as a way to keep the code tidy and stop any lines from wrapping around. They are also efficient because each string is used twice. These are the assignments:

```
var swap = "ChainThis('VisibilityToggle(\"#1\")')"
var fast = "ZoomToggle('#1', #2, #3,  1, #4, 0)"
var slow = "ZoomToggle('#1', #2, #3, #4, #5, 0)"
```

The variable swap is assigned a string suitable for enabling the VisibilityToggle() recipe to be used in a chain (by implementing it via the ChainThis() recipe). The strings fast and slow contain strings to place calls to the ZoomToggle() recipe, one of them taking 1 millisecond (and therefore being virtually instantaneous) and the other taking a specified time.

The #1, #2, and so on within the strings are variable or value placeholders. When these strings are passed to the InsVars() recipe, these placeholders will be replaced by the values or variables also passed to it.

The final call in the recipe is to the Chain() recipe, passing it a sequence of six commands, which are all passed through the InsVars() recipe to combine the strings with the variables, like this:

```
Chain(Array(
    InsVars(slow, id1, w, h, msecs / 2, pad),
    InsVars(fast, id2, w, h,            pad),
    InsVars(swap, id2                      ),
    InsVars(slow, id2, w, h, msecs / 2, pad),
    InsVars(swap, id1                      ),
    InsVars(fast, id1, w, h,            pad)
))
```

I have spaced out the code into columns so you can more clearly see the values being passed. The sequence of commands performs the following six steps:

1. **Zoom id1 down over half the time specified in msecs** This performs the first half of the flip animation.

2. **Zoom id2 down over the course of 1 millisecond** This ensures that id2 is quickly zoomed down so that can be zoomed up shortly at normal speed.

3. **Toggle id2's visibility (from hidden to visible)** After id2 has been zoomed down, this makes it safe to make it visible, ready for zooming up.

4. **Zoom id2 up over half the time specified in msecs** This performs the second half of the flip animation.

5. **Toggle id1's visibility (from visible to hidden)** This tidies up after the flip by making id1 invisible.

6. **Zoom id1 up over the course of 1 millisecond** Once invisible, id1 is zoomed back up again, and the objects are then in a state where the flip can be reversed.

How to Use It

To create a flip animation, you need to first have two objects of equal dimensions. They must then be overlaid on each other, with the second object's visibility property turned off, using code such as this:

```
ids = Array('a', 'b')
Locate(ids, ABS, 10, 10)
VisibilityToggle('b')
Flip('a', 'b', 1, 0, 1000, 0)
```

This code takes two objects that have been given the IDs of 'a' and 'b', places their names in the array ids, and then locates them at the absolute position 10,10 with a call to the Locate() recipe. Object 'b' then has its visibility turned off by the VisibilityToggle() recipe. Finally, the Flip() recipe is called with the two objects and set to flip only the width (so that the flip will twist around the vertical axis). A time of 1000 milliseconds is specified and padding is not used.

Here's an example that creates a mini web page on the subject of general relativity with a photo of Albert Einstein that flips when you pass the mouse over it, revealing more information on the reverse side:

```
<img id='a' src='einstein1.png' />
<img id='b' src='einstein2.png' />
<div id='c'><font size='5'><b>General Relativity</b></font>
<p align='justify'>General relativity is a theory of gravitation
developed by Einstein in the years 1907-1915. The development of
general relativity began with the equivalence principle, under
which the states of accelerated motion and being at rest in a
gravitational field (for example when standing on the surface of
the Earth) are physically identical. The upshot of this is that
free fall is inertial motion; an object in free fall is falling
because that is how objects move when there is no force being
exerted on them, instead of this being due to the force of gravity
as is the case in classical mechanics.</p></div>

<script>
OnDOMReady(function()
{
    Hide('c')
    width  = GetWindowWidth()
    Resize('c', width - 220, 260)
    Show('c')
    ids = Array('a', 'b')
    Locate(ids, ABS, width - 205, 5)
```

```
      Resize(ids, 200, 264)
      VisibilityToggle('b')
      O('a').onmouseover = function() { Flip('a', 'b', 1, 0, 250, 0) }
      O('b').onmouseout  = function() { Flip('b', 'a', 1, 0, 250, 0) }
   })
</script>
```

The HTML section displays the two images along with a div containing the article text. The `<script>` section then hides the text with a call to `Hide()` because it is going to be resized. If it didn't do this, the Internet Explorer browser would return the wrong browser width in the next command because it would prepare for possibly requiring a scroll bar. After resizing the article text, the `Show()` recipe is called to display it again, and now that it has its dimensions reduced to fit within the current window, Internet Explorer will not try to leave a gap for a scroll bar in case it should need it.

Next, the `ids` array is populated with the image IDs and is passed to the `Locate()` recipe to place them at the top-right corner of the browser. The `Resize()` recipe is also called because, unfortunately, odd widths and heights sometimes cause a slight 1-pixel disturbance to animations depending on the browser used (something to do with the way they handle rounding), so ensuring that both dimensions of objects passed to `Flip()` are even is the easiest way to get the best results. It also ensures that both images have the same dimensions and will flip neatly.

Next, the second object is set to invisible before setting up the mouse events to call `Flip()`. This *must* be done because the two images are overlaid on each other and could have varying `zIndex` values, so you must ensure the correct one is at the front by making the other one invisible.

In the final two lines, the `onmouseover` event of object 'a' is attached to a flip from object 'a' to 'b', while the `onmouseout` event of object 'b' is attached to a flip from object 'b' to 'a'.

Before any flips, object 'a' will be visible, so passing the mouse over it will start the flip. After the flip has finished, object 'b' will be visible and the mouse will still be over it (unless the user quickly moved it away), which is why the `onmouseout` event of object 'b' is attached: so the animation will flip back again when the mouse moves away.

Objects as Well as Images

Although images give the best flip results, you can pass any kind of object, such as a div or table and so on, to the `Flip()` recipe. This means you could, for example, have an e-mail button that flips over when the mouse passes over it to reveal a small form for entering your e-mail address to subscribe to newsletters. If you do this, text and objects will flow in and out of the object rather than rotate the way an image does, so you get a slightly different—but still interesting—effect.

You can also use `Flip()` to swap sections of HTML according to the selection of radio buttons or the clicking of links. And don't forget that you can flip objects horizontally and vertically, or you can even do both at the same time to create a zoom-away-and-back-again effect. Try changing the values in the `Flip()` calls of the last two lines of the example and see what different results you get.

NOTE *As already mentioned, when using objects that have an odd value for one or more dimensions, you may see a slight 1-pixel jitter occur either horizontally or vertically during a flip. This happens because there are differences between the way different browsers round fractional numbers and is fixed by the recipe remembering the object's positions before a flip and restoring them afterwards. Even though it's almost imperceptible, if you wish to avoid this tiny disturbance, you should work only with dimensions that have even values. It's quite easy to ensure this with a call to the* `Resize()` *recipe prior to using* `Flip()`.

The Recipe

```
function Flip(id1, id2, w, h, msecs, pad)
{
    if (O(id1).ZO_Flag || O(id2).ZO_Flag) return

    var swap = "ChainThis('VisibilityToggle(\"#1\")')"
    var fast = "ZoomToggle('#1', #2, #3,  1, #4, 0)"
    var slow = "ZoomToggle('#1', #2, #3, #4, #5, 0)"

    Chain(Array(
        InsVars(slow, id1, w, h, msecs / 2, pad),
        InsVars(fast, id2, w, h,            pad),
        InsVars(swap, id2                      ),
        InsVars(slow, id2, w, h, msecs / 2, pad),
        InsVars(swap, id1                      ),
        InsVars(fast, id1, w, h,            pad)
    ))
}
```

59 HoverSlide()

This recipe places an object on one of the edges of the browser, with a small portion of it revealed and the remainder hidden. When you pass your mouse over it, the object slides out into the window to reveal itself and then slides back in again when you move the mouse away.

Figure 17-8 shows an object that has been attached to the top of a browser, showing only the keys of a piano. In Figure 17-9, the mouse has passed over the keyboard and slid the object into the browser to reveal itself.

About the Recipe

This recipe places an object across one edge of a browser boundary with most of it unseen, outside the browser, and a small area showing that you can pass the mouse over to make the object slide in and out. It requires the following arguments:

- **id** Either an object or an object ID—this cannot be an array of objects.
- **where** The edge to which the object should be attached out of 'top', 'left', 'right', and 'bottom'.

FIGURE 17-8 An object is attached to the browser top showing only its bottom.

- **offset** The amount by which the object should be offset from the left or top of the edge—if `offset` is a number, the amount is an exact offset in pixels, but if it is a string prefaced with a % symbol (such as "%50"), then the object is to be placed that percent along the edge.

- **showing** The number of pixels by which the object must poke into the browser.

- **msecs** The number of milliseconds it should take for the object to slide either in or out.

FIGURE 17-9 After moving the mouse over the object, it slides into view.

Variables, Arrays, and Functions

w and h	Local variables containing the furthest positions along and down an edge that id can be placed
o	Local variable containing the position in pixels along or down the edge at which to display id
t	Local variable containing the portion of the object in pixels that isn't displayed when id is slid out
u	Local variable containing the number of steps in the animation
x, y	Local variable containing the coordinates of the top-left corner of id
s	Local variable containing the amount by which to move id for each step when it is sliding
ox, oy	Local variables used while updating the HS_X and HS_Y properties of id
HS_X, HS_Y	Properties of id containing its top-left coordinates
HS_IID	Property of id used for clearing repeating interrupts set up by setInterval()
INTERVAL	Global variable containing the value 30
TP, BM, LT, RT	Global variables standing for 'top', 'bottom', 'left', and 'right'
onmouseover	Event attached to id when the mouse passes over it
onmouseout	Event attached to id when the mouse passes out of it
Math.max()	Function to return the maximum of two values
Math.min()	Function to return the minimum of two values
setInterval()	Function to start repeating interrupts
clearInterval()	Function to end repeating interrupts
substr()	Function to return part of a string
GetWindowWidth()	Function to return the width of the browser
GetWindowHeight()	Function to return the height of the browser
W()	Function to return the width of an object
H()	Function to return the height of an object
GoTo()	Function to move an object to a new location
SlideIn()	Subfunction to start id sliding into the browser
SlideOut()	Subfunction to start id sliding out of the browser
DoSlideIn()	Sub-subfunction to perform the slide in animation
DoSlideOut()	Sub-subfunction to perform the slide out animation

How It Works

This recipe begins by finding the farthest possible position along or down an edge that id can be placed by taking the browser width, subtracting the width of id from it, and placing the result into w. The variable h is also calculated for the vertical edges, as follows:

```
var w = GetWindowWidth()  - W(id)
var h = GetWindowHeight() - H(id)
```

Next, the variable o is set to zero if `offset` is a number, or if `offset` is a string beginning with the % character, o is given the value resulting from dividing the numeric part of the argument by 100. In the first instance, the value of zero will indicate later that an exact offset in pixels has been passed in `offset`, but in the second case, a percentage distance along the edge has been specified for where `id` should be located, and that value is now in o. Here is the code that does this:

```
var o = offset[0] != '%' ? 0 : offset.substr(1) / 100
```

If the Left or Right Edge Has Been Chosen
Next, the recipe needs to determine which edge is going to be used, so it first tests the value where against the global variables LT and RT (which contain the strings 'left' and 'right'). If it is one of these, then the following code is executed:

```
var t = W(id) - showing
var u = Math.min(t, msecs / INTERVAL)
var x = where == LT ? -t : w + t
var y = o ? h * o : offset
var s = t / u
```

This assigns the amount of `id` that isn't shown by default to t, then u is assigned the number of steps the animation requires to complete in `msecs` milliseconds. After this, the x and y coordinates are determined by checking the where argument again to see if it contains 'left' (the value of LT). If it does, it means the left edge is being used, so x is set to -t, which places `id` sufficiently offscreen so that only showing pixels of the object are visible. Otherwise, x is set to move the object off the right-hand edge of the screen in a similar fashion.

The y variable is similarly calculated, being set either to the value in `offset` if o is zero (in other words, an absolute offset along the edge was requested), or set to h * o because o is a fractional value representing the percent along the edge that the object should be located, and h is the maximum distance down the edge that the object may appear.

Finally, s, the step distance by which `id` should be moved for each frame of a slide, is calculated by dividing t (the amount of `id` that isn't shown by default) by u (the number of steps required to make the animation last `msecs` milliseconds). These variables will all be used during the animation stages of the recipe.

If the Top or Bottom Edge Has Been Chosen
If either the top or bottom edge has been chosen for the object's placement, a very similar set of calculations is made to obtain the values required for t, u, x, y, and s, as follows:

```
var t = H(id) - showing
var u = Math.min(t, msecs / INTERVAL)
var x = o ? w * o : offset
var y = where == TP ? -t : h + t
var s = t / u
```

Setting Up the Events

The final few lines of code in the setup section move id to the location x,y; store a copy of each in the HS_X and HS_Y properties; and set up the onmouseover and onmouseout events to call up the SlideIn() and SlideOut() subfunctions, respectively:

```
GoTo(id, x, y)
O(id).HS_X = x
O(id).HS_Y = y
O(id).onmouseover = SlideIn
O(id).onmouseout  = SlideOut
```

The SlideIn() Subfunction

The job of this function is to slide the object into view when the mouse passes over any part of it. The first thing it does is cancel any previously running regular interrupts (for instance, if the object was in the process of sliding out) with a call to clearInterval(), and then it sets up a new regular interrupt to the DoSlideIn() sub-subfunction, like this:

```
if (O(id).HS_IID) clearInterval(O(id).HS_IID)
O(id).HS_IID = setInterval(DoSlideIn, INTERVAL)
```

This sub-subfunction is where all the animation takes place. First, though, to make use of smaller, more manageable variable names, ox and oy are given the values in the HS_X and HS_Y properties of id. These are the location of the top-left corner of id:

```
var ox = O(id).HS_X
var oy = O(id).HS_Y
```

Next, a group of if… else if… statements test for whether the edge being used is the top, bottom, left, or right by checking the argument where against the global variables TP, BM, LT, and RT. Then, as long as id still has further to move, the value of either ox or oy is incremented or decremented by the step value in s. Otherwise, if there is no further movement to make, the clearInterval() function is called to stop the repeating interrupts, like this:

```
if      (where == TP && oy < 0) oy = Math.min(0, oy + s)
else if (where == BM && oy > h) oy = Math.max(h, oy - s)
else if (where == LT && ox < 0) ox = Math.min(0, ox + s)
else if (where == RT && ox > w) ox = Math.max(w, ox - s)
else clearInterval(O(id).HS_IID)
```

Finally, the object is moved to the new location in ox and oy, and the HS_X and HS_Y properties are assigned these values, as follows:

```
GoTo(id, ox, oy)
O(id).HS_X = ox
O(id).HS_Y = oy
```

The SlideOut() Subfunction

The job of this function is to slide the object away again when the mouse passes out of it. The first thing it does is cancel any previously running regular interrupts (for instance, if the object was in the process of sliding in) with a call to clearInterval(). Then, it sets up a new regular interrupt to the DoSlideOut() sub-subfunction, like this:

```
if (O(id).HS_IID) clearInterval(O(id).HS_IID)
O(id).HS_IID = setInterval(DoSlideOut, INTERVAL)
```

As with the similar function DoSlideIn(), copies of the properties used are first placed into shorter variable names, like this:

```
var ox = O(id).HS_X
var oy = O(id).HS_Y
```

Then, if the movement hasn't completed, the values of ox and oy are modified as necessary depending upon which edge is being used; otherwise, the repeating interrupt is canceled, as follows:

```
if        (where == TP && oy > y) oy = Math.max(y, oy - s)
else if (where == BM && oy < y) oy = Math.min(y, oy + s)
else if (where == LT && ox > x) ox = Math.max(x, ox - s)
else if (where == RT && ox < x) ox = Math.max(x, ox + s)
else clearInterval(O(id).HS_IID)
```

Finally, the object is moved to the new location in ox and oy, and the HS_X and HS_Y properties are assigned these values, as follows:

```
GoTo(id, ox, oy)
O(id).HS_X = ox
O(id).HS_Y = oy
```

NOTE *HoverSlide() is one of the more complicated recipes, but it does create great effects, so it's worth reading the preceding explanation a few times if any parts aren't clear at first.*

How to Use It

To use the HoverSlide() recipe, you pass it an object and then tell it where the object should be placed (out of the 'top', 'bottom', 'left', or 'right' edges), whereabouts on the edge to place it, how much of the object to show, and the speed of the sliding animation in milliseconds, as in these two examples:

```
HoverSlide('myobject', 'top', '%50', 60, 1000)
HoverSlide('myobject2', 'right', 15, 20, 1000)
```

The first statement places an object at the top edge of the browser, exactly 50 percent along, with 60 pixels showing, and with a sliding time of 1 second. The second one does the same for another object, but it is attached to the right edge, starting 15 pixels down and with only 20 pixels showing.

Before you call the recipe, it's important to give the object a style position of either 'absolute' or 'fixed', as in these statements:

```
Position(object, FIX)
Position('mydiv', ABS)
```

The first of these has a fixed position (FIX) and places the object in the browser so that even if you scroll right through the web page, the object will remain on screen exactly where it was placed. The second has an absolute position (ABS) and places the object absolutely within a web page so it will start off looking exactly the same as a fixed object but will move with the page when you scroll it.

Here's a fun example using a fixed object to create a dynamic menu for a music store:

```
<table id='a' width='375' height='160'
    cellpadding='0' cellspacing='0' bgcolor='black'>
    <tr height='20'>
        <td colspan='3'>
            <font color='white' face='Verdana' size='5'>
                <center>
                    <b>I'll Be Bach Music Store</b>
                </center>
            </font>
        </td>
    </tr>
    <tr height='80'>
        <td width='150' align='right'>
            <img src='instruments.png'>
        </td>
        <td>
             
        </td>
        <td width='315' valign='middle'>
            <center>
                <font face='Verdana' color='yellow'>
                    <u>New! - Special Offers</u><br />
                    <u>View our Guestbook</u><br />
                    <u>Follow us on Twitter</u><br />
                    <u>Read our Blog</u>
                </font>
            </center>
        </td>
    </tr>
    <tr height='60'>
        <td colspan='3'>
            <img id='a' src='piano.png' />
        </td>
    </tr>
</table>

<br /><br /><br />
<font face='Verdana'>
    <center>
        <font color='purple' size=5>
            <b>The "I'll Be Bach" Music Store</b>
```

```
     </font>
  </center>
  <br />
  We pride ourselves in having the widest selection of instruments
  of any music store, ranging from pianos, violins, flutes, and
  other classical and band instruments, to the latest electric
  guitars, keyboards, synthesizers and mixing equipment.
</font>

<script>
OnDOMReady(function()
{
   Position('a', FIX)
   HoverSlide('a', 'top', '%50', 60, 300)
})


</script>
```

The vast majority of this example is plain HTML, which is intentional, because I wanted to illustrate how easy it is to set up such a feature on your web site with only a couple of lines of JavaScript; the first one of which sets the style position of the object, and the second displays the object with just the piano keyboard graphic image showing. By the way, the links shown in the slide menu are, of course, only for illustrative purposes and cannot be clicked.

For an even more interesting effect, you could try changing the opacity of the div, like this:

```
Opacity('a', 80)
```

Now that you have available the full power of chaining and other interactive techniques, in the next chapter I'll show you some amazing menu and navigation effects that will really help your web pages stand out from the crowd.

The Recipe

```
function HoverSlide(id, where, offset, showing, msecs)
{
   var w = GetWindowWidth()   - W(id)
   var h = GetWindowHeight()  - H(id)
   var o = offset[0] != '%' ? 0 : offset.substr(1) / 100

   if (where == LT || where == RT)
   {
      var t = W(id) - showing
      var u = Math.min(t, msecs / INTERVAL)
      var x = where == LT ? -t : w + t
      var y = o ? h * o : offset
      var s = t / u
   }
   else
   {
      var t = H(id) - showing
      var u = Math.min(t, msecs / INTERVAL)
```

```
        var x = o ? w * o : offset
        var y = where == TP ? -t : h + t
        var s = t / u
    }

GoTo(id, x, y)
O(id).HS_X = x
O(id).HS_Y = y
O(id).onmouseover = SlideIn
O(id).onmouseout  = SlideOut

function SlideIn()
{
    if (O(id).HS_IID) clearInterval(O(id).HS_IID)
    O(id).HS_IID = setInterval(DoSlideIn, INTERVAL)

    function DoSlideIn()
    {
       var ox = O(id).HS_X
       var oy = O(id).HS_Y

       if      (where == TP && oy < 0) oy = Math.min(0, oy + s)
       else if (where == BM && oy > h) oy = Math.max(h, oy - s)
       else if (where == LT && ox < 0) ox = Math.min(0, ox + s)
       else if (where == RT && ox > w) ox = Math.max(w, ox - s)
       else clearInterval(O(id).HS_IID)

       GoTo(id, ox, oy)
       O(id).HS_X = ox
       O(id).HS_Y = oy
    }
}

function SlideOut()
{
    if (O(id).HS_IID) clearInterval(O(id).HS_IID)
    O(id).HS_IID = setInterval(DoSlideOut, INTERVAL)

    function DoSlideOut()
    {
       var ox = O(id).HS_X
       var oy = O(id).HS_Y

       if      (where == TP && oy > y) oy = Math.max(y, oy - s)
       else if (where == BM && oy < y) oy = Math.min(y, oy + s)
       else if (where == LT && ox > x) ox = Math.max(x, ox - s)
       else if (where == RT && ox < x) ox = Math.max(x, ox + s)
       else clearInterval(O(id).HS_IID)

       GoTo(id, ox, oy)
       O(id).HS_X = ox
       O(id).HS_Y = oy
    }
}
}
```

CHAPTER 18

Menus and Navigation

As web sites try to offer a better look and feel than their competitors, new ways of navigating through large numbers of pages are being devised all the time. Menus and navigation are probably the areas that make the most use of JavaScript for this purpose.

In the early days of JavaScript, the interaction was mainly limited to instant changes of location and color as the mouse passed over a menu. But nowadays, savvy web users expect much more fluid and appealing designs with fades, transitions, and more.

The recipes in this chapter give you a variety of solutions that you can use as is, or that you can employ as a foundation to create more sophisticated systems. They range from sliding menus to popup and dropdown menus, folding and context menus, and even a dock bar similar to the one used in Mac OS X.

HoverSlideMenu()

This recipe expands on the final one in Chapter 17, HoverSlide(), to build a complete menu system, rather than just a single slideable menu. With it you can select a group of objects that will be attached to one of the edges of the browser and which will slide into view when the mouse passes over the part showing. In Figure 18-1, two almost identical sets of objects containing links have been attached to the top and bottom of the browser.

About the Recipe

This recipe takes an array of objects and then lines them all up along one of the browser edges where they become a collection of slide-in menus. The following arguments are required:

- **ids** An array of objects and/or object IDs.
- **where** The edge the objects should be attached to, either 'top', 'left', 'right', or 'bottom'.
- **offset** How far along the edge to locate the objects—if offset begins with a % symbol, the position will be that percent from the start; otherwise, it will be offset pixels from the start.

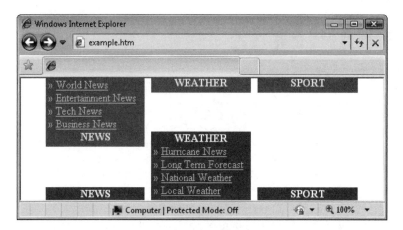

Figure 18-1   This recipe creates slide-in menus on any edge of the browser.

- **showing**   The number of pixels to leave showing of each object so the mouse can pass over them to cause the menu to slide in.
- **gap**   The number of pixels to leave between each object.
- **msecs**   The number of milliseconds each object should take to slide in or out.

Variables, Arrays, and Functions

len	Local variable containing the number of objects in ids
total	Local variable containing the total width or height that all the objects take up when brought together, including gaps
start	Local variable containing the position along or down an edge where the first object should be placed
a	Local array containing the width or height of each object
jump	Local variable containing the progressive width of each object and the gaps while positioning the objects
j	Local variable for indexing into the a array to save the width or height of each object
TP and BM	Global variables containing the values 'top' and 'bottom'
W()	Function to return the width of an object
H()	Function to return the height of an object
GetWindowWidth()	Function to return the width of the browser
GetWindowHeight()	Function to return the height of the browser
HoverSlide()	Function to slide an object in and out from a browser edge

How It Works

The first thing this recipe does is assign values to some local variables, like this:

```
var len    = ids.length
var total  = gap * (len - 1)
var start  = (offset[0] != '%') ? 0 : offset.substr(1) / 100
var a      = []
var jump   = 0
```

The variable `len` is assigned the number of items in the `ids` array, and `total` is assigned the width in pixels of all the gaps. Next, `start` is set to either 0 or the value of `offset / 100` if it begins with the character %. Later, if `start` is 0, the value in `offset` will be used to align the objects in their required positions at exact positions. Otherwise, `start` contains a percentage value for the start point.

After this, the array `a` is created to hold the widths of the objects and `jump` is initialized to 0. It will store the current widths and gaps so far encountered as each object is given its location.

Next, there are two sections of code, the first of which is executed if either the top or bottom of the browser is to be used for the menu:

```
if (where == TP || where == BM)
{
   for (var j = 0 ; j < len ; ++j)
   {
      a[j]    = W(ids[j])
      total += a[j]
   }

   start = start ? (GetWindowWidth() - total) * start : offset * 1
}
```

The first line compares the `where` argument with `TP` and `BM` (global variables containing the values 'top' and 'bottom'). If `where` is one of these values, the menu will be laid out horizontally, so the `for()` loop places all the widths of the objects in the a array by fetching them with the `W()` recipe. The variable `total` is also incremented by this value so that when the loop has finished it will contain the sum of all the object widths and all the gap widths (the latter having been assigned earlier).

Then, if `start` is not zero, it contains the percentage value that was previously assigned, so the width of the browser, as returned by `GetWindowWidth()` less the value in `total`, is multiplied by `start` (which is a fractional value less than 1), and the result is placed in `start`. This value represents the percent offset from the start of the edge. However, if `start` is 0, then offset contains the exact number of pixels the menus should be located from the edge. Because this value may be a string, it is multiplied by 1 to turn it into an integer. The result is then placed in `start`.

The second part of the `if()` statement repeats the procedure, substituting values applicable for the left- or right-hand edge of the screen, like this:

```
else
{
   for (var j = 0 ; j < len ; ++j)
```

```
{
   a[j]    = H(ids[j])
   total += a[j]
}

   start = start ? (GetWindowHeight() - total) * start : offset * 1
}
```

Finally, another `for()` loop iterates through the `ids` array and calls the `HoverSlide()` plug-in for each object, placing them all in their correct positions based on the value of `start`, plus that in `jump`. Initially, `jump` is zero so there is no additional offset, but as each object is added to the menu, `jump` is incremented by the previous object width and the size of the gap so that each additional object is located at the correct distance from the previous one.

How to Use It

To use this recipe, you need to create an object for each of the sliding menu parts. A div is perfect for the job. Fill each with the images, links, and any other contents you need, and make sure the edge of the div is a suitable tab that will make people want to pass their mouse over it. Now all you need to do is call the recipe, like this:

```
HoverSlideMenu(ids1, 'top', '%50', 20, 10, 200)
```

In this example, the objects in the array `ids` are passed to the recipe, telling it to place the menus at the browser top, 50 percent along the edge (therefore in the middle), with 20 pixels poking into the browser, 10 pixels space between each object, and a slide in and out time of 200 milliseconds.

Here's an example that places such a set of menus at the top of the screen:

```
<div id='m1'>
 &raquo; <u>World News</u><br />
 &raquo; <u>Entertainment News</u><br />
 &raquo; <u>Tech News</u><br />
 &raquo; <u>Business News</u><br />
<center><b><font color='yellow'>NEWS</font></b></center></div>

<div id='m2'>
 &raquo; <u>Hurricane News</u><br />
 &raquo; <u>Long Term Forecast</u><br />
 &raquo; <u>National Weather</u><br />
 &raquo; <u>Local Weather</u><br />
<center><b><font color='yellow'>WEATHER</font></b></center></div>

<div id='m3'>
 &raquo; <u>Football News</u><br />
 &raquo; <u>Baseball News</u><br />
 &raquo; <u>Soccer News</u><br />
 &raquo; <u>Hockey News</u><br />
<center><b><font color='yellow'>SPORT</font></b></center></div>

<script>
OnDOMReady(function()
```

```
{
    ids = Array('m1', 'm2', 'm3')
    Hide(ids)
    Resize(ids, 150, 100)
    Position(ids, FIX)
    S(ids, 'background', 'red')
    S(ids, 'color',      'cyan')
    Show(ids)
    HoverSlideMenu(ids, 'top', '%50', 21, 10, 200)
})
</script?>
```

This example creates three divs and places simulated links in them using `<u>` tags—in the real world, you might use `<a href...>` tags here. Each object is also given a unique ID. Also, the `&raquo;` HTML entity creates pairs of right-pointing brackets.

Then, in the `<script>` section, the `ids` array is populated with the object names and the `Hide()` recipe makes them invisible so they will display neatly when the menus have been created—and you shouldn't see them jump around. It also helps to hide any content that might make some browsers return a value that makes room for a potential horizontal scroll bar, thus ensuring that everything centers correctly.

After resizing the objects, setting style positions, and assigning their colors, it's then safe to show the objects again with `Show()`. In fact, you *must* do so in order for the recipe to be able to look up their dimensions. Finally, the `HoverSlideMenu()` recipe is called and the menus are displayed.

NOTE *It isn't necessary to give all objects the same dimensions—they will still line up neatly, spaced from each other by the value passed in the gap argument. You can also specify a value of 0 for the gap if you want all the menus to align directly next to each other. Also, don't forget that if you use a style position of 'absolute', your menus will scroll with the page, but if you use 'fixed', they will stay where you put them, even if the page is scrolled.*

The Recipe

```
function HoverSlideMenu(ids, where, offset, showing, gap, msecs)
{
    var len    = ids.length
    var total  = gap * (len - 1)
    var start  = (offset[0] != '%') ? 0 : offset.substr(1) / 100
    var a      = []
    var jump   = 0

    if (where == TP || where == BM)
    {
        for (var j = 0 ; j < len ; ++j)
        {
            a[j]   = W(ids[j])
            total += a[j]
        }
    }
```

```
      start = start ? (GetWindowWidth() - total) * start : offset * 1
   }
   else
   {
      for (var j = 0 ; j < len ; ++j)
      {
         a[j]    = H(ids[j])
         total += a[j]
      }

      start = start ? (GetWindowHeight() - total) * start :
         offset * 1
   }

   for (var j = 0 ; j < len ; ++j)
   {
      HoverSlide(ids[j], where, start + jump, showing, msecs)
      jump += a[j] + gap
   }
}
```

RECIPE 61   PopDown()

With this function, you can remove an object from the browser using a variety of different transitions. This recipe is especially good for menu effects, as you'll see in other recipes in this chapter. Figure 18-2 shows four avatars from the resource web site *art.eonworks.com*. Each avatar has a different PopDown() style attached to its onmouseover event and will disappear in different ways as you pass your mouse over them.

FIGURE 18-2   Attaching four different PopDown() effects to avatars

About the Recipe

This recipe takes an object and then removes it from the browser in one of a variety of styles. It requires the following arguments:

- **id**   An object or object ID or an array of objects and/or object IDs.
- **type**   The type of pop-down—out of 'fade', 'inflate', 'zoom', or 'instant'.
- **w**   If `true` or 1, the width of the object (where applicable) will reduce.
- **h**   If `true` or 1, the height of the object (where applicable) will reduce.
- **msecs**   The number of milliseconds the transition should take, except for the type 'instant', which uses no timing.
- **interruptible**   If `true` or 1, the recipe can be interrupted with another call on the same object.

Variables, Arrays, and Functions

j	Local variable for iterating though `id` if it is an array
PO_IsUp	Property of `id` that is `false` if it is popped down; otherwise, it is popped up
FadeOut()	Function to fade out an object over time
Deflate()	Function to reduce an object's dimensions over time
ZoomDown()	Function to zoom down an object around its center point
Hide()	Function to hide an object so it does not appear in the browser
InsVars()	Function to insert values into a string

How It Works

This recipe starts with the standard code that iterates through `id` if it is an array and recursively passes each element back to itself to be dealt with individually, as follows:

```
if (id instanceof Array)
{

   for (var j = 0 ; j < id.length ; ++j)
      PopDown(id[j], type, w, h, msecs, interruptible)
   return
}
```

Next, a group of four `if()` ... `else if()` statements check for the different types of pop-down requested in the argument type, like this:

```
if (type == 'fade')
{
   FadeOut(id, msecs, interruptible,
      InsVars("Hide('#1')", id))
}
else if() ...
```

This first section calls the `FadeOut()` recipe and passes the callback function name of `Hide()`, with `id` as its argument, so that the object will be hidden after it has faded. The other sections call up `Deflate()` and `ZoomDown()` in the same way and with the same callback string, with the final section simply calling the `Hide()` recipe when the type of pop-down requested is 'instant'.

Finally, the `PO_IsUp` property of `id` is set to `false` to indicate to other recipes that the object is (or is in the process of being) popped down.

How to Use It

Using this recipe is as simple as passing an object (or an array of objects), along with the pop-down type you want, out of 'fade', 'inflate', 'zoom', or 'instant'. If `type` is either 'inflate' or 'zoom', you also need to specify whether the width or height (or both) dimensions should be modified. If `type` is either 'fade' or 'instant', you can pass any values for these arguments, such as 0 or `null`, as they will be ignored. Finally, you specify the length of time in milliseconds the pop-down should take (if it's not 'instant') and whether the recipe can be interrupted.

Here's an example that displays four images and attaches a different style of pop-down to each:

```
<center><a href=example61.htm>Reload</a><br /><br />
<img id='a1' src='avatar1.jpg' />   
<img id='a2' src='avatar2.jpg' />   
<img id='a3' src='avatar3.jpg' />   
<img id='a4' src='avatar4.jpg' /></center>

<script>
OnDOMReady(function()
{
    O('a1').onmouseover=function() {PopDown('a1','fade',    1,1,500,0)}
    O('a2').onmouseover=function() {PopDown('a2','inflate',1,0,500,0)}
    O('a3').onmouseover=function() {PopDown('a3','zoom',    1,1,500,0)}
    O('a4').onmouseover=function() {PopDown('a4','instant',1,1,500,0)}
})
</script>
```

The HTML section centers a group of four images and gives them unique IDs. A link is also made to reload the page. Next, in the `<script>` section, four different calls to `PopDown()` are attached to the different `onmouseover` events of the images.

When you pass your mouse over any image, it will pop down and then hide, and the other images will all move in to take up the space it previously occupied. This is why there is the "Reload" link above them, so you can reload the example and watch it again.

Take some time to play with each type of pop-down and note what's different about them. For example, the `Deflate()` recipe reduces the object's dimensions in real time, causing the other objects to reposition as the object is deflating, whereas the `ZoomDown()` recipe first zooms the object down and then collapses its width and height. You may also wish to experiment with the `w` and `h` arguments to see how they change the type of pop-down effect.

The Recipe

```
function PopDown(id, type, w, h, msecs, interruptible)
{
   if (id instanceof Array)
   {
      for (var j = 0 ; j < id.length ; ++j)
         PopDown(id[j], type, w, h, msecs, interruptible)


      return
   }

   if (type == 'fade')
   {
      FadeOut(id, msecs, interruptible,
         InsVars("Hide('#1')", id))
   }
   else if (type == 'inflate')
   {
      Deflate(id, w, h, msecs, interruptible,
         InsVars("Hide('#1')", id))
   }
   else if (type == 'zoom')
   {
      ZoomDown(id, w, h, msecs, 1, interruptible,
         InsVars("Hide('#1')", id))
   }
   else if (type == 'instant') Hide(id)

   O(id).PO_IsUp = false
}
```

PopUp()

This is the partner recipe for PopDown(). With it, you can pop an object up that has previously been popped down. Figure 18-3 extends the one in the PopDown() recipe by providing four spans, which you can pass the mouse over and out of to pop an object down and back up again.

About the Recipe

This recipe takes an object and then restores its state using one of a variety of styles. It requires the following arguments:

- **id** An object or object ID, or an array of objects and/or object IDs.
- **type** The type of pop-up, out of 'fade', 'inflate', 'zoom', or 'instant'.
- **w** If true or 1, the width of the object (where applicable) will expand.
- **h** If true or 1, the height of the object (where applicable) will expand.

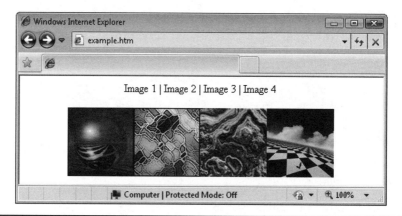

Figure 18-3 With this recipe, you can pop objects back up again.

- **msecs** The number of milliseconds the transition should take, except for the type 'instant', which uses no timing.
- **interruptible** If `true` or 1, the recipe can be interrupted with another call on the same object.

Variables, Arrays, and Functions

`j`	Local variable for iterating though `id` if it is an array
`PO_IsUp`	Property of `id` that is `false` if it is popped down; otherwise, it is popped up
`FadeIn()`	Function to fade in an object over time
`Reflate()`	Function to expand an object's dimensions over time
`ZoomRestore()`	Function to zoom up an object around its center point
`Hide()`	Function to show an object that has been hidden
`InsVars()`	Function to insert values into a string

How It Works

This recipe has the usual code at the start that iterates through `id` if it is an array and recursively passes each element back to itself to be dealt with individually, as follows:

```
if (id instanceof Array)
{
   for (var j = 0 ; j < id.length ; ++j)
      PopUp(id[j], type, w, h, msecs, interruptible)
   return
}
```

Next, since the object will previously have been hidden using the `Hide()` recipe, it is shown by calling `Show()`:

```
Show(id)
```

This is all that needs to be done at this point if `type` is 'instant'. If it isn't, a group of `if ()` ... `else if ()` statements call one of the `FadeIn()`, `Reflate()`, or `ZoomRestore()` recipes, depending on the value in `type`, as follows:

```
if (type == 'fade')
   FadeIn(id, msecs, interruptible)
else if (type == 'inflate')
   Reflate(id, w, h, msecs, interruptible)
else if (type == 'zoom')
   ZoomRestore(id, w, h, msecs, 1, interruptible)
```

Finally, the `PO_IsUp` property of `id` is set to `true` to indicate to other recipes that the object is (or is in the process of being) popped up.

```
O(id).PO_IsUp = true
```

How to Use It

You use this recipe in the same manner as `PopDown()` to restore an object to its original state. Following is an example that expands on the `PopDown()` recipe to make the images pop both down and up again:

```
<center>
<span id='l1'>Image 1</span> |
<span id='l2'>Image 2</span> |
<span id='l3'>Image 3</span> |
<span id='l4'>Image 4</span>

<br /><br /><div id='d'>
<img id='a1' src='avatar1.jpg' align='left' />
<img id='a2' src='avatar2.jpg' align='left' />
<img id='a3' src='avatar3.jpg' align='left' />
<img id='a4' src='avatar4.jpg' align='left' /></div></center>

<script>
OnDOMReady(function()
{
   Position('d', 'absolute')
   CenterX('d')

   O('l1').onmouseover=function() {PopDown('a1','fade',    1,1,500,1)}
   O('l2').onmouseover=function() {PopDown('a2','inflate',1,0,500,1)}
   O('l3').onmouseover=function() {PopDown('a3','zoom',    1,1,500,1)}
   O('l4').onmouseover=function() {PopDown('a4','instant',1,1,500,1)}

   O('l1').onmouseout =function() {PopUp('a1','fade',    1,1,500,1)}
   O('l2').onmouseout =function() {PopUp('a2','inflate',1,0,500,1)}
   O('l3').onmouseout =function() {PopUp('a3','zoom',    1,1,500,1)}
   O('l4').onmouseout =function() {PopUp('a4','instant',1,1,500,1)}
})
</script>
```

As well as displaying the four images, the HTML section now includes four spans that you can pass the mouse over and out of to make the associated images pop down and back up again. The images have their alignment set to make them line up beside each other, and they are placed in a div that is centered by a statement in the `<script>` section.

Also, in the `<script>` section, there are four more statements that attach `PopUp()` recipes to the `onmouseout` events of the spans.

The Recipe

```
function PopUp(id, type, w, h, msecs, interruptible)
{
   if (id instanceof Array)
   {
      for (var j = 0 ; j < id.length ; ++j)
         PopUp(id[j], type, w, h, msecs, interruptible)
      return
   }

   Show(id)

   if (type == 'fade')
      FadeIn(id, msecs, interruptible)
   else if (type == 'inflate')
      Reflate(id, w, h, msecs, interruptible)
   else if (type == 'zoom')
      ZoomRestore(id, w, h, msecs, 1, interruptible)

   O(id).PO_IsUp = true
}
```

 ## PopToggle()

With this recipe, you can cut down on a lot of code by calling it whenever you want to reverse the pop-down or pop-up state of an object. Figure 18-4 shows the result of optimizing the code from the `PopUp()` recipe section to use only this recipe.

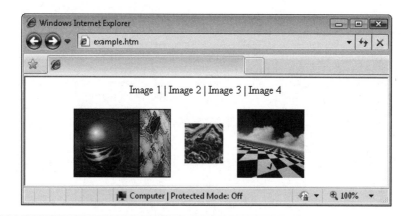

FIGURE 18-4 With `PopToggle()`, you can substantially optimize your code.

About the Recipe

This recipe takes an object and then toggles its state between popped up and down using one of a variety of styles. It requires the following arguments:

- **id**   An object or object ID, or an array of objects and/or object IDs.
- **type**   The type of pop-up or pop-down, out of 'fade', 'inflate', 'zoom', or 'instant'.
- **w**   If true or 1, the width of the object (where applicable) will be modified.
- **h**   If true or 1, the height of the object (where applicable) will be modified.
- **msecs**   The number of milliseconds the transition should take, except for the type 'instant', which uses no timing.
- **interruptible**   If true or 1, the recipe can be interrupted with another call on the same object.

Variables, Arrays, and Functions

j	Local variable for iterating though id if it is an array
PO_IsUp	Property of id that is false if it is popped down; otherwise, it is popped up
PopDown()	Function to pop down an object
PopUp()	Function to pop up an object

How It Works

This recipe starts with the code used by many recipes to iterate though id if it is an array and recursively pass each element back to itself to be processed individually, like this:

```
if (id instanceof Array)
{
   for (var j = 0 ; j < id.length ; ++j)
      PopToggle(id[j], type, w, h, msecs, interruptible)
   return
}
```

Next, the PO_IsUp property of id is tested to see whether it has a value. If its type is UNDEF (or 'undefined'), then it doesn't, and the object has to be popped down (since it hasn't been popped down yet), so PO_IsUp is set to true, like this:

```
if (typeof O(id).PO_IsUp == UNDEF)
   O(id).PO_IsUp = true
```

Then, a check is again made on PO_IsUp now that it must have a value of either true or false. If it is true, the PopDown() recipe is called; otherwise, the object is already popped down so the PopUp() recipe is called, as follows:

```
if (O(id).PO_IsUp) PopDown(id, type, w, h, msecs, interruptible)
else               PopUp(id, type, w, h, msecs, interruptible)
```

How to Use It

To use this recipe, pass it an object and the type of pop-up and pop-down effect to use, out of 'fade', 'inflate', 'zoom', or 'instant'. Then decide whether the width, height, or both dimensions will resize (if applicable), how long the transition should take, and whether it can be interrupted, like this:

```
PopToggle('object', 'inflate', 0, 1, 500, 0)
```

Here's an example that rewrites the code used in the previous pop-in example to significantly shorten it:

```
<center>
<span id='l1'>Image 1</span> |
<span id='l2'>Image 2</span> |
<span id='l3'>Image 3</span> |
<span id='l4'>Image 4</span>

<br /><br /><div id='d'>

<img id='a1' src='avatar1.jpg' align='left' />
<img id='a2' src='avatar2.jpg' align='left' />
<img id='a3' src='avatar3.jpg' align='left' />
<img id='a4' src='avatar4.jpg' align='left' /></div></center>

<script>
OnDOMReady(function()
{
    Position('d', ABS)
    CenterX('d')

    O('l1').onmouseover = O('l1').onmouseout = fade
    O('l2').onmouseover = O('l2').onmouseout = inflate
    O('l3').onmouseover = O('l3').onmouseout = zoom
    O('l4').onmouseover = O('l4').onmouseout = instant

    function fade()    { PopToggle('a1', 'fade',    1, 1, 500, 1) }
    function inflate() { PopToggle('a2', 'inflate', 1, 0, 500, 1) }
    function zoom()    { PopToggle('a3', 'zoom',    1, 1, 500, 1) }
    function instant() { PopToggle('a4', 'instant', 1, 1, 500, 1) }
})
</script>
```

The HTML section is unchanged, but the `<script>` uses a technique I haven't shown you yet, which is to assign both the onmouseover and onmouseout events to the same function, using a single statement, like this:

```
O('l1').onmouseover = O('l1').onmouseout = fade
```

This works because these events are readable as well as writable, so the onmouseout event is first assigned to the fade() function, and the onmouseover event is then assigned to the value in the onmouseout event.

This means only four statements are used in place of eight. Likewise, because `PopToggle()` can replace both the `PopDown()` and `PopUp()` recipes, only four functions are required to manage eight actions.

In fact, the functions can be attached to the events using inline anonymous functions, but the line lengths would become rather long and less easy to edit.

The Recipe

```
function PopToggle(id, type, w, h, msecs, interruptible)
{
   if (id instanceof Array)
   {
      for (var j = 0 ; j < id.length ; ++j)
         PopToggle(id[j], type, w, h, msecs, interruptible)
      return
   }

   if (typeof O(id).PO_IsUp == UNDEF)
      O(id).PO_IsUp = true

   if (O(id).PO_IsUp) PopDown(id, type, w, h, msecs, interruptible)
   else                PopUp(id, type, w, h, msecs, interruptible)
}
```

RECIPE 64 FoldingMenu()

Using the pop-up and down features of the preceding recipes, it's possible to create professional-looking folding menus, which is what this recipe offers. With it, you can create a wide variety of different folding menus with different transition styles. For example, Figure 18-5 shows a folding menu with four headings, each with different sets of contents.

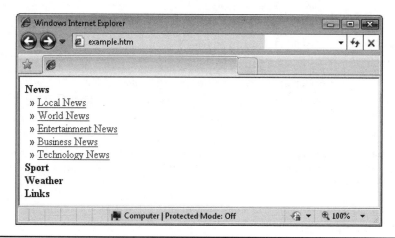

FIGURE 18-5   Creating a folding menu side bar

About the Recipe

The recipe requires a pair of arrays of heading and contents objects and then displays a folding menu based on the styles and actions you supply. It takes the following arguments:

- `headings`   An array of objects and/or object IDs.
- `contents`   An array of objects and/or object IDs.
- `action`   The menu action type, either 'hover' or 'click'.
- `type`   The type of transitions to use, out of 'fade', 'inflate', 'zoom', or 'instant'.
- `multi`   If `true` or 1, more than one contents section can be open at a time.
- `w` and `h`   If `type` is 'inflate' or 'zoom', these arguments specify whether the width, height, or both dimensions will be modified during transitions.
- `msecs1`   The transition time in milliseconds of popping down.
- `msecs2`   The transition time in milliseconds of popping up.
- `interruptible`   If `true` or 1, the `PopUp()` and `PopDown()` recipe can be interrupted by another call on the same `id`.

Variables, Arrays, and Functions

`j`	Local variable for iterating through the `headings` array
`FO_C`	Property of each heading containing the object in the `contents` array to which it refers
`PO_IsUp`	Property of each object in the contents array, which is `false` when an object is popped down; otherwise, the object is popped up
`cursor`	Property of each heading's style object used for changing the mouse pointer when over the heading
`onmouseover`	Event of each heading
`onmouseout`	Event of each heading
`slice()`	Function to return a subsection of an array
`PopUp()`	Function to pop up an object
`PopDown()`	Function to pop down an object
`PopToggle()`	Function to toggle the popped state of an object
`DoFoldingMenu()`	Subfunction to perform the transition

How It Works

The first thing this recipe does is pop down all the objects in the contents array except for the first one, which must remain popped up—and which has its `PO_IsUp` property set to true to indicate this, as follows:

```
PopDown(contents.slice(1), type, w, h, 1, 0)
O(contents[0]).PO_IsUp = true
```

The `slice()` function is used with a value of 1 to pass to `PopDown()` all elements from the second element onward (because the first element of an array is 0). The `msecs` argument to PopDown() is 1 so that the transition is set to take only 1 millisecond and is therefore virtually instantaneous.

Next, the headings and contents arrays are iterated through in a for() loop, using j as an index into them, like this:

```
for (var j = 0 ; j < headings.length ; ++j)
{
   O(headings[j]).FO_C    = contents[j]
   S(headings[j]).cursor = 'pointer'

   if (action == 'hover') O(headings[j]).onmouseover = DoFoldingMenu
   else                    O(headings[j]).onclick    = DoFoldingMenu
}
```

Each heading has its FO_C property assigned the object in the associated contents array. This will pop up and down the contents associated with a heading. Then, each heading has its cursor property set to 'pointer' so that the mouse pointer will change when it passes over the heading.

After that, the action argument is tested. If it is 'hover', the DoFoldingMenu() subfunction is attached to the current heading's onmouseover event so it will be called up by passing the mouse over it.

Otherwise, the subfunction is attached to the current heading's onclick event so that it will only be called up when the heading is clicked.

The DoFoldingMenu() Subfunction

Once all the various properties and events are set up for the recipe, the DoFoldingMenu() subfunction will be called up whenever a change to the menus is required.

When this happens, the first statement in the function checks the multi argument. If it is true or 1, it means that more than one set of contents can be popped up at a time; in fact, all of them can be up (or down) at the same time.

By setting the multi argument, each onmouseover or onclick event of a heading will toggle the pop-up or pop-down state of the associated contents object with the PopToggle() recipe, like this:

```
if (multi) PopToggle(this.FO_C, type, w, h, msecs1, interruptible)
```

If multi is not set, then only one contents object can be popped up at a time, so when a new one is selected to be popped up, the previously popped-up one must be popped down. This is worked out by iterating through the headings array in a for() loop, like this:

```
for (j = 0 ; j < headings.length ; ++j)
   if (O(O(headings[j]).FO_C).PO_IsUp && O(headings[j]) != this)
      PopDown(O(headings[j]).FO_C, type, w, h, msecs1, interruptible)
```

The variable j iterates through each element in the headings array and checks each one's associated contents object PO_IsUp property. If it is true or 1, the contents object is currently popped up, so the heading object is compared with this, which refers to the current heading that was either clicked or had the mouse passed over it. If they match, they are one and the same and nothing happens since the currently selected contents object will be set to a popped-up state a couple of lines later in the code.

However, if the `contents` object that has been found to be popped up is different from the current heading's `contents` object, then it is the one that was previously popped up, so it is popped down with a call to `PopDown()`. The time setting used here is from the argument `msecs1`.

Finally, the currently selected `contents` object is set to a popped-up state (if it isn't already popped up), like this:

```
if (!O(this.FO_C).PO_IsUp)
    PopUp(this.FO_C, type, w, h, msecs2, interruptible)
```

This pop-up action is given its own time setting in `msecs2` so that different folding effects can be achieved by using differing values for `msecs1` and `msecs2`.

How to Use It

There are two main ways to use this recipe. The first is within an accordion or folding menu, and the other is to separate out the headings from the contents to have the control objects in a different place from the displayed contents. The first is most suited to being operated by mouse clicks because, as the transitions occur, new elements could pass under the mouse cursor, and if `onmouseover` were used, unwanted selections could be made.

Here's an example of an accordion-style menu driven by mouse clicks:

```
<span id='h1'><b>News</b></span><br /><div id='c1'>
 &raquo;<a href='local.htm'>Local News</a><br/ >
 &raquo;<a href='world.htm'>World News</a><br/ >
 &raquo;<a href='entertainment.htm'>Entertainment News</a><br/ >
 &raquo;<a href='business.htm'>Business News</a><br/ >
 &raquo;<a href='technology.htm'>Technology News</a><br/ ></div>

<span id='h2'><b>Sport</b></span><br /><div id='c2'>
 &raquo;<a href='football.htm'>Football</a><br/ >
 &raquo;<a href='baseball.htm'>Baseball</a><br/ >
 &raquo;<a href='hockey.htm'>Hockey</a><br/ >
 &raquo;<a href='soccer.htm'>Soccer</a><br/ ></div>

<span id='h3'><b>Weather</b></span><br /><div id='c3'>
 &raquo;<a href='movies.htm'>Movies</a><br/ >
 &raquo;<a href='music.htm'>Music</a><br/ >
 &raquo;<a href='televison.htm'>Television</a><br/ ></div>

<span id='h4'><b>Links</b></span><br /><div id='c4'>
 &raquo;<a href='index.htm'>Home Page</a><br/ >
 &raquo;<a href='articles.htm'>Articles</a><br/ >
 &raquo;<a href='videos.htm'>Videos</a><br/ >
 &raquo;<a href='podcasts.htm'>Podcasts</a><br/ ></div>

<script>
OnDOMReady(function()
{
    headings = Array('h1', 'h2', 'h3', 'h4')
    contents = Array('c1', 'c2', 'c3', 'c4')
```

```
        FoldingMenu(headings,contents,'click','inflate',0,1,1,200,300,1)
})
</script>
```

I designed this and most other recipes in such a way that they do not rely on you using CSS other than to style the menus in the way you want them. Of course, CSS can be used to apply different styles when the mouse passes over an object, but the goal of this book is to enable you to set up objects in standard HTML that you control with a small section of JavaScript.

Therefore, the HTML in this example creates four heading spans, each of which has a span section of links underneath, although the contents could be any type of HTML or object, such as images and so on. In addition to the four headings, there are four contents sections.

I have specifically chosen spans here because browsers automatically know their dimensions based on their contents. Divs are different in that their width is effectively infinite (at least to the browser edge), so you cannot deflate a div's width dimension unless you set it, for example, using the `ResizeWidth()` recipe.

The `<script>` section is very simple. Two arrays are created, one for the headings and one for the contents. Next, the `FoldingMenu()` recipe is called, with an `action` argument of 'click', a `style` argument of 'inflate', and a `multi` argument of 0. The w and h arguments are set to 0 and 1 so that only the height of an object will be adjusted during transitions.

After this, `msecs1` and `msecs2` are set to 200 and 300 so that popping down will take 200 milliseconds and popping up will take 300. This provides a more interesting effect than if they are given the same values. I recommend you try altering them yourself, giving first `msecs1` the larger value and then `msecs2`. You'll find you can create a wide range of interesting effects.

You can also have a lot of fun by changing the `type` to another value, such as 'fade', 'zoom', or 'instant'. You may also want to experiment with modifying the w and h arguments to change the width and height (or both). Don't forget that you can also change `multi` to `true` or 1 and have a quite different type of menu in which the headings toggle their contents between being popped up and down.

Using the 'hover' Action

If you plan to offer a hover effect, you'll need to lay out your HTML slightly differently so that when objects pop up they don't do so under the mouse and then cause an automatic (and unwanted) mouseover event to occur—which could result in popping up the wrong section.

Here's one way you can modify the HTML to use the 'hover' action of the `FoldingMenu()` recipe:

```
<span id='h1'><b>News</b></span> |
<span id='h2'><b>Sport</b></span> |
<span id='h3'><b>Weather</b></span> |
<span id='h4'><b>Links</b></span><br />

<span id='c1'>
  &raquo; <a href='local.htm'>Local News</a>
  <a href='world.htm'>World News</a>
  <a href='entertainment.htm'>Entertainment News</a>
```

```
  <a href='business.htm'>Business News</a>
  <a href='technology.htm'>Technology News</a></span>

<span id='c2'>
  &raquo; <a href='football.htm'>Football</a>
  <a href='baseball.htm'>Baseball</a>
  <a href='hockey.htm'>Hockey</a>
  <a href='soccer.htm'>Soccer</a></span>

<span id='c3'>
  &raquo; <a href='movies.htm'>Movies</a>
  <a href='music.htm'>Music</a>
  <a href='televison.htm'>Television</a></span>

<span id='c4'>
  &raquo; <a href='index.htm'>Home Page</a>
  <a href='articles.htm'>Articles</a>
  <a href='videos.htm'>Videos</a>
  <a href='podcasts.htm'>Podcasts</a></span>

<script>
OnDOMReady(function()
{
    headings = Array('h1', 'h2', 'h3', 'h4')
    contents = Array('c1', 'c2', 'c3', 'c4')

    FoldingMenu(headings,contents,'click','inflate',0,1,1,200,300,1)
})
</script>
```

The script section is identical to the previous example. Only the HTML has been changed to place all the headings at the top, with the contents sections underneath them as shown in Figure 18-6.

The Recipe
```
function FoldingMenu(headings, contents, action, type, multi,
    w, h, msecs1, msecs2, interruptible)
```

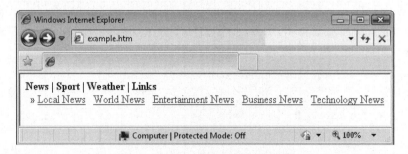

FIGURE 18-6 The recipe is now used to create 'hover' action menus.

```
{
   PopDown(contents.slice(1), type, w, h, 1, 0)
   O(contents[0]).PO_IsUp = true

   for (var j = 0 ; j < headings.length ; ++j)
   {
      O(headings[j]).FO_C   = contents[j]
      S(headings[j]).cursor = 'pointer'

      if (action == 'hover')
           O(headings[j]).onmouseover = DoFoldingMenu
      else O(headings[j]).onclick     = DoFoldingMenu
   }

   function DoFoldingMenu()
   {
      if (multi) PopToggle(this.FO_C,type,w,h,msecs1,interruptible)
      else
      {
         for (j = 0 ; j < headings.length ; ++j)
            if (O(O(headings[j]).FO_C).PO_IsUp &&
                  O(headings[j]) != this)
               PopDown(O(headings[j]).FO_C, type, w, h,
                  msecs1, interruptible)

         if (!O(this.FO_C).PO_IsUp)
            PopUp(this.FO_C, type, w, h, msecs2, interruptible)
      }
   }
}
```

ContextMenu()

With this recipe, you can replace the standard mouse right-click menu with your own. Much more than a way to block casual users from viewing the source of a page, the `ContextMenu()` recipe lets you create entire sections of HTML and pop them up at the mouse cursor position when the user clicks the right mouse button. In Figure 18-7, a simple menu for a hardware store has been popped up with a right-click.

About the Recipe

This recipe requires an object that, when right-clicked, should pop up a menu, which you also pass to it. It takes the following arguments:

- **id**   An object to which the right-click should be attached—generally, you will attach to the `document` object, but you can be more specific and attach different context menus to different objects (arrays of objects are not supported).

- **contents**   An object containing the menu to be displayed.

- **type**   The type of transition effect for popping the menu up and down, out of 'fade', 'inflate', 'zoom', or 'instant'.

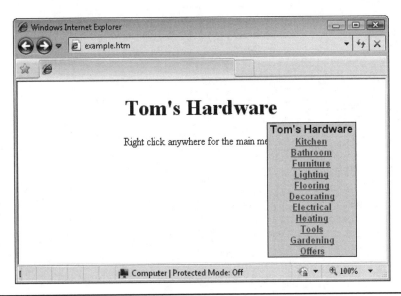

FIGURE 18-7 Now you can create your own right-click menus.

- **w** If applicable and this argument is `true` or 1, the object's width will be modified during the transition.
- **h** If applicable and this argument is `true` or 1, the object's height will be modified during the transition.
- **msecs** The number of milliseconds the pop-up transition should take.

Variables, Arrays, and Functions

`x` and `y`	Local variables containing the left and top edges of the location of `content`
`MOUSE_X` and `MOUSE_Y`	Global variables containing the current mouse `x` and `y` coordinates
`PO_IsUp`	Property of `id` that is false if it is popped down; otherwise, it is popped up
`FA_Flag`	Property of `id` set by the `Fade()` recipe when a fade is in progress on `id`
`DF_Flag`	Property of `id` set by the `Deflate` or `Inflate()` recipe when a deflate or reflate is in progress on `id`
`zIndex`	Style property of `contents` containing its depth location from front (highest) to back (lowest)
`Context_IID`	Property of `id` returned by calling `setInterval()` to later be used by `clearInterval()`
`SetInterval()`	Function to start repeating interrupts
`clearInterval()`	Function to stop repeating interrupts

Locate()	Function to set an object's style position and coordinates
PopUp()	Function to pop up a previously popped-down object
PopDown()	Function to pop down an object
W() and H()	Functions to return the width and height of an object
ContextUp()	Subfunction to pop up contents when the mouse is right-clicked
ContextDown()	Subfunction of ContextUp() to check whether the mouse has moved out of the space occupied by contents, and if so, to remove it

How It Works

This recipe first releases the contents object from its position in the HTML document by using the Locate() recipe to give it a style position of ABS (a global variable with the value 'absolute'). Next, it moves it offscreen to a location thousands of pixels away, removing it from the browser as quickly as possible so as not to appear within your page.

Next, contents is popped down, ready to be popped up when required, and the oncontextmenu event of id is attached to the ContextUp() subfunction, which will pop up contents when id is right-clicked. Here are the three lines of code that do this:

```
Locate(contents, ABS, -10000, -10000)
PopDown(contents, type, 1, 1, 1, 0)
O(id).oncontextmenu = ContextUp
```

The ContextUp() Subfunction

The purpose of this subfunction is to react to a right-click event on id. The first thing it does, though, is check whether it can go ahead by examining the state of flags created by the PopUp(), PopDown(), Fade(), Deflate(), and Reflate() recipes, like this:

```
if (O(contents).PO_IsUp ||
    O(contents).FA_Flag ||
    O(contents).DF_Flag) return false
```

If any of these flags is true, then either contents is already popped up or one of the transition types is already in action on contents, so the recipe returns.

If the recipe can proceed, it next sets the local variables x and y to the current coordinates of the mouse cursor and then moves the popped-down contents to that location with a call to GoTo(). It calls PopUp() to pop it up, like this:

```
var x = MOUSE_X
var y = MOUSE_Y
GoTo(contents, x, y)
PopUp(contents, type, w, h, msecs, 1)
```

Next, it's necessary to ensure that any objects that have been created or had their zIndex property changed since the contents div was created will not appear in front of it so the object's zIndex property is set to the value in ZINDEX plus 1. ZINDEX is the global variable that tracks the highest zIndex property so far used by an object, so adding 1 to this value ensures that `contents` will appear on top of every other object in the browser. Here's the statement that does this:

```
S(contents).zIndex = ZINDEX + 1
```

The recipe needs a way to determine whether the mouse has moved out of the area occupied by `contents`, and therefore whether it needs to be popped down. You might think that attaching to the `onmouseout` event of `contents` would do the trick, but sadly it won't do so reliably and in all cases. The reason for this is if you include a form input or other elements within `contents`, when the mouse passes over them the browser will think it has passed out of being over the contents object and will prematurely trigger the `onmouseout` event.

Therefore, it is necessary to track the position of the mouse and pop the object down only if it moves out of the object's bounds. To do this, a repeating interrupt is created to call up the subfunction `ContextDown()` every `INTERVAL` milliseconds to see whether the mouse is still inside the object, as follows:

```
O(id).Context_Iid = setInterval(ContextDown, INTERVAL)
```

Finally, the `return` statement returns a value of `false` to tell the browser to cancel pulling up the standard right-click menu:

```
return false
```

The ContextDown() Sub-subfunction

This function monitors the position of the mouse by checking the `MOUSE_X` and `MOUSE_Y` global variables:

```
if (MOUSE_X < x || MOUSE_X > (x + W(contents)) ||
    MOUSE_Y < y || MOUSE_Y > (y + H(contents)))
```

If the mouse pointer is not within the bounds of `contents`, the object is popped down and the repeating interrupts are stopped with a call to `clearInterval()`, passing it the value in the property `Context_IID` that was saved when `setInterval()` was called. Also, the property `PO_IsUp` is set to `false` because `contents` has now been popped down:

```
PopDown(contents, type, w, h, msecs, 1)
clearInterval(O(id).Context_IID)
O(contents).PO_IsUp = false
```

If the mouse is still within the bounds of `contents`, the function returns to be called again in another `INTERVAL` milliseconds.

NOTE *With a little tweaking, this recipe could easily be adapted to create a slight buffer around the context menu so the menu won't disappear if the mouse goes slightly outside the boundary.*

How to Use It

To use this recipe, use HTML (and CSS if you wish) to create an attractive menu (or whatever object you want the right-click to call up) and pass it to the recipe, along with the object to which it should be attached, the type of pop-up transition to use, and the time the transition should take.

Here's an example that creates a simple menu for a hardware store:

```
<center><h1>Tom's Hardware</h1>
Right-click anywhere for the main menu</center>

<span id='menu'><center>
<font face='Arial' size='2'><b>
<font size='3' color='#0b0d7d'>
 Tom's Hardware </font><br />
<a href='#'>Kitchen</a><br />
<a href='#'>Bathroom</a><br />
<a href='#'>Furniture</a><br />
<a href='#'>Lighting</a><br />
<a href='#'>Flooring</a><br />
<a href='#'>Decorating</a><br />
<a href='#'>Electrical</a><br />
<a href='#'>Heating</a><br />
<a href='#'>Tools</a><br />
<a href='#'>Gardening</a><br />
<a href='#'>Offers</a>
</b></font></center></span>

<script>
OnDOMReady(function()
{
    S('menu').background = '#abeceb'
    S('menu').border     = 'solid 1px'
    ContextMenu(document, 'menu', 'fade', 0, 0, 300)
})
</script>
```

The HTML section displays a simple heading and instructional sentence, followed by a span with the ID 'menu', which contains a few links. Of course, the links go nowhere because they only contain a # symbol, but they display as if they do contain a link.

The `<script>` section sets the background color of the menu, gives it a solid border, and then calls up `ContextMenu()` to prepare the browser for handling right-clicks.

You might want to play with this example by trying different `style` arguments, such as 'inflate', 'zoom', and 'instant'. You can also play with the w and h arguments, as well as the timing in `msecs`.

Something else you can try is to create an object and attach the menu to that rather than the entire `document`. Or, try making a couple of different menus for different objects—once you have this recipe in your web toolkit, you are on your way to creating some highly dynamic and interactive web sites.

The Recipe

```
function ContextMenu(id, contents, type, w, h, msecs)
{
    Locate(contents, ABS, -10000, -10000)
    PopDown(contents, type, 1, 1, 1, 0)
    O(id).oncontextmenu = ContextUp
```

```
function ContextUp()
{
   if (O(contents).PO_IsUp ||
       O(contents).FA_Flag ||
       O(contents).DF_Flag) return false

   var x = MOUSE_X
   var y = MOUSE_Y
   GoTo(contents, x, y)
   PopUp(contents, type, w, h, msecs, 1)
   S(contents).zIndex = ZINDEX + 1
   O(id).Context_IID  = setInterval(ContextDown, INTERVAL)
   return false

   function ContextDown()
   {
      if (MOUSE_X < x || MOUSE_X > (x + W(contents)) ||
          MOUSE_Y < y || MOUSE_Y > (y + H(contents)))
      {
         PopDown(contents, type, w, h, msecs, 1)
         clearInterval(O(id).Context_IID)
         O(contents).PO_IsUp = false
      }
   }
}
```

RECIPE 66 DockBar()

This recipe adds a dock bar to the browser similar to the one used by Mac OS X. It's easily configurable and can be attached to any of the browser's four edges. Figure 18-8 shows six dock bar icons attached to the bottom edge of a browser using this recipe, with one in the process of zooming up.

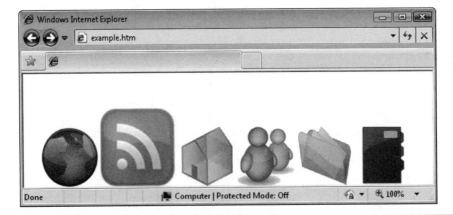

FIGURE 18-8   Use this recipe to create impressive dock bars.

About the Recipe

This recipe takes a containing object and list of elements within the object and turns them into a dock bar that you can affix to any edge of the browser. It requires the following arguments:

- **id** A containing object such as a div or span that holds the individual dock bar elements—this cannot be an array.
- **items** An array of objects located within id, usually comprising images.
- **where** The edge to which the bar should be attached, out of 'top', 'bottom', 'left', or 'right'.
- **increase** The percentage by which an item should enlarge when the mouse passes over it.
- **msecs** The number of milliseconds the transition should take.

Variables, Arrays, and Functions

j	Local variable used for iterating through the items array
oldw and oldh	Local variables containing the original width and height of an item
TP and BM	Global variables containing the strings 'top' and 'bottom'
verticalAlign	Style property of the elements of the items array
align	Property of the elements of the items array
cursor	Style property of the elements of the items array to set the mouse cursor icon
DB_Parent	Property of each element of the items array containing a copy of id
DB_Where	Property of each element of the items array containing a copy of where
DB_Name	Property of each element of the items array containing a copy of the element
DB_OldW and DB_OldH	Properties of each element of the items array containing the original width and height of the element
DB_NewW and DB_NewH	Properties of each element of the items array containing the enlarged width and height of the element
onmouseover	Event of each element of the items array used for attaching to DockUp()
onmouseout	Event of each element of the items array used for attaching to DockDown()
Math.round()	Function to turn a floating point number into an integer
Position()	Function to change the style position of an object
GoToEdge()	Function to move an object to a browser edge
Zoom()	Function to zoom an object down or up
DockUp()	Subfunction to zoom up an object
DockDown()	Subfunction to zoom down an object

How It Works

This recipe starts by releasing the containing object in `id` from the browser and giving it a style position of 'fixed' to ensure that the dock bar will stay in place even if the browser is scrolled, as follows (`FIX` being a global variable with the value 'fixed'):

```
Position(id, FIX)
```

Then, all the elements in the items array are iterated through in a `for()` loop with the local variable `j` as the index pointer, and the first statements within the loop set the alignment of each element, like this:

```
for (var j = 0 ; j < items.length ; ++j)
{
   if (where[1] == TP || where == BM)
      S(items[j]).verticalAlign = where
   else        O(items[j]).align = where
```

If the argument `where` has either of the values 'top' or 'bottom' (tested by the global variables `TP` and `BM`), then the `verticalAlign` style property of the element is set to the value in `where`. Otherwise, `where` must have a value of either 'left' or 'right' so the `align` property of the element is given that value.

Next, each element's original width and height is extracted from the `W()` and `H()` recipes and placed in the local variables `oldw` and `oldh`, like this:

```
var oldw = W(items[j])
var oldh = H(items[j])
```

After that, the cursor to display whenever the mouse is over an element is set to 'pointer' and several properties are created, as follows:

```
S(items[j]).cursor      = 'pointer'
O(items[j]).DB_Parent = id
O(items[j]).DB_Where  = where
O(items[j]).DB_OldW   = oldw
O(items[j]).DB_OldH   = oldh
O(items[j]).DB_NewW   = Math.round(oldw + oldw * increase / 100)
O(items[j]).DB_NewH   = Math.round(oldh + oldh * increase / 100)
```

This causes information about the element and the containing object it is located within to be stored as new properties of the elements. These properties can then be referenced by the following `DockUp()` and `DockDown()` subfunctions, and also be referenced from within the `Zoom()` recipe, which this one relies on.

First, the `id` object is copied to the `DB_Parent` property. Next, the value in `where` is copied so that `Zoom()` will know where to place the element as it zooms it, and `oldw` and `oldh` are added as properties to tell `Zoom()` where to zoom up from. The width and height that an element should be zoomed up to are also calculated by increasing the original width and height by the percentage value in `increase`, which is placed in the `DB_NewW` and `DB_NewH` properties.

The final two statements in this loop attach the `DockUp()` and `DockDown()` subfunctions to the element's `onmouseover` and `onmouseout` events, respectively, as follows:

```
O(items[j]).onmouseover = DockUp
O(items[j]).onmouseout  = DockDown
```

Finally, in the setup section of code, the containing object `id` is moved to the edge indicated by the value in `where`, like this:

```
GoToEdge(id, where, 50)
```

The DockUp() and DockDown() Subfunctions

These two functions trigger either the popping up or the popping down of an element by passing the various properties of the pseudo-object `this` to the `Zoom()` recipe (`this` being a keyword that represents the object that triggered the event that called the function).

The two functions are very similar and simply swap the positions of the original and larger dimensions of the element. Here's the statement that zooms an object up:

```
Zoom(this, 1, 1, O(this).DB_OldW, O(this).DB_OldH,
   O(this).DB_NewW, O(this).DB_NewH, msecs, 0, 1)
```

And this one zooms it back down again:

```
Zoom(this, 1, 1, O(this).DB_NewW, O(this).DB_NewH,
   O(this).DB_OldW, O(this).DB_OldH, msecs, 0, 1)
```

How to Use It

To use this recipe to create a dock bar, you first need to create an HTML object to contain the various elements. Usually a simple span or div is all you need. Next, place the elements that comprise the dock bar in that container. Generally, you will want to use images, but you can use objects if you wish.

Here's an example that creates a six-icon dock bar:

```
<span id='dock'>
<img id='i1' src='i1.gif' />
<img id='i2' src='i2.gif' />
<img id='i3' src='i3.gif' />
<img id='i4' src='i4.gif' />
<img id='i5' src='i5.gif' />
<img id='i6' src='i6.gif' />
</span>

<script>
OnDOMReady(function()
{
   Position('dock', FIX)
   ids = Array('i1', 'i2', 'i3', 'i4', 'i5', 'i6')
   DockBar('dock', ids, 'bottom', 32, 256)
})
</script>
```

As you can see, it's all very simple and easy to assemble. I placed only the images in the span, but you will probably want to enclose each image within an `<a href... > ... </a>` pair of tags to give them a click action.

In this instance, I placed the dock bar at the bottom, but a quick change to the `where` argument from 'bottom' to 'top' will move it to the top of the browser.

If you wish to place a dock bar on the left or right edge of the browser, you'll need to slightly alter the HTML, like this:

```
<span id='dock'>
<img id='i1' src='i1.gif' /><br clear='all' />
<img id='i2' src='i2.gif' /><br clear='all' />
<img id='i3' src='i3.gif' /><br clear='all' />
<img id='i4' src='i4.gif' /><br clear='all' />
<img id='i5' src='i5.gif' /><br clear='all' />
<img id='i6' src='i6.gif' />
</span>
```

Notice that all I added are some `<br clear='all' />` statements to ensure that the elements line up one below the other. Now you can change the `where` argument in the `<script>` section to either 'left' or 'right' to attach the dock bar to the left or right edge.

TIP *You can apply a background or gradient to the enclosing span to provide a greater effect.*

The Recipe

```
function DockBar(id, items, where, increase, msecs)
{
    Position(id, FIX)

    for (var j = 0 ; j < items.length ; ++j)
    {
        if (where == TP || where == BM)
            S(items[j]).verticalAlign = where
        else        O(items[j]).align = where

        var oldw = W(items[j])
        var oldh = H(items[j])

        S(items[j]).cursor    = 'pointer'
        O(items[j]).DB_Parent = id
        O(items[j]).DB_Where  = where
        O(items[j]).DB_OldW   = oldw
        O(items[j]).DB_OldH   = oldh
        O(items[j]).DB_NewW   = Math.round(oldw + oldw * increase / 100)
        O(items[j]).DB_NewH   = Math.round(oldh + oldh * increase / 100)

        O(items[j]).onmouseover = DockUp
        O(items[j]).onmouseout  = DockDown
    }

    GoToEdge(id, where, 50)
```

```
function DockUp()
{
   Zoom(this, 1, 1, O(this).DB_OldW, O(this).DB_OldH,
      O(this).DB_NewW, O(this).DB_NewH, msecs, 0, 1)
}

function DockDown()
{
   Zoom(this, 1, 1, O(this).DB_NewW, O(this).DB_NewH,
      O(this).DB_OldW, O(this).DB_OldH, msecs, 0, 1)
}
}
```

RollOver()

You've almost certainly seen and used rollover images that change as the mouse passes over them, but what about making rollover objects do the same? That's what this recipe does. With it, rollovers can contain HTML, images, and anything else you like, making them much more powerful than simple image rollovers.

Figure 18-9 shows an advertisement from a classified ads site.

When you mouse over the ad, it rolls over to show the new details in Figure 18-10.

About the Recipe

This recipe takes two objects that can be images, divs, or spans containing HTML and/or images. It creates a rollover so that the second object is displayed when the mouse passes across the first. It requires the following arguments:

- **ro1**   An object or object ID, or an array of objects and/or object IDs—if it is an array, then ro2 must also be an array with the same number of elements.

- ro2   An object or object ID, or an array of objects and/or object IDs—this should only be an array if ro1 is an array.

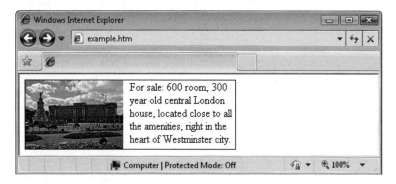

FIGURE 18-9   A rollover has been attached to this "for sale" classified ad.

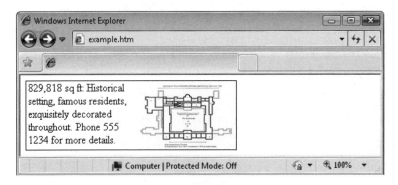

FIGURE 18-10 When the mouse passes over, the second object is displayed.

Variables, Arrays, and Functions

a	Local array containing the objects in `ro1` and `ro2`
w and h	Local variable containing the width and height of the objects
X and y	Local variable containing the top-left corner coordinates of the objects
iid	Local variable containing the result of calling `setInterval()`, used later for calling `clearInterval()`
MOUSE_X and MOUSE_Y	Global variables containing the current horizontal and vertical positions of the mouse pointer
Hide()	Function to hide an object
HideToggle()	Function to toggle the hidden/shown state of an object
Locate()	Function to move an object to another location and assign it a style position property such as 'relative' or 'absolute', and so on
onmouseover	Event of `ro1` that calls up the `DoRoll()` subfunction
DoRoll()	Subfunction to perform a rollover from `ro1` to `ro2` and then set up a repeating interrupt to the `RollCheck()` sub-subfunction to see if the mouse has moved away yet
RollCheck()	Sub-subfunction that returns every `INTERVAL` milliseconds when it is called—unless the mouse has moved away from `ro2`, in which case the objects are rolled back again

How It Works

This recipe supports arrays as well as single objects and is almost unique among all the recipes in that if the first argument is an array, then the second one must also be an array. Usually, if the first argument is an array, the second argument (a single object) is assigned to all elements of the array, but this recipe requires either two single objects or two arrays.

In the former case, the first object is rolled over with the second. In the latter case, each element of the first array will roll over with each matching element in the second array.

The first few lines of code facilitate recursively passing on the elements of both arrays as individual items back to the same function to be processed as individual items (there is no error checking, so make sure you pass two matching arrays or two objects):

```
if (ro1 instanceof Array)
{
    for (var j = 0 ; j < id.length ; ++j)
        RollOver(ro1[j], ro2[j])
    return
}
```

Next, the local array a is assigned elements ro1 and ro2 to make them easier for later functions to access them. Then, the width and height and horizontal and vertical locations of the objects are saved in the local variables w, h, x, and y, like this:

```
var a = Array(ro1, ro2)
var w = W(ro1) + 1
var h = H(ro1) + 1
var x = X(ro1)
var y = Y(ro1)
```

The width and height each have a pixel added to resolve issues in some browsers where there might otherwise be an anomaly at the edge boundary, which could cause the rollover to cycle rapidly.

The final three lines of the main setup section hide ro2 so that only ro1 is visible, then both ro1 and ro2 are located relative to their enclosing object at an offset of 0,0, so that they are on top of each other. Finally, an onmouseover event attaches the DoRoll() subfunction to the onmouseover event of ro1, as follows:

```
Hide(ro2)
Locate(a, REL, 0, 0)
O(ro1).onmouseover = DoRoll
```

The DoRoll() Subfunction

This function swaps the two objects' visibility properties so that ro2 becomes visible and ro1 becomes hidden. Then it sets up a repeating interrupt to call the RollCheck() sub-subfunction every INTERVAL milliseconds, like this:

```
HideToggle(a)
var iid = setInterval(RollCheck, INTERVAL)
```

The local variable iid is given the value returned by setInterval(), which will later be used by clearInterval() to cancel the repeating interrupts.

The RollCheck() Sub-subfunction

This function simply checks whether the mouse has moved out of the space occupied by the objects. If it has, it swaps the two objects back so that ro1 is visible and ro2 is again hidden. Then it cancels the repeating interrupts with a call to clearInterval(), like this:

```
if (MOUSE_X < x || MOUSE_X > x + w ||
    MOUSE_Y < y || MOUSE_Y > y + h)
```

```
{
   HideToggle(a)
   clearInterval(iid)
}
```

Why Not Use onmouseout Instead of RollCheck()?

Much as I would like to use onmouseout instead of RollCheck(), it's not possible to do so on an object that contains many different items because passing the mouse cursor between these items will often trigger an unwanted onmouseout event. Therefore, the simplest—and also a 100 percent reliable solution—is to check whether the mouse has moved out of the area and then call the code that you would otherwise have attached to an onmouseout event.

How to Use It

To use this recipe, you need to prepare two objects that have the same width and height. You can then pass them as arguments. Or, if you prefer, you can create several sets of matching pairs to use as rollovers and pass two arrays to the recipe. This saves repeated calls to the recipe if you have many sets to create.

Here's an example that uses two single objects to create a rollover effect for a classified ad:

```
<div id='r1'>
<img id='p1' src='palace.png' align='left'>
For sale: 600 room, 300 year old central London house, located
close to all the amenities, right in the heart of Westminster city.</div>

<div id='r2'>
<img id='p2' src='plan.png' align='right'>
829,818 sq ft: Historical setting, famous residents, exquisitely
decorated throughout. Phone 555 1234 for more details.</div>

<script>
OnDOMReady(function()
{
   rolls = Array('r1', 'r2')
   S(rolls, 'border', 'solid 1px')
   Resize(rolls, 320, 100)
   S('p1').paddingRight = Px(10)
   S('p2').paddingLeft  = Px(10)
   RollOver('r1', 'r2')
})
</script>
```

The HTML section creates two divs and places some text and an image in each. Then the <script> section creates the array rolls, which adds a border to each object and resizes them both to 320 by 100 pixels.

A couple of calls to the S() recipe sets up some padding around the images so that the text doesn't align right up against them, and then the RollOver() recipe is called to combine the two objects into a single rollover.

The Recipe

```
function RollOver(ro1, ro2)
{
   if (ro1 instanceof Array)
   {
      for (var j = 0 ; j < id.length ; ++j)
         RollOver(ro1[j], ro2[j])
      return
   }

   var a = Array(ro1, ro2)
   var w = W(ro1) + 1
   var h = H(ro1) + 1
   var x = X(ro1)
   var y = Y(ro1)

   Hide(ro2)
   Locate(a, REL, 0, 0)
   O(ro1).onmouseover = DoRoll

   function DoRoll()
   {
      HideToggle(a)
      var iid = setInterval(RollCheck, INTERVAL)

      function RollCheck()
      {
         if (MOUSE_X < x || MOUSE_X > x + w ||
             MOUSE_Y < y || MOUSE_Y > y + h)
         {
            HideToggle(a)
            clearInterval(iid)
         }
      }
   }
}
```

Breadcrumbs()

This recipe provides an automatic trail of "breadcrumbs" leading from a web site's home page to the current page. With it, users can backtrack to any location between the current page and the home page with a single click. Figure 18-11 shows the recipe being used on a page in a local file system on a Windows PC.

About the Recipe

This recipe returns the HTML to create a breadcrumb trail from the current web page back to the home page. It requires the following argument:

- **spacer** A string of characters to place between each breadcrumb.

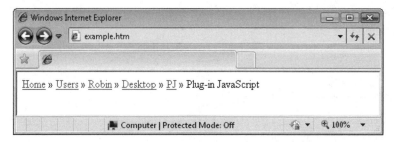

FIGURE **18-11**   Breadcrumbs provide a quick and easy web site navigation aid.

Variables, Arrays, and Functions

`parts`	Local array containing the URL of the current page split into parts
`crumbs`	Local array that builds the breadcrumbs
`title`	Local variable containing the title of the current web page, if any
`url`	Local variable containing the URL of the web site
`display`	Local variable containing the main HTML to return to
`j`	Local variable for iterating through different arrays
`push()`	Function to push a value onto an array
`InsVars()`	Function to insert values into a string

How It Works

This recipe fetches the path to the current page from `self.location.href` and splits it at the `?` character (if there is one) to extract the main URL from any query string. Then, the half before the `?` is split again at every `/` character, with the result being placed in the array `parts`.

After that, the `crumbs` array is created, which will be built up to contain the path. It is assigned an initial value of `parts[0]` (which will be `http:` or `ftp:` and so on), followed by the string `'//'`, like this:

```
var parts  = self.location.href.split('?')[0].split('/')
var crumbs = Array(parts[0] + '//')
```

Next a `for()` loop iterates through all but the first two elements of the `parts` array to reassemble the URL into the `crumbs` array using the `push()` function, as follows:

```
for (var j = 2 ; j < parts.length ; ++j)
{
   if (parts[j] == '') crumbs[0] += '/'
   else crumbs.push(parts[j])
}
```

The next three lines of code extract the title of the page (if any), the main URL of the web site, and the first breadcrumb, named 'Home', like this:

```
var title   = document.title ? document.title : parts[j - 1]
var url     = crumbs[0] + crumbs[1]
var display = InsVars("<a href='#1'>Home</a>", url)
```

The InsVars() recipe inserts the value in url into the string display, replacing the #1. If no title is found, the filename of the current page is used instead. Then, if no argument was supplied for the spacer to place between each breadcrumb, spacer is given the default value of a single space:

```
if (typeof spacer == UNDEF) gap = ' '
```

After this, another for() loop extracts each element from the crumbs array and attaches it (prefaced with a / character) to the display string with suitable HTML anchor tags, like this:

```
for (j = 2 ; j < crumbs.length - 1 ; ++j)
{
   url     += '/' + crumbs[j]
   display += spacer + InsVars("<a href='#1'>#2</a>", url, crumbs[j])
}
```

Finally, the contents of display are returned and prepended to another spacer string, followed by the page title:

```
return display + spacer + title
```

How to Use It

To use this recipe, pass it a string to use as a spacer between the breadcrumbs, and the breadcrumb string will be returned. Here's a simple example to do just that:

```
<div id='bc'></div>

<script>
OnDOMReady(function()
{
   O('bc').innerHTML = Breadcrumbs(" &raquo; ")
})
</script>
```

The HTML section creates a div in which the result will be placed, while the <script> section makes a single call and places the result into the innerHTML property of the div. Because simple plain HTML is returned, you can use CSS to style the returned string to make it fit with your web page design.

The Recipe

```
function Breadcrumbs(spacer)
{
    var parts  = self.location.href.split('?')[0].split('/')
    var crumbs = Array(parts[0] + '//')

    for (var j = 2 ; j < parts.length ; ++j)
    {
        if (parts[j] == '') crumbs[0] += '/'
        else crumbs.push(parts[j])
    }

    var title   = document.title ? document.title : parts[j - 1]
    var url     = crumbs[0] + crumbs[1]
    var display = InsVars("<a href='#1'>Home</a>", url)

    if (typeof spacer == UNDEF) gap = ' '

    for (j = 2 ; j < crumbs.length - 1 ; ++j)
    {
        url     += '/' + crumbs[j]
        display += spacer + InsVars("<a href='#1'>#2</a>",
            url, crumbs[j])
    }

    return display + spacer + title
}
```

BrowserWindow( )

Didn't you just hate pop-ups before browsers came with blockers? In my view, there is nothing wrong with the concept of pop-ups; it's just that it was too easy for web sites to inundate you with them, and once everyone started using them it turned into a nightmare.

However, when I set up an Internet radio station in the 1990s, I used pop-ups to good effect by implementing them as an audio player console so that people could listen to the radio while they continued to surf in the main browser window. Perhaps partly due to the novelty, most of the web site's visitors kept these pop-ups open for long periods as they listened to our shows.

Even though they have a bad name nowadays, pop-ups do have plenty of sensible uses, such as providing alerts and instant message notifications, for example. This recipe provides a versatile in-browser pop-up that's more user-friendly than opening a new browser window pop-up—which will generally only get blocked anyway. It also gives the user full control, as it can be moved around the screen and is easily dismissible.

With this recipe, you can ask a user for their login details, display private messages from another user in a forum, provide a selection of options, and so on. Or, as in Figure 18-12, you can pop up a window to provide further details when a user clicks a link. The great thing about it is that the user has full control. They can keep the window raised and move it around to reveal any content it was covering, or they can simply close it.

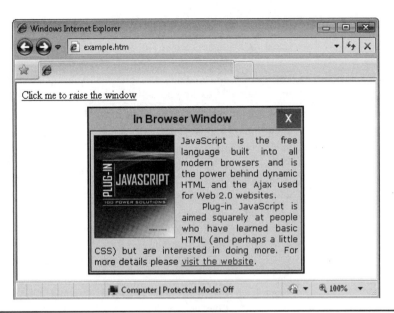

FIGURE 18-12   Creating an in-browser pop-up window

About the Recipe

This recipe creates an in-browser pop-up window that can be moved about by the user and also popped back down again. It requires the following arguments:

- **id**   An object or object ID identifying the main container—this may not be an array.
- **headerid**   An object or object ID identifying the draggable header.
- **closeid**   An object or object ID identifying the close button.
- **x** and **y**   The top-left coordinates of the pop-up.
- **bounds**   If true, the pop-up is forced to stay within the browser window; otherwise, it may be moved off the edges.
- **type**   The type of transition to use when popping the pop-up up or down, either 'fade', 'inflate', 'zoom', or 'instant'.
- **w** and **h**   If type is either 'inflate' or 'zoom', w and h specify which dimension(s) will be modified; otherwise, these values will be ignored.
- **msecs**   The number of milliseconds a pop-up or pop-down should take (unless type is 'instant').
- **interruptible**   If true, the pop-up can be interrupted by a pop-down call during its pop-up transition.

PART III

Variables, Arrays, and Functions

browserw and browserh	Local variables containing the width and height of the browser
borderw and borderh	Local variables containing the total widths of the left and right and top and bottom borders of the pop-up
popupw and popuph	Local variables containing the width and height of the pop-up
xoffset and yoffset	Local variables of the BWMove() subfunction containing the differences between the pop-up location and the current mouse positions
x and y	Local variables of the DoBWMove() sub-subfunction containing the differences between the current and saved mouse positions
r and b	Local variables of the DoBWMove() sub-subfunction containing the right and bottom maximum allowable coordinates for the pop-up if bounds is true
cursor	Style property of closeid set to 'pointer' when the mouse passes over it
onclick	Event of id attached to the BWToFront() subfunction, and event of closeid attached to the BWCloseWindow() subfunction
onmousedown	Event of headerid attached to the BWMove() subfunction
MOUSE_X, MOUSE_Y	Global variables containing the coordinates of the mouse cursor
MOUSE_DOWN	Global variable set to true when the mouse button is down
MOUSE_IN	Global variable set to true when the mouse cursor is within the bounds of the browser
SCROLL_X and SCROLL_Y	Global variables containing the number of pixels the document has been scrolled in the horizontal and vertical directions
setInterval()	Function to start repeated interrupts
clearInterval()	Function to stop repeated interrupts
Math.max()	Function to return the maximum of two values
Math.min()	Function to return the minimum of two values
PreventAction()	Function to stop an event from occurring
GoTo()	Function to move an object to a new location
PopUp()	Function to pop up a previously popped-down object
PopDown()	Function to pop down an object
BWToFront()	Subfunction to bring a pop-up window to the front
BWCloseWindow()	Subfunction to close a pop-up window
BWMove()	Subfunction to prepare to move a pop-up when it is dragged
DoBWMove()	Sub-subfunction to move a pop-up when it is dragged

How It Works

The first thing this recipe does is move the pop-up to its correct location and initiate the pop-up process, like this:

```
GoTo(id, x, y)
PopUp(id, type, w, h, msecs, interruptible)
```

Next, some local variables are assigned values to keep track of the browser's dimensions, the borders (if any) of the pop-up, and its width and height, as follows:

```
var browserw = GetWindowWidth()
var browserh = GetWindowHeight()
var borderw  = NoPx(S(id).borderLeftWidth) +
               NoPx(S(id).borderRightWidth)
var borderh  = NoPx(S(id).borderTopWidth)  +
               NoPx(S(id).borderBottomWidth)
var popupw   = W(id)
var popuph   = H(id)
```

The mouse cursor is then set to become a pointer when it passes over the `closeid` object, which is used as the close button. After that, the `BWToFront()` subfunction is assigned to the `onclick` event of the pop-up so that whenever you click anywhere on the pop-up, if it is partially obscured by another, it is brought to the front.

In addition, the `closeid` object is assigned to the `BWCloseWindow()` subfunction so that clicking the close button will pop the window down, and the `BWMove()` subfunction is attached to the `headerid` object so that you can click and drag the header to move the pop-up about, like this:

```
S(closeid).cursor        = 'pointer'
O(id).onclick            = BWToFront
O(closeid).onclick       = BWCloseWindow
O(headerid).onmousedown  = BWMove
```

The last couple of lines in the main setup section of code use the `PreventAction()` recipe to disable the 'select' event on the `headerid` and `closeid` objects. If this is not done, dragging the pop-up quickly may highlight parts of the header text because the pop-up will drag behind the pointer. This unsightly behavior is prevented like this:

```
PreventAction(headerid, 'select', true)
PreventAction(closeid,  'select', true)
```

The BWToFront() and BWCloseWindow() Subfunctions

The `BWToFront()` function simply changes the style `zIndex` property of the pop-up so that it is brought to the front, like this:

```
S(id).zIndex = ++ZINDEX
```

Every time an in-browser window such as `id` is clicked, this function is called, moving it to the front, and updating the value in `ZINDEX`.

The `BWCloseWindow()` function pops the pop-up down, like this:

```
PopDown(id, type, w, h, msecs, interruptible)
```

The BWMove Subfunction

The job of this function is to prepare the pop-up for being dragged around. First, the pop-up is brought to the front with a call to `BWToFront()` and the mouse cursor is changed to the operating system's icon for moving a window, like this:

```
BWToFront()
S(headerid).cursor = 'move'
```

Next, it makes copies of the current difference between the top-left corner of the pop-up and the current mouse position, placing them in `xoffset` and `yoffset`, and `setInterval()` is called to create repeating interrupts to the `DoBWMove()` sub-subfunction every 10 milliseconds to allow the object to be dragged about, as follows:

```
var xoffset = MOUSE_X - X(id)
var yoffset = MOUSE_Y - Y(id)
var iid     = setInterval(DoBWMove, 10)
```

The DoBWMove() Sub-subfunction

This is the function that actually moves the pop-up about. It starts by giving the local variables x and y the difference between the current mouse location and the location that was stored in `xoffset` and `yoffset` when `BWMove()` was initially called, like this:

```
var x = MOUSE_X - xoffset
var y = MOUSE_Y - yoffset
```

Then, the `bounds` argument is tested. If it is `true` or 1, then the pop-up must stay within the main browser window, and the farthest horizontal and vertical locations the pop-up may go to are placed in the local variables r and b (for right and bottom). These values are then used to calculate the new values of x and y, using the `Math.min()` and `Math.max()` functions to ensure the pop-up stays in bounds, like this:

```
var r = browserw - popupw - borderw + SCROLL_X
var b = browserh - popuph - borderh + SCROLL_Y
x     = Math.max(0, Math.min(x, r))
y     = Math.max(0, Math.min(y, b))
```

Next, the current mouse position is tested to see whether it is outside the bounds of the browser window or if the mouse button is no longer down. In any of these cases, dragging of the pop-up must be terminated so the `clearInterval()` function is called to stop the repeating interrupts and the mouse cursor icon for the `headerid` object is restored to the default, like this:

```
if (MOUSE_X < 0 || MOUSE_X > (browserw + SCROLL_X) ||
    MOUSE_Y < 0 || MOUSE_Y > (browserh + SCROLL_Y) ||
    !MOUSE_DOWN || !MOUSE_IN)
```

```
{
  clearInterval(iid)
  S(headerid).cursor = 'default'
}
```

Finally, whether or not the interrupts have been stopped, a call is made to `GoTo()` to update the location of the pop-up, like this:

```
GoTo(id, x, y)
```

If the interrupts have not been turned off, `DoBWMove()` will be called again in another 10 milliseconds, and so on, until dragging the object has stopped.

The use of `SCROLL_X` and `SCROLL_Y` means that as long as they have the style `position` property of 'absolute', these windows can be made to pop up anywhere within a document, not just within the viewable area.

How to Use It

To use this recipe, you must first create an object that will be the main container for the recipe. This can be a div, a span, or even a table. Then, you need to place a couple of different elements within this container, namely a header that will drag the pop-up about and also a close button for dismissing the pop-up. Once this is done, you can place anything else you want in your pop-up and it will be ready to be called up.

The following is an example that uses a table to create the various elements. Many people will say this is not the correct use for tables and that I should use CSS. However, my aim in this example is to avoid styling as much as possible and provide the bare bones to keep it easy to follow. A simple table is easy to understand and uses less code than CSS styling would take:

```
<div id='click'><u>Click me to raise the window</u></div>

<table id='window' bgcolor='lightblue' cellpadding='5'>
  <tr>
    <td id='header' width='310' align='center'>
      <font face='Arial'><b>In Browser Window</b></font>
    </td>
    <td id='close' width='20' bgcolor='red' align='center'>
      <font face='Arial' color='white'><b>X</b></font>
    </td>
  </tr>
  <tr>
    <td id='content' colspan='2' bgcolor='#eeeeee'>
      <img id='image' src='pijsmall.png' align='left' />
      <font face='Verdana' size='2'>
        JavaScript is the free language built into all modern
        browsers and is the power behind dynamic HTML and the
        Ajax used for Web 2.0 websites. <br />    this
        book is aimed squarely at people who have learned
        basic HTML (and perhaps a little CSS) but are interested
        in doing more. For more details please <a href=
        'http://webdevelopmentcookbook.com' target='New'>visit
        the website</a>.
      </font>
```

PART III

```
        </td>
    </tr>
</table>

<script>
OnDOMReady(function()
{
    Hide('window')
    x = (GetWindowWidth()  - 330) / 2
    y = (GetWindowHeight() - 245) / 2

    S('window').border = 'solid 2px'
    Position('window', ABS)
    PopDown('window', 'fade', null, null, 1, false)
    Resize('window', 330, 245)

    S('click').cursor       = 'pointer'
    S('image').paddingRight = Px(10)
    S('content').border     = 'solid 1px'
    S('content').textAlign  = 'justify'

    O('click').onclick = function()
    {
        BrowserWindow('window', 'header', 'close', x, y, true,
            'fade', null, null, 500, false)
    }
})
</script>
```

The HTML section starts by creating a div that you can click to raise the pop-up. Underneath this is a table with three sections: a header, a close button, and a content section.

The `<script>` section of code starts by calculating the correct coordinates to place the pop-up in the center of the browser. It also gives the pop-up a solid border with a width of 2 pixels, and uses the `Position()` recipe to give the pop-up a style `position` of 'absolute', which releases it from its place within the HTML so that it can be moved anywhere within the document. You can use a style `position` of 'fixed' if you prefer to limit the pop-up to staying only within the browser's viewport into the document.

The `PopDown()` recipe is then called with a value of 1 millisecond to quickly hide the pop-up away. It's important to use the transition type of 'fade' to later pop the window up because the transition types must match or you will get strange errors.

The window is then resized to ensure that it is of set dimensions. Also, to prevent content overflowing from the pop-up, its `overflow` style property is set to 'hidden'.

Next, four style properties are set to give the first div a mouse pointer cursor, to give a little padding to the image, to provide a 1-pixel border between the header and the content, and to set the text to full justification. None of these things are necessary, but they are included to show how you can add a little styling from JavaScript as easily as you can from a `<style>` section of HTML.

Finally, the `onclick` event of the div is set to call the `BrowserWindow()` recipe.

NOTE *Because I used a table as the container object for this pop-up, it does not handle the 'deflate' or 'zoom' transitions well at all since table dimensions are fixed and will not collapse on demand. If you wish to create a pop-up window that uses either of these transition types, you will need to build your container object using divs, spans, and CSS.*

The Recipe

```
function BrowserWindow(id, headerid, closeid, x, y, bounds,
   type, w, h, msecs, interruptible)
{
   GoTo(id, x, y)
   PopUp(id, type, w, h, msecs, interruptible)

   var browserw = GetWindowWidth()
   var browserh = GetWindowHeight()
   var borderw  = NoPx(S(id).borderLeftWidth) +
                  NoPx(S(id).borderRightWidth)
   var borderh  = NoPx(S(id).borderTopWidth)  +
                  NoPx(S(id).borderBottomWidth)
   var popupw   = W(id)
   var popuph   = H(id)

   S(closeid).cursor      = 'pointer'
   O(id).onclick          = BWToFront
   O(closeid).onclick     = BWCloseWindow
   O(headerid).onmousedown = BWMove

   PreventAction(headerid, 'select', true)
   PreventAction(closeid,  'select', true)

   function BWToFront()
   {
      S(id).zIndex = ++ZINDEX
   }

   function BWCloseWindow()
   {
      PopDown(id, type, w, h, msecs, interruptible)
   }

   function BWMove()
   {
      BWToFront()
      S(headerid).cursor = 'move'

      var xoffset = MOUSE_X - X(id)
      var yoffset = MOUSE_Y - Y(id)
      var iid     = setInterval(DoBWMove, 10)

      function DoBWMove()
      {
         var x = MOUSE_X - xoffset
         var y = MOUSE_Y - yoffset
```

```
if (bounds)
{
    var r = browserw - popupw - borderw + SCROLL_X
    var b = browserh - popuph - borderh + SCROLL_Y
    x     = Math.max(0, Math.min(x, r))
    y     = Math.max(0, Math.min(y, b))
}

if (MOUSE_X < 0 || MOUSE_X > (browserw + SCROLL_X) ||
    MOUSE_Y < 0 || MOUSE_Y > (browserh + SCROLL_Y) ||
    !MOUSE_DOWN || !MOUSE_IN)
{
    clearInterval(iid)
    S(headerid).cursor = 'default'
}

GoTo(id, x, y)
        }
    }
}
```

CHAPTER 19

Text Effects

This chapter provides you with a wide range of recipes offering text manipulation features. For example, you can enable text scrolling, either to the left or right, and you can choose both its speed and how many times the scroll should repeat.

There are also typewriter and "matrix" effects to make text appear and disappear, as well as color fading text, flying text into position, and even fancy ripple effects for drawing attention to important text.

RECIPE 70 TextScroll()

With this recipe, you can scroll selected text either left or right at a speed of your choosing and for a set number of times. Figure 19-1 shows two phrases. The top one is scrolling left over the course of three seconds, and the bottom one is scrolling right over a period of one second.

About the Recipe

This recipe takes an object that contains text and then scrolls it. It requires the following arguments:

- **id** An object, object ID, or array of objects and/or object IDs.
- **dir** The direction of scrolling, either 'left' or 'right'.
- **number** The number of times to repeat the scroll, with 0 indicating infinite repeats.
- **msecs** The number of milliseconds a full scroll should take.

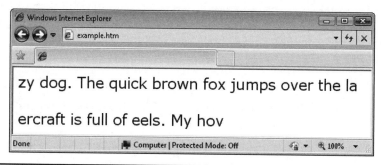

FIGURE 19-1 Scrolling text is easy with this recipe.

Variables, Arrays, and Functions

`j`	Local variable for iterating through `id` if it is an array
`copy`	Local copy of the HTML contents of `id`
`len`	Local variable containing the length of `copy`
`freq`	Local variable containing the period in milliseconds between each call to `DoTextScroll()`
`ctr1` and `ctr2`	Local counters for counting the characters in a string and the number of scroll iterations
`iid`	Local variable returned from the call to `setInterval()`, to be used when calling `clearInterval()`
`innerText`	Property of `id` in non-Firefox browsers containing the object's text
`textContent`	Property of `id` in Firefox browsers containing the object's text
`TS_Flag`	Property of `id` that is `true` when a scroll is in progress on it
`LT`	Global variable with the value 'left'
`Math.round()`	Function to turn a floating point number into an integer
`substr()`	Function to return a substring
`SetInterval()`	Function to start repeating interrupts
`clearInterval()`	Function to stop repeating interrupts
`DoTextScroll()`	Subfunction to perform the text scrolling
`Html()`	Function to return the HTML content of an object

How It Works

This recipe begins by iterating through `id` if it is an array, recursively calling itself to individually deal with each element, like this:

```
if (id instanceof Array)
{
   for (var j = 0 ; j < id.length ; ++j)
      TextScroll(id[j], dir, number, msecs)
   return
}
```

The `TS_Flag` property of `id` is then tested. If it's true, a scroll is already operating on the object so the function returns. Otherwise, the property is set to `true` to indicate that a scroll is in action on the `id`, as follows:

```
if (O(id).TS_Flag) return
else O(id).TS_Flag = true
```

Next, some local variables are set up to hold the following: the text content of `id`; the length of the text; the frequency at which the `DoTextScroll()` subfunction must be called in order for the scroll to take msecs milliseconds; and a couple of counters. Finally, the repeating interrupts are set up with a call to setInterval() using these statements:

```
var copy = Html(id)
var len  = copy.length
var freq = Math.round(msecs / len)
var ctr1 = 0
var ctr2 = 0
var iid  = setInterval(DoTextScroll, freq)
```

The DoTextScroll Subfunction

This function is called repeatedly at a frequency that will ensure that a full scroll of the text will take msecs milliseconds. It first determines whether to scroll left or right by checking the dir argument and then modifying the string copy accordingly. If scrolling left, characters are removed from the beginning of the string and added to the end. If scrolling right, characters are removed from the end of the string and added to the beginning, like this:

```
if (dir == LT) copy = copy.substr(1) + copy[0]
else           copy = copy[len - 1] + copy.substr(0, len - 1)
```

Another test must then be made due to differences between browsers. If the browser supports the innerText property of an object, then that is assigned the value in copy; otherwise, the textContent property is assigned the value, as follows:

```
if (O(id).innerText) O(id).innerText = copy
else                 O(id).textContent = copy
```

Next, an if() statement increments ctr1. If the incremented value equals the value in len, then the contents of the statement are executed because a full scroll has completed; otherwise, the function returns to be called again in freq milliseconds. The code looks like this:

```
if (++ctr1 == len)
{
```

Inside the statement, ctr1 is reset to 0, ready for the next scroll (if there is one). Then ctr2 is incremented in another if() statement. If that value equals the one in the argument number, all scrolling is complete, and the TS_Flag property of id is set to false and the repeated interrupts are stopped with a call to clearInterval(), like this:

```
ctr1 = 0

if (++ctr2 == number)
{
   O(id).TS_Flag = false
   clearInterval(iid)
}
```

How to Use It

To use this recipe, pass it an object such as a div or span that has some text in it, tell it whether to scroll left or right, and decide how many times the scroll should repeat and how long it should take.

Here's an example that creates two divs with different sentences in the HTML section, and then in the `<script>` section scrolls them in different directions, a different number of times, and at differing speeds:

```
<font face='Verdana' size='5'>
<div id='t1'>The quick brown fox jumps over the lazy dog. </div>
<br /><div id='t2'>My hovercraft is full of eels. </div>
</font>

<script>
OnDOMReady(function()
{
   TextScroll('t1', LT, 2, 1000)
   TextScroll('t2', RT, 1, 2000)
})
</script>
```

The divs have IDs of t1 and t2, respectively, and the LT and RT arguments are global variables with the values 'left' and 'right'.

The Recipe

```
function TextScroll(id, dir, number, msecs)
{
    if (id instanceof Array)
    {
      for (var j = 0 ; j < id.length ; ++j)
         TextScroll(id[j], dir, number, msecs)
      return
    }

    if (O(id).TS_Flag) return
    else O(id).TS_Flag = true

    var copy = Html(id)
    var len  = copy.length
    var freq = Math.round(msecs / len)
    var ctr1 = 0
    var ctr2 = 0
    var iid  = setInterval(DoTextScroll, freq)
```

```
function DoTextScroll()
{
   if (dir == LT) copy = copy.substr(1) + copy[0]
   else           copy = copy[len - 1]  + copy.substr(0, len - 1)

   if (O(id).innerText) O(id).innerText   = copy
   else                 O(id).textContent = copy

   if (++ctr1 == len)
   {
      ctr1 = 0

      if (++ctr2 == number)
      {
         O(id).TS_Flag = false
         clearInterval(iid)
      }
   }
}
```

TextType()

This recipe emulates an old-fashioned typewriter or a teletype machine by outputting the text contents of an object one character at a time, over a period of time specified by you. Figure 19-2 shows a phrase being displayed with this recipe.

About the Recipe

This recipe takes an object that contains text and then displays it one character at a time. It requires the following arguments:

- **id**   An object, object ID, or array of objects and/or object IDs.
- **number**   The number of times to repeat the process, with 0 indicating infinite repeats.
- **msecs**   The number of milliseconds it should take to type out the text.

FIGURE 19-2   You can emulate a teletype machine or typewriter with this recipe.

Variables, Arrays, and Functions

`j`	Local variable that iterates through `id` if it is an array
`html`	Local variable containing the HTML content of `id`
`len`	Local variable containing the length of `html`
`freq`	Local variable containing the period in milliseconds between each call to `DoTextScroll()`
`ctr1` and `ctr2`	Local counters for counting the characters in a string and the number of scroll iterations
`iid`	Local variable returned from the call to `setInterval()`, to be used when calling `clearInterval()`
`str`	Substring of `html` used for displaying the characters so far "typed"
`innerText`	Property of `id` in non-Firefox browsers containing the object's text
`textContent`	Property of `id` in Firefox browsers containing the object's text
`TT_Flag`	Property of `id` that is `true` when a call to `TextType()` is already in progress on it
`Math.round()`	Function to turn a floating point number into an integer
`substr()`	Function to return a substring
`SetInterval()`	Function to start repeating interrupts
`clearInterval()`	Function to stop repeating interrupts
`Html()`	Function to return the HTML content of an object
`DoTextType()`	Subfunction to perform the "typing"

How It Works

This recipe begins by iterating through `id` if it is an array, recursively calling itself to individually process each element, like this:

```
if (id instanceof Array)
{
   for (var j = 0 ; j < id.length ; ++j)
      TextType(id[j], number, msecs)
   return
}
```

The `TT_Flag` property of `id` is then tested. If it's true, a call to this recipe is already operating on the object, so it returns. Otherwise, the property is set to `true` to indicate that a call is in progress on the `id`, as follows:

```
if (O(id).TT_Flag) return
else O(id).TT_Flag = true
```

Next, some local variables are set up to hold the following: the text content of `id`; the length of the text; the frequency at which the `DoTextType()` subfunction must be called in order for the typing to take msecs milliseconds; and a couple of counters. Finally, the repeating interrupts are set up with a call to setInterval() using these statements:

```
var html = Html(id)
var len  = html.length
var freq = Math.round(msecs / len)
var ctr1 = 0
var ctr2 = 0
var iid  = setInterval(DoTextType, freq)
```

The DoTextType() Subfunction

This function starts by assigning the characters so far typed to the local variable str. Next, an underline character is placed at the end to simulate a cursor, like this:

```
var str = html.substr(0, ctr1) + '_'
```

After that, the ctr1 counter is tested against the value in len. If they match, the text has completed being typed; otherwise, there is more yet to be typed, so ctr1 is incremented, like this:

```
if (ctr1++ == len)
{
```

Inside the if() statement, ctr1 is reset to 0, making it ready for the next repeat (if there is one), and ctr2 is incremented within another if() statement and compared with the value in the number argument. If they match, then all repeats have finished and the TT_Flag property of id is set to false, the repeating interrupts are canceled with a call to clearInterval(), and the final underline character (which was previously appended to str) is stripped from it using a call to substr(), as follows:

```
ctr1 = 0

if (++ctr2 == number)
{
   O(id).TT_Flag = false
   clearInterval(iid)
   str = str.substr(0, len)
}
```

Next, because different browsers use different properties for the value, if the browser supports the innerText property, it is assigned the value in str; otherwise, the textContent property of id is assigned the value, like this:

```
if (O(id).innerText)
    O(id).innerText = str
else Html(id, str)
```

Then, the function returns, and if the repeating interrupts have not been cleared, it will be called up again in another freq milliseconds.

How to Use It

To use this recipe, put some text in a container, such as a div or span, and pass that container to the recipe along with the number of repeats required and the length of time it should take to complete the typing.

Here's a simple example that types out a simple phrase once, over a period of five seconds:

```
<font face='Courier New' size='6'><b>
<div id='text'>The quick brown fox jumps over the lazy dog.</div>
</b></font>

<script>
OnDOMReady(function()
{
   TextType('text', 1, 5000)
})
</script>
```

The Recipe

```
function TextType(id, number, msecs)
{
    if (id instanceof Array)
    {
      for (var j = 0 ; j < id.length ; ++j)
         TextType(id[j], number, msecs)
      return
    }

    if (O(id).TT_Flag) return
    else O(id).TT_Flag = true

    var html = Html(id)
    var len  = html.length
    var freq = Math.round(msecs / len)
    var ctr1 = 0
    var ctr2 = 0
    var iid  = setInterval(DoTextType, freq)

    function DoTextType()
    {
      var str = html.substr(0, ctr1) + '_'

      if (ctr1++ == len)
      {
         ctr1 = 0

         if (++ctr2 == number)
         {
            O(id).TT_Flag = false
            clearInterval(iid)
            str = str.substr(0, len)
         }
      }
```

```
        if (O(id).innerText)
            O(id).innerText = str
        else Html(id, str)
    }
}
```

MatrixToText()

This recipe provides an effect similar to the one used in the *Matrix* movies to make text slowly appear from a random collection of characters. Figure 19-3 shows some text halfway through being revealed using this recipe.

About the Recipe

This recipe takes an object containing some text and replaces it with random characters, then slowly changes them to reveal the original text. It requires the following arguments:

- **id**   An object, object ID, or array of objects and/or object IDs.
- **msecs**   The number of milliseconds it should take to reveal the text.

Variables, Arrays, and Functions

j	Local variable that iterates through `id` if it is an array
html	Local variable containing the HTML content of `id`
len	Local variable containing the length of `html`
freq	Local variable containing the period in milliseconds between each call to `DoMatrixTotext()`
matrix	Local string variable originally containing scrambled text
count	Local variable for counting the steps of the transformation
chars	Local string variable containing all the upper- and lowercase letters and the digits 0 to 9
iid	Local variable returned from the call to `setInterval()`; to be used when calling `clearInterval()`
innerText	Property of `id` in non-Firefox browsers containing the object's text
textContent	Property of `id` in Firefox browsers containing the object's text
innerHTML	Property of `id` containing its HTML
INTERVAL	Global variable with the value 30
MT_Flag	Property of `id` that is `true` when a call to `MatrixToText()` is already in progress on it
substr()	Function to return a substring
Math.round()	Function to turn a floating point number into an integer, rounding the number up or down, whichever is closest

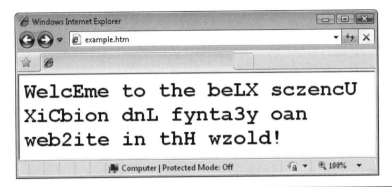

FIGURE 19-3   This recipe creates an interesting text reveal effect.

`Math.floor()`	Function to turn a floating point number into an integer, always rounding the number down
`Math.random()`	Function to return a random number between 0 and 1
`SetInterval()`	Function to start repeating interrupts
`clearInterval()`	Function to stop repeating interrupts
`Html()`	Function to return the HTML of an object
`DoMatrixToText()`	Function to reveal the original text

How It Works

This recipe begins by iterating through `id` if it is an array, recursively calling itself to individually process each element, like this:

```
if (id instanceof Array)
{
   for (var j = 0 ; j < id.length ; ++j)
     MatrixToText(id[j], msecs)
   return
}
```

The `MT_Flag` property of `id` is then tested. If it's true, a call to this recipe is already operating on the object, so it returns. Otherwise, the property is set to `true` to indicate that a call is in progress on the `id`, as follows:

```
if (O(id).MT_Flag) return
else O(id).MT_Flag = true
```

Next, `html` is given the HTML contents of `id`, `len` (its length), and `freq` (the frequency with which the `DoMatrixToText()` subfunction needs to be called in order for the transition to take `msecs` milliseconds). In addition, the following are created: string variable `matrix`, which will hold the random text as it is slowly revealed; `count`, the counter for each step, which is initialized to 0; and chars, the string containing all possible characters for scrambling the text, which is populated with the characters a–z, A–Z, and 0–9, as follows:

```
var html   = Html(id)
var len    = html.length
var freq   = Math.round(msecs / INTERVAL)
var matrix = ''
var count  = 0
var chars  = 'ABCDEFGHIHJKLMOPQRSTUVWXYZ' +
             'abcdefghijklmnopqrstuvwxyz' +
             '0123456789'
```

Next, a for() loop iterates through each character in html, replacing it with a random character from chars (if it is not a newline or space), like this:

```
for (var j = 0 ; j < len ; ++j)
{
   if (html[j] == '\n' || html[j] == ' ') matrix += html[j]
   else matrix += chars[Math.floor(Math.random() * chars.length)]
}
```

The value in matrix is then assigned to either the innerText or textContent property of id, according to which one is supported by the current browser. The regular interrupts to the subfunction that will perform the reveal are then set up, like this:

```
if (O(id).innerText) O(id).innerText   = matrix
else                 O(id).textContent = matrix
var iid = setInterval(DoMatrixToText, freq)
```

The DoMatrixToText() Subfunction

This function does the revealing by using a for() loop each time it is called up to replace len / 20 characters in the string matrix with the correct values. This is sufficient to change only enough for each step so that the transition will take msecs milliseconds, as follows:

```
for (j = 0 ; j < len / 20 ; ++j)
{
   var k  = Math.floor(Math.random() * len)
   matrix = matrix.substr(0, k) +
            html[k] + matrix.substr(k + 1)
}
```

The value of 20 was determined by performing several tests with strings of different sizes and timing them. It's not an exact value, so you might find you want to tweak it. The new value in matrix is then assigned to the correct property of id in order to display it:

```
if (O(id).innerText) O(id).innerText   = matrix
else                 O(id).textContent = matrix
```

Finally, the count variable is incremented within an if() statement. If the new value is the same as INTERVAL, the transition has completed, so the MT_Flag property of id is set to false to indicate that the transition is over. Its innerHTML property is then restored to its original value, and the repeating interrupts are canceled, like this:

```
if (++count == INTERVAL)
{
   O(id).MT_Flag = false
   O(id).innerHTML = html
   clearInterval(iid)
}
```

The function then returns and, if there are still characters to be revealed, it is called up again in freq milliseconds time, and so forth, until the transition has finished.

How to Use It

To use this recipe, pass it an object, such as a div or span that contains some text, and tell it how long the reveal transition should take, as with this example:

```
<font face='Courier New' size='6'><b>
<div id='text'>Welcome to the best science fiction and fantasy fan
website in the world!</div>
</b></font>

<script>
OnDOMReady(function()
{
   MatrixToText('text', 3000)
})
</script>
```

The Recipe

```
function MatrixToText(id, msecs)
{
   if (id instanceof Array)
   {
     for (var j = 0 ; j < id.length ; ++j)
        MatrixToText(id[j], msecs)
     return
   }

   if (O(id).MT_Flag) return
   else O(id).MT_Flag = true

   var html   = Html(id)
   var len    = html.length
   var freq   = Math.round(msecs / INTERVAL)
   var matrix = ''
   var count  = 0
   var chars  = 'ABCDEFGHIHJKLMOPQRSTUVWXYZ' +
                'abcdefghijklmnopqrstuvwxyz' +
                '0123456789'

   for (var j = 0 ; j < len ; ++j)
```

```
{
   if (html[j] == '\n' || html[j] == ' ') matrix += html[j]
   else matrix += chars[Math.floor(Math.random() * chars.length)]
}

if (O(id).innerText) O(id).innerText   = matrix
else                  O(id).textContent = matrix

var iid = setInterval(DoMatrixToText, freq)

function DoMatrixToText()
{
   for (j = 0 ; j < len / 20 ; ++j)
   {
      var k   = Math.floor(Math.random() * len)
      matrix = matrix.substr(0, k) +
               html[k] + matrix.substr(k + 1)
   }

   if (O(id).innerText) O(id).innerText   = matrix
   else                  O(id).textContent = matrix


   if (++count == INTERVAL)
   {
      O(id).MT_Flag = false
      O(id).innerHTML = html
      clearInterval(iid)
   }
}
}
```

TextToMatrix()

This recipe provides the inverse functionality to the MatrixToText() recipe. It takes some text and slowly scrambles it over a period of time specified by you. Figure 19-4 shows some text that has been fully scrambled with this recipe.

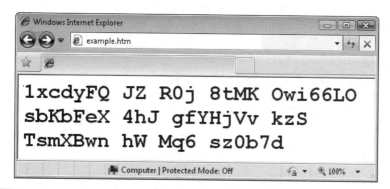

FIGURE 19-4   This recipe slowly scrambles text over a specified length of time.

About the Recipe

This recipe takes an object containing some text and replaces it with random characters over a time period you specify. It requires the following arguments:

- **id**   An object, object ID, or array of objects and/or object IDs.
- **msecs**   The number of milliseconds it should take to scramble the text.

Variables, Arrays, and Functions

j	Local variable that iterates through id if it is an array
text	Local variable containing the HTML content of id
len	Local variable containing the length of html
freq	Local variable containing the period in milliseconds between each call to DoMatrixTotext()
count	Local variable for counting the steps of the transformation
chars	Local string variable containing all the upper- and lowercase letters and the digits 0 to 9
iid	Local variable returned from the call to setInterval(); to be used when calling clearInterval()
innerText	Property of id in non-Firefox browsers containing the object's text
textContent	Property of id in Firefox browsers containing the object's text
INTERVAL	Global variable with the value 30
TM_Flag	Property of id that is true when a call to TextToMatrix() is already in progress on it
substr()	Function to return a substring
Math.floor()	Function to turn a floating point number into an integer, always rounding the number down
Math.random()	Function to return a random number between 0 and 1
SetInterval()	Function to start repeating interrupts
clearInterval()	Function to stop repeating interrupts
Html()	Function to return the HTML of an object
DoTextToMatrix()	Function to scramble the original text

How It Works

This recipe works in almost the same fashion as the MatrixToText() recipe except that the string text is slowly scrambled over time and assigned to the id object to display it—a full explanation can be found in the notes in the MatrixToText() function, JavaScript Recipe 72.

How to Use It

To use this recipe, pass it an object, such as a div or span that contains some text, and tell it how long the scramble transition should take, as with this example:

```
<font face='Courier New' size='6'><b>
<div id='text'>Welcome to the best science fiction and fantasy fan
website in the world!</div>
</b></font>

<script>
OnDOMReady(function()
{
   TextToMatrix('text', 3000)
   FadeOut('text', 3000)
})
</script>
```

Note that I snuck in a call to the FadeOut() recipe in this example, as it makes for an interesting combined effect of the scrambling text slowly fading away—this is just one example of how you can combine these recipes to produce even more complex and interesting results.

You may also notice that I omitted the interruptible argument to FadeOut(). This therefore passes a value of 'undefined' for that argument to the function, which will be treated as if it was the value false, thus saving you some typing.

The Recipe

```
function TextToMatrix(id, msecs)
{
    if (id instanceof Array)
    {
      for (var j = 0 ; j < id.length ; ++j)
         TextToMatrix(id[j], msecs)
      return
    }

    if (O(id).TM_Flag) return
    else O(id).TM_Flag = true

    var text  = Html(id)
    var len   = text.length
    var freq  = Math.round(msecs / INTERVAL)
    var count = 0
    var chars = 'ABCDEFGHIHJKLMOPQRSTUVWXYZ' +
                'abcdefghijklmnopqrstuvwxyz' +
                '0123456789'
    var iid   = setInterval(DoTextToMatrix, freq)

    function DoTextToMatrix()
    {
      for (var j = 0 ; j < len / 20 ; ++j)
      {
         var k = Math.floor(Math.random() * len)
         var l = Math.floor(Math.random() * chars.length)

         if (text[k] != '\n' && text[k] != '\r' && text[k] != ' ')
            text = text.substr(0, k) + chars[l] + text.substr(k + 1)
      }
```

```
        if (O(id).innerText) O(id).innerText   = text
        else                 O(id).textContent = text

        if (++count == INTERVAL)
        {
           O(id).TM_Flag = false
           clearInterval(iid)
        }
     }
  }
}
```

74 ColorFade()

This recipe provides a very smooth transition effect between two different colors, and you can use it with either an object's text or its background colors. Figure 19-5 shows two elements that have been set to fade colors. The first continuously alternates between yellow and blue text and background colors, while the second fades from black to light blue when the mouse is passed over it.

About the Recipe

This recipe changes the text or background color of the contents of an object over a specified period of time. It requires the following arguments:

- **id**   An object or object ID, or an array of objects and/or object IDs.
- **color1**   The start color expressed as a six-digit hexadecimal number.
- **color2**   The end color expressed as a six-digit hexadecimal number.
- **what**   The property to change, either 'text' for the text color, or 'back' (or anything other than 'text') for the background color.
- **msecs**   The number of milliseconds the transition should take.
- **number**   The number of times the transition should repeat, with 0 meaning infinite repeats.

Figure 19-5   This recipe is great for banners and mouseover highlights.

Variables, Arrays, and Functions

j	Local variable that indexes into `id` if it is an array, and for splitting the colors into triplets
step	Local variable containing the amount of change between each transition frame
index	Local variable used as a multiplier for generating color values
count	Local variable containing a counter for counting the repeats
direc	Local variable containing the direction of color change, either 1 or –1
cols[]	Local array containing the 'from' color triplets
steps[]	Local array containing the step between each color triplet
prop	Local variable containing the property to change, either `color` or `background`
iid	Local variable containing the value returned by `setInterval()`; to be used later by `clearInterval()`
temp	Local variable used for building up each transition color
CF_Flagtext	Property of `id` that is `true` if a color change transition is in effect on it
CF_Flagback	Property of `id` that is `true` if a background color change transition is in effect on it
INTERVAL	Global variable with the value 30
DoColorFade()	Subfunction to perform the color changes
ZeroToFF()	Sub-subfunction to ensure values are integers between 0 and 255 (equal to 00 to FF hexadecimal)
DecHex()	Function to convert a decimal value to hexadecimal
setInterval()	Function to set up repeating interrupts
clearInterval()	Function to stop repeating interrupts
Math.round()	Function to turn a floating point number into a integer
Math.max()	Function to return the maximum of two values
Math.min()	Function to return the minimum of two values

How It Works

This function starts by iterating through `id` if it is an array, recursively calling itself to process each element individually, like this:

```
if (id instanceof Array)
{
   for (var j = 0 ; j < id.length ; ++j)
      ColorFade(id[j], color1, color2, what, msecs, number)
   return
}
```

Next, a pair of flags is checked to see whether a fade is already in process on id. If the argument what has the value 'text', then the CF_Flagtext property of id is tested or set. Otherwise, if it is 'back', its CF_Flagback property is tested or set, like this:

```
if (O(id)['CF_Flag' + what])
{
    if (!O(id)['CF_Int' + what]) return
    else clearInterval(O(id)['CF_IID' + what])
}
else O(id)['CF_Flag' + what] = true
```

If a fade is running and the recipe is not set to interruptible, the recipe returns; otherwise, any current repeating interrupts are halted, ready for new ones to be set up. If the flag is not set, it is assigned the value true to indicate that a fade is in progress.

After this, if either of the colors was passed without the preceding required # character, it is added:

```
if (color1[0] == '#') color1 = color1.substr(1)
if (color2[0] == '#') color2 = color2.substr(1)
```

Next, various local variables are assigned values that will be used later:

```
var step  = Math.round(msecs / INTERVAL)
var index = 0
var count = 0
var direc = 1
var cols  = []
var steps = []
```

The last five are simple initializations, while the first one gives step a value that will calculate the difference between transition frames so that the whole effect will take msecs milliseconds.

After this, the cols[] array is populated with the triplet color values, and the steps[] array with the step values for each triplet between each frame, like this:

```
for (var j = 0 ; j < 3 ; ++j)
{
    var tmp  = HexDec(color2.substr(j * 2, 2))
    cols[j]  = HexDec(color1.substr(j * 2, 2))
    steps[j] = (tmp - cols[j]) / step
}
```

The local variable prop is then assigned a property name, either color or background, depending on the value in the argument what:

```
if (what == 'text') var prop = 'color'
else                var prop = 'background'
```

This is what makes the recipe dual functional: either the foreground or background color will be changed.

Finally, in the setup section of code, the value in `interruptible` is saved, and the `setInterval()` function is called to set up repeating interrupts to the `DoColorFade()` subfunction every `INTERVAL` milliseconds. The value returned by the function is then stored in `IID` to be used later when `clearInterval()` is called:

```
O(id)['CF_Int' + what] = interruptible
O(id)['CF_IID' + what] = setInterval(DoColorFade, INTERVAL)
```

The DoColorFade Subfunction

This function starts off by preparing the variable `temp` with an initial # character to start a color string. A `for()` loop then iterates through the `cols[]` array, calculating the current frame's color values, converting them to hexadecimal, and then appending them to `temp`. After that, the value in `temp` is assigned to the property of `id` stored in `prop`:

```
var temp ='#'

for (var j = 0 ; j < 3 ; ++j)
    temp += DecHex(ZeroToFF(cols[j] + index * steps[j]))

S(id)[prop] = temp
```

After this, the `index` variable is incremented by the value in `direc`. If `direc` is 1, `index` increases by 1; if it is –1, it decreases by 1, like this:

```
if ((index += direc) > step || index < 0)
```

If the new value of `index` is either greater than `step` or less than 0, the transition is complete, so the following code is executed to reverse the direction of fade by negating `direc`. Then, if all repeats are finished, it cancels the repeating interrupts:

```
direc = -direc

if (++count == number)
{
    O(id)['CF_Flag' + what] = false
    clearInterval(O(id)['CF_IID' + what])
}
```

The ZeroToFF() Sub-subfunction

This function takes the value passed to it in `num` and uses the `Math.max()` function to ensure it is not less than 0, uses the `Math.min()` function to ensure it isn't greater than 255, and uses the `Math.round()` function to turn it into an integer, like this:

```
return Math.round(Math.min(255, Math.max(0, num)))
```

How to Use It

To use this recipe, pass it an object, such as a div or span that contains some text; provide starting and ending values in strings such as '#123456'; decide whether to change the text or background color by setting an argument for what of 'text' or 'back'; choose a length of time in milliseconds for the transition; and, finally, decide how many times you want the transition to repeat.

Here's an example that uses the recipe in two different ways. One highlights some text by constantly transitioning it between the two colors supplied, and the other reacts to onmouseover and onmouseout events to fade between the two colors:

```
<center>
    <b>
        <font face='Verdana' size='6'>
            <span id='t'>New - See our latest offers!</span><br />
            <span id='m'>Mouseover Me</span>
        </font>
    </b>
</center>

<script>
OnDOMReady(function()
{
    ColorFade('t', '#ffffff', '#0000ff', 'text', 2000, 0)
    ColorFade('t', '#ff0000', '#ffff00', 'back', 2000, 0)

    O('m').onmouseover = function() { fade('#000000', '#0088ff') }
    O('m').onmouseout  = function() { fade('#0088ff', '#000000') }

    function fade(a, b)
    {
        ColorFade('m', a, b, 'text', 200, 1)
    }
})
</script>
```

The text section creates two spans with the IDs 't' and 'm'. In the <script> section, the first two commands set both the background and text colors of 't' to transition between yellow (#ffff00) and blue (#0000ff). Because a number argument of 0 is passed, the transitions continue infinitely.

Below this, the 'm' span has its onmouseover and onmouseout events attached to a small function called fade() that calls ColorFade() with a number argument of 1 so that each transition happens only once. This means that when the mouse passes over, the color fades to light blue (#0000ff), and when the mouse moves away, it fades back to black (#000000).

Pass your mouse over the second span to see the smooth fading mouseover effect you can achieve for links and other elements.

NOTE *Odd transitions change the color of an object from the first to the second color, while even ones change it back again. This means that number argument values of 1, 3, 5, and so on will leave the second color on display, while 2, 4, 6, and so on will restore the first color after all transitions are over.*

The Recipe

```
function ColorFade(id, color1, color2, what, msecs, number, interruptible)
{
   if (id instanceof Array)
   {
      for (var j = 0 ; j < id.length ; ++j)
         ColorFade(id[j], color1, color2, what, msecs, number)
      return
   }

   if (O(id)['CF_Flag' + what])
   {
      if (!O(id)['CF_Int' + what]) return
      else clearInterval(O(id)['CF_IID' + what])
   }
   else O(id)['CF_Flag' + what] = true

   if (color1[0] == '#') color1 = color1.substr(1)
   if (color2[0] == '#') color2 = color2.substr(1)

   var step  = Math.round(msecs / INTERVAL)
   var index = 0
   var count = 0
   var direc = 1
   var cols  = []
   var steps = []

   for (var j = 0 ; j < 3 ; ++j)
   {
      var tmp  = HexDec(color2.substr(j * 2, 2))
      cols[j]  = HexDec(color1.substr(j * 2, 2))
      steps[j] = (tmp - cols[j]) / step
   }

   if (what == 'text') var prop = 'color'
   else                var prop = 'background'

   O(id)['CF_Int' + what] = interruptible
   O(id)['CF_IID' + what] = setInterval(DoColorFade, INTERVAL)

   function DoColorFade()
   {
      var temp ='#'

      for (var j = 0 ; j < 3 ; ++j)

         temp += DecHex(ZeroToFF(cols[j] + index * steps[j]))

      S(id)[prop] = temp

      if ((index += direc) > step || index < 0)
      {
         direc = -direc
```

```
        if (++count == number)
        {
           O(id)['CF_Flag' + what] = false
           clearInterval(O(id)['CF_IID' + what])
        }
     }

     function ZeroToFF(num)
     {
        return Math.round(Math.min(255, Math.max(0, num)))
     }
   }
}
```

FlyIn()

With this recipe, you can make text (or any object) fly into its position in a document from any location you choose and at whatever speed you wish. Figure 19-6 shows a list of five items set to fly in from the bottom of the browser, one per second over the course of five seconds.

About the Recipe

This recipe flies an object into its final location over a time you specify. It requires these arguments:

- **id** An object or object ID, or an array of objects and/or object IDs.
- **x** If specified, the relative horizontal offset at which the animation should start—it may be a positive or negative value.
- **y** If specified, the relative vertical offset at which the animation should start—it may be a positive or negative value.
- **msecs** The number of milliseconds the animation should take.

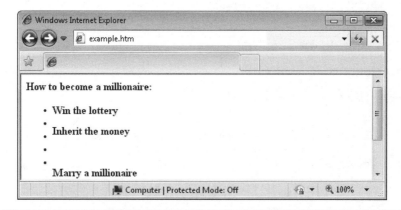

FIGURE 19-6 Instead of having static objects, why not fly them in at the start?

Variables, Arrays, and Functions

j	Local variable to iterate through `id` if it is an array
`tox` and `toy`	Local variables containing the original (and final) location of `id`
`fromx` and `fromy`	Local variables containing the start location of `id` for the animation
`xstep` and `ystep`	Local variables containing the amount by which to move `id` in each frame
`count`	Local variable to count the animation frames
`ABS`	Global variable with the value 'absolute'
`FI_Flag`	Property of `id` that is true if a fly-in is already in progress on it
`setInterval()`	Function to start repeating interrupts
`clearInterval()`	Function to end repeating interrupts
`DoFlyIn()`	Subfunction to perform the animation
`Position()`	Function to set the style position property of an object
`GoTo`	Function to move an object to a new location

How It Works

This recipe starts by using `j` to iterate through `id` if it is an array, recursively calling itself to individually process each element:

```
if (id instanceof Array)
{
   for (var j = 0 ; j < id.length ; ++j)
      FlyIn(id[j], x, y, msecs)
   return
}
```

Next, the `FI_Flag` property of `id` is checked. If it is true, a fly-in is already in progress on the object, so it returns. Otherwise, the property is given the value `true` to indicate that a fly-in is running on `id`, like this:

```
if (O(id).FI_Flag) return
else O(id).FI_Flag = true
```

After that, the various local variables that will be used by the `DoFlyIn()` subfunction are set up, as follows:

```
var tox   = X(id)
var toy   = Y(id)
var fromx = tox + x
var fromy = toy + y
var xstep = x / (msecs / INTERVAL)
var ystep = y / (msecs / INTERVAL)
var count = 0
```

The variables `tox` and `toy` save the current location of the object as a record of where to fly it into. The start location for the animation is then placed in `fromx` and `fromy`, the step value for each dimension of each frame is stored in `xstep` and `ystep`, and the counter `count` is initialized.

Finally, in the setup section, the `id` object is released from the HTML and given a style position property of 'absolute', using the global variable `ABS`. This allows it to be moved anywhere within the document. Next, the `setInterval()` function is called to start repeating interrupts to the `DoFlyIn()` subfunction every `INTERVAL` milliseconds. The result of calling the function is saved in `iid` to be used later when `clearInterval()` is called:

```
Position(id, ABS)
var iid = setInterval(DoFlyIn, INTERVAL)
```

The DoFlyIn() Subfunction

This function simply uses the `GoTo()` recipe to move `id` to each location in the animation, like this:

```
GoTo(id, fromx - xstep * count, fromy - ystep * count)
```

An `if()` statement then checks `count` to see whether it has a value greater than or equal to `msecs / INTERVAL`. If it does, the fly-in has completed and the following code is executed, but whether it does or doesn't equal that value, `count` is incremented after the test is made, like this:

```
if (count++ >= msecs / INTERVAL)
{
```

If the fly-in has finished, the `FI_Flag` property of `id` is set to `false` to indicate this, `GoTo()` is called to ensure that `id` is placed at exactly the correct location (because `xstep` and `ystep` will usually be floating point values and the final values calculated using them could be off by a pixel or two). Then, the repeating interrupts are stopped with a call to `clearInterval()`, like this:

```
O(id).FI_Flag = false
GoTo(id, tox, toy)
clearInterval(iid)
```

The function then returns, and if the fly-in hasn't yet finished, it will be called again in `INTERVAL` milliseconds, and so on until the animation has completed.

How to Use It

To use this recipe, pass it an object and specify where you wish the object to fly in from by providing relative horizontal and vertical coordinates in the next two arguments. You also have to tell the recipe how long the animation should take in milliseconds.

Here's an example that flies some list elements up from the browser bottom, with each arriving at its destination one second after the one above it:

```
<b>How to become a millionaire:<ul>
   <li><span id='a'>Win the lottery</span></li>
   <li><span id='b'>Inherit the money</span></li>
   <li><span id='c'>Marry a millionaire</span></li>
   <li><span id='d'>Become a movie or pop star</span></li>
   <li><span id='e'>Invest $130/month for 40 years!</span></li>
</ul></b>
```

```
<script>
OnDOMReady(function()
{
   h = GetWindowHeight()

   FlyIn('a',  0,  h,  1000)
   FlyIn('b',  0,  h,  2000)
   FlyIn('c',  0,  h,  3000)
   FlyIn('d',  0,  h,  4000)
   FlyIn('e',  0,  h,  5000)
})
</script>
```

This HTML section creates a simple list and places its element within spans. The `<script>` section then places the height of the browser into the variable h and issues five calls to `FlyIn()` with the different object IDs, a start location just under the bottom of the screen, and animation periods from 1 to 5 seconds.

You can just as easily fly the elements in from the browser top by specifying a y value of –20 or so, or from the left or right edges by using values of `-W('object')` `-50` for the x argument when flying in from the left, or `GetWindowWidth()` for the x argument if flying in from the right. In fact, you can specify any relative x and y coordinates you like so objects can fly in at any angle.

TIP *Because objects have to be given a style position property of 'absolute' in order to move them about, if you have not enclosed the object (or a set of objects) in a suitable container with set dimensions such as a div or span, other elements of the HTML could move themselves to fill in the space previously occupied by the object (or objects). Tables are also good placeholders for objects that you will be flying in.*

The Recipe

```
function FlyIn(id, x, y, msecs)
{
   if (id instanceof Array)
   {
      for (var j = 0 ; j < id.length ; ++j)
         FlyIn(id[j], x, y, msecs)
      return
   }

   if (O(id).FI_Flag) return
   else O(id).FI_Flag = true

   var tox   = X(id)
   var toy   = Y(id)
   var fromx = tox + x
   var fromy = toy + y
   var xstep = x / (msecs / INTERVAL)
   var ystep = y / (msecs / INTERVAL)
   var count = 0
```

```
Position(id, ABS)
var iid = setInterval(DoFlyIn, INTERVAL)

function DoFlyIn()
{
   GoTo(id, fromx - xstep * count, fromy - ystep * count)

   if (count++ >= msecs / INTERVAL)
   {
      O(id).FI_Flag = false
      GoTo(id, tox, toy)
      clearInterval(iid)
   }
}
}
```

76 TextRipple()

This recipe gives an interesting ripple effect to text, changing the size of characters next to each other to provide a wave that runs from the start to the end of the string. Figure 19-7 shows the list elements from the previous recipe, FlyIn(), but here they have their onmouseover events attached to this recipe.

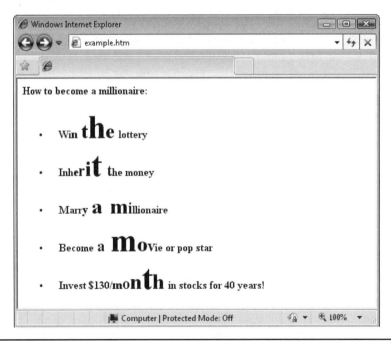

FIGURE 19-7   This recipe provides a great effect for drawing people's attention.

About the Recipe

This recipe performs a wave or ripple effect from start to end of a portion of text contained within an object. It requires the following arguments:

- **id**   An object, object ID, or an array of objects and/or object IDs.
- **number**   The number of times to repeat the ripple—infinite, if number is 0.
- **msecs**   The number of milliseconds the ripple should take.

Variables, Arrays, and Functions

j	Local variable used for iterating through id if it is an array
html	Local variable containing the HTML content of id
len	Local variable containing the length of html
freq	Local variable containing the time between each call to DoTextRipple() in milliseconds, such that the ripple will take msecs milliseconds to complete
ctr1 and ctr2	Local variables for counting each character in a ripple, and each repeat of the animation, respectively
iid	Local variable containing the result of calling setInterval(); to be used later when calling clearInterval()
temp	Local variable that holds the HTML for each step of the animation
innerHTML	Property of id containing its HTML
innerText	Property of id in non-Firefox browsers containing its text content
textContent	Property of id in Firefox browsers containing its text content
TR_Flag	Property of id that is true when a ripple is in process on it
Html()	Function to return the HTML content of an object
InsVars()	Function to insert values into a string
DoTextRipple()	Subfunction to perform the animation
setInterval()	Function to set up repeating interrupts
clearInterval()	Function to stop repeating interrupts
substr()	Function to return a substring

How It Works

This recipe starts by using j to iterate through id if it is an array, recursively calling itself to individually process each element:

```
if (id instanceof Array)
{
   for (var j = 0 ; j < id.length ; ++j)
     TextRipple(id[j], number, msecs)
   return
}
```

Next, the TR_Flag property of id is checked. If it is true, a ripple is already in progress on the object and it returns. Otherwise, the property is given the value true to indicate that a ripple is running on id, like this:

```
if (O(id).TR_Flag) return
else O(id).TR_Flag = true
```

After that, the local variable html is given a copy of the HTML content of id; len is set to its length; freq is assigned the time in milliseconds between each call to DoTextRipple() such that the ripple will take msecs milliseconds; two counters, ctr1 and ctr2, are initialized; and setInterval() is called to set up repeating interrupts to the DoTextRipple() subfunction every freq milliseconds, like this:

```
var html = Html(id)
var len  = html.length
var freq = msecs / len
var ctr1 = 0
var ctr2 = 0
var iid  = setInterval(DoTextRipple, freq)
```

The variable iid is given the value returned by setInterval(), which will be used later when clearInterval() is called.

The DoTextRipple() Subfunction

This function starts off by assigning temp the left-hand part of html, prior to any font size changes, with ctr1 indexing the point at which the fonts will be manipulated:

```
var temp = html.substr(0, ctr1)
```

Next, each character in html that will have its font size changed is processed within a for() loop such that the outside characters of the group are the smallest, the characters just in from them are larger, and the largest character is in the center, as follows:

```
for (var j = 0 ; j < 7 ; ++j)
   temp += InsVars("<font size='+#1'>#2</font>",
      4 - Math.abs(j - 3), html.substr(ctr1 + j, 1))
```

The part that determines this is 4 - Math.abs(j - 3), which, for the values 0 through 6 of j, gives the following font size values (because the Math.abs() function makes all negative numbers positive): 1, 2, 3, 4, 3, 2, 1.

Once all the font sizes have been calculated and stored in temp using the InsVars() recipe to insert the values into a string containing <font size= ...> statements, the innerHTML property of id is assigned this string to display it, along with the remaining, unchanged portion of html:

```
Html(id, temp + html.substr(ctr1 + j))
```

An if() statement then increments ctr1 and checks whether it equals the value in len. If so, the animation has finished and the following code is executed:

```
if (++ctr1 == len)
{
```

If the ripple is finished, then ctr1 is reset and another if() statement checks whether there are any more repeats of the interrupt remaining, like this:

```
ctr1 = 0

if (++ctr2 == number)
{
    if (O(id).innerText) O(id).innerText    = html
    else                 O(id).textContent = html

    O(id).TR_Flag = false
    clearInterval(iid)
}
```

If the repeats have finished, the value in html is saved back into id as text, not HTML (otherwise, unwanted extra HTML tags would be added by the browser—the time for saving HTML to the property is only when the font sizes are being changed).

Next, the TR_Flag property of id is set to false to indicate that all ripples have completed, and the clearInterval() function is called to stop any future calls to the subfunction, passing it the value previously stored in iid.

The function then returns but will be called up again in freq milliseconds if there are still outstanding animation frames to display.

How to Use It

To use this animation, pass it an object such as a div or span containing only text with no HTML markup or other tags; tell it the number of times to repeat the ripple; and give it the length of time in milliseconds that the animation should take.

Here's an example that takes the list from the FlyIn() recipe and attaches each entry to an onmouseover event to trigger the ripple:

```
<b>How to become a millionaire:<ul>
    <li><font size='+4'> </font>
      <span id='a'>Win the lottery</span></li>
    <li><font size='+4'> </font>
      <span id='b'>Inherit the money</span></li>
    <li><font size='+4'> </font>
      <span id='c'>Marry a millionaire</span></li>
    <li><font size='+4'> </font>
      <span id='d'>Become a movie or pop star</span></li>
    <li><font size='+4'> </font>
      <span id='e'>Invest $130/month for 40 years!</span></li>
</ul></b>
```

```
<script>
OnDOMReady(function()
{
   O(Array('a', 'b', 'c', 'd', 'e'), 'onmouseover', ripple)

   function ripple()
   {
      TextRipple(this, 1, 500)
   }
})
</script>
```

To prevent the text from moving down on the page as the larger characters in a ripple increase its height, each line on which a ripple can be triggered has the html `<font size='+4'> </font>` immediately preceding it. This ensures that the height of the line is always set to the maximum +4 size of font used by the recipe. You can also use CSS styling, tables, and other methods to enclose lines that will be rippled and prevent them moving themselves or other elements about.

The `<script>` section passes an array of the objects to the `O()` recipe, along with the 'onmouseover' event name as a string, and the name of the function `ripple` below it. The `ripple` function then uses the `this` keyword, which acts as a pseudo-object representing the object that triggered the event. This saves having to pass arguments to the function, keeping the code short and simple.

The Recipe

```
function TextRipple(id, number, msecs)
{
   if (id instanceof Array)
   {
      for (var j = 0 ; j < id.length ; ++j)
         TextRipple(id[j], number, msecs)
      return
   }

   if (O(id).TR_Flag) return
   else O(id).TR_Flag = true

   var html = Html(id)
   var len  = html.length
   var freq = msecs / len
   var ctr1 = 0
   var ctr2 = 0
   var iid  = setInterval(DoTextRipple, freq)

   function DoTextRipple()
   {
      var temp = html.substr(0, ctr1)
```

```
    for (var j = 0 ; j < 7 ; ++j)
        temp += InsVars("<font size='+#1'>#2</font>",
            4 - Math.abs(j - 3), html.substr(ctr1 + j, 1))

    O(id).innerHTML = temp + html.substr(ctr1 + j)



    if (++ctr1 == len)
    {
        ctr1 = 0

        if (++ctr2 == number)
        {
            if (O(id).innerText) O(id).innerText   = html
            else                 O(id).textContent = html

            O(id).TR_Flag = false
            clearInterval(iid)
        }
    }
    }
}
```

CHAPTER 20

Audio and Visual Effects

This chapter contains a number of handy recipes, which you can use for creating light boxes and slide shows (or combining the two), making rotating billboards for placing advertising or news updates, or making objects pulsate as you pass the mouse over them. There are also recipes to help you create professional-looking charts with the help of Google Charts, present YouTube videos in a variety of ways with a single function call, and play sounds in response to events or for any other reason.

RECIPE 77 | Lightbox()

With this recipe, you can display an image or any object in the center of the browser with the outside darkened and made transparent by amounts you can specify. Your users can then view these objects with minimum distraction and simply click them to dismiss the light box. Figure 20-1 shows a photograph being displayed using this recipe.

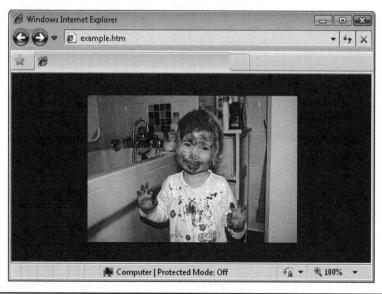

Figure 20-1   Show off your favorite photographs with this light box recipe.

About the Recipe

This recipe displays a photo (or other object) centered in the browser, with a darkened frame over the web page behind it. It requires the following arguments:

- **id** An object or object ID—this may not be an array.
- **col1** A starting color for the frame.
- **col2** An ending color for the frame.
- **opacity** The final opacity of the frame.
- **msecs** The time in milliseconds the transition should take.

Variables, Arrays, and Functions

newdiv	New div object created to use for the frame
LB_DIV	Object ID of the new div
cursor	Style property of id that sets the mouse cursor to a pointer when it is over id, indicating that it is clickable
overflow	Style property of document.body set to 'hidden' during the display of id to prevent scrolling
zIndex	Style properties of both the frame and id, set to bring them to the forefront of the browser
onclick	Event of id set to dismiss the light box if clicked
HID	Global variable with the value 'hidden'
ABS	Global variable with the value 'absolute'
ZINDEX	Global variable containing the highest zIndex property used so far
DismissLB()	Subfunction to dismiss the light box
Hide()	Function to hide an object
Show()	Function to show a previously hidden object
Position()	Function to set an object's style position property
Locate()	Function to set an object's style position property and move it to a new location
Resize()	Function to resize an object
Opacity()	Function to set an object's opacity
Center()	Function to center an object in the browser
GetWindowWidth()	Function to return the width of the browser
GetWindowHeight()	Function to return the height of the browser
Fade()	Function to fade the opacity of an object to a new level
FadeIn()	Function to fade the opacity of an object to 100
FadeOut()	Function to fade the opacity of an object to 0
ColorFade()	Function to fade the color of an object between two colors

Chain	Function to chain two or more recipes in a sequence
InsVars()	Function to insert values into a string
createElement()	Function to create a new HTML element
setAttribute()	Function to set an attribute of an HTML element
appendChild()	Function to append a child HTML element

How It Works

This recipe starts off by setting the mouse cursor when over id into a pointer to indicate that it is clickable (doing so dismisses the light box), like this:

```
S(id).cursor = 'pointer'
```

Then, if this is the first time the recipe has been called, a new div object with the ID of 'LB_DIV' is created and appended to the HTML for use as the darkened frame around id—otherwise, the div has previously been created so this code is skipped:

```
if (!O('LB_DIV'))
{
    var newdiv = document.createElement('div')
    newdiv.setAttribute('id', 'LB_DIV')
    document.body.appendChild(newdiv)
}
```

Next, the overflow property of the document.body is set to 'hidden' to disable scrolling the web page, then both the frame and id are hidden with a call to Hide(). This is so that they can both be moved about and otherwise modified without these actions being seen by the user.

After that, the frame is moved to the top left of the browser and resized to fill the entire window, and its zIndex property is set to the highest value used so far (held in ZINDEX), like this:

```
S(document.body).overflow = HID
Hide(Array(id, 'LB_DIV'))
Locate('LB_DIV', ABS, 0, 0)
Resize('LB_DIV', GetWindowWidth(), GetWindowHeight())
S('LB_DIV').zIndex = ZINDEX
```

Having set up the frame, id is processed next by setting its opacity to 0, which releases it from the HTML by calling Position() to set its style position attribute to 'absolute'. Next, its zIndex is set to a value that is 1 higher than the frame's, and the ZINDEX global variable is also incremented to contain this higher value:

```
Opacity(id, 0)
Position(id, ABS)
S(id).zIndex = ++ZINDEX
```

With both objects now prepared, the Show() recipe is called to re-enable the objects in the browser, and id is centered. Next, the new div (with the ID 'LB_DIV') is faded to the value in `opacity` over `msecs` milliseconds, `id` is faded in to an opacity of 100, and the background color of the frame is faded between `col1` and `col2` over the same time period, like this (remembering that `FadeIn()` fades an object from 0 percent to 100 percent opacity):

```
Show(Array(id, 'LB_DIV'))
Center(id)
Fade('LB_DIV', 0, opacity, msecs)
FadeIn(id, msecs, 0)
ColorFade('LB_DIV', col1, col2, 'back', msecs, 1)
```

Finally, in the display section of code, the `onclick` event of `id` is set to call up the `DismissLB()` subfunction when clicked, as follows:

```
O(id).onclick = DismissLB
```

The DismissLB() Subfunction

This function is called whenever `id` is clicked. The first thing it does is fade the frame's opacity back down to 0 and its background color from `col2` back to `col1`, like this:

```
Fade('LB_DIV', opacity, 0, msecs)
ColorFade('LB_DIV', col2, col1, 'back', msecs, 1)
```

At the same time, a chain is created to perform three actions in sequence: first, fade out `id`; second, hide `id`; and third, restore any scroll bars to `document.body`, as follows:

```
Chain(Array(
    InsVars("FadeOut(Array('#1', 'LB_DIV'), #2, 0)", id, msecs),
    InsVars("Hide(Array('#1', 'LB_DIV'))", id),
    "S(document.body, 'overflow', 'auto')"
```

How to Use It

To use this recipe, you need to have an image (or any other object) already prepared. Most likely you will also have set its `style.display` attribute to 'none' so that it is not visible in the web page, like this:

```
<img id='photo' src='photo6.jpg' border='1' style='display:none'>
```

Next, you can attach the recipe to an event such as an `onclick` or `onmouseover` to pop the object up in a light box. Here's an example that uses an `onclick` event:

```
<button id='link' type='button'>Click Me</button>
<img id='photo' src='photo6.jpg' border='1' style='display:none'>

<script>
OnDOMReady(function()
{
    O('link').onclick = function()
    {
        Lightbox('photo', '#888888', '000000', 80, 500, 1)
```

```
    }
})
</script>
```

The HTML section of this example creates a button with a link to the anonymous inline function, along with an image object with the ID 'photo'. The `<script>` section simply contains the function that calls up the `Lightbox()` recipe.

When a light box is in use, none of the elements underneath it that are usually clickable (or have `onmouseover` events attached) will work until the light box is removed. This is because the div object it creates covers the entire browser window and has a higher `zIndex` value than everything except the light box contents, which makes it especially useful when you wish to force the user to focus only on one thing, such as entering login details or accepting notification of an error, and so on.

TIP *The reason for requiring the two color arguments of* `col1` *and* `col2` *is to allow for web pages of any color background, which can then be faded to any other color of your choice for the light box frame. If your web site has standard black text on a white background, I recommend you try fading the light box between the color values #888888 (midgray) and #000000 (black). Or, you can be creative and fade between contrasting colors for an even more eye-catching effect. The value you choose for the* `opacity` *argument will also greatly change the transition effect.*

The Recipe

```
function Lightbox(id, col1, col2, opacity, msecs)
{
    S(id).cursor = 'pointer'

    if (!O('LB_DIV'))
    {
        var newdiv = document.createElement('div')
        newdiv.setAttribute('id', 'LB_DIV')
        document.body.appendChild(newdiv)
    }

    S(document.body).overflow = HID
    Hide(Array(id, 'LB_DIV'))
    Locate('LB_DIV', ABS, 0, 0)
    Resize('LB_DIV', GetWindowWidth(), GetWindowHeight())
    S('LB_DIV').zIndex = ZINDEX

    Opacity(id, 0)
    Position(id, ABS)
    S(id).zIndex = ++ZINDEX

    Show(Array(id, 'LB_DIV'))
    Center(id)
    Fade('LB_DIV', 0, opacity, msecs)
    FadeIn(id, msecs, 0)
    ColorFade('LB_DIV', col1, col2, 'back', msecs, 1)
```

```
O(id).onclick = DismissLB

function DismissLB()
{
   Fade('LB_DIV', opacity, 0, msecs)
   ColorFade('LB_DIV', col2, col1, 'back', msecs, 1)
   Chain(Array(
      InsVars("FadeOut(Array('#1', 'LB_DIV'), #2, 0)", id, msecs),
      InsVars("Hide(Array('#1', 'LB_DIV'))", id),
      "S(document.body, 'overflow', 'auto')"
   ))
   }
}
```

RECIPE 78 — Slideshow()

With this recipe, you can display a sequence of images in a slide show. Figure 20-2 shows this recipe being used in conjunction with the previous recipe, Lightbox(), to create a slide show on a darkened background.

About the Recipe

This recipe takes an empty container such as a div or span and displays a continuously rotating sequence of images that fade into each other. It requires the following arguments:

- **id** An object or object ID—this may not be an array.
- **images** An array of images (preferably of the same dimensions).

FIGURE 20-2 With this recipe, one image fades into another.

- **msecs**   The time each fade transition should take in milliseconds.
- **wait**   The time in milliseconds to wait between each transition—if this value is set to the string 'stop', it tells the recipe to stop any current slide show and exit.

Variables, Arrays, and Functions

index	Local variable used for indexing the array of images
newimg	Local variable containing a new image object
SS_Stop	Property of id, which, if true, stops the slide show
SS_IMG1 and SS_IMG2	Object IDs of the two new image objects
src	Property of each image object containing its source file
ABS	Global variable with the value 'absolute'
setTimeout()	Function to set up an interrupt to a function after a specified period
DoSlideshow()	Subfunction to perform the fade transitions
Locate()	Function to set an object's style position property and move it to a new location
Opacity()	Function to set an object's opacity
FadeIn()	Function to center an object in the browser
FadeBetween()	Function to fade between two objects
createElement()	Function to create a new HTML element
setAttribute()	Function to set an attribute of an HTML element
appendChild()	Function to append a child HTML element

How It Works

This recipe begins by setting len to the number of items in images and setting the SS_Stop attribute of id to either true or false, depending on whether the wait argument contains the string 'stop'. If it does, the value true is assigned so the subfunction will know to stop the fade transitions. The line of code looks like this:

```
var len      = images.length
O(id).SS_Stop = (wait == 'stop') ? true : false
```

As well as checking the wait arguments to see if it has the value 'stop', the SS_Flag property of id is tested; if it is true, a slide show is already in operation on this id, so the following code is not executed:

```
if (!O(id).SS_Stop && !O(id).SS_Flag)
```

Otherwise, as long as the wait argument contains a number, the following code is then entered.

Here, if there is no object with the ID 'SS_IMG1', this is the first time the recipe has been called, so it populates the id container object with two new image objects having the IDs

'SS_IMG1' and 'SS_IMG2'. It then overlays these objects over each other by locating the second one in the same position as the first, like this:

```
var newimg = document.createElement('img')
newimg.setAttribute('id', 'SS_IMG1')
O(id).appendChild(newimg)

newimg = document.createElement('img')
newimg.setAttribute('id', 'SS_IMG2')
O(id).appendChild(newimg)

Locate('SS_IMG2', ABS, 0, 0)
```

These lines illustrate how you can add new elements to a DOM tree at any point. First, use document.createElement() to create a new element object, then set any attributes using setAttribute(), and finally, use appendChild() to append the new element to the DOM.

Next, the variable index is initialized to 0; this will be used later to index the next image in a slide show. The first image object is then assigned the contents of the first element in the images array, which will be the location of a photo or other image:

```
var index       = 0
O('SS_IMG1').src = images[0]
O(id).SS_Flag    = true
```

The SS_Flag property is also set to true to indicate that a slide show is in progress. After that, the second image has its opacity set to 0 to make it invisible, and the first image is faded in over a period of msecs milliseconds:

```
Opacity('SS_IMG2', 0)
FadeIn('SS_IMG1', msecs, 0)
```

Finally, in the setup section of code, the setTimeout() function is called to set up an interrupt to call the DoSlideshow() subfunction after a period of msecs + wait milliseconds. This accounts for the time it will take the first image to fade in, plus the time required for the wait:

```
setTimeout(DoSlideshow, msecs + wait)
```

The DoSlideshow() Subfunction

The job of this function is to transition a fade between two images and then initiate an interrupt to call itself again when the next transition is due (unless it is canceled).

The first thing this function does is load the first image with the current value in the images array, as indexed by index. The first time it calls this, nothing happens since the same image has already been loaded. However, on all future transitions it has the effect of taking the picture that is being displayed in the second image and duplicating it in the first, so that they both are showing the same picture:

```
O('SS_IMG1').src = images[index]
```

Since both images are showing the same picture, it is safe to set the first one to be fully visible and the second one to be invisible, like this:

```
Opacity('SS_IMG1', 100)
Opacity('SS_IMG2', 0)
```

Having made this swap, the `index` variable is incremented to point to the next picture in the slide show, and if it becomes larger than the number of images in the `images` array, it is reset to 0 (using the `%` operator) to start again at the beginning, as follows:

```
index = ++index % len
```

Next, it's time to load in the next picture listed in the `images` array into the second image (because the first image is the one currently being displayed, and the second has been made invisible, ready to load the next picture in):

```
O('SS_IMG2').src = images[index]
```

I will explain the following statement shortly, but here it is for reference:

```
var next = InsVars("O('SS_IMG1').src = '#1'",
   images[(index + 1) % len])
```

Now that each image holds a different picture, it's a simple matter to call the `FadeBetween()` recipe to fade between the two, like this:

```
FadeBetween('SS_IMG1', 'SS_IMG2', msecs, next)
```

This makes the second image the visible one and the first one invisible. At this point, the image states are the same as at the start of the subfunction.

The value of the `next` argument in the `FadeBetween()` call is a string containing a callback function, which is mostly used by chains to link them together. However, in this case it is just passing a statement to be executed once the recipe completes its work.

The contents of `next`, which I previously glossed over, creates a statement that will load the next picture in the slide show into the first image once the fade between the two images is finished and the first image is now invisible (and available for use in this way).

This is done to preload the picture so it is cached in the browser, and next time around the loop, when the picture is loaded into image 2, it will be fetched from the cache without any delays while it is downloaded from the server.

This means program execution is ready to go around the loop again. However, the next interrupt call to the subfunction is only set up if the `SS_Stop` property of `id` is `false`, because if it is `true`, then a call has been made requesting the slide show to stop:

```
if (!O(id).SS_Stop) setTimeout(DoSlideshow, msecs + wait)
```

Otherwise, if the slide show is stopped, the `SS_Flag` property of `id` is set to `false` to indicate this:

```
else O(id).SS_Flag = false
```

How to Use It

To use this recipe, prepare an empty div or span and pass it to the recipe along with an array containing the URLs of the images for the show and two timers: the first for how long each fade transition should take and the second for the length of pause between changing images, both in milliseconds.

Here's an example that combines this recipe with the previous one, Lightbox(), to create a slide show in a light box:

```
<button id='link' type='button'>Click Me</button>
<div id='show'></div>

<script>
OnDOMReady(function()
{
    Resize('show', 320, 240)
    Hide('show')
    photos = Array('photo1.jpg', 'photo2.jpg',
        'photo3.jpg', 'photo4.jpg', 'photo5.jpg')

    O('link').onclick = function()
    {
        Slideshow('show', photos, 500, 2000)
        Lightbox('show', '#888888', '000000', 80, 500, 1)
    }
})
</script>
```

In the HTML section, a button is created that will call the anonymous, inline function when clicked, while underneath it there's an empty div. In the <script> section, the div is resized (with a call to Resize()) to the dimensions required so that the Slideshow() function can center it correctly. Without these dimensions, if the contents of the div are not ready when the Center() call is made, the object might appear off-center.

The div is also hidden with a call to Hide() because now that it has dimensions it will push any content below it out of the way. Then, the array photos is populated with the URLs of five photos, and the function calls both Slideshow() and Lightbox() to merge the two recipes together.

Because the Lightbox() recipe dismisses its contents when you click it, the slide show will not stop, even though it isn't visible. If you click the button again, the Slideshow() recipe will realize that it is still running and simply continue the slide show.

If you want to turn the slide show off, you need to set the SS_Stop property of 'show' to 1 or true, and the next time a slide change is due, it will stop:

```
O('show').SS_Stop = true
```

TIP *This recipe is designed so you can place the containing object anywhere you like and the slide show will occur at that position; you don't have to use it in a light box if you don't want to.*

The Recipe

```
function Slideshow(id, images, msecs, wait)
{
   var len       = images.length
   O(id).SS_Stop = (wait == 'stop') ? true : false

   if (!O(id).SS_Stop && !O(id).SS_Flag)
   {
      if (!O('SS_IMG1'))
      {
         var newimg = document.createElement('img')
         newimg.setAttribute('id', 'SS_IMG1')
         O(id).appendChild(newimg)

         newimg = document.createElement('img')
         newimg.setAttribute('id', 'SS_IMG2')
         O(id).appendChild(newimg)

         Locate('SS_IMG2', ABS, 0, 0)
      }

      var index       = 0
      O('SS_IMG1').src = images[0]
      Opacity('SS_IMG2', 0)
      FadeIn('SS_IMG1', msecs, 0)
      setTimeout(DoSlideshow, msecs + wait)
   }

   function DoSlideshow()
   {
      O('SS_IMG1').src = images[index]
      Opacity('SS_IMG1', 100)
      Opacity('SS_IMG2', 0)

      index = ++index % images.length
      O('SS_IMG2').src = images[index]
      var next = InsVars("O('SS_IMG1').src = '#1'",
          images[(index + 1) % len])
      FadeBetween('SS_IMG1', 'SS_IMG2', msecs, 0, next)

      if (!O(id).SS_Stop) setTimeout(DoSlideshow, msecs + wait)
      else O(id).SS_Flag = false
   }
}
```

PART III

Billboard()

This recipe is similar to the `Slideshow()` recipe in that it fades between objects in a sequence. The difference is that the `Billboard()` recipe allows you to put any objects in a show, and they must already exist in the document (whereas the `Slideshow()` recipe pulls images in by their URLs only when needed).

A great use for this recipe is to rotate banners or other advertisements, which can be images, divs, spans, or other objects. Figure 20-3 shows one image in a sequence being displayed using this recipe.

About the Recipe

This recipe takes a containing object such as a div or span and an array of objects held within it, which it then rotates like an automated billboard. It requires the following arguments:

- **id** An object or object ID—this cannot be an array.
- **objects** An array of objects or object IDs.
- **random** If `true`, the objects will be displayed in random order.
- **msecs** The time in milliseconds that each fade between objects should take.
- **wait** The time in milliseconds to wait before fading to the next object.

Variables, Arrays, and Functions

j	Local variable used as an index to iterate through the `objects` array
len	Local variable containing the number of items in the `objects` array
index	Local variable used to reference each object to be displayed
h	Local variable containing the cumulative height of each object for locating them in their required locations
rand	Local variable containing a random number between 0 and `len − 1`

FIGURE 20-3 This recipe creates a billboard of rotating objects and/or images.

BB_Ready	Property of id that is true if the objects have already been positioned in their places
BB_Stop	Property of id that is true if the billboard rotation is disabled
REL	Global variable with the value 'relative'
FadeOut()	Function to fade out an object
FadeIn()	Function to fade in an object
Locate()	Function to apply a style position and location to an object
H()	Function to return an object's height
DoBillboard()	Subfunction to rotate the contents of the billboard
setTimeout()	Function to set up an interrupt to a function in the future
clearTimeout()	Function to stop any timeout that has been set
slice()	Function to return a portion of an array
Math.floor()	Function to turn a floating point number into a rounded down integer
Math.random()	Function to return a random number

How It Works

This recipe begins by setting the local variable len to the number of items in the objects array:

```
var len = objects.length
```

Next, it checks whether it has already been called by examining the BB_Ready property of id. If it is not true, then the objects have not yet been moved to their required locations, so the following code is executed, which begins with setting up some variables.

First, len is assigned the number of items in objects, and then the O(id).BB_Index property of id and the local variable h are initialized to 0, like this:

```
var h        = 0
O(id).BB_Index = 0
```

After setting up the local variables, the BB_Ready property of id is set to true so that future calls to the recipe will know that the objects have been properly located. Then all items in objects other than the first are faded out by passing them through the slice() function to split them off, and a value of 1 millisecond is used for the transition to make it virtually instantaneous. This has the effect of leaving only the first item visible:

```
O(id).BB_Ready = true
FadeOut(objects.slice(1), 1, 0)
```

After that, a for() loop iterates through all but the first item in objects, subtracting the height of each previous object from the local variable h. Each object is then released from its position in the web page and given a style position attribute of 'relative' (using the global variable REL).

Each object's x coordinate is set to 0 to line it up with the left-hand side of the first one, and its y coordinate is set to h, which is a negative number containing the sum of all the heights of the objects above the current one, thus moving the object up the browser and placing it directly on top of the first one:

```
for (j = 1 ; j < len ; ++j)
{
   h -= H(O(objects[j-1]))
   Locate(O(objects[j]), REL, 0, h)
}
```

Next, if the `wait` argument has the value 'stop', the `BB_Stop` property of `id` is set to `true`, indicating that the billboard transitions should stop; otherwise, it is assigned the value `false`:

```
O(id).BB_Stop = (wait == 'stop') ? true : false
```

After that, as long as `BB_Stop` is not `true` and as long as the billboard is not already running (the `BB_Flag` property of `id` will be `true` if it is), an interrupt is set to call the `DoBillboard()` subfunction in `msecs` + `wait` milliseconds:

```
if (!O(id).BB_Stop && !O(id).BB_Flag)
   O(id).BB_IID = setTimeout(DoBillboard, msecs + wait)
```

The result retuned by the call is placed in the `BB_IID` property of `id` for use when calling `clearTimeout()`.

The DoBillboard() Subfunction

This function starts by setting the `BB_Flag` property of `id` to `true` to indicate that the billboard is running:

```
O(id).BB_Flag = true
```

It then checks the `BB_Stop` property of `id` to see whether it can continue or should stop:

```
if (O(id).BB_Stop)
{
   O(id).BB_Flag = false
   clearTimeout(O(id).BB_IID)
   return
}
```

If `BB_Stop` is `true`, then a request has been made to stop the transition, so the function will reset `BB_Flag` to `false`, stop any timeout that is due, and return. No more interrupts will occur on it, unless the recipe is called again—at which time the transitions pick up from where they left off. This allows you to, for example, pause the transitions if the mouse passes over an object and resume them again when it leaves.

Otherwise, the function continues running and the next thing to happen is the currently displayed object gets faded out:

```
else FadeOut(objects[O(id).BB_Index], msecs, 0)
```

Then, if the argument `random` is `true` (or 1), the subsequent object to display should be selected at random, which is done by this code:

```
var rand = O(id).BB_Index
while (rand == O(id).BB_Index )
   rand = Math.floor(Math.random() * len)
O(id).BB_Index = rand
```

Here `rand` is assigned the value of the `O(id).BB_Index` property, which points to the currently displayed object. Then, a `while()` statement repeatedly selects random numbers, placing them in the variable `rand`, until it is *not* the same as `O(id).BB_Index`. This ensures that the next object displayed in the billboard won't be the same as the current one.

Once a value is found, it is placed in `O(id).BB_Index`. Otherwise, if `random` is not true, the objects are displayed in sequential order and `O(id).BB_Index` is incremented. If it becomes greater than the number of items in the `objects` array, it is reset to 0 (using the `%` operator):

```
else O(id).BB_Index = ++O(id).BB_Index  % len
```

At this point, `O(id).BB_Index` represents the next object to be displayed, so a call is made to the `FadeIn()` recipe to fade it in:

```
FadeIn(objects[O(id).BB_Index], msecs, 0)
```

Finally, any currently pending interrupt is canceled and another interrupt is set up to call the subfunction again in `msecs + wait` milliseconds, giving enough time for both the fade transition and the wait period to pass:

```
clearTimeout(O(id).BB_IID)
O(id).BB_IID = setTimeout(DoBillboard, msecs + wait)
```

How to Use It

To use this recipe, you need to first prepare a containing object to hold all the items that will be rotated in the billboard. Then, place the subobjects within it, and you're ready to call the recipe from JavaScript.

Here's an example that combines the divs used in Recipe 67, `RollOver()`, with a new image of the same dimensions:

```
<div id='billb' style='display:none'>

   <div id='b1'><img id='p1' src='palace.png' align='left' style=
   'padding-right:10px'>For sale: 600 room, 300 year old central
   London house, located close to all the amenities, right in the
   heart of Westminster city.</div>

   <div id='b2'><img id='p2' src='plan.png' align='right' style=
   'padding-left:10px'>829,818 sq ft: Historical setting, famous
   residents, exquisitely decorated throughout. Phone 555 1234 for
   more details.</div>
```

```
    <img id='b3' src='london.png' />

</div>

<script>
OnDOMReady(function()
{
    S('billb').border = 'solid 1px'
    Resize('billb', 320, 100)
    objects = Array('b1', 'b2', 'b3')
    Resize(objects, 320, 100)
    S(objects, 'background.Color', '#ffffff')
    Show('billb')
    Billboard('billb', objects, 1, 500, 3000)

    O('billb').onmouseover = pause
    O('billb').onmouseout  = resume

    function pause()
    {
        Billboard('billb', '', '', '', 'stop')
    }

    function resume()
    {
        Billboard('billb', objects, 1, 500, 3000)
    }
})
</script>
```

I laid out the HTML so you can clearly see the three subobjects within the main containing object (with the ID 'billb'), which has its style display attribute set to 'hidden' so as not to show the subobjects.

In the <script> section, the containing object is given a solid 1-pixel border (which is not necessary but improves the look) and resized it to 320 by 100 pixels. The subobjects are then also resized to those dimensions so that all elements are the same, then Show() is called to re-enable the displaying of the container div, and then the Billboard() recipe is called to start things.

Next, the onmouseover and onmouseout events of 'billb' are attached to the functions pause() and resume(). The pause() function needs only to pass the argument names of 'billb' to reference the container object and the value 'stop' in the wait argument. In this instance, all other arguments will be ignored, so they have been set to the empty string. The resume() function, however, should be identical to the initial call made to start the billboard in the first place.

As you pass your mouse over the billboard, it will stop rotating, but it will resume once you move it away. Of course, the objects in this example are not linked to anything, but you will probably use this recipe for advertising and make them clickable; you can even include forms within the objects.

NOTE *To place all the subobjects in the same location, they must start off lined up underneath each other in the browser. In the case of divs, this will already be the case, but spans and images may require a <br /> tag placed after them to ensure the correct positioning. The* Billboard() *recipe then subtracts the height of all previous objects to place each consecutive one over the first. Should you forget to line them all up this way, some of the objects will not display correctly, if at all.*

The Recipe

```
function Billboard(id, objects, random, msecs, wait)
{
    var len = objects.length

    if (!O(id).BB_Ready)
    {
        var h        = 0
        O(id).BB_Index = 0

        O(id).BB_Ready = true
        FadeOut(objects.slice(1), 1, 0)

        for (j = 1 ; j < len ; ++j)
        {
            h -= H(O(objects[j-1]))
            Locate(O(objects[j]), REL, 0, h)
        }
    }

    O(id).BB_Stop = (wait == 'stop') ? true : false

    if (!O(id).BB_Stop && !O(id).BB_Flag)
        O(id).BB_IID = setTimeout(DoBillboard, msecs + wait)

    function DoBillboard()
    {
        O(id).BB_Flag = true

        if (O(id).BB_Stop)
        {
            O(id).BB_Flag = false
            clearTimeout(O(id).BB_IID)
            return


        }
        else FadeOut(objects[O(id).BB_Index], msecs, 0)

        if (random)
        {
            var rand = O(id).BB_Index
            while (rand == O(id).BB_Index )
                rand = Math.floor(Math.random() * len)
```

```
        O(id).BB_Index = rand
    }
    else O(id).BB_Index = ++O(id).BB_Index  % len

    FadeIn(objects[O(id).BB_Index], msecs, 0)
    clearTimeout(O(id).BB_IID)
    O(id).BB_IID = setTimeout(DoBillboard, msecs + wait)
  }
}
```

GoogleChart()

Among many other products, Google offers a great program for creating and displaying charts. However, to make the best use of it there are many options you need to set up and a lot of documentation to be read. This recipe distills the main features of the service into a set of basic arguments you can pass to it, making the service extra easy to use. Figure 20-4 shows the recipe being used to display a 3D pie chart.

About the Recipe

This recipe takes a container such as a div or span and inserts an image into it, which it fetches from the Google Charts service. It requires the following arguments:

- **id**   An object or object ID—this cannot be an array.
- **title**   The chart title.
- **tcolor**   The title color.

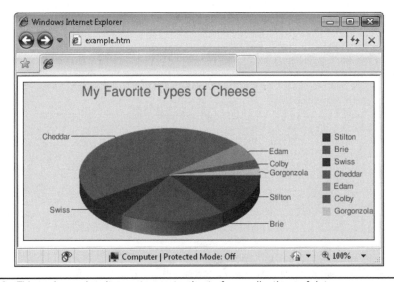

FIGURE 20-4   This recipe makes it easy to create charts from collections of data.

Type Value	Chart Type
'line'	Standard line chart
'vbar'	Vertical bar chart
'hbar'	Horizontal bar chart
'gometer'	Google Go Meter
'pie'	Standard pie chart
'pie3d'	3D pie chart
'venn'	Venn diagram
'radar'	Radar chart

TABLE 20-1 The Supported Values for the type Argument and the Charts They Create

- **tsize** The title font size.
- **type** The type of chart, any of 'line', 'vbar', 'hbar', 'gometer', 'pie', 'pie3d', 'venn', or 'radar'—see Table 20-1 for more details (and see Figure 20-5 for some example chart types).
- **bwidth** The bar width if the chart is a bar chart.
- **labels** A string of data labels, separated by | characters.
- **legends** A string of data legends, separated by | characters.
- **colors** A string of colors, one for each item of data, in six-digit hex values, separated by commas.
- **bgfill** The background fill color as a six-digit hex string.
- **data** The data, as a string of numeric values, separated by commas.

Variables, Arrays, and Functions

types	Local associative array used to turn values in the type argument into the keywords required by Google Charts
t1	Local variable containing the escaped title
t2	Local variable containing the type of chart as a Google Charts keyword
tail	Local variable containing the query string for sending to Google
innerHTML	Property of id containing its HTML
UNDEF	Global variable containing the string 'undefined'
escape()	Function to escape a string, making it suitable for use in a query string

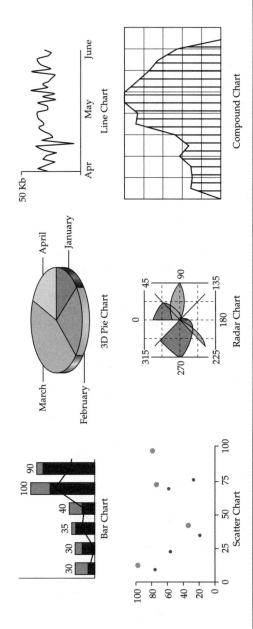

Figure 20-5 Some of the chart types supported by Google Charts

How It Works

This recipe begins by populating the associative array `types` with the eight types of chart names as used by the recipe and their corresponding keywords, as passed on to Google Charts, like this:

```
var types =
{
    'line'    : 'lc',
    'vbar'    : 'bvg',
    'hbar'    : 'bhg',
    'gometer' : 'gom',
    'pie'     : 'p',
    'pie3d'   : 'p3',
    'venn'    : 'v',
    'radar'   : 'r'
}
```

Next, the `type` argument is tested to see if it has a value. If not, it is given the value 'pie', which therefore becomes the default when no type is given:

```
if (typeof type == UNDEF) type = 'pie'
```

Then, `title` is passed through the `escape()` function to make it suitable for passing in a query string URL tail, and `title` is then placed in the variable `t1`. Meanwhile, the keyword for the chart type to send to Google is looked up by referencing the `type` argument in the `types` array, as follows (such that if, for example, `type` has the value 'hbar', `t2` will be assigned the value 'bhg', and so on):

```
var t1 = escape(title)
var t2 = types[type]
```

After this, a selection of arguments that are required for most charts (such as the chart's title, width, height, and so on) are assembled into the variable `tail`, each separated by an & entity, like this:

```
var tail = 'chtt='        + t1
        + '&amp;cht='     + t2
        + '&amp;chs='     + width + 'x' + height
        + '&amp;chbh='    + bwidth
        + '&amp;chxt=x,y'
        + '&amp;chd=t:'   + data
```

Then, if values for them have been passed to the recipe, a set of five `if()` statements adds other arguments to `tail`:

```
if (tcolor && tsize) tail += '&amp;chts='    + tcolor + ',' + tsize
if (labels)          tail += '&amp;chl='     + labels
if (legends)         tail += '&amp;chdl='    + legends
if (colors)          tail += '&amp;chco='    + colors
if (bgfill)          tail += '&amp;chf=bg,s,' + bgfill
```

With `tail` now containing the completed query string, it is appended to the Google Charts URL and then placed in an `<img ... >` tag, which is then assigned to the HTML of `id`:

```
Html(id, "<img src='http://chart.apis.google.com/chart?" +
   tail + "' />")
```

This results in the chart displaying within the `id` container object.

How to Use It

To use this recipe, start with an empty div, span, or other container that has an `innerHTML` property, and then pass this object along with all the required parameters to the recipe, as in this example:

```
<div id='chart'></div>

<script>
OnDOMReady(function()
{
  title   = 'My Favorite Types of Cheese'
  tcolor  = 'FF0000'
  tsize   = '20'
  type    = 'pie3d'
  width   = '530'
  height  = '230'
  bwidth  = ''
  labels  = 'Stilton|Brie|Swiss|Cheddar|Edam|Colby|Gorgonzola'
  legends = labels
  colors  = 'BD0000,DE6B00,284B89,008951,9D9D9D,A5AB4B,8C70A4,FFD200'
  bgfill  = 'EEEEFF'
  data    = '14.9,18.7,7.1,47.3,6.0,3.1,2.1'

  GoogleChart('chart', title, tcolor, tsize, type, bwidth, labels,
      legends, colors, bgfill, width, height, data)

  Resize('chart', width, height)
  S('chart').border = 'solid 1px'
})
</script>
```

To simplify this example, all the arguments have been separately assigned to variables, which are then passed to the recipe. Also, the containing div is resized to the width and height of the chart and is given a one-pixel solid border. This results in a fully self-contained div, displaying the chart as returned by Google. You can get more information about Google Charts at *code.google.com/apis/chart/*.

TIP *The Google Charts API has a limit of 50,000 calls per day from each web site, so if your site is making that many calls or more, you should run the recipe once in your browser, right-click, save the image, and upload it to your web server. That way, you can display it as often as you like using* `<img>` *tags.*

The Recipe

```
function GoogleChart(id, title, tcolor, tsize, type, bwidth,
   labels, legends, colors, bgfill, width, height, data)
{
   var types =
   {
      'line'    : 'lc',
      'vbar'    : 'bvg',
      'hbar'    : 'bhg',
      'gometer' : 'gom',
      'pie'     : 'p',
      'pie3d'   : 'p3',
      'venn'    : 'v',
      'radar'   : 'r'
   }

   if (typeof type == UNDEF) type = 'pie'

   var t1                     = escape(title)
   var t2                     = types[type]
   var tail                   = 'chtt='        + t1
                              + '&amp;cht='     + t2
                              + '&amp;chs='     + width  + 'x'
                                                + height
                              + '&amp;chbh='    + bwidth
                              + '&amp;chxt=x,y'
                              + '&amp;chd=t:'   + data

   if (tcolor && tsize) tail += '&amp;chts='    + tcolor + ','
                                                + tsize
   if (labels)          tail += '&amp;chl='     + labels
   if (legends)         tail += '&amp;chdl='    + legends
   if (colors)          tail += '&amp;chco='    + colors
   if (bgfill)          tail += '&amp;chf=bg,s,' + bgfill

   Html(id, "<img src='http://chart.apis.google.com/chart?" +
      tail + "' />")
}
```

PlaySound( )

This recipe lets you play a sound as a result of a mouse move or button event, a keyboard event, or any other reason. Figure 20-6 reintroduces the avatars used in previous chapters, but this time their onmouseover events are attached to this recipe.

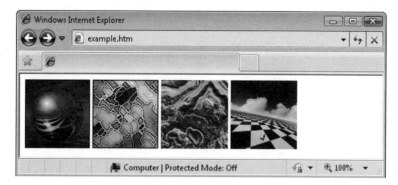

FIGURE 20-6   When you pass the mouse over these images, a sound will play.

About the Recipe

This recipe takes an empty container such as a div or span and embeds an audio player in it to play a sound. It requires the following arguments:

- **id**   An object or object ID—this cannot be an array.
- **file**   The URL of an audio file, generally a WAV or similar file.
- **loop**   If 'true', the sound will loop continuously; if 'stop', it will stop a previously playing sound; any other value will play the sound once.

Variables, Arrays, and Functions

innerHTML	Property of id containing its HTML
Resize()	Function to resize an object
Locate()	Function to set an object's style position and location
InsVars()	Function to insert values into a string

How It Works

This recipe first resizes id so it has no width or height and then gives it an 'absolute' style position so it cannot affect any other objects in the web page, like this:

```
Resize(id, 0, 0)
Locate(id, ABS, 0, 0)
```

Next, if the argument loop contains the string value 'stop', then any currently playing sound is stopped by setting the innerHTML property of id to the empty string, thus removing any previously embedded sound player:

```
if (loop == 'stop') O(id).innerHTML = ''
```

Otherwise, the `innerHTML` property of `id` is assigned the correct HTML to embed a sound player and auto start the sound playing, looping it if `loop` contains the string value 'true', like this:

```
else O(id).innerHTML =
    InsVars("<embed src='#1' hidden='true' " +
        "autostart='true' loop='#2' />", file, loop)
```

How to Use It

Playing a sound is as easy as passing an empty container such as a div or span to the recipe, along with the URL of the sound to play and, if required, the value 'true' in the argument `loop`. Here's an example that attaches the recipe to the onmouseover events of four images:

```
<span id='sound'></span>

<img id='a1' src='avatar1.jpg'>
<img id='a2' src='avatar2.jpg'>
<img id='a3' src='avatar3.jpg'>
<img id='a4' src='avatar4.jpg'>

<script>
OnDOMReady(function()
{
    ids = Array('a1', 'a2', 'a3', 'a4')
    O(ids, 'onmouseover', bloop)

    function bloop()
    {
        PlaySound('sound', 'bloop.wav', 0)
    }
})
</script>
```

NOTE *This recipe relies on the browser having a plug-in already installed to play sounds, which is true in the majority of cases. Browsers without a sound plug-in will simply ignore this code. Also, there may be a slight delay before some sounds begin playing, so this recipe works best when immediate playback is not essential. If you do need instant sounds, the most robust way to accomplish this is probably to write a Flash script, or obtain a Flash sound player and embed it. Also, small files will play quicker than large ones.*

The Recipe

```
function PlaySound(id, file, loop)
{
    Resize(id, 0, 0)
    Locate(id, ABS, 0, 0)

    if (loop == 'stop') O(id).innerHTML = ''
```

```
      else O(id).innerHTML =
        InsVars("<embed src='#1' hidden='true' " +
          "autostart='true' loop='#2' />", file, loop)
}
```

EmbedYouTube( )

With this recipe, you can forget about all the HTML and other code needed to display a YouTube video because it's all handled for you with a single function call. Figure 20-7 shows the Emmy Award–winning movie *Dr. Horrible's Sing-Along Blog* being played using this recipe.

About the Recipe

This recipe returns the HTML code required to embed a YouTube video. It requires the following arguments:

- **video**   A YouTube video identifier such as 'apEZpYnN_1g'.
- **width** and **height**   The width and height at which to display the video.
- **high**   If 'true' or 1 (and it is available), the video is played in high quality.
- **full**   If 'true' or 1, the video is allowed to be viewed in full screen mode.
- **auto**   If 'true' or 1, the video starts playing automatically.

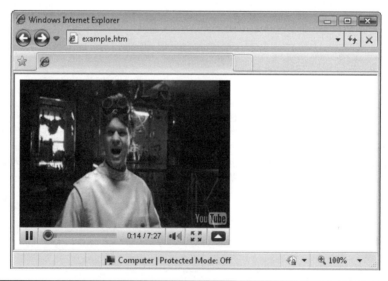

FIGURE 20-7   Displaying YouTube videos is easy with this recipe.

Variables, Arrays, and Functions

`iframe.src`	Property of `iframe` containing the URL
`S(iframe).class`	Property of `iframe` containing the class name
`createElement()`	Function to create a new element
`appendChild()`	Function to append an element to a document
`Resize()`	Function to resize an object
`InsVars()`	Function to insert values into a string

How It Works

This code first ensures that the video has valid width and height dimensions, like this:

```
if (width && !height) height = width  * 0.7500
if (!width && height) width  = height * 1.3333
if (!width)           width  = 480
if (!height)          height = 385
```

If only one dimension is entered, the other is scaled accordingly to keep the average ratio of 4:3, while if no dimensions are passed, defaults of 480 by 385 pixels are chosen. If you know the dimensions of a video, it's always best to use them to ensure the best playback quality.

After this, the code checks whether `full` has a value of 1 and, if so, sets `fs` to the value `allowfullscreen`, which will be appended to the end of the `<iframe>` tag to enable full screen playback, like this:

```
fs = (full) ? 'allowfullscreen' : '';
```

Then, if the parameter `high` has a value of 1, the string `hd` is set to the value `?hd=1`, which is later tacked onto the URL of the video to enable it to be played in high-quality video (if available), as follows:

```
hd = (high) ? '?hd=1' : '';
```

After this, the string variable `as` is set either to ? if `high` is not 1, or to & if it is. This prepares the correct symbol to place before the part of the query string used to make a video auto play. If it is the first argument in the query string, it must be prefaced by a ? symbol; otherwise, a & symbol should be used. It will be the first argument if there is no argument to set high definition; otherwise, it will be the second argument, like this:

```
as = (hd) ? '?' : '&';
```

The `ap` variable is then set to either the null string or the relevant value to cause the video to auto play, like this:

```
ap = (auto) ? "as" . 'autoplay=1' : '';
```

The result is that the recipe creates the `<iframe>` element required for displaying the YouTube player and installs the video into it, as follows:

```
iframe          = document.createElement('iframe');
S(iframe).class = 'youtube-player'
iframe.src      = InsVars('http://www.youtube.com/embed/#1#2#3 #4',
   video, hd, ap, fs))
```

This code uses the `createElement()` function to create the `<iframe>`, then gives it the class name that YouTube requires (`youtube-player`), and provides the URL to the player via the object's `src` property using the `InsVars()` function to insert all the required parameters in their correct places, signified by the tokens #1 through #4.

The `Resize()` function then resizes the `<iframe>` to the correct dimensions. It is then appended to the web document using the `appendChild()` function:

```
Resize(iframe, width, height)
document.body.appendChild(iframe)
```

For this to work, there must be a `<body>` tag in the document.

How to Use It

To use this recipe, simply call the function with the required attributes for the video to be played, like this:

```
<script>
OnDOMReady(function()
{
   EmbedYouTube('apEZpYnN_1g', 320, 240, 'true', 'true', 1))
})
</script>
```

All you have to decide is the width and height for the video and whether to allow high quality, full screen, and auto starting. At the most basic, you can issue a simple call such as the following to place the video in a web page, ready for the user to click its Play button:

```
EmbedYouTube('apEZpYnN_1g')
```

You must insert the call to this function in the part of your web page in which you want the video to be displayed, since the new `<iframe>` object is appended to the document at that position.

HINT *If you wish to display videos using YouTube's recommended default dimensions, then select a width and height of 480 × 385 for a 4:3 video, or 640 × 385 for a 16:9 video.*

The Recipe

```
function EmbedYouTube(video, width, height, high, full, auto)
{
   if (width && !height) height = width  * 0.7500
```

```
    if (!width && height) width  = height * 1.3333
    if (!width)           width  = 480
    if (!height)          height = 385

    fs = (full) ? 'allowfullscreen' : ''
    hd = (high) ? '?hd=1'           : ''
    as = (hd)   ? '?'               : '&'
    ap = (auto) ? as + 'autoplay=1' : ''

    iframe          = document.createElement('iframe');
    S(iframe).class = 'youtube-player'
    iframe.src      = InsVars('http://www.youtube.com/embed/#1#2#3 #4',
       video, hd, ap, fs)
    Resize(iframe, width, height)
    document.body.appendChild(iframe)
}
```

PulsateOnMouseover( )

With this recipe, you can create an onmouseover hover effect for an object, which slowly fades the object in and out again, over a specified time and by an amount that you choose. Figure 20-8 shows the same image attached to this recipe using three different levels of fading and transition times.

About the Recipe

This recipe takes an object and attaches to its onmouseover and onmouseout events to create a pulsating effect. It requires the following arguments:

- **id**   An object or object ID, or an array of objects and/or object IDs.
- **op1**   The default opacity for the object, between 0 and 100.

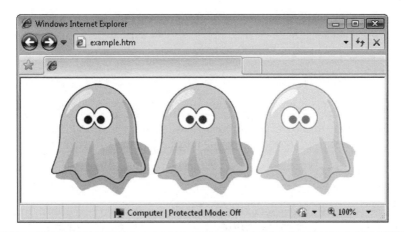

FIGURE 20-8   Attach this recipe to an object and it will pulsate when the mouse passes over it.

- **op1**   The opacity to which the object should be faded, between 0 and 100.
- **msecs**   The number of milliseconds each full cycle should take.

Variables, Arrays, and Functions

j	Local variable used to index into id if it is an array
finish	Local variable set to true if the pulsating stops
faded	Local variable set to true when the object is faded (or fading); otherwise, false
iid	Local variable assigned the result of calling setInterval() to be used later when clearInterval() is called
FA_Level	Property of id used by the Fade() recipe to set its opacity
FA_Flag	Property of id used by the Fade() recipe and set to true to indicate that a fade transition is in progress; otherwise, it is false or 'undefined'
onmouseover	Event attached to id that is triggered when the mouse passes over
onmouseout	Event attached to id that is triggered when the mouse passes out
PulseateOn()	Subfunction that sets up the main variables
DoPulsate()	Sub-subfunction that performs the transitions
Fade()	Function to fade an object from one opacity level to another
setInterval()	Function to set up repeating interrupts to another function
clearInterval()	Function to stop the repeating interrupts

How It Works

This recipe begins by checking whether id is an array. If it is, it iterates through it and recursively calls itself, separately passing each element of the array to be processed individually, like this:

```
if (id instanceof Array)
{
   for (var j = 0 ; j < id.length ; ++j)
      PulsateOnMouseover(id[j], op1, op2, msecs)
   return
}
```

Next, the variable finish is set to false—it will later be set to true whenever the mouse passes out of an object and the pulsating has to stop. The iid variable is also declared, which will be used to store the value returned by the setInterval() function:

```
var finish = false
var iid
```

After this, the opacity of id is set to the level in the argument op1, to which the FA_Level property of id is also set. This property is used by the Fade() recipe, but this recipe needs to access it in order to know when an object has faded in or out by the correct amount:

```
Opacity(id, op1)
O(id).FA_Level = op1
```

Finally, in the setup section, the mouse events of `id` are attached to the `PulsateOn()` subfunction for starting the pulsations and to an inline anonymous function that sets the variable `finish` to `true` when the mouse moves away from an object, like this:

```
O(id).onmouseover = PulsateOn
O(id).onmouseout  = function() { finish = true }
```

The PulsateOn() Subfunction

This function's job is to set up the variables required prior to calling the `DoPulsate()` sub-subfunction. It first declares the variable `faded` and assigns it the value of `false`, indicating that the object is faded in—it will be `true` when it is faded out. The `finish` variable is also set to `false` in case the recipe has been restarted after having been previously stopped:

```
var faded = false
finish    = false
```

If the variable `iid` has a value, a previous call has been made to the recipe, so it is passed to the `clearInterval()` function to stop any repeating interrupts that may currently be in place. After that, `setInterval()` is called to set up repeating interrupts to the `DoPulsate()` recipe every `INTERVAL` milliseconds, like this:

```
if (iid) clearInterval(iid)
iid = setInterval(DoPulsate, INTERVAL)
```

The DoPulsate() Sub-subfunction

This function is where the pulsating is made to occur. It is in two parts: one for fading out and the other for fading in. The first part checks the `faded` variable, and if it is not `true`, the object is not faded out. Next, it checks the `FA_Level` property of `id` and, if it is the same as the value in `op1`, then `id` is at its default opacity and is ready to be faded out. Here is the line of code that performs these two tests:

```
if (!faded && O(id).FA_Level == op1)
```

Inside the `if()` statement, a further check is made to see whether the `finish` variable has been set to `true`. If it has, rather than fade the object out, it's necessary to stop the repeating interrupts, like this:

```
if (finish) clearInterval(iid)
```

When the function next returns, it will not be called up again unless a new set of repeating interrupts is triggered by another `onmouseover` event.

However, if `finish` is not `true`, then it's business as usual for the function, which instigates a fade out by calling the `Fade()` recipe with a final opacity value of `op2`.

The variable `faded` is also set to `true` to indicate that the object is faded or is in the process of doing so, like this:

```
Fade(id, op1, op2, msecs / 2, 0)
faded = true
```

The transition duration of `msecs / 2` is used because there are two transitions in each full cycle, so each transition must take only half the value in `msecs` to complete.

In the second part of this function, if the variable `faded` is `true`, the `FA_Flag` property of `id` is tested. This property is set to `true` by the `Fade()` recipe whenever a fade transition is in progress, and it is set to `false` once a transition has completed. If `FA_Flag` is `true`, the function will return because a fade is in progress, and it must not be interrupted:

```
else if (!O(id).FA_Flag)
```

Otherwise, the code within the `if()` statement will be executed, as follows:

```
Fade(id, op2, op1, msecs / 2, 0)
faded = false
```

Here, a call to `Fade()` is made with a final opacity value of `op1` to fade the object back to its default opacity level, and the variable `faded` is set to `false` to indicate that the object is faded in or is in the process of doing so.

How to Use It

The recipe is written so that it will always fade back to the default opacity for an object when the mouse is moved away. To use it, attach it to any objects that you would like to pulsate when the mouse passes over them. These can be images, divs, spans, or anything that has an opacity property that can be changed.

Here's an example that uses the same image three times, with each attached to the recipe using different arguments:

```
<img id='a' src='ghost.png' />
<img id='b' src='ghost.png' />
<img id='c' src='ghost.png' />

<script>
OnDOMReady(function()
{
    PulsateOnMouseover('a', 100, 66,  500)
    PulsateOnMouseover('b', 66, 100,  750)
    PulsateOnMouseover('c', 100,  0, 1000)
})
</script>
```

The first image is set to pulsate between opacity levels of 100 and 66, so it will lighten by a third and back again on each pulsation, over a duration of 500 milliseconds. The second one starts with a default opacity level of 66 and a fade value of 100, so rather than fade out, it will in fact darken by about a third and lighten back again during each pulsation, which will take three quarters of a second to complete. The final image simply fades between full and zero opacity and back again over the course of a second.

The Recipe

```
function PulsateOnMouseover(id, op1, op2, msecs)
{
    if (id instanceof Array)
    {
        for (var j = 0 ; j < id.length ; ++j)
            PulsateOnMouseover(id[j], op1, op2, msecs)
        return
    }

    var finish = false
    var iid

    Opacity(id, op1)
    O(id).FA_Level    = op1
    O(id).onmouseover = PulsateOn
    O(id).onmouseout  = function() { finish = true }

    function PulsateOn()
    {
        var faded = false
        finish    = false

        if (iid) clearInterval(iid)
        iid = setInterval(DoPulsate, INTERVAL)

        function DoPulsate()
        {
            if (!faded && O(id).FA_Level == op1)
            {
                if (finish) clearInterval(iid)

                else
                {
                    Fade(id, op1, op2, msecs / 2, 0)
                    faded = true
                }
            }
            else if (!O(id).FA_Flag)
            {
                Fade(id, op2, op1, msecs / 2, 0)
                faded = false
            }
        }
    }
}
```

CHAPTER 21

Cookies, Ajax, and Security

When developing with JavaScript, you often need ways to store and retrieve data from both the user's web browser and the web server. This chapter provides you with the recipes you need to manage the transfer of cookies between the web document and browser and to handle Ajax calls between the browser and web server.

There are also a couple of recipes you can use to bust a web page out of frames if it has been loaded inside one and to allow you to put your e-mail address in a web document in such a way that it is easily clickable or copyable by a surfer, but not by web bots that harvest e-mail addresses for spamming.

ProcessCookie()

With this recipe, you can save cookies to a user's computer and read them back again later. This lets you keep track of usernames, shopping carts, or any data you need to keep current as a user browses your site and changes pages. Figure 21-1 shows the cookie 'username' being read back and its value displayed using an `alert()` message.

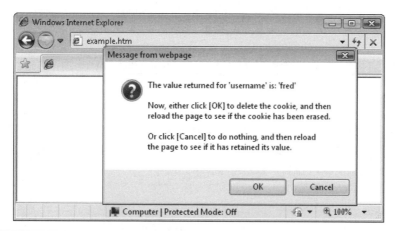

FIGURE 21-1 Setting and reading cookie values with this recipe

About the Recipe

This recipe can save a cookie, read it in from the computer, or delete it. It requires the following arguments:

- **action**   The action to take with the cookie, out of 'save', 'read', or 'erase'.
- **name**   The cookie's name.
- **value**   The value to be stored in the cookie.
- **seconds**   The number of seconds after which the cookie should expire.
- **path**   The domain and path to which the cookie applies.
- **domain**   The domain name of the web site, such as *mydomain.com*.
- **secure**   If this has the value 1, the browser should use SSL when sending the cookie.

Variables, Arrays, and Functions

date	Local variable containing a new date object
expires	Local variable containing the expiry time and date
start	Local variable set to point to the start of cookie data
end	Local variable set to point to the end of cookie data
document.cookie	The cookie property of the document use for accessing the cookie
toGMTString()	Function to convert a date to Greenwich Mean Time
Date()	Function to return a new date object
setTime()	Function to set a time
getTime()	Function to return a time
indexOf()	Function to return the location of one string within another
substring()	Function to return a portion of a string
escape()	Function to encode a string to a form suitable for transferring over the Internet
unescape()	Function to decode an escaped string

How It Works

This program is in three parts. The first is executed when the action argument contains the value 'save'. It creates a new date object and sets it to the current time and date, like this:

```
var date = new Date()
date.setTime(date.getTime() + seconds * 1000)
```

Saving a Cookie

Next, the expires variable is given the correct value to make the cookie expire in seconds seconds, the path variable is assigned the path on the server to which the cookie applies, the domain and secure arguments are added (if they have values), and the cookie is set by assigning these values to document.cookie, as follows:

```
var expires    = seconds ? '; expires=' + date.toGMTString() : ''
path           = path    ? '; path='    + path              : ''
domain         = domain  ? '; domain='  + domain            : ''
secure         = secure  ? '; secure='  + secure            : ''
document.cookie = name + '=' + escape(value) + expires + path
```

Reading a Cookie

In the next section, a cookie is read back from the computer, starting by checking whether there are any cookies on the computer to search; if there are not, the value `false` is returned:

```
if (!document.cookie.length) return false
```

Otherwise, the cookie is looked up by setting the variable `start` to point to the string containing the value in `name` followed by the = sign, by using a call to `indexOf()`. If it is not found, a value of –1 is returned, so the value `false` is returned by the recipe:

```
var start = document.cookie.indexOf(name + '=')
if (start == -1) return false
```

If both these tests pass, then the cookie has been found, so `start` is set to point to the portion of the cookie string directly after the `name` and = sign:

```
start += name.length + 1
```

The variable `end` is then set to the end of the string by finding the character `;` that terminates all cookie strings bar the last one:

```
var end = document.cookie.indexOf(';', start)
```

If it is not found, it means this was the last cookie and it is the end of the string. Therefore, the following line of code returns either the location of the following `;` or the end of the string and places it back in `end`:

```
end = (end == -1) ? document.cookie.length : end
```

Finally, the cookie value is returned:

```
return unescape(document.cookie.substring(start, end))
```

Erasing a Cookie

The code to erase a cookie makes use of a recursive call by passing the cookie name and a value of the empty string, along with a time one minute in the past, back to itself with an `action` argument of 'save':

```
ProcessCookie('save', name, '', -60)
```

How to Use It

To use this recipe, put the action in the `action` argument, which should be a value of 'save', 'read', or 'erase', and then pass the cookie's name and any other values needed.

For example, to set the cookie 'password' to the value 'mypass' with an expiry date of one hour from now, you would use the following:

```
ProcessCookie('save', 'password', 'mypass', 60 * 60, '/')
```

Once a cookie has been set, you can read it back like this:

```
value = ProcessCookie('read', 'password', '', '', '/')
```

Or, you can delete a cookie like this:

```
ProcessCookie('erase', 'password', '', '', '/')
```

The final path argument specifies which part of the server the cookie applies to. The value of '/' means that every spot, from the document root upward, can access the cookie. However, you can restrict the scope by, for example, changing the path to a subfolder such as '/chat'. Or you can simply omit the argument to give the same scope as if it had the value '/'. If you do so, you can also shorten the calls used to read and erase the cookie, like this:

```
value = ProcessCookie('read', 'password')
ProcessCookie('erase', 'password')
```

Remember that the path (or no path) you use must be the same for all accesses to the same cookie; otherwise, you will not be able to reliably read and write it. Also, you will probably not need to use the domain and secure arguments, which is why I omitted them from the preceding examples, but if you do, they are available.

Here's an example that lets you test that cookies are being reliably transferred:

```
<script>
OnDOMReady(function()
{
   value = ProcessCookie('read', 'username')
   if (value != false)
      alert("The value returned for 'username' is: '" + value + "'")
   else alert("The cookie 'username' has no value.")

   alert("Click OK to store cookie 'username' with the value 'fred'")
   ProcessCookie('save', 'username', 'fred', 60 * 60 * 24)

   alert("Click OK to retrieve the cookie")
   value = ProcessCookie('read', 'username')

   if (confirm("The value returned for 'username' is: '" + value    +
       "'\n\nNow, either click [OK] to delete the cookie, and then\n"+
       "reload the page to see if the cookie has been erased.\n\nOr "+
       "click [Cancel] to do nothing, and then reload\nthe page to " +

       "see if it has retained its value.\n"))
      ProcessCookie('erase', 'username')
})
</script>
```

This JavaScript first fetches the cookie 'username', and if it has a value, it is displayed. The first time you load this page, that cookie won't exist, so an alert will pop up and tell you so.

Next, the cookie is created and assigned the value 'fred', with alert messages before and after so you can see the result of each action.

Finally, a confirm dialog is called up in which you can click either the OK button to erase the cookie or the Cancel button to leave it alone. I suggest you click OK and then reload the page to see that the cookie has been erased. Then, follow through the alerts again, but this time click the Cancel button and reload the page, and you'll see that the cookie's value has been retained.

The Recipe

```
function ProcessCookie(action, name, value, seconds, path,
   domain, secure)
{
   if (action == 'save')
   {
      var date = new Date()
      date.setTime(date.getTime() + seconds * 1000)

      var expires     = seconds ? '; expires='+date.toGMTString(): ''
      path            = path   ? '; path='   + path      : ''
      domain          = domain ? '; domain=' + domain    : ''
      secure          = secure ? '; secure=' + secure    : ''
      document.cookie = name + '=' + escape(value) + expires + path
   }
   else if (action == 'read')
   {
      if (!document.cookie.length) return false
      else
      {
         var start = document.cookie.indexOf(name + '=')

         if (start == -1) return false
         else
         {
            start += name.length + 1
            var end = document.cookie.indexOf(';', start)
            end     = (end == -1) ? document.cookie.length : end

            return unescape(document.cookie.substring(start, end))
         }
      }
   }
   else if (action == 'erase')
      ProcessCookie('save', name, '', -60)
}
```

CreateAjaxObject()

Ajax is the power behind the vastly improved user interaction of Web 2.0. It stands for
Asynchronous JavaScript and XML, which is really a contrived acronym for a background
call made to a web server. Using this recipe, you can easily create a new Ajax object that can
be used to send and request information to and from a web server in the background,
without the user being aware of it.

Unlike in the past, when a POST or GET stopped action in the browser until it completed,
with Ajax the browser handles the request without disrupting the web application.

Figure 21-2 shows a simple HTML file that has been fetched from the web server and
inserted into a div, using this recipe in conjunction with the next one, GetAjaxRequest().

About the Recipe

This recipe creates an Ajax object ready for making background calls to the web server. It
requires the following argument:

- **callback**   The function to pass the returned data to once it has been retrieved.

Variables, Arrays, and Functions

ajax	Local Ajax object
readyState	Property of ajax containing its state
status	Property of ajax containing its status
responseText	Property of ajax containing the text returned by the Ajax call
XMLHttpRequest()	Function used by non-Microsoft browsers to create an Ajax object
ActiveXObject()	Function used by Microsoft browsers to create an Ajax object

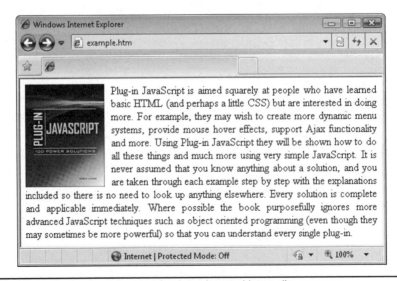

FIGURE 21-2   The contents of a web page have been inserted into a div.

How It Works

Since the Ajax request object has to be created in different ways for different browsers, this recipe uses pairs of `try ... catch()` statements to try each method in turn until one works or until all have been tried and `false` is returned, like this:

```
try
{
    var ajax = new XMLHttpRequest()
}
catch(e1)
{
    try
    {
        ajax = new ActiveXObject("Msxml2.XMLHTTP")
    }
    catch(e2)
    {
        try
        {
            ajax = new ActiveXObject("Microsoft.XMLHTTP")
        }
        catch(e3)
        {
            ajax = false
        }
    }
}
```

The first `try` works with any browser but Internet Explorer version 6 or earlier, the second is for Internet Explorer 6, and the third is for Internet Explorer 5. Therefore, the tests are made roughly in order of popular browser usage.

Assuming one of the `try` statements succeeds, `ajax` is a new Ajax object; otherwise, it contains the value `false`. If it isn't an object, then the recipe will return `false`; otherwise, the following code attaches an inline anonymous function to the `onreadystatechange` event of `ajax`, as follows:

```
if (ajax) ajax.onreadystatechange = function()
{
    if (this.readyState   == 4   &&
        this.status       == 200 &&
        this.responseText != null)
        callback.call(this.responseText)
}
```

```
return ajax
```

This subfunction is called every time the `readyState` property of `ajax` changes and checks whether it has a value of 4, the `status` property has a value of 200, and the `responseText` property is not `null`. If all these tests are satisfied, it means an Ajax request was successful, so the function passed in the `callback` argument is called, passing it the data returned in `this.responseText`.

The actual Ajax call is not made by this recipe. It merely catches the event ready to populate id with the value that is returned by an Ajax call. The Ajax call itself is made in the next two recipes, GetAjaxRequest() and PostAjaxRequest().

How to Use It
Generally, you will not use this function directly if you call either GetAjaxRequest() or PostAjaxRequest() to handle your Ajax calls, because they will call it for you, as in the following code, which loads some data into a div:

```
<div id='a'>The data returned by Ajax will replace this text</div>

<script>
OnDOMReady(function()
{
    url = 'ajaxtest.htm'
    GetAjaxRequest(todiv, url, '')

    function todiv()
    {
        Html('a', this)
    }
})
</script>
```

The function todiv() is passed to the recipe (note that parentheses have been omitted from the function; otherwise, only the value returned by it would be passed) and is later called back by it when the returned data is ready. At that point, it retrieves the data using the this keyword and assigns it to the innerHTML property of the div using the Html() recipe.

You need to know that Ajax is a tightly controlled process to prevent hackers from using it to inject malevolent code from other servers. Therefore, only files or programs on the same server as the one containing the Ajax can be accessed. For example, if you wanted to pull a copy of the Google home page into a div on your web site, it would not be possible and the Ajax call would fail.

Therefore, the preceding example will not work if you test it on another server unless you also copy the *ajaxtest.htm* file to it. However, you can verify that it works by calling the script up from the companion web site, using this URL:

webdeveloperscookbook.com/JS/example85.htm

The Recipe
```
function CreateAjaxObject(callback)
{
    try
    {
        var ajax = new XMLHttpRequest()
    }
```

```
catch(e1)
{
   try
   {
      ajax = new ActiveXObject("Msxml2.XMLHTTP")
   }
   catch(e2)
   {
      try
      {
         ajax = new ActiveXObject("Microsoft.XMLHTTP")
      }
      catch(e3)
      {
         ajax = false
      }
   }
}

if (ajax) ajax.onreadystatechange = function()
{
   if (this.readyState  == 4   &&
       this.status      == 200 &&
       this.responseText != null)
      callback.call(this.responseText)
}

return ajax
}
```

GetAjaxRequest()

This recipe uses the previous one, CreateAjaxObject(), to load the Wikipedia home page into a div. Of course, Ajax can be used for much more than grabbing web pages, such as checking whether a username is taken when signing up to a web site or updating news feeds, reader comments, or chat and so on. However, I decided to pull in a web page for the sake of simplicity so that you can quickly verify that these recipes are working for you, as shown in Figure 21-3.

About the Recipe

This recipe fetches data from a web site in the background. It requires the following arguments:

- **callback** The function to pass the returned data to once it has been retrieved.
- **url** The URL with which to communicate.
- **args** Any arguments to pass to the URL.

FIGURE 21-3 The Wikipedia home page has been inserted into a div.

Variables, Arrays, and Functions

nocache	Local variable assigned a random string to prevent caching
ajax	Local variable assigned an Ajax object
CreateAjaxObject()	Function to return a new Ajax object
open()	Method of ajax for opening a request
send()	Method of ajax for sending a request
Math.random()	Function to return a random number

How It Works

This recipe uses the GET method to communicate with a server, which passes data in the tail of the URL (called a query string). However, browser caching will often interfere with repeated requests of this type, serving up only the cached data from previous requests. Therefore, the variable nocache is created and assigned a random string to ensure that no two GET calls will be the same and therefore will not be cached:

```
var nocache = '&nocache=' + Math.random() * 1000000
```

Next, the variable ajax is assigned the new Ajax object returned by calling CreateAjaxObject(), and if the result is not true (meaning the call was unsuccessful), a value of false is returned:

```
var ajax = new CreateAjaxObject(callback)

if (!ajax) return false
```

If execution reaches this point, the Ajax object was successfully created, so the open method of ajax is called, passing it the string 'GET' for the type of request. This is followed by a string comprising the URL to be called that was passed in url, the arguments supplied in args, the nocache string just created, and the value true to tell the browser to make an asynchronous call (a value of false would tell it to make a synchronous call):

```
ajax.open('GET', url + '?' + args + nocache, true)
```

Finally, the call is made and the value true is returned to indicate success:

```
ajax.send(null)
return true
```

How to Use It

To use this recipe, decide what data you wish to load and from where, then call the recipe, passing it a function to call back when the data has been retrieved and any arguments that require passing.

The following example is somewhat interesting in that it gets around the problem of being unable to access web sites other than the one the Ajax web page came from by calling a PHP script on the server, which then fetches the requested data without a hitch:

```
<div id='a'>The data returned by Ajax will replace this text</div>

<script>
OnDOMReady(function()
{
    url  = 'ajaxget.php'
    args = 'url=http://wikipedia.org/'
    GetAjaxRequest(todiv, url, args)

    function todiv()
    {
        Html('a', this)
    }
})
</script>
```

The *ajaxget.php* program is a very simple one-liner that looks like this:

```
<?php if (isset($_GET['url'])) echo file_get_contents($_GET['url']); ?>
```

If your server supports PHP (and most do), you can use the same script on it to check whether the server has been sent a query string looking something like *url=http://website .com?args=vals*. (In the case of the preceding example, the *args=vals* section is specified in the line that assigns the string *url=http://wikipedia.org* to the args variable).

The *ajaxget.php* script then uses the file_get_contents() PHP function to fetch the requested data (in this case, the Wikipedia home page), This is returned using the PHP echo command, which outputs the data it just fetched.

The todiv() callback function, which was passed to GetAjaxRequest(), is then called back and passed the retrieved data, which it then promptly inserts into the innerHTML property of the div.

As with the previous Ajax example, the restrictions put in place by browsers require that the example and PHP files reside on the same server, so here's a link you can try it out with:

webdeveloperscookbook.com/JS/example86.htm

The Recipe

```
function GetAjaxRequest(callback, url, args)
{
    var nocache = '&nocache=' + Math.random() * 1000000
    var ajax    = new CreateAjaxObject(callback)
    if (!ajax) return false

    ajax.open('GET', url + '?' + args + nocache, true)
    ajax.send(null)
    return true
}
```

RECIPE 87 PostAjaxRequest()

This recipe is very similar to GetAjaxRequest() except that it uses a POST request to interact with the web server. In Figure 21-4, the weather at the airport in Anchorage, Alaska, has been extracted from the *weather.gov* RSS feed. Here it is displayed in raw form, but you can easily write some JavaScript to use only the items of data you want and format them to your requirements.

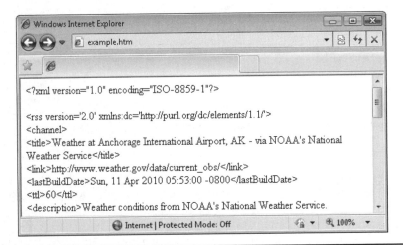

FIGURE 21-4 Using this recipe to extract data from an RSS feed into a div element.

About the Recipe

This recipe fetches data from a web site in the background. It requires the following arguments:

- **callback**   The function to pass the returned data to once it has been retrieved.
- **url**   The URL with which to communicate.
- **args**   Any arguments to pass to the URL.

Variables, Arrays, and Functions

contenttype	Local variable containing the content type used for URL-encoded forms
ajax	Local variable assigned an Ajax object
CreateAjaxObject()	Function to return a new Ajax object
open()	Method of ajax for opening a request
setRequestHeader()	Method of ajax for setting various headers
send()	Method of ajax for sending a request
Math.random()	Function to return a random number

How It Works

This recipe is as simple as GetAjaxRequest(). It starts by setting the content type of the date in the request being sent to that of a URL-encoded form. It then creates the Ajax object with a call to CreateAjaxObject(), and if the result is not true, it returns the value false since it cannot proceed any further:

```
var contenttype = 'application/x-www-form-urlencoded'
var ajax        = new CreateAjaxObject(callback)
if (!ajax) return false
```

If the object creation was successful, it goes on to open up the request, passing a type of 'POST', the URL, and the value true, for an asynchronous request:

```
ajax.open('POST', url, true)
```

Next, the content type, content length, and connection headers are sent:

```
ajax.setRequestHeader('Content-type',   contenttype)
ajax.setRequestHeader('Content-length', args.length)
ajax.setRequestHeader('Connection',     'close')
```

Finally, the request is sent and the value true is returned to indicate success:

```
ajax.send(args)
return true
```

How to Use It

You call this recipe in exactly the same way as `GetAjaxRequest()`—it's just that the process used by the recipe to perform the Ajax is a POST, not a GET request. Therefore, the target of the request also needs to respond to the POST request, as is the case with the following example, which fetches the weather details at the airport in Anchorage, Alaska:

```
<div id='a'>The data returned by Ajax will replace this text</div>

<script>
OnDOMReady(function()
{
   url  = 'ajaxpost.php'
   args = 'url=http://www.weather.gov/xml/current_obs/PANC.rss'
   PostAjaxRequest(todiv, url, args)

   function todiv()
   {
      var rss = this.replace(/\</g, '&lt;')
      rss     = rss.replace(/\>/g, '&gt;')
      rss     = rss.replace(/\n/g, '<br />')
      Html('a', rss)
   }
})
</script>
```

The URL supplied to the recipe is the PHP script *ajaxpost.php,* which is in the same folder as the example file. It's another simple one-line PHP script, which looks like this:

```
<?php if (isset($_POST['url'])) echo file_get_contents($_POST['url']); ?>
```

This is almost the same as the *ajaxget.php* script except that it processes POST requests. You can copy it to your own server, where it should work fine if it supports PHP.

This example is a little more interesting than the previous two in that an RSS feed is fetched. It's no different than a web page as far as Ajax is concerned, but displaying it after it has been retrieved poses a problem, in that it contains several XML tags that won't show up under HTML.

To correct this, the callback function `todiv()` has been modified to change all occurrences of the < and > symbols with their HTML entity equivalents < and > and all linefeed characters are changed to <br /> tags.

For reasons previously stated, the PHP example should be in the same folder of the same server, so here's a URL you can use to test the code:

webdeveloperscookbook.com/JS/example87.htm

NOTE *With XML, you would probably want to parse the tree to extract just the elements you want, but if you are fetching only text or HTML, you have all the tools you need to easily make all types of Ajax calls and act appropriately on the data they return.*

The Recipe

```
function PostAjaxRequest(callback, url, args)
{
   var contenttype = 'application/x-www-form-urlencoded'
   var ajax        = new CreateAjaxObject(callback)
   if (!ajax) return false

   ajax.open('POST', url, true)
   ajax.setRequestHeader('Content-type',   contenttype)
   ajax.setRequestHeader('Content-length', args.length)
   ajax.setRequestHeader('Connection',     'close')
   ajax.send(args)
   return true
}
```

FrameBust()

This is a simple but always useful recipe that checks whether it is running inside a frame, and if it is, busts out of it, placing the current page in its own parent page. This can be useful when you find that other sites link to your pages but bury them inside iframes so that they do not display at their best. Figure 21-5 shows one web page embedded within another and displaying an optional confirm dialog, offering to bust out of the frame.

About the Recipe

This recipe can close any embedding frame, making a web page the parent web page for the current tab or window. It supports the following optional argument:

- **message**   If this has a value, it will be displayed in a confirm dialog window offering the user the option to click OK to close the surrounding frame. If it doesn't have a value, the recipe will automatically and silently close the embedding frame.

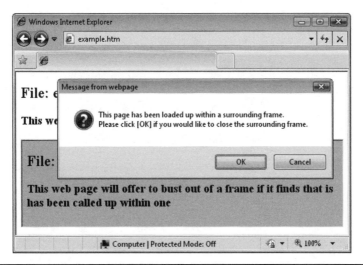

FIGURE 21-5   With this recipe, you can bust your web pages out of embedding frames.

Variables, Arrays, and Functions

`top`	Object representing the outermost of any frame set
`self`	Object representing the current document
`top.location`	Property of `top` containing the URL of its document
`self.location.href`	Property of `self.location` containing its URL
`confirm()`	Function to offer a yes/no confirm dialog

How It Works

This recipe either makes the current document the top one by setting its URL to that of the top object's, or it displays a message (if the message argument has a value) that offers the user the choice of breaking out of frames or leaving them as they are.

How to Use It

To use this recipe, either call it without an argument if you never want your pages to be embedded in frames, or pass a message for a confirm dialog, to which the response is to click OK to bust out of frames or choose Cancel to keep the pages as they are. Here's an example of passing a message:

```
<script>
FrameBust("This page has been loaded up within a surrounding " +
    "frame.\nPlease click [OK] if you would like to close the " +
    "surrounding frame.")
</script>
```

You can use \n or other escaped characters in the message to control the way it displays.

If you don't wish to provide a message and want all pages to bust out of frames, just leave the message string out of the call to `FrameBust()`.

The Recipe

```
function FrameBust(message)
{
   if (top != self)
   {
      if (message)
      {
         if (confirm(message))
            top.location.replace(self.location.href)
      }
      else top.location.replace(self.location.href)
   }
}
```

ProtectEmail()

Spamming these days is worse than ever now that the spammers have access to huge botnets of hacked computers and use automated programs to continuously trawl the web looking for e-mail addresses to harvest. However, e-mail is still extremely important, and you usually need to display your e-mail address prominently on your site.

Thankfully, with this recipe you can display your e-mail address in such a way that your users can click or copy it, yet it will be obfuscated from automatic e-mail harvesters, as shown in Figure 21-6, where the e-mail address is both copyable and clickable but doesn't actually appear as a whole in the web page.

About the Recipe

This recipe obfuscates an e-mail address in such a way that spam harvesting programs should not be able to find it. It requires as many arguments as you like because you break your e-mail address into multiple strings and then pass them all as parameters.

Variables, Arrays, and Functions

j	Local variable used to iterate through the `arguments` array
a	Local variable containing the e-mail address to display
`arguments`	Array containing all the arguments passed to a function

How It Works

This is a simple function that relies on the fact that all arguments sent to a function can be accessed via the `arguments` array. What it does is piece together all the arguments it is sent back together to reconstruct an e-mail address using a `for()` loop, like this:

```
var a = ''
for (var j=0 ; j < arguments.length ; ++j)
   a += arguments[j]
```

The variable a is then used to create a hyperlink to the e-mail address, with the code itself using segmented strings to further obfuscate matters. The result is then returned, like this:

```
return "<a hr" + "ef" + "='mai" + "lt" + "o:" + a + "'>" + a + "</a>"
```

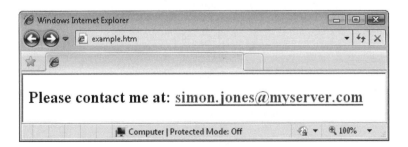

FIGURE 21-6   Use this recipe to keep your e-mail address visible but unharvestable.

How to Use It

To use this recipe, break your e-mail address up into multiple strings and then pass them all to it. Here's an example showing how to do this for the e-mail address *simon.jones@myserver.com.*

```
<h2>Please contact me at: <span id='email'></span>.</h2>

<script>
OnDOMReady(function()
{
   Html('email', ProtectEmail('sim', 'on.j', 'ones',
      '@myserv', 'er.c', 'om'))
})
</script>
```

Where you wish the e-mail address to be shown, just place an empty span and give it an ID. You can then insert the e-mail address into the innerHTML property of the span from within a section of JavaScript. If you ensure that the e-mail address is completely broken into parts, it is doubtful that any known automatic harvester will be able to extract it for spamming purposes.

The Recipe

```
function ProtectEmail()
{
   var a = ''

   for (var j=0 ; j < arguments.length ; ++j)
      a += arguments[j]

   return "<a hr" + "ef" + "='mai" + "lt" + "o:" + a + "'>" +
      a + "</a>"
}
```

CHAPTER 22

Forms and Validation

Form validation is something you must do on your web server to ensure that you receive the data that is required and to remove, as much as possible, any vulnerabilities to hacking or the possibility of your server being compromised, as well as the data on it. However, it is very helpful to your users if you also provide validation directly in the browser.

For example, it can be particularly helpful to provide extra assistance when a user is filling in a form to save it from having to be re-presented to them if it fails validation at the server. It also cuts down on your bandwidth usage and keeps the optimum number of concurrent users on the server.

This chapter includes recipes to provide extra hints for blank form fields that must be filled out, to provide the ability to resize text area inputs if a user types more than the expected amount of text, to check that e-mail addresses and passwords are valid, to clean up user input strings, and to check that credit card number checksums validate.

FieldPrompt()

When a form field hasn't been entered, there's a large blank area of white space that isn't being used. With this recipe, you can display a prompt in the field that disappears as soon as the user starts typing into it. Figure 22-1 shows two empty input fields containing prompts that were created using this recipe.

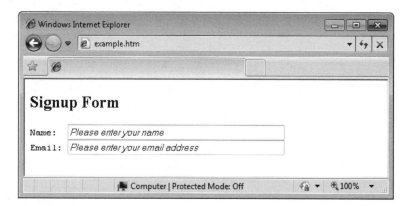

FIGURE 22-1 This recipe provides additional information to your users.

About the Recipe

This recipe takes a form input object and, if it is blank, displays a prompt of your choosing. It requires the following arguments:

- `id`   An object or object ID—this cannot be an array.
- `prompt`   The prompt string to display.
- `inputcolor`   The color to use for displaying user input.
- `promptcolor`   The color in which to display the font.
- `promptstyle`   The font style to use for the prompt, such as 'italic'.

Variables, Arrays, and Functions

`FP_Empty`	Property of `id` that is `true` when the input field doesn't contain any input; otherwise, `false`
`value`	Property of `id` containing its contents
`fontStyle`	Style property of `id` containing the font style of the field
`color`	Style property of `id` containing the color of the field text
`FP_Off()`	Subfunction called when the user moves the cursor into the field
`FP_On()`	Subfunction called when the user moves out of a field

How It Works

This recipe starts by giving the input and prompt colors and styles default values if none have been passed to it, like this:

```
inputcolor  = inputcolor  ? inputcolor  : '#000000'
promptcolor = promptcolor ? promptcolor : '#888888'
promptstyle = promptstyle ? promptstyle : 'italic'
```

Next, the `FP_On()` subfunction is called to display the supplied prompt if the field is empty, and the onfocus and onblur events of `id` are attached to the `FP_Off()` and `FP_On()` subfunctions so that the prompt can be switched in and out according to whether the user has clicked within the field or outside of it:

```
if (BROWSER == 'Opera' || BROWSER == 'Chrome')
   ResizeWidth(id, W(id))

FP_On()
O(id).onfocus = FP_Off
O(id).onblur  = FP_On
```

The first line of the preceding code is for the Opera and Chrome browsers. It forces the width of the input to the current width to prevent these browsers changing the width as they switch between normal and italic text.

The FP_Off() Subfunction

This function is called when the field gains focus. It first checks the value property of id to see whether it contains the prompt string. If it does, then the prompt needs to be removed so the user can type in some input, like this:

```
O(id).FP_Empty  = true
O(id).value     = ''
S(id).fontStyle = ''
S(id).color     = inputcolor
```

Here, the FP_Empty property of id is set to true to indicate that the field is empty, the field's value is set to the empty string, any font style is turned off, and the field text color is set to the value in the inputcolor argument.

If the field doesn't contain the value in prompt, then the FP_Empty property is set to false.

The FP_On() Subfunction

This function displays the value in prompt as long as the field doesn't already have a value entered by the user, which it checks by examining the value property of id. It also allows the code within to be executed if the field contains the prompt string. The reason for this is that if the user reloads the page while a prompt is displayed, the value property will already be set to the prompt before this function runs. This is the code that inserts the prompt:

```
O(id).FP_Empty  = true
O(id).value     = prompt
S(id).fontStyle = promptstyle
S(id).color     = promptcolor
```

Here, the FP_Empty property is first set to true to indicate that there isn't any user-entered text in the field, value is assigned the string in prompt, and the fontStyle and color properties of the prompt are set.

However, if the value property does contain text entered by the user, the FP_Empty property of id is set to false to indicate this.

How to Use It

To use this recipe, pass it a form field object, a prompt string, and optional color and style arguments. Here's an example that creates two fields, both displaying different prompts:

```
<h2>Signup Form</h2>
<pre>
Name:  <input id='name'  type='text' size='50'/>
Email: <input id='email' type='text' size='50'/>
</pre>

<script>
OnDOMReady(function()
{
   FieldPrompt('name', "Please enter your name",
      '#000000', '#444444', 'italic')
```

```
    FieldPrompt('email', "Please enter your email address",
        '#000000', '#444444', 'italic')
})
</script>
```

The two calls to `FieldPrompt()` can also use the recipe's default values, like this:

```
FieldPrompt('name', "Please enter your name")
FieldPrompt('email', "Please enter your email address")
```

The Recipe

```
function FieldPrompt(id, prompt, inputcolor,
    promptcolor, promptstyle)
{
    inputcolor  = inputcolor  ? inputcolor  : '#000000'
    promptcolor = promptcolor ? promptcolor : '#888888'
    promptstyle = promptstyle ? promptstyle : 'italic'

    if (BROWSER == 'Opera' || BROWSER == 'Chrome')
        ResizeWidth(id, W(id))

    FP_On()

    O(id).onfocus = FP_Off
    O(id).onblur  = FP_On

    function FP_Off()
    {
        if (O(id).value == prompt)
        {
            O(id).FP_Empty  = true
            O(id).value     = ''
            S(id).fontStyle = ''
            S(id).color     = inputcolor
        }
        else O(id).FP_Empty = false
    }

    function FP_On()
    {
        if (O(id).value == '' || O(id).value == prompt)
        {
            O(id).FP_Empty  = true
            O(id).value     = prompt
            S(id).fontStyle = promptstyle
            S(id).color     = promptcolor
        }
        else O(id).FP_Empty = false
    }
}
```

ResizeTextarea()

When you offer a textarea field in a form in which users can enter more than a single line of input, it can be difficult to decide how large to make it. If it is too small, users will have to scroll back and forth through it when making revisions. On the other hand, if it is too large, it wastes space and can look intimidating, implying that a large amount of text is expected to be input.

This recipe provides the solution by allowing you to specify minimum and maximum vertical heights within which the textarea is allowed to expand or contract, according to the amount of text entered. In Figure 22-2, a 64-by-3 column textarea is displayed, in which some text is being entered.

Then, in Figure 22-3, a total of eight lines of text have been input, and the textarea has expanded accordingly.

About the Recipe

This recipe adjusts the height of a textarea field according to the amount of text it contains, within bounds that you specify. It requires the following arguments:

- **id** An object or object ID or an array of objects and/or object IDs.
- **min** Optional argument specifying the minimum height that id can be reduced to.
- **max** Optional argument specifying the maximum height that id can be enlarged to.

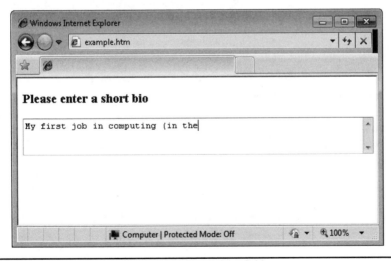

FIGURE 22-2 Some text is being entered into a textarea form field.

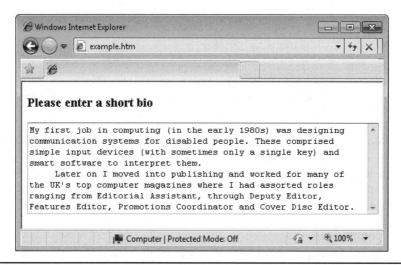

FIGURE 22-3   After several more lines are entered, the textarea expands accordingly.

Variables, Arrays, and Functions

j	Local variable for iterating through id if it is an array
onmouseup	Event of id that calls the subfunction after a mouse click
onkeyup	Event of id that calls the subfunction after a key press
scrollHeight	Property of id containing its total height in pixels
clientHeight	Property of id containing its visible height in pixels
rows	Property of id containing its number of rows
DoResizeTextarea()	Subfunction to resize the height of id

How It Works

This recipe starts by calling itself recursively if id is an array, passing each element to be processed individually, like this:

```
if (id instanceof Array)
{
   for (var j = 0 ; j < id.length ; ++j)
      ResizeTextarea(id[j], min, max)
   return
}
```

Next, if min and max have not been passed values, they are assigned defaults of 0 and 100 lines, respectively:

```
min = min ? min : 0
max = max ? max : 100
```

Finally, in the setup section, the onmouseup and onkeyup events of id are assigned to the DoResizeTextarea() subfunction:

```
O(id).onmouseup = DoResizeTextarea
O(id).onkeyup   = DoResizeTextarea
```

The DoResizeTextarea() Subfunction

This function contains just two while() loops. The first one continuously increases the number of rows that id has until either the text in the textarea is fully visible, or the maximum number of rows in the argument max is reached:

```
while (O(id).scrollHeight > O(id).clientHeight && O(id).rows < max)
   ++O(id).rows
```

The second while() loop performs the inverse, reducing the height of the textarea so that it is only as large as the text it contains or until it reaches the minimum height supplied in the argument min:

```
while (O(id).scrollHeight < O(id).clientHeight && O(id).rows > min)
   --O(id).rows
```

NOTE *While automatically expanding and reducing the textarea seems to work fine on most major browsers, once the* clientHeight *property in Firefox has been increased it doesn't seem to reduce it back down again if text is deleted, so the textarea will not shrink.*

How to Use It

To use this recipe, prepare the textarea by setting it to the width and height you need, then pass it to the recipe, along with an optional minimum and maximum height. This example shows how:

```
<h3>Please enter a short bio</h3>
<textarea id='ta' rows='3' cols=64'></textarea>

<script>
OnDOMReady(function()
{
   ResizeTextarea('ta', 3, 8)
})
</script>
```

In this example, a minimum height of 3 and a maximum height of 8 rows have been passed. However, you can omit one or both of these arguments, in which case minimum and maximum values of 0 and 10 will be used.

The Recipe

```
function ResizeTextarea(id, min, max)
{
   if (id instanceof Array)
   {
      for (var j = 0 ; j < id.length ; ++j)
         ResizeTextarea(id[j], min, max)
      return
   }

   min = min ? min : 0
   max = max ? max : 10

   O(id).onmouseup = DoResizeTextarea
   O(id).onkeyup   = DoResizeTextarea

   function DoResizeTextarea()
   {
      while (O(id).scrollHeight > O(id).clientHeight && O(id).rows < max)
         ++O(id).rows

      while (O(id).scrollHeight < O(id).clientHeight && O(id).rows > min)
         --O(id).rows
   }
}
```

RECIPE 92 ValidateEmail()

With this recipe, you can make a quick test on a supplied e-mail address to determine whether it is legally structured. This lets you filter out typos, as well as keep people from simply entering nonsense to see what will happen. Figure 22-4 shows the result of testing the fictitious e-mail address *bill@gates.com*, which validates since it is correctly formed.

About the Recipe

This recipe checks whether an e-mail address is correctly structured and in a valid format. It requires the following argument:

- **email**   A string containing the e-mail address to validate.

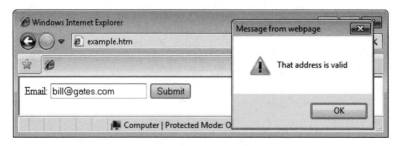

FIGURE 22-4   This recipe tests whether an e-mail address validates.

Variables, Arrays, and Functions

at	Local variable containing the position of the @ sign in email
left	Local variable containing the part of email before the @
right	Local variable containing the part of email after the @
llen	Local variable containing the length of left
rlen	Local variable containing the length of right
test()	Function to test for a match in a string
indexOf()	Function to locate the first occurrence of one string in another

How It Works

This function tests various aspects of a supplied string to check whether it conforms to the correct standards for an e-mail address. It starts off by seeing if there is an @ symbol in the string, using a call to indexOf():

```
var at = email.indexOf('@')
```

Then, if there is no @ or the argument contains characters that are not word characters (a–z, A–Z, or 0–9), hyphens, periods, or the @, underline or plus symbols, the recipe returns false, because it has already been determined that the e-mail address is invalid, as follows:

```
if (at == -1 || /[^\w\-\.\@\_\+]/.test(email)) return false
```

Next, the variables left and right are assigned the string on either side of the @ symbol, and the variables llen and rlen are then set to the lengths of each, like this:

```
var left  = email.substr(0, at)
var right = email.substr(at + 1)
var llen  = left.length
var rlen  = right.length
```

Using these values, if left is less than 1 or greater than 64 characters, or right is less than 4 or greater than 254 characters, or if there is no period after the @ symbol, then the e-mail address is invalid, and so the recipe returns false:

```
if (llen < 1 || llen > 64 || rlen < 4 || rlen > 254 ||
    right.indexOf('.') == -1) return false
```

After all these tests, the format of the e-mail address appears to be valid, so the value true is returned:

```
return true
```

NOTE A valid e-mail address should be of the form 1–64 characters@4–254 characters. It can contain the letters a–z or A–Z, the digits 0–9, and the hyphen, period, underline, and plus characters. No other characters are recommended, even though some may seem to be supported, as they could conflict with shell scripts or other programs used to process e-mails. If you need to support other characters, place them into the regular expression passed to the test() function in the second line of the recipe. Also, there should always be a period after the @ symbol to divide the domain name from the top-level domain extension.

How to Use It

To use this recipe, pass it a string containing an e-mail address, and it will return either true or false, depending on whether the e-mail address is valid. Here's an example that will let you test the recipe by entering different e-mail addresses:

```
Email: <input id='email' type='text' name='email' />
<button id='button'>Submit</button>

<script>
OnDOMReady(function()
{
    O('button').onclick = function()
    {
        if (ValidateEmail(O('email').value))
            alert("That address is valid")
        else alert("That email address is invalid")
    }
})
</script>
```

The HTML section creates an input field and then places a button after it. The <script> section then attaches an anonymous inline function to the button via its onclick event, which validates the e-mail address each time it is clicked.

The Recipe

```
function ValidateEmail(email)
{
    var at = email.indexOf('@')

    if (at == -1 || /[^\w\-\.\@\_\+]/.test(email)) return false

    var left  = email.substr(0, at)
    var right = email.substr(at + 1)
    var llen  = left.length
    var rlen  = right.length

    if (llen < 1 || llen > 64 || rlen < 4 || rlen > 254 ||
        right.indexOf('.') == -1) return false

    return true
}
```

ValidatePassword()

To help your users pick more secure passwords, you may wish to require them to be of a certain format, such as including both upper- and lowercase characters, as well as digits and punctuation. With this recipe, you can choose any or all of these and the recipe will return `true` or `false`, depending on whether the user has satisfied your requirements. In Figure 22-5, the password that has been entered has not verified.

About the Recipe

This recipe takes a password string and then returns either `true` or `false`, depending on whether it satisfies the conditions also passed as arguments. It requires the following arguments:

- **pass**   The password to validate.
- **min**   The minimum password length.
- **max**   The maximum password length.
- **upper**   If `true` or 1, at least one uppercase character must be in `pass`.
- **lower**   If `true` or 1, at least one lowercase character must be in `pass`.
- **dig**   If `true` or 1, at least one digit must be in `pass`.
- **punct**   If `true` or 1, at least one nonalphanumeric character must be in `pass`.

Variables, Arrays, and Functions

`len`	Local variable containing the length of `pass`
`valid`	Local variable that is `true` if `pass` validates; otherwise, `false`
`test()`	Function to test for a match in a string

How It Works

This recipe first assigns the length of the password to `len` and initializes `valid` with the value `true`, which it will retain if it passes the tests to determine its validity:

```
var len   = pass.length
var valid = true
```

Figure 22-5   Ensure your users enter strong passwords with this recipe.

Next, pass is checked to ensure it is within the lengths required by the min and max arguments, and valid is assigned the value false if not:

```
if (len < min || len > max) valid = false
```

The following four tests are made only if the argument they work from is true or has the value 1. For example, the following statement returns false if the argument upper is true or 1 *and* there is not at least one uppercase letter in pass:

```
else if (upper && !/[A-Z]/.test(pass)) valid = false
```

The following three statements do the same for lowercase letters, digits, and punctuation (nonalphanumeric) characters:

```
else if (lower  && !/[a-z]/.test(pass))        valid = false
else if (dig    && !/[0-9]/.test(pass))        valid = false
else if (punct  && !/[^a-zA-Z0-9]/.test(pass)) valid = false
```

If pass meets all these tests, then valid will retain its initial value of true, which is then returned; otherwise, one of the tests will set valid to false, and that value will be returned:

```
return valid
```

How to Use It

To use this recipe, pass it a password string and the arguments you want for the password to meet your security requirements. The following example uses the strictest policy the recipe supports, in which the password must include at least one each of upper- and lowercase letters, digits, and punctuation. It also requires passwords to be at least 8 characters long (but no more than 16):

```
Password: <input id='pass' type='password' name='pass' />
<button id='button'>Submit</button>

<script>
OnDOMReady(function()
{
    O('button').onclick = function()
    {
        if (ValidatePassword(O('pass').value, 8, 16, 1, 1, 1, 1))
            alert("That password is valid")
        else alert("That password is invalid")
    }
})
</script>
```

The Recipe

```
function ValidatePassword(pass, min, max, upper, lower, dig, punct)
{
   var len   = pass.length
   var valid = true

   if      (len < min || len > max)             valid = false
   else if (upper  && !/[A-Z]/.test(pass))      valid = false
   else if (lower  && !/[a-z]/.test(pass))      valid = false
   else if (dig    && !/[0-9]/.test(pass))      valid = false
   else if (punct  && !/[^a-zA-Z0-9]/.test(pass)) valid = false

   return valid
}
```

94 CleanupString()

This recipe provides a number of string manipulation functions that often come in handy. For example, don't you hate it when you enter a credit card or phone number into a web form, only to be told you aren't allowed to use spaces and must enter it again? If your content management system doesn't like spaces either, this recipe can remove them before they arrive at your server. It can also remove all digits, text, or punctuation, convert from lower- to uppercase text (and vice versa), and even change all groups of multiple spaces into just a single space. Figure 22-6 shows a credit card number being entered into a web form, including spaces.

Figure 22-7 shows the input after the user has clicked the Submit button—all the spaces are now removed, leaving only the card number behind.

About the Recipe

This recipe takes a string and can perform one or more of several actions on it. It requires the following arguments:

- **string**   The string to clean up.
- **allspaces**   If true or 1, all spaces in string are removed.
- **alldigs**   If true or 1, all digits in string are removed.

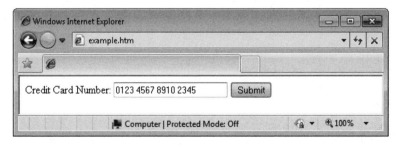

FIGURE 22-6   A user has entered a sequence of credit card numbers with spaces.

FIGURE 22-7   This recipe has automatically stripped out the spaces.

- **alltext** If `true` or 1, all text in `string` is removed.
- **allpunct** If `true` or 1, all punctuation in `string` is removed.
- **uptolow** If `true` or 1, all uppercase characters in `string` are converted to lowercase.
- **lowtoup** If `true` or 1, all lowercase characters in `string` are converted to uppercase.
- **spacestosingle** If `true` or 1, all groups of multiple spaces in `string` are reduced to a single space.

Variables, Arrays, and Functions

`replace()`	Function to replace one value with another in a string

How It Works

This recipe goes through each of the arguments it is supplied in turn. If the argument has the value `true` or 1, then the matching `replace()` function is performed on the string. For example, the following statement removes all spaces from `string` when the `allspaces` argument is 1 or `true`:

```
if (allspaces) string = string.replace(/[\s]/g, '')
```

All the remaining statements are very similar, differing only by the regular expressions used for testing.

How to Use It

To use this recipe, pass it a string along with the arguments needed to perform the changes required on the string. The modified string will then be returned. Here's an example that cleans up a credit card number by removing all spaces, text, and punctuation from it:

```
Credit Card Number:
<input id='ccnum' type='text' name='ccnum' size='24' />
<button id='button'>Submit</button>
```

```
<script>
OnDOMReady(function()
{
   O('button').onclick = function()
   {
      O('ccnum').value =
         CleanupString(O('ccnum').value , 1 ,0 ,1, 1, 0, 0, 0)
   }
})
</script>
```

To use this in a web form, you could change the onclick event used in this example to the onsubmit event of your form. If you do, make sure that when the recipe has finished execution, the function you point the event to returns true, because any other value will likely cancel the form submission, and a return value of false certainly will cancel it.

The Recipe

```
function CleanupString(string, allspaces, alldigs, alltext, allpunct,
   uptolow, lowtoup, spacestosingle)
{
   if (allspaces)       string = string.replace(/[\s]/g, '')
   if (alldigs)         string = string.replace(/[\d]/g, '')
   if (alltext)         string = string.replace(/[a-zA-Z]/g, '')
   if (allpunct)        string = string.replace(/[^\sa-zA-Z0-9]/g, '')
   if (uptolow)         string = string.toLowerCase()
   if (lowtoup)         string = string.toUpperCase()
   if (spacestosingle)  string = string.replace(/[\s]/g, ' ')

   return string
}
```

ValidateCreditCard()

With this recipe, you can check that a credit card number you are given by a user at least has the correct format, and the right checksum, before submitting it to a card processing company. Figure 22-8 shows a set of made-up credit card details that did not pass the validation.

About the Recipe

This recipe takes details about a credit card and returns true or false depending on whether the card passes checksum and date verification. It requires the following arguments:

- **number** A credit card number.
- **month** The card's expiry month.
- **year** The card's expiry year.

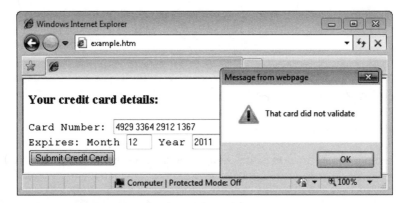

FIGURE 22-8 Checking whether credit card details match basic requirements

Variables, Arrays, and Functions

`left`	Local variable containing the first four digits of `number`
`cclen`	Local variable containing the number of digits in `number`
`chksum`	Local variable containing the card's checksum
`date`	Local date object
`substr()`	Function to return a portion of a string
`getTime()`	Function to get the current time and date
`getFullYear()`	Function to get the year as a four-digit number
`getMonth()`	Function to get the month

How It Works

This function first ensures that all three parameters passed to it are strings by adding the null string to them, like this:

```
number += ''
month  += ''
year   += ''
```

Next, each argument is processed through the `CleanupString()` recipe to ensure that they are in the formats required:

```
number = CleanupString(number, true, false, true, true)
month  = CleanupString(month,  true, false, true, true)
year   = CleanupString(year,   true, false, true, true)
```

After this, the variable `left` is assigned the first four digits of number, `cclen` is set to the card number's length, and `chksum` is initialized to 0:

```
var left     = number.substr(0, 4)
var cclen    = number.length
var chksum   = 0
```

Next, several `if()` ... `else if()` statements check that `left` contains a valid sequence that matches a known brand of credit card, and if it does, that the card number length in `cclen` is correct for the card type. If `left` doesn't match a known card—or it matches one, but `cclen` is the wrong length—then the recipe returns `false` to indicate that the card didn't verify.

If these initial tests are passed, the card's checksum is then calculated using an algorithm invented by IBM scientist Hans Peter Luhn (for further details, see *en.wikipedia.org/wiki/Luhn_algorithm*), like this:

```
for (var j = 1 - (cclen % 2) ; j < cclen ; j += 2)
   if (j < cclen) chksum += number[j] * 1

for (j = cclen % 2 ; j < cclen ; j += 2)
{
   if (j < cclen)
   {
      d = number[j] * 2
      chksum += d < 10 ? d : d - 9
   }
}

if (chksum % 10 != 0) return false
```

Finally, the date is looked up and compared to the values supplied to the recipe, so that even if the card has validated this far, the recipe will still return `false` if the card has expired:

```
var date = new Date()
date.setTime(date.getTime())
if (year.length == 4) year = year.substr(2, 2)

   if (year > 50)                              return false
   else if (year < (date.getFullYear() - 2000)) return false
   else if ((date.getMonth() + 1) > month)     return false
   else                                        return true
```

How to Use It

To use this recipe, pass it a card number, expiry date, and month, and it will return `true` or `false`. Of course, this algorithm tests only whether the card meets certain requirements and not whether the user has entered a genuine card or whether the card has been revoked or is over the user's credit limit, and so on. The purpose of the recipe is mainly to catch typing errors and people entering random data to see what happens.

```
This example shows how you might use the recipe:
<h3>Your credit card details:</h3>
<font face='Courier New'>
Card Number: <input id='ccnum' type='text' name='n' size='24' /><br/>
Expires: Month <input id='ccmonth' type='text' name='m' size='2' />
Year <input id='ccyear' type='text' name='y' size='4'  /><br />
<button id='button'>Submit Credit Card</button>
```

```
<script>
OnDOMReady(function()
{
   O('button').onclick = function()
   {
      if (ValidateCreditCard(O('ccnum').value,
          O('ccmonth').value, O('ccyear').value))
             alert("That card validated successfully")
      else alert("That card did not validate")
   }
})
</script>
```

When incorporating the recipe with your own code, you will probably want to replace the onclick event attachment used in the example with a function attached to the onsubmit event of your form. Also, make sure that when you do this your function returns true if the card verifies so as to allow the form submission to complete, and false (along with probably displaying an error message) if the card doesn't validate, in order to stop the form submission going through.

NOTE *Only years up to 2050 are currently supported in order to base card dates around the years 1950 to 2050. If you are reading a well-thumbed copy of this book and it's coming up to mid-century, and JavaScript is still being used, well, you may wish to increase the value 50 in the fourth to last line to a higher value a few years ahead of the current year.*

The Recipe

```
function ValidateCreditCard(number, month, year)
{
   number      += ''
   month       += ''
   year        += ''
   number       = CleanupString(number, true, false, true, true)
   month        = CleanupString(month,  true, false, true, true)
   year         = CleanupString(year,   true, false, true, true)
   var left     = number.substr(0, 4)
   var cclen    = number.length
   var chksum   = 0

   if (left >= 3000 && left <= 3059 ||
       left >= 3600 && left <= 3699 ||
       left >= 3800 && left <= 3889)
   { // Diners Club
      if (cclen != 14) return false
   }
   else if (left >= 3088 && left <= 3094 ||
       left >= 3096 && left <= 3102 ||
       left >= 3112 && left <= 3120 ||
       left >= 3158 && left <= 3159 ||
       left >= 3337 && left <= 3349 ||
       left >= 3528 && left <= 3589)
   { // JCB
```

```
      if (cclen != 16) return false
   }
   else if (left >= 3400 && left <= 3499 ||
      left >= 3700 && left <= 3799)
   { // American Express
      if (cclen != 15) return false
   }
   else if (left >= 3890 && left <= 3899)
   { // Carte Blanche
      if (cclen != 14) return false
   }
   else if (left >= 4000 && left <= 4999)
   { // Visa
      if (cclen != 13 && cclen != 16) return false
   }
   else if (left >= 5100 && left <= 5599)
   { // MasterCard

      if (cclen != 16) return false
   }
   else if (left == 5610)
   { // Australian BankCard
      if (cclen != 16) return false
   }
   else if (left == 6011)
   { // Discover
      if (cclen != 16) return false
   }
   else return false // Unrecognized Card

   for (var j = 1 - (cclen % 2) ; j < cclen ; j += 2)
      if (j < cclen) chksum += number[j] * 1

   for (j = cclen % 2 ; j < cclen ; j += 2)
   {
      if (j < cclen)
      {
         d = number[j] * 2
         chksum += d < 10 ? d : d - 9
      }
   }

   if (chksum % 10 != 0) return false

   var date = new Date()
   date.setTime(date.getTime())

   if (year.length == 4) year = year.substr(2, 2)

   if (year > 50)                                 return false
   else if (year  < (date.getFullYear() - 2000)) return false
   else if ((date.getMonth() + 1) > month        return false
   else                                          return true
}
```

CHAPTER 23

Solutions to Common Problems

A number of JavaScript recipes didn't fit clearly within any of the previous chapters in this section, so I've included them here. They offer features such as keeping your copyright notices current each new year; creating a less intrusive in-browser alert window that doesn't prevent you from accessing the rest of the current document; a function to provide tooltips for any object; the ability to add cursor trails to the mouse pointer; and a way to make a web page touch-enabled for use with tablet computers and other touch devices.

RollingCopyright( )

RECIPE 96

This simple recipe is worth using on any pages where a copyright notice is included, because no matter how many years ago you last updated the page, it will always display the current year, as shown by the screen grab in Figure 23-1.

About the Recipe

This recipe takes a start year for when the copyright began and returns a copyright string using that and the current year. It requires the following argument:

- **start**   The start year as a four-digit number.

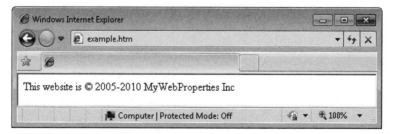

FIGURE 23-1   Keep your copyright notices up to date with this recipe.

Variables, Arrays, and Functions

date	Local date object
Date()	Function to return a new date object
getFullYear()	Function to return a four-digit year

How It Works

This recipe creates a new date object and assigns it the current year as a four-digit number, like this:

```
var date = new Date()
date      = date.getFullYear()
```

Then, the two dates are returned, preceded by a copyright symbol:

```
return '&copy; ' + start + "-" + date
```

How to Use It

To use this recipe, pass it the starting year for the copyright and then assign the string it returns to an element in your document, as in the following example:

```
<span id='copy'></span>

<script>
OnDOMReady(function()
{
    Html('copy', InsVars("This website is #1 MyWebProperties Inc",
        RollingCopyright(2005)))
})
</script>
```

The HTML section creates a span that will be used to display the copyright message, and then the `<script>` section uses the `InsVars()` recipe to insert the result of calling `RollingCopyright()` into a sentence, which is then assigned to the `innerHTML` property of the span.

The Recipe

```
function RollingCopyright(start)
{
    var date = new Date()
    date      = date.getFullYear()

    return '&copy; ' + start + "-" + date
}
```

97 Alert()

The built-in JavaScript `alert()` function is great for help with debugging or for alerting users about something important. However, the function is a *modal* dialog, which means that it takes over the browser, preventing access to anything within it other than the alert window. What's worse, if a web page calls `alert()` in a loop, it will effectively lock you out of the browser, even preventing you from closing it.

This recipe provides a handy replacement for the function that is much more user-friendly in that it is not modal, and all other parts of the browser remain accessible while it is displayed. It also features smart scrolling. Unlike the regular `alert()` window that just gets bigger and bigger depending on the size of the message, this recipe will provide scroll bars instead, so that it always remains the same size. Figure 23-2 shows a standard `alert()` dialog.

Figure 23-3 shows this recipe used to display the same message as Figure 23-2. It is fairly similar to the Internet Explorer alert window, but it also uses some styling similar to that used by Firefox and other web browsers, so it should look good on all major browsers.

About the Recipe

This recipe takes a message and displays it in an in-browser alert dialog. It requires the following argument:

- **value** A string, value, or expression to display.

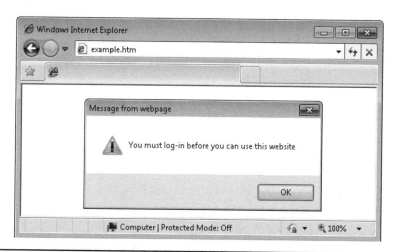

Figure 23-2 A standard Internet Explorer alert message

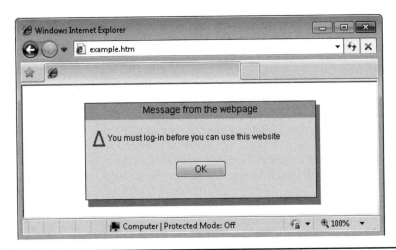

Figure 23-3   A message displayed by the Alert() recipe

Variables, Arrays, and Functions

`divs`	Local array containing the IDs of the two main divs
`newdiv`	Local object used for creating new divs
`warn`	Local variable containing the HTML for the warning triangle
`ok`	Local variable containing the HTML for the OK button
`mess`	Local variable containing the HTML of the message
`html`	Local variable containing the HTML for the alert contents

`ALERT_DIV,`
`SHADOW_DIV,`
`ALERT_TITLE,`
`ALERT_MESSAGE,`
`and ALERT_OK`
	IDs of the various elements created by this recipe

`innerHTML`	Property of various objects containing their HTML
`backgroundColor`	Property of various objects containing their background colors
`fontFamily`	Property of various objects containing their fonts
`fontSize`	Property of various objects containing their font sizes
`padding`	Property of the message area containing its padding
`paddingTop`	Property of the title area containing its top padding
`textAlign`	Property of the title containing its text alignment
`overflow`	Property of the message area containing its overflow setting
`border`	Property of the main div containing its border setting
`onclick`	Event of the OK button attached to `AlertHide()`
`AlertHide()`	Subfunction to hide the alert

`Position()`	Function to set an object's style position property
`Resize()`	Function to resize an object
`Center()`	Function to center an object both vertically and horizontally
`GoTo()`	Function to move an object to a new position
`Opacity()`	Function to set the opacity of an object
`visible()`	Function to make an object visible
`Invisible()`	Function to make an object invisible
`createElement()`	Function to create a new HTML element
`setAttribute()`	Function to set an attribute of an HTML element
`appendChild()`	Function to append a child object to an element

How It Works

This recipe starts by creating an array of the main two divs it uses, then four strings are created to hold the warning triangle HTML, the OK button, the alert message itself, and two new subdivs that will contain the alert's title and message HTML:

```
var divs = Array('ALERT_DIV', 'SHADOW_DIV')
var warn = "<font color=red size=6 style='vertical-align:middle;'>" +
           "&#916;</font> "
var ok   = "<center><input id='ALERT_OK' type='submit' /></center>"
var mess = warn + value + '<br /><br />' + ok
var html = "<div id='ALERT_TITLE'></div>" +
           "<div id='ALERT_MESSAGE'></div>"
```

Next, if the object with the ID 'ALERT_DIV' doesn't exist, it means this is the first time the recipe has been called, so the two main divs are created, like this:

```
var newdiv = document.createElement('div')
newdiv.id  = 'SHADOW_DIV'
document.body.appendChild(newdiv)
newdiv     = document.createElement('div')
newdiv.id  = 'ALERT_DIV'
document.body.appendChild(newdiv)
```

These statements create new divs with the IDs 'ALERT_DIV' and 'SHADOW_DIV', attaching them to the document body. The divs are then released from their location in the HTML, resized, and centered, and the shadow div has its opacity set to 50 percent, as follows:

```
Position(divs, ABS)
Resize('ALERT_DIV',   350, 140)
Resize('SHADOW_DIV',  354, 146)
Center('ALERT_DIV')
GoTo('SHADOW_DIV', X('ALERT_DIV') + 4, Y('ALERT_DIV') + 6)
Opacity('SHADOW_DIV', 50)
```

Next, the divs are hidden with a call to the subfunction AlertHide(), and the main div's innerHTML property is assigned the value of html, which contains the HTML with which to create the two subdivs, both of which are then resized:

```
AlertHide()
Html('ALERT_DIV', html)
Resize('ALERT_TITLE',    350, 22)
Resize('ALERT_MESSAGE', 330, 98)
```

After this, a number of style elements are set up, and the innerHTML of the title and message divs are assigned, like this:

```
Html('ALERT_TITLE', 'Message from the webpage')
Html('ALERT_MESSAGE', mess)

S('ALERT_TITLE').background    = '#acc5e0'
S('ALERT_TITLE').fontFamily    = 'Arial'
S('ALERT_TITLE').paddingTop    = '2px'
S('ALERT_TITLE').textAlign     = 'center'
S('ALERT_TITLE').fontSize      = '14px'
O('ALERT_MESSAGE').innerHTML   = mess
S('ALERT_MESSAGE').fontFamily  = 'Arial'
S('ALERT_MESSAGE').fontSize    = '12px'
S('ALERT_MESSAGE').padding     = '10px'
S('ALERT_MESSAGE').overflow    = 'auto'
S('ALERT_DIV').background      = '#f0f0f0'
S('ALERT_DIV').border          = 'solid #444444 1px'
S('SHADOW_DIV').background      = '#444444'
O('ALERT_OK').value            = '       OK       '
```

These statements set the correct colors, fonts, alignments, padding, and borders for the elements, and the message alert has its overflow property set to 'auto' so that larger messages will have scroll bars added if necessary to scroll through the content.

Finally, the onclick event of the OK button is attached to the AlertHide() subfunction, and the divs are made visible, like this:

```
O('ALERT_OK').onclick = AlertHide
Visible(divs)
```

The recipe ends with the AlertHide() subfunction, which is called when the OK button is clicked:

```
function AlertHide()
{
    Invisible(divs)
}
```

How to Use It

You use this recipe in the same manner as the built-in `alert()` function: by simply passing a value or expression to display, like this:

```
Alert("You must log in before you can use this website")
```

Or, here's an example that combines a string and an expression:

```
Alert("The product of 6 and 7 is " + 6 * 7)
```

One of the best things about this recipe is that you can use it to watch values changing in real time without having to click OK after each alert message, as you would with the standard `alert()` function. Here's an example you can try that creates repeating interrupts to call the recipe and display the current mouse coordinates, which change as you move the mouse about:

```
OnDOMReady(function()
{
    setInterval(mousecoords, INTERVAL)

    function mousecoords()
    {
        Alert("Mouse X = " + MOUSE_X + " | Mouse Y = " + MOUSE_Y)
    }
}
```

In this particular example, because the calls to `Alert()` repeat continuously, nothing will happen if you click the OK button to dismiss the message, because another `Alert()` call is made `INTERVAL` milliseconds later. If you want to test the recipe with a single call, just try a command such as this:

```
Alert("This is a test alert message")
```

> **NOTE** *Don't confuse the two functions because they use the same letters. The original JavaScript function starts with a lowercase letter 'a', and is called* `alert()`, *while the new recipe begins with an uppercase letter 'A' and is called* `Alert()`.

The Recipe

```
function Alert(value)
{
    var divs = Array('ALERT_DIV', 'SHADOW_DIV')
    var warn = "<font color=red size=6 " +
               "style='vertical-align:middle;'>" +
               "&#916;</font> "
    var ok   = "<center><input id='ALERT_OK' type='submit' />" +
               "</center>"
    var mess = warn + value + '<br /><br />' + ok
    var html = "<div id='ALERT_TITLE'></div>" +
```

```
                "<div id='ALERT_MESSAGE'></div>"

   if (!O('ALERT_DIV'))
   {
      var newdiv = document.createElement('div')
      newdiv.id  = 'SHADOW_DIV'
      document.body.appendChild(newdiv)
      newdiv     = document.createElement('div')
      newdiv.id  = 'ALERT_DIV'
      document.body.appendChild(newdiv)

      Position(divs, ABS)
      Resize('ALERT_DIV',   350, 140)
      Resize('SHADOW_DIV', 354, 146)
      Center('ALERT_DIV')
      GoTo('SHADOW_DIV', X('ALERT_DIV') + 4, Y('ALERT_DIV') + 6)
      Opacity('SHADOW_DIV', 50)
   }

   AlertHide()
   Html('ALERT_DIV', html)
   Resize('ALERT_TITLE',    350, 22)
   Resize('ALERT_MESSAGE', 330, 98)
   Html('ALERT_TITLE', 'Message from the webpage')
   Html('ALERT_MESSAGE', mess)

   S('ALERT_TITLE').background   = '#acc5e0'
   S('ALERT_TITLE').fontFamily   = 'Arial'
   S('ALERT_TITLE').paddingTop   = '2px'
   S('ALERT_TITLE').textAlign    = 'center'
   S('ALERT_TITLE').fontSize     = '14px'
   S('ALERT_MESSAGE').fontFamily = 'Arial'
   S('ALERT_MESSAGE').fontSize   = '12px'
   S('ALERT_MESSAGE').padding    = '10px'
   S('ALERT_MESSAGE').overflow   = 'auto'
   S('ALERT_DIV').background     = '#f0f0f0'
   S('ALERT_DIV').border         = 'solid #444444 1px'
   S('SHADOW_DIV').background     = '#444444'
   O('ALERT_OK').value           = '        OK        '
   O('ALERT_OK').onclick         = AlertHide

   Visible(divs)

   function AlertHide()
   {
      Invisible(divs)
   }
}
```

ReplaceAlert()

If you like the `Alert()` recipe, you can use this one to replace the default JavaScript `alert()` with it and use it all the time. Figure 23-4 shows the `alert()` function being called to display the mouse's current coordinates, but in fact the `Alert()` recipe is handling the message display since it has now replaced the default function.

About the Recipe

This is probably the shortest recipe in the book, and it requires no arguments to change the default action of `alert()` to use the new `Alert()` recipe.

Variables, Arrays, and Functions

alert	Property of the `window` object specifying which code to use for handling alerts

How It Works

This recipe simply attaches the `Alert()` recipe to the `alert` event of the `window` object, like this:

```
window.alert = Alert
```

How to Use It

To replace the default JavaScript `alert()` function with the new `Alert()` recipe, just call `ReplaceAlert()`. The following example is modified from the one used in the previous recipe, `Alert()`, to call the default `alert()` function, which has been diverted to use the new `Alert()` recipe:

```
OnDOMReady(function()
{
   ReplaceAlert()
   setInterval(mousecoords, INTERVAL)

   function mousecoords()
   {
      alert("Mouse X = " + MOUSE_X + " | Mouse Y = " + MOUSE_Y)
   }
})
```

The Recipe

```
function ReplaceAlert()
{
   window.alert = Alert
}
```

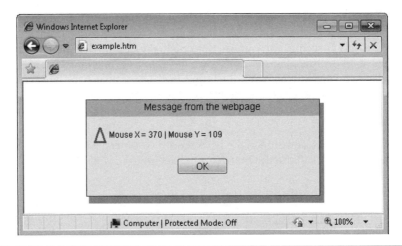

Figure 23-4 With this recipe, all calls to `alert()` will use the new `Alert()` recipe.

 # ToolTip()

With this recipe, you can add tooltips that fade in and out over a period to any object, with a range of fully configurable display options. Figure 23-5 shows a tooltip that has been attached to the Home link of a web page.

About the Recipe

This recipe displays a tooltip when the mouse passes over an attached object. It requires the following arguments:

- **id** An object or object ID—this cannot be an array.
- **tip** The tip message to display, which may contain HTML.
- **font** The font to use.

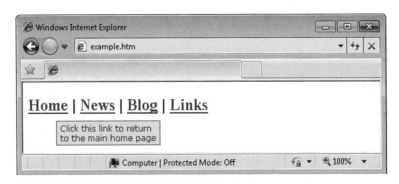

Figure 23-5 Use this recipe to attach smoothly fading tooltips to objects.

- **size** The font size to use.
- **textc** The text color to use.
- **backc** The background color to use.
- **bordc** The border color to use.
- **bstyle** The border style to use.
- **bwidth** The border width to use, in pixels.
- **msecs** The time each fade out or in should take in milliseconds.
- **timeout** The time after which the tooltip will automatically fade out in milliseconds; if 0 or not passed, the tooltip will not automatically fade out.

Variables, Arrays, and Functions

tt	Local variable containing the string 'TT_' concatenated with the ID name of id
newdiv	Local variable containing the new div object
MOUSE_X	Global variable containing the current horizontal location of the mouse cursor
MOUSE_Y	Global variable containing the current vertical location of the mouse cursor
ZINDEX	Global variable containing the highest zIndex value so far used
Hidden	Property of the new div: true when the tooltip is hidden; otherwise, false
IID	Property of the new div used to cancel any pending interrupt that may have been set using setTimeout()
zIndex	Property of the new div set to bring it to the front of all objects
fontFamily	Property of the new div containing its font family
fontSize	Property of the new div containing its font size
padding	Property of the new div containing its padding
color	Property of the new div containing its text color
backgroundColor	Property of the new div containing its background color
bordercolor	Property of the new div containing its border color
borderStyle	Property of the new div containing its border style
borderWidth	Property of the new div containing its border width
innerHTML	Property of the new div containing its HTML
onmouseover	Event of id attached to DoToolTip()
onmouseout	Event of id attached to ToolTipHide()
DoToolTip()	Subfunction to display a tooltip
ToolTipHide()	Subfunction to hide a tooltip
FadeIn()	Function to fade an object in
FadeOut()	Function to fade out an object
Px()	Function to add the suffix 'px' to a number
setTimeout()	Function to set up an interrupt to a function at a future time
clearTimeout()	Function to cancel an interrupt set by setTimeout()

How It Works

This recipe first creates a new div for each different tooltip, with an ID comprising the string 'TT_' and an ID name of id, and then creates a local variable to hold this ID, like this:

```
var tt = 'TT_' + O(id).id
```

Next, if the div for the tooltip for id hasn't yet been created, this is done using the following code:

```
var newdiv = document.createElement('div')
newdiv.id  = tt
document.body.appendChild(newdiv)
```

The opacity of the new div is then set to 0 to hide it, and it is released from the HTML by giving it a style position attribute of 'absolute', using the global variable ABS:

```
Opacity(tt, 0)
Position(tt, ABS)
```

Next, all the arguments that have not been given a value are given default values:

```
font   = font   ? font   : 'Arial'
size   = size   ? size   : 'small'
textc  = textc  ? textc  : '#884444'
backc  = backc  ? backc  : '#ffff88'
bordc  = bordc  ? bordc  : '#aaaaaa'
bstyle = bstyle ? bstyle : 'dotted'
bwidth = bwidth ? bwidth : 1
msecs  = msecs  ? msecs  : 250
```

After that, various style settings based on these values are applied to the new div, and the contents of the tip argument are placed in its innerHTML property, as follows:

```
S(tt).fontFamily  = font
S(tt).fontSize    = size
S(tt).padding     = '3px 5px 3px 5px'
S(tt).color       = textc
S(tt).background  = backc
S(tt).borderColor = bordc
S(tt).borderStyle = bstyle
S(tt).borderWidth = Px(bwidth)
```

```
Html(tt, tip)
```

Finally, in the setup section, the DoToolTip() and ToolTipHide() subfunctions are attached to the onmouseover and onmouseout events of id, and the Hidden property of id is set to false to indicate that the tooltip is not currently visible:

```
O(id).onmouseover = DoToolTip
O(id).onmouseout  = ToolTipHide
O(tt).Hidden      = false
```

The DoToolTip() Subfunction

This function moves the tooltip div referred to by `tt` to a location 15 pixels to the right and 15 down from the mouse position, sets its `zIndex` property to the highest value used so far plus 1 (to ensure it displays above all other elements), fades the tooltip in, and sets the tooltip's `Hidden` attribute to `false` to indicate that it is now visible:

```
GoTo(tt, MOUSE_X + 15, MOUSE_Y + 15)
O(tt).zIndex = ZINDEX + 1
FadeIn(tt, msecs)
O(tt).Hidden = false
```

With the tooltip now displayed, if a timeout has been specified, then `setTimeout()` is called to create an interrupt call to the `ToolTipHide()` subfunction in `timeout` milliseconds, to fade it away again (after first canceling any timeout that may currently be in place), like this:

```
if (O(tt).IID) clearTimeout(O(tt).IID)
O(tt).IID = setTimeout(ToolTipHide, timeout)
```

The ToolTipHide() Subfunction

This function simply checks whether the tooltip is currently hidden. If it is, it has nothing to do and returns; otherwise, it fades out the tooltip and sets its `Hidden` attribute to `true` to indicate the new setting:

```
FadeOut(tt, msecs)
O(tt).Hidden = true
```

How to Use It

To use this recipe, all you need to do is pass it an object and the tip message to display, like this:

```
ToolTip('home', 'Visit the Home page')
```

You can also pass any or all of the other supported arguments to tailor the output. The following example illustrates attaching a tooltip to a link using all the available options:

```
<h2>
<a id='home'  href='/'      >Home</a> |
<a id='news'  href='/news' >News</a> |
<a id='blog'  href='/blog' >Blog</a> |
<a id='links' href='/links'>Links</a>
</h2>

<script>
OnDOMReady(function()
{
   tip = 'Click this link to return<br />to the main home page'
   ToolTip('home', tip, 'Verdana', '12px', '#444444', '#eeeeff',
```

PART III

```
        '#008888', 'solid', '1', 500, 5000)
   O('links').title = tip
})
</script>
```

The HTML section sets up four links and gives them IDs. Then, the <script> section attaches a tooltip to the first link. As you can see by the <br /> included in the string assigned to tip, HTML is supported, enabling you to configure the tooltip any way you like.

There is also a standard title tag attached to the final link so you can compare the way it displays with this recipe by passing the mouse over that link, too.

The Recipe

```
function ToolTip(id, tip, font, size, textc, backc, bordc,
   bstyle, bwidth, msecs, timeout)
{
   var tt = 'TT_' + O(id).id

   if (!O(tt))
   {
      var newdiv = document.createElement('div')
      newdiv.id  = tt
      document.body.appendChild(newdiv)
      Opacity(tt, 0)
      Position(tt, ABS)

      font   = font   ? font   : 'Arial'
      size   = size   ? size   : 'small'
      textc  = textc  ? textc  : '#884444'
      backc  = backc  ? backc  : '#ffff88'
      bordc  = bordc  ? bordc  : '#aaaaaa'
      bstyle = bstyle ? bstyle : 'dotted'
      bwidth = bwidth ? bwidth : 1
      msecs  = msecs  ? msecs  : 250

      S(tt).fontFamily  = font
      S(tt).fontSize    = size
      S(tt).padding     = '3px 5px 3px 5px'
      S(tt).color       = textc
      S(tt).background  = backc
      S(tt).borderColor = bordc
      S(tt).borderStyle = bstyle
      S(tt).borderWidth = Px(bwidth)
      O(tt).innerHTML   = tip
   }

   O(id).onmouseover = DoToolTip
   O(id).onmouseout  = ToolTipHide
   O(tt).Hidden      = false

   function DoToolTip()
   {
      GoTo(tt, MOUSE_X + 15, MOUSE_Y + 15)
```

```
      O(tt).zIndex = ZINDEX + 1
      FadeIn(tt, msecs)
      O(tt).Hidden = false

      if (timeout)
      {
         if (O(tt).IID) clearTimeout(O(tt).IID)
         O(tt).IID = setTimeout(ToolTipHide, timeout)
      }
   }

   function ToolTipHide()
   {

      if (!O(tt).Hidden)
      {
         FadeOut(tt, msecs)
         O(tt).Hidden = true
      }
   }
}
```

CursorTrail()

This recipe can provide a great visual aid for your users, or you can use it as a special effect. It leaves a trail of 10 images behind the mouse cursor, with each image a little more faded out than the one in front of it, so that it gives a smoother flowing appearance than, for example, the built-in Windows cursor trail utility. It also allows you to select your own images for the trail. Figure 23-6 shows a cursor trail created using the mouse pointer image supplied with this recipe.

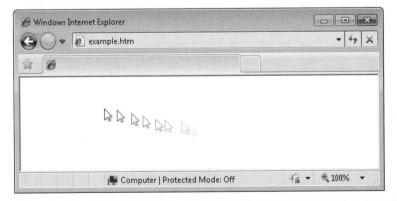

FIGURE 23-6   Add cursor trails to the mouse pointer by calling this recipe.

About the Recipe

This recipe creates a trail of images that follow the mouse pointer. It requires the following arguments:

- **image**   The URL of an image to use for the trail.
- **length**   The length of the trail, with smaller numbers being shorter.
- **state**   If 1 or `true`, the trails are turned on; a value of 0 or `false` turns them off.

Variables, Arrays, and Functions

j	Local variable for iterating through the 10 images
w	Local variable containing the width of the browser
h	Local variable containing the height of the browser
c	Local variable containing the string 'CT_'
newimg	Local variable containing each new image as it is created
zIndex	Property of each image set to bring them in front of all other elements
ABS	Global variable with the value 'absolute'
MOUSE_X and MOUSE_Y	Global variables containing the horizontal and vertical mouse coordinates
ZINDEX	Global variable containing the highest zIndex property so far used
GoTo()	Function to move an object to a new location
Hide()	Function to hide an object
Show()	Function to show an object that has been hidden
Position()	Function to set the style position property of an object
Opacity()	Function to set the opacity of an object
GetWindowWidth()	Function to return the width of the browser
GetWindowHeight()	Function to return the height of the browser
createElement()	Function to create a new HTML element
setAttribute()	Function to set an attribute of an object
appendChild()	Function to attach a child object to an object
setInterval()	Function to start repeating interrupts to another function
clearInterval()	Function to stop repeating interrupts

How It Works

To start with, this recipe saves the width and height of the browser in w and h, and sets c to the string 'CT_', a prefix that will be used when assigning IDs to the image objects that will be created:

```
var w = GetWindowWidth()
var h = GetWindowHeight()
var c = 'CT_'
```

Next, if state is not 1 or true, any repeating interrupts are canceled and the recipe returns, which turns off the mouse trails:

```
if (!state) return clearInterval(CT_IID)
```

At the next line of code, if no object has the ID 'TT_0', it means this is the first time the recipe has been called, so all the image objects are created and set to style positions of 'absolute' (so that they can be moved about). In addition, their opacity is set to different levels so that the ones furthest away from the mouse cursor are the most faded, the images are loaded from the URL supplied in image, and the X and Y properties of each image are assigned starting values of –9999 to place them well offscreen, as follows:

```
if (!O('TT_0'))
{
   for (var j = 0 ; j < 10 ; ++j)
   {
      var newimg = document.createElement('img')
      newimg.id  = c + j)
      document.body.appendChild(newimg)
      Position(newimg, ABS)
      Opacity(newimg, (j + 1) * 9)
      newimg.src = image
      O(c + j).X = -9999
      O(c + j).Y = -9999
   }
}
```

With everything prepared, the final command in the setup section starts the repeating interrupts to the DoCurTrail() subfunction:

```
CT_IID = setInterval(DoCurTrail, length)
```

The DoCurTrail() Subfunction
This function performs the moving of all the trail images, which it manages with a for() loop, within which the first command moves the image for the current iteration to its new position:

```
for (var j = 0 ; j < 10 ; ++j)
{
   GoTo(c + j, O(c + j).X + 2, O(c + j).Y + 2)
```

For example, when j has the value 5, the image with the ID calculated with the expression c + j is manipulated, which is 'CT_5'. The number 2 in the code places the images down and to the right by two pixels.

Next, the zIndex property of the image is set to the maximum zIndex so far used plus 1, to ensure that it will display on top of all other elements:

```
S(c + j).zIndex = ZINDEX + 1
```

PART III

Then, if the image is set to display directly under the mouse pointer, the image is hidden. If it wasn't hidden, the user could never click a link because a trail image would be between the mouse pointer and the clickable object underneath it:

```
if (O(c + j).X == MOUSE_X && O(c + j).Y == MOUSE_Y) Hide(c + j)
```

Otherwise, if the image is away from the mouse pointer, it is shown:

```
else Show(c + j)
```

Next, as long as j has a value greater than 0 (and therefore is indexing the nine trail images above the first), the image location of the image one behind the current one is set to that of the current image:

```
if (j > 0)
{
   O(c + (j - 1)).X = O(c + j).X
   O(c + (j - 1)).Y = O(c + j).Y
}
```

Finally, the highest numbered image (with the ID 'CT_9') is set either to the current mouse location or, if the mouse is offscreen, to a position well off the start of the screen (with the values 12 and 20 representing the width and height of the mouse pointer):

```
O(c + 9).X = MOUSE_X < (w - 12) ? MOUSE_X : -9999
O(c + 9).Y = MOUSE_Y < (h - 20) ? MOUSE_Y : -9999
```

Only this highest numbered image needs to be given the mouse coordinates, because each time around the loop the coordinates of each item are copied down to the one behind it. For example, the next time around, the image with the ID 'CT_8' will be passed the values in the image with the ID 'CT_9', and so on.

How to Use It

To use this recipe, pass it the URL of an image to display as the trail, a value for how long the trail should be (with 1 being the smallest), and a value of `true` or 1 for the `state` argument, like this:

```
CursorTrail('mousepointer.gif', 20, 1)
```

To turn the effect off, just change the `state` argument to 0 or `false`, like this:

```
CursorTrail('mousepointer.gif', 20, 0)
```

For example, Figure 23-7 shows the file *snowflake.gif* being used in place of *mousepointer.gif*, with the following code:

```
<script>
OnDOMReady(function()
{
    CursorTrail('snowflake.gif', 20, 1)
})
</script>
```

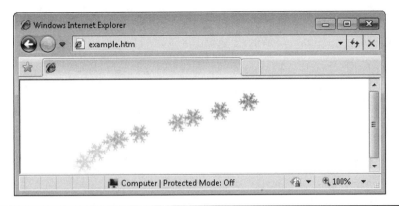

FIGURE 23-7   You can use this recipe to provide seasonal or festive cursor trails.

TIP   For an even more interesting effect, try displaying animated GIFs in the cursor trail instead of static ones.

The Recipe

```
function CursorTrail(image, length, state)
{
    var w = GetWindowWidth()
    var h = GetWindowHeight()
    var c = 'CT_'

    if (!state) return clearInterval(CT_IID)

    if (!O('TT_0'))
    {
        for (var j = 0 ; j < 10 ; ++j)
        {
            var newimg = document.createElement('img')
            newimg.id  = c + j
            document.body.appendChild(newimg)
            Position(newimg, ABS)
            Opacity(newimg, (j + 1) * 9)
            newimg.src = image
            O(c + j).X = -9999
            O(c + j).Y = -9999
        }
    }

    CT_IID = setInterval(DoCurTrail, length)

    function DoCurTrail()
    {
        for (var j = 0 ; j < 10 ; ++j)
```

```
    {
       GoTo(c + j, O(c + j).X + 2, O(c + j).Y + 2)
       S(c + j).zIndex = ZINDEX + 1

       if (O(c + j).X == MOUSE_X && O(c + j).Y == MOUSE_Y)
             Hide(c + j)
       else Show(c + j)

       if (j > 0)
       {
          O(c + (j - 1)).X = O(c + j).X
          O(c + (j - 1)).Y = O(c + j).Y
       }
    }

    O(c + 9).X = MOUSE_X < (w - 12) ? MOUSE_X : -9999
    O(c + 9).Y = MOUSE_Y < (h - 20) ? MOUSE_Y : -9999
  }


}
```

TouchEnable()

Here's the final JavaScript recipe, which allows you to touch-enable a web page. Figure 23-8 shows a copy of the web page in which a small frame has been attached to the top of the browser window with links to turn touch-enabling on and off.

About the Recipe

This recipe changes the mouse click action so that a click and drag operation becomes a scroll operation, allowing users of touch-enabled screens to scroll a document up, down, left, and right simply by touching the screen and moving their finger (or a stylus) about, in the same manner they would use an iPhone, iPad, Android phone, or other touch device. It requires the following argument:

- **state**   If 1 or `true`, touch-enabling is turned on; otherwise, it is turned off.

Variables, Arrays, and Functions

db	Local variable used as shorthand for `document.body`
iid	Local variable containing the result of calling `setInterval()` to be used later when calling `clearInterval()`
flag	Local variable set to `true` when touch-enabling is on
oldmousex and oldmousey	Temporary copies of MOUSE_X and MOUSE_Y to save the mouse position when `StartTE()` is called
tempmousex and tempmousey	Temporary copies of MOUSE_X and MOUSE_Y used in `DoTE()` to see if the mouse has moved

MOUSE_X and MOUSE_Y	Global variables containing the location of the mouse cursor
MOUSE_IN	Global variable set to `true` if the mouse is within the bounds of the browser; otherwise, `false`
onmousedown and onmouseup	Events of the document body that trigger when the mouse is clicked and released
StartTE()	Subfunction to begin touch-enabling
DoTE()	Sub-subfunction to scroll the document as required
StopTE()	Subfunction to turn off touch-enabling
PreventAction()	Function to prevent the default action of an event
setInterval()	Function to set up repeated interrupts to another function
clearInterval()	Function to stop repeated interrupts
scrollBy()	Function to scroll the document body by a specified amount

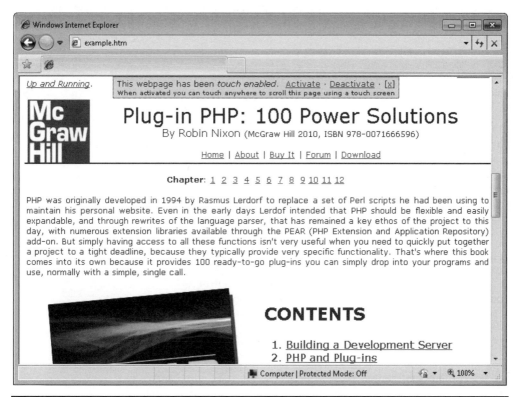

FIGURE 23-8 With this recipe, you can touch-enable your web pages.

How It Works

This recipe starts by making a copy of document.body in the local variable db, thus creating a shorthand reference to shorten the code:

```
var db = document.body
```

The state argument is then tested, and if it is 1 or true, touch-enabling is being turned on, so the variables iid and flag are initialized, PreventAction() is called to disable the default actions for drag and select operations on the document body, and the onmousedown and onmouseup events of the document body are attached to the StartTE() and StopTE() subfunctions, as follows:

```
var iid  = null
var flag = false
PreventAction(db, 'both', true)
db.onmousedown = StartTE
db.onmouseup   = StopTE
```

If state is 0 or false, then touch-enabling is to be turned off, so PreventAction() is called to restore the default actions for drag and select operations on the document body, its onmousedown and onmouseup event hooks are removed, and the recipe returns:

```
PreventAction(db, 'both', false)
db.onmousedown = ''
db.onmouseup   = ''
return
```

The StartTE() Subfunction

This function first checks the flag variable to see whether touch control has already been enabled. If it has, false is returned; otherwise, copies of the mouse cursor position are placed in temporary variables to compare later to see if the document body should be scrolled, like this:

```
var oldmousex  = MOUSE_X
var oldmousey  = MOUSE_Y
var tempmousex = MOUSE_X
var tempmousey = MOUSE_Y
```

Next, flag is set to true to indicate that touch control has been enabled, and setInterval() is called to set up repeating interrupts to DoTE():

```
flag = true
iid  = setInterval(DoTE, 10)
```

The DoTE() Sub-subfunction

This function first checks whether the mouse button is currently held down and is within the bounds of the browser, like this:

```
if (MOUSE_DOWN && MOUSE_IN)
```

If the mouse button is either not down or not within the browser's bounds, the `StopTE()` subfunction is called to release the current scroll. Otherwise, a test is made to see whether the mouse has moved from the position that was stored in the variables `tempmousex` and `tempmousey` when `StartTE()` was first called:

```
if (MOUSE_X != tempmousex || MOUSE_Y != tempmousey)
```

If the mouse has moved, `tempmousex` and `tempmousey` are updated to the new mouse location, like this:

```
tempmousex = MOUSE_X
tempmousey = MOUSE_Y
```

Next, the window is scrolled by the difference between the current mouse location and the one that was stored in `oldmousex` and `oldmousey` when `StartTE()` was first called, like this:

```
window.scrollBy(oldmousex - MOUSE_X, oldmousey - MOUSE_Y)
```

This causes `oldmousex` and `oldmousey` to retain the location of the mouse at the point when the mouse button was clicked, and this location is compared to the current mouse location to determine the amount by which the document body should be scrolled.

However, the variables `tempmousex` and `tempmousey` are used only to see whether the mouse has moved since the last interrupt to the `DoTE()` sub-subfunction and to decide whether a scroll is required. The scrolling is always relative to the values stored in `oldmousex` and `oldmousey`, not those in `tempmousex` and `tempmousey`.

The StopTE() Subfunction

This function simply sets the `flag` variable to `false` to indicate that a scroll is not currently in operation and clears the repeating intervals. The document will not scroll again until the mouse button is held down once more—the same action as touching a touchscreen.

How to Use It

To use this recipe, call it up with a value of 1 or `true`, like this:

```
TouchEnable(1)
```

To turn it off again, call it with a value of 0 or `false`, like this:

```
TouchEnable(0)
```

The following example shows how you can embed on and off controls for this feature in a web page in a similar way to the one shown in Figure 23-8:

```
<div id='enabled'><font size='2' face='Verdana'>
This webpage has been <i>touch-enabled</i>.  
<a href="javascript:TouchEnable(1)"
title="Turn on touchscreen control">Activate</a> &#183;
<a href="javascript:TouchEnable(0)"
title="Turn off touchscreen control">Deactivate</a> &#183;
```

```
[<a href="javascript:ZoomDown('enabled', 1, 1, 1000);
FadeOut('enabled', 1000)"title="Remove this panel">x</a>]</font>
<br /><font size='1' face='Verdana'>
When activated, you can touch anywhere to scroll this page
using a touchscreen</font></div>

<script>
Locate('enabled', 'fixed', 0, -100)
S('enabled').backgroundColor = '#eeeeaa'
S('enabled').padding         = '2px 5px 2px 5px'
S('enabled').border          = 'dotted black 1px'
Opacity('enabled', 0)
GoToEdge('enabled', 'top', 50)
FadeIn('enabled', 1000)
</script>
```

Just add this code to any existing web page that is long enough to require scrolling.

The Recipe

```
function TouchEnable(state)
{
   var db = document.body

   if (state)
   {
      var iid  = null
      var flag = false

      PreventAction(db, 'both', true)

      db.onmousedown = StartTE
      db.onmouseup   = StopTE
   }
   else
   {
      PreventAction(db, 'both', false)

      db.onmousedown = ''
      db.onmouseup   = ''

      return
   }

   function StartTE(e)
   {
      if (!flag)
      {
         var oldmousex  = MOUSE_X
         var oldmousey  = MOUSE_Y
         var tempmousex = MOUSE_X
         var tempmousey = MOUSE_Y

         flag = true
```

```
        iid  = setInterval(DoTE, 10)
    }

    return false

    function DoTE()
    {
        if (MOUSE_DOWN && MOUSE_IN)
        {
            if (MOUSE_X != tempmousex || MOUSE_Y != tempmousey)
            {
                tempmousex = MOUSE_X
                tempmousey = MOUSE_Y
                window.scrollBy(oldmousex - MOUSE_X,
                    oldmousey - MOUSE_Y)
            }
        }
        else StopTE()
    }
}

function StopTE()
{
    flag = false
    clearInterval(iid)
}
}
```

PART IV
CSS Classes

CHAPTER 24

Manipulating Objects

This chapter introduces 19 groups of CSS classes you can use in your web pages to manage the positioning of elements, change text and background colors, add gradient fills and box shadows, alter transparency, and do a whole lot more.

Using the supplied *WDC.css* file (available at *webdeveloperscookbook.com*), you can simply add class names to your HTML class declarations to apply any of a wide range of styling to an element, without having to write any CSS yourself.

And because modern browsers support the use of multiple class names in a declaration, you can supply as many classes as you like to style elements exactly how you want them. This means that with over 880 classes to draw on in this chapter alone, you can concentrate on creating great web pages without the hassle of writing and tweaking CSS rules.

Positioning

The positioning classes let you decide the type of positioning to use for an object between the four types available (absolute, fixed, relative, and static), each of which changes the way CSS properties will affect objects using them. For example, Figure 24-1 shows two sections of text that have been given vertical offsets of 25 pixels, but because one has absolute positioning and the other is fixed, when the document is scrolled, one of them scrolls and the other remains where it is.

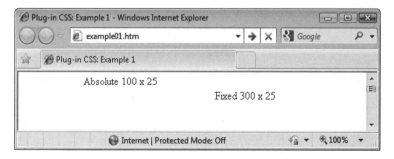

FIGURE 24-1   Different positioning types behave in different ways.

Classes and Properties

absolute abs	Class to assign absolute positioning to an object, plus a shorthand version to save on typing
fixed fix	Class to assign fixed positioning to an object, plus a shorthand version to save on typing
relative rel	Class to assign relative positioning to an object, plus a shorthand version to save on typing
static sta	Class to assign static positioning to an object, plus a shorthand version to save on typing
position	Property containing the type of object positioning to use out of absolute, fixed, relative, or static

About the Classes

The four classes in this group are absolute, relative, fixed, and static, and they have the following effects:

- **absolute**   When this position property is assigned to an object, it can be removed from the normal flow of the document to any other part. When it is moved, any other objects that are able to will move in to occupy the space released. Absolute objects can be placed behind or in front of other objects, and their coordinates are relative to the first parent object that has a position other than static.

- **fixed**   This type of positioning is similar to absolute, except that the object's coordinates are based on the browser window, such that if the document is scrolled, any fixed objects remain where they are and do not scroll with it.

- **relative**   An object that is given relative positioning has its coordinates based on the location it occupied when the document was fully loaded.

- **static**   Static positioning is the default for all elements and indicates that an object is to remain at the position within a document that it first occupied when the document was fully loaded.

How to Use Them

To use these classes, you reference them from HTML, like this:

```
<span class='absolute'>Example text</span>
```

Here's an example HTML page illustrating use of the absolute and fixed classes:

```
<!DOCTYPE html>
<html>
    <head>
        <title>Recipe CSS: Example 1</title>
        <link rel='stylesheet' type='text/css' href='WDC.css' />
        <script src='WDC.js'></script>
    </head>
    <body>
```

```
      <span class='absolute' style='left:100px; top:25px;'>
         Absolute 100 x 25
      </span>
      <span class='fixed'    style='left:300px; top:25px;'>
         Fixed 300 x 25
      </span>
      <br /><br /><br /><br /><br /><br /><br /><br /><br /><br />
      <br /><br /><br /><br /><br /><br /><br /><br /><br /><br />
   </body>
</html>
```

Here, two files are included in the <head> section of the web page:

- **WDC.css**   The CSS rules for the recipes in this part of the book.
- **WDC.js**   The JavaScript recipes from Part II of this book, and JavaScript-enhanced CSS from Part III.

To ensure all the CSS examples in this part of the book work correctly, you should include both files, in the manner shown in the preceding example (shown in bold). I will not show you this code again because I will assume you will include it if you enter the examples to try them for yourself, or you can download them from the companion web site at *webdeveloperscookbook.com*.

In the example, one span has been made absolute and moved to a position 100 pixels across by 25 down from the document start, while the other is fixed at an offset of 300 pixels across and 25 down from the top-left corner of the browser window.

The <br /> tags that follow create 22 blank lines so that if you open this code in a small browser window, it will create a scroll bar at the right side which, if you scroll it, will move the text with absolute positioning, but the fixed text will remain in place.

You probably have noticed the use of inline styles in this example, such as style='left:100px; top:25px;'. These are required to assign the coordinates to each element. Later on, you will see how you can use much simpler classes instead of direct CSS rules.

Also, to save on typing, instead of using the longhand class names of absolute, relative, fixed, and static, you can use the alternate shorthand names of abs, fix, rel, and sta instead (there are handy shorthand versions for many of the more commonly used classes in this book).

NOTE *Because this is the first example, I have shown you a complete HTML web page including all the lines you need at the start, such as the document type and the "saved from" comment used to stop Internet Explorer from displaying errors when a page is viewed on a local file system. I have also shown the page title and the HTML required to load in the style sheet and JavaScript files. However, in future examples I will show only the main HTML.*

The Classes

```
.absolute,  .abs { position:absolute; }
.fixed,     .fix { position:fixed;    }
.relative,  .rel { position:relative; }
.static,    .sta { position:static;   }
```

Floating

RECIPE 2

The float property makes it possible for you to choose to place an object at either the right or left of a section of HTML and have accompanying text flow around it. To enable you to do this without writing any CSS rules, you can use the ready-made ones supplied with this recipe.

In Figure 24-2, both the `leftfloat` and `rightfloat` classes have been used to display boats on either side of the screen with text flowing around them.

Classes and Properties

`leftfloat` `lf`	Class to float an object to the left and make text and other elements flow around it (plus shorthand version)
`leftfloat_h` `lf_h`	The same as `leftfloat`, but this style is only applied when the mouse is over the element to which it applies (plus shorthand version)
`rightfloat` `rf`	Class to float an object to the left and make text and other elements flow around it (plus shorthand version)
`rightfloat_h` `rf_h`	The same as `rightfloat`, but this style is only applied when the mouse is over the element to which it applies (plus shorthand version)
`nofloat` `nf`	Class to unfloat a previously floated object (plus shorthand version)
`nofloat_h` `nf_h`	The same as `unfloat`, but this style is applied only when the mouse is over the element to which it applies (plus shorthand version)
`float`	Property to float an object, which accepts the values `left`, `right`, or `none`

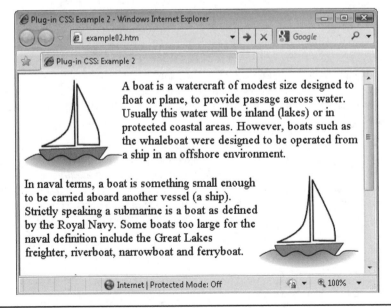

FIGURE 24-2 Using the leftfloat and rightfloat classes

About the Classes

This group has three main classes:

- **leftfloat** This class floats an object to the left, with other elements flowing around it. The flowing can be exited by issuing a `<br clear='left'>` tag, which causes all following HTML to appear under the floated object.

- **rightfloat** This class floats an object to the right, with other elements flowing around it. The flowing can be exited by issuing a `<br clear='right'>` tag, which causes all following HTML to appear under the floated object.

- **nofloat** Using this class will unfloat an object that has previously been floated.

As well as the shorthand versions of these class names, there is another group of classes that have the suffix _h appended to their names. This is one of the more powerful features of the recipes in this book in that (where it makes logical sense) each class also has an accompanying hover class denoted by the _h suffix. When these hover classes are used, their styles will be applied only when the mouse is over the object to which they refer. This makes it easy for you to apply rollover and other dynamic effects without writing a single line of either CSS or JavaScript.

How to Use Them

To use these classes, you refer to them from any section of HTML to which you wish them applied. For example, the following HTML creates two floats—one on the left and one on the right—with text flowing around them (as shown in Figure 24-2):

```
<font size='4'>
<img class='lf' src='boat.png'>A boat is a watercraft of modest size
designed to float or plane, to provide passage across water. Usually
this water will be inland (lakes) or in protected coastal areas.
However, boats such as the whaleboat were designed to be operated from
a ship in an offshore environment.<br clear='left'>

<img class='rf' src='boat.png'>In naval terms, a boat is something small
enough to be carried aboard another vessel (a ship). Strictly speaking
a submarine is a boat as defined by the Royal Navy. Some boats too large
for the naval definition include the Great Lakes freighter, riverboat,
narrowboat and ferryboat.<br clear='right'>
```

Note the use of the `<br clear='...'>` tags to end the floating at specific places in the HTML. As well as these specific tags, if you want to ensure that no floats are applied to a section of text, you can also issue the tag `<br clear='all'>` to clear any and all left or right floats. You will also see that I have used the `lf` and `rf` shorthand versions of the class names, instead of having to type in the longer class names of `leftfloat` and `rightfloat`.

NOTE *As mentioned in the previous recipe group, the start and end portions of the HTML file are not shown here since they will usually all be exactly the same as each other. Therefore, only the main HTML is shown in this and all future examples.*

Using the Hover Classes

To change the float property of an object when the mouse passes over it, you can use one of the class names with the _h suffix, like this:

```
<img class='lf_h' src='boat.png'>This text will display below the boat
image by default. But when the mouse is passed over the boat it will
move up to flow around the image.
```

In the following and in many other recipe groups, you will see how this feature particularly comes into its own.

NOTE   *Although it's not likely that you would often want to change the float property of an element when it is hovered over, it is certainly possible that this feature could be required for certain applications and, as it takes only a few extra characters of CSS to support, there's no reason to omit the feature.*

The Classes

```
.leftfloat,    .leftfloat_h:hover,   .lf,  .lf_h:hover { float:left;  }
.rightfloat,   .rightfloat_h:hover,  .rf,  .rf_h:hover { float:right; }
.nofloat,      .nofloat_h:hover,     .nf,  .nf_h:hover { float:none;  }
```

3   Background Colors

This group of classes illustrates the power of the recipes because they provide six different ways of changing the background color of an object to any of 21 different colors. Figure 24-3 shows six objects, with each using one of the different methods of changing the background color. In the first three, the entire element is modified, while in the second three only links that are contained within the element are affected.

As you hover over and/or click the different links, you will see the color change for the whole element in lines 2 and 3, but only for the link part in lines 5 and 6. As with all the examples, the one used to create this screen grab is downloadable from the companion web site.

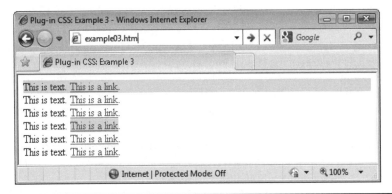

FIGURE 24-3   This recipe group offers many different ways of changing background colors.

Classes and Properties

aqua_b aqua_ba aqua_bh aqua_lb aqua_lba aqua_lbh	Class to change the background color of an object to aqua (aqua_b), plus classes to do so only if the object is actively being clicked (aqua_ba) or hovered over (aqua_bh), and another three classes to change the background of any links within the object (aqua_lb), any links within the object that are actively being clicked (aqua_lba), and any links within the object that are being hovered over (aqua_lbh)
black_b (etc...)	Classes – as aqua_b (etc...) but for black
blue_b (etc...)	Classes – as aqua_b (etc...) but for blue
brown_b (etc...)	Classes – as aqua_b (etc...) but for brown
fuchsia_b (etc...)	Classes – as aqua_b (etc...) but for fuchsia
gold_b (etc...)	Classes – as aqua_b (etc...) but for gold
gray_b (etc...)	Classes – as aqua_b (etc...) but for gray
green_b (etc...)	Classes – as aqua_b (etc...) but for green
khaki_b (etc...)	Classes – as aqua_b (etc...) but for khaki
lime_b (etc...)	Classes – as aqua_b (etc...) but for lime
maroon_b (etc...)	Classes – as aqua_b (etc...) but for maroon
navy_b (etc...)	Classes – as aqua_b (etc...) but for navy
olive_b (etc...)	Classes – as aqua_b (etc...) but for olive
orange_b (etc...)	Classes – as aqua_b (etc...) but for orange
pink_b (etc...)	Classes – as aqua_b (etc...) but for pink
purple_b (etc...)	Classes – as aqua_b (etc...) but for purple
red_b (etc...)	Classes – as aqua_b (etc...) but for red
silver_b (etc...)	Classes – as aqua_b (etc...) but for silver
teal_b (etc...)	Classes – as aqua_b (etc...) but for teal
white_b (etc...)	Classes – as aqua_b (etc...) but for white
yellow_b (etc...)	Classes – as aqua_b (etc...) but for yellow
background	Property containing background settings

About the Classes

This recipe group has 21 main classes, with six different types of each that can be selected by choosing the required suffix. The preceding *Classes and Properties* table lists the available colors. Here is what the suffixes do:

- **_b** Used to refer to a background property.
- **_ba** Used to refer only to the background property of an object that is active (in other words, that is in the process of being clicked).
- **_bh** Used to refer only to the background property of an object that the mouse is hovering over.
- **_lb** Used to refer only to the background property of a link within the object.

- **_lba** Used to refer only to the background property of a link within the object that is actively being clicked.

- **_lbh** Used to refer only to the background property of a link within the object over which the mouse is hovering.

How to Use Them

When you wish to change the background color of an object, first choose the color out of the 21 in the *Classes and Properties* table, and then decide when the color should be applied. So, let's assume you want to change the background color of an object to gold. To do this, you only need to use some simple HTML such as this:

```
<div class='gold_b'>This element has a gold background</div>
```

Or, if you wish the background color to change to orange, but only when the mouse is over it, you might use the following code:

```
<div class='orange_bh'>This element turns orange when moused over</div>
```

Then again, perhaps you would like the background to change color only when it is clicked. In which case, you might use code such as this:

```
<div class='purple_ba'>This element turns purple when clicked</div>
```

Or you can be really creative and combine all three effects into one, like this:

```
<div class='gold_b orange_bh purple_ba'>This element has a gold
background that turns orange when hovered over and purple when
clicked</div>
```

Changing Links Within the Object

Sometimes you won't want to change the background color of an entire object, but may wish to do so for any links it contains, and you can do this using HTML such as the following:

```
<div class='gold_lb'>This element has a plain background.
<a href='#'>And this link has a gold background</a></div>
```

Or all three types of color change can be applied to just the links within an object, like this:

```
<div class='gold_lb orange_lbh purple_lba'>This element has a plain
background. <a href='#'>And this link has a gold background that
turns orange when hovered over and purple when clicked</a></div>
```

Here's the HTML used to create the screen grab in Figure 24-3:

```
<div class='aqua_b'  >This is text. <a href='#'>This is a link</a>.</div>
<div class='aqua_ba' >This is text. <a href='#'>This is a link</a>.</div>
<div class='aqua_bh' >This is text. <a href='#'>This is a link</a>.</div>
<div class='aqua_lb' >This is text. <a href='#'>This is a link</a>.</div>
<div class='aqua_lba'>This is text. <a href='#'>This is a link</a>.</div>
<div class='aqua_lbh'>This is text. <a href='#'>This is a link</a>.</div>
```

As you can see, these classes provide a great deal of interactive functionality, with no need for writing JavaScript programs or creating your own CSS rules.

TIP *Try downloading the example file from the companion web site and clicking (and hovering over) different parts of each element to get a feel for how the different suffixes work.*

The Classes

`.aqua_b,`	`.aqua_ba:active,`	`.aqua_bh:hover,`	
`.aqua_lb a,`	`.aqua_lba a:active,`	`.aqua_lbh a:hover`	`{background:#0ff}`
`.black_b,`	`.black_ba:active,`	`.black_bh:hover,`	
`.black_lb a,`	`.black_lba a:active,`	`.black_lbh a:hover`	`{background:#000}`
`.blue_b,`	`.blue_ba:active,`	`.blue_bh:hover,`	
`.blue_lb a,`	`.blue_lba a:active,`	`.blue_lbh a:hover`	`{background:#00f}`
`.brown_b,`	`.brown_ba:active,`	`.brown_bh:hover,`	
`.brown_lb a,`	`.brown_lba a:active,`	`.brown_lbh a:hover`	`{background:#c44}`
`.fuchsia_b,`	`.fuchsia_ba:active,`	`.fuchsia_bh:hover,`	
`.fuchsia_lb a,`	`.fuchsia_lba a:active,`	`.fuchsia_lbh a:hover`	`{background:#f0f}`
`.gold_b,`	`.gold_ba:active,`	`.gold_bh:hover,`	
`.gold_lb a,`	`.gold_lba a:active,`	`.gold_lbh a:hover`	`{background:#fc0}`
`.gray_b,`	`.gray_ba:active,`	`.gray_bh:hover,`	
`.gray_lb a,`	`.gray_lba a:active,`	`.gray_lbh a:hover`	`{background:#888}`
`.green_b,`	`.green_ba:active,`	`.green_bh:hover,`	
`.green_lb a,`	`.green_lba a:active,`	`.green_lbh a:hover`	`{background:#080}`
`.khaki_b,`	`.khaki_ba:active,`	`.khaki_bh:hover,`	
`.khaki_lb a,`	`.khaki_lba a:active,`	`.khaki_lbh a:hover`	`{background:#cc8}`
`.lime_b,`	`.lime_ba:active,`	`.lime_bh:hover,`	
`.lime_lb a,`	`.lime_lba a:active,`	`.lime_lbh a:hover`	`{background:#0f0}`
`.maroon_b,`	`.maroon_ba:active,`	`.maroon_bh:hover,`	
`.maroon_lb a,`	`.maroon_lba a:active,`	`.maroon_lbh a:hover`	`{background:#800}`
`.navy_b,`	`.navy_ba:active,`	`.navy_bh:hover,`	
`.navy_lb a,`	`.navy_lba a:active,`	`.navy_lbh a:hover`	`{background:#008}`
`.olive_b,`	`.olive_ba:active,`	`.olive_bh:hover,`	
`.olive_lb a,`	`.olive_lba a:active,`	`.olive_lbh a:hover`	`{background:#880}`
`.orange_b,`	`.orange_ba:active,`	`.orange_bh:hover,`	
`.orange_lb a,`	`.orange_lba a:active,`	`.orange_lbh a:hover`	`{background:#f80}`
`.pink_b,`	`.pink_ba:active,`	`.pink_bh:hover,`	
`.pink_lb a,`	`.pink_lba a:active,`	`.pink_lbh a:hover`	`{background:#f88}`
`.purple_b,`	`.purple_ba:active,`	`.purple_bh:hover,`	
`.purple_lb a,`	`.purple_lba a:active,`	`.purple_lbh a:hover`	`{background:#808}`
`.red_b,`	`.red_ba:active,`	`.red_bh:hover,`	
`.red_lb a,`	`.red_lba a:active,`	`.red_lbh a:hover`	`{background:#f00}`
`.silver_b,`	`.silver_ba:active,`	`.silver_bh:hover,`	
`.silver_lb a,`	`.silver_lba a:active,`	`.silver_lbh a:hover`	`{background:#ccc}`
`.teal_b,`	`.teal_ba:active,`	`.teal_bh:hover,`	
`.teal_lb a,`	`.teal_lba a:active,`	`.teal_lbh a:hover`	`{background:#088}`
`.white_b,`	`.white_ba:active,`	`.white_bh:hover,`	
`.white_lb a,`	`.white_lba a:active,`	`.white_lbh a:hover`	`{background:#fff}`
`.yellow_b,`	`.yellow_ba:active,`	`.yellow_bh:hover,`	
`.yellow_lb a,`	`.yellow_lba a:active,`	`.yellow_lbh a:hover`	`{background:#ff0}`

PART IV

Gradients

Most modern browsers already support graduated background fills (with the surprising exception of Opera, which is usually very good at supporting web standards). Therefore, the classes in this group can be used to easily create gradient effects. And even Opera doesn't look too bad because it defaults to a single color average of the gradient.

Figure 24-4 shows a selection of gradients being applied to objects with the same suffixes as used by the solid color background classes (such as `aqua_b`).

Classes and Properties

carrot1 carrot1_a carrot1_h carrot1_l carrot1_la carrot1_lh	Class to change the background gradient of an object to the range of colors you would see in a carrot (`carrot1`), plus classes to do so only if the object is actively being clicked (`carrot1_a`) or hovered over (`carrot1_h`), and another three classes to change the background of any links within the object (`carrot1_l`), any links within the object that are actively being clicked (`carrot1_la`), and any links within the object that are being hovered over (`carrot1_lh`)
chrome1 (etc...)	Classes – as `carrot1` but for a range of chrome steel colors
coffee1 (etc...)	Classes – as `carrot1` but for a range of coffee brown colors
dusk1 (etc...)	Classes – as `carrot1` but for a range of dusky blue colors
earth1 (etc...)	Classes – as `carrot1` but for a range of brown earth colors
fire1 (etc...)	Classes – as `carrot1` but for a range of yellow orange fire colors
grass1 (etc...)	Classes – as `carrot1` but for a range of fresh green grass colors
iron1 (etc...)	Classes – as `carrot1` but for a range of metallic iron colors
plum1 (etc...)	Classes – as `carrot1` but for a range of purple plum colors
rose1 (etc...)	Classes – as `carrot1` but for a range of red rose colors
sky1 (etc...)	Classes – as `carrot1` but for a range of blue sky colors
sunset1 (etc...)	Classes – as `carrot1` but for a range of orangy sunset colors
tin1 (etc...)	Classes – as `carrot1` but for a range of metallic tin colors
water1 (etc...)	Classes – as `carrot1` but for a range of clear blue water colors
wine1 (etc...)	Classes – as `carrot1` but for a range of deep red wine colors
background	Property to which the gradient (or solid color) is applied
Filter	Property used by Internet Explorer for creating gradients and other effects

About the Classes

This recipe group has 15 main classes, with six different types of each that can be selected by choosing the required suffix. The preceding *Classes and Properties* table lists the available gradients. Here is what the suffixes do:

- **(no suffix)**   Without a suffix, the object's background gradient will be set to the color supplied.

- **_a**   This suffix is used to refer only to the background gradient of an object that is active (in other words, that is in the process of being clicked).

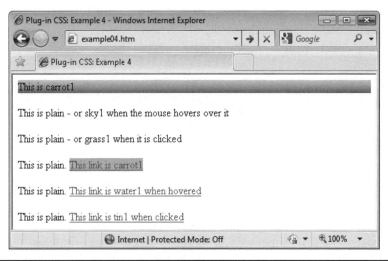

FIGURE 24-4   Applying gradient backgrounds is easy with these classes.

- **_h**   This suffix is used to refer only to the background gradient of an object that the mouse is hovering over.

- **_l**   This suffix is used to refer only to the background gradient of a link within the object.

- **_la**   This suffix is used to refer only to the background gradient of a link within the object that is actively being clicked.

- **_lh**   This suffix is used to refer only to the background gradient of a link within the object over which the mouse is hovering.

There is no _b suffix since gradients are background-only properties anyway. Therefore, all the other suffixes are a little shorter than those used for the solid colors in the previous recipe group.

The property used to achieve the gradient (or solid fallback color) background is the background property. In the case of the Apple Safari and Google Chrome browsers, it is passed a string that looks like this:

```
background:-webkit-gradient(linear, left top, left bottom,
    from(#f44), to(#922));
```

This tells those browsers to create a linear gradient fill, starting at the top left of the object and continuing to the bottom left, starting with the color #f44, slowly graduating to the color #922.

Firefox and other Mozilla-based browsers require the following string format to be applied to the property:

```
background:-moz-linear-gradient(top, #f44, #922);
```

While all other browsers (and all future browsers once it is made the international standard) should send a string such as this:

```
background:linear-gradient(left top, #f44, #922);
```

Microsoft, often the odd one out, takes quite a different approach, so it is necessary to pass a string such as the following to its `filter` property:

```
filter:progid:DXImageTransform.Microsoft.Gradient(
    startColorstr='#f04040', endColorstr='#902020');
```

Also, for those browsers that do not support gradients, a simple solid color string such as #d33 is provided before any of the preceding lines, so that if all the gradient rules fail, at least the simple color setting will remain active.

The downside of all this, as you will often see as you progress through this book, is that all the browsers have to be catered to and therefore all the different strings must be applied for each gradient. This means that the CSS rules end up quite large. But then again, because all the work has already been done for you, all you need to do is include the CSS file and use simple class names in your HTML—you can forget about how cumbersome some of the rules are.

How to Use Them

You apply a gradient in much the same way as a solid background color. For example, to set the background gradient of an object to the `water1` gradient, you might use HTML such as this:

```
<div class='water1'>This is the water1 gradient</div>
```

As with the solid-colored backgrounds, you can also choose when a gradient is to be applied according to whether an object is moused over or clicked, and also whether the object contains any links that should have their gradients changed.

Here's the HTML code used to create the screen grab in Figure 24-1:

```
<div class='carrot1'>This is carrot1</div><br />

<div class='sky1_h'>This is plain - or sky1 when the mouse hovers over
it</div><br />

<div class='grass1_a'>This is plain - or grass1 when it is
clicked</div><br />

<div class='carrot1_l'>This is plain. <a href='#'>This link is
carrot1</a></div><br />

<div class='water1_lh'>This is plain. <a href='#'>This link is
water1 when hovered</a></div><br />

<div class='tin1_la'>This is plain. <a href='#'>This link is
tin1 when clicked</a></div>
```

It is very similar to the example in the previous recipe group, in that the first three objects have their entire background gradient set, while the second three have only the links contained within them changed.

Incidentally, if you are wondering why all these class names end with the number 1, it's because there's a complementary set of gradients that fade in the other vertical direction, in the following recipe group.

NOTE *These classes degrade gracefully, so older browsers that do not support gradient backgrounds will simply show a solid background representative of the average gradient color when you use them.*

The Classes

```
.carrot1,      .carrot1_a:active,    .carrot1_h:hover,
.carrot1_l a, .carrot1_la a:active, .carrot1_lh a:hover {
   background:#ea4;
   background:-webkit-gradient(linear, left top, left bottom,
             from(#fd8), to(#c60));
   background:-moz-linear-gradient(top, #fd8, #c60);
   background:linear-gradient(left top, #fd8, #c60);
   filter    :progid:DXImageTransform.Microsoft.Gradient(
             startColorstr='#f0d080', endColorstr='#c06000');
}
.chrome1,      .chrome1_a:active,    .chrome1_h:hover,
.chrome1_l a, .chrome1_la a:active, .chrome1_lh a:hover {
   background:#ddd;
   background:-webkit-gradient(linear, left top, left bottom,
             from(#fff), to(#aaa));
   background:-moz-linear-gradient(top, #fff, #aaa);
   background:linear-gradient(left top, #fff, #aaa);
   filter    :progid:DXImageTransform.Microsoft.Gradient(
             startColorstr='#f0f0f0', endColorstr='#a0a0a0');
}
.coffee1,      .coffee1_a:active,    .coffee1_h:hover,
.coffee1_l a, .coffee1_la a:active, .coffee1_lh a:hover {
   background:#c94;
   background:-webkit-gradient(linear, left top, left bottom,
             from(#fc6), to(#752));
   background:-moz-linear-gradient(top, #fc6, #752);
   background:linear-gradient(left top, #fc6, #752);
   filter    :progid:DXImageTransform.Microsoft.Gradient(
             startColorstr='#f0c060', endColorstr='#705020');
}
.dusk1,      .dusk1_a:active,    .dusk1_h:hover,
.dusk1_l a, .dusk1_la a:active, .dusk1_lh a:hover {
   background:#79c;
   background:-webkit-gradient(linear, left top, left bottom,
             from(#8ad), to(#357));
   background:-moz-linear-gradient(top, #8ad, #357);
   background:linear-gradient(left top, #8ad, #357);
```

```
    filter      :progid:DXImageTransform.Microsoft.Gradient(
                  startColorstr='#80a0d0', endColorstr='#305070');
}
.earth1,        .earth1_a:active,       .earth1_h:hover,
.earth1_l a,    .earth1_la a:active,    .earth1_lh a:hover {
    background:#a86;
    background:-webkit-gradient(linear, left top, left bottom,
                  from(#db8), to(#532));
    background:-moz-linear-gradient(top, #db8, #532);
    background:linear-gradient(left top, #db8, #532);
    filter      :progid:DXImageTransform.Microsoft.Gradient(
                  startColorstr='#d0b080', endColorstr='#503020');
}
.fire1,         .fire1_a:active,        .fire1_h:hover,
.fire1_l a,     .fire1_la a:active,     .fire1_lh a:hover {
    background:#db3;
    background:-webkit-gradient(linear, left top, left bottom,
                  from(#ef5), to(#b40));
    background:-moz-linear-gradient(top, #ef5, #b40);
    background:linear-gradient(left top, #ef5, #b40);
    filter      :progid:DXImageTransform.Microsoft.Gradient(
                  startColorstr='#e0f050', endColorstr='#b04000');
}
.grass1,        .grass1_a:active,       .grass1_h:hover,
.grass1_l a,    .grass1_la a:active,    .grass1_lh a:hover {
    background:#7b6;
    background:-webkit-gradient(linear, left top, left bottom,
                  from(#ae9), to(#160));
    background:-moz-linear-gradient(top, #ae9, #160);
    background:linear-gradient(left top, #ae9, #160);
    filter      :progid:DXImageTransform.Microsoft.Gradient(
                  startColorstr='#a0e090', endColorstr='#106000');
}
.iron1,         .iron1_a:active,        .iron1_h:hover,
.iron1_l a,     .iron1_la a:active,     .iron1_lh a:hover {
    background:#777;
    background:-webkit-gradient(linear, left top, left bottom,
                  from(#999), to(#333));
    background:-moz-linear-gradient(top, #999, #333);
    background:linear-gradient(left top, #999, #333);
    filter      :progid:DXImageTransform.Microsoft.Gradient(
                  startColorstr='#909090', endColorstr='#303030');
}
.plum1,         .plum1_a:active,        .plum1_h:hover,
.plum1_l a,     .plum1_la a:active,     .plum1_lh a:hover {
    background:#969;
    background:-webkit-gradient(linear, left top, left bottom,
                  from(#b8a), to(#636));
    background:-moz-linear-gradient(top, #b8a, #636);
    background:linear-gradient(left top, #b8a, #636);
    filter      :progid:DXImageTransform.Microsoft.Gradient(
                  startColorstr='#b080a0', endColorstr='#603060');
}
```

```
.rose1,        .rose1_a:active,      .rose1_h:hover,
.rose1_l a,    .rose1_la a:active,   .rose1_lh a:hover {
   background:#e45;
   background:-webkit-gradient(linear, left top, left bottom,
             from(#f67), to(#b12));
   background:-moz-linear-gradient(top, #f67, #b12);
   background:linear-gradient(top, #f67, #b12);
   filter   :progid:DXImageTransform.Microsoft.Gradient(
             startColorstr='#f06070', endColorstr='#b01020');
}
.sky1,         .sky1_a:active,       .sky1_h:hover,
.sky1_l a,     .sky1_la a:active,    .sky1_lh a:hover {
   background:#abe;
   background:-webkit-gradient(linear, left top, left bottom,
             from(#cdf), to(#68c));
   background:-moz-linear-gradient(top, #cdf, #68c);
   background:linear-gradient(left top, #cdf, #68c);
   filter   :progid:DXImageTransform.Microsoft.Gradient(
             startColorstr='#c0d0f0', endColorstr='#6080c0');
}
.sunset1,      .sunset1_a:active,    .sunset1_h:hover,
.sunset1_l a,  .sunset1_la a:active, .sunset1_lh a:hover {
   background:#ed3;
   background:-webkit-gradient(linear, left top, left bottom,
             from(#fe4), to(#ca0));
   background:-moz-linear-gradient(top, #fe4, #ca0);
   background:linear-gradient(left top, #fe4, #ca0);
   filter   :progid:DXImageTransform.Microsoft.Gradient(
             startColorstr='#f0e040', endColorstr='#c0a000');
}
.tin1,         .tin1_a:active,       .tin1_h:hover,
.tin1_l a,     .tin1_la a:active,    .tin1_lh a:hover {
   background:#aaa;
   background:-webkit-gradient(linear, left top, left bottom,
             from(#bbb), to(#777));
   background:-moz-linear-gradient(top, #bbb, #777);
   background:linear-gradient(left top, #bbb, #777);
   filter   :progid:DXImageTransform.Microsoft.Gradient(
             startColorstr='#b0b0b0', endColorstr='#707070');
}
.water1,       .water1_a:active,     .water1_h:hover,
.water1_l a,   .water1_la a:active,  .water1_lh a:hover {
   background:#ace;
   background:-webkit-gradient(linear, left top, left bottom,
             from(#eff), to(#58c));
   background:-moz-linear-gradient(top, #eff, #58c);
   background:linear-gradient(left top, #eff, #58c);
   filter   :progid:DXImageTransform.Microsoft.Gradient(
             startColorstr='#e0f0f0', endColorstr='#5080c0');
}
.wine1,        .wine1_a:active,      .wine1_h:hover,
.wine1_l a,    .wine1_la a:active,   .wine1_lh a:hover {
   background:#d33;
```

```
background:-webkit-gradient(linear, left top, left bottom,
         from(#f44), to(#922));
background:-moz-linear-gradient(top, #f44, #922);
background:linear-gradient(left top, #f44, #922);
filter   :progid:DXImageTransform.Microsoft.Gradient(
         startColorstr='#f04040', endColorstr='#902020');
}
```

Inverse Gradients

The classes in this recipe group are the inverse of the ones in the previous section in that they create background gradient fills that look as if the previous fills were flipped from top to bottom. They are particularly useful as mouseover or button click effects, as can be seen in Figure 24-5, which is an updated version of the example in the previous recipe group that now alternates gradients when clicked and/or hovered over.

Notice how the second set of links does not show any gradients. This is due to an unfortunate bug in Internet Explorer (the browser used for the screen grab), and serves to illustrate how these classes will degrade gracefully when they cannot be applied to their fullest effect. In any case, with a little extra HTML, it is easy to work around this IE bug by using only the first three types of classes that assign gradients to an entire object—then Opera will be the only browser unable to show them (but it will at least still display a solid color representative of the gradient).

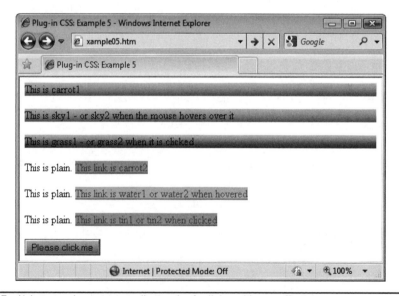

FIGURE 24-5 Using complementary gradient pairs for link and hover effects

Classes and Properties

carrot2 (etc...)	Classes – as carrot1 but reversed from top to bottom
chrome2 (etc...)	Classes – as chrome1 but reversed from top to bottom
coffee2 (etc...)	Classes – as coffee1 but reversed from top to bottom
dusk2 (etc...)	Classes – as dusk1 but reversed from top to bottom
earth2 (etc...)	Classes – as earth1 but reversed from top to bottom
fire2 (etc...)	Classes – as fire1 but reversed from top to bottom
grass2 (etc...)	Classes – as grass1 but reversed from top to bottom
iron2 (etc...)	Classes – as iron1 but reversed from top to bottom
plum2 (etc...)	Classes – as plum1 but reversed from top to bottom
rose2 (etc...)	Classes – as rose1 but reversed from top to bottom
sky2 (etc...)	Classes – as sky1 but reversed from top to bottom
sunset2 (etc...)	Classes – as sunset1 but reversed from top to bottom
tin2 (etc...)	Classes – as tin1 but reversed from top to bottom
water2 (etc...)	Classes – as water1 but reversed from top to bottom
wine2 (etc...)	Classes – as wine1 but reversed from top to bottom
background	Property to which the gradient (or solid color) is applied
filter	Property used by Internet Explorer for creating gradients and other effects

About the Classes

These classes are almost identical to those in the previous recipe group except that they have a number 2 in them instead of a 1, and they display gradients that are the inverse from top to bottom.

How to Use Them

You can use these classes in the same way as the first set of gradients, or use them to make cool mouseover effects like in the following example, which is an extension of the one in the previous recipe group that swaps the gradients when moused over and/or clicked:

```
<div class='carrot2'>This is carrot2</div><br />

<div class='sky1 sky2_h'>This is sky1 - or sky2 when the mouse hovers
over it</div><br />

<div class='grass1 grass2_a'>This is grass1 - or grass2 when it is
clicked</div><br />

<div class='carrot2_l'>This is plain. <a href='#'>This link is
carrot2</a></div><br />

<div class='water1_l water2_lh'>This is plain. <a href='#'>This link is
water1 or water2 when hovered</a></div><br />

<div class='tin1_l tin2_la'>This is plain. <a href='#'>This link is
tin1 or tin2 when clicked</a></div>
```

PART IV

Already, these are some quite impressive effects, but now take a look at what you can do with the HTML <button> tag:

```
<button class='sky1 sky2_a'>Please click me</button>
```

When you click buttons that use gradient classes in this way, they appear to depress even more than normal and produce a highly professional-looking effect.

CAUTION *Unfortunately, Microsoft Internet Explorer has a bug—one of many, in fact—such that the second set of three objects (in which links within an object are addressed) will not show as gradients. For some reason, Internet Explorer balks at CSS rules like* `.classname a { filter:…; }`*, and refuses to apply the filter (although it will apply other styles), so only the background solid color will be applied for these objects. Curiously, IE works fine with rules such as* `.classname { filter:…; }`*. Anyway, until it is corrected, this is one example of how the classes sometimes have to gracefully degrade in certain situations.*

The Classes

```
.carrot2,        .carrot2_a:active,      .carrot2_h:hover,
.carrot2_l a, .carrot2_la a:active, .carrot2_lh a:hover {
    background:#d93;
    background:linear-gradient(left top, #c60, #fd8);
    background:-webkit-gradient(linear, left top, left bottom,
               from(#c60), to(#fd8));
    background:-moz-linear-gradient(top, #c60, #fd8);
    filter   :progid:DXImageTransform.Microsoft.Gradient(
               startColorstr='#c06000', endColorstr='#f0d080');
}
.chrome2,        .chrome2_a:active,      .chrome2_h:hover,
.chrome2_l a, .chrome2_la a:active, .chrome2_lh a:hover {
    background:#ccc;
    background:linear-gradient(left top, #aaa, #fff);
    background:-webkit-gradient(linear, left top, left bottom,
               from(#aaa), to(#fff));
    background:-moz-linear-gradient(top, #aaa, #fff);
    filter   :progid:DXImageTransform.Microsoft.Gradient(
               startColorstr='#a0a0a0', endColorstr='#f0f0f0');
}
.coffee2,        .coffee2_a:active,      .coffee2_h:hover,
.coffee2_l a, .coffee2_la a:active, .coffee2_lh a:hover {
    background:#b83;
    background:linear-gradient(left top, #752, #fc6);
    background:-webkit-gradient(linear, left top, left bottom,
               from(#752), to(#fc6));
    background:-moz-linear-gradient(top, #752, #fc6);
    filter   :progid:DXImageTransform.Microsoft.Gradient(
               startColorstr='#705020', endColorstr='#f0c060');
}
```

```
.dusk2,        .dusk2_a:active,    .dusk2_h:hover,
.dusk2_l a,    .dusk2_la a:active, .dusk2_lh a:hover {
   background:#68b;
   background:linear-gradient(left top, #357, #8ad);
   background:-webkit-gradient(linear, left top, left bottom,
              from(#357), to(#8ad));
   background:-moz-linear-gradient(top, #357, #8ad);
   filter    :progid:DXImageTransform.Microsoft.Gradient(
              startColorstr='#305070', endColorstr='#80a0d0');
}
.earth2,       .earth2_a:active,    .earth2_h:hover,
.earth2_l a,   .earth2_la a:active, .earth2_lh a:hover {
   background:#975;
   background:linear-gradient(left top, #532, #db8);
   background:-webkit-gradient(linear, left top, left bottom,
              from(#532), to(#db8));
   background:-moz-linear-gradient(top, #532, #db8);
   filter    :progid:DXImageTransform.Microsoft.Gradient(
              startColorstr='#503020', endColorstr='#d0b080');
}
.fire2,        .fire2_a:active,    .fire2_h:hover,
.fire2_l a,    .fire2_la a:active, .fire2_lh a:hover {
   background:#ca2;
   background:linear-gradient(left top, #b40, #ef5);
   background:-webkit-gradient(linear, left top, left bottom,
              from(#b40), to(#ef5));
   background:-moz-linear-gradient(top, #b40, #ef5);
   filter    :progid:DXImageTransform.Microsoft.Gradient(
              startColorstr='#b04000', endColorstr='#e0f050');
}
.grass2,       .grass2_a:active,    .grass2_h:hover,
.grass2_l a,   .grass2_la a:active, .grass2_lh a:hover {
   background:#6a5;
   background:linear-gradient(left top, #160, #ae9);
   background:-webkit-gradient(linear, left top, left bottom,
              from(#160), to(#ae9));
   background:-moz-linear-gradient(top, #160, #ae9);
   filter    :progid:DXImageTransform.Microsoft.Gradient(
              startColorstr='#106000', endColorstr='#aaee99');
}
.iron2,        .iron2_a:active,    .iron2_h:hover,
.iron2_l a,    .iron2_la a:active, .iron2_lh a:hover {
   background:#666;
   background:linear-gradient(left top, #333, #999);
   background:-webkit-gradient(linear, left top, left bottom,
              from(#333), to(#999));
   background:-moz-linear-gradient(top, #333, #999);
   filter    :progid:DXImageTransform.Microsoft.Gradient(
              startColorstr='#303030', endColorstr='#909090');
}
.plum2,        .plum2_a:active,    .plum2_h:hover,
.plum2_l a,    .plum2_la a:active, .plum2_lh a:hover {
```

```
        background:#858;
        background:linear-gradient(left top, #636, #b8a);
        background:-webkit-gradient(linear, left top, left bottom,
                   from(#636), to(#b8a));
        background:-moz-linear-gradient(top, #636, #b8a);
        filter    :progid:DXImageTransform.Microsoft.Gradient(
                   startColorstr='#603060', endColorstr='#b080a0');
}
.rose2,        .rose2_a:active,     .rose2_h:hover,
.rose2_l a,    .rose2_la a:active,  .rose2_lh a:hover {
        background:#d34;
        background:linear-gradient(left top, #b12, #f67);
        background:-webkit-gradient(linear, left top, left bottom,
                   from(#b12), to(#f67));
        background:-moz-linear-gradient(top, #b12, #f67);
        filter    :progid:DXImageTransform.Microsoft.Gradient(
                   startColorstr='#b01020', endColorstr='#f06070');
}
.sky2,         .sky2_a:active,      .sky2_h:hover,
.sky2_l a,     .sky2_la a:active,   .sky2_lh a:hover {
        background:#9ad;
        background:linear-gradient(left top, #68c, #cdf);
        background:-webkit-gradient(linear, left top, left bottom,
                   from(#68c), to(#cdf));
        background:-moz-linear-gradient(top, #68c, #cdf);
        filter    :progid:DXImageTransform.Microsoft.Gradient(
                   startColorstr='#6080c0', endColorstr='#c0d0f0');
}
.sunset2,      .sunset2_a:active,   .sunset2_h:hover,
.sunset2_l a,  .sunset2_la a:active, .sunset2_lh a:hover {
        background:#dc2;
        background:linear-gradient(left top, #ca0, #fe4);
        background:-webkit-gradient(linear, left top, left bottom,
                   from(#ca0), to(#fe4));
        background:-moz-linear-gradient(top, #ca0, #fe4);
        filter    :progid:DXImageTransform.Microsoft.Gradient(
                   startColorstr='#c0a000', endColorstr='#f0e040');
}
.tin2,         .tin2_a:active,      .tin2_h:hover,
.tin2_l a,     .tin2_la a:active,   .tin2_lh a:hover {
        background:#999;
        background:linear-gradient(left top, #777, #bbb);
        background:-webkit-gradient(linear, left top, left bottom,
                   from(#777), to(#bbb));
        background:-moz-linear-gradient(top, #777, #bbb);
        filter    :progid:DXImageTransform.Microsoft.Gradient(
                   startColorstr='#707070', endColorstr='#b0b0b0');
}
.water2,       .water2_a:active,    .water2_h:hover,
.water2_l a,   .water2_la a:active, .water2_lh a:hover {
        background:#9bd;
        background:linear-gradient(left top, #58c, #eff);
        background:-webkit-gradient(linear, left top, left bottom,
                   from(#58c), to(#eff));
```

```
    background:-moz-linear-gradient(top, #58c, #eff);
    filter    :progid:DXImageTransform.Microsoft.Gradient(
              startColorstr='#5080c0', endColorstr='#e0f0f0');
}
.wine2,        .wine2_a:active,      .wine2_h:hover,
.wine2_l a,    .wine2_la a:active,   .wine2_lh a:hover {
    background:#c22;
    background:linear-gradient(left top, #922, #f44);
    background:-webkit-gradient(linear, left top, left bottom,
              from(#922), to(#f44));
    background:-moz-linear-gradient(top, #922, #f44);
    filter    :progid:DXImageTransform.Microsoft.Gradient(
              startColorstr='#902020', endColorstr='#f04040');
}
```

6 Box Shadows

Adding a shadow effect underneath images and other objects helps them stand out. Using the classes in this recipe group, you can add box shadows of five different lightnesses in six different ways.

Figure 24-6 shows a photograph repeated six times. The first copy has no box shadow, while the other five range from the lightest to the darkest box shadow. This screen grab was taken using Internet Explorer, which doesn't support blurring. All other browsers blur and round the edges of box shadows, providing a smoother effect.

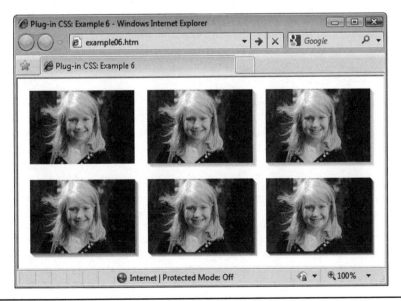

FIGURE 24-6   Adding box shadows makes objects stand out from the page.

Classes and Properties

boxshadow boxshadow_a boxshadow_h boxshadow_l boxshadow_la boxshadow_lh	Class to add a box shadow to an object (boxshadow), plus classes to do so only if the object is actively being clicked (boxshadow_a) or hovered over (boxshadow_h), and another three classes to add a box shadow only to any links within the object (boxshadow_l), any links within the object that are actively being clicked (boxshadow_la), and any links within the object that are being hovered over (boxshadow_lh)
lightestboxshadow (etc...)	Class – as boxshadow but with the lightest shadow
lightboxshadow (etc...)	Class – as boxshadow but with a lighter shadow
darkboxshadow (etc...)	Class – as boxshadow but with a darker shadow
darkestboxshadow (etc...)	Class – as boxshadow but with the darkest shadow
-moz-box-shadow	Property to create a box shadow on Firefox and other Mozilla browsers
-webkit-box-shadow	Property to create a box shadow on Safari and Chrome
filter	Property to create box shadows and other effects on Internet Explorer
box-shadow	Property to create a box shadow on all other browsers

About the Classes

This group has five classes, each of which is supplied with the standard suffixes used to change the way they act: _a for active, _h for hover, _l for a link, _la for an active link, and _lh for a hovered link.

The box shadow is applied using the box-shadow CSS property, or -moz-box-shadow for Mozilla-based browsers such as Firefox, or -webkit-box-shadow for Safari and Chrome. In all cases, the values passed are the shadow color, its vertical and horizontal offset from the object, and the amount of blurring to use. So a typical box shadow rule looks like this:

```
box-shadow:#444444 4px 4px 6px;
```

On Internet Explorer, box shadowing is handled by the filter property and the equivalent CSS rule is as follows:

```
filter:progid:DXImageTransform.Microsoft.Shadow(color='#444444',
Direction=135, Strength=6);
```

TIP *If you are interested in tweaking the WDC.css file, there is also a DropShadow filter argument available in Internet Explorer that provides a different effect and which is identical in use to the Shadow argument, except for the extra four letters preceding the word Shadow. You could therefore use it in the following way:*

```
filter:progid:DXImageTransform.Microsoft.DropShadow(color='#444444',
Direction=135, Strength=6);
```

How to Use Them

To add a box shadow to an object, enter its class name into some HTML, like this:

```
<img class='boxshadow' src='photo1.jpg' />
```

You can also choose any of the four lighter or darker variants, or add one of the action suffixes to change the way the box shadow is implemented. For example, to add a darker box shadow to an object when it is being hovered over, you might do this:

```
<img class='darkboxshadow_h' src='photo1.jpg' />
```

Or you could combine the two to give an object a lighter box shadow that changes to a darker one when hovered over, like this:

```
<img class='lightboxshadow darkboxshadow_h ' src='photo1.jpg' />
```

Here is the HTML that was used to create the screen grab in Figure 24-6.

```
<div class='black_bh' style='padding:10px;'>
    <img                            src='photo1.jpg' />    
    <img class='lightestboxshadow'  src='photo1.jpg' />    
    <img class='lightboxshadow'     src='photo1.jpg' /> <br /><br />
    <img class='boxshadow'          src='photo1.jpg' />    
    <img class='darkboxshadow'      src='photo1.jpg' />    
    <img class='darkestboxshadow'   src='photo1.jpg' />
</div>
```

In this example, there are six instances of a photo: one with no box shadow, and five more with shadows of varying lightness. A few   and <br /> tags are used to neatly space them out.

Enclosing these photos is a <div> tag that has been set to change its background color to black when hovered over (using the black_bh class), so you can pass the mouse over it and see the effect of the lighter shadows when used on a dark background.

The Classes

```
.boxshadow,                       .boxshadow_a:active,
.boxshadow_h:hover,               .boxshadow_l a,
.boxshadow_la a:active,           .boxshadow_lh a:hover {
    -moz-box-shadow    :#888888 4px 4px 6px;
    -webkit-box-shadow:#888888 4px 4px 6px;
    box-shadow         :#888888 4px 4px 6px;
    filter             :progid:DXImageTransform.Microsoft.Shadow(
                        color='#888888', Direction=135, Strength=6);
}
.lightestboxshadow,               .lightestboxshadow_a:active,
.lightestboxshadow_h:hover,       .lightestboxshadow_l a,
.lightestboxshadow_la a:active,   .lightestboxshadow_lh a:hover {
    -moz-box-shadow    :#ffffff 4px 4px 6px;
    -webkit-box-shadow:#ffffff 4px 4px 6px;
    box-shadow         :#ffffff 4px 4px 6px;
    filter             :progid:DXImageTransform.Microsoft.Shadow(
                        color='#cccccc', Direction=135, Strength=6);
```

```
}
.lightboxshadow,                      .lightboxshadow_a:active,
.lightboxshadow_h:hover,              .lightboxshadow_l a,
.lightboxshadow_la a:active,          .lightboxshadow_lh a:hover {
   -moz-box-shadow    :#cccccc 4px 4px 6px;
   -webkit-box-shadow:#cccccc 4px 4px 6px;
   box-shadow         :#cccccc 4px 4px 6px;
   filter             :progid:DXImageTransform.Microsoft.Shadow(
                         color='#cccccc', Direction=135, Strength=6);
}
.darkboxshadow,                       .darkboxshadow_a:active,
.darkboxshadow_h:hover,               .darkboxshadow_l a,
.darkboxshadow_la a:active,           .darkboxshadow_lh a:hover {
   box-shadow         :#444444 4px 4px 6px;
   -moz-box-shadow    :#444444 4px 4px 6px;
   -webkit-box-shadow:#444444 4px 4px 6px;
   filter             :progid:DXImageTransform.Microsoft.Shadow(
                         color='#444444', Direction=135, Strength=6);
}
.darkestboxshadow,                    .darkestboxshadow_a:active,
.darkestboxshadow_h:hover,            .darkestboxshadow_l a,
.darkestboxshadow_la a:active,        .darkestboxshadow_lh a:hover {
   -moz-box-shadow    :#000000 4px 4px 6px;
   -webkit-box-shadow:#000000 4px 4px 6px;
   box-shadow         :#000000 4px 4px 6px;
   filter             :progid:DXImageTransform.Microsoft.Shadow(
                         color='#000000', Direction=135, Strength=6);
}
```

Padding

When you need to quickly add some padding around an object, as long as you're happy to use values of 2, 5, 8, 11, or 15 pixels, you can simply drop one of the class names in this group into your HTML.

For example, Figure 24-7 shows the example from the previous recipe group modified so that each picture has a different amount of padding. A border has been added to each to make it clear how much padding has been applied.

Classes and Properties

padding padding_a padding_h padding_l padding_la padding_lh	Class to add 8 pixels of padding around an object (padding), plus classes to do so only if the object is actively being clicked (padding_a) or hovered over (padding_h), and another three classes to add padding only to any links within the object (padding_l), any links within the object that are actively being clicked (padding_la), and any links within the object that are being hovered over (padding_lh)
smallestpadding (etc...)	Class – as padding but with 2 pixels of padding
smallpadding (etc...)	Class – as padding but with 5 pixels of padding

largepadding (etc...)	Class – as `padding` but with 11 pixels of padding
largestpadding (etc...)	Class – as `padding` but with 15 pixels of padding
padding	Property to set an object's padding

About the Classes

This group has five classes, and each is supplied with the standard suffixes used to change the way they act: `_a` for active, `_h` for hover, `_l` for a link, `_la` for an active link, and `_lh` for a hovered link. Padding is applied using the `padding` CSS property, with values of 2px, 5px, 8px, 11px, or 15px, like this:

```
padding:8px;
```

How to Use Them

Using the padding classes is as easy as choosing the size you need and using that classname in a `class='...'` argument, like this:

```
<img class='padding' src='photo1.jpg' />
```

You can add padding to most objects, not just images. You can also choose to use any of the dynamic versions of these classes. For example, to give an object a small padding and then enlarge it when the mouse hovers over it, you could use code such as this:

```
<img class='smallpadding largepadding_h' src='photo1.jpg' />
```

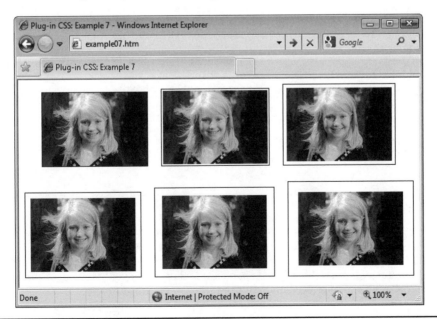

FIGURE 24-7 Applying different padding classes to a photograph

Or to change the padding only when the object is clicked, you could use:

```
<img class='smallpadding largepadding_a' src='photo1.jpg' />
```

And, of course, there are also the classes for modifying only links within an object, like the following, which applies a small padding to any such links, and which changes to a larger padding when the link is hovered over:

```
<img class='smallpadding_l largepadding_lh' src='photo1.jpg' />
```

Here is the HTML used to create the page shown in Figure 24-7:

```
<img border='1'                         src='photo1.jpg' />    
<img border='1' class='smallestpadding' src='photo1.jpg' />    
<img border='1' class='smallpadding'    src='photo1.jpg' /> <br /><br />
<img border='1' class='padding'         src='photo1.jpg' />    
<img border='1' class='largepadding'    src='photo1.jpg' />    
<img border='1' class='largestpadding'  src='photo1.jpg' />
```

The Classes

```
.padding,                          .padding_a:active,
.padding_h:hover,                  .padding_l a,
.padding_la a:active,              .padding_lh a:hover
    { padding:8px;   }
.smallestpadding,                  .smallestpadding_a:active,
.smallestpadding_h:hover,          .smallestpadding_l a,
.smallestpadding_la a:active,      .smallestpadding_lh a:hover
    { padding:2px;   }
.smallpadding,                     .smallpadding_a:active,
.smallpadding_h:hover,             .smallpadding_l a,
.smallpadding_la a:active,         .smallpadding_lh a:hover
    { padding:5px;   }
.largepadding,                     .largepadding_a:active,
.largepadding_h:hover,             .largepadding_l a,
.largepadding_la a:active,         .largepadding_lh a:hover
    { padding:11px; }
.largestpadding,                   .largestpadding_a:active,
.largestpadding_h:hover,           .largestpadding_l a,
.largestpadding_la a:active,       .largestpadding_lh a:hover
    { padding:15px; }
```

Rounded Borders

You can create rounded borders in many ways, from using images and image parts, to table cells, nested elements, and so on. Generally, they are quite complicated to use, but thankfully the new CSS 3 `border-radius` command is supported on all browsers except Internet Explorer, and even that browser can handle them from version 9 on, as can be seen in Figure 24-8, which shows a screen grab from the IE 9 Platform Preview.

FIGURE 24-8   These rounded borders work on all modern browsers, including IE 9.

Classes and Properties

round round_a round_h round_l round_la round_lh	Class to add a 10-pixel rounded border radius to an object (round), plus classes to do so only if the object is actively being clicked (round_a) or hovered over (round_h), and another three classes to add the border only to any links within the object (round_l), any links within the object that are actively being clicked (round_la), and any links within the object that are being hovered over (round_lh)
smallestround (etc...)	Class – as round but creates a 2-pixel radius rounded border
smallround (etc...)	Class – as round but creates a 5-pixel radius rounded border
largeround (etc...)	Class – as round but creates a 15-pixel radius rounded border
largestround (etc...)	Class – as round but creates a 20-pixel radius rounded border
-moz-border-radius	Property to create a rounded border on Firefox and other Mozilla browsers
-webkit-border-radius	Property to create a rounded border on Safari and Chrome
border-radius	Property to create a rounded border on all other browsers

About the Classes

This group has five classes, each of which is supplied with the standard suffixes used to change the way they act: _a for active, _h for hover, _l for a link, _la for an active link, and _lh for a hovered link.

The rounded border is applied using the box-shadow CSS property, or –moz-border-radius for Mozilla-based browsers such as Firefox, or –webkit-border-radius for Safari and Chrome. In all cases, a pixel value is passed, like this CSS rule:

```
border-radius:10px;
```

Interestingly, Internet Explorer was late to the game in supporting rounded borders, but today it actually does a better job than the other browsers because if the object is an image it also gets slightly rounded at the corners, whereas other browsers leave the images untouched. I suppose it could be argued that this is a case of Microsoft doing things in a nonstandard way again, but I like their approach to this feature.

How to Use Them

To add a rounded border to an object, you must first ensure that a border has been enabled. This can be done the old-fashioned way in images with an argument such as `border='1'`, or via CSS such as `border:1px solid;` (or using the border classes later in this chapter).

Once a border is visible, you can round it off by including one of the classes, like this:

```
<img border='1' class='round padding' src='photo1.jpg' />
```

This will add a rounded border with a radius of 10 pixels. You can choose smaller or larger radii and also use the various standard suffixes to change the border only when clicked or hovered over, or only when it is part of a link within the current object.

Here is the HTML used to create Figure 24-8:

```
<img border='1' class='padding'                src='photo1.jpg' />  
<img border='1' class='smallestround padding'  src='photo1.jpg' />  
<img border='1' class='smallround padding'     src='photo1.jpg' />
<br /><br />
<img border='1' class='round padding'          src='photo1.jpg' />  
<img border='1' class='largeround padding'     src='photo1.jpg' />  
<img border='1' class='largestround padding'   src='photo1.jpg' />
```

The Classes

```
.round,                    .round_a:active,
.round_h:hover,            .round_l a,
.round_la a:active,        .round_lh a:hover {
   border-radius        :10px;
   -moz-border-radius   :10px;
   -webkit-border-radius:10px;
}
.smallestround,            .smallestround_a:active,
.smallestround_h:hover,    .smallestround_l a,
.smallestround_la a:active, .smallestround_lh a:hover {
   border-radius        :2px;
   -moz-border-radius   :2px;
   -webkit-border-radius:2px;
}
.smallround,               .smallround_a:active,
.smallround_h:hover,       .smallround_l a,
.smallround_la a:active,   .smallround_lh a:hover {
   border-radius        :5px;
   -moz-border-radius   :5px;
   -webkit-border-radius:5px;
}
```

```
.largeround,                 .largeround_a:active,
.largeround_h:hover,         .largeround_l a,
.largeround_la a:active,     .largeround_lh a:hover {
   border-radius          :15px;
   -moz-border-radius     :15px;
   -webkit-border-radius  :15px;
}
.largestround,               .largestround_a:active,
.largestround_h:hover,       .largestround_l a,
.largestround_la a:active,   .largestround_lh a:hover {
   border-radius          :20px;
   -moz-border-radius     :20px;
   -webkit-border-radius  :20px;
}
```

Transparency

The ability to change the transparency of an object opens up a wide range of professional effects, and the classes in this recipe group make doing so very easy. For example, Figure 24-9 shows a photograph displayed at 11 different levels of transparency.

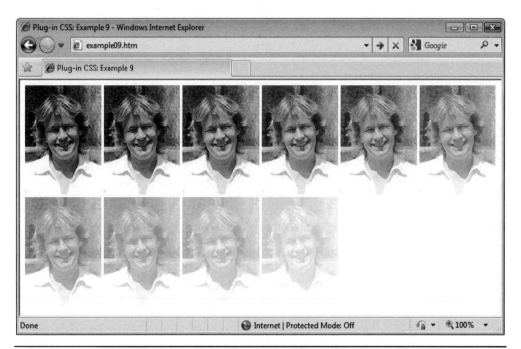

FIGURE 24-9   You can vary the transparency of objects with these classes.

Classes and Properties

`trans00`
`trans00_a`
`trans00_h`
`trans00_l`
`trans00_la`
`trans00_lh`
	Class to set the transparency of an object to 0%, or no transparency (`trans00`), plus classes to do so only if the object is actively being clicked (`trans00_a`) or hovered over (`trans00_h`), and another three classes to set the transparency only for any links within the object (`trans00_l`), any links within the object that are actively being clicked (`trans00_la`), and any links within the object that are being hovered over (`trans00_lh`)

`trans01 - trans10` (etc...)	Classes to change the transparency of an object in steps of 10 percent, including `_a`, `_h`, `_l`, `_la`, and `_lh` suffixes for each
`opacity`	Property used by all modern browsers for changing the opacity (and therefore the transparency) of an object
`filter`	Property used by Internet Explorer for opacity and other features

About the Classes

Transparency, or more precisely the inverse of it, opacity, is one area that most of the browser developers caught up with a while ago, so there is no need to use property names such as `-moz-opacity` or `-webkit-opacity`. Instead, the single property `opacity` is all that is required, as in the following CSS rule, which sets the opacity of an object to 50 percent:

`opacity:0.5;`

Of course, Microsoft always likes to be different, so Internet Explorer uses the filter property instead, like this (with a value between 0 and 100, rather than 0 and 1):

`filter:alpha(opacity = '50');`

How to Use Them

You can change the opacity of an object by selecting the class name you want out of the 11 levels between 0 and 100 percent. Then, you can optionally choose a suffix to determine how the change should be made, as with the following code, which sets the transparency of a photograph to 70 percent:

```
<img class='trans05' src='photo2.jpg' />
```

A neat trick you can utilize for highlighting photos is to also provide a different level of transparency when a picture is hovered over, as with the following example, which changes the transparency of the photo to zero percent (or solid) when the mouse passes over it:

```
<img class='trans05 trans00_h' src='photo2.jpg' />
```

You can also use the other standard suffixes to change the transparency when an object is clicked, or only for links within an object.

Here is the HTML used to create Figure 24-9:

```
<img class='trans00'            src='photo2.jpg' />
<img class='trans01 trans00_h' src='photo2.jpg' />
<img class='trans02 trans01_h' src='photo2.jpg' />
<img class='trans03 trans02_h' src='photo2.jpg' />
<img class='trans04 trans03_h' src='photo2.jpg' />
<img class='trans05 trans04_h' src='photo2.jpg' />
<img class='trans06 trans05_h' src='photo2.jpg' />
<img class='trans07 trans06_h' src='photo2.jpg' />
<img class='trans08 trans07_h' src='photo2.jpg' />
<img class='trans09 trans08_h' src='photo2.jpg' />
<img class='trans10 trans09_h' src='photo2.jpg' />
```

With the exception of the first, when you pass the mouse over the pictures, they darken by 10 percent.

The Classes

```
.trans00,      .trans00_a:active,     .trans00_h:hover,
.trans00_l a, .trans00_la a:active, .trans00_lh a:hover {
   opacity:1;
   filter :alpha(opacity = '100');
}
.trans01,      .trans01_a:active,     .trans01_h:hover,
.trans01_l a, .trans01_la a:active, .trans01_lh a:hover {
   opacity:0.9;
   filter :alpha(opacity = '90');
}
.trans02,      .trans02_a:active,     .trans02_h:hover,
.trans02_l a, .trans02_la a:active, .trans02_lh a:hover {
   opacity:0.8;
   filter :alpha(opacity = '80');
}
.trans03,      .trans03_a:active,     .trans03_h:hover,
.trans03_l a, .trans03_la a:active, .trans03_lh a:hover {
   opacity:0.7;
   filter :alpha(opacity = '70');
}
.trans04,      .trans04_a:active,     .trans04_h:hover,
.trans04_l a, .trans04_la a:active, .trans04_lh a:hover {
   opacity:0.6;
   filter :alpha(opacity = '60');
}
.trans05,      .trans05_a:active,     .trans05_h:hover,
.trans05_l a, .trans05_la a:active, .trans05_lh a:hover {
   opacity:0.5;
   filter :alpha(opacity = '50');
}
.trans06,      .trans06_a:active,     .trans06_h:hover,
.trans06_l a, .trans06_la a:active, .trans06_lh a:hover {
   opacity:0.4;
   filter :alpha(opacity = '40');
}
.trans07,      .trans07_a:active,     .trans07_h:hover,
.trans07_l a, .trans07_la a:active, .trans07_lh a:hover {
```

```
   opacity:0.3;
   filter :alpha(opacity = '30');
}
.trans08,     .trans08_a:active,    .trans08_h:hover,
.trans08_l a, .trans08_la a:active, .trans08_lh a:hover {
   opacity:0.2;
   filter :alpha(opacity = '20');
}
.trans09,     .trans09_a:active,    .trans09_h:hover,
.trans09_l a, .trans09_la a:active, .  a:hover {
   opacity:0.1;
   filter :alpha(opacity = '10');
}
.trans10,     .trans10_a:active,    .trans10_h:hover,
.trans10_l a, .trans10_la a:active, .trans10_lh a:hover {
   opacity:0;
   filter :alpha(opacity = '0');
}
```

 ## Visibility and Display

The classes in this recipe group provide different ways of presenting objects, including making them visible or invisible, hidden (a different type of invisible), or positioning them either inline or as a block.

Figure 24-10 shows three images in which the first is presented normally using the visible class (which is the default for all objects). The second uses the invisible class, which retains its dimensions, as can be seen by the caption still in the correct place. The third image uses the hidden class, so it has been completely removed from display, as can be seen by the caption, which has collapsed inward to occupy the space released.

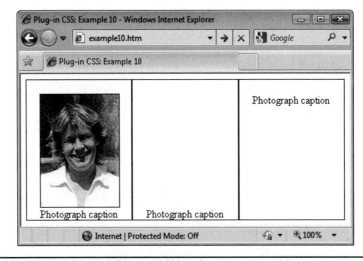

Figure 24-10 Using the visible, invisible, and hidden classes to present images

Classes and Properties

`visible`	Class to make an object visible
`invisible`	Class to make an object invisible but retain its dimensions
`hidden`	Class to hide an object, reducing its dimensions to zero
`block`	Class to make an object visible and to give it the properties of a `<div>` element—it will display underneath the preceding object and force following objects to display under it
`inline`	Class to make an object visible and to give it the properties of a `<span>` element—it will display to the right of the preceding object (if there's room) and following objects will display to the right of it (if there's room)
`table-cell`	Class to give an object the attributes of a table cell
`valigntop`	Class to vertically align an object to the top of the containing object (used mainly for `tablecell` classes)
`valignmid`	Class to vertically align an object to the middle of the containing object (used mainly for `tablecell` classes)
`valignbot`	Class to vertically align an object to the bottom of the containing object (used mainly for `tablecell` classes)
`visibility`	Property to set the visibility and invisibility of an object
`display`	Property to set the hidden, block, and inline display of an object

About the Classes

Unlike the transparency class of `trans10` (which makes an object totally transparent but keeps its position and dimensions), when an object uses either the `invisible` or `hidden` classes, it also has no associated actions and therefore cannot be hovered over or clicked. If you try to do these things on an invisible object, the browser will ignore them. As for hidden objects, they are removed from the web page so other elements that can will move in to occupy the space released.

Therefore, none of the usual suffix versions of these classes are available. If they were, they would be completely useless. For example, if a hover class was created for hiding an object, as soon as the object disappeared a mouse-out event would trigger and the object would reappear again and the process would start all over, resulting in the object appearing to flicker.

How to Use Them

The `visible`, `invisible`, and `hidden` classes are mostly of use for assigning initial settings to objects that you may change later using JavaScript. For example, you may wish to hide an element that should display only at the correct time, when a certain action is performed.

Here's some HTML that shows the effects of using the different classes:

```
<div style='padding:20px; border:1px solid; width:120px; height:164px;'
   class='leftfloat'>
   <img border='1' class='visible' src='photo2.jpg' />Photograph caption
</div>
<div style='padding:20px; border:1px solid; width:120px; height:164px;'
```

PART IV

```
  class='leftfloat'>
    <img border='1' class='invisible' src='photo2.jpg'/>Photograph caption
</div>
<div style='padding:20px; border:1px solid; width:120px; height:164px;'
    class='leftfloat'>
    <img border='1' class='hidden' src='photo2.jpg' />Photograph caption
</div>
```

Each image is embedded within a <div> that has 20 pixels of padding, a solid border, and is floated to the left. These act as placeholders. Then, within each <div> there is one instance each of a visible, invisible, and hidden class, each followed by a picture caption. The result is the screen grab in Figure 24-10.

Using the block and inline Classes

The other two classes in this group have the effect of giving an object either the positioning properties of a <div> for the block class, or those of a <span> for the inline class.

Objects with a block display property start on a new line, and objects that follow them also start on a new line. Objects with an inline display property follow on from the right of the previous object, only dropping to the next line if they would extend past the right margin. Also, if there's room, objects following after an inline object will also display to the right of it.

The tablecell and valign Classes

Sometimes it can be helpful to give an object the properties of a table cell. For example, when used in a table cell, the vertical-align property mimics the deprecated HTML valign property, so it can be used to vertically center objects inside other objects, like this:

```
<div class='tablecell valignmid'>
    This text is vertically centered
</div>
```

You can also use the valigntop and valignbot classes in table cells.

The Classes

```
.visible   { visibility:visible;       }
.invisible { visibility:hidden;        }
.hidden    { display    :none;         }
.block     { display    :block;        }
.inline    { display    :inline;       }
.tablecell { display    :table-cell;   }
.valigntop { vertical-align:top;       }
.valignmid { vertical-align:middle;    }
.valignbot { vertical-align:bottom;    }
```

Scroll Bars

Using the recipes in this group, you can decide whether and how to display scroll bars on an object that supports them. In Figure 24-11, an excerpt from a poem by William Blake is displayed in three different ways. The first instance uses forced vertical and horizontal scroll bars, the second uses no scroll bars, and the third uses automatic scroll bars—therefore, only the vertical scroll bar is visible.

Classes and Properties

scroll scroll_a scroll_h scroll_l scroll_la scroll_lh scroll_f	Class to set the overflow property (and hence the scrolling) of an object (scroll), plus classes to do so only if the object is actively being clicked (scroll_a) or hovered over (scroll_h), and another three classes to set the scroll bars only for any links within the object (scroll_l), any links within the object that are actively being clicked (scroll_la), and any links within the object that are being hovered over (scroll_lh), or when the object has focus (scroll_f)
noscroll (etc...)	Class to set the overflow property of an object to hidden, and therefore remove any scroll bars
nooverflow (etc...)	Class that is an alias of noscroll, and does exactly the same
autoscroll (etc...)	Class to set the overflow property of an object to auto, and therefore show only those scroll bars needed to view the object's contents
overflow (etc...)	Class that is an alias of autoscroll, and does exactly the same
overflow	Property of an object to specify whether contents are allowed to overflow, and if so, how

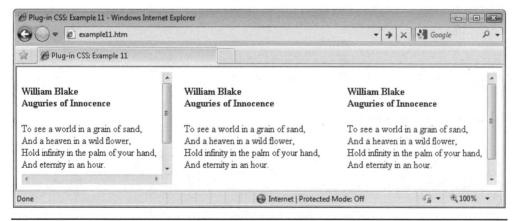

FIGURE 24-11 Use these classes to choose the types of scroll bars you want.

About the Classes

These classes let you specify what to do with any content that would otherwise overflow the bounds of its containing object. You can choose to force the display of both vertical and horizontal scroll bars with the scroll class, to hide any overflow with the noscroll (or nooverflow) class, or to let the browser choose whether and which scroll bars to use with the autoscroll (or overflow) class.

The standard suffixes of _a, _h, _l, _la, and _lh are also supported to apply the change only when the mouse is hovering over an object or it is being clicked, or to apply the setting only to links within the object. There is also a new suffix available that hasn't been seen before, _f, which is available on classes such as this that may apply to input elements. With it, you can apply the setting only to an element that has focus, such as an <input> or <textarea> that has been clicked.

How to Use Them

There are three different types of scroll bar classes: scroll, noscroll (also called nooverflow), and autoscroll (also called overflow). Once you have decided which to apply to an object and (optionally) whether to use any suffix to control the way the setting is applied, simply embed the class name as an argument in the class='...' section of the object declaration, like this:

```
<div class='autoscroll'>
   The contents goes here
</div>
```

Alternatively, scroll bars are actually only required on an object when you want to scroll it, so you could choose to only display them when the mouse passes over scrollable text, like this:

```
<div class='autoscroll_h'>
   The contents goes here
</div>
```

Or maybe you have created a <textarea> field and only want scroll bars to appear when the user clicks into it to begin typing, which you can do using the _f suffix, like this:

```
<textarea rows='5' cols='50' class='noscroll autoscroll_f'>
   The contents goes here
</textarea>
```

In this case, it's important that the noscroll class is used in conjunction with autoscroll_f so that the scroll bars will disappear when the object no longer has focus.

Here's the HTML used to produce the screen grab in Figure 24-11:

```
<div class='scroll leftfloat' style='width:250px; height:180px;'>
   <h4>William Blake<br />Auguries of Innocence</h4>
   To see a world in a grain of sand,<br />
   And a heaven in a wild flower,<br />
   Hold infinity in the palm of your hand,<br />
   And eternity in an hour.<br /><br />
```

```
   A robin redbreast in a cage<br />
   Puts all heaven in a rage.
</div>

<div class='noscroll autoscroll_h leftfloat'
   style='width:250px; height:180px; padding-left:20px'>
   <h4>William Blake<br />Auguries of Innocence</h4>
   To see a world in a grain of sand,<br />
   And a heaven in a wild flower,<br />
   Hold infinity in the palm of your hand,<br />
   And eternity in an hour.<br /><br />
   A robin redbreast in a cage<br />
   Puts all heaven in a rage.
</div>

<div class='autoscroll'
   style='width:250px; height:180px; padding-left:20px'>
   <h4>William Blake<br />Auguries of Innocence</h4>
   To see a world in a grain of sand,<br />
   And a heaven in a wild flower,<br />
   Hold infinity in the palm of your hand,<br />
   And eternity in an hour.<br /><br />
   A robin redbreast in a cage<br />
   Puts all heaven in a rage.
</div>
```

The first instance of the poem has forced scroll bars, the second has none (but if the mouse is passed over it, an automatic vertical scroll bar will appear), and the third has an automatic vertical scroll bar.

The Classes

```
.scroll,              .scroll_a:active,      .scroll_h:hover,
.scroll_l a,          .scroll_la a:active,   .scroll_lh a:hover,
.scroll_f:focus
   { overflow:scroll; }
.noscroll,            .noscroll_a:active,    .noscroll_h:hover,
.noscroll_l a,        .noscroll_la a:active, .noscroll_lh a:hover,
.nooverflow,          .nooverflow_a:active,  .nooverflow_h:hover,
.nooverflow_l a,      .nooverflow_la a:active, .nooverflow_lh a:hover,
.noscroll_f:focus,    .nooverflow_f:focus
   { overflow:hidden; }
.autoscroll,          .autoscroll_a:active,  .autoscroll_h:hover,
.autoscroll_l a,      .autoscroll_la a:active, .autoscroll_lh a:hover,
.overflow,            .overflow_a:active,    .overflow_h:hover,
.overflow_l a,        .overflow_la a:active, .overflow_lh a:hover,
.autoscroll_f:focus,  .overflow_f:focus
   { overflow:auto;   }
```

Maximum Sizes

Using these classes, you can resize an object to better fill the amount of space allocated to it by its containing object. For example, in Figure 24-12 a 250 by 167–pixel photograph is displayed in four different ways within a 500 by 100–pixel boundary, using the `nooverflow` class to prevent any part of the image from leaking outside of the boundary.

The first image is displayed using its default dimensions, but as it is taller than 100 pixels, the bottom half is cut off.

The second image has had its width increased to that of the containing object and, because no new size was specified for its height, the image has also been resized vertically by the browser to retain the same relative dimensions. This time most of the image is now missing.

The third image has had its height set to that of the containing object and its width has been accordingly reduced by the browser. Since the photo's width is less than the width of the containing object, the entire image is visible.

Lastly, the final image has been resized to the width and height of the containing object and, while the whole image is in view, it has been horizontally stretched.

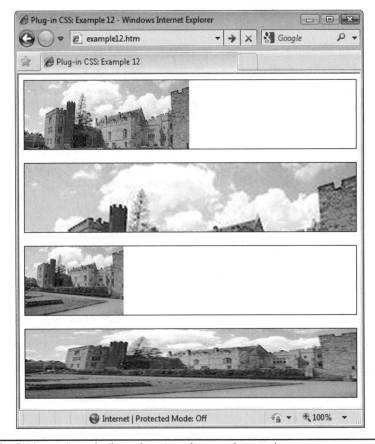

Figure 24-12 Setting an image's dimensions to various maximum values

Classes and Properties

maxwidth maxwidth_a maxwidth_h maxwidth_l maxwidth_la maxwidth_lh	Class to set an object's width to that of its containing object (maxwidth), plus classes to do so only if the object is actively being clicked (maxwidth_a) or hovered over (maxwidth_h), and another three classes to set the width only for any links within the object (maxwidth_l), any links within the object that are actively being clicked (maxwidth_la), and any links within the object that are being hovered over (maxwidth_lh)
maxheight (etc...)	Class to set an object's height to that of its containing object
maxsize (etc...)	Class to set both an object's width and height to those of its containing object
width	Property for changing the width of an object
height	Property for changing the height of an object

About the Classes

These classes apply a value of 100 percent to whichever property they refer, allowing you to set the width, height, or both dimensions to those of the containing object. Where the object being resized is an image, if only one dimension is resized, the other will be automatically resized by the browser to retain the same aspect ratio.

The CSS rules used are either or both of the following:

```
width:100%;
height:100%;
```

You can also use the standard suffixes to apply the change only when an object is hovered over or clicked, or only to links within an object.

How to Use Them

To change any dimensions of an object to those of its containing object, use one of the maxwidth, maxheight, or maxsize classes, like this:

```
<img src='photo3.jpg' class='maxwidth' />
```

Or, for example, if you want the object to change only its height when hovered over, you would use code such as this:

```
<img src='photo3.jpg' class='maxheight_h' />
```

To change both dimensions at once, you would use the maxsize class, like this:

```
<img src='photo3.jpg' class='maxsize' />
```

Here's the HTML used to create Figure 24-12:

```
<div class='nooverflow' style='width:500px; height:100px;
   border:1px solid;'>
   <img src='photo3.jpg' />
</div><br />
```

PART IV

```
<div class='nooverflow' style='width:500px; height:100px;
    border:1px solid;'>
    <img src='photo3.jpg' class='maxwidth' />
</div><br />

<div class='nooverflow' style='width:500px; height:100px;
    border:1px solid;'>
    <img src='photo3.jpg' class='maxheight' />
</div><br />

<div class='nooverflow' style='width:500px; height:100px;
    border:1px solid;'>
    <img src='photo3.jpg' class='maxsize' />
</div>
```

As always, this example file and its images are available for download from the companion web site at *webdeveloperscookbook.com*.

The Classes

```
.maxwidth,          .maxwidth_a:active,     .maxwidth_h:hover,
.maxwidth_l a,      .maxwidth_la a:active,  .maxwidth_lh a:hover
    { width :100%; }
.maxheight,         .maxheight_a:active,    .maxheight_h:hover
.maxheight_l a,     .maxheight_la a:active, .maxheight_lh a:hover
    { height:100%; }
.maxsize,           .maxsize_a:active,      .maxsize_h:hover,
.maxsize_l a,       .maxsize_la a:active,   .maxsize_lh a:hover
    { height:100%; width:100%; }
```

Location

The classes in recipe group 13 offer a variety of absolute and relative positioning functions. For example, in Figure 24-13 the `totop`, `tobottom`, `toleft`, and `toright` classes have been used to place four images in the corners of their containing object.

Classes and Properties

totop	Class to move an object to the top edge of its container
tobottom	Class to move an object to the bottom edge of its container
toleft	Class to move an object to the left edge of its container
toright	Class to move an object to the right edge of its container
leftby0 leftby0_h	Class to move an object left by 0 pixels (or move it to the left edge of the containing object); the _h suffix is used for applying the property only when it is hovered over
leftby5 – leftby100 (etc...)	Classes to move an object left by a value of 5 or from 10 through 100 pixels in steps of 10; the _h suffix is used for applying the property only when it is hovered over

rightby0 – rightby100 (etc...)	Classes – as the leftby... classes but moves the object right
upby0 – upby100 (etc...)	Classes – as the leftby... classes but moves the object up
downby0 – downby100 (etc...)	Classes – as the leftby... classes but moves the object down
top	Property for changing the vertical distance of an object from the top of its container, or for moving an object by relative vertical amounts
bottom	Property for changing the vertical distance of an object from the bottom of its container, or for moving an object by relative vertical amounts
left	Property for changing the vertical distance of an object from the left of its container, or for moving an object by relative horizontal amounts
right	Property for changing the vertical distance of an object from the right of its container, or for moving an object by relative horizontal amounts

About the Classes

These classes access the top, bottom, left, and right properties of an object to either place it in an absolute position or move it by a relative amount. The _h suffix of the class names is supported to apply the change only when an object is hovered over, while the other suffixes are not supported, since it is unlikely they would ever be used.

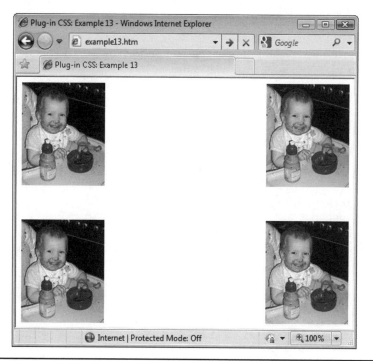

FIGURE 24-13   Moving images to the four corners of their containing object

Some of the CSS rules used are similar to the following examples:

```
top:20px;
left:-5px;
right:0px;
bottom:50px;
```

How to Use Them

To position an object against one or more edges of its containing object, you can use code such as the following, which was used to create Figure 24-13:

```
<div class='relative' style='width:500px; height:350px;'>
    <img class='absolute toleft totop'    src='photo4.jpg' />
    <img class='absolute toright totop'   src='photo4.jpg' />
    <img class='absolute toleft tobottom' src='photo4.jpg' />
    <img class='absolute toright tobottom' src='photo4.jpg' />
</div>
```

This example creates a container out of a <div>, which is given a position property of relative so it is no longer static (the default). Therefore, all the absolute objects within it will place themselves relative to it.

Inside the <div>, the classes are used in pairs to place each of the photographs in the four corners of the parent object.

Moving Objects by Relative Amounts

You can also move objects relative to their current position by 5 pixels, or any amount between 10 and 100 pixels in steps of 10, like this:

```
<img class='rightby50 downby50' src='image.jpg' />
```

This example moves the object down and to the right by 50 pixels. If the object doesn't already have a position, it will be placed 50 pixels down from the top and in from the left edge of its containing object.

The Classes

```
.totop,     .totop_h:hover   { top    :0px; }
.tobottom,  .tobottom_h:hover { bottom:0px; }
.toleft,    .toleft_h:hover  { left   :0px; }
.toright,   .toright_h:hover { right  :0px; }

.leftby0,   .leftby0_h:hover,
.rightby0,  .rightby0_h:hover { left:0px;   }
.leftby5,   .leftby5_h:hover  { left:-5px;  }
.leftby10,  .leftby10_h:hover { left:-10px; }
.leftby20,  .leftby20_h:hover { left:-20px; }
.leftby30,  .leftby30_h:hover { left:-30px; }
.leftby40,  .leftby40_h:hover { left:-40px; }
.leftby50,  .leftby50_h:hover { left:-50px; }
.leftby60,  .leftby60_h:hover { left:-60px; }
```

```
.leftby70,   .leftby70_h:hover  { left:-70px;  }
.leftby80,   .leftby80_h:hover  { left:-80px;  }
.leftby90,   .leftby90_h:hover  { left:-90px;  }
.leftby100,  .leftby100_h:hover { left:-100px; }

.rightby5,   .rightby5_h:hover    { left:5px;    }
.rightby10,  .rightby10_h:hover   { left:10px;   }
.rightby20,  .rightby20_h:hover   { left:20px;   }
.rightby30,  .rightby30_h:hover   { left:30px;   }
.rightby40,  .rightby40_h:hover   { left:40px;   }
.rightby50,  .rightby50_h:hover   { left:50px;   }
.rightby60,  .rightby60_h:hover   { left:60px;   }
.rightby70,  .rightby70_h:hover   { left:70px;   }
.rightby80,  .rightby80_h:hover   { left:80px;   }
.rightby90,  .rightby90_h:hover   { left:90px;   }
.rightby100, .rightby100_h:hover  { left:100px;  }

.upby0,    .upby0_h:hover,
.downby0,  .downby0_h:hover  { top:0px;    }
.upby5,    .upby5_h:hover    { top:-5px;   }
.upby10,   .upby10_h:hover   { top:-10px;  }
.upby20,   .upby20_h:hover   { top:-20px;  }
.upby30,   .upby30_h:hover   { top:-30px;  }
.upby40,   .upby40_h:hover   { top:-40px;  }
.upby50,   .upby50_h:hover   { top:-50px;  }
.upby60,   .upby60_h:hover   { top:-60px;  }
.upby70,   .upby70_h:hover   { top:-70px;  }
.upby80,   .upby80_h:hover   { top:-80px;  }
.upby90,   .upby90_h:hover   { top:-90px;  }
.upby100,  .upby100_h:hover  { top:-100px; }

.downby5,   .downby5_h:hover    { top:5px;    }
.downby10,  .downby10_h:hover   { top:10px;   }
.downby20,  .downby20_h:hover   { top:20px;   }
.downby30,  .downby30_h:hover   { top:30px;   }
.downby40,  .downby40_h:hover   { top:40px;   }
.downby50,  .downby50_h:hover   { top:50px;   }
.downby60,  .downby60_h:hover   { top:60px;   }
.downby70,  .downby70_h:hover   { top:70px;   }
.downby80,  .downby80_h:hover   { top:80px;   }
.downby90,  .downby90_h:hover   { top:90px;   }
.downby100, .downby100_h:hover  { top:100px;  }
```

Selective Margins

Using the classes in this group of recipes, you can specify or change any of the four margins of an object by 5 pixels, or by any amount between 10 and 100 pixels, in steps of 10. In Figure 24-14, 11 <div> tags have been created, each one resting on the left edge of the browser, but using classes of leftmargin5_h through leftmargin100_h to indent them by the specified amount when the mouse passes over. In the screen grab, the mouse is currently over the <div> using the leftmargin70_h class.

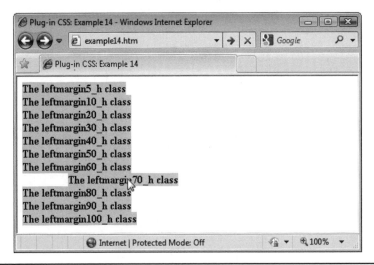

FIGURE 24-14   A collection of objects set to indent by differing amounts when hovered over

Classes and Properties

leftmargin0 leftmargin0_h	Class to set the left margin of an object to zero pixels, the _h suffix is used for applying the property only when it is hovered over
leftmargin5 – lefmargin100 (etc...)	Classes to set the left margin of an object to 5 pixels, or from 10 through 100 pixels in steps of 10
rightmargin0 (etc...)	Class – as leftmargin0 but for the right margin
topmargin0 (etc...)	Class – as leftmargin0 but for the top margin
bottommargin0 (etc...)	Class – as leftmargin0 but for the bottom margin
margin-left	Property to change an object's left margin
margin-right	Property to change an object's right margin
margin-top	Property to change an object's top margin
margin-bottom	Property to change an object's bottom margin

About the Classes

With these classes, you can change the margins of an object by amounts between 0 and 100 pixels, in steps of 10, and also by 5 pixels. The _h suffix for the classes is supported to change a property only when it is being hovered over. The other standard suffixes are not available since they are highly unlikely to be used.

Some of the CSS rules used are similar to the following examples:

```
margin-left:10px;
margin-right:-10px;
margin-top:20px;
margin-bottom:0px;
```

How to Use Them

To use these classes, refer to the one you need by placing its name in the `class='...'` argument of an HTML tag, like this:

```
<div class='leftmargin30'>This text is indented by 30 pixels</div>
```

You can also apply the hover versions of these classes, for example, enabling you to create professional-looking animations for menus, like this:

```
<div class='leftmargin10 leftmargin20_h'>Menu Item 1</div>
<div class='leftmargin10 leftmargin20_h'>Menu Item 2</div>
<div class='leftmargin10 leftmargin20_h'>Menu Item 3</div>
```

Following is the code used to create the screen shown in Figure 24-14:

```
<span class='leftmargin5_h lime_b'>The leftmargin5_h class</span><br />
<span class='leftmargin10_h lime_b'>The leftmargin10_h class</span><br />
<span class='leftmargin20_h lime_b'>The leftmargin20_h class</span><br />
<span class='leftmargin30_h lime_b'>The leftmargin30_h class</span><br />
<span class='leftmargin40_h lime_b'>The leftmargin40_h class</span><br />
<span class='leftmargin50_h lime_b'>The leftmargin50_h class</span><br />
<span class='leftmargin60_h lime_b'>The leftmargin60_h class</span><br />
<span class='leftmargin70_h lime_b'>The leftmargin70_h class</span><br />
<span class='leftmargin80_h lime_b'>The leftmargin80_h class</span><br />
<span class='leftmargin90_h lime_b'>The leftmargin90_h class</span><br />
<span class='leftmargin100_h lime_b'>The leftmargin100_h class</span>
```

Each item has a background fill color of lime green, is aligned with the left side of the browser, and indents by the number of pixels specified in the class name it uses when the mouse passes over it.

Margins are external to objects and are therefore invisible, as can be seen in Figure 24-14, where the lime green background color has not been apportioned to the margin area of the hovered element.

The Classes

```
.leftmargin0,     .leftmargin0_h:hover    { margin-left:0px;    }
.leftmargin5,     .leftmargin5_h:hover    { margin-left:5px;    }
.leftmargin10,    .leftmargin10_h:hover   { margin-left:10px;   }
.leftmargin20,    .leftmargin20_h:hover   { margin-left:20px;   }
.leftmargin30,    .leftmargin30_h:hover   { margin-left:30px;   }
.leftmargin40,    .leftmargin40_h:hover   { margin-left:40px;   }
.leftmargin50,    .leftmargin50_h:hover   { margin-left:50px;   }
.leftmargin60,    .leftmargin60_h:hover   { margin-left:60px;   }
.leftmargin70,    .leftmargin70_h:hover   { margin-left:70px;   }
.leftmargin80,    .leftmargin80_h:hover   { margin-left:80px;   }
.leftmargin90,    .leftmargin90_h:hover   { margin-left:90px;   }
.leftmargin100,   .leftmargin100_h:hover  { margin-left:100px;  }

.rightmargin0,    .rightmargin0_h:hover   { margin-right:0px;   }
.rightmargin5,    .rightmargin5_h:hover   { margin-right:5px;   }
.rightmargin10,   .rightmargin10_h:hover  { margin-right:10px;  }
```

PART IV

```
.rightmargin20,   .rightmargin20_h:hover   { margin-right:20px;   }
.rightmargin30,   .rightmargin30_h:hover   { margin-right:30px;   }
.rightmargin40,   .rightmargin40_h:hover   { margin-right:40px;   }
.rightmargin50,   .rightmargin50_h:hover   { margin-right:50px;   }
.rightmargin60,   .rightmargin60_h:hover   { margin-right:60px;   }
.rightmargin70,   .rightmargin70_h:hover   { margin-right:70px;   }
.rightmargin80,   .rightmargin80_h:hover   { margin-right:80px;   }
.rightmargin90,   .rightmargin90_h:hover   { margin-right:90px;   }
.rightmargin100,  .rightmargin100_h:hover  { margin-right:100px;  }

.topmargin0,      .topmargin0_h:hover      { margin-top:0px;      }
.topmargin5,      .topmargin5_h:hover      { margin-top:5px;      }
.topmargin10,     .topmargin10_h:hover     { margin-top:10px;     }
.topmargin20,     .topmargin20_h:hover     { margin-top:20px;     }
.topmargin30,     .topmargin30_h:hover     { margin-top:30px;     }
.topmargin40,     .topmargin40_h:hover     { margin-top:40px;     }
.topmargin50,     .topmargin50_h:hover     { margin-top:50px;     }
.topmargin60,     .topmargin60_h:hover     { margin-top:60px;     }
.topmargin70,     .topmargin70_h:hover     { margin-top:70px;     }
.topmargin80,     .topmargin80_h:hover     { margin-top:80px;     }
.topmargin90,     .topmargin90_h:hover     { margin-top:90px;     }
.topmargin100,    .topmargin100_h:hover    { margin-top:100px;    }

.bottommargin0,    .bottommargin0_h:hover    { margin-bottom:0px;    }
.bottommargin5,    .bottommargin5_h:hover    { margin-bottom:5px;    }
.bottommargin10,   .bottommargin10_h:hover   { margin-bottom:10px;   }
.bottommargin20,   .bottommargin20_h:hover   { margin-bottom:20px;   }
.bottommargin30,   .bottommargin30_h:hover   { margin-bottom:30px;   }
.bottommargin40,   .bottommargin40_h:hover   { margin-bottom:40px;   }
.bottommargin50,   .bottommargin50_h:hover   { margin-bottom:50px;   }
.bottommargin60,   .bottommargin60_h:hover   { margin-bottom:60px;   }
.bottommargin70,   .bottommargin70_h:hover   { margin-bottom:70px;   }
.bottommargin80,   .bottommargin80_h:hover   { margin-bottom:80px;   }
.bottommargin90,   .bottommargin90_h:hover   { margin-bottom:90px;   }
.bottommargin100,  .bottommargin100_h:hover  { margin-bottom:100px;  }
```

Selective Padding

You've already seen the basic padding classes provided in Recipe 7. You can also use this collection of classes to give you even greater control over which edges to pad and by how much.

In Figure 24-15, a collection of <span> objects have been given varying `leftpadding.._h` properties. The mouse is currently over the one assigned a value of 90 pixels, which has therefore been indented by that amount.

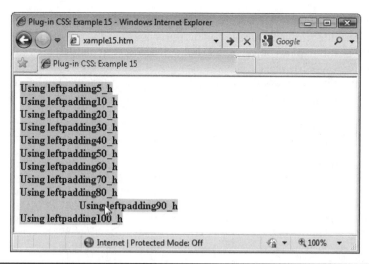

FIGURE 24-15   The left padding of these objects is set to differing amounts when hovered over.

Classes and Properties

leftpadding0 leftpadding0_h	Class to set the left padding of an object to zero pixels; the _h suffix is used for applying the property only when it is hovered over
leftpadding5 – lefpadding100 (etc...)	Classes to set the left padding of an object to 5 pixels, or from 10 through 100 pixels in steps of 10
rightpadding0 (etc...)	Class – as leftpadding0 but for the right padding
toppadding0 (etc...)	Class – as leftpadding0 but for the top padding
bottompadding0 (etc...)	Class – as leftpadding0 but for the bottom padding
padding-left	Property to change an object's left padding
padding-right	Property to change an object's right padding
padding-top	Property to change an object's top padding
padding-bottom	Property to change an object's bottom padding

About the Classes

With these classes, you can change the padding of an object by amounts between 0 and 100 pixels in steps of 10, and also by 5 pixels. The _h suffix for the classes is supported to change a property only when it is being hovered over. The other standard suffixes are not available since they are highly unlikely to be used.

Here are some examples of the CSS rules used by these classes:

```
padding-left:5px;
padding-right:20px;
padding-top:0px;
padding-bottom:-10px;
```

How to Use Them

These classes provide similar results to the margin classes in the previous recipe group, except that the padding of an object is internal to it and so the padded area assumes the properties of the rest of the object. This can be seen in Figure 24-15, in which the 90 pixels–wide padding that has been applied to the left side of the indented span has assumed the lime green background color of the object. Here is the code used to create the screen grab:

```
<span class='leftpadding5_h   lime_b'>Using leftpadding5_h  </span><br />
<span class='leftpadding10_h  lime_b'>Using leftpadding10_h </span><br />
<span class='leftpadding20_h  lime_b'>Using leftpadding20_h </span><br />
<span class='leftpadding30_h  lime_b'>Using leftpadding30_h </span><br />
<span class='leftpadding40_h  lime_b'>Using leftpadding40_h </span><br />
<span class='leftpadding50_h  lime_b'>Using leftpadding50_h </span><br />
<span class='leftpadding60_h  lime_b'>Using leftpadding60_h </span><br />
<span class='leftpadding70_h  lime_b'>Using leftpadding70_h </span><br />
<span class='leftpadding80_h  lime_b'>Using leftpadding80_h </span><br />
<span class='leftpadding90_h  lime_b'>Using leftpadding90_h </span><br />
<span class='leftpadding100_h lime_b'>Using leftpadding100_h</span>
```

Because of the padding property's ability to seem to stretch an object, you will see this feature used to good effect in Chapter 33, in conjunction with animated transitions to smoothly move menu items in and out again as the mouse hovers over them.

The Classes

```
.leftpadding0,     .leftpadding0_h:hover   { padding-left:0px;    }
.leftpadding5,     .leftpadding5_h:hover   { padding-left:5px;    }
.leftpadding10,    .leftpadding10_h:hover  { padding-left:10px;   }
.leftpadding20,    .leftpadding20_h:hover  { padding-left:20px;   }
.leftpadding30,    .leftpadding30_h:hover  { padding-left:30px;   }
.leftpadding40,    .leftpadding40_h:hover  { padding-left:40px;   }
.leftpadding50,    .leftpadding50_h:hover  { padding-left:50px;   }
.leftpadding60,    .leftpadding60_h:hover  { padding-left:60px;   }
.leftpadding70,    .leftpadding70_h:hover  { padding-left:70px;   }
.leftpadding80,    .leftpadding80_h:hover  { padding-left:80px;   }
.leftpadding90,    .leftpadding90_h:hover  { padding-left:90px;   }
.leftpadding100,   .leftpadding100_h:hover { padding-left:100px;  }

.rightpadding0,    .rightpadding0_h:hover   { padding-right:0px;    }
.rightpadding5,    .rightpadding5_h:hover   { padding-right:5px;    }
.rightpadding10,   .rightpadding10_h:hover  { padding-right:10px;   }
.rightpadding20,   .rightpadding20_h:hover  { padding-right:20px;   }
.rightpadding30,   .rightpadding30_h:hover  { padding-right:30px;   }
.rightpadding40,   .rightpadding40_h:hover  { padding-right:40px;   }
.rightpadding50,   .rightpadding50_h:hover  { padding-right:50px;   }
.rightpadding60,   .rightpadding60_h:hover  { padding-right:60px;   }
.rightpadding70,   .rightpadding70_h:hover  { padding-right:70px;   }
.rightpadding80,   .rightpadding80_h:hover  { padding-right:80px;   }
.rightpadding90,   .rightpadding90_h:hover  { padding-right:90px;   }
.rightpadding100,  .rightpadding100_h:hover { padding-right:100px;  }
```

```
.toppadding0,      .toppadding0_h:hover    { padding-top:0px;     }
.toppadding5,      .toppadding5_h:hover    { padding-top:5px;     }
.toppadding10,     .toppadding10_h:hover   { padding-top:10px;    }
.toppadding20,     .toppadding20_h:hover   { padding-top:20px;    }
.toppadding30,     .toppadding30_h:hover   { padding-top:30px;    }
.toppadding40,     .toppadding40_h:hover   { padding-top:40px;    }
.toppadding50,     .toppadding50_h:hover   { padding-top:50px;    }
.toppadding60,     .toppadding60_h:hover   { padding-top:60px;    }
.toppadding70,     .toppadding70_h:hover   { padding-top:70px;    }
.toppadding80,     .toppadding80_h:hover   { padding-top:80px;    }
.toppadding90,     .toppadding90_h:hover   { padding-top:90px;    }
.toppadding100,    .toppadding100_h:hover  { padding-top:100px;   }

.bottompadding0,     .bottompadding0_h:hover    { padding-bottom:0px;    }
.bottompadding5,     .bottompadding5_h:hover    { padding-bottom:5px;    }
.bottompadding10,    .bottompadding10_h:hover   { padding-bottom:10px;   }
.bottompadding20,    .bottompadding20_h:hover   { padding-bottom:20px;   }
.bottompadding30,    .bottompadding30_h:hover   { padding-bottom:30px;   }
.bottompadding40,    .bottompadding40_h:hover   { padding-bottom:40px;   }
.bottompadding50,    .bottompadding50_h:hover   { padding-bottom:50px;   }
.bottompadding60,    .bottompadding60_h:hover   { padding-bottom:60px;   }
.bottompadding70,    .bottompadding70_h:hover   { padding-bottom:70px;   }
.bottompadding80,    .bottompadding80_h:hover   { padding-bottom:80px;   }
.bottompadding90,    .bottompadding90_h:hover   { padding-bottom:90px;   }
.bottompadding100,   .bottompadding100_h:hover  { padding-bottom:100px;  }
```

RECIPE 16 Border Style

Using the classes in this recipe, you can choose exactly the kind of border you want for an object. For example, Figure 24-16 shows two rows of objects, the first of which has one of each different border style, while the second is the same but the border styles are activated only when the mouse passes over them. In the screen grab, the mouse is currently hovering over the object with grooved borders in the second row.

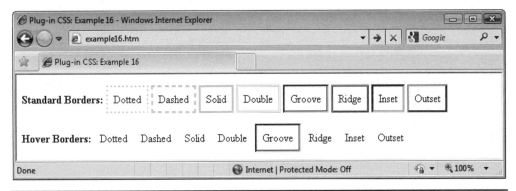

FIGURE 24-16   The eight different border style classes and their hover equivalents

Classes and Properties

bdotted bdotted_h	Classes to set an object's border style to dotted either immediately, or when hovered over
bdashed bdashed_h	Classes to set an object's border style to dashed either immediately, or when hovered over
bsolid bsolid_h	Classes to set an object's border style to solid either immediately, or when hovered over
bdouble bdouble_h	Classes to set an object's border style to double either immediately, or when hovered over
bgroove bgroove_h	Classes to set an object's border style to groove either immediately, or when hovered over—this effect depends on the border color
bridge bridge_h	Classes to set an object's border style to ridge either immediately, or when hovered over—this effect depends on the border color
binset binset_h	Classes to set an object's border style to inset either immediately, or when hovered over—this effect depends on the border color
boutset boutset_h	Classes to set an object's border style to outset either immediately, or when hovered over—this effect depends on the border color
border-style	Property for changing an object's border style

About the Classes

These classes enable the selection of all eight different types of border styles, which can be applied immediately, or only when hovered over. They achieve this effect using the border-style property, like this:

border-style:dashed;

How to Use Them

As soon as you choose a border style for an object, the border will be displayed, but some of the classes only show these styles at their best when a mid-range color is also supplied (see the border color recipe group).

To add a border to an object, refer to the border style in a class, like this:

```
<span class='bdouble'>Double</span>
```

Following is the HTML used to create the screen grab in Figure 24-16:

```
<br /><b>Standard Borders:</b>
<span class='bdotted padding blime'>Dotted</span>
<span class='bdashed padding blime'>Dashed</span>
<span class='bsolid  padding blime'>Solid </span>
<span class='bdouble padding blime'>Double</span>
<span class='bgroove padding blime'>Groove</span>
<span class='bridge  padding blime'>Ridge </span>
<span class='binset  padding blime'>Inset </span>
<span class='boutset padding blime'>Outset</span>
```

```
<br /><br /><br /><b>Hover Borders:</b>
<span class='bdotted_h padding blime'>Dotted</span>
<span class='bdashed_h padding blime'>Dashed</span>
<span class='bsolid_h  padding blime'>Solid </span>
<span class='bdouble_h padding blime'>Double</span>
<span class='bgroove_h padding blime'>Groove</span>
<span class='bridge_h  padding blime'>Ridge </span>
<span class='binset_h  padding blime'>Inset </span>
<span class='boutset_h padding blime'>Outset</span>
```

To create space around the text, the padding class has been used, as has the class blime (explained a little further on), which sets the border color to lime green in order to clearly display the different border types that rely on color.

The first set of objects displays the borders immediately, while the second does so only when hovered over.

The Classes

```
.bdotted, .bdotted_h:hover { border-style:dotted; }
.bdashed, .bdashed_h:hover { border-style:dashed; }
.bsolid,  .bsolid_h:hover  { border-style:solid;  }
.bdouble, .bdouble_h:hover { border-style:double; }
.bgroove, .bgroove_h:hover { border-style:groove; }
.bridge,  .bridge_h:hover  { border-style:ridge;  }
.binset,  .binset_h:hover  { border-style:inset;  }
.boutset, .boutset_h:hover { border-style:outset; }
```

Border Width

With these recipe classes, you can specify 10 different border widths either immediately or when the mouse hovers over an object. Figure 24-17 shows the same code from the previous example except that all the borders have been given widths of 10 pixels.

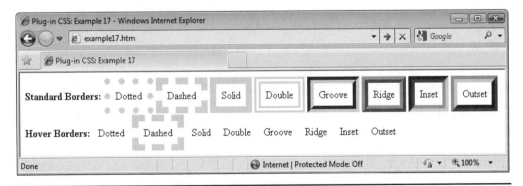

FIGURE 24-17   You can specify up to 10 different border widths with these classes.

Classes and Properties

`bwidth1` `bwidth1_h`	Classes to set an object's border width to 1 pixel either immediately or when hovered over
`bwidth2` `bwidth2_h`	Classes to set an object's border width to 2 pixels either immediately or when hovered over
`bwidth3` `bwidth3_h`	Classes to set an object's border width to 3 pixels either immediately or when hovered over
`bwidth4` `bwidth4_h`	Classes to set an object's border width to 4 pixels either immediately or when hovered over
`bwidth5` `bwidth5_h`	Classes to set an object's border width to 5 pixels either immediately or when hovered over
`bwidth10` `bwidth10_h`	Classes to set an object's border width to 10 pixels either immediately or when hovered over
`bwidth15` `bwidth15_h`	Classes to set an object's border width to 15 pixels either immediately or when hovered over
`bwidth20` `bwidth20_h`	Classes to set an object's border width to 20 pixels either immediately or when hovered over
`bwidth25` `bwidth25_h`	Classes to set an object's border width to 25 pixels either immediately or when hovered over
`bwidth50` `bwidth50_h`	Classes to set an object's border width to 50 pixels either immediately or when hovered over
`border-width`	Property for changing the width of a border

About the Classes

These classes let you change the width of a border to a value from 1 through 5 pixels, 10 through 25 pixels in steps of 5, or 50 pixels. You can also use the hover versions of the classes to apply the change only when an object is being hovered over by the mouse.

To achieve this effect, the classes use the `border-width` property, like this:

border-width:20px;

How to Use Them

Simply use the name of the class you need for the width you want in your HTML, like this:

```
<span class='bsolid'>This object has a solid border</span>
```

You can also use the hover versions of these classes, as with the following HTML, which was used to create Figure 24-17:

```
<br /><b>Standard Borders:</b>
<span class='bdotted bwidth10 padding blime'>Dotted</span>
<span class='bdashed bwidth10 padding blime'>Dashed</span>
<span class='bsolid  bwidth10 padding blime'>Solid </span>
<span class='bdouble bwidth10 padding blime'>Double</span>
<span class='bgroove bwidth10 padding blime'>Groove</span>
```

```
<span class='bridge  bwidth10 padding blime'>Ridge </span>
<span class='binset  bwidth10 padding blime'>Inset </span>
<span class='boutset bwidth10 padding blime'>Outset</span>

<br /><br /><br /><b>Hover Borders:</b>
<span class='bdotted_h bwidth10 padding blime'>Dotted</span>
<span class='bdashed_h bwidth10 padding blime'>Dashed</span>
<span class='bsolid_h  bwidth10 padding blime'>Solid </span>
<span class='bdouble_h bwidth10 padding blime'>Double</span>
<span class='bgroove_h bwidth10 padding blime'>Groove</span>
<span class='bridge_h  bwidth10 padding blime'>Ridge </span>
<span class='binset_h  bwidth10 padding blime'>Inset </span>
<span class='boutset_h bwidth10 padding blime'>Outset</span>
```

In each of these objects, a different border style is specified, with a width of 10 pixels and standard padding. Once again, the `blime` class (see the next section) has been used to set a border color that will show all the styles to their best effect.

The Classes

```
.bwidth1,   .bwidth1_h:hover  { border-width:1px;  }
.bwidth2,   .bwidth2_h:hover  { border-width:2px;  }
.bwidth3,   .bwidth3_h:hover  { border-width:3px;  }
.bwidth4,   .bwidth4_h:hover  { border-width:4px;  }
.bwidth5,   .bwidth5_h:hover  { border-width:5px;  }
.bwidth10,  .bwidth10_h:hover { border-width:10px; }
.bwidth15,  .bwidth15_h:hover { border-width:15px; }
.bwidth20,  .bwidth20_h:hover { border-width:20px; }
.bwidth25,  .bwidth25_h:hover { border-width:25px; }
.bwidth50,  .bwidth50_h:hover { border-width:50px; }
```

RECIPE 18 Border Color

With this final group of border classes, you can choose any of 21 different colors to apply to a border either immediately, or when it is moused over. Figure 24-18 expands on the example in the previous section to present two rows of objects using a variety of different border styles, widths, and colors. The second row of classes applies only when the mouse passes over an object. In the figure, it is currently over the Inset object.

Classes and Properties

baqua baqua_h bblack bblack_h bblue bblue_h bbrown bbrown_h bfuchsia bfuchsia_h bgold bgold_h bgray bgray_h bgreen bgreen_h bkhaki bkhaki_h blime blime_h bmaroon bmaroon_h bnavy bnavy_h bolive bolive_h borange borange_h bpink bpink_h bpurple bpurple_h bred bred_h bsilver bsilver_h bteal bteal_h bwhite bwhite_h byellow byellow_h	Classes to change the border color of an object either immediately or when it is moused over
Border-color	Property to change the border color of an object

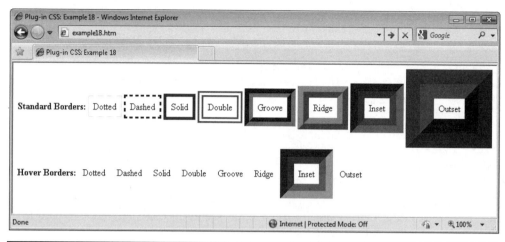

FIGURE 24-18   A selection of the different border types, widths, and colors available

About the Classes

These classes provide a wide range of colors that you can apply to borders either immediately or when they are moused over. The property that is manipulated is `border-color`, like this:

```
border-color:#c44;
```

How to Use Them

Using these color classes is as easy as putting their names within an object's `class='...'` argument, like this:

```
<span class='bbrown'>This object has a brown border</span>
```

In the following example HTML (which was used to create Figure 24-18), a variety of different colors has been used, along with different border styles and widths:

```
<br /><br /><br /><b>Standard Borders:</b>
<span class='bdotted bwidth1  padding baqua'>Dotted</span>
<span class='bdashed bwidth3  padding bblack'  >Dashed</span>
<span class='bsolid  bwidth5  padding bblue'   >Solid </span>
<span class='bdouble bwidth10 padding bbrown'  >Double</span>
<span class='bgroove bwidth15 padding bfuchsia'>Groove</span>
<span class='bridge  bwidth20 padding bgold'   >Ridge </span>
<span class='binset  bwidth25 padding bgray'   >Inset </span>
<span class='boutset bwidth50 padding bgreen'  >Outset</span>

<br /><br /><br /><br /><br /><br /><b>Hover Borders:</b>
<span class='bdotted_h bwidth1  padding bkhaki' >Dotted</span>
<span class='bdashed_h bwidth3  padding bmaroon'>Dashed</span>
<span class='bsolid_h  bwidth5  padding bnavy'  >Solid </span>
```

```
<span class='bdouble_h bwidth10 padding bolive' >Double</span>
<span class='bgroove_h bwidth15 padding borange'>Groove</span>
<span class='bridge_h  bwidth20 padding bpurple'>Ridge </span>
<span class='binset_h  bwidth25 padding bpink'  >Inset </span>
<span class='boutset_h bwidth50 padding bred'   >Outset</span>
```

The Classes

```
.baqua,     .baqua_h:hover    { border-color:#0ff; }
.bblack,    .bblack_h:hover   { border-color:#000; }
.bblue,     .bblue_h:hover    { border-color:#00f; }
.bbrown,    .bbrown_h:hover   { border-color:#c44; }
.bfuchsia,  .bfuchsia_h:hover { border-color:#f0f; }
.bgold,     .bgold_h:hover    { border-color:#fc0; }
.bgray,     .bgray_h:hover    { border-color:#888; }
.bgreen,    .bgreen_h:hover   { border-color:#080; }
.bkhaki,    .bkhaki_h:hover   { border-color:#cc8; }
.blime,     .blime_h:hover    { border-color:#0f0; }
.bmaroon,   .bmaroon_h:hover  { border-color:#800; }
.bnavy,     .bnavy_h:hover    { border-color:#008; }
.bolive,    .bolive_h:hover   { border-color:#880; }
.borange,   .borange_h:hover  { border-color:#f80; }
.bpink,     .bpink_h:hover    { border-color:#f88; }
.bpurple,   .bpurple_h:hover  { border-color:#808; }
.bred,      .bred_h:hover     { border-color:#f00; }
.bsilver,   .bsilver_h:hover  { border-color:#ccc; }
.bteal,     .bteal_h:hover    { border-color:#088; }
.bwhite,    .bwhite_h:hover   { border-color:#fff; }
.byellow,   .byellow_h:hover  { border-color:#ff0; }
```

RECIPE 19 No Outline

To enable people to tab through a document more easily, some browsers display a dotted outline around the object being focused on, as well as highlight it. This certainly helps make it clear which object has the focus, but as you can see in Figure 24-19 where Button 2 has the focus, the dotted border inset into the button destroys much of the button's 3D gradient effect.

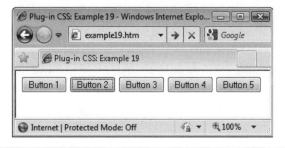

Figure 24-19   Button 2 shows a highlight and a dotted outline.

On the other hand, in Figure 24-20, Button 3 is now focused on, and because it is using the `nooutline` class, there is no dotted outline. As you can see, there is still a highlight around the button, which is sufficient to inform you that the button has the focus, and the button itself looks much cleaner as a result. And on a color monitor (rather than a grayscale printed page like this), it looks even better.

Classes and Properties

`nooutline`	Class to remove the dotted border from an object that has focus
`outline`	Property used by most browsers to enable or disable the outline
`border`	Property used by Firefox and other Mozilla-based browsers (in conjunction with the `::-moz-focus-inner` pseudo-class) to enable or disable the outline

About the Class

When applied to an object, this class prevents it from displaying a dotted outline when it has focus. This is achieved on most browsers with the `:focus` pseudo-class and the `outline` property, like this:

```
.nooutline:focus { outline:none; }
```

However, Firefox and other Mozilla-based browsers need to be handled differently, so the following alternative is used:

```
.nooutline::-moz-focus-inner { border:none; padding:1px 3px; }
```

When the outline is removed in a Firefox browser, it reduces the size of a button by the amount of the removed outline, so the padding property is updated to increase the button's size back again.

How to Use It

To prevent an object that has focus from displaying a dotted outline, just insert the `nooutline` class into the object's `class='...'` argument, like this:

```
<button class='nooutline'>Click me</button>
```

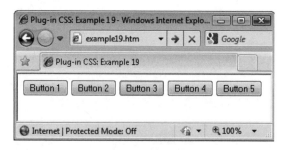

FIGURE 24-20   The dotted outline has been removed from Button 3, leaving only the highlight.

Here is the HTML used to create Figures 3-19 and 3-20. If you press the TAB key several times or click the buttons, you'll see that Button 3 does not show the dotted outline that the others display:

```
<button>Button 1</button>
<button>Button 2</button>
<button class='nooutline'>Button 3</button>
<button>Button 4</button>
<button>Button 5</button>
```

The Class

```
.nooutline:focus              { outline:none; }
.nooutline::-moz-focus-inner  { border :none; padding:1px 3px; }
```

CHAPTER 25

Text and Typography

This chapter features a wide range of powerful recipes for managing most aspects of using and presenting fonts. These include quick access to font families, embedding any of an additional 19 fonts courtesy of Google, changing text size alignment and styles, and adding colors and drop shadows.

There are also handy classes to transform your text, automatically add icons and other characters such as quotation marks, create professional drop-cap effects, and more. Between them, there are over 720 classes for doing almost everything you could want to do with text, without having to write your own CSS rules.

Fonts

Choosing a font for displaying text is very easy using the classes in this recipe group, as you only need to enter a short name into the `class` argument of an object. Plus, each font offers fallback fonts so that systems without the exact font you choose will display the closest match that they have. You can also decide when to enable the fonts since there are six versions of each class.

In Figure 25-1, all the available font classes have been used twice: once to display the associated fonts immediately, and again for mouse hover versions. In the second group of fonts, "Lucida Grande" is currently being hovered over.

FIGURE 25-1   A typical collection of fonts on a Windows computer

Classes and Properties

arial arial_a arial_h arial_l arial_la arial_lh	Classes to assign a font to an object (arial), to do so only when it is actively being clicked (arial_a), or when it is being hovered over (arial_h); also three classes to enable a font only for a link within the object (arial_l), a link within the object that is being clicked (arial_la), or a link within the object that is being hovered over (arial_lh)
arialb (etc...)	Class – the same as Arial, but for Arial Bold
arialn (etc...)	Class – the same as Arial, but for Arial Narrow
avant (etc...)	Class – the same as Arial, but for Avant Garde
bookman (etc...)	Class – the same as Arial, but for Bookman
century (etc...)	Class – the same as Arial, but for Century Gothic
copper (etc...)	Class – the same as Arial, but for Copperplate
comic (etc...)	Class – the same as Arial, but for Comic Sans MS
courier (etc...)	Class – the same as Arial, but for Courier
couriern (etc...)	Class – the same as Arial, but for Courier New
garamond (etc...)	Class – the same as Arial, but for Garamond
gill (etc...)	Class – the same as Arial, but for Gill Sans MT
georgia (etc...)	Class – the same as Arial, but for Georgia
helvetica (etc...)	Class – the same as Arial, but for Helvetica
impact (etc...)	Class – the same as Arial, but for Impact
lucida (etc...)	Class – the same as Arial, but for Lucida
lucidac (etc...)	Class – the same as Arial, but for Lucida Console
palatino (etc...)	Class – the same as Arial, but for Palatino
tahoma (etc...)	Class – the same as Arial, but for Tahoma
times (etc...)	Class – the same as Arial, but for Times
timesnr (etc...)	Class – the same as Arial, but for Times New Roman
trebuchet (etc...)	Class – the same as Arial, but for Trebuchet MS
verdana (etc...)	Class – the same as Arial, but for Verdana
font-family	Property used for changing font

About the Classes

These classes use the CSS font-family property to assign the font you choose. Fallback fonts are provided for each to ensure that if a computer doesn't have a particular font, it can at least display the closest one it does have.

For example, the copper class uses the following rule:

```
font-family:"Copperplate", "Copperplate Gothic Light", serif;
```

How to Use Them

To use a font class, enter its name in the `class` argument of an object. For example, to change to the Impact font, you could use HTML such as this:

```
<span class='impact'>Impact</span>
```

Or, to change a font only when the mouse hovers over the object, you might use this:

```
<span class='impact_h'>Impact</span>
```

Or you can combine classes so that, for example, to change the font of an object to Verdana, and then to Georgia when it is hovered over, you might use this:

```
<span class='verdana Georgia_h'>Impact</span>
```

You can also use the other class suffixes to enable a font only when it is actively clicked (*classname*_a), or when it is a link that is part of the object (*classname*_l), or when it is a clicked link that is part of the object (*classname*_la), or when it is a hovered link that is part of the object (*classname*_lh).

Here is the code used to create Figure 25-1:

```
<span class='arial'     >Arial</span>,
<span class='arialb'    >Arial Bold</span>,
<span class='arialn'    >Arial Narrow</span>,
<span class='avant'     >Avant Garde</span>
<span class='bookman'   >Bookman</span>
<span class='century'   >Century Gothic</span>
<span class='copper'    >Copperplate</span>
<span class='comic'     >Comic Sans MS</span>
<span class='courier'   >Courier</span>
<span class='couriern'  >Courier New</span>
<span class='garamond'  >Garamond</span>
<span class='gill'      >Gill Sans</span>
<span class='georgia'   >Georgia</span>
<span class='helvetica' >Helvetica</span>
<span class='impact'    >Impact</span>
<span class='lucida'    >Lucida Grande</span>
<span class='lucidacon' >Lucida Console</span>
<span class='palatino'  >Palatino</span>
<span class='tahoma'    >Tahoma</span>
<span class='times'     >Times</span>
<span class='timesnr'   >Times New Roman</span>
<span class='trebuchet' >Trebuchet MS</span>
<span class='verdana'   >Verdana</span><br /><br />

<span class='arial_h'    >Arial</span>,
<span class='arialb_h'   >Arial Bold</span>,
<span class='arialn_h'   >Arial Narrow</span>,
<span class='avant_h'    >Avant Garde</span>
<span class='bookman_h'  >Bookman</span>
<span class='century_h'  >Century Gothic</span>
<span class='copper_h'   >Copperplate</span>
<span class='comic_h'    >Comic Sans MS</span>
```

```
<span class='courie_hr'  >Courier</span>
<span class='couriern_h' >Courier New</span>
<span class='garamond_h' >Garamond</span>
<span class='gill_h'     >Gill Sans</span>
<span class='georgia_h'  >Georgia</span>
<span class='helvetica_h'>Helvetica</span>
<span class='impact_h'   >Impact</span>
<span class='lucida_h   '>Lucida Grande</span>
<span class='lucidacon_h'>Lucida Console</span>
<span class='palatino_h' >Palatino</span>
<span class='tahoma_h'   >Tahoma</span>
<span class='times_h'    >Times</span>
<span class='timesnr_h'  >Times New Roman</span>
<span class='trebuchet_h'>Trebuchet MS</span>
<span class='verdana_h'  >Verdana</span>
```

The Classes

```
.arial,         .arial_a:active,      .arial_h:hover,
.arial_l a,     .arial_la a:active,   .arial_lh a:hover
   { font-family:"Arial", sans-serif; }
.arialb,        .arialb_a:active,     .arialb_h:hover,
.arialb_l a,    .arialb_la a:active,  .arialb_lh a:hover
   { font-family:"Arial Black", sans-serif; }
.arialn,        .arialn_a:active,     .arialn_h:hover,
.arialn_l a,    .arialn_la a:active,  .arialbn_lh a:hover
   { font-family:"Arial Narrow", sans-serif; }
.avant,         .avant_a:active,      .avant_h:hover,
.avant_l a,     .avant_la a:active,   .avant_lh a:hover
   { font-family:"Avant Garde", sans-serif; }
.bookman,       .bookman_a:active,    .bookman_h:hover,
.bookman_l a,   .bookman_la a:active, .bookman_lh a:hover
   { font-family:"Bookman", "Bookman Old Style", serif; }
.century,       .century_a:active,    .century_h:hover,
.century_l a,   .century_la a:active, .century_lh a:hover
   { font-family:"Century Gothic", sans-serif; }
.copper,        .copper_a:active,     .copper_h:hover,
.copper_l a,    .copper_la a:active,  .copper_lh a:hover
   { font-family:"Copperplate", "Copperplate Gothic Light", serif; }
.comic,         .comic_a:active,      .comic_h:hover,
.comic_l a,     .comic_la a:active,   .comic_lh a:hover
   { font-family:"Comic Sans MS", cursive; }
.courier,       .courier_a:active,    .courier_h:hover,
.courier_l a,   .courier_la a:active, .courier_lh a:hover
   { font-family:"Courier", monospace; }
.couriern,      .couriern_a:active,   .couriern_h:hover,
.couriern_l a,  .couriern_la a:active, .couriern_lh a:hover
   { font-family:"Courier New", monospace; }
.garamond,      .garamond_a:active,   .garamond_h:hover,
.garamond_l a,  .garamond_la a:active, .garamond_lh a:hover
   { font-family:"Garamond", serif; }
.gill,          .gill_a:active,       .gill_h:hover,
.gill_l a,      .gill_la a:active,    .gill_lh a:hover
   { font-family:"Gill Sans", "Gill Sans MT", sans-serif; }
```

```
.georgia,        .georgia_a:active,      .georgia_h:hover,
.georgia_l a,    .georgia_la a:active,   .georgia_lh a:hover
   { font-family:"Georgia", serif; }
.helvetica,      .helvetica_a:active,    .helvetica_h:hover,
.helvetica_l a, .helvetica_la a:active, .helvetica_lh a:hover
   { font-family:"Helvetica", sans-serif; }
.impact,         .impact_a:active,       .impact_h:hover,
.impact_l a,     .impact_la a:active,    .impact_lh a:hover
   { font-family:"Impact", fantasy; }
.lucida,         .lucida_a:active,       .lucida_h:hover,
.lucida_l a,     .lucida_la a:active,    .lucida_lh a:hover
   { font-family:"Lucida Grande", "Lucida Sans Unicode", sans-serif; }
.lucidac,        .lucidac_a:active,      .lucidac_h:hover,
.lucidac_l a,    .lucidac_la a:active,   .lucidac_lh a:hover
   { font-family:"Lucida Console", monospace; }
.palatino,       .palatino_a:active,     .palatino_h:hover,
.palatino_l a,   .palatino_la a:active,  .palatino_lh a:hover
   { font-family:"Palatino", "Palatino Linotype", serif; }
.tahoma,         .tahoma_a:active,       .tahoma_h:hover,
.tahoma_l a,     .tahoma_la a:active,    .tahoma_lh a:hover
   { font-family:"Tahoma", sans-serif; }
.times,          .times_a:active,        .times_h:hover,
.times_l a,      .times_la a:active,     .times_lh a:hover
   { font-family:"Times", serif; }
.timesnr,        .timesnr_a:active,      .timesnr_h:hover,
.timesnr_l a,    .timesnr_la a:active,   .timesnr_lh a:hover
   { font-family:"Times New Roman", serif; }
.trebuchet,      .trebuchet_a:active,    .trebuchet_h:hover,
.trebuchet_l a, .trebuchet_la a:active, .trebuchet_lh a:hover
   { font-family:"Trebuchet MS", sans-serif; }
.verdana,        .verdana_a:active,      .verdana_h:hover,
.verdana_l a,    .verdana_la a:active,   .verdana_lh a:hover
   { font-family:"Verdana", sans-serif; }
```

Font Styles

Choosing font styles with CSS can involve up to three different properties. But when you want to choose font styles such as bold, italic, or underline, these classes are much simpler. Figure 25-2 shows the various styles being applied one at a time until all are employed.

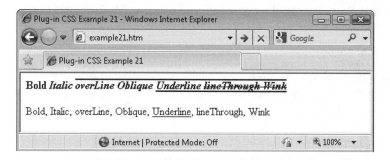

FIGURE 25-2   The various font styles supported by these classes

(Internet Explorer doesn't support the `blink` property, so on that browser, any blinking text is shown in bold).

In the second row, the text is set to change its font only when hovered over, as is the case with the word Underline.

Classes and Properties

b b_a b_h b_l b_la b_lh	Classes to assign a font to bold (b), to do so only when it is actively being clicked (b_a), or when it is being hovered over (b_h); also three classes to enable bold for a link within the object (b_l), a link within the object that is being clicked (b_la), or a link within the object that is being hovered over (b_lh)
i (etc...)	Class – as b but to enable italic text
l (etc...)	Class – as b but to enable overline text
n (etc...)	Class – as b but to restore normal styles
o (etc...)	Class – as b but to enable oblique text
u (etc...)	Class – as b but to enable underlined text
t (etc...)	Class – as b but to enable linethrough text
w (etc...)	Class – as b but to enable winking (or blinking) text, or bold in Internet Explorer
font-weight	Property for changing the weight of a font
font-style	Property for changing the style of a font
text-decoration	Property for adding a decoration to a font

About the Classes

These classes use three different CSS rules to create different font styles. They also support the suffixes such as _h to apply the new style only when an object is hovered over, and so on. For example, here are the CSS rules used to restore a font's styling to normal:

```
font-style:normal;
font-weight:normal;
text-decoration:none;
```

Out of all modern browsers, only Internet Explorer will not display blinking text, so the bold attribute is selected instead. This is achieved using a CSS "hack" that only Internet Explorer can see, like this:

```
font-weight:bold\0;
```

By adding the \0 to the end of the rule, all browsers except Internet Explorer will ignore the rule, while IE will accept the rule and ignore the \0. This is also the case with the current preview version of IE 9.

How to Use Them

These font class names have been kept to single letters because they are frequently used, so it saves on typing and keeps class arguments short. To use them, just add the class letter (or letter plus suffix) to a class argument, like the following, which sets both an Arial font and italic styling:

```
<span class='arial i'>This text is in an italic Arial font</span>
```

This is the HTML used to create the screen grab in Figure 25-2:

```
<span class='b'>Bold
<span class='i'>Italic
<span class='l'>overLine
<span class='o'>Oblique
<span class='u'>Underline
<span class='t'>lineThrough
<span class='w'>Wink
</span></span></span></span></span></span></span><br /><br />

<span class='b_h'>Bold</span>,
<span class='i_h'>Italic</span>,
<span class='l_h'>overLine</span>,
<span class='o_h'>Oblique</span>,
<span class='u_h'>Underline</span>,
<span class='t_h'>lineThrough</span>,
<span class='w_h'>Wink</span>
```

The Classes

```
.b,       .b_a:active,     .b_h:hover,
.b_l a, .b_la a:active, .b_lh a:hover { font-weight:bold; }
.i,       .i_a:active,     .i_h:hover,
.i_l a, .i_la a:active, .i_lh a:hover { font-style:italic; }
.l,       .l_a:active,     .l_h:hover,
.l_l a, .l_la a:active, .l_lh a:hover { text-decoration:overline; }
.n,       .n_a:active,     .n_h:hover,
.n_l a, .n_la a:active, .n_lh a:hover { font-style:normal;
                                        font-weight:normal;
                                        text-decoration:none; }
.o,       .o_a:active,     .o_h:hover,
.o_l a, .o_la a:active, .o_lh a:hover { font-style:oblique; }
.u,       .u_a:active,     .u_h:hover,
.u_l a, .u_la a:active, .u_lh a:hover { text-decoration:underline; }
.t,       .t_a:active,     .t_h:hover,
.t_l a, .t_la a:active, .t_lh a:hover { text-decoration:line-through; }
.w,       .w_a:active,     .w_h:hover,
.w_l a, .w_la a:active, .w_lh a:hover { text-decoration:blink;
                                        font-weight:bold\0;  /* IE */ }
```

Text Alignment

With these classes, you can choose between applying left, center, right, or full justification, as shown in Figure 25-3, which includes one example of each type of justification (taken from Charles Dickens' novel, *A Tale of Two Cities*):

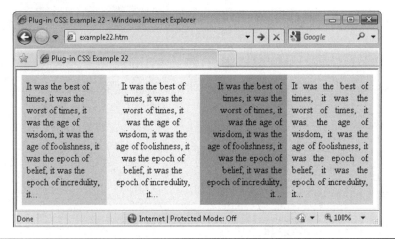

FIGURE 25-3   The four different types of text justification: left, center, right, and full.

Classes and Properties

`leftjustify`
`leftjustify_a`
`leftjustify_h`
`leftjustify_l`
`leftjustify_la`
`leftjustify_lh`
`lj lj_a lj_h lj_l lj_la lj_lh`
	Classes to left-align text—the default—(`leftjustify`), to do so only when it is actively being clicked (`leftjustify_a`), or when it is being hovered over (`leftjustify_h`); also three classes to enable bold for a link within the object (`leftjustify_l`), a link within the object that is being clicked (`leftjustify_la`), or a link within the object that is being hovered over (`leftjustify_lh`), plus six shorthand versions (`lj...`)

`center` (etc...) `c` (etc...)	Class – as `leftjustify` but for centered text
`rightjustify` (etc...) `rj` (etc...)	Class – as `leftjustify` but for right-justified text
`justify` (etc...) `j` (etc...)	Class – as `leftjustify` but for fully justified text
`text-align`	Property used for aligning text

About the Classes

These classes use the `text-align` property to set the alignment of some text, like this:

`text-align``:right;`

How to Use Them

You can use these classes to change the justification of text by entering their names into the `class` argument of an object, like this:

```
<span class='justify'>This text is fully justified</span>
```

Or you may prefer the shorthand class names, like this:

```
<span class='j'>This text is fully justified</span>
```

You can also use the standard suffixes to change the justification only when the text is hovered over, like this:

```
<span class=c_h'>This text is centered when hovered over</span>
```

Here is the HTML used for the screen grab in Figure 25-3:

```
<div style='width:125px' class='leftfloat padding lime_b'>
<div class='leftjustify'>It was the best of times, it was the worst of
times, it was the age of wisdom, it was the age of foolishness, it was
the epoch of belief, it was the epoch of incredulity, it...</div></div>

<div style='width:138px' class='leftfloat padding yellow_b'>
<div class='center'>It was the best of times, it was the worst of
times, it was the age of wisdom, it was the age of foolishness, it was
the epoch of belief, it was the epoch of incredulity, it...</div></div>

<div style='width:125px' class='leftfloat padding pink_b'>
<div class='rightjustify'>It was the best of times, it was the worst of
times, it was the age of wisdom, it was the age of foolishness, it was
the epoch of belief, it was the epoch of incredulity, it...</div></div>

<div style='width:125px' class='leftfloat padding aqua_b'>
<div class='justify'>It was the best of times, it was the worst of
times, it was the age of wisdom, it was the age of foolishness, it was
the epoch of belief, it was the epoch of incredulity, it...</div></div>
```

Each <div> is set to a width of 125 pixels, except for the second one, which has to be a little wider since centered text takes up more space. Also each one is given a different background color for clarity, and they are floated to the left so they line up in a row.

The Classes

```
.leftjustify,          .leftjustify_a:active,        .leftjustify_h:hover,
.leftjustify_l a,      .leftjustify_la a:active,     .leftjustify_lh a:hover,
.lj,                   .lj_a:active,                 .lj_h:hover,
.lj_l a,               .lj_la a:active,              .lj_lh a:hover
   { text-align:left;     }
.center,               .center_a:active,             .center_h:hover,
.center_l a,           .center_la a:active,          .center_lh a:hover,
.c,                    .c_a:active,                  .c_h:hover,
.c_l a,                .c_la a:active,               .c_lh a:hover
   { text-align:center;   }
.rightjustify,         .rightjustify_a:active,       .rightjustify_h:hover,
.rightjustify_l a,     .rightjustify_la a:active,    .rightjustify_lh a:hover,
.rj,                   .rj_a:active,                 .rj_h:hover,
.rj_l a,               .rj_la a:active,              .rj_lh a:hover
   { text-align:right;    }
.justify,              .justify_a:active,            .justify_h:hover,
```

```
.justify_l a,        .justify_la a:active,      .justify_lh a:hover,
.j,                  .j_a:active,               .j_h:hover,
.j_l a,              .j_la a:active,            .j_lh a:hover
   { text-align:justify; }
```

Text Point Size

The classes in this group let you specify the point size for text from 1 to 100 points with varying intervals: 1–20 in steps of 1 point, 25–50 in steps of 5 points, and 60–100 in steps of 10 points.

In Figure 25-4, there are two rows of text. The first contains three immediately set font sizes, and the second uses the classes to set the font size only when an object is hovered over, as is the case with the text 25pt.

Classes and Properties

pt1 pt1_a pt1_h pt1_l pt1_la pt1_lh	Class to change the text size to 1 point (pt1), plus classes to do so only if the object is actively being clicked (pt1_a) or hovered over (pt1_h), and another three classes to change the point size of any links within the object (pt1_l), any links within the object that are actively being clicked (pt1_la), and any links within the object that are being hovered over (pt1_lh)
pt2 – pt20 (etc...)	Classes – in steps of 1 point, as pt1
pt25 – pt50 (etc...)	Classes – in steps of 5 points, as pt1
pt60 – pt100 (etc...)	Classes – in steps of 10 points, as pt1
font-size	Property containing the text font size

About the Classes

You can change the size of a font in many ways, such as by using ems or pixels and so on, but one of the most common is to use point size, and so the most useful sizes have been

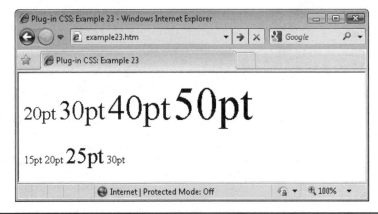

FIGURE 25-4   A variety of font sizes applied using these classes

given class names of pt1 through pt20, pt25 through pt50 in steps of 5 points, and pt60 through pt100 in steps of 10 points. These are applied using the font-size class, like this:

```
font-size:45pt;
```

How to Use Them

To set the point size of some text, place the matching class name in the class argument of the object containing the text, like this:

```
<span class='pt14'>This is 14pt text</span>
```

You can also use the standard class suffixes to specify when the font size is applied, such as the font size hover class, like this:

```
<span class='pt20_h'>This is 20pt text when hovered over</span>
```

And you can combine the class, too. For example, the following code sets the enclosed text to 10pt, or 14pt when hovered, and to 12pt when clicked:

```
<span class='pt10 pt14_h pt12_a'>Hover over and click me</span>
```

Here is the code used to create the screen grab in Figure 25-4:

```
<span class='pt20'>20pt</span>
<span class='pt30'>30pt</span>
<span class='pt40'>40pt</span>
<span class='pt50'>50pt</span><br /><br />

<span class='pt15_h'>15pt</span>
<span class='pt20_h'>20pt</span>
<span class='pt25_h'>25pt</span>
<span class='pt30_h'>30pt</span>
```

The Classes

```
.pt1,        .pt1_a:active,     .pt1_h:hover,
.pt1_l a,    .pt1_la a:active,  .pt1_lh a:hover   { font-size:1pt;  }
.pt2,        .pt2_a:active,     .pt2_h:hover,
.pt2_l a,    .pt2_la a:active,  .pt2_lh a:hover   { font-size:2pt;  }
.pt3,        .pt3_a:active,     .pt3_h:hover,
.pt3_l a,    .pt3_la a:active,  .pt3_lh a:hover   { font-size:3pt;  }
.pt4,        .pt4_a:active,     .pt4_h:hover,
.pt4_l a,    .pt4_la a:active,  .pt4_lh a:hover   { font-size:4pt;  }
.pt5,        .pt5_a:active,     .pt5_h:hover,
.pt5_l a,    .pt5_la a:active,  .pt5_lh a:hover   { font-size:5pt;  }
.pt6,        .pt6_a:active,     .pt6_h:hover,
.pt6_l a,    .pt6_la a:active,  .pt6_lh a:hover   { font-size:6pt;  }
.pt7,        .pt7_a:active,     .pt7_h:hover,
.pt7_l a,    .pt7_la a:active,  .pt7_lh a:hover   { font-size:7pt;  }
.pt8,        .pt8_a:active,     .pt8_h:hover,
.pt8_l a,    .pt8_la a:active,  .pt8_lh a:hover   { font-size:8pt;  }
.pt9,        .pt9_a:active,     .pt9_h:hover,
```

```
.pt9_l a,    .pt9_la a:active,    .pt9_lh a:hover   { font-size:9pt;  }
.pt10,       .pt10_a:active,      .pt10_h:hover,
.pt10_l a,   .pt10_l a:active,    .pt10_lh a:hover  { font-size:10pt; }
.pt11,       .pt11_a:active,      .pt11_h:hover,
.pt11_l a,   .pt11_la a:active,   .pt11_lh a:hover  { font-size:11pt; }
.pt12,       .pt12_a:active,      .pt12_h:hover,
.pt12_l a,   .pt12_la a:active,   .pt12_lh a:hover  { font-size:12pt; }
.pt13,       .pt13_a:active,      .pt13_h:hover,
.pt13_l a,   .pt13_la a:active,   .pt13_lh a:hover  { font-size:13pt; }
.pt14,       .pt14_a:active,      .pt14_h:hover,
.pt14_l a,   .pt14_la a:active,   .pt14_lh a:hover  { font-size:14pt; }
.pt15,       .pt15_a:active,      .pt15_h:hover,
.pt15_l a,   .pt15_la a:active,   .pt15_lh a:hover  { font-size:15pt; }
.pt16,       .pt16_a:active,      .pt16_h:hover,
.pt16_l a,   .pt16_la a:active,   .pt16_lh a:hover  { font-size:16pt; }
.pt17,       .pt17_a:active,      .pt17_h:hover,
.pt17_l a,   .pt17_la a:active,   .pt17_lh a:hover  { font-size:17pt; }
.pt18,       .pt18_a:active,      .pt18_h:hover,
.pt18_l a,   .pt18_la a:active,   .pt18_lh a:hover  { font-size:18pt; }
.pt19,       .pt19_a:active,      .pt19_h:hover,
.pt19_l a,   .pt19_la a:active,   .pt19_lh a:hover  { font-size:19pt; }
.pt20,       .pt20_a:active,      .pt20_h:hover,
.pt20_l a,   .pt20_la a:active,   .pt20_lh a:hover  { font-size:20pt; }
.pt25,       .pt25_a:active,      .pt25_h:hover,
.pt25_l a,   .pt25_la a:active,   .pt25_lh a:hover  { font-size:25pt; }
.pt30,       .pt30_a:active,      .pt30_h:hover,
.pt30_l a,   .pt30_la a:active,   .pt30_lh a:hover  { font-size:30pt; }
.pt35,       .pt35_a:active,      .pt35_h:hover,
.pt35_l a,   .pt35_la a:active,   .pt35_lh a:hover  { font-size:35pt; }
.pt40,       .pt40_a:active,      .pt40_h:hover,
.pt40_l a,   .pt40_la a:active,   .pt40_lh a:hover  { font-size:40pt; }
.pt45,       .pt45_a:active,      .pt45_h:hover,
.pt45_l a,   .pt45_la a:active,   .pt45_lh a:hover  { font-size:45pt; }
.pt50,       .pt50_a:active,      .pt50_h:hover,
.pt50_l a,   .pt50_la a:active,   .pt50_lh a:hover  { font-size:50pt; }
.pt60,       .pt60_a:active,      .pt60_h:hover,
.pt60_l a,   .pt60_la a:active,   .pt60_lh a:hover  { font-size:60pt; }
.pt70,       .pt70_a:active,      .pt70_h:hover,
.pt70_l a,   .pt70_la a:active,   .pt70_lh a:hover  { font-size:70pt; }
.pt80,       .pt80_a:active,      .pt80_h:hover,
.pt80_l a,   .pt80_la a:active,   .pt80_lh a:hover  { font-size:80pt; }
.pt90,       .pt90_a:active,      .pt90_h:hover,
.pt90_l a,   .pt90_la a:active,   .pt90_lh a:hover  { font-size:90pt; }
.pt100,      .pt100_a:active,     .pt100_h:hover,
.pt100_l a,  .pt100_la a:active,  .pt100_lh a:hover { font-size:100pt;}
```

Text Colors

In Chapter 24, a number of classes were provided that let you change the background color of an object. These classes partner them by letting you change the text color. The same set of 21 colors is supported, along with all the usual suffixes to control how they are applied.

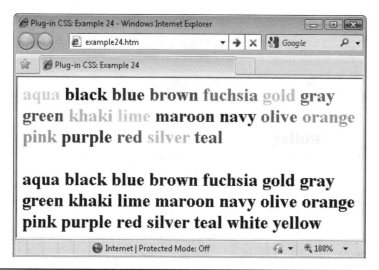

FIGURE 25-5   The 21 different colors supported by these classes, followed by the same colors as hover-over classes

In Figure 25-5, all the colors are shown twice: the first set uses the main text color class names to immediately apply the color, while the second set uses the _h suffix so the color is only applied when the mouse passes over an object, as it has over the word lime in the screen grab.

Classes and Properties

aqua aqua_a aqua_h aqua_l aqua_la aqua_lh	Class to change the background color of an object to aqua (aqua), plus classes to do so only if the object is actively being clicked (aqua_a) or hovered over (aqua_h), and another three classes to change the background of any links within the object (aqua_l), any links within the object that are actively being clicked (aqua_la), and any links within the object that are being hovered over (aqua_lh)
black (etc...)	Classes – as aqua but for black
blue (etc...)	Classes – as aqua but for blue
brown (etc...)	Classes – as aqua but for brown
fuchsia (etc...)	Classes – as aqua but for fuchsia
gold (etc...)	Classes – as aqua but for gold
gray (etc...)	Classes – as aqua but for gray
green (etc...)	Classes – as aqua but for green
khaki (etc...)	Classes – as aqua but for khaki
lime (etc...)	Classes – as aqua but for lime
maroon (etc...)	Classes – as aqua but for maroon
navy (etc...)	Classes – as aqua but for navy
olive (etc...)	Classes – as aqua but for olive

orange (etc...)	Classes – as aqua but for orange
pink (etc...)	Classes – as aqua but for pink
purple (etc...)	Classes – as aqua but for purple
red (etc...)	Classes – as aqua but for red
silver (etc...)	Classes – as aqua but for silver
teal (etc...)	Classes – as aqua but for teal
white (etc...)	Classes – as aqua but for white
yellow (etc...)	Classes – as aqua but for yellow
color	Property containing text color settings

About the Classes

The reason for using the _b suffix for the background colors in Chapter 24 is now clear: It's because the text colors in this recipe group have the non-_b names. As with the background classes, there are 21 color choices, and six different ways of applying them using the standard class suffixes such as _h to apply a color to an object only when it is being hovered over by the mouse.

The property being manipulated is color, like this:

```
color:#580;
```

How to Use Them

To change the color of a section of text, enter the matching class name (and any optional suffix) in the class argument of the object's HTML tag, like this:

```
<span class='gold'>This text is gold</span>
```

You can also use the standard dynamic suffixes so that, for example, a section of text can be changed to navy when it is hovered over like this:

```
<span class='navy_h'>This text is navy when hovered over</span>
```

Here is the code used to create the image in Figure 25-5:

```
<div class='b pt20'>
    <span class='aqua'      >aqua    </span>
    <span class='black'     >black   </span>
    <span class='blue'      >blue    </span>
    <span class='brown'     >brown   </span>
    <span class='fuchsia'   >fuchsia</span>
    <span class='gold'      >gold    </span>
    <span class='gray'      >gray    </span>
    <span class='green'     >green   </span>
    <span class='khaki'     >khaki   </span>
    <span class='lime'      >lime    </span>
    <span class='maroon'    >maroon  </span>
    <span class='navy'      >navy    </span>
```

```
<span class='olive'    >olive  </span>
<span class='orange'   >orange </span>
<span class='pink'     >pink   </span>
<span class='purple'   >purple </span>
<span class='red'      >red    </span>
<span class='silver'   >silver </span>
<span class='teal'     >teal   </span>
<span class='white'    >white  </span>
<span class='yellow'   >yellow </span><br /><br />

<span class='aqua_h'   >aqua   </span>
<span class='black_h'  >black  </span>
<span class='blue_h'   >blue   </span>
<span class='brown_h'  >brown  </span>
<span class='fuchsia_h'>fuchsia</span>
<span class='gold_h'   >gold   </span>
<span class='gray_h'   >gray   </span>
<span class='green_h'  >green  </span>
<span class='khaki_h'  >khaki  </span>
<span class='lime_h'   >lime   </span>
<span class='maroon_h' >maroon </span>
<span class='navy_h'   >navy   </span>
<span class='olive_h'  >olive  </span>
<span class='orange_h' >orange </span>
<span class='pink_h'   >pink   </span>
<span class='purple_h' >purple </span>
<span class='red_h'    >red    </span>
<span class='silver_h' >silver </span>
<span class='teal_h'   >teal   </span>
<span class='white_h'  >white  </span>
<span class='yellow_h' >yellow </span>
</div>
```

For clarity, the pair of color sets is enclosed in a `<div>` that sets the text to bold 20 point.

The Classes

.aqua,	**.aqua_a**:active,	**.aqua_h**:hover,	
.aqua_l a,	**.aqua_la** a:active,	**.aqua_lh** a:hover	{ **color**:#0ff; }
.black,	**.black_a**:active,	**.black_h**:hover,	
.black_l a,	**.black_la** a:active,	**.black_lh** a:hover	{ **color**:#000; }
.blue,	**.blue_a**:active,	**.blue_h**:hover,	
.blue_l a,	**.blue_la** a:active,	**.blue_lh** a:hover	{ **color**:#00f; }
.brown,	**.brown_a**:active,	**.brown_h**:hover,	
.brown_l a,	**.brown_la** a:active,	**.brown_lh** a:hover	{ **color**:#c44; }
.fuchsia,	**.fuchsia_a**:active,	**.fuchsia_h**:hover,	
.fuchsia_l a,	**.fuchsia_la** a:active,	**.fuchsia_lh** a:hover	{ **color**:#f0f; }
.gold,	**.gold_a**:active,	**.gold_h**:hover,	
.gold_l a,	**.gold_la** a:active,	**.gold_lh** a:hover	{ **color**:#fc0; }
.gray,	**.gray_a**:active,	**.gray_h**:hover,	
.gray_l a,	**.gray_la** a:active,	**.gray_lh** a:hover	{ **color**:#888; }
.green,	**.green_a**:active,	**.green_h**:hover,	
.green_l a,	**.green_la** a:active,	**.green_lh** a:hover	{ **color**:#080; }
.khaki,	**.khaki_a**:active,	**.khaki_h**:hover,	

```
.khaki_l a,      .khaki_la a:active,    .khaki_lh a:hover     { color:#cc8; }
.lime,           .lime_a:active,        .lime_h:hover,
.lime_l a,       .lime_la a:active,     .lime_lh a:hover      { color:#0f0; }
.maroon,         .maroon_a:active,      .maroon_h:hover,
.maroon_l a,     .maroon_la a:active,   .maroon_lh a:hover    { color:#800; }
.navy,           .navy_a:active,        .navy_h:hover,
.navy_l a,       .navy_la a:active,     .navy_lh a:hover      { color:#008; }
.olive,          .olive_a:active,       .olive_h:hover,
.olive_l a,      .olive_la a:active,    .olive_lh a:hover     { color:#880; }
.orange,         .orange_a:active,      .orange_h:hover,
.orange_l a,     .orange_la a:active,   .orange_lh a:hover    { color:#f80; }
.pink,           .pink_a:active,        .pink_h:hover,
.pink_l a,       .pink_la a:active,     .pink_lh a:hover      { color:#f88; }
.purple,         .purple_a:active,      .purple_h:hover,
.purple_l a,     .purple_la a:active,   .purple_lh a:hover    { color:#808; }
.red,            .red_a:active,         .red_h:hover,
.red_l a,        .red_la a:active,      .red_lh a:hover       { color:#f00; }
.silver,         .silver_a:active,      .silver_h:hover,
.silver_l a,     .silver_la a:active,   .silver_lh a:hover    { color:#ccc; }
.teal,           .teal_a:active,        .teal_h:hover,
.teal_l a,       .teal_la a:active,     .teal_lh a:hover      { color:#088; }
.white,          .white_a:active,       .white_h:hover,
.white_l a,      .white_la a:active,    .white_lh a:hover     { color:#fff; }
.yellow,         .yellow_a:active,      .yellow_h:hover,
.yellow_l a,     .yellow_la a:active,   .yellow_lh a:hover    { color:#ff0; }
```

Text Shadows

Using these classes, you can apply shadows of varying strengths underneath sections of text. Figure 25-6 shows two sets of shadowed text. The first has used the main class names to immediately apply the shadows, while the second has used the hover versions of the classes to apply the shadows only when the objects are hovered over, as is currently the case with the second instance of the phrase "Medium Shadow."

FIGURE 25-6 Applying shadows to text using the standard and hover versions of the classes

This grab was taken using Internet Explorer, and the `filter` property used for creating these shadows is much harsher than those created in most other modern browsers, which also blur and round the shadows for a softer effect.

Classes and Properties

shadow shadow_a shadow_h shadow_l shadow_la shadow_lh	Class to place a shadow underneath some text (shadow), plus classes to do so only if the object is actively being clicked (shadow_a) or hovered over (shadow_h), and another three classes to place the shadow under any links within the object (shadow_l), any links within the object that are actively being clicked (shadow_la), and any links within the object that are being hovered over (shadow_lh)
lightestshadow (etc...)	Class – as shadow but creates the lightest shadow
lightshadow (etc...)	Class – as shadow but creates a light shadow
darkshadow (etc...)	Class – as shadow but creates a dark shadow
darkestshadow (etc...)	Class – as shadow but creates the darkest shadow
text-shadow	Property to apply a shadow to text
filter	Property used by Internet Explorer to apply shadows and many other features to objects

About the Classes

These classes apply shadows to text using the CSS `text-shadow` property or the Microsoft proprietary `filter` property in Internet Explorer, like this:

```
text-shadow:#888888 3px 3px 4px;
filter     :progid:DXImageTransform.Microsoft.Shadow(
            color='#888888', Direction=135, Strength=5);
```

How to Use Them

To use these classes, enter their names into the `class` argument of the containing object for some text. I recommend you use only the <div> tag when you want shadowed text (since Internet Explorer—even the version 9 preview—refuses to add shadows to text within a <span> or any other inline object), like this:

```
<div class='shadow'>This text is shadowed</div>
```

Alternatively, Internet Explorer *will* add shadows if a <span> is floated, as in the following, which uses the `lf` class (short for `leftfloat`):

```
<span class='shadow lf'>Shadowed text, floated left</span>
```

You can also use the hover and other forms of classes, as in the following, which adds the shadow only when hovered over:

```
<div class='shadow_h'>This text is shadowed when hovered</div>
```

Following is the HML used to create Figure 25-6. In it, the <span> tags all use the lf class to float them so that Internet Explorer will be able to create shadows.

```
<div class='b pt20'>
   <span class='lightestshadow lf gray_bh'>Lightest Shadow  </span>
   <span class='lightshadow lf gray_bh'>Light Shadow  </span>
   <span class='shadow lf gray_bh'>Medium Shadow  </span>
   <span class='darkshadow lf gray_bh'>Dark Shadow  </span>
   <span class='darkestshadow lf gray_bh'>Darkest Shadow  </span>
</div><br clear='left'>

<div class='b pt20'>
   <span class='lightestshadow_h lf'>Lightest Shadow  </span>
   <span class='lightshadow_h lf'>Light Shadow  </span>
   <span class='shadow_h lf'>Medium Shadow  </span>
   <span class='darkshadow_h lf'>Dark Shadow  </span>
   <span class='darkestshadow_h lf'>Darkest Shadow  </span>
</div>
```

When you hover over the first five elements, the background changes to gray (using the gray_bh class) so you can see the effect of the different lightnesses of shadow on different backgrounds. If you hover over the second set of five elements, the shadow will be applied only as the mouse passes over them.

The Classes

```
.shadow,                        .shadow_a:active,
.shadow_h:hover,                .shadow_l a,
.shadow_la a:active,            .shadow_lh a:hover {
   text-shadow:#888888 3px 3px 4px;
   filter     :progid:DXImageTransform.Microsoft.Shadow(
               color='#888888', Direction=135, Strength=5);
}
.lightestshadow,                .lightestshadow_a:active,
.lightestshadow_h:hover,        .lightestshadow_l a,
.lightestshadow_la a:active, .lightestshadow_lh a:hover {
   text-shadow:#ffffff 3px 3px 4px;
   filter     :progid:DXImageTransform.Microsoft.Shadow(
               color='#ffffff', Direction=135, Strength=5);
}
.lightshadow,                   .lightshadow_a:active,
.lightshadow_h:hover,           .lightshadow_l a,
.lightshadow_la a:active,       .lightshadow_lh a:hover {
   text-shadow:#cccccc 3px 3px 4px;
   filter     :progid:DXImageTransform.Microsoft.Shadow(
               color='#cccccc', Direction=135, Strength=5);
}
.darkshadow,                    .darkshadow_a:active,
.darkshadow_h:hover,            .darkshadow_l a,
.darkshadow_la a:active,        .darkshadow_lh a:hover {
   text-shadow:#444444 3px 3px 4px;
   filter     :progid:DXImageTransform.Microsoft.Shadow(
               color='#444444', Direction=135, Strength=5);
```

```
}
.darkestshadow,            .darkestshadow_a:active,
.darkestshadow_h:hover,    .darkestshadow_l a,
.darkestshadow_la a:active,  .darkestshadow_lh a:hover {
   text-shadow:#000000 3px 3px 4px;
   filter     :progid:DXImageTransform.Microsoft.Shadow(
               color='#000000', Direction=135, Strength=5);
}
```

Text Transformations

When you need to quickly change the case of a section of text, you can simply apply one of the classes in this recipe group. Figure 25-7 shows the four different transformations being used on a famous Albert Einstein quotation.

Classes and Properties

caps caps_a caps_h caps_l caps_la caps_lh	Class to change the first letter of each word in a section of text to a capital letter (caps), plus classes to do so only if the object is actively being clicked (caps_a) or hovered over (caps_h), and another three classes to change the case of any links within the object (caps_l), any links within the object that are actively being clicked (caps_la), and any links within the object that are being hovered over (caps_lh)
scaps (etc...)	Class – as caps but changes the entire text to small capital letters
lower (etc...)	Class – as caps but changes the entire text to all lowercase
upper (etc...)	Class – as caps but changes the text to all uppercase
text-transform	Property to capitalize text or change it to lower- or uppercase
font-variant	Property to implement a font variant such as small capital letters

About the Classes

These classes make use of the text-transform and font-variant properties to change a selection of text, like this:

```
text-transform:capitalize;
font-variant:small-caps;
```

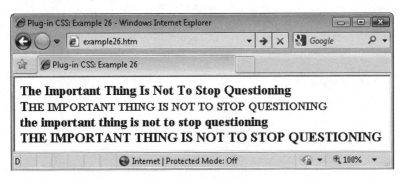

FIGURE 25-7 These classes provide a quick means of transforming sections of text.

How to Use Them

You can transform a section of text by using one of these classes in the `class` argument of the containing object, like this:

```
<span class='scaps'>This text displays in small capital letters</span>
```

The standard suffixes are also available for transforming the text only under certain conditions, such as when the mouse hovers over it, like this:

```
<span class='scaps_h'>Small caps when hovered over</span>
```

Here is the HTML used for the screen grab in Figure 25-7:

```
<div class='b pt15'>
  <div class='caps' >The important thing is not to stop questioning</div>
  <div class='scaps'>The important thing is not to stop questioning</div>
  <div class='lower'>The important thing is not to stop questioning</div>
  <div class='upper'>The important thing is not to stop questioning</div>
</div>
```

The Classes

```
.caps,        .caps_a:active,      .caps_h:hover,
.caps_l a,  .caps_la a:active,   .caps_lh a:hover
   { text-transform:capitalize; }
.scaps,       .scaps_a:active,     .scaps_h:hover,
.scaps_l a, .scaps_la a:active,  .scaps_lh a:hover
   { font-variant  :small-caps; }
.lower,       .lower_a:active,     .lower_h:hover,
.lower_l a, .lower_la a:active,  .lower_lh a:hover
   { text-transform:lowercase;  }
.upper,       .upper_a:active,     .upper_h:hover,
.upper_l a, .upper_la a:active,  .upper_lh a:hover
   { text-transform:uppercase;  }
```

Encapsulation

Encapsulation is a neat trick that you can use to enclose a section of text within other text or objects. In this case, it is used to automatically add quotation marks and other symbols before and after a section of text, as shown in Figure 25-8, in which a phrase is repeated five times, each using a different encapsulation class.

Classes and Properties

quotes quotes_h	Classes to place curly quotation marks before and after a section of text (quotes), or only when the text is hovered over (quotes_h)
parens (etc...)	Class – as quotes but for parentheses
brackets (etc...)	Class – as quotes but for brackets

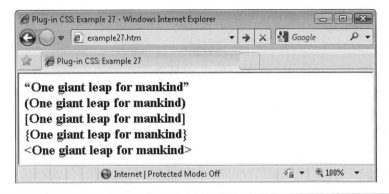

Figure 25-8   Enclosing a section of text with symbols using the encapsulation classes

braces (etc...)	Class – as `quotes` but for braces
chevrons (etc...)	Class – as `quotes` but for chevrons
content	Property used to insert content before and after some text

About the Classes

These classes use the pseudo-classes `:before` and `:after` to insert characters before and after a section of text using the `content` property, as in the following, which places curly quotation marks before and after the text:

```
.quotes:before { content:'\201c'; }
.quotes:after  { content:'\201d'; }
```

How to Use Them

When you want to encapsulate some text, enter the class needed into the `class` argument of the text's container, like this:

```
<div class='quotes'>This will have quotes added to it</div>
```

Or, you could add the quotes only when the mouse hovers over the text, for example, like this:

```
<div class='quotes_h'>This has quotes added when hovered over</div>
```

The other dynamic suffixes (such as _a, and so on) are not supported by these classes since they would almost certainly never be used.

The Classes

```
.quotes:before, .quotes_h:hover:before { content:'\201c'; }
.quotes:after,  .quotes_h:hover:after  { content:'\201d'; }
.parens:before, .parens_h:hover:before { content:'('; }
.parens:after,  .parens_h:hover:after  { content:')'; }
```

```
.brackets:before,  .brackets_h:hover:before { content:'['; }
.brackets:after,   .brackets_h:hover:after  { content:']'; }
.braces:before,    .braces_h:hover:before   { content:'{'; }
.braces:after,     .braces_h:hover:after    { content:'}'; }
.chevrons:before,  .chevrons_h:hover:before { content:'<'; }
.chevrons:after,   .chevrons_h:hover:after  { content:'>'; }
```

Google Fonts

Google has kindly placed a number of fonts on their servers that can be easily included in your web pages by referencing them in the class arguments of this recipe group.

Figure 25-9 shows all the Google fonts being used at the same time. This is something you may not want to do normally, since each font takes a second or two to download and install. Generally, you will only want two or three fonts on a page anyway, or it will begin to look too cluttered.

Classes and Properties

cantarell cantarell_a cantarell_h cantarell_l cantarell_la cantarell_lh	Class to select a Google font (cantarell), plus classes to do so only if the object is actively being clicked (cantarell_a) or hovered over (cantarell_h), and another three classes to change the font of any links within the object (cantarell_l), any links within the object that are actively being clicked (cantarell_la), and any links within the object that are being hovered over (cantarell_lh)
cardo crimson droidsans droidsansm droidserif imfell inconsolata josefin lobster molengo neuton nobile oflsorts oldstandard reenie tangerine vollkorn yanone	Classes – as cantarell but for different font faces
font-family	Property for specifying a font to apply

About the Classes

These classes provide a shorthand way of using the Google fonts. They access the font-family CSS property to do so, like this:

```
font-family:"Droid Serif", serif;
```

How to Use Them

To use the Google fonts, you will need to include a line such as the following for every Google font you plan to use:

```
<link rel='stylesheet' type='text/css'
 href='http://fonts.googleapis.com/css?family=fontfamily'>
```

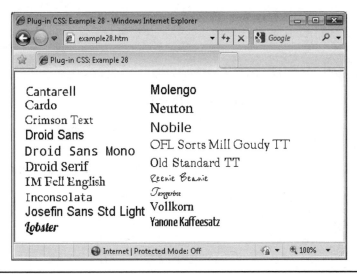

Figure 25-9 The 19 Google fonts supported by these classes

The class names and their respective font family names to use in place of *fontfamily* are listed in Table 25-1. Note that the + symbol is used instead of spaces.

Table 25-1 The Google Font Families and Recipe Class Names

Class Name	Font Name for Use in the Link
cardo	Cardo
cantarell	Cantarell
crimson	Crimson+Text
droidsans	Droid+Sans
droidsansm	Droid+San+Mono
droidserif	Droid+Serif
imfell	IM+Fell+English
inconsolata	Inconsolata
josefin	Josefin+Sans+Std+Light
lobster	Lobster
molengo	Molengo
neuton	Neuton
nobile	Nobile
oflsorts	OFL+Sorts+Mill+Goudy+TT
oldstandard	Old+Standard+TT
reenie	Reenie+Beanie
tangerine	Tangerine
vollkorn	Vollkorn
yanone	Yanone+Kaffeesatz

PART IV

To load in the Crimson Text font, for example, you would use the following code in the <head> section of a web page:

```
<link rel='stylesheet' type='text/css'
 href='http://fonts.googleapis.com/css?family=Crimson+Text'>
```

Then, in the page's body you can use the font like this:

```
<span class='tangerine'>This text uses the Tangerine Font</span>
```

The following is the <head> code used to create Figure 25-9. It's a little long-winded because it loads in every single font (you will probably only want a few of them):

```
<link rel='stylesheet' type='text/css'
   href='http://fonts.googleapis.com/css?family=Cantarell'>
<link rel='stylesheet' type='text/css'
   href='http://fonts.googleapis.com/css?family=Cardo'>
<link rel='stylesheet' type='text/css'
   href='http://fonts.googleapis.com/css?family=Crimson+Text'>
<link rel='stylesheet' type='text/css'
   href='http://fonts.googleapis.com/css?family=Droid+Sans'>
<link rel='stylesheet' type='text/css'
   href='http://fonts.googleapis.com/css?family=Droid+Sans+Mono'>
<link rel='stylesheet' type='text/css'
   href='http://fonts.googleapis.com/css?family=Droid+Serif'>
<link rel='stylesheet' type='text/css'
   href='http://fonts.googleapis.com/css?family=IM+Fell+English'>
<link rel='stylesheet' type='text/css'
   href='http://fonts.googleapis.com/css?family=Inconsolata'>
<link rel='stylesheet' type='text/css'
   href='http://fonts.googleapis.com/css?family=Josefin+Sans+Std+Light'>
<link rel='stylesheet' type='text/css'
   href='http://fonts.googleapis.com/css?family=Lobster'>
<link rel='stylesheet' type='text/css'
   href='http://fonts.googleapis.com/css?family=Molengo'>
<link rel='stylesheet' type='text/css'
   href='http://fonts.googleapis.com/css?family=Neuton'>
<link rel='stylesheet' type='text/css'
   href='http://fonts.googleapis.com/css?family=Nobile'>
<link rel='stylesheet' type='text/css'
   href='http://fonts.googleapis.com/css?family=OFL+Sorts+Mill+Goudy+TT'>
<link rel='stylesheet' type='text/css'
   href='http://fonts.googleapis.com/css?family=Old+Standard+TT'>
<link rel='stylesheet' type='text/css'
   href='http://fonts.googleapis.com/css?family=Reenie+Beanie'>
<link rel='stylesheet' type='text/css'
   href='http://fonts.googleapis.com/css?family=Tangerine'>
<link rel='stylesheet' type='text/css'
   href='http://fonts.googleapis.com/css?family=Vollkorn'>
<link rel='stylesheet' type='text/css'
   href='http://fonts.googleapis.com/css?family=Yanone+Kaffeesatz'>
```

And here is the code from the body of the example:

```
<div class='pt15 lf padding'>
    <div class='cantarell'  >Cantarell            </div>
    <div class='cardo'      >Cardo                </div>
    <div class='crimson'    >Crimson Text         </div>
    <div class='droidsans'  >Droid Sans           </div>
    <div class='droidsansm' >Droid Sans Mono      </div>
    <div class='droidserif' >Droid Serif          </div>
    <div class='imfell'     >IM Fell English      </div>
    <div class='inconsolata'>Inconsolata          </div>
    <div class='josefin'    >Josefin Sans Std Light </div>
    <div class='lobster'    >Lobster              </div></div>
<div class='pt15 padding'>
    <div class='molengo'    >Molengo              </div>
    <div class='neuton'     >Neuton               </div>
    <div class='nobile'     >Nobile               </div>
    <div class='oflsorts'   >OFL Sorts Mill Goudy TT</div>
    <div class='oldstandard'>Old Standard TT      </div>
    <div class='reenie'     >Reenie Beanie        </div>
    <div class='tangerine'  >Tangerine            </div>
    <div class='vollkorn'   >Vollkorn             </div>
    <div class='yanone'     >Yanone Kaffeesatz</div></div>
```

NOTE *In Chapter 30, I'll introduce a method you can use to automate all this, as long as your users have JavaScript, but the method in this recipe will allow you to display Google fonts to all users of recent browsers, regardless of having JavaScript or not.*

The Classes

```
.cantarell,       .cantarell_a:active,   .cantarell_h:hover,
.cantarell_l a,   .cantarell_la a:active .cantarell_lh a:hover
    { font-family:"Cantarell", sans-serif; }
.cardo,           .cardo_a:active,       .cardo_h:hover,
.cardo_l a,       .cardo_la a:active     .cardo_lh a:hover
    { font-family:"Cardo", serif; }
.crimson,         .crimson_a:active,     .crimson_h:hover,
.crimson_l a,     .crimson_la a:active   .crimson_lh a:hover
    { font-family:"Crimson Text", serif; }
.droidsans,       .droidsans_a:active,   .droidsans_h:hover,
.droidsans_l a,   .droidsans_la a:active .droidsans_lh a:hover
    { font-family:"Droid Sans", sans-serif; }
.droidsansm,      .droidsansm_a:active,  .droidsansm_h:hover,
.droidsansm_l a,  .droidsansm_la a:active .droidsansm_lh a:hover
    { font-family:"Droid Sans Mono", monospace; }
.droidserif,      .droidserif_a:active,  .droidserif_h:hover,
.droidserif_l a,  .droidserif_la a:active .droidserif_lh a:hover
    { font-family:"Droid Serif", serif; }
.imfell,          .imfell_a:active,      .imfell_h:hover,
.imfell_l a,      .imfell_la a:active    .imfell_lh a:hover
    { font-family:"IM Fell English", serif; }
.inconsolata,     .inconsolata_a:active, .inconsolata_h:hover,
.inconsolata_l a, .inconsolata_la a:active .inconsolata_lh a:hover
```

```
          { font-family:"Inconsolata", monospace; }
.josefin,             .josefin_a:active,       .josefin_h:hover,
.josefin_l a,         .josefin_la a:active     .josefin_lh a:hover
    { font-family:"Josefin Sans Std Light", sans-serif; }
.lobster,             .lobster_a:active,       .lobster_h:hover,
.lobster_l a,         .lobster_la a:active     .lobster_lh a:hover
    { font-family:"Lobster", fantasy, serif; }
.molengo,             .molengo_a:active,       .molengo_h:hover,
.molengo_l a,         .molengo_la a:active     .molengo_lh a:hover
    { font-family:"Molengo", sans-serif; }
.neuton,              .neuton_a:active,        .neuton_h:hover,
.neuton_l a,          .neuton_la a:active      .neuton_lh a:hover
    { font-family:"Neuton", sans-serif; }
.nobile,              .nobile_a:active,        .nobile_h:hover,
.nobile_l a,          .nobile_la a:active      .nobile_lh a:hover
    { font-family:"Nobile", sans-serif; }
.oflsorts,            .oflsorts_a:active,      .oflsorts_h:hover,
.oflsorts_l a,        .oflsorts_la a:active    .oflsorts_lh a:hover
    { font-family:"OFL Sorts Mill Goudy TT", serif; }
.oldstandard,         .oldstandard_a:active,   .oldstandard_h:hover,
.oldstandard_l a,     .oldstandard_la a:active .oldstandard_lh a:hover
    { font-family:"Old Standard TT", serif; }
.reenie,              .reenie_a:active,        .reenie_h:hover,
.reenie_l a,          .reenie_la a:active      .reenie_lh a:hover
    { font-family:"Reenie Beanie", cursive, serif; }
.tangerine,           .tangerine_a:active,     .tangerine_h:hover,
.tangerine_l a,       .tangerine_la a:active   .tangerine_lh a:hover
    { font-family:"Tangerine", cursive, serif; }
.vollkorn,            .vollkorn_a:active,      .vollkorn_h:hover,
.vollkorn_l a,        .vollkorn_la a:active    .vollkorn_lh a:hover
    { font-family:"Vollkorn", serif; }
.yanone,              .yanone_a:active,        .yanone_h:hover,
.yanone_l a,          .yanone_la a:active      .yanone_lh a:hover
    { font-family:"Yanone Kaffeesatz", sans-serif; }
```

Drop Cap

Placing a drop-cap at the start of an article is a mainstay of print design, but it's also easy to achieve on the Web with this recipe, as shown in Figure 25-10, which features a famous quotation from Shakespeare's play, *Macbeth*.

Classes and Properties

dropcap dropcap_h	Classes to turn the contents of an object into a drop capital (dropcap), or do so only when the object is hovered over (dropcap_h)
font-size	Property to change the font size of text
line-height	Property to change the line height of text
margin-right	Property to change an object's right margin width
margin-bottom	Property to change an object's bottom margin width
float-left	Property to float an object to the left

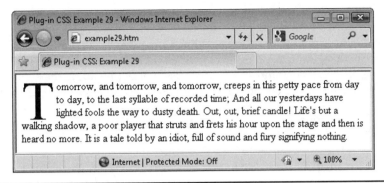

FIGURE 25-10 This recipe makes it easy to add drop-caps to your text.

About the Class

This class enlarges the text within it by five times and lines it up with the following text to create a drop-cap. This is achieved by setting the font-size property to 500 percent. Also, to neatly align the drop-cap, the line-height, margin-right, and margin-bottom of the object are tweaked. Finally, the object is floated to the left using the float property to let the following text flow around it.

How to Use It

To use this class, you should place the initial letter of some text within a <span> and use the dropcap class in the class argument, like this:

```
<span class='dropcap'>T</span>omorrow, and tomorrow, and tomorrow,
creeps in this petty pace from day to day, to the last syllable of
recorded time; And all our yesterdays have lighted fools the way to
dusty death. Out, out, brief candle! Life's but a walking shadow, a
poor player that struts and frets his hour upon the stage and then is
heard no more. It is a tale told by an idiot, full of sound and fury
signifying nothing.
```

A hover version of the class (dropcap_h) is also available, although the other dynamic versions such as _a are not, as they are most unlikely to be used.

The Class

```
.dropcap, .dropcap_h:hover {
    font-size:500%;
    line-height:0.8em;
    margin-right:0.04em;
    margin-bottom:-0.15em;
    float:left;
}
```

Columns

If you would like to present your text in columns to many of your users, these classes will automatically lay them out for you using between two and five columns inclusive. I say *many* of your users because, unfortunately, no version of IE (including the preview of version 9) supports the web standard for columns, and neither does the Opera browser.

Nevertheless, on all other modern browsers columns work well, as shown by Figure 25-11, which shows these classes being used and displayed in the Google Chrome browser.

Classes and Properties

columns2 columns2_h	Classes to reformat text into two columns (columns2), or to do so only when the text is hovered over (columns2_h)
columns3 (etc...)	Class – as columns2 but for three columns
columns4 (etc...)	Class – as columns2 but for four columns
Columns5 (etc...)	Class – as columns2 but for five columns
-moz-column-rule	Property to specify the type of ruled line between columns on Firefox and other Mozilla browsers
-webkit-column-rule	Property to specify the type of ruled line between columns on Safari and Google Chrome
-o-column-rule	Property to specify the type of ruled line between columns on Opera (when/if it is supported)
column-rule	Property to specify the type of ruled line between columns on all other browsers (but not IE)
-moz-column-gap	Property to specify the gap between columns on Firefox and other Mozilla browsers
-webkit-column-gap	Property to specify the gap between columns on Safari and Google Chrome
-o-column-gap	Property to specify the gap between columns on Opera (when/if it is supported)
column-gap	Property to specify the gap between columns on all other browsers (but not IE)
-moz-column-count	Property to specify the number of columns on Firefox and other Mozilla browsers
-webkit-column-count	Property to specify the number of columns on Safari and Google Chrome
-o-column-count	Property to specify the number of columns on Opera (when/if it is supported)
column-count	Property to specify the number of columns on all other browsers (but not IE)

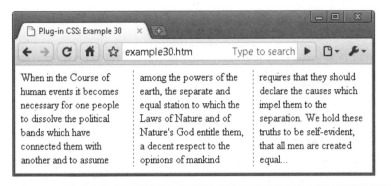

FIGURE 25-11   Create multiple columns on browsers that support the feature.

About the Classes

These classes display text in the number of columns you choose, between two and five inclusive, using the CSS column rules, as in the following example, which creates a two-column display:

```
column-rule:dashed 1px #888888;
column-gap:20px;
column-count:2;
```

Firefox and other Mozilla-based browsers require –moz placed before these properties, and Apple Safari and Google Chrome require –webkit. Although Opera doesn't yet support columns, it seems likely that the browser will do so soon, so to future-proof the classes, versions of the properties prefaced with –o are also included.

How to Use Them

To use these classes, decide the number of columns you want and place the relevant class in the class argument of the text's container, like the following, which was used to create the screen grab in Figure 25-11:

```
<div class='columns3'>When in the Course of human events it becomes
necessary for one people to dissolve the political bands which have
connected them with another and to assume among the powers of the earth,
the separate and equal station to which the Laws of Nature and of
Nature's God entitle them, a decent respect to the opinions of mankind
requires that they should declare the causes which impel them to the
separation. We hold these truths to be self-evident, that all men are
created equal...</div>
```

Neither Opera nor Microsoft Internet Explorer has caught up with the rest of the Web on this feature, so the text will simply display in a single column on those browsers. If you wish to have them also display columns, you will need to create an alternative section of HTML, which might look something like this:

```
<div style='width:160px' class='lf padding'>When in the Course of human
events it becomes necessary for one people to dissolve the political
bands which have connected them with another and to assume</div>

<div style='width:160px; class='lf padding'>among the powers of the
earth, the separate and equal station to which the Laws of Nature and
of Nature's God entitle them, a decent respect to the opinions of
mankind</div>

<div style='width:160px' class='lf padding'>requires that they should
declare the causes which impel them to the separation. We hold these
truths to be self-evident, that all men are created equal...</div>
```

The Classes

```
.columns2, .columns2_h:hover {
   -moz-column-rule:      dashed 1px #888888;
   -webkit-column-rule:   dashed 1px #888888;
   -o-column-rule:        dashed 1px #888888;
   column-rule:           dashed 1px #888888;
   -moz-column-gap:       20px;
   -webkit-column-gap:    20px;
   -o-column-gap:         20px;
   column-gap:            20px;
   -moz-column-count:     2;
   -webkit-column-count:2;
   -o-column-count:       2;
   column-count:          2;
}
.columns3, .columns3_h:hover {
   -moz-column-rule:      dashed 1px #888888;
   -webkit-column-rule:   dashed 1px #888888;
   -o-column-rule:        dashed 1px #888888;
   column-rule:           dashed 1px #888888;
   -moz-column-gap:       20px;
   -webkit-column-gap:    20px;
   -o-column-gap:         20px;
   column-gap:            20px;
   -moz-column-count:     3;
   -webkit-column-count:3;
   -o-column-count:       3;
   column-count:          3;
}
.columns4, .columns4_h:hover {
   -moz-column-rule:      dashed 1px #888888;
   -webkit-column-rule:   dashed 1px #888888;
   -o-column-rule:        dashed 1px #888888;
   column-rule:           dashed 1px #888888;
   -moz-column-gap:       20px;
```

```
  -webkit-column-gap:    20px;
  -o-column-gap:         20px;
  column-gap:            20px;
  -moz-column-count:     4;
  -webkit-column-count:4;
  -o-column-count:       4;
  column-count:          4;
}
.columns5, .columns5_h:hover {
  -moz-column-rule:      dashed 1px #888888;
  -webkit-column-rule:  dashed 1px #888888;
  -o-column-rule:        dashed 1px #888888;
  column-rule:           dashed 1px #888888;
  -moz-column-gap:       20px;
  -webkit-column-gap:    20px;
  -o-column-gap:         20px;
  column-gap:            20px;
  -moz-column-count:     5;
  -webkit-column-count:5;
  -o-column-count:       5;
  column-count:          5;
}
```

Text Indent

Indenting the first line of a paragraph is an alternative to separating paragraphs with extra line breaks. It is commonly used in print typography. You can easily implement this feature too using these classes, as shown in Figure 25-12, in which three different indent classes have been applied to the same piece of text.

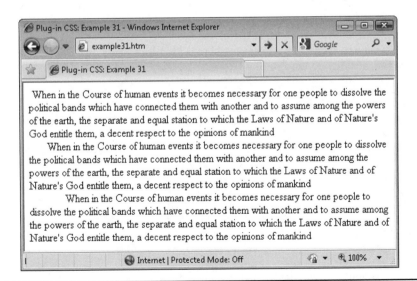

FIGURE 25-12   These classes enable indenting the first line of paragraphs by different amounts.

Classes and Properties

indent1 indent1_h	Classes to indent the first line of a section of text by 1 percent of the containing object's width (indent1), or to do so only when the text is hovered over (indent1_h)
indent2 - indent10 (etc...)	Class – as indent1 for 2 to 10 percent indent
text-indent	Property for indenting the first line of a section of text

About the Classes

These classes use the CSS text-indent property to indent the first line of a section of text by between 1 and 10 percent of the width of the containing object, like this:

text-indent:3%;

Percentage values are used to make the classes scalable for all font sizes.

How to Use Them

When you want the first line of a section of text to be indented, use one of these classes in the class argument of the text's container, like the following, which indents the first line by 5 percent:

```
<div class='indent5'>When in the Course of human events it becomes
necessary for one people to dissolve the political bands which have
connected them with another and to assume among the powers of the
earth, the separate and equal station to which the Laws of Nature and
of Nature's God entitle them, a decent respect to the opinions of
mankind</div>
```

Or more likely you will use the class within a <p> tag, like this:

```
<p class='indent5'>When in the Course of human events (etc...) </p>
```

The hover version suffix of these classes (_h) is also supported, but the other dynamic variants are not, as they are very unlikely to ever be used.

TIP *If you do use <p> tags with these classes, you may wish to modify the top and/or bottom margins for this tag since paragraphs will be separated and identified by indentation, rather than by spacing.*

The Classes

```
.indent1,   .indent1_h:hover   { text-indent:1%;  }
.indent2,   .indent2_h:hover   { text-indent:2%;  }
.indent3,   .indent3_h:hover   { text-indent:3%;  }
.indent4,   .indent4_h:hover   { text-indent:4%;  }
.indent5,   .indent5_h:hover   { text-indent:5%;  }
.indent6,   .indent6_h:hover   { text-indent:6%;  }
.indent7,   .indent7_h:hover   { text-indent:7%;  }
```

```
.indent8,  .indent8_h:hover  { text-indent:8%;  }
.indent9,  .indent9_h:hover  { text-indent:9%;  }
.indent10, .indent10_h:hover { text-indent:10%; }
```

Symbols

The final recipes in this chapter provide easy access to four commonly used icons: checkmark, cross, e-mail, and star. Figure 25-13 shows the icons automatically attached to a set of four buttons. A second set uses the hover versions of the classes in which the icons are initially lighter, but darken when hovered over (although, unfortunately, not in Internet Explorer when used on a button).

Classes and Properties

check check_h	Classes to preface text (or any object) with a checkmark icon (check), or to do so only when the text is hovered over (check_h)
cross	Class – as check but for a cross icon
email	Class – as check but for an e-mail icon
star	Class – as check but for a star icon
font-family	Property to change the font
font-weight	Property to change the weight of a font
color	Property to change the color of text
content	Property to add content to an object
opacity	Property used by non-IE browsers for opacity setting
filter	Property used by Internet Explorer for opacity and other features

About the Classes

These classes use the content property to place an icon before the text (or any object) that uses them. The text is also set to Courier with the font-family property, bold using the font-weight property, with colors set to green for check, red for cross, blue for email, and yellow for star, using the color property.

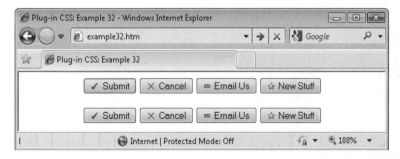

Figure 25-13 Use these classes to automatically add icons to text.

To create the hover effect, the opacity property is set to 50 percent, or 100 percent when hovered over. Microsoft browsers use the alternate filter property for this.

How to Use Them

To use these classes, simply refer to them in the class argument of an object, as with the following HTML, which was used to create Figure 25-13, and also utilizes the hover versions of the classes:

```
<center>
   <button class='check'>Submit</button>
   <button class='cross'>Cancel</button>
   <button class='email'>Email Us</button>
   <button class='star'>New Stuff</button><br /><br />

   <button class='check_h'>Submit</button>
   <button class='cross_h'>Cancel</button>
   <button class='email_h'>Email Us</button>
   <button class='star_h'>New Stuff</button>
</center>
```

The Classes

```
.check:before,  .check_h:before,  .check_h:hover:before {
   font-family:Courier;
   font-weight:bold;
   content:'\2713 ';
   color:#008800;
}
.cross:before,  .cross_h:before,  .cross_h:hover:before {
   font-family:Courier;
   font-weight:bold;
   content:'\2715 ';
   color:#ff0000;
}
.email:before,  .email_h:before,  .email_h:hover:before {
   font-family:Courier;
   content:'\2709 ';
   color:#0066ff;
}
.star:before,  .star_h:before,  .star_h:hover:before {
   font-family:Courier;
   content:'\2730 ';
   color:#888800;
}
.check_h:before,  .cross_h:before,  .email_h:before,  .star_h:before {
   opacity:.5;
   filter :alpha(opacity = '50');
}
.check_h:hover:before,  .cross_h:hover:before,  .email_h:hover:before,
.star_h:hover:before {
   opacity:1;
   filter :alpha(opacity = '100');
}
```

CHAPTER 26

Menus and Navigation

This chapter explores a range of classes used for creating buttons and vertical and horizontal menus, and for implementing top and bottom dock bars similar to those used by Mac OS X.

There's also a handy class for creating tooltips that you can format in a variety of different ways. Between them, you can provide a professional range of menuing and navigation aids for your web visitors.

RECIPE 33

Buttons

These classes make it a simple matter to quickly create buttons when you need them. In Figure 26-1, an Internet Explorer and Safari web browser have been placed next to each other, showing the same web page. IE displays the different button sizes but cannot manage the rounded borders, whereas Safari displays the buttons well. As you can see, even though IE is missing the rounded corners, it degrades gracefully.

Classes and Properties

`button`	Class to create a medium-sized button
`smallbutton`	Class to create a small button
`largebutton`	Class to create a large button
`Padding`	Property to change an object's padding
`border`	Property containing border details such as width and color
`font-size`	Property to change the size of a font
`text-align`	Property to align text to the left, right, or center, or make it fully justified
`width`	Property containing the width of an object
`overflow`	Property for setting whether and how objects overflow their boundaries

About the Classes

Three classes are available in this recipe for creating medium, small, or large buttons. They also use the `:hover` pseudo-class to provide professional effects when clicked or hovered over. To do this, they change the object's `border`, `font-size`, `text-align`, `width`, and `overflow` properties.

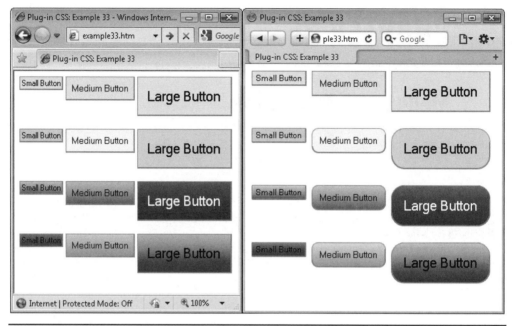

Figure 26-1 These classes make it easy to create great-looking buttons.

Hovered versions of the buttons change the border, while clicking them moves the button text down and to the right to emulate a 3D press.

How to Use Them

You can use these classes with any objects, but they work best with `<input type='submit'>` and `<button>` tags. In conjunction with other classes, you can give the buttons rounded borders, different background colors, gradients that change when clicked or hovered over, add shadow effects, and more.

Here is the HTML used to create the screen grabs in Figure 26-1:

```
<input type='submit' class='smallbutton'
    value='Small Button' />
<input type='submit' class='button'
    value='Medium Button' />
<input type='submit' class='largebutton'
    value='Large Button' /><br /><br />

<input type='submit' class='smallbutton smallestround lime_b'
    value='Small Button' />
<input type='submit' class='button round yellow_b'
    value='Medium Button' />
<input type='submit' class='largebutton largestround aqua_b'
    value='Large Button' /><br /><br />
```

```
<input type='submit' class='smallbutton smallestround carrot1 carrot2_a'
   value='Small Button' />
<input type='submit' class='button round sky1 sky2_a'
   value='Medium Button' />
<input type='submit' class='largebutton largestround wine1 wine2_a white'
   value='Large Button' /><br /><br/>

<input type='submit' class='smallbutton smallestround rose1 rose2_a
   white_h' value='Small Button' />
<input type='submit' class='button round sunset1 sunset2_a white_h'
   value='Medium Button' />
<input type='submit' class='largebutton largestround grass1 grass2_a
   white_h' value='Large Button' /><br /><br/>
```

The first row of buttons offers plain features, while the second row adds rounded borders and background colors. In the third row, the background colors have been replaced with gradient fills that reverse when the buttons are clicked, while the fourth row adds a hover color of white to each button.

As I have already noted a few times, different browsers have different features, so they will fall back gracefully when one isn't supported. For example, Internet Explorer will not display rounded borders, but Firefox, Opera, Safari, and Chrome will. There again, Opera won't display gradient background fills, and so on.

Even so, these button classes go a long way toward producing more engaging web sites, and as browsers implement the missing features, these classes will display better, without you having to change anything.

The Classes

```
.button {
   padding:8px;
}
.button:hover {
   border:2px solid #666666;
   padding:7px 8px 8px 7px;
}
.button:active {
   border-width:2px 1px 1px 2px;
   padding:9px 7px 7px 9px;
}
.smallbutton {
   font-size:75%;
   padding:2px;
}
.smallbutton:hover {
   border:2px solid #666666;
   padding:1px 2px 2px 1px;
}
.smallbutton:active {
   border-width:2px 1px 1px 2px;
   padding:3px 1px 1px 3px;
}
```

```
.largebutton {
   font-size:125%;
   padding:15px;
}
.largebutton:hover {
   border:2px solid #666666;
   padding:14px 15px 15px 14px;
}
.largebutton:active {
   border-width:2px 1px 1px 2px;
   padding:16px 14px 14px 16px;
}
.button, .smallbutton, .largebutton {
   text-align:center;
   border-color:#999999;
   border-width:1px 2px 2px 1px;
   vertical-align:top;
   border-style:solid; /* Required by Opera */
   width:auto;         /* Required by IE to not pad the sides */
   overflow:visible;
}
```

RECIPE 34 Vertical Menu

This recipe creates a dynamic vertical menu using only unordered lists. In Figure 26-2, three levels of menus have been created, with each overlaying and offset from the previous, and with each submenu set to overlay the chevron submenu indicator of its parent.

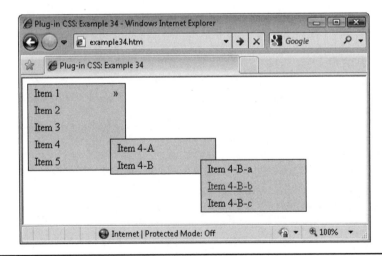

FIGURE 26-2   With this recipe, you can create professional-looking vertical menus.

Classes and Properties

`vmenu`	Class to create a set of vertical menus
`width`	Property containing the width of an object
`height`	Property containing the height of an object
`display`	Property used to set the display type of an object, such as block, inline, or none
`text-decoration`	Property containing the decoration for a section of text, such as underlines
`border`	Property containing all the border parameters of an object
`margin`	Property containing all the margin parameters of an object
`padding`	Property containing all the padding parameters of an object
`line-height`	Property containing the height of a section of text
`list-style`	Property containing the type of list
`left`	Property containing the offset of an object from the left of its containing object
`top`	Property containing the offset of an object from the top of its containing object
`z-index`	Property controlling how far behind or in front the object is compared to others
`float`	Property used to float an object to the right or left
`position`	Property used to manage the position of an object, such as relative or absolute
`content`	Property used to add content to an object from a CSS rule

About the Class

This class manipulates a large number of CSS properties in order to create menus and submenus that dynamically appear and disappear as required. The way it works is to make all second- and third-level menus (if any) invisible, and then it unhides them when they are due to appear.

The submenus are also given absolute positioning so they can be placed alongside the parent menu, starting at the item that calls them up, and covering over the chevron symbol that indicates a submenu is available.

How to Use It

To use this class, create a menu structure using unordered lists. The simplest of which might look like this:

```
<div class='vmenu aqua_b black_l blue_lh u_lh'>

   <ul>  <!-- Beg Level 1 -->
     <li><a href='url'>Item 1</a></li>
     <li><a href='url'>Item 2</a></li>
     <li><a href='url'>Item 3</a></li>
     <li><a href='url'>Item 4</a></li>
     <li><a href='url'>Item 5</a></li>
   </ul>  <!-- End Level 1 -->

</div>
```

The entire menu is enclosed in a `<div>` with the class name of `vmenu`. This div has its background color set to aqua, text within links set to black (or blue when hovered over), and

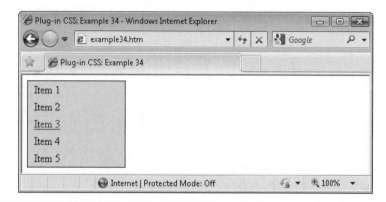

FIGURE 26-3 A single-level menu created with this class

underlines in links are enabled when hovered over. Inside this there are five list elements within an unordered list, and each of these elements contains a link.

For clarity, I have left a line break before and after the section labeled with `<!—Beg Level 1 -->` and `<!—End Level 1 -->` comments. These breaks indicate a complete section. When you open this HTML in a web browser, it looks like Figure 26-3, in which the third menu entry is currently being hovered over.

Creating a Two-Level Menu

Using almost the same structure, it's easy to add a second level of menus, as with the following example, which has taken the previous HTML and expanded it to add three second-level menus:

```
<div class='vmenu aqua_b black_l blue_lh u_lh'>

    <ul>  <!-- Beg Level 1 -->
        <li class='vmenu1'>
            <a href='url'>Item 1</a>

            <ul class='aqua_b'>  <!-- Beg Level 2 -->
                <li><a href='url'>Item 1-A</a></li>
                <li><a href='url'>Item 1-B</a></li>
                <li><a href='url'>Item 1-C</a></li>
            </ul>                 <!-- End Level 2 -->

        </li>
        <li><a href='url'>Item 2</a></li>
        <li><a href='url'>Item 3</a></li>
        <li class='vmenu1'>
            <a href='url' >Item 4</a>

            <ul class='aqua_b'>  <!-- Beg Level 2 -->
                <li><a href='url'>Item 4-A</a></li>
                <li><a href='url'>Item 4-B</a></li>
            </ul>                 <!-- End Level 2 -->
```

```
    </li>
    <li class='vmenu1'>
       <a href='url'>Item 5</a>

       <ul class='aqua_b'>   <!-- Beg Level 2 -->
          <li><a href='url'>Item 5-A</a></li>
          <li><a href='url'>Item 5-B</a></li>
          <li><a href='url'>Item 5-C</a></li>
       </ul>                 <!-- End Level 2 -->

    </li>
  </ul> <!-- End Level 1 -->

</div>
```

When viewed in a browser, this example looks like Figure 26-4, in which the first of the three menus has been opened by hovering over Item 1 in the main menu.

To add each second-level menu, the `<li>` and `</li>` tags surrounding the entry to which the menus are attached have been altered. The `<li>` tag has become `<li class='vmenu1'>` and the `</li>` has been moved to after the position where the new menu was added. In other words, the line...

```
<li><a href='url'>Item 1</a></li>
```

...has become the following section of code (the new code being marked by the comments):

```
<li class='vmenu1'>
   <a href='url'>Item 1</a>

   <ul class='aqua_b'>   <!-- Beg Level 2 -->
      <li><a href='url'>Item 1-A</a></li>
      <li><a href='url'>Item 1-B</a></li>
      <li><a href='url'>Item 1-C</a></li>
   </ul>                 <!-- End Level 2 -->

</li>
```

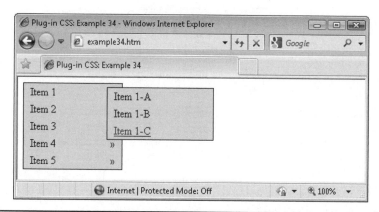

FIGURE 26-4   A two-level menu created with this class

Creating a Three-Level Menu

You can take the process a step further by adding another level of menus, like the following code, which was used to create Figure 26-2:

```html
<div class='vmenu aqua_b black_l blue_lh u_lh'>

   <ul>  <!-- Beg Level 1 -->
     <li class='vmenu1'>
        <a href='url'>Item 1</a>

        <ul class='aqua_b'>  <!-- Beg Level 2 -->
           <li class='vmenu1'>
             <a href='url'>Item 1-A</a>

             <ul class='aqua_b'>  <!-- Beg Level 3 -->
                <li><a href='url'>Item 1-A-a</a></li>
                <li><a href='url'>Item 1-A-b</a></li>
             </ul>              <!-- End Level 3 -->

           </li>
           <li><a href='url'>Item 1-B</a></li>
           <li><a href='url'>Item 1-C</a></li>
        </ul>                 <!-- End Level 2 -->

     </li>
     <li><a href='url'>Item 2</a></li>
     <li><a href='url'>Item 3</a></li>
     <li class='vmenu1'>
        <a href='url'>Item 4</a>

        <ul class='aqua_b'>  <!-- Beg Level 2 -->
           <li><a href='url'>Item 4-A</a></li>
           <li class='vmenu1'>
             <a href='url'>Item 4-B</a>

             <ul class='aqua_b'>  <!-- Beg Level 3 -->
                <li><a href='url'>Item 4-B-a</a></li>
                <li><a href='url'>Item 4-B-b</a></li>
                <li><a href='url'>Item 4-B-c</a></li>
             </ul>             <!-- End Level 3 -->

           </li>
        </ul>                 <!-- End Level 2 -->

     </li>
     <li class='vmenu1'>
        <a href='url'>Item 5</a>
```

```
            <ul class='aqua_b'>   <!-- Beg Level 2 -->
                <li class='vmenu1'>
                    <a href='url'>Item 5-A</a>

                    <ul class='aqua_b'>   <!-- Beg Level 3 -->
                        <li><a href='url'>Item 5-A-a</a></li>
                        <li><a href='url'>Item 5-A-b</a></li>
                    </ul>                 <!-- End Level 3 -->

                </li>
                <li><a href='url'>Item 5-B</a></li>
                <li><a href='url'>Item 5-C</a></li>
            </ul>                 <!-- End Level 2 -->

        </li>
    </ul> <!-- End Level 1 -->

</div>
```

Here, one of the second-level items has been split into a menu in the same way the
first-level item was split into a second-level menu.

This example is now quite long, so to make its working clearer, the following is the
underlying set of nested unordered list items as they would appear without the CSS styling,
as you can determine for yourself by not importing the *WDC.css* style sheet file:

```
Item 1
    Item 1-A
        Item 1-A-a
        Item 1-A-b
    Item 1-B
    Item 1-C
Item 2
Item 3
Item 4
    Item 4-A
    Item 4-B
        Item 4-B-a
        Item 4-B-b
        Item 4-B-c
Item 5
    Item 5-A
        Item 5-A-a
        Item 5-A-b
    Item 5-B
    Item 5-C
```

If you study the following CSS rules, you'll see references to an hmenu class. This is
because the following horizontal menu recipe shares many of the same styles, so bringing
them into the same rules is more efficient than including them twice.

By the way, a fourth (or any deeper) level of menus is not supported by this recipe.

The Class

```css
.vmenu, .hmenu {
    width:150px;
}
.vmenu a, .hmenu a {
    display:table-cell;
    width:150px;
    text-decoration:none;
}
.vmenu ul, .hmenu ul {
    border:1px solid #000;
    margin:0px;
    padding:0px;
}
.vmenu ul li, .hmenu ul li {
    height:25px;
    line-height:25px;
    list-style:none;
    padding-left:10px;
}
.vmenu ul li:hover, .hmenu ul li:hover {
    position:relative;
}
.vmenu ul ul, .hmenu ul ul {
    display:none;
    position:absolute;
}
.vmenu ul ul {
    left:125px;
    top:5px;
}
.vmenu ul li:hover ul, .hmenu ul li:hover ul {
    z-index:1;
}
.vmenu ul li:hover ul {
    display:block;
}
.vmenu ul ul li, .hmenu ul ul li {
    width:150px;
    float:left;
}
.vmenu ul ul li {
    display:block;
}
.vmenu li:hover ul li ul, .hmenu li:hover ul li ul {
    display:none;
}
.vmenu ul ul li ul, .hmenu ul ul li ul {
    left:137px;
}
.vmenu ul ul li:hover ul, .hmenu ul ul li:hover ul {
    z-index:1;
}
```

```
.vmenu ul ul li:hover ul {
   display:block;
}
.vmenu1:after, .hmenu1:after {
   position:relative;
   top:-25px;
   float:right;
   z-index:0;
   margin-right:10px;
   content:'\0bb';
}
```

Horizontal Menu

Using this class, it is equally easy to create a horizontal menu. In fact, by swapping the class names vmenu and vmenu1 in the previous recipe for hmenu and hmenu1 in this one, the menu completely reorientates itself, as shown by Figure 26-5, which uses exactly the same unordered list structure.

Classes and Properties

vmenu	Class to create a set of horizontal menus
width	Property containing the width of an object
height	Property containing the height of an object
display	Property used to set the display type of an object, such as block, inline, or none
text-decoration	Property containing the decoration for a section of text, such as underlines
border	Property containing all the border parameters of an object
margin	Property containing all the margin parameters of an object
padding	Property containing all the padding parameters of an object
line-height	Property containing the height of a section of text
list-style	Property containing the type of list
left	Property containing the offset of an object from the left of its containing object
top	Property containing the offset of an object from the top of its containing object
z-index	Property controlling how far behind or in front an object is compared to others
float	Property used to float an object to the right or left
position	Property used to manage the position of an object, such as relative or absolute
content	Property used to add content to an object from a CSS rule

About the Class

This class is almost the same as for the vertical menu, except that a few CSS rules have been modified to display the menus inline so they line up horizontally. It also moves the submenus to slightly different relative locations.

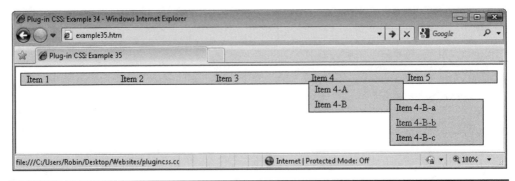

Figure 26-5 You can get a horizontal menu by using the hmenu classes instead of vmenu.

How to Use It

You use this class in exactly the same way as the vertical menu class, just change the class names used from vmenu and vmenu1 to hmenu and hmenu1. Please refer to the earlier Vertical Menu recipe section for full details.

Following are the additional tweaks made to the class in the previous section to provide horizontal menus.

The Class

```
.hmenu, .hmenu ul, .hmenu ul li, .hmenu ul li:hover ul, .hmenu ul ul li,
.hmenu ul ul li:hover ul {
    display:inline;
}
.hmenu ul ul {
    left:5px;
    top:15px;
}
.hmenu ul ul li ul {
    top:5px;
}
```

Top Dock Bar

Recipe 36 provides a static dock bar that can be placed at the top of a web page for use as a menu or navigation aid. Figure 26-6 shows such a dock bar created from six icons, the fourth of which is currently being hovered over and has expanded under the mouse pointer.

Classes and Properties

topdockbar	Class for creating a dock bar container
topdockitem	Class for assigning an icon to a top dock bar
position	Class for assigning an icon to a top dock bar
left	Class for assigning an icon to a top dock bar

margin-left	Class for assigning an icon to a top dock bar
vertical-align	Class for assigning an icon to a top dock bar
width	Class for assigning an icon to a top dock bar
height	Class for assigning an icon to a top dock bar
-moz-transition	Property used by Mozilla and other Mozilla browsers to transition between two sets of property values
-webkit-transition	Property used by Safari and Chrome to transition between two sets of property values
-o-transition	Property used by Opera to transition between two sets of property values
transition	Property used by all other browsers except for Internet Explorer

About the Classes

This recipe has two classes: the first (topdockbar) is used to create a container for the dock bar items, and the second is for attaching to icons used in the dock bar (topdockitem).

The topdockbar class moves the object that uses it to the top of the browser and centers it. The object's position is also fixed so it will not move when the browser scrolls.

The topdockitem class attaches a transition to the object so that any changes made to it will transition over the time period specified (on browsers that support transitions). It also aligns each item to the top of the dock bar so that passing the mouse over it will enlarge the image but keep it top-aligned.

A :hover pseudo-class is then used to enlarge the icons when moused over and restore them when the mouse passes away.

How to Use Them

To use these classes, you need to have six icons that are 86 by 86 pixels in size. If they are different sizes or a different number, you may need to modify the code in the *PC.css* file.

These images are then resized to 50 by 50 pixels for the initial display (so that they can be enlarged to their full dimensions when moused over).

Then, write some HTML to contain all the images, such as this:

```
<div class='topdockbar'>
    <img class='topdockitem' src='i1.gif'>
    <img class='topdockitem' src='i2.gif'>
    <img class='topdockitem' src='i3.gif'>
    <img class='topdockitem' src='i4.gif'>
    <img class='topdockitem' src='i5.gif'>
    <img class='topdockitem' src='i6.gif'>
</div>
```

When you use this HTML in a web page, you get the result seen in Figure 26-6. Of course, you will also attach links to the images to give each a function. When you do, a border may be displayed around the images, which you can remove by adding the argument border='0' to the <img...> tag. You may also wish to use CSS Recipe 19 (No Outline) to remove the dotted focus outline added to clicked elements.

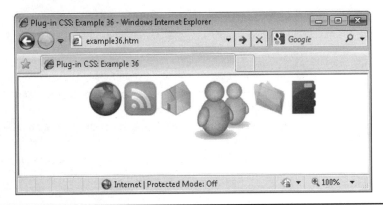

FIGURE 26-6   Using this class, you can create a top dock bar.

NOTE   *In Internet Explorer, when the icons are hovered over, they will instantly enlarge, and reduce down again in size when the mouse passes away. But on all of Opera 10, Firefox 4, Safari 5, and the Chrome 5 web browsers (or better), the enlarging and reduction are animated using CSS transitions, which automatically generate and display a sequence of frames between a start and end set of style settings.*

Changing the Number of Icons and/or Icon Sizes

In the following CSS rules, note the value assigned to the `margin-left` property in order to center the dock bar. If you change the icon sizes or number of icons, you should calculate a new value for this property, using this formula:

```
(Reduced image size x Number of images) / 2
   +
(Actual width - Reduced width) / 4
```

So, for example, if you intend to use five 100 by 100–pixel images with a reduced size of 80 by 80 pixels, this is the calculation:

```
(5 x 100) / 2
   +
(100 - 80) / 4
```

This would give you a new value of 5 multiplied by 100 (which is 500), divided by 2 (which is 250), plus 100 – 80 (which is 20), divided by 4 (which is 5), which equals 250 plus 5, or a value of 255 pixels.

You will also see mention of a `bottomdockbar` class in these rules. This is because the following recipe shares much of the CSS, so it also shares some of the CSS rule assignments in order to keep from repeating the code.

The Classes

```
.topdockbar, .bottomdockbar {
  position:fixed;
  left:50%;
  margin-left:-159px;    /* Set to (total width of reduced images) / 2 */
                         /*      + (actual width -  reduced width) / 4 */
}
.topdockitem, .bottomdockitem {
  -moz-transition:   all .2s;
  -webkit-transition:all .2s;
  -o-transition:     all .2s;
  transition:        all .2s;
  vertical-align:top;
  width: 50px;          /* Set to reduced image width  */
  height:50px;          /* Set to reduced image height */
}
.topdockitem:hover, .bottomdockitem:hover {
  width: 86px;          /* Set to actual image width  */
  height:86px;          /* Set to actual image height */
}
```

Bottom Dock Bar

RECIPE 37

Recipe 37 lets you create a bottom dock bar in the same way you created the top dock bar in the previous recipe. Figure 26-7 shows the classes being used in the Apple Safari browser.

Classes and Properties

bottomdockbar	Class for creating a bottom dock bar container
bottomdockitem	Class for assigning an icon to a bottom dock bar
position	Property specifying whether an object has absolute or relative positioning, and so on
left	Property containing an object's left offset
margin-left	Property containing an object's left margin
vertical-align	Property containing an object's vertical alignment
width	Property containing an object's width
height	Property containing an object's height
-moz-transition	Property used by Mozilla and other Mozilla browsers to transition between two sets of property values
-webkit-transition	Property used by Safari and Chrome to transition between two sets of property values
-o-transition	Property used by Opera to transition between two sets of property values
transition	Property used by all other browsers except for Internet Explorer

FIGURE 26-7   Creating a bottom dock bar in the Apple Safari browser

About the Classes

These classes work in exactly the same manner as the `topdockbar` and `topdockitem` classes, only replacing those class names with `bottomdockbar` and `bottomdockitem`.

How to Use Them

Using these items is identical to creating a top dock bar, except for swapping the class names to `bottomdockbar` and `bottomdockitem`. Therefore, please refer to the previous recipe for details.

Following are the additional CSS rules required to create bottom dock bars. If you change the height of any images, you will also need to change the `margin-top` property to the new height plus 7 pixels, and `padding-top` to the difference in pixels between the actual height of the images and their reduced heights.

The Classes

```css
.bottomdockbar {
  top:100%;
  margin-top:-93px;      /* Set to -(actual image height + 7) */
}
.bottomdockitem {
  padding-top:36px;      /* Set to (actual height) - (reduced height) */
}
.bottomdockitem:hover {
  padding-top:0px;
}
```

Tooltip and Tooltip Fade

These classes let you add tooltips (most of whose dimensions and HTML you can decide) to any object. In Figure 26-8, the word *gravity* has been assigned a short tooltip, briefly providing an explanation for the term. Tooltips can also be applied to links and any other objects.

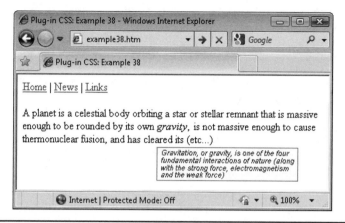

Figure 26-8   With this class, you can add tooltips to any object.

Classes and Properties

tooltip	Class to display a tooltip when the mouse passes over an object
tooltipfade	Class to fade in a tooltip when the mouse passes over an object (for browsers that support transitions)
text-decoration	Property for changing text decorations such as underlines
position	Property containing an objects' position, such as absolute or relative
display	Property containing the way an object displays, such as block or inline
top	Property containing the vertical offset of an object from the top of its container
left	Property containing the horizontal offset of an object from the left of its container
white-space	Property used to disallow word wrapping at spaces
background	Property containing an object's background settings
border	Property containing an object's border settings
color	Property containing an object's text color
font-family	Property specifying the font to use
font-size	Property specifying the font size to use
line-height	Property specifying the line height of a font
padding	Property containing an object's padding settings
opacity	Property used to control an object's opacity (or transparency)
-moz-transition	Property for creating transitions on Firefox and other Mozilla browsers
-webkit-transition	Property for creating transitions on Safari and Chrome
-o-transition	Property for creating transitions on Opera
transition	Property for creating transitions on all other browsers (except IE)
filter	Property used by IE for opacity and other features

About the Classes

The tooltip class takes a <span> that must be provided alongside the object being given a tooltip and then hides it away to be displayed only when the mouse passes over the object.

The tooltipfade class is identical except that (where supported) it uses CSS transitions to slide and fade a tooltip into place.

How to Use Them

To use either of these classes, you must place a <span> directly following the object to be given the tooltip, in which you should place the tip to be displayed, like this:

```
<a class='tooltip' href='/'>Home<span>Go to the Home page</span></a>
```

The <span> is then lifted from the flow of the web page and made invisible, to appear only when the object is moused over.

Here is the code used to create Figure 26-8, showing the two different variants of the class in action:

```
<a href='/'>Home</a> |
<a href='/news/'>News</a> |
<a class='tooltip' href='/links/'>Links<span>Click here for a<br />
collection of great links</span></a><br /><br />

A planet is a celestial body orbiting a star or stellar remnant that is
massive enough to be rounded by its own
<span class='tooltipfade i'>gravity<span>Gravitation, or gravity, is one
of the four<br />fundamental interactions of nature (along<br />with the
strong force, electromagnetism<br />and the weak force)</span></span>,
is not massive enough to cause thermonuclear fusion, and has (etc...)
```

The first use of these classes is of the tooltip class in the third link from the top, and the second is of the tooltipfade class in the text below it. The class argument of 'tooltipfade i' tells the browsers to display the text within the tooltip in italics. When displayed in the Opera 10, Firefox 4, Safari 5, or Chrome 5 browsers (or better), the tooltip attached to the word *gravity* will slide down into place, smoothly fading in at the same time. On Internet Explorer, the tooltip will simply appear and disappear as the mouse hovers over the object and moves away again.

These classes disallow automatic wrapping at white space so that the width of each tooltip can be specified according to where the <br /> tags are placed, and therefore the final width is that of the widest line.

NOTE *The text and background colors of the tooltips are fixed, so if you want different ones, you'll need to alter the WDC.css file accordingly.*

The Classes

```css
.tooltip:hover, .tooltipfade:hover {
  text-decoration:none;
  position:relative;
}
.tooltip span {
  display:none;
}
.tooltip:hover span {
  display:block;
  position:absolute;
  top:40px;
  left:0px;
  white-space:nowrap;
  background:#ffffdd;
  border:1px solid #888888;
  color:#444444;
  font-family:Arial, Helvetica, sans-serif;
  font-size:8pt;
  line-height:95%;
  padding:2px 5px;
}
.tooltipfade span {
  position:absolute;
  white-space:nowrap;
  font-family:Arial, Helvetica, sans-serif;
  font-size:8pt;
  line-height:95%;
  padding:2px 5px;
  top:0px;
  top:-10000px\0; /* IE hack to keep it out of the way */
  left:0px;
  background:#ffffdd;
  border:1px solid #888888;
  color:#444444;
  opacity:0;
  filter:alpha(opacity = '0');
}
.tooltipfade:hover span {
  -moz-transition    :all .5s linear;
  -webkit-transition:all .5s linear;
  -o-transition      :all .5s linear;
  transition         :all .5s linear;
  opacity:1;
  filter:alpha(opacity = '100');
  top:40px;
}
```

CHAPTER 27

Page Layout

The recipes in this chapter provide classes for making your web pages appear as similar as possible when displayed on different web browsers; to emphasize sections of text and HTML using boxouts, sidebars, and quotes; and to format a web page so it looks its best when printed.

Reset CSS

When you plan a lot of style changes, sometimes it is easier to reset all the settings so that whichever browser is used the styles will be the same (or as close as possible). By resetting all the styles, when you view a web page during development it should become clear when you haven't created a style for an element, since it gives you a visual reminder.

Also, when you rely on the browser for default styles, you have no guarantee that all other browsers will use the same default setting. So by resetting all the properties, you are forced to create your own styling—which will be the same across all browsers.

For example, in Figure 27-1, I have displayed the same small segment of HTML in each of the Firefox, Internet Explorer, Chrome, Opera, and Safari web browsers.

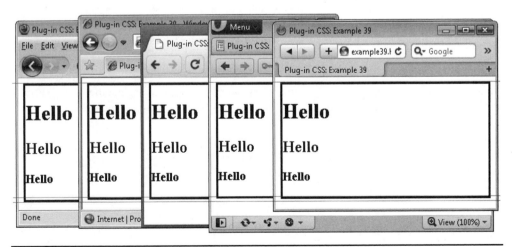

FIGURE 27-1   A simple section of HTML displayed in five different browsers

The HTML each displays is the following, which simply creates a `<div>` with a solid one-pixel border, placing three headings within it:

```
<div class='bsolid'>
    <h1>Hello</h1>
    <h2>Hello</h2>
    <h3>Hello</h3>
</div>
```

You might think that such a tiny piece of HTML would display exactly the same way in all web browsers, but take a look at the figure and note the light line I have drawn across the top border of the `<div>` in each browser. As you can see, all the browsers have been aligned so that the top border of each `<div>` is against the line.

Now look at the bottom border of each `<div>`. Using a graphics program, I counted the difference in pixels and can report that the Internet Explorer `<div>` is three pixels shorter than the Firefox one. If you look at the two other light lines I drew—under the lowest and over the highest of the bottom borders—you can easily see this discrepancy. Also, the headings are one, one, and two pixels higher up, respectively in IE.

Turning to Google Chrome, it has exactly the same appearance as IE and therefore is also different from Firefox in the same ways. The Opera `<div>`, on the other hand, is one pixel shorter than these two, and therefore four pixels shorter than the one in Firefox one. Also, its headings are zero, one, and one pixel higher than IE and Chrome, or one, two, and three pixels higher than Firefox.

Finally, Apple Safari has the same height `<div>` as IE and Chrome. Therefore, it is three pixels shorter than Firefox—and its headings are also slightly higher than Firefox.

Perhaps you never realized how different all the browsers are—and this example uses only a couple of elements. But by using the `reset` class, you can remove all these different attributes and start again with your own settings.

Classes and Properties

reset	Class to reset all the major properties of an object—can be applied to a document to reset all of the document's properties
(numerous properties)	Properties of an object that are too numerous to mention here

About the Class

This class resets every property of an object that sensibly can be reset, leaving them ready for you to assign your own values. These will then be the same on all browsers.

How to Use It

You can use this class in a couple of ways. First, to reset only the properties of an object and its subobjects, you might use code such as this:

```
<div id='obj' class='reset'>Everything in this div is reset</div>
```

You would then need to write CSS rules for the ID `obj` to create the property values you want, such as:

```
#obj p {
    display:block;
    Margin:1.12em;
}
```

Alternatively (and probably the most useful method), you can attach the class to the
<html> tag, like this:

```
<html class='reset'>
```

Once you do this, your whole web page will lose almost all its styling, making it ready
for you to provide the styles you need.

The Class

```
.reset a,          .reset abbr,       .reset acronym,
.reset address,    .reset applet,     .reset big,
.reset blockquote, .reset body,       .reset caption,
.reset cite,       .reset code,       .reset dd,
.reset del,        .reset dl,         .reset dfn,
.reset div,        .reset dt,         .reset em,
.reset fieldset,   .reset font,       .reset form,
.reset h1,         .reset h2,         .reset h3,
.reset h4,         .reset h5,         .reset h6,
.reset html,       .reset iframe,     .reset img,
.reset ins,        .reset kbd,        .reset label,
.reset legend,     .reset li,         .reset object,
.reset ol,         .reset p,          .reset pre,
.reset span,       .reset q,          .reset s,
.reset samp,       .reset small,      .reset strike,
.reset strong,     .reset sub,        .reset sup,
.reset table,      .reset tbody,      .reset td,
.reset tfoot,      .reset th,         .reset thead,
.reset tr,         .reset tt,         .reset ul,
.reset var {
    margin         :0;
    padding        :0;
    border         :0;
    outline        :0;
    font-family    :inherit;
    font-style     :inherit;
    font-weight    :inherit;
    font-size      :100%;
    vertical-align :baseline;
}
.reset address,    .reset ar,         .reset caption,
.reset cite,       .reset code,       .reset dfn,
.reset em,         .reset strong,     .reset th,
.reset v {
    font-style     :normal;
    font-weight    :normal;
}
.reset h1,         .reset h2,         .reset h3,
.reset h4,         .reset h5,         .reset h6 {
```

```
   font-weight     :normal;
   font-size       :100%;
}
.reset blockquote:after, .reset blockquote:before,
.reset q:after,          .reset q:before {
   content         :'';
}
.reset caption,    .reset th,       .reset td {
   font-weight     :normal;
   text-align      :left;
}
.reset              .reset fieldset, .reset img {
   border          :0;
}
.reset abbr,        .reset acronym {
   border          :0;
}
.reset ol,          .reset ul {
   list-style      :none;
}
.reset body {
   line-height     :1;
   background      :#ffffff;
   color           :#000000;
}
.reset table {
   border-collapse :separate;
   border-spacing  :0;
}
.reset:focus {
   outline         :0;
}
```

Default CSS

As an alternative to resetting all the CSS values, you can use this class, which creates a set of default property values, as recommended by the World Wide Web Consortium (*w3.org/TR/CSS2/sample.html*).

Figure 27-2 shows the same code as in the previous recipe, displayed in the same browsers, with a single difference—the `default` class has been attached to the `<html>` tag. Now that all the browsers are using the same settings, their display is much more similar.

However, some slight differences still remain. This is because it is necessary to allow fonts and margins to scale up or down, so relative em measurements have been used for their values and, due to the different ways each browser calculates them, there is still a slight difference between them. Overall, however, you have a lot more control over a web page's display using this class, instead of relying on each browser's default settings.

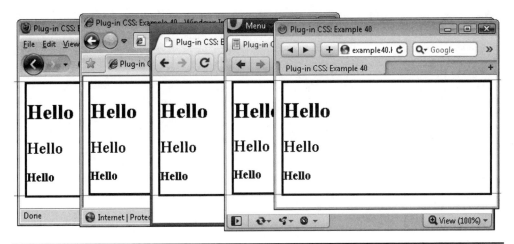

Figure 27-2   Using the `default` class, the differences in display between browsers are reduced.

Classes and Properties

default	Class to reset all the major properties of an object—can be applied to a document to reset all of the document's properties
(numerous properties)	Properties of an object that are too numerous to mention here

About the Class

This class resets every property of an object to sensible defaults, as recommended by *w3.org*, the web standards body, so your pages look much more alike on different browsers.

How to Use It

You can use this class in a couple of ways. First, to set default styles only for the properties of an object and its subobjects, you might use code such as this:

```
<div id='obj' class='default'>This div has default settings</div>
```

Alternatively, you might be more likely to attach the class to the <html> tag, like this:

```
<html class='default'>
```

Tip   *In the case of both the* `reset` *and* `default` *classes, you may prefer to extract the CSS rules for these classes from the* WDC.css *file into separate CSS style sheets that you can import before any others. In which case, use a search and replace facility to remove all instances of* .reset *for the* reset *class or* .default *for the* default *class, and then the styles will apply to the entire document, not just to classes using those names. For example, the rule* .default h1 *applies only to* <h1> *tags with an element ID of* default. *But by removing the* .default *prior to the* h1, *the rule will apply to* all *instances of the* <h1> *tag anywhere in a web page.*

The Class

```
.default address,    .default blockquote,  .default body,
.default center,     .default dd,          .default dir,
.default div,        .default dl,          .default dt,
.default fieldset,   .default form,        .default frame,
.default frameset,   .default h1,          .default h2,
.default h3,         .default h4,          .default h5,
.default h6,         .default hr,          .default html,
.default menu,       .default noframes,    .default ol,
.default p,          .default pre,         .default ul
    { display:block; }
.default blockquote, .default dir,         .default dl,
.default fieldset,   .default form,        .default h4,
.default menu,       .default ol,          .default p,
.default ul
    { margin:1.12em 0; }
.default b,          .default h1,          .default h2,
.default h3,         .default h4,          .default h5,
.default h6,         .default strong
    { font-weight:bolder; }
.default address,    .default cite,        .default em,
.default i,          .default var
    { font-style:italic; }
.default code,       .default kbd,         .default pre,
.default samp,       .default tt
    { font-family:monospace; }
.default dd,         .default dir,         .default menu,
.default ol,         .default ul
    { margin-left:40px; }
.default button,     .default input,       .default select,
.default textarea
    { display:inline-block; }
.default ol ol,      .default ol ul,       .default ul ol,
.default ul ul
    { margin-top:0; margin-bottom:0; }
.default del,        .default s,           .default strike
    { text-decoration:line-through; }
.default small,      .default sub,         .default sup
    { font-size:0.83em; }
.default tbody,      .default tfoot,       .default thead
    { vertical-align :middle; }
.default td,         .default th,          .default tr
    { vertical-align :inherit; }
.default ins,        .default u
    { text-decoration:underline; }
.default td,         .default th
    { display:table-cell; padding:2px; }
.default a:active,   .default a:link
    { text-decoration:underline; color:#0000ff; }
.default big
    { font-size:1.17em; }
.default blockquote
    { margin-left:40px; margin-right:40px; }
```

```
.default body
   { margin:8px; }
.default br:before
   { content:"\A"; white-space:pre-line; }
.default caption
   { display:table-caption; text-align:center; }
.default center
   { text-align:center; }
.default col
   { display:table-column; }
.default colgroup
   { display:table-column-group; }
.default h1
   { font-size:2em; margin:0.7em 0; }
.default h2
   { font-size:1.5em; margin:0.75em 0; }
.default h3
   { font-size:1.17em; margin:0.83em 0; }
.default h5
   { font-size:0.83em; margin:1.5em 0; }
.default h6
   { font-size:0.75em; margin:1.67em 0; }
.default head
   { display:none; }
.default hr
   { border:1px inset; }
.default li
   { display:list-item; }
.default ol
   { list-style-type:decimal; }
.default table
   { display:table; }
.default tbody
   { display:table-row-group; }
.default tfoot
   { display:table-footer-group; }
.default th
   { font-weight:bolder; text-align:center; }
.default thead
   { display:table-header-group;   }
.default tr
   { display:table-row; }
.default pre
   { white-space:pre; }
.default sub
   { vertical-align:sub;   }
.default sup
   { vertical-align:super; }
.default table
   { border-spacing:2px; }
.default a:visited
   { color:#800080; }
.default :focus
   { outline:thin dotted invert; }
```

Boxout

With the boxout class, you can easily place a section of HTML within a special boxout to make it stand out from the rest of the page. Figure 27-3 shows the class being used to emphasize some information in an article on global warming (taken from *wikipedia.org*).

Classes and Properties

boxout boxout_h	Class to create a boxout around a section of HTML (boxout), or to do so only when the text is hovered over (boxout_h)
margin	Property containing the various margin settings of an object
padding	Property containing the various padding settings of an object
border	Property containing the various border settings of an object
background	Property containing the various background settings of an object

About the Classes

These classes create a professional-looking boxout around any section of HTML. They do so either immediately or only when hovered over, and completely restyle the HTML by altering the margin, padding, border, and background properties of an object.

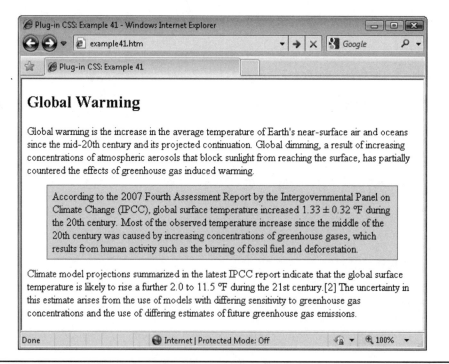

FIGURE 27-3   The boxout class helps add emphasis to important sections of a page.

How to Use Them

To place a section of HTML into a boxout, you would use HTML such as this:

```
<div class='boxout'>This text will appear in a boxout</div>
```

Or you can choose to make the boxout appear only when the HTML is hovered over, like this:

```
<div class='boxout_h'>This is a boxout when hovered over</div>
```

TIP *If you use the hover version of the class, it's a good idea to ensure the section is already separated from the text above and below; otherwise, the change when hovered over may be too much on the eye.*

Following is the HTML used to create Figure 27-3. As you can see, when writing, it's easy to drop the class into a section of text without distracting you from your creative flow:

```
<h2>Global Warming</h2>
Global warming is the increase in the average temperature of Earth's
near-surface air and oceans since the mid-20th century and its projected
continuation. Global dimming, a result of increasing concentrations of
atmospheric aerosols that block sunlight from reaching the surface, has
partially countered the effects of greenhouse gas induced warming.

<div class='boxout_h'>
According to the 2007 Fourth Assessment Report by the Intergovernmental
Panel on Climate Change (IPCC), global surface temperature increased
1.33 +/- 0.32 &deg;F during the 20th century. Most of the observed
temperature increase since the middle of the 20th century was caused by
increasing concentrations of greenhouse gases, which results from human
activity such as the burning of fossil fuel and deforestation.</div>

Climate model projections summarized in the latest IPCC report indicate
that the global surface temperature is likely to rise a further 2.0 to
11.5 &deg;F during the 21st century. The uncertainty in this estimate
arises from the use of models with differing sensitivity to greenhouse
gas concentrations and the use of differing estimates of future
greenhouse gas emissions.
```

The Classes

```
.boxout, .boxout_h:hover {
  margin:2% 5%;
  padding:1% 1.4%;
  border:1px solid #888;
  background:#eeeeee;
}
```

Quote

Another great way to emphasize a section of text is to change the font style to something like italic and add a faded-out icon behind it, as with the `quote` class. In Figure 27-4, an article about the poet William Wordsworth (from *wikipedia.org*) has been displayed, with a few lines from one of his poems shown using this class.

Classes and Properties

quote quote_h	Class to enclose a section of HTML in a quote (quote), or to do so only when the text is hovered over (quote_h)
margin	Property containing the various margin settings of an object
padding	Property containing the various padding settings of an object
font-style	Property containing the style of a font
font-size	Property containing the size of a font
content	Property for adding content via CSS
position	Property specifying an object's position, such as absolute or relative
left	Property containing the offset from the left of an object
top	Property containing the offset from the top of an object
line-height	Property specifying the line height of a font
margin-bottom	Property specifying the bottom margin height
color	Property containing the text color
opacity	Property specifying the opacity (or transparency) of an object (except IE)
float	Property used to float an object to the left or right

About the Classes

These classes present a section of text in such a way that it is clearly obvious the text is a quotation. They do so by changing the text font to italic and resizing the margins and padding. Then, a large pale opening quotation mark symbol is placed at the top left of, and behind, the text.

Internet Explorer refuses to use the `filter` property to change the large quotation mark's opacity. For some reason, `filter` seems to not like operating within a `:before` or `:after` pseudo-class. Therefore, an IE-specific hack is used to set the color of the symbol to very light gray instead.

How to Use Them

To use these classes, simply mention one or the other in the `class` argument of an object, like this:

```
<div class='quote'>This text will appear as a quote</div>
```

Or you can choose to make the quote appear only when the HTML is hovered over, like this:

```
<div class='quote_h'>This appears as a quote when hovered over</div>
```

Here is the HTML used for the screen grab in Figure 27-4:

```
<h2>William Wordsworth</h2>
William Wordsworth (7 April 1770 - 23 April 1850) was a major English
Romantic poet who, with Samuel Taylor Coleridge, helped to launch the
Romantic Age in English literature with the 1798 joint publication
Lyrical Ballads.

<div class='quote'><h3>I Wandered Lonely As A Cloud</h3>
I wandered lonely as a cloud That floats on high o'er vales and hills,
When all at once I saw a crowd, A host of golden daffodils; Beside the
lake, beneath the trees, Fluttering and dancing in the breeze.</div>

Wordsworth's magnum opus is generally considered to be The Prelude, a
semiautobiographical poem of his early years which he revised and
expanded a number of times. It was posthumously titled and published,
prior to which it was generally known as the poem "to Coleridge."
Wordsworth was Britain's Poet Laureate from 1843 until his death in 1850.
```

You can change the quotation mark to one of many different styles by changing the font-family assignment in the following class in the *WDC.css* file (available at *webdeveloperscookbook.com*). You may find you also need to play with the padding and left properties if you do so, since different fonts display at different sizes and in different ways.

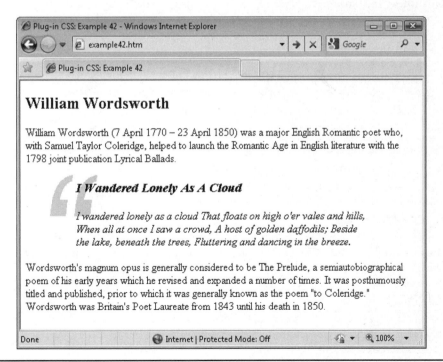

FIGURE 27-4   Using the quote class automatically sets up an appealing style.

The Classes

```
.quote, .quote_h {
   margin:2% 10%;
   padding:1% 3%;
   font-style:italic
}
.quote:before, .quote_h:hover:before  {
   font-size:1500%;
   font-family:Arial, serif;
   content:'\201c';
   position:relative;
   left:-15%;
   top:-1%;
   line-height:0.7em;
   margin-bottom:-2em;
   color:#dddddd\0;    /* hack for IE only */
   opacity:.1;
   float:left;
}
```

Left Sidebar

Another way of emphasizing a section of HTML is to move it to one side as a boxout and let the main article flow around it. Figure 27-5 shows this class being used to do exactly that on the example from the previous recipe.

Classes and Properties

leftsidebar	Class to float a section of HTML to the left of the main text
padding	Property containing all the padding settings of an object
margin-right	Property specifying the width of an object's right margin
border	Property containing all the border settings of an object
background	Property containing all the background settings of an object
width	Property specifying an object's width
float	Property for floating an object to the left or right

About the Class

This class floats a section of HTML to the left using the float property, and then adds padding around it, as well as a suitable margin to the right. The background is set to very light gray, and the object's width is set to 25 percent of its containing object.

How to Use It

To use this class, decide exactly where in the flow of your HTML you would like it to appear, and then enclose the section for placement in the sidebar in a <div> using the class name leftsidebar, like this:

```
<div class='leftsidebar'>This text will appear in a left sidebar</div>
```

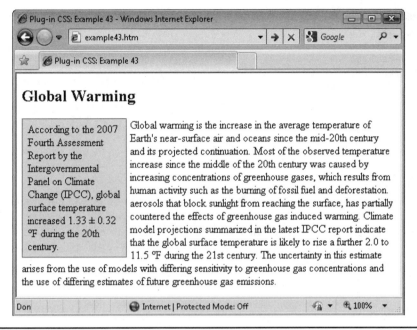

FIGURE 27-5   Sidebars are another great way to make your text more interesting.

For example, here is the HTML used to create Figure 27-5, with the sidebar starting at the same vertical position as the main text:

```
<h2>Global Warming</h2>
<div class='leftsidebar'>
According to the 2007 Fourth Assessment Report by the Intergovernmental
Panel on Climate Change (IPCC), global surface temperature increased
1.33 +/- 0.32 &deg;F during the 20th century.</div>
```

```
Global warming is the increase in the average temperature of Earth's
near-surface air and oceans since the mid-20th century and its projected
continuation. Most of the observed temperature increase since the middle
of the 20th century was caused by increasing concentrations of greenhouse
gases, which result from human activity such as the burning of fossil
fuel and deforestation. Aerosols that block sunlight from reaching the
surface, have partially countered the effects of greenhouse-gas-induced
warming. Climate model projections summarized in the latest IPCC report
indicate that the global surface temperature is likely to rise a further
2.0 to 11.5 &deg;F during the 21st century. The uncertainty in this
estimate arises from the use of models with differing sensitivity to
greenhouse gas concentrations and the use of differing estimates of
future greenhouse gas emissions.
```

PART IV

The Class

```
.leftsidebar {
    padding:1% 1.4%;
    margin-right:1%;
    border:1px solid #888;
    background:#eeeeee;
    width:25%;
    float:left;
}
```

Right Sidebar

This is the partner class to Left Sidebar. It works in exactly the same way but moves the sidebar to the right-hand side of the main text. Figure 27-6 shows the same example used in the previous recipe, with only the class used being changed to rightsidebar:

Classes and Properties

rightsidebar	Class to float a section of HTML to the right of the main text
padding	Property containing all the padding settings of an object
margin-right	Property specifying the width of an object's right margin
border	Property containing all the border settings of an object
background	Property containing all the background settings of an object
width	Property specifying an object's width
float	Property for floating an object to the left or right

About the Class

This class floats a section of HTML to the left using the float property, and then adds padding around it and a suitable margin to the left. The background is very light gray, and the object's width is set to 25 percent of its containing object.

How to Use It

To use this class, decide exactly where in the flow of your HTML you would like it to appear and then enclose the section for placement in the sidebar in a <div>, with the class name rightsidebar, like this:

```
<div class='leftsidebar'>This text will appear in a right sidebar</div>
```

For example, here is the HTML used to create Figure 27-6, with the sidebar starting at the same vertical position as the main text (since the article text is identical to that in the previous recipe, only the first five lines are shown):

```
<h2>Global Warming</h2>
<div class='rightsidebar'>
According to the 2007 Fourth Assessment Report by the Intergovernmental
Panel on Climate Change (IPCC), global surface temperature increased
1.33 +/- 0.32 &deg;F during the 20th century.</div>
(etc...)
```

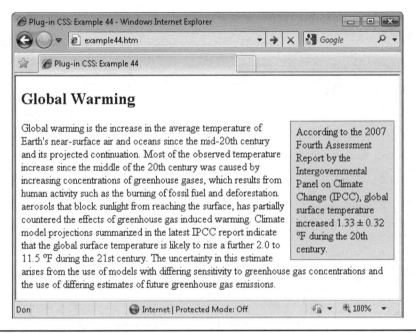

FIGURE 27-6   You can also create a sidebar on the right if you prefer.

The Class

```
.rightsidebar {
    padding:1% 1.4%;
    margin-left:1%;
    border:1px solid #888;
    background:#eeeeee;
    width:25%;
    float:right;
}
```

Page Break

This is a short and sweet class that you will find useful when visitors print out a web page, because with it you can specify where the page breaks should be located, so the printout will look much cleaner than web pages printed without using such a feature. For example, although the text is too small to read clearly, Figure 27-7 shows a copy of the Wikipedia Computer Printers page being viewed using Internet Explorer's Print Preview mode.

Immediately, you may notice that a couple of things could be improved here, such as the heading near the bottom left of the first page, which would be better moved over to the top of the following page. At the same time, there's a heading at the bottom of the second page that currently isn't too short, but if the first heading is moved to that page, it will become so. Therefore, it could also be moved to the following page.

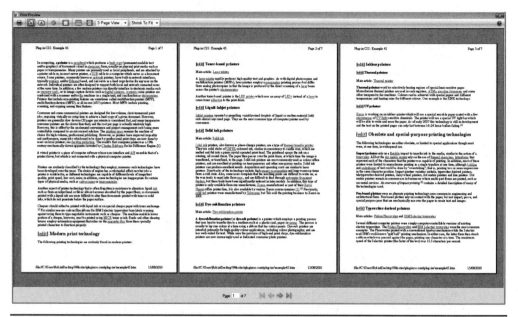

FIGURE 27-7 A copy of Wikipedia's Computer Printers page in Print Preview mode

However, in Figure 27-8, by placing a `<br />` tag containing this class just before each of the headings, you can see that the page layout is clearer—without headings commencing too near the bottom of any page.

After adding these two page breaks, it looks like a page break should also be forced at the start of the short paragraph at the bottom of the third page in Figure 27-8.

Classes and Properties

break	Class to force a page break at the current location when it is printed
page-break-before	Property to set up page breaks for printing purposes

About the Class

This class is acted on only when a web page is being printed (or print previewed). With it, you specify where you want printing to continue on a new page of paper. To do this, the recipe makes use of the `page-break-before` property.

How to Use It

The best way to use this class is to drop it in at the start of a heading you would like to ensure appears on a new sheet of paper when printed, like this:

```
<h1 class='break'>This is a heading</h1>
```

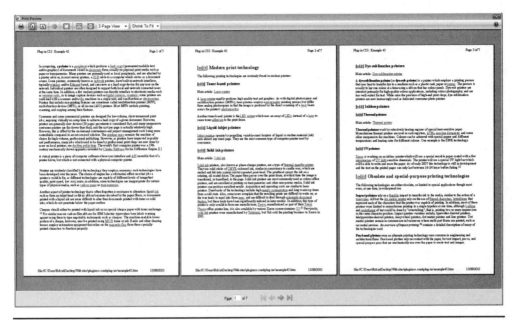

FIGURE 27-8   Using this class, printouts can be made much easier to read.

Or you may wish to attach it to a `<p>` or `<br />` tag, like this:

```
<p class='break'>The start of a paragraph...
<br class='break' />Text after a line break...
```

CAUTION   *Usually, it's best to add this class to an existing tag because if you add it to a new `<p>` or other tag, you may see unwanted extra line breaks or other styling when the web page is viewed normally.*

The Class

```
.break { page-break-before:always; }
```

CHAPTER 28

Visual Effects

This chapter provides a wide range of visual effects such as star ratings (similar to those used on the Amazon web site), progress bars or bar ratings, the scaling of images up or down, animating transitions at different speeds (and using different types of motion), viewing enlarged versions of thumbnail images, captioning and the rotation of images, changing the mouse pointer, and alternating the text and background colors of table rows.

Between them, you'll find you can build an amazing variety of different effects just by applying the right classes to the right elements, all without JavaScript or having to write your own CSS (unless you want to).

Star Rating

Many sites use rating systems composed of stars, the most notable probably being Amazon with its five-star ratings. Using this class, you can easily achieve a similar effect, as shown in Figure 28-1, in which a 65 percent popularity rating is displayed.

Classes and Properties

starrating starrating_h	Classes to display a star rating of between 0 and 100 percent (starrating), or to do so only when hovered over (starrating_h)
position	Property specifying an object's position, such as absolute or relative
color	Property containing the text color of an object
width	Property containing the width of an object
font-size	Property containing the font size
display	Property specifying how to display an object, such as block, inline, or none
overflow	Property specifying what to do with any text that overflows the object's boundaries
top	Property containing an object's vertical offset from the top of its container
left	Property containing an object's horizontal offset from the left of its container

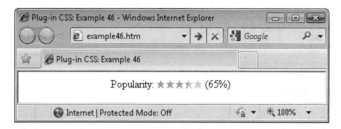

FIGURE 28-1   Using this class makes it easy to display star ratings.

About the Classes

These classes display a star rating using a star symbol already available as a character; therefore, they need no external image. This is achieved by overlaying two sets of stars. The first is a set of five very light stars, and the second is a set of darker stars truncated to the right at whatever percent value is to be displayed.

How to Use Them

To use these classes, embed a <div> (whose width is set using a style argument to the percent value to display) within another container such as a <span>, like this:

```
<span class='starrating'>&#9733;&#9733;&#9733;&#9733;&#9733;
    <div style='width:65%'>&#9733;&#9733;&#9733;&#9733;&#9733;</div>
</span>
```

The ★ HTML entity represents the solid star symbol, and the width parameter of the style argument restricts the width of the inner <div> to only 65 percent of the outer <span>.

You can also choose to display the rating only when hovered over by using the starrating_h class instead of starrating. Also, because of the simplicity of this recipe's design, you can easily use other characters instead of stars.

The Classes

```
.starrating, .starrating_h {
    position:relative;
    color:#ffddcc;
    width:65px;
    font-size:10pt;
}
.starrating_h div {
    display:none;
}
.starrating div, .starrating_h:hover div {
    display:block;
    position:absolute;
    overflow:hidden;
    color:#ff9900;
    top:0px;
    left:0px;
}
```

Star Rating Using Images

In much the same way that you can use different characters instead of the star in the previous recipe, with this recipe you can use images of your choice. In Figure 28-2, this class has been used with a pair of star images for a more interesting effect, due to the range of colors an image can use.

Classes and Properties

starratingi starratingi_h	Classes to display a star rating of between 0 and 100 percent using gif images (starratingi), or to do so only when hovered over (starratingi_h)
position	Property specifying an object's position, such as absolute or relative
width	Property containing the width of an object
height	Property containing the height of an object
background	Property containing an object's various background settings
top	Property containing an object's vertical offset from the top of its container
left	Property containing an object's horizontal offset from the left of its container

About the Classes

These classes display a star rating using an image. This is achieved by using images for the backgrounds of two objects that are overlaid on each other. The first is a set of five very light stars, and the second is a set of darker stars with the right cut off at whatever percent value is to be displayed.

How to Use Them

To use these classes, embed a <div> (whose width is set to the percent value to display) within another <div> (not a <span>), like this:

```
<div class='starratingi'><div style='width:52%'></div></div>
```

Figure 28-2 Using images for the stars provides greater color depth.

In this example, the `width` parameter of the `style` argument restricts the width of the inner `<div>` to only 52 percent of the outer `<div>`. You can also choose to display the rating only when hovered over by using the `starratingi_h` class instead of `starratingi`.

You can change the images for any others of your choosing by altering the *PC.css* file (by either editing the `starratingi` class, or copying it and creating a new one), but if they will have dimensions other than 13 × 12 pixels, you will need to also alter the `width` and `height` properties in the class definition to the new image width (multiplied by the number of images used) and height. You will also need to change the filenames if you aren't using *star1.gif* and *star2.gif*. Don't forget that all the examples, classes, and images are available for download at *webdeveloperscookbook.com*.

The Classes

```
.starratingi, .starratingi_h {
    position:relative;
    width:65px;
    height:12px;
    background:url(star1.gif) 0 0 repeat-x;
}
.starratingi div, .starratingi_h:hover div {
    position:absolute;
    height:12px;
    background:url(star2.gif) 0 0 repeat-x;
    top:0px;
    left:0px;
}
```

 ## Progress Bar

By relying on changing only an object's background color, the class in this recipe lets you create a progress or rating bar you can use to indicate how far a particular action has progressed, or the rating given to something, as shown in Figure 28-3, which shows 65 percent progress of a loading action.

FIGURE 28-3   Show how far an action has progressed with this recipe.

Classes and Properties

progress progress_h	Classes to display a progress bar of between 0 and 100 percent using background colors (progress), or to do so only when hovered over (progress_h)
position	Property specifying an object's position, such as absolute or relative
width	Property containing the width of an object
height	Property containing the height of an object
top	Property containing an object's vertical offset from the top of its container
left	Property containing an object's horizontal offset from the left of its container

About the Classes

These classes display a progress bar using only the background colors of two objects that are overlaid on each other.

How to Use Them

To display a progress bar <div> inside another and give each a background color or perhaps a gradient fill using a suitable class (and use the style argument to set the width of the inner <div>), you would use code such as this:

```
<div class='progress yellow_b'>
   <div class='red_b' style='width:65%'></div>
</div>
```

In this example, a yellow progress bar is created with a red bar on top of it showing 65 percent progress. Or here's an example that uses gradient fills:

```
<div class='progress sunset1'>
   <div class='sky1' style='width:23%'></div>
</div>
```

You can also use the progress_h class to show the progress only when the object is hovered over by the mouse.

As you can see, you can specify both colors and the percentage to indicate directly from HTML. But, if you would like to have a progress bar with dimensions other than 120×15 pixels, you'll need to modify the class rules in the *WDC.css* file.

The Classes

```
.progress, .progress_h {
   position:relative;
   width:120px;
   height:15px;
}
.progress div, .progress_h:hover div {
   position:absolute;
   height:15px;
   top:0px;
   left:0px;
}
```

Scale Up

These classes let you scale an object up by between 110 and 200 percent. Rather than simply changing the width and height of an object, these classes scale it in place, without pushing other objects around to make room. Therefore, they are great for special effects such as rollovers.

Figure 28-4 shows 10 instances of a 100 × 100–pixel image displayed at dimensions between 110 × 110 and 200 × 200 pixels. As you can see, none of them has affected the location of any of the other images.

Classes and Properties

`scaleup1` `scaleup1_h`	Classes to scale up an image by 110 percent (`scaleup1`), or to do so only when hovered over (`scaleup1_h`)
`scaleup2` – `scaleup10` (etc...)	Class—as `scaleup1` but for scaling between 120 and 200 percent
`-moz-transform`	Property for transforming an object in Firefox and other Mozilla browsers
`-webkit-transform`	Property for transforming an object in Safari and Chrome
`-o-transform`	Property for transforming an object in Opera
`transform`	Property for transforming an object in all other browsers (except IE)
`filter`	Property for transforming an image in Internet Explorer

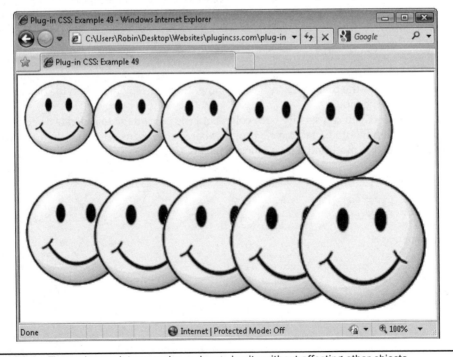

FIGURE 28-4   These classes let you resize an image in situ without affecting other objects.

About the Classes

These classes are particularly useful in that they create effects you don't often see so easily implanted. What they do is use the CSS `transform` property (or browser-specific versions of it) along with the `scale()` argument, like this:

```
transform:scale(1.5);
```

CAUTION *On Internet Explorer, the* `filter` *property is used instead of* `transform` *to achieve a similar effect. However, this means that, on IE, only images can be scaled (whereas you can scale* <div>, <span>, *and other objects with other browsers). And there's another couple of provisos: While all other browsers scale using the object's center, IE scales from the top left. It also scales objects up* behind *other objects. Therefore, elements that may be scaled up should be separated from others that could obscure it, or vice versa. There is more on this topic in CSS Recipe 51.*

How to Use Them

To use these classes, place them in the `class` argument of an object to be scaled, as in the following example, which was used to create Figure 28-4:

```
<img src='smiley.gif' class='scaleup1' />
<img src='smiley.gif' class='scaleup2' />
<img src='smiley.gif' class='scaleup3' />
<img src='smiley.gif' class='scaleup4' />
<img src='smiley.gif' class='scaleup5' /><br /><br /><br />

<img src='smiley.gif' class='scaleup6' />
<img src='smiley.gif' class='scaleup7' />
<img src='smiley.gif' class='scaleup8' />
<img src='smiley.gif' class='scaleup9' />
<img src='smiley.gif' class='scaleup10' />
```

You can also use the _h hover versions of the classes to resize an object only when it is hovered over, like this:

```
<img src='smiley.gif' class='scaleup5_h' />
```

NOTE *When scaling up an object in the Opera or Firefox browsers, if the new size of the object will place its boundaries outside the browser's borders, scroll bars will be added to the browser. This behavior does not occur on other browsers.*

The Classes

```
.scaleup1, .scaleup1_h:hover {
   -moz-transform    :scale(1.1);
   -webkit-transform:scale(1.1);
   -o-transform      :scale(1.1);
   transform         :scale(1.1);
   filter            :progid:DXImageTransform.Microsoft.Matrix(
                      SizingMethod='auto expand', M11='1.1', M22='1.1');
}
```

```
.scaleup2, .scaleup2_h:hover {
    -moz-transform    :scale(1.2);
    -webkit-transform:scale(1.2);
    -o-transform      :scale(1.2);
    transform         :scale(1.2);
    filter            :progid:DXImageTransform.Microsoft.Matrix(
                       SizingMethod='auto expand', M11='1.2', M22='1.2');
}
.scaleup3, .scaleup3_h:hover {
    -moz-transform    :scale(1.3);
    -webkit-transform:scale(1.3);
    -o-transform      :scale(1.3);
    transform         :scale(1.3);
    filter            :progid:DXImageTransform.Microsoft.Matrix(
                       SizingMethod='auto expand', M11='1.3', M22='1.3');
}
.scaleup4, .scaleup4_h:hover {
    -moz-transform    :scale(1.4);
    -webkit-transform:scale(1.4);
    -o-transform      :scale(1.4);
    transform         :scale(1.4);
    filter            :progid:DXImageTransform.Microsoft.Matrix(
                       SizingMethod='auto expand', M11='1.4', M22='1.4');
}
.scaleup5, .scaleup5_h:hover {
    -moz-transform    :scale(1.5);
    -webkit-transform:scale(1.5);
    -o-transform      :scale(1.5);
    transform         :scale(1.5);
    filter            :progid:DXImageTransform.Microsoft.Matrix(
                       SizingMethod='auto expand', M11='1.5', M22='1.5');
}
.scaleup6, .scaleup6_h:hover {
    -moz-transform    :scale(1.6);
    -webkit-transform:scale(1.6);
    -o-transform      :scale(1.6);
    transform         :scale(1.6);
    filter            :progid:DXImageTransform.Microsoft.Matrix(
                       SizingMethod='auto expand', M11='1.6', M22='1.6');
}
.scaleup7, .scaleup7_h:hover {
    -moz-transform    :scale(1.7);
    -webkit-transform:scale(1.7);
    -o-transform      :scale(1.7);
    transform         :scale(1.7);
    filter            :progid:DXImageTransform.Microsoft.Matrix(
                       SizingMethod='auto expand', M11='1.7', M22='1.7');
}
.scaleup8, .scaleup8_h:hover {
    -moz-transform    :scale(1.8);
    -webkit-transform:scale(1.8);
    -o-transform      :scale(1.8);
    transform         :scale(1.8);
```

```
   filter              :progid:DXImageTransform.Microsoft.Matrix(
                         SizingMethod='auto expand', M11='1.8', M22='1.8');
}
.scaleup9, .scaleup9_h:hover {
   -moz-transform      :scale(1.9);
   -webkit-transform:scale(1.9);
   -o-transform        :scale(1.9);
   transform           :scale(1.9);
   filter              :progid:DXImageTransform.Microsoft.Matrix(
                         SizingMethod='auto expand', M11='1.9', M22='1.9');
}
.scaleup10, .scaleup10_h:hover {
   -moz-transform      :scale(2);
   -webkit-transform:scale(2);
   -o-transform        :scale(2);
   transform           :scale(2);
   filter              :progid:DXImageTransform.Microsoft.Matrix(
                         SizingMethod='auto expand', M11='2', M22='2');
}
```

50 Scale Down

RECIPE

These classes offer the inverse functionality to the previous recipe group, in that they reduce an object down by between 10 and 100 percent, as shown in Figure 28-5, in which 10 instances of an image have been reduced by these amounts.

As with the previous group of Scale Up classes, these classes do not alter the position of surrounding objects.

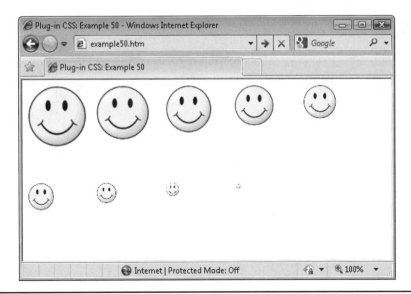

FIGURE 28-5   These classes let you scale objects down to as little as 0 percent in size.

Classes and Properties

scaledown1 scaledown1_h	Classes to scale down an image by 10 percent (scaledown1), or to do so only when hovered over (scaledown1_h)
scaledown2 – scaledown10 (etc…)	Classes — as scaleup1 but for scaling down between 20 and 100 percent
-moz-transform	Property for transforming an object in Firefox and other Mozilla browsers
-webkit-transform	Property for transforming an object in Safari and Chrome
-o-transform	Property for transforming an object in Opera
transform	Property for transforming an object in all other browsers (except IE)
filter	Property for transforming an image in Internet Explorer

About the Classes

These classes use the CSS transform property (or browser-specific versions of it) along with the scale() argument, like this:

transform:scale(0.5);

On Internet Explorer, the filter property achieves a similar effect. However, this means that on IE only images can be scaled. Also, while all other browsers scale using the object's center, IE scales from the top left.

How to Use Them

To use these classes, place them in the class argument of an object to be scaled, as in the following example, which was used to create Figure 28-5:

```
<img src='smiley.gif' class='scaledown1' />
<img src='smiley.gif' class='scaledown2' />
<img src='smiley.gif' class='scaledown3' />
<img src='smiley.gif' class='scaledown4' />
<img src='smiley.gif' class='scaledown5' /><br /><br /><br />

<img src='smiley.gif' class='scaledown6' />
<img src='smiley.gif' class='scaledown7' />
<img src='smiley.gif' class='scaledown8' />
<img src='smiley.gif' class='scaledown9' />
<img src='smiley.gif' class='scaledown10' />
```

You can also use the _h hover versions of the classes to resize an object only when it is hovered over, like this:

```
<img src='smiley.gif' class='scaledown5_h' />
```

The Classes

```
.scaledown1, .scaledown1_h:hover {
   -moz-transform    :scale(0.9);
   -webkit-transform:scale(0.9);
```

```
   -o-transform      :scale(0.9);
   transform         :scale(0.9);
   filter            :progid:DXImageTransform.Microsoft.Matrix(
                      SizingMethod='auto expand', M11='0.9', M22='0.9');
}
.scaledown2, .scaledown2_h:hover {
   -moz-transform    :scale(0.8);
   -webkit-transform:scale(0.8);
   -o-transform      :scale(0.8);
   transform         :scale(0.8);
   filter            :progid:DXImageTransform.Microsoft.Matrix(
                      SizingMethod='auto expand', M11='0.8', M22='0.8');
}
.scaledown3, .scaledown3_h :hover {
   -moz-transform    :scale(0.7);
   -webkit-transform:scale(0.7);
   -o-transform      :scale(0.7);
   transform         :scale(0.7);
   filter            :progid:DXImageTransform.Microsoft.Matrix(
                      SizingMethod='auto expand', M11='0.7', M22='0.7');
}
.scaledown4, .scaledown4_h:hover {
   -moz-transform    :scale(0.6);
   -webkit-transform:scale(0.6);
   -o-transform      :scale(0.6);
   transform         :scale(0.6);
   filter            :progid:DXImageTransform.Microsoft.Matrix(
                      SizingMethod='auto expand', M11='0.6', M22='0.6');
}
.scaledown5, .scaledown5_h:hover {
   -moz-transform    :scale(0.5);
   -webkit-transform:scale(0.5);
   -o-transform      :scale(0.5);
   transform         :scale(0.5);
   filter            :progid:DXImageTransform.Microsoft.Matrix(
                      SizingMethod='auto expand', M11='0.5', M22='0.5');
}
.scaledown6, .scaledown6_h:hover {
   -moz-transform    :scale(0.4);
   -webkit-transform:scale(0.4);
   -o-transform      :scale(0.4);
   transform         :scale(0.4);
   filter            :progid:DXImageTransform.Microsoft.Matrix(
                      SizingMethod='auto expand', M11='0.4', M22='0.4');
}
.scaledown7, .scaledown7_h:hover {
   -moz-transform    :scale(0.3);
   -webkit-transform:scale(0.3);
   -o-transform      :scale(0.3);
   transform         :scale(0.3);
   filter            :progid:DXImageTransform.Microsoft.Matrix(
                      SizingMethod='auto expand', M11='0.3', M22='0.3');
}
```

```
.scaledown8, .scaledown8_h:hover {
   -moz-transform    :scale(0.2);
   -webkit-transform:scale(0.2);
   -o-transform      :scale(0.2);
   transform         :scale(0.2);
   filter            :progid:DXImageTransform.Microsoft.Matrix(
                      SizingMethod='auto expand', M11='0.2', M22='0.2');
}
.scaledown9, .scaledown9_h:hover {
   -moz-transform    :scale(0.1);
   -webkit-transform:scale(0.1);
   -o-transform      :scale(0.1);
   transform         :scale(0.1);
   filter            :progid:DXImageTransform.Microsoft.Matrix(
                      SizingMethod='auto expand', M11='0.1', M22='0.1');
}
.scaledown10, .scaledown10_h:hover {
   -moz-transform    :scale(0);
   -webkit-transform:scale(0);
   -o-transform      :scale(0);
   transform         :scale(0);
   filter            :progid:DXImageTransform.Microsoft.Matrix(
                      SizingMethod='auto expand', M11='0', M22='0');
}
```

Transition All

For browsers that support the new `transition` property, including Opera 10, Firefox 4, Apple Safari 5, and Google Chrome 5 (but, sadly, not Internet Explorer), you can use this recipe to make any changes made to an object transition smoothly, over a time between 0.1 and 2.0 seconds. Browsers that do not support transitions ignore these classes and will change properties immediately rather than transitioning.

In Figure 28-6 (a screen grab taken using the Apple Safari browser), the mouse is currently hovering over the middle smiley in the bottom row, which has smoothly enlarged—and it will gently shrink back down in size when the mouse moves away.

However, a word of caution when using scaling... In Figure 28-7 (a screen grab taken using Internet Explorer), the object has correctly enlarged (but not transitioned, as IE doesn't support it), and you can see the reason for the warning I gave in Recipe 49 about ensuring objects that may be scaled up in an IE window are separated from each other (since scaled-up objects appear *behind* others in IE). Other browsers do, however, correctly bring an object to the front when scaled and move it back to its previous position when not scaled.

NOTE   *Unfortunately, Internet Explorer is currently out of the picture as far as CSS 3 transitions go, with even IE9 not supporting them. So users of this browser will simply see instant changes rather than animated transitions. Let's hope that this powerful feature is added to IE soon.*

FIGURE 28-6 Combining the `transitionall` and `scale8_h` classes to create a rollover effect

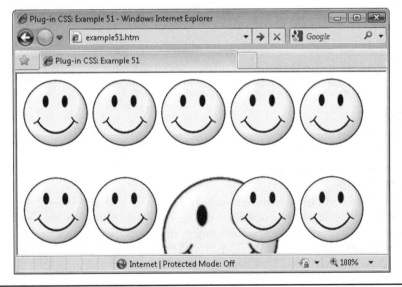

FIGURE 28-7 If you do not separate objects that are scalable, they can obscure each other when viewed in Internet Explorer.

Classes and Properties

transitionall transitionall_1	Classes for applying transitions of 0.7 seconds duration to all changed properties of an object (transitionall), or to do so but with linear rather than easing movement (transitionall_1)
transitionallslowest transitionallslow transitionallfast transitionallfastest	Classes—as transitionall and transitionall_1, but for durations of 2.0, 1.5, 0.3, and 0.1 seconds duration, including _1 versions for linear movement
-moz-transition	Property for transitioning properties of an object over a set duration in Firefox and other Mozilla browsers
-webkit-transition	Property for transitioning properties of an object over a set duration in Safari and Chrome
-o-transition	Property for transitioning properties of an object over a set duration in Opera
transition	Property for transitioning properties of an object over a set duration in all other browsers (except IE)

About the Classes

These classes apply transitions to all of an object's properties that change. This change is usually a result of the :hover pseudo-class, as used by the _h versions of the classes in this book, or it can be a change instigated through the use of JavaScript, as implemented in the remaining chapters.

The transition is applied to an object using a CSS rule such as the following (or browser-specific variants of the property name like those that begin -moz, -webkit-, or -o-):

```
transition:all .7s;
```

Browsers that do not support transitions will ignore this and just change properties immediately, without transitioning.

How to Use Them

To use these classes, add them to the class argument of an object and forget about them. Then, when any properties of the object are changed that can transition, they will be animated over the period of time specified, rather than changing immediately.

For example, here's the example HTML from CSS Recipe 49, but modified to change all the hover effects to transitions of differing durations:

```
<img src='smiley.gif' class='scaleup1_h transitionallslowest' />
<img src='smiley.gif' class='scaleup2_h transitionallslow' />
<img src='smiley.gif' class='scaleup3_h transitionall' />
<img src='smiley.gif' class='scaleup4_h transitionallfast' />
<img src='smiley.gif' class='scaleup5_h transitionallfastest' />
<br /><br /><br />

<img src='smiley.gif' class='scaleup6_h transitionallslowest_1' />
<img src='smiley.gif' class='scaleup7_h transitionallslow_1' />
```

```
<img src='smiley.gif' class='scaleup8_h transitionall_l' />
<img src='smiley.gif' class='scaleup9_h transitionallfast_l' />
<img src='smiley.gif' class='scaleup10_h transitionallfastest_l' />
```

The first set of five images uses the default easing transition, in which the animation starts slowly, increases in speed, and then slows again at the end. The second set uses the _l versions of the recipes to specify linear motion for the animation, where there is no speeding up and slowing down.

TIP *You will find you can add transitions to a wide range of the classes in this book that provide _h hover versions. This includes changing colors, position, dimensions, shadows, opacity, borders, and many more properties. Users of Internet Explorer won't get to see these nice transitions (yet), but for the sake of adding a simple extra class to your HTML, all other browser users will enjoy a much more sophisticated environment on their web pages. Incidentally, if transitions are added to IE it is likely they will use the –ms- prefix, so it will be a simple matter for you to add the lines required (such as* -ms-transition:all .7s; *in the first class) to the WDC.css file yourself.*

The Classes

```
.transitionall {
    -moz-transition    :all .7s;
    -webkit-transition:all .7s;
    -o-transition      :all .7s;
    transition         :all .7s;
}
.transitionallslowest {
    -moz-transition    :all 2s;
    -webkit-transition:all 2s;
    -o-transition      :all 2s;
    transition         :all 2s;
}
.transitionallslow {
    -moz-transition    :all 1.5s;
    -webkit-transition:all 1.5s;
    -o-transition      :all 1.5s;
    transition         :all 1.5s;
}
.transitionallfast {
    -moz-transition    :all .3s;
    -webkit-transition:all .3s;
    -o-transition      :all .3s;
    transition         :all .3s;
}
.transitionallfastest {
    -moz-transition    :all .1s;
    -webkit-transition:all .1s;
    -o-transition      :all .1s;
    transition         :all .1s;
}
.transitionall_l {
    -moz-transition    :all .7s linear;
```

```
    -webkit-transition:all .7s linear;
    -o-transition     :all .7s linear;
    transition        :all .7s linear;
}
.transitionallslowest_1 {
    -moz-transition    :all 2s linear;
    -webkit-transition:all 2s linear;
    -o-transition      :all 2s linear;
    transition         :all 2s linear;
}
.transitionallslow_1 {
    -moz-transition    :all 1.5s linear;
    -webkit-transition:all 1.5s linear;
    -o-transition      :all 1.5s linear;
    transition         :all 1.5s linear;
}
.transitionallfast_1 {
    -moz-transition    :all .3s linear;
    -webkit-transition:all .3s linear;
    -o-transition      :all .3s linear;
    transition         :all .3s linear;
}
.transitionallfastest_1 {
    -moz-transition    :all .1s linear;
    -webkit-transition:all .1s linear;
    -o-transition      :all .1s linear;
    transition         :all .1s linear;
}
```

Thumb View

This class provides a simple and effective way for users to browse large versions of photo thumbnails. In Figure 28-8, six thumbnails are displayed and the mouse is currently hovering over the second, which has caused the large version of the image to be displayed.

Classes and Properties

thumbview	Class to display a larger image of a thumbnail
position	Property containing the position of an object, such as relative or absolute
top	Property containing the vertical offset of an object from the top of its container
left	Property containing the horizontal offset of an object from the left of its container
display	Property specifying how an object is displayed, such as inline or block

About the Class

This class displays the contents of a <span> that accompanies a thumbnail image by hiding it using the opacity property and by scaling it to zero dimensions—until the mouse passes over the image, when the <span> is scaled back up again and the opacity is restored to reveal it. The <span> is set to appear inset from the left of the container and down from the top by 30 pixels.

FIGURE 28-8   Use these classes to create a simple viewer for thumbnail images.

For some reason, the Opera browser doesn't vertically offset the same way that the other browsers do, so a browser-specific hack is used to change the `top` property of the `<span>` to a different value.

How to Use It

Although this recipe is intended mainly for displaying a large version of a thumbnail image, because it simply hides and displays a `<span>` on demand, you can place anything you like in it, meaning you can use it to display information on an image or other details.

Here is the HTML used for Figure 28-8:

```
<span class='thumbview'>
   <img class='bwidth1 bblack bsolid' src='t1.jpg' />
   <span><img class='bwidth2 bblack bsolid' src='i1.jpg' /></span>
</span>
<span class='thumbview'>
   <img class='bwidth1 bblack bsolid' src='t2.jpg' />
   <span><img class='bwidth2 bblack bsolid' src='i2.jpg' /></span>
</span>
<span class='thumbview'>
   <img class='bwidth1 bblack bsolid' src='t3.jpg' />
   <span><img class='bwidth2 bblack bsolid' src='i3.jpg' /></span>
</span><br />

<span class='thumbview'>
   <img class='bwidth1 bblack bsolid' src='t4.jpg' />
```

```
    <span><img class='bwidth2 bblack bsolid' src='i4.jpg' /></span>
</span>
<span class='thumbview'>
    <img class='bwidth1 bblack bsolid' src='t5.jpg' />
    <span><img class='bwidth2 bblack bsolid' src='i5.jpg' /></span>
</span>
<span class='thumbview'>
    <img class='bwidth1 bblack bsolid' src='t6.jpg' />
    <span><img class='bwidth2 bblack bsolid' src='i6.jpg' /></span>
</span>
```

The outer container of each thumbnail and image is a <span>, but it could equally be a <div> or other container. Within each container is an image followed by a <span>, in which a large version of each thumbnail image is placed. When the mouse passes over the outer container, the inner one is set to display, and when the mouse passes out, the inner one is hidden again.

NOTE *In Internet Explorer, what has been described here is pretty much what you will see. But on Opera 10, Firefox 4, Apple Safari 5, and Google Chrome 5 (or higher), the images (or whatever is contained in the inner <span>) will fade and zoom in at the same time (and out again when the mouse passes away) due to the combined use of transitions, scaling, and opacity. If you can, try to view it in one of these browsers to see the impressive effect that results.*

The Class

```css
.thumbview {
  position:relative;
}
.thumbview span {
    position:absolute;
    top:-30px;
    left:30px;
    -moz-transition    :all .3s linear;
    -webkit-transition:all .3s linear;
    -o-transition      :all .3s linear;
    transition         :all .3s linear;
    -moz-transform     :scale(0);
    -webkit-transform :scale(0);
    -o-transform       :scale(0);
    transform          :scale(0);
    opacity            :0;
    z-index            :0;
    filter             :progid:DXImageTransform.Microsoft.Matrix(
                        SizingMethod='auto expand', M11='0', M22='0');
}
.thumbview:hover span {
    -moz-transform     :scale(1);
    -webkit-transform :scale(1);
    -o-transform       :scale(1);
    transform          :scale(1);
    opacity            :1;
    z-index            :100;
```

```
    filter                     :progid:DXImageTransform.Microsoft.Matrix(
                               SizingMethod='auto expand', M11='1', M22='1');
}

@media all and (-webkit-min-device-pixel-ratio:10000), /* Only  Opera */
    not all and (-webkit-min-device-pixel-ratio:0) { /* sees this hack */
    .thumbview span { top:30px; }
}
```

Caption Image

Using this recipe, you can present your images with neat white borders and a shadowed caption on a thicker border at the picture's bottom. In Figure 28-9, the HTML from the previous example has been reused, with this class added to provide captions, and without the previous borders, since this class provides its own.

The screen grab was taken using Google Chrome, which is representative of the results you'll get with most browsers in that there is a smooth transition, the border of the photo is white and shadowed, and the caption is shadowed text on a translucent background.

However, in Internet Explorer it's not possible to achieve quite the same effect, mainly because IE dislikes using many of its features within a `content` property that is part of a pseudo-class such as `:before`, or `:after`. Nevertheless, as you can see in Figure 28-10, it degrades reasonably well thanks to a few (unfortunately necessary) CSS hacks.

Figure 28-9   Use this class to add captions and interesting effects to images.

FIGURE 28-10 Displaying an image using a caption class in Internet Explorer

Classes and Properties

`caption` `caption_h`	Classes to add a caption and other embellishments to an image (`caption`), or to do so only when the object is hovered over (`caption_h`)
`position`	Property containing the position of an object, such as absolute or relative
`background`	Property containing an object's background settings
`padding`	Property containing an object's padding settings
`border`	Property containing an object's border settings
`color`	Property containing the text color of an object
`top`	Property containing the vertical offset of an object from the top of its container
`bottom`	Property containing the vertical offset of an object from the bottom of its container
`left`	Property containing the horizontal offset of an object from the left of its container
`height`	Property containing the height of an object
`line-height`	Property containing the line height of an object
`text-align`	Property containing the alignment of the text in an object, such as left or right
`font-size`	Property containing the font size of an object
`font-weight`	Property containing the font weight of an object
`font-family`	Property containing the font family of an object
`content`	Property for adding content to an object from CSS
`opacity`	Property containing the opacity (or invisibility) of an object

About the Classes

These classes frame and caption an image in a professional manner by changing various properties, such as its borders, and by adding content taken from the `alt` argument.

The `caption_h` class applies the caption only when the mouse passes over the associated image, while the `caption` class applies it as soon as the larger image is displayed.

A few hacks must be used in the CSS to get Internet Explorer to display anything at all! These consist of affixing the `\0` suffix to any rules that only IE should see. Also, to create the light ribbon behind the captions, the Unicode character 2588 (a solid block) is repeated 50 times in a `:before` set of rules. This block character string should be enough for reasonably wide pictures, but you can easily increase it if it isn't. Non-IE browsers do not see these `:before` rules.

How to Use Them

To use these classes, you need to provide a caption for the image in the `alt` argument of its container (such as a `<div>` or `<span>`), and then use either the `caption` or `caption_h` class in the `class` argument, like this:

```
<span class='caption_h' alt='A caption'>
   <img src='myimage.jpg' />
</span>
```

For example, following is the HTML used for Figures 28-9 and 28-10, which combines the `thumbview` class with both the `caption` and `caption_h` classes:

```
<span class='thumbview'>
   <img class='bwidth1 bblack bsolid' src='t1.jpg' />
   <span class='caption' alt='San Francisco, Pier 39 Seals'>
      <img src='i1.jpg' />
   </span>
</span>
<span class='thumbview'>
   <img class='bwidth1 bblack bsolid' src='t2.jpg' />
   <span class='caption' alt='San Francisco Bay Bridge'>
      <img src='i2.jpg' />
   </span>
</span>
<span class='thumbview'>
   <img class='bwidth1 bblack bsolid' src='t3.jpg' />
   <span class='caption' alt='The San Francisco Peaks'>
      <img src='i3.jpg' />
   </span>
</span><br />

<span class='thumbview'>
   <img class='bwidth1 bblack bsolid' src='t4.jpg' />
   <span class='caption_h' alt='San Francisco Peaks Forest'>
      <img src='i4.jpg' />
   </span>
</span>
```

```
<span class='thumbview'>
   <img class='bwidth1 bblack bsolid' src='t5.jpg' />
   <span class='caption_h' alt='San Francisco Park Lake'>
      <img src='i5.jpg' />
   </span>
</span>
<span class='thumbview'>
   <img class='bwidth1 bblack bsolid' src='t6.jpg' />
   <span class='caption_h' alt='Las Vegas At Night'>
      <img src='i6.jpg' />
   </span>
</span>
```

The captions are immediately displayed when the larger version is shown of any of the top row of thumbnails, but the bottom row of icons only open up the large image. You need to move the mouse into this image to be shown the caption, too.

The Classes

```
.caption, .caption_h {
   position:relative;
}
.caption img, .caption_h img {
   background:#000000;
   padding:3px;
}
.caption img, .caption_h:hover img {
   padding:0px;
   border:3px solid #ffffff;
   border:3px solid #eeeeee\0;                    /* IE hack */
   -moz-box-shadow    :3px 5px 9px #444;
   -webkit-box-shadow:3px 5px 9px #444;
   box-shadow         :3px 5px 9px #444;
}
.caption:before\0, .caption_h:hover:before\0 { /* IE hack section */
   position:absolute\0;
   color:#eeeeee\0;
   top:auto\0;
   bottom:3px\0;
   left:0px\0;
   font-size:20pt\0;
   font-weight:bold\0;
   font-family:Impact\0;
   content: '\2588\2588\2588\2588\2588\2588\2588\2588\2588\2588\2588
   \2588\2588\2588\2588\2588\2588\2588\2588\2588\2588\2588\2588\2588
   \2588\2588\2588\2588\2588\2588\2588\2588\2588\2588\2588\2588\2588
   \2588\2588\2588\2588\2588\2588\2588\2588\2588\2588'; /* 1 long line */
}
.caption:after, .caption_h:hover:after {
   position:absolute;
   background:#ffffff;
```

```
    color:#000000;
    top:auto;
    bottom:3px;
    left:0px;
    width:100%;
    text-align:center;
    height:30px;
    line-height:30px;
    font-size:8pt;
    text-shadow:#888888 2px 2px 2px;
    font-weight:bold;
    font-family:Verdana, Helvetica, sans-serif;
    content:attr(alt);
    opacity:.9;
}
```

Pointer

This pointer class is useful for making the mouse cursor change from an arrow to a pointing finger when it passes over an object, and is especially useful for attaching to buttons (which generally don't have this cursor behavior).

In Figure 28-11, two screen grabs have been taken with the mouse pointer enabled, and then merged to show the effect of passing the cursor over one object not using this class and another that is. In the figure, the mouse cursor has changed to a pointing finger as it passes over the second button.

Classes and Properties

pointer	Class to change the mouse cursor to a pointing finger when it passes over an object
cursor	Property for changing the mouse cursor

About the Class

This short and sweet class simply sets the cursor property of an object to the value pointer so that the mouse cursor will change to a pointing finger when it passes over the object.

How to Use It

Following is the HTML used for Figure 28-11, in which the class has been assigned to one of two buttons:

```
<button>This is a normal button</button>
<button class='pointer'>This button causes a pointing finger cursor
</button>
```

The Class

```
.pointer { cursor:pointer; }
```

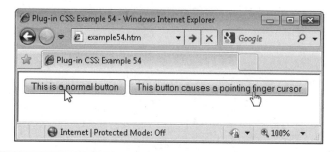

FIGURE 28-11 This class lets you alert users that an object is clickable.

Rotation

With these classes, you can rotate an image by 90, 180, or 270 degrees, as shown in Figure 28-12 in which a smiley face appears 12 times. The first four instances are the four possible clockwise rotations (the first being unrotated); the second group is the same, except that the rotation occurs only when the mouse passes over an image; and the third is the same as the second group, except that the rotations are counterclockwise. In the figure, the second smiley on the third row is currently being hovered over and has rotated counterclockwise by 90 degrees.

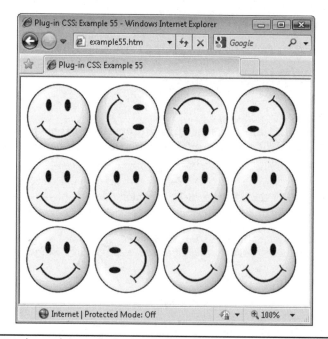

FIGURE 28-12 These classes let you display images in any of four different rotations.

TIP If you need to rotate by different amounts than intervals of 90 degrees, see Chapter 29 for a JavaScript-aided solution.

Classes and Properties

rotatec90 rotatec90_h	Classes to rotate an image clockwise by 90 degrees (rotatec90), or to do so only when the object is hovered over (rotatec90_h)
rotatec180 rotatec270 (etc...)	Classes—as rotatec90 but for rotating an object by 180 or 270 degrees, including _h classes for doing so only when hovered over
rotatea90 rotatea270 (etc...)	Classes—as rotatec90 but for rotating an object counterclockwise by 180 or 270 degrees, including _h classes for doing so only when hovered over
-moz-transform	Property used by Firefox and other Mozilla browsers to transform an object
-webkit-transform	Property used by Safari and Chrome to transform an object
-o-transform	Property used by Opera to transform an object
transform	Property used by all other browsers to transform an object (but not IE)
filter	Property used by IE to rotate an image, among many other features

About the Classes

These classes take an object and apply a rotation of 90, 180, or 270 degrees to it. The transforms used rotate in either a clockwise or counterclockwise direction so, for example, the rotatec90 class uses this CSS rule:

```
transform:rotate(90deg);
```

...and the rotatea90 class uses this rule:

```
transform:rotate(-90deg);
```

The reason for providing both clockwise and counterclockwise methods is to allow the use of the transitionall classes (CSS Recipe 51) with these classes. When combined on browsers that support transitions, the image will rotate smoothly in the direction supplied, rather than immediately change.

The Internet Explorer browser doesn't support transitions but does change the object to the required rotation.

How to Use Them

To use these classes, enter them into the class argument of an object, like this:

```
<img class='rotatec90' src='myphoto.jpg' />
```

Browsers other than Internet Explorer support the rotating of any object such as a <span> or <div>, which means complete sections of text and HTML can be rotated. But IE is limited to only images.

Here is the HTML used to create Figure 28-12:

```
<img src='smiley.gif' />
<img class='rotatec90' src='smiley.gif' />
<img class='rotatec180' src='smiley.gif' />
<img class='rotatec270' src='smiley.gif' /><br />

<img src='smiley.gif' />
<img class='transitionall rotatec90_h' src='smiley.gif' />
<img class='transitionall rotatec180_h' src='smiley.gif' />
<img class='transitionall rotatec270_h' src='smiley.gif' /><br />

<img src='smiley.gif' />
<img class='transitionall_l rotatea90_h' src='smiley.gif' />
<img class='transitionall_l rotatea180_h' src='smiley.gif' />
<img class='transitionall_l rotatea270_h' src='smiley.gif' />
```

The first group instantly rotates the images, and the second one rotates them only when the mouse hovers over an image. This group also implements the transitionall class so that browsers that support it will animate the rotation.

The final group is the same as the second except that the images rotate counterclockwise, and the transitionall_l class is used for a linear, rather than easing, movement to the animation.

The Classes

```
.rotatec90,.rotatec90_h:hover {
    -webkit-transform:rotate(90deg);
    -moz-transform    :rotate(90deg);
    -o-transform      :rotate(90deg);
    transform         :rotate(90deg);
    filter:progid:DXImageTransform.Microsoft.BasicImage(rotation=1);
}
.rotatec180, .rotatec180_h:hover {
    -webkit-transform:rotate(180deg);
    -moz-transform    :rotate(180deg);
    -o-transform      :rotate(180deg);
    transform         :rotate(180deg);
    filter:progid:DXImageTransform.Microsoft.BasicImage(rotation=2);
}
.rotatec270, .rotatec270_h:hover {
    -webkit-transform:rotate(270deg);
    -moz-transform    :rotate(270deg);
    -o-transform      :rotate(270deg);
    transform         :rotate(270deg);
    filter:progid:DXImageTransform.Microsoft.BasicImage(rotation=3);
}
.rotatea90,.rotatea90_h:hover {
    -webkit-transform:rotate(-90deg);
```

```
   -moz-transform      :rotate(-90deg);
   -o-transform        :rotate(-90deg);
   transform           :rotate(-90deg);
   filter:progid:DXImageTransform.Microsoft.BasicImage(rotation=3);
}
.rotatea180, .rotatea180_h:hover {
   -webkit-transform:rotate(-180deg);
   -moz-transform      :rotate(-180deg);
   -o-transform        :rotate(-180deg);
   transform           :rotate(-180deg);
   filter:progid:DXImageTransform.Microsoft.BasicImage(rotation=2);
}
.rotatea270, .rotatea270_h:hover {
   -webkit-transform:rotate(-270deg);
   -moz-transform      :rotate(-270deg);
   -o-transform        :rotate(-270deg);
   transform           :rotate(-270deg);
   filter:progid:DXImageTransform.Microsoft.BasicImage(rotation=1);
}
```

RECIPE 56 Odd and Even Text Colors

When you wish to present a table in a more easy-to-read format, you can use the classes in this recipe to alternate the color of each row by adding a class to the <table> tag, as shown in Figure 28-13 (a screen grab from Google Chrome), where the text color in the odd rows has been changed to green.

These classes work in all the latest browsers except for Internet Explorer (even IE9), which will simply display tables the normal way.

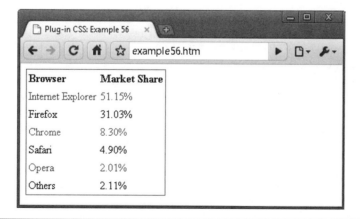

FIGURE 28-13   Using these classes to create alternately colored rows of text in tables

Classes and Properties

aqua_o aqua_e	Classes to change the text color of either all odd rows in a table to aqua (aqua_o) or all even rows (aqua_e)
black blue brown fuchsia gold gray green khaki lime maroon navy olive orange pink purple red silver teal white yellow (etc...)	Classes—as aqua_o and aqua_e, but for the colors shown
nth-child()	Pseudo-class used with the values odd or even for accessing odd- or even-numbered rows
color	Property containing the text color of an object

About the Classes

These classes change the text color of either the odd- or even-numbered rows in a table by using the nth-child pseudo-class, like this:

```
.aqua_o tr:nth-child(odd) { color:#0ff; }
```

For example, this rule sets the class aqua_o to change the text color of all odd table rows to aqua, using the tr: part of the rule, in conjunction with the :nth-child(odd) pseudo-class. For even rows, the odd parameter is changed to even.

How to Use Them

To use these classes, simply mention them in the class argument of a table, as in the following, which will change the text color of all even rows to green:

```
<table class='green_e'>
```

Here's the HTML used to create Figure 28-13:

```
<table class='bsolid bwidth1 green_e' cellspacing='0' cellpadding='3'>
   <tr class='green_e'>
      <td><b>Browser</b></td>
      <td><b>Market Share</b></td>
   </tr>
   <tr>
      <td>Internet Explorer</td>
      <td>51.15%</td>
   </tr>
   <tr>
      <td>Firefox</td>
      <td>31.03%</td>
   </tr>
   <tr>
      <td>Chrome</td>
      <td>8.30%</td>
   </tr>
   <tr>
```

```
      <td>Safari</td>
      <td>4.90%</td>
   </tr>
   <tr>
      <td>Opera</td>
      <td>2.01%</td>
   </tr>
   <tr>
      <td>Others</td>
      <td>2.11%</td>
   </tr>
</table>
```

This example displays the state of the market share of the main web browsers as of July 2010 according to Wikipedia. It starts by creating a solid black border around the table with a width of one pixel, and then uses the green_e class to set the color of all even rows in the table to green. The table's cellspacing and cellpadding arguments are also set to 0 and 3, respectively, for improved styling.

A color class with the suffix _o could also be used if the odd row color needed changing from the default of black.

The Classes

```
.aqua_o     tr:nth-child(odd),    .aqua_e     tr:nth-child(even)
   { color:#0ff }
.black_o    tr:nth-child(odd),    .black_e    tr:nth-child(even)
   { color:#000 }
.blue_o     tr:nth-child(odd),    .blue_e     tr:nth-child(even)
   { color:#00f }
.brown_o    tr:nth-child(odd),    .brown_e    tr:nth-child(even)
   { color:#c44 }
.fuchsia_o  tr:nth-child(odd),    .fuchsia_e  tr:nth-child(even)
   { color:#f0f }
.gold_o     tr:nth-child(odd),    .gold_e     tr:nth-child(even)
   { color:#fc0 }
.gray_o     tr:nth-child(odd),    .gray_e     tr:nth-child(even)
   { color:#888 }
.green_o    tr:nth-child(odd),    .green_e    tr:nth-child(even)
   { color:#080 }
.khaki_o    tr:nth-child(odd),    .khaki_e    tr:nth-child(even)
   { color:#cc8 }
.lime_o     tr:nth-child(odd),    .lime_e     tr:nth-child(even)
   { color:#0f0 }
.maroon_o   tr:nth-child(odd),    .maroon_e   tr:nth-child(even)
   { color:#800 }
.navy_o     tr:nth-child(odd),    .navy_e     tr:nth-child(even)
   { color:#008 }
.olive_o    tr:nth-child(odd),    .olive_e    tr:nth-child(even)
   { color:#880 }
.orange_o   tr:nth-child(odd),    .orange_e   tr:nth-child(even)
   { color:#f80 }
.pink_o     tr:nth-child(odd),    .pink_e     tr:nth-child(even)
   { color:#f88 }
.purple_o   tr:nth-child(odd),    .purple_e   tr:nth-child(even)
   { color:#808 }
```

```
.red_o      tr:nth-child(odd),   .red_e      tr:nth-child(even)
   { color:#f00 }
.silver_o  tr:nth-child(odd),   .silver_e  tr:nth-child(even)
   { color:#ccc }
.teal_o     tr:nth-child(odd),   .teal_e     tr:nth-child(even)
   { color:#088 }
.white_o    tr:nth-child(odd),   .white_e    tr:nth-child(even)
   { color:#fff }
.yellow_o  tr:nth-child(odd),   .yellow_e  tr:nth-child(even)
   { color:#ff0 }
```

57 Odd and Even Background Colors

These classes complement those in the previous recipe by enabling the changing of a table row's odd or even background colors as shown in Figure 28-14, in which the background colors have been styled to alternate between lime green and aqua.

As with the odd and even text color classes, these classes will not work with Internet Explorer, which will simply display as normal; therefore, you may wish to apply a standard background color to your tables as a fallback.

Classes and Properties

aqua_bo aqua_be	Classes to change the background color of either all odd rows in a table to aqua (aqua_bo) or all even rows (aqua_be)
black blue brown fuchsia gold gray green khaki lime maroon navy olive orange pink purple red silver teal white yellow (etc...)	Classes—as aqua_bo and aqua_be, but for the colors shown
nth-child()	Pseudo-class used with the values odd or even for accessing odd- or even-numbered rows
background	Property containing the background color of an object

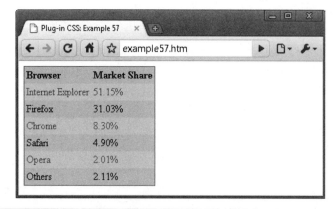

FIGURE 28-14 The table from the previous recipe, now styled with alternating background colors

About the Classes

These classes work in the same way as those in the previous recipe group, except that they change the background instead of the color property.

How to Use Them

To use these classes, simply mention them in the class argument of a table as in the following, which will change the background color of all even rows to aqua:

```
<table class='aqua_be'>
```

Here's the HTML used to create Figure 28-14:

```
<table class='bsolid bwidth1 green_e aqua_be lime_bo'
    cellspacing='0' cellpadding='3'>
    <tr class='green_e'>
        <td><b>Browser</b></td>
        <td><b>Market Share</b></td>
    </tr>
    <tr>
        <td>Internet Explorer</td>
        <td>51.15%</td>
    </tr>
    <tr>
        <td>Firefox</td>
        <td>31.03%</td>
    </tr>
    <tr>
        <td>Chrome</td>
        <td>8.30%</td>
    </tr>
    <tr>
        <td>Safari</td>
        <td>4.90%</td>
    </tr>
    <tr>
        <td>Opera</td>
        <td>2.01%</td>
    </tr>
    <tr>
        <td>Others</td>
        <td>2.11%</td>
    </tr>
</table>
```

This example adds the classes aqua_be and lime_bo to the previous example to change the background colors of the table rows. Although the colors in this example may look garish when you run them on your computer, I chose them because they convert well to the monochrome print used in this book—and it's easy enough for you to change them anyway.

NOTE *This concludes the standard CSS recipes. In the next chapter, I'll introduce Dynamic classes and show what you can do when you add a little JavaScript to your CSS.*

The Classes

```
.aqua_bo     tr:nth-child(odd), .aqua_be     tr:nth-child(even)
   { background:#0ff }
.black_bo    tr:nth-child(odd), .black_be    tr:nth-child(even)
   { background:#000 }
.blue_bo     tr:nth-child(odd), .blue_be     tr:nth-child(even)
   { background:#00f }
.brown_bo    tr:nth-child(odd), .brown_be    tr:nth-child(even)
   { background:#c44 }
.fuchsia_bo  tr:nth-child(odd), .fuchsia_be  tr:nth-child(even)
   { background:#f0f }
.gold_bo     tr:nth-child(odd), .gold_be     tr:nth-child(even)
   { background:#fc0 }
.gray_bo     tr:nth-child(odd), .gray_be     tr:nth-child(even)
   { background:#888 }
.green_bo    tr:nth-child(odd), .green_be    tr:nth-child(even)
   { background:#080 }
.khaki_bo    tr:nth-child(odd), .khaki_be    tr:nth-child(even)
   { background:#cc8 }
.lime_bo     tr:nth-child(odd), .lime_be     tr:nth-child(even)
   { background:#0f0 }
.maroon_bo   tr:nth-child(odd), .maroon_be   tr:nth-child(even)
   { background:#800 }
.navy_bo     tr:nth-child(odd), .navy_be     tr:nth-child(even)
   { background:#008 }
.olive_bo    tr:nth-child(odd), .olive_be    tr:nth-child(even)
   { background:#880 }
.orange_bo   tr:nth-child(odd), .orange_be   tr:nth-child(even)
   { background:#f80 }
.pink_bo     tr:nth-child(odd), .pink_be     tr:nth-child(even)
   { background:#f88 }
.purple_bo   tr:nth-child(odd), .purple_be   tr:nth-child(even)
   { background:#808 }
.red_bo      tr:nth-child(odd), .red_be      tr:nth-child(even)
   { background:#f00 }
.silver_bo   tr:nth-child(odd), .silver_be   tr:nth-child(even)
   { background:#ccc }
.teal_bo     tr:nth-child(odd), .teal_be     tr:nth-child(even)
   { background:#088 }
.white_bo    tr:nth-child(odd), .white_be    tr:nth-child(even)
   { background:#fff }
.yellow_bo   tr:nth-child(odd), .yellow_be   tr:nth-child(even)
   { background:#ff0 }
```

CHAPTER 29

Dynamic Objects

Powerful as CSS is, it isn't really a language, as shown by the recipes in this book having to repeat large chunks of code where only a minor change is required between each, such as a color or width. A language, on the other hand, is very good at repeating things based on only a few lines of code. And that's where JavaScript fits in, because with it you can bring the dynamic interaction of a web page up an order of magnitude.

What's more, many of the classes in this chapter allow you to enter values as parameters to create exactly the result you want, including moving objects about in the browser, loading images in only when (or if) they are scrolled into view, fading images in and out over user-definable periods, resizing and rotating objects by any amount, and changing an object's text and background colors to all possible values.

NoJS (nojs) and OnlyJS (onlyjs)

There is a downside to employing JavaScript-aided classes because some people have JavaScript turned off, generally due to a habit they got into when pop-up windows became so prevalent. But with the advent of pop-up blocking in all modern browsers, the percent of users with JavaScript disabled has dropped from a height of around 12–15 percent a decade ago to an estimated 2 percent or so nowadays. It may not be a large number of users, but it's still enough that, where possible, care should be taken to offer fallback features for these users. And that's what this first dynamic recipe helps with, providing you with an easy way to offer fallback HTML for browsers on which the dynamic classes fail.

You can use the `<noscript>` tag for this, but it requires you to place all the fallback sections of code within pairs of these tags, and there's no simple solution for hiding standard HTML from non-JavaScript browsers. However, by using the `nojs` class for any block of code that should be viewable only to non-JavaScript browsers, no extra tags are required. You simply use the name in the `class` argument of an object, and the `onlyjs` class is used to make any section of HTML visible only to JavaScript-enabled browsers.

For example, the screen grab in Figure 29-1 shows a sentence enclosed within a `<div>` using the `nojs` class, making the sentence visible only to users without JavaScript, or those who have JavaScript disabled.

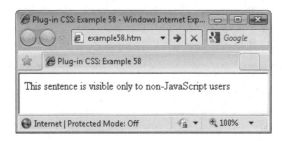

FIGURE 29-1   The sentence in this window will be seen only on browsers without JavaScript.

TIP *JavaScript can be disabled and reenabled in Internet Explorer by pressing ALT+T, selecting Internet Options, choosing the Security tab, clicking the Custom level button, and then scrolling down and checking Active Scripting: Disable or Enable. Different commands are required to do this on other browsers.*

Alternatively, in Figure 29-2, JavaScript is running in the browser and so a section of text for JavaScript-enabled browsers only is displayed.

Variables, Functions, and Properties

classname	String variable containing the name of the class—used by all these recipes so not mentioned again
thistag	Object referring to the current object—used by all these recipes so not mentioned again
search()	JavaScript function to search one string for another—used by all these recipes so not mentioned again
Hide()	Function to hide an object
Show()	Function to show an object

About the Classes

These classes provide complementary functionality to each other. The nojs class is ignored on non-JavaScript browsers; therefore, any object using the class is viewable. But on JavaScript-enabled browsers, the nojs class is acted upon by JavaScript and any object using it is hidden, so users who have JavaScript will not see any objects using the nojs class.

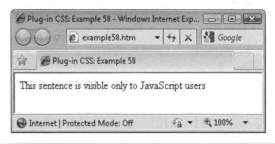

FIGURE 29-2   With JavaScript enabled, a different sentence becomes visible.

On the other hand, the onlyjs class should be used in conjunction with a style argument to hide an object from non-JavaScript browsers, but browsers with JavaScript enabled detect the class and unhide such objects so they become visible.

How to Use Them

You will generally use these classes in pairs, so you can offer one set of HTML to users with JavaScript and another to those without, like this:

```
<div style='display:none;' class='onlyjs'>
   This sentence is visible only to JavaScript users
</div>
<div class='nojs'>
   This sentence is visible only to non-JavaScript users
</div>
```

In the first `<div>`, both the arguments `style='display:none'` and `class='onlyjs'` must be applied in order to make its contents visible only to browsers with JavaScript enabled.

For non-JavaScript browsers, you simply attach the argument `class='nojs'` to an object to ensure that only users without JavaScript enabled can see it.

About the JavaScript

Don't worry if you don't program, because you can ignore these JavaScript code segments and skip to the next recipe—they are included simply for programmers who may be interested in how they work.

The following partial JavaScript listing shows the main setup JavaScript code for all of the classes in the remainder of this book. It starts with initializing the *WDC.js* JavaScript library, which is available as part of the download at *webdeveloperscookbook.com*.

```
OnDOMReady(function()
{
   var gfurl     = 'http://fonts.googleapis.com/css?family='
   var wheight   = GetWindowHeight()
   var tags      = document.getElementsByTagName("*")
   var numtags   = tags.length
   var font      = ''
   var elems     = []
   var gfonts    = []
   var cites     = []
   var refers    = []
   var sclasses  = []
   var gfindex   = 0
   var cindex    = 0
   var demand    = false
   var index, index2, thistag, regex, oldclassname

   loadsclasses(sclasses)

   for (index = 0 ; index < numtags ; ++ index)
   {
```

```
thistag       = tags[index]
var tagname   = thistag.tagName.toLowerCase()
var tagtype   = (thistag.type) ? thistag.type.toLowerCase() : ''
var classname = thistag.className.toLowerCase()
var cnamecopy = classname
var origcname = thistag.className
var repeat    = true
```

First the OnDOMReady() function is called, which sets up the code after it in such a way that the classes become active only once the entire web page is loaded (but before any images or other embedded objects), so that all objects in it can then be referenced at the earliest possible opportunity.

After that, a number of variables used by JavaScript are declared. If you load the code into an editor, you can issue a quick search to see which variables are used by which routines.

Next, the superclasses referred to in Chapter 33 are loaded using the loadsclasses() function, and then the main loop controlling the dynamic classes begins, in which every single class= argument in the web page is examined one at a time, and if it matches one of the new dynamic classes, the code to handle it is activated.

In the case of the two classes in this recipe group, the code used follows. It simply employs a regular expression to find the class names (highlighted in bold), and if found, acts on them by calling either the Hide() function to hide the object using the class, or the Show() function to reveal it. The variable thistag refers to the current object whose class argument is being examined.

TIP *Remember that to function correctly, all the files used by the recipes must be loaded in at the start of each web page within <head> tags, like the following example, which pulls in the WDC.css style sheet and the WDC.js JavaScript library:*

```
<head>
    <link rel='stylesheet' type='text/css' href='WDC.css' />
    <script src='WDC.js'></script>
</head>
```

The JavaScript

```
if (classname.search(/\bnojs\b/, 0)   != -1) Hide(thistag)

if (classname.search(/\bonlyjs\b/, 0) != -1) Show(thistag)
```

Middle (middle)

This class is particularly suitable in cases when standard CSS doesn't have the effect you want because instead of using values of auto, it calculates the correct margins by querying the dimension of the parent object and uses those values to force the desired behavior (as do the middle, center, top, bottom, left, and right recipe classes).

What this class does is vertically align an object by finding out the height of the object immediately enclosing it (its parent) and then placing it directly between the upper and lower boundaries. In Figure 29-3, a 300 × 100–pixel <div> contains another object that has been vertically centered using this class.

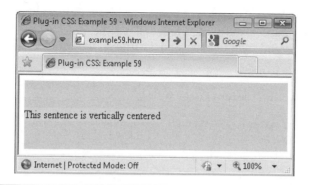

FIGURE 29-3   Vertically centering one object inside another

Variables, Functions, and Properties

parentNode	Object containing the parent of the current object
H()	Function to return the height of an object
O()	Function to return an object—used by most of these dynamic classes and therefore will not be mentioned again
Px()	Function to add the suffix px to a value—used by many of these dynamic classes and therefore will not be mentioned again
marginTop	Property containing the object's top margin
marginBottom	Property containing the object's bottom margin

About the Class

After looking up the height of the parent object, this class then sets the marginTop and marginBottom JavaScript equivalents of the CSS margin-top and margin-bottom properties to equal values sufficient to display the object exactly in the middle.

NOTE   *Wherever you see a JavaScript property that starts with a lowercase letter and has an uppercase one in the middle, you can convert it to a CSS property by changing the uppercase letter to lowercase and placing a hyphen before it. Therefore, marginBottom becomes margin-bottom, and so on.*

How to Use It

In order to use this class, the parent object needs to already have a position other than static, such as relative or absolute, and the object to be moved should be given an absolute position, like this:

```
<div style='width:400px; height:100px;' class='relative lime_b'>
   <div class='absolute aqua_b middle'>
      This sentence is vertically centered
   </div>
</div>
```

This example sets the outer <div> to a width of 400 and a height of 100 pixels, gives it relative positioning, and sets the background to lime. The inner <div> is given absolute positioning, a background color of aqua, and is assigned the middle class.

The JavaScript

```
if (classname.search(/\bmiddle\b/, 0) != -1)
{
    S(thistag).marginTop = S(thistag).marginBottom =
        Px((H(thistag.parentNode) - H(thistag)) / 2)
}
```

60 Center (center)

This class is similar to the middle class, but it centers an object horizontally. In Figure 29-4, the previous example has been extended to also center the inner object using this class.

Variables, Functions, and Properties

parentNode	Object containing the parent of the current object
W()	Function to return the width of an object
marginLeft	Property containing the object's left margin
marginRight	Property containing the object's right margin

About the Class

By looking up the width of the parent object, this class then sets the marginLeft and marginRight properties of the object to equal values sufficient to display the object exactly in the center.

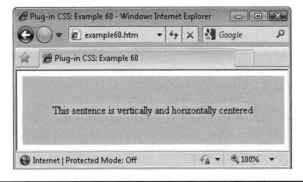

FIGURE 29-4   The example from the previous recipe is now also centered horizontally.

How to Use It

In order to use this class, the parent object needs to already have a position other than `static`, such as `relative` or `absolute`, and the object to be moved should be given an `absolute` position, like this:

```
<div style='width:400px; height:100px;' class='relative lime_b'>
   <div class='absolute middle center aqua_b'>
      This sentence is vertically and horizontally centered
   </div>
</div>
```

This example sets the outer `<div>` to a width of 400 and a height of 100 pixels, gives it relative positioning, and sets the background to lime. The inner object is given absolute positioning, a background color of aqua, and is assigned both the `center` and `middle` classes.

The JavaScript

```
if (classname.search(/\bcenter\b/, 0) != -1)
{
   S(thistag).marginLeft = S(thistag).marginRight =
      Px((W(thistag.parentNode) - W(thistag)) / 2)
}
```

Top (top)

This class attaches an object to the top of its parent, as shown in Figure 29-5, in which the previous example is top- instead of middle-aligned.

Variables, Functions, and Properties

parentNode	Object containing the parent of the current object
H()	Function to return the height of an object
marginTop	Property containing the object's top margin
marginBottom	Property containing the object's bottom margin

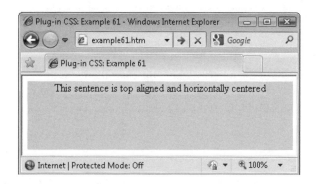

FIGURE 29-5   The inner object is top-aligned using this class.

About the Class

By looking up the height of the parent object, this class then sets the `marginTop` property to 0 pixels and the `marginBottom` property of the object to the value required to ensure it stays at the top of its containing object.

How to Use It

In order to use this class, the parent object needs to already have a position other than static, such as relative or absolute, and the object to be moved should be given an absolute position, like this:

```
<div style='width:400px; height:100px;' class='relative lime_b'>
   <div class='absolute top center aqua_b'>
      This sentence is top-aligned and horizontally centered
   </div>
</div>
```

Here, the inner object is given absolute positioning, a background color of aqua, and is assigned both the `top` and `center` classes.

The JavaScript

```
if (classname.search(/\btop\b/, 0) != -1)
{
    S(thistag).marginTop    = '0px';
    S(thistag).marginBottom = Px(H(thistag.parentNode) -H(thistag))
}
```

Bottom (bottom)

This class attaches an object to the bottom of its parent, as shown in Figure 29-6, in which the previous example is bottom- instead of top-aligned.

Variables, Functions, and Properties

parentNode	Object containing the parent of the current object
H()	Function to return the height of an object
marginTop	Property containing the object's top margin
marginBottom	Property containing the object's bottom margin

About the Class

By looking up the height of the parent object, this class then sets the `marginBottom` property to 0 pixels and the `marginTop` property of the object to the value required to ensure it stays at the bottom of its containing object.

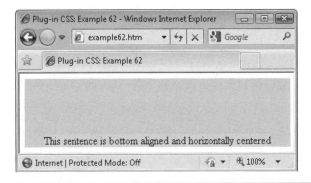

FIGURE 29-6   The inner object is bottom-aligned using this class.

How to Use It

The following example is the same as the previous one, with just one class change:

```
<div style='width:400px; height:100px;' class='relative lime_b'>
   <div class='absolute bottom center aqua_b'>
      This sentence is bottom-aligned and horizontally centered
   </div>
</div>
```

Here, the inner `object` is assigned both the `bottom` and `center` classes.

The JavaScript

```
if (classname.search(/\bbottom\b/, 0) != -1)
{
    S(thistag).marginTop    = Px(H(thistag.parentNode) -H(thistag))
    S(thistag).marginBottom = '0px';
}
```

Left (left)

This class is similar to the `center` class, but it aligns an object to the left. In Figure 29-7, the previous example has been modified to left-align the inner object using this class, rather than centering it. The object is also middle-aligned vertically.

Variables, Functions, and Properties

parentNode	Object containing the parent of the current object
W()	Function to return the width of an object
marginLeft	Property containing the object's left margin
marginRight	Property containing the object's right margin

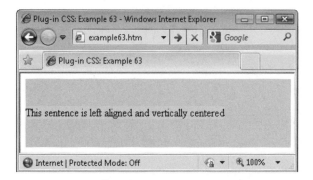

FIGURE 29-7   The example from the previous recipe is now left-aligned and centered vertically.

About the Class

By looking up the width of the parent object, this class then sets the `marginLeft` property to 0 pixels and the `marginRight` property of the object to the value required to ensure it stays at the left of its containing object.

How to Use It

The following example is the same as the previous one, with just one class change:

```
<div style='width:400px; height:100px;' class='relative lime_b'>
   <div class='absolute left middle aqua_b'>
        This sentence is left-aligned and vertically centered
   </div>
</div>
```

Here, the inner `object` is assigned both the `left` and `middle` classes.

The JavaScript

```
if (classname.search(/\bleft\b/, 0) != -1)
{
   S(thistag).marginLeft  = '0px';
   S(thistag).marginRight = Px(W(thistag.parentNode) - W(thistag))
}
```

Right (right)

This class is similar to the `left` class, but it aligns an object to the right. In Figure 29-8, the previous example has been modified to right-align the inner object using this class, rather than left-aligning it.

Variables, Functions, and Properties

parentNode	Object containing the parent of the current object
W()	Function to return the width of an object
marginLeft	Property containing the object's left margin
marginRight	Property containing the object's right margin

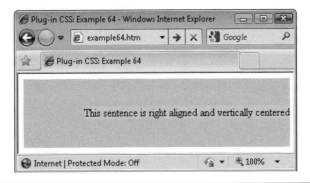

FIGURE 29-8   The example from the previous recipe is now right-aligned.

About the Class

By looking up the width of the parent object, this class then sets the `marginRight` property to 0 pixels and the `marginLeft` property of the object to the value required to ensure it stays at the right of its containing object.

How to Use It

The following example is the same as the previous one, with just one class change:

```
<div style='width:400px; height:100px;' class='relative lime_b'>
    <div class='absolute right middle aqua_b'>
         This sentence is right-aligned and vertically centered
    </div>
</div>
```

Here, the inner `object` is assigned both the `right` and `middle` classes.

The JavaScript

```
if (classname.search(/\bright\b/, 0) != -1)
{
    S(thistag).marginLeft  = Px(W(thistag.parentNode) - W(thistag))
    S(thistag).marginRight = '0px';
}
```

On Demand (ondemand)

Have you noticed how Flash programs and movies generally don't load until you scroll them into view? The idea behind this is to save on downloading data unnecessarily, thus decreasing the provider's bandwidth fees and speeding up your browsing.

Well, with this class you can provide the same feature for your images. When you use it, only those images already in view when a page loads are downloaded. Then, as you scroll, when each new image comes into view it is quickly downloaded and displayed. And, because only one image is fetched at a time, rather than as part of the initial flurry of downloads accompanying a page load, it's actually very fast and looks good too since they fade into view.

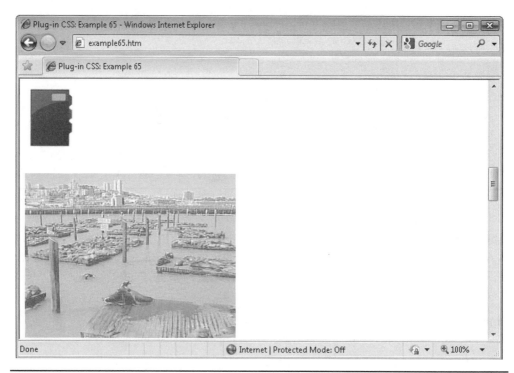

With it, you'll save on your bandwidth bills and speed up your web pages at the same time, as shown in Figure 29-9, in which the photo is being faded in after being scrolled into view.

Variables, Functions, and Properties

`tagname`	String variable containing the name of the tag, such as `img`
`SCROLL_Y`	Global integer variable containing the amount by which the browser has scrolled (global variables are always all uppercase in this program)
`wheight`	Integer variable containing the height of the browser viewport
`index`	Integer variable used for iterating through all the classes found in a web page
`elems[]`	String array containing the sources of all images yet to be loaded
`thistag.alt`	String variable (and a property of `thistag`) containing the alternate text for the current image
`thistag.src`	String variable (and a property of `thistag`) containing the source of the current image

demand	Integer variable used as a flag and set to `true` if the `ondemand` class is being used on a web page
`setTimeout()`	JavaScript function to call a function after a set period
`DoOnDemand()`	Function to keep an eye on images and decide whether to load them
`Opacity()`	Function to set the opacity of an object
`Y()`	Function to return the height of an object
`FadeIn()`	Function to fade an object in over a set time

About the Class

This class checks all images in a web page to see whether they are using the `ondemand` class. Any that do have their position in the web page are examined to see if they are within view. If they are, then the image locations are loaded in from the `alt` arguments and placed in the `src` arguments to download them. But any that are not yet in view have their opacity set to zero so that the broken image icon will not display.

Later in the program, a function will be set up to keep an eye on these images and download and fade them in gently as they come into view.

How to Use It

To use this class, all you need to do is attach the `ondemand` class to any images you have decided should use this feature, and use the `alt` argument for the image URL *not* the *src* argument (this is important), like this:

```
<img class='ondemand' alt='myphoto.jpg' />
```

The image will then only be downloaded and faded in when it is scrolled into view.

For programmers interested in the JavaScript code that later monitors the images (toward the end of the *WDC.js* file), here it is (nonprogrammers can skip ahead to the next recipe):

```
if (demand) setTimeout(DoOnDemand, 10)
```

This line checks whether the variable `demand` has a value of `true`. If so, then the `ondemand` class has been used at least once in the web page and so the function `DoOnDemand()` is set to be called in 10 milliseconds. That function looks like this:

```
function DoOnDemand()
{
   demand = false

   for (index = 0 ; index < numtags ; ++index)
   {
      thistag = tags[index]

      if (elems[index])
      {
         demand = true
```

```
        if (Y(thistag) < (SCROLL_Y + wheight))
        {
            thistag.onload = function() { FadeIn(this, 500) }
            thistag.src    = elems[index]
            elems[index]   = ''
        }
    }
}

if (demand) setTimeout(DoOnDemand, 10)
}
```

What it does is iterate through the array elems[], which has previously been assigned the locations of all ondemand images, and checks whether the image is in view. If so, then the FadeIn() function is set to be called as soon as the image is loaded, and then the image's src= argument is given the location of the image, so it can be fetched. Once an image is loaded, its entry in the elems[] array is removed so it won't be looked up again.

After this, if the variable demand is true, then the interrupt is set up to call the function in a further 10 milliseconds (and so on until all images are downloaded). If it is not true, then no more images require loading in, and so no more calls are made to the interrupt function.

Following is the initial code that locates instances of the ondemand class and acts on them.

CAUTION *Remember that you must use the ALT attribute of an image not its src attribute when using the ondemand class. This is to prevent fast browsers that may have already parsed the full HTML from trying to load images in until the program lets it. With no URLs in the src arguments, the browser will skip them.*

The JavaScript

```
if (classname.search(/\bondemand\b/, 0) != -1 && tagname == 'img')
{
    if (Y(thistag) > (SCROLL_Y + wheight))
    {
        elems[index] = thistag.alt
        demand       = true
        Opacity(thistag, 0)
    }
    else thistag.src = thistag.alt
}
```

Fadein (fadein[*n*])

Using this recipe, you can fade in an object over a length of time of your choosing. This is the first dynamic recipe in which you'll see how to pass values to those classes that use them. For example, the image in Figure 29-10 has been set to fade in over 2,000 milliseconds (or 2 seconds) and is now in the process of fading.

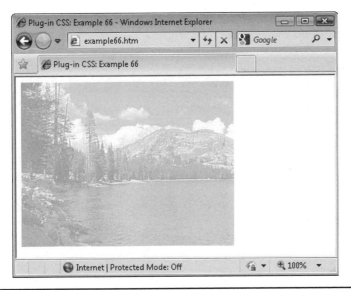

FIGURE 29-10   Using this class to fade in images over a period of time

Variables, Functions, and Properties

arguments[1]	JavaScript array element containing the duration value
cnamecopy	String variable containing a copy of the class name
replace()	JavaScript function to replace values found in a string with other values
Opacity()	Function to set the opacity of an object
FadeIn()	Function to fade an object in over a set time

About the Class

This class uses the JavaScript replace() function on a copy of the class name and specifies an anonymous inline function for handling the replacement. But, rather than replacing it, the function only wants access to the matched string, which it receives in the array element arguments[1]. It then sets the opacity of the object to 0 and calls the FadeIn() function (from *WDC.js*), passing it the object to fade and the value in arguments[1], which is the number of milliseconds the fade should take.

How to Use It

To make an object fade in, use this dynamic class in its class argument, as in the following (ensuring that the duration of the fade in milliseconds is placed within a pair of square brackets):

```
<img class='fadein[2000]' src='i5.jpg' />
```

Any value from 0 upward is acceptable for the duration length, and the argument and square brackets may not be omitted.

The JavaScript

```
if (classname.search(/\bfadein\b/, 0) != -1)
{
    cnamecopy.replace(/fadein\[([^\]]*)\]/, function()
    {
        Opacity(thistag, 0);
        FadeIn(thistag, arguments[1])
    } )
}
```

 Fadeout (fadeout[*n*])

This class offers the inverse functionality to the `fadein[]` class by fading out an object over a set period of time, as shown in Figure 29-11, in which a photo is in the process of fading out using this class.

Variables, Functions, and Properties

`arguments[1]`	JavaScript array element containing the fade duration length
`cnamecopy`	String variable containing a copy of the class name
`replace()`	JavaScript function to replace values found in a string with other values
`Opacity()`	Function to set the opacity of an object
`FadeOut()`	Function to fade out object over a set time

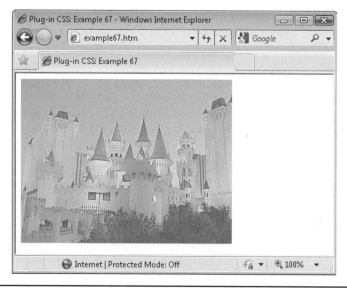

FIGURE 29-11   You can also fade out objects with the fadeout class.

About the Class

This class uses the JavaScript `replace()` function in the same way as the `fadein[]` recipe to pass a duration interval to the `FadeOut()` function.

How to Use It

To make an object fade out, use this dynamic class in its `class` argument, like this (ensuring that the duration of the fade in milliseconds is placed within a pair of square brackets):

```
<img class='fadeout[2000]' src='i6.jpg' />
```

Any value from 0 upward is acceptable for the duration length, and the argument and square brackets may not be omitted.

TIP *You can fade out any object, not just images. Beware, however, because Internet Explorer removes the ClearType setting on any text that has its opacity changed, making it appear more jagged. One solution is to fade a white object in and out that you place over such text, which will then appear to fade out and in, and no fonts will be affected.*

The JavaScript

```
if (classname.search(/\bfadeout\b/, 0) != -1)
{
    cnamecopy.replace(/fadeout\[([^\]]*)\]/, function()
    {
        FadeOut(thistag, arguments[1])
    } )
}
```

68 Resize Textarea (resizeta[n|n])

Choosing the right dimensions for a `<textarea>` input tag can be difficult. Make it too small and there is not much room for the user. But if it's too large, it may appear daunting to the user, who will feel they need to fill the space.

Thankfully, the `resizeta[]` class provides an answer, allowing you to set up a `<textarea>` with an initial number of rows. This class will then monitor it for the minimum and maximum values you give it, contracting and expanding the area according to how many lines of text have been input, as shown in Figure 29-12.

Variables, Functions, and Properties

`tagname`	String variable containing the name of the tag, such as `img`
`cnamecopy`	String variable containing a copy of the class name
`arguments[1]`	JavaScript array element containing the minimum number of rows
`arguments[2]`	JavaScript array element containing the maximum number of rows
`replace()`	JavaScript function to replace values found in a string with other values
`ResizeTextarea()`	Function to automatically resize a textarea as necessary

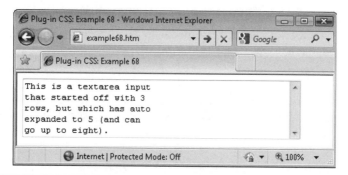

FIGURE **29-12**   A textarea that was originally three rows high has expanded to five.

About the Class

This class uses the JavaScript `replace()` function on a copy of the class name, and specifies an anonymous inline function for handling the replacement. But, rather than replacing it, the function only wants access to the matched string, which it receives in the array elements `arguments[1]` and `arguments[2]`. It then passes these values to the `ResizeTextarea()` function, which continuously monitors the textarea, contracting and expanding it as necessary.

How to Use It

To use this class, set up a `<textarea>` tag with the required number of rows and columns, then place the `resizeta[]` class in the class argument and provide the minimum and maximum number of rows within the square brackets. These two values must be separated with a | symbol, which is the standard way to separate values passed in classes. The result looks like this:

```
<textarea class='resizeta[3|8]' rows='3' cols='50'></textarea>
```

This example creates a three-row by 50-column `<textarea>`, which can expand up to eight and retract back to three rows.

The JavaScript

```
if (classname.search(/\bresizeta\b/, 0) != -1 &&
    tagname == 'textarea')
{
    cnamecopy.replace(/resizeta\[([^\|]*)\|([^\]]*)\]/, function()
    {
        ResizeTextarea(thistag, arguments[1], arguments[2])
    } )
}
```

Rotate (rotate[*n*])

This class starts to use a little meatier code. It's a more powerful version of the `rotatec...` and `rotatea...` classes from CSS Recipe 55 in Chapter 28, because it supports rotating an object between 1 and 359 degrees or –1 and –359 degrees.

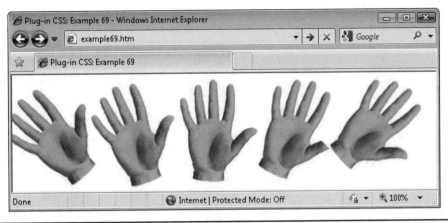

FIGURE 29-13   Using this class, you can rotate any object clockwise or counterclockwise, by any amount.

For example, the image of the hand in Figure 29-13 has been rotated by −45, −22.5, 0, 22.5, and 45 degrees, respectively.

Variables, Functions, and Properties

cnamecopy	String variable copy of the class name
arguments[1]	JavaScript array element containing the amount of rotation
r	Array copy of the JavaScript arguments[] array, the amount by which to rotate the object
rad cosrad sinrad	Floating point variables used for calculating rotation values for Internet Explorer
w h	Integer variables containing the width and height of the object
REL	Global string variable containing the value "relative"
replace()	JavaScript function to replace values found in a string with other values
W()	Function to get the width of an object
H()	Function to get the height of an object
S()	Function to set the style properties of an object
Locate()	Function to move an object to a new location
MozTransform	Property for setting up a transformation on Firefox and other Mozilla-based browsers
WebkitTransform	Property for setting up a transformation on the Safari and Chrome browsers
OTransform	Property for setting up a transformation on the Opera browser
transform	Property for setting up a transformation on all other browsers (except IE)
filter	Property used by Internet Explorer for image transformations, among other features

About the Class

This class uses the JavaScript `replace()` function on a copy of the class name, and specifies an anonymous inline function for handling the replacement. However, rather than replacing it, the function only wants access to the matched string, which it receives in the array element `arguments[1]`. If the browser is not Internet Explorer, it then passes this value to the `S()` function to modify the correct transform property for the browser.

If the browser is IE (determined by checking for the existence of the `filter` property), a series of calculations are made to determine the correct values for the matrix function IE uses to rotate an object. The matrix is then applied by assigning it to the `filter` property using the `S()` function, and then the object is moved to a relative location that will make the rotation appear to have occurred around its center (to match the way all other browsers rotate).

How to Use It

To use this class, enter its name in the `class` argument of the object to be rotated, ensuring you pass the amount of rotation required within a pair of square brackets, like the following, which rotates the image clockwise by 17 degrees:

```
<img class='rotate[17]' src='image.jpg' />
```

Here, for example, is the HTML used to create Figure 29-13:

```
<img class='rotate[-45]'   src='hand.jpg' />
<img class='rotate[-22.5]' src='hand.jpg' />
<img                       src='hand.jpg' />
<img class='rotate[22.5]'  src='hand.jpg' />
<img class='rotate[45]'    src='hand.jpg' />
```

CAUTION *On all recent browsers other than Internet Explorer, you can rotate any object. But because IE has to use the* `filter` *property for this effect, it will only work on images.*

The JavaScript

```
if (classname.search(/\brotate\b/, 0) != -1)
{
    cnamecopy.replace(/rotate\[([^\]]*)\]/, function()
    {
      var r = arguments[1]

      S(thistag).MozTransform    = 'rotate(' + r + 'deg)'
      S(thistag).WebkitTransform = 'rotate(' + r + 'deg)'
      S(thistag).OTransform      = 'rotate(' + r + 'deg)'
      S(thistag).transform       = 'rotate(' + r + 'deg)'

      if (typeof S(thistag).filter != UNDEF)
      {
         var rad    = r * (Math.PI * 2 / 360)
         var cosrad = Math.cos(rad)
         var sinrad = Math.sin(rad)
```

```
        var w       = W(thistag)
        var h       = H(thistag)
        var filter = 'progid:DXImageTransform.Microsoft.' +
           'Matrix(M11=' + cosrad + ', M12=' + -sinrad    +
           ',       M21=' + sinrad + ', M22=' +  cosrad    +
           ", SizingMethod='auto expand')"

        S(thistag).filter = filter
        Locate(thistag, REL, -((W(thistag) - w) / 2),
                             -((H(thistag) - h) / 2))
      }
   } )
}
```

Width (w[*n*])

Throughout this book, there have been examples where the width of an object has required changing, and this has been achieved using a `style` attribute. However, with this class you can specify the width of an object as a dynamic class parameter, as shown in Figure 29-14, in which the width of the `<div>` has been set to 450 pixels.

Variables, Functions, and Properties

cnamecopy	String variable copy of the class name
arguments[1]	JavaScript array element containing the new width
replace()	JavaScript function to replace one section of a string with another
S()	Function to modify a style property of an object
width	Property containing the width of an object

About the Class

This class uses the `rename()` function to pass the width from the class argument to the `S()` function in order to modify the object's width by changing the `width` property.

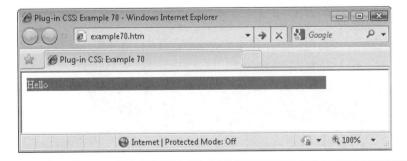

FIGURE 29-14   Using this class to change the width of an object

How to Use It

To use this class, enter the width amount in pixels within square brackets after the class name like this, which sets the width of the <div> to 450 pixels:

```
<div class='w[450] yellow red_b'>Hello</div>
```

No measurements other than pixels are supported, and you must enter a number greater than 0 in the square brackets.

The JavaScript

```
if (classname.search(/\bw\b/, 0) != -1)
{
    cnamecopy.replace(/w\[([^\]]*)\]/, function()
    {
        S(thistag).width = Px(arguments[1])
    } )
}
```

Height (h[*n*])

With this class, you can specify the height of an object as a dynamic class parameter, as in the case of Figure 29-15, in which the example in the previous recipe has also had its height set to 70 pixels.

Variables, Functions, and Properties

cnamecopy	String variable copy of the class name
arguments[1]	JavaScript array element containing the new height
replace()	JavaScript function to replace one section of a string with another
S()	Function to modify a style property of an object
height	Property containing the height of an object

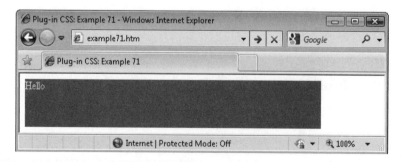

FIGURE 29-15   Using this class to change the height of an object

About the Class

This class uses the `replace()` function to pass the width from the class argument to the `S()` function in order to modify the object's height by changing the `height` property.

How to Use It

To use this class, enter the height amount in pixels within square brackets after the class name like this, which sets the height of the `<div>` to 70 pixels:

```
<div class='h[70] yellow red_b'>Hello</div>
```

No measurements other than pixels are supported, and you must enter a number greater than 0 in the square brackets.

The JavaScript

```
if (classname.search(/\bh\b/, 0) != -1)
{
    cnamecopy.replace(/h\[([^\]]*)\]/, function()
    {
        S(thistag).height = Px(arguments[1])
    } )
}
```

72 X (x[n])

Once you free an object from the flow of a web page by giving it a position other than static (such as relative or absolute), you can move it where you like on a page (or within its containing object). Using this class, you can change an object's horizontal position on the page, as shown in Figure 29-16, in which a 115 × 115–pixel object has been inset from the left of the browser by 475 pixels.

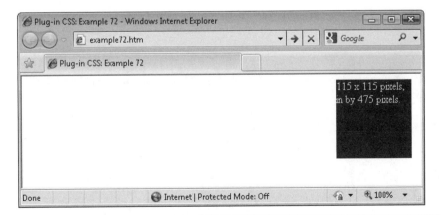

FIGURE 29-16 The box has been inset from the left by 475 pixels using this class.

Variables, Functions, and Properties

cnamecopy	String variable copy of the class name
arguments[1]	JavaScript array element containing the new offset
replace()	JavaScript function to replace one section of a string with another
S()	Function to modify a style property of an object
left	Property containing the left offset of the object

About the Class

This class uses the rename() function to pass the horizontal location from the class argument to the S() function in order to modify the object's left offset by changing its left property.

How to Use It

To use this class, enter the left offset amount in pixels within square brackets after the class name like this, which sets the left offset of the <div> to 475 pixels (and also sets the width and height to 115 pixels each):

```
<div class='absolute w[115] h[115] x[475] yellow blue_b'>
   115 x 115 pixels, in by 475 pixels.
</div>
```

No measurements other than pixels are supported, and you must enter a number greater than 0 in the square brackets.

The JavaScript

```
if (classname.search(/\bx\b/, 0) != -1)
{
   cnamecopy.replace(/x\[([^\]]*)\]/, function()
   {
      S(thistag).left = Px(arguments[1])
   } )
}
```

73 Y (y[n])

This is the partner class for x[]; it moves an object down by the amount specified in the parameter in square brackets. Figure 29-17 shows the example from the previous recipe, but with its vertical offset set to 53 pixels.

Variables, Functions, and Properties

cnamecopy	String variable copy of the class name
arguments[1]	JavaScript array element containing the new offset
replace()	JavaScript function to replace one section of a string with another
S()	Function to modify a style property of an object
top	Property containing the top offset of the object

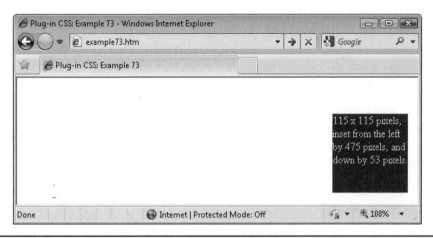

FIGURE 29-17   The object has now been moved down by 53 pixels.

About the Class

This class uses the `replace()` function to pass the vertical location from the class argument to the `S()` function in order to modify the object's top offset by changing its `top` property.

How to Use It

To use this class, enter the top offset amount in pixels within square brackets after the class name like this, which sets the top offset of the `<div>` to 53 pixels (and also sets the width and height to 115 pixels each and the left offset to 475 pixels):

```
<div class='absolute w[115] h[115] x[475] y[53] yellow blue_b'>
   115 x 115 pixels, inset from the left by 475 pixels, and
   down by 53 pixels.
</div>
```

No measurements other than pixels are supported, and you must enter a number greater than 0 in the square brackets.

TIP You can also use negative values on objects with relative position to move them both to the left and up in the browser.

The JavaScript

```
if (classname.search(/\by\b/, 0) != -1)
{
   cnamecopy.replace(/y\[([^\]]*)\]/, function()
   {
      S(thistag).top = Px(arguments[1])
   } )
}
```

PART IV

Text Color (color[*colorname*/*#nnnnnn*/*#nnn*])

Although previous chapters have introduced a basic set of 21 color names that you can use within classes, sometimes you need much finer color control, which is what this class provides. With it, you can choose any color value from #000000 through to #ffffff (or the #000 to #fff short forms), as well as any predefined color names that browsers understand, such as blue, green, or violet. In Figure 29-18, six different color values have been selected using this class.

Variables, Functions, and Properties

cnamecopy	String variable copy of the class name
arguments[1]	JavaScript array element containing the new color
replace()	JavaScript function to replace one section of a string with another
S()	Function to modify a style property of an object
color	Property containing the text color of an object

About the Class

This class uses the replace() function to pass the color value from the class argument to the S() function in order to modify the object's color by changing its color property.

How to Use It

To use this class to change the color of some text, place it in the class argument of the containing object and enter the color value you want within a pair of square brackets following the class name, as in the following HTML, which was used for the screen grab in Figure 29-18:

```
<span class='pt40'>
   <span class='color[#456789]'>#456789</span>
   <span class='color[#ca8]   '>#ca8    </span>
   <span class='color[#987654]'>#987654</span><br />
   <span class='color[green]'  >green  </span>
   <span class='color[violet]' >violet </span>
   <span class='color[magenta]'>magenta</span>
</span>
```

The JavaScript

```
if (classname.search(/\bcolor\b/, 0) != -1)
{
   cnamecopy.replace(/color\[([^\]]*)\]/, function()
   {
      S(thistag).color = arguments[1]
   } )
}
```

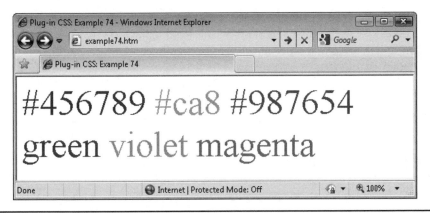

Figure 29-18   The result of using this class on six different values

Background Color (bcolor[#*nnnnnn*])

This class provides the same functionality as the color[] class, except for changing the background color of an object, as shown in Figure 29-19, in which the same six color values from the previous example have now been applied to the background properties of the objects.

Variables, Functions, and Properties

cnamecopy	String variable copy of the class name
arguments[1]	JavaScript array element containing the new color
replace()	JavaScript function to replace one section of a string with another
S()	Function to modify a style property of an object
backgroundColor	Property containing the background color of an object

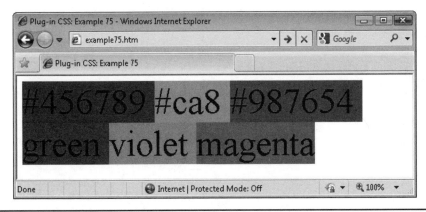

Figure 29-19   This class lets you change the background of any object to any color.

About the Class

This class uses the `replace()` function to pass the color value from the class argument to the `S()` function in order to modify the object's background color by changing its `backgroundColor` property.

How to Use It

To use this class to change the background color of some text, place it in the `class` argument of the containing object and enter the color value you want within a pair of square brackets following the class name, as in the following HTML, which was used for the screen grab in Figure 29-19:

```
<span class='pt40'>
   <span class='bcolor[#456789]'>#456789 </span>
   <span class='bcolor[#ca8]'    >#ca8    </span>
   <span class='bcolor[#987654]'>#987654 </span><br />
   <span class='bcolor[green]'  >green   </span>
   <span class='bcolor[violet]' >violet  </span>
   <span class='bcolor[magenta]'>magenta </span>
</span>
```

The JavaScript

```
if (classname.search(/\bbcolor\b/, 0) != -1)
{
   cnamecopy.replace(/bcolor\[([^\]]*)\]/, function()
   {
      S(thistag).backgroundColor = arguments[1]
   } )
}
```

CHAPTER 30

Dynamic Text and Typography

This chapter explores a range of dynamic classes for enhancing the way you use text in a web page, including a typewriter or teletype effect, a way of cleaning up strings by removing unwanted characters and whitespace, a class for automatically loading Google fonts in from the Google servers when you reference them, one for vertically aligning text within an object, and another for creating glow effects by cycling the foreground and background colors of objects.

Typetext (typetext[n])

This class displays the contents of an object as if it is being typed out on a typewriter or teletype machine. The class also takes a parameter specifying the duration of the animation so you can specify the exact time you require.

For example, in Figure 30-1 the poem "The Tyger" by William Blake is being typed to the screen over the course of 60 seconds.

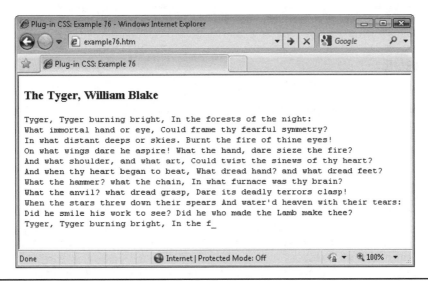

FIGURE 30-1 Display a poem as if typed in a typewriter with this recipe.

Variables, Functions, and Properties

cnamecopy	String variable copy of the class name
arguments[1]	JavaScript array element containing the animation duration
replace()	JavaScript function to replace one section of a string with another
TextType()	Function to modify a style property of an object

About the Class

This class removes the contents of the object it applies to and then replaces those contents over a time duration passed to it.

How to Use It

To use this class, enter its name into the class argument of the containing object, along with the animation duration within square brackets, as with the following example, which was used for the screen grab in Figure 30-1:

```
<pre><div class='typetext[60000]'>
Tyger, Tyger burning bright, In the forests of the night:
What immortal hand or eye, Could frame thy fearful symmetry?
In what distant deeps or skies. Burnt the fire of thine eyes!
On what wings dare he aspire! What the hand, dare sieze the fire?

And what shoulder, and what art, Could twist the sinews of thy heart?
And when thy heart began to beat, What dread hand? and what dread feet?
What the hammer? what the chain, In what furnace was thy brain?
What the anvil? what dread grasp, Dare its deadly terrors clasp!

When the stars threw down their spears And water'd heaven with their ears:
Did he smile his work to see? Did he who made the Lamb make thee?
Tyger, Tyger burning bright, In the forests of the night:
What immortal hand or eye, Dare frame thy fearful symmetry?</div></pre>
```

The JavaScript

```
if (classname.search(/\btypetext\b/, 0) != -1)
{
    cnamecopy.replace(/typetext\[(([^\]]*)\]/, function()
    {
        TextType(thistag, 1, arguments[1])
    } )
}
```

Digits Only (digitsonly)

This class removes any characters from an input field that are not digits or whitespace. For example, in Figure 30-2 the user has been asked for their credit card number and has also entered some irrelevant text.

But in Figure 30-3, as soon as the user moves the mouse away, all the erroneous characters are automatically removed, leaving behind only the numbers and whitespace.

FIGURE 30-2   The user has input more than just a card number.

Variables, Functions, and Properties

onchange	JavaScript event that triggers when the contents of a field change
onmouseout	JavaScript event that triggers when the mouse moves away from an object
onsubmit	JavaScript event that triggers when a form is submitted
CleanupString()	Function to clean up a string in a variety of different ways
this.value	Property containing the contents of the input field

About the Class

This class is triggered whenever the mouse moves out of the object employing it, at which point it calls the CleanupString() function (from the *WDC.js* library) to strip out all characters that are not digits or whitespace.

How to Use It

When you want to ensure that an input field contains only digits or whitespace, place this class name in the class argument of the element, like this:

```
<input name='creditcard' class='digitsonly' size='30' />
```

The field will be automatically cleaned up for you with no further effort on your part.

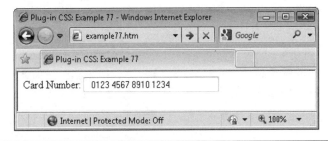

FIGURE 30-3   The unwanted characters have now been removed.

The JavaScript

```
if (classname.search(/\bdigitsonly\b/, 0) != -1)
{
    thistag.onchange = thistag.onmouseout =
        thistag.onsubmit = function()
    {
        this.value = CleanupString(this.value, 0, 0, 1, 1)
    }
}
```

Text Only (textonly)

This class is similar to the previous one in that it removes all characters that are not text or whitespace from an input field. For example, in Figure 30-4 the user has entered some numbers into the field, which are not allowed.

However, in Figure 30-5 only the text and whitespace remain once the mouse is moved out of the field.

Variables, Functions, and Properties

onchange	JavaScript event that triggers when the contents of a field change
onmouseout	JavaScript event that triggers when the mouse moves away from an object
onsubmit	JavaScript event that triggers when a form is submitted
CleanupString()	Function to clean up a string in a variety of different ways
this.value	Property containing the contents of the input field

About the Class

This class is triggered whenever the mouse moves out of the object employing it, at which point it calls the CleanupString() function to strip out all characters that are not text or whitespace.

How to Use It

When you want to ensure that an input field contains only text or whitespace, place this class name in the class argument of the element, like this:

```
<input name='name' class='textonly' size='30' />
```

The field will be automatically cleaned up for you with no further effort on your part.

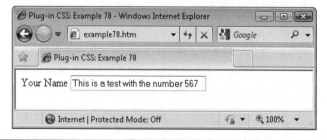

FIGURE 30-4   The user has entered numbers, which are not allowed.

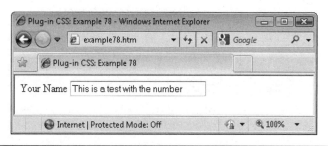

FIGURE 30-5   The field has been cleaned up by removing the numbers.

The JavaScript

```
if (classname.search(/\btextonly\b/, 0) != -1)
{
   thistag.onchange = thistag.onmouseout =
      thistag.onsubmit = function()
   {
      this.value = CleanupString(this.value, 1, 1, 0, 1)
   }
}
```

No Spaces (nospaces)

With this class, you can remove all the spaces from an input field. It is probably most useful for stripping spaces out of credit card numbers. For example, how often have you entered your credit card online only to have a form re-presented to you advising that the input was invalid because spaces are not allowed? It's certainly happened a few times to me, and it's so unnecessary because it's an easy problem to fix on behalf of the user. For example, in Figure 30-6 a credit card number has been entered with spaces.

However, once the user moves the mouse away, clicks into another field, or submits the form, the whitespace is removed (see Figure 30-7).

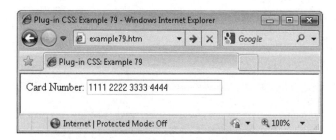

FIGURE 30-6   A credit card number containing spaces has been entered.

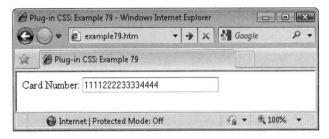

FIGURE 30-7   Now the spaces have been automatically removed.

Variables, Functions, and Properties

onchange	JavaScript event that triggers when the contents of a field change
onmouseout	JavaScript event that triggers when the mouse moves away from an object
onsubmit	JavaScript event that triggers when a form is submitted
CleanupString()	Function to clean up a string in a variety of different ways
this.value	Property containing the contents of the input field

About the Class

This class is triggered whenever the mouse moves out of the object employing it, at which point it calls the CleanupString() function to strip out all whitespace from it.

How to Use It

To remove the whitespace from a field, place this class name in the class argument of the element, as in the following example, in which both the digitsonly and nospaces classes have been used (they generally go well together when used for inputting credit card details):

```
<input name='creditcard' class='digitsonly nospaces' size='30'/>
```

The field will be automatically cleaned up for you by removing all non-digits and all whitespace.

The JavaScript

```
if (classname.search(/\bnospaces\b/, 0) != -1)
{
   thistag.onchange = thistag.onmouseout =
      thistag.onsubmit = function()
   {
      this.value = CleanupString(this.value, 1)
   }
}
```

Figure 30-8   This input contains several punctuation characters.

No Punctuation (nopunct)

Sometimes you want just the bare text to be posted to a web form, and not any punctuation like exclamation points and question marks. You can do this easily with Recipe 80, which strips them all out for you.

For example, in Figure 30-8 the user is being prompted for a reminder phrase that will be used to prompt them if they forget their password.

But in Figure 30-9, the user has moved the mouse away and so the punctuation has been automatically filtered out.

Variables, Functions, and Properties

onchange	JavaScript event that triggers when the contents of a field change
onmouseout	JavaScript event that triggers when the mouse moves away from an object
onsubmit	JavaScript event that triggers when a form is submitted
CleanupString()	Function to clean up a string in a variety of different ways
this.value	Property containing the contents of the input field

Figure 30-9   The punctuation has now been removed.

About the Class

This class is triggered whenever the mouse moves out of the object employing it, at which point it calls the `CleanupString()` function to strip out all punctuation characters from it.

How to Use It

To remove the punctuation characters from a field, place this class name in the `class` argument of the element, as in the following example:

```
<input name='reminder' class='nopunct' size='30'/>
```

The field will be automatically cleaned up for you by removing all the punctuation.

The JavaScript

```
if (classname.search(/\bnopunct\b/, 0) != -1)
{
    thistag.onchange = thistag.onmouseout =
        thistag.onsubmit = function()
    {
        this.value = CleanupString(this.value, 0, 0, 0, 1)
    }
}
```

RECIPE 81 Minimum Whitespace (minwhitespace)

Using this class, you can remove all the additional whitespace characters users sometimes enter, replacing any groups of more than one whitespace character with a single space.

For example, in Figure 30-10 a `<textarea>` has been created in which a user is entering their bio, with a somewhat messy use of whitespace.

However, after passing the mouse away, the extra whitespace is removed, leaving much better formatted text (see Figure 30-11).

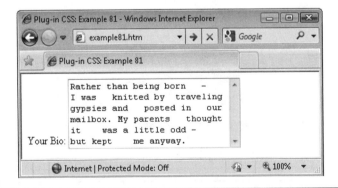

FIGURE 30-10 This `<textarea>` contains a lot of unnecessary whitespace.

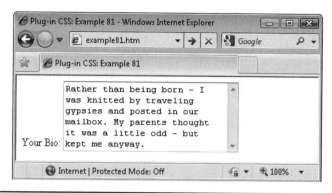

FIGURE 30-11   Now the text has been stripped of unnecessary extra whitespace.

Variables, Functions, and Properties

onchange	JavaScript event that triggers when the contents of a field change
onmouseout	JavaScript event that triggers when the mouse moves away from an object
onsubmit	JavaScript event that triggers when a form is submitted
CleanupString()	Function to clean up a string in a variety of different ways
this.value	Property containing the contents of the input field

About the Class

This class is triggered whenever the mouse moves out of the object employing it, at which point it calls the CleanupString() function to strip out all extra whitespace characters from it.

How to Use It

To remove the extra whitespace from a field, place this class name in the class argument of the element, as in the following example:

```
<textarea class='minwhitespace' rows='6' cols='30'></textarea>
```

The field will be automatically cleaned up for you by removing all the extra whitespace.

The JavaScript

```
if (classname.search(/\bminwhitespace\b/, 0) != -1)
{
   thistag.onchange = thistag.onmouseout =
      thistag.onsubmit = function()
   {
      this.value = CleanupString(this.value, 0, 0, 0, 0, 0, 0, 1)
   }
}
```

Google Font (gfont[n])

In CSS Recipe 28 of Chapter 25, you saw how to incorporate Google fonts into your web pages. Unfortunately, you have to fiddle around with it a bit since you must add a `<link rel...>` tag for every font you include. But using this class, you simply mention a Google font by name, and if it hasn't been loaded in yet, it is fetched automatically for you.

Figure 30-12 is similar to Figure 25-9 but was achieved using this recipe and without having to manually load in all the fonts.

Variables, Functions, and Properties

`arguments[1]`	JavaScript array element containing the font name to use
`font`	String variable containing the full font name
`window[font]`	Array attached to the window object instead of using a global array, containing the value `true` if a Google font is already due to be loaded
`gfonts`	Local array containing the Google fonts to be loaded
`gfindex`	Integer variable containing the number of Google fonts to load
`index`	Integer variable used for iterating through an array
`newcss`	Object containing a new style sheet to append to the DOM
`replace()`	JavaScript function to replace a section of one string with another
`createElement()`	JavaScript function to create a new element object
`appendChild()`	JavaScript function to add a new element to the DOM
`fontFamily`	Property containing the font family of an object
`window.opera`	Property only set in the Opera browser; used for determining whether the browser requires a redraw
`document.body.style`	Property that, if changed, forces a browser redraw in Opera

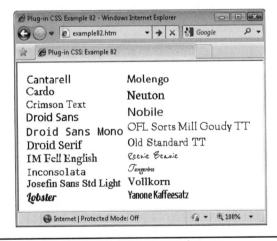

FIGURE 30-12   This class makes using Google fonts even easier.

About the Class

This is a very easy class to use but a little complicated to explain. If you are interested only in how you can use it, then skip to the next section.

This class works by making a note of every `class` argument you use that mentions the `gfont[]` class name. Then, if the font required has not been marked to be fetched from Google's servers, the full font name is added to the `gfonts[]` array, and the `fontFamily` property is set to the font to use.

Later on, the fonts are all loaded in from Google's servers, but only after all the dynamic functions have been processed. This is because the act of loading in the new style sheets changes the DOM by adding new elements to it, which, if done before the HTML processing is complete, would corrupt the array of elements to be processed each time a new font is fetched.

How to Use It

To use this class to access Google's fonts, just mention it in a class argument, supplying the shorthand name of the font from Table 30-1 in the following square brackets, like this:

```
<div class='gfont[crimson]'>Crimson Text</div>
```

Shorthand	Font Name
cardo	Cardo
cantarell	Cantarell
crimson	Crimson Text
droidsans	Droid Sans
droidsansm	Droid Sans Mono
droidserif	Droid Serif
imfell	IM Fell English
inconsolata	Inconsolata
josefin	Josefin Sans Std Light
lobster	Lobster
molengo	Molengo
neuton	Neuton
nobile	Nobile
oflsorts	OFL Sorts Mill Goudy TT
oldstandard	Old Standard TT
reenie	Reenie Beanie
tangerine	Tangerine
vollkorn	Vollkorn
yanone	Yanone Kaffeesatz

TABLE 30-1   The Google Font Families and Shorthand Class Argument Names

About the JavaScript

Once all the dynamic classes used in a web page have been processed, the following JavaScript code is run to load in all the Google fonts from Google's servers that were accessed in the page:

```
for (index = 0 ; index < gfindex ; ++index)
{
   var newcss  = document.createElement('link')
   newcss.href = gfurl + escape(gfonts[index])
   newcss.rel  = 'stylesheet'
   newcss.type = 'text/css'
   document.getElementsByTagName('head')[0].appendChild(newcss)
}
```

With the fonts loaded, all browsers that support these fonts will be displaying them, with the exception of Opera, which requires a nudge to redraw the browser contents, like this:

```
if (gfindex && window.opera) setTimeout(function()
   { document.body.style += "" }, 1)
```

Following is the code used in the main section of JavaScript to process just the gfont [] class.

The JavaScript

```
if (classname.search(/\bgfont\b/, 0) != -1)
{
   cnamecopy.replace(/gfont\[([^\]]*)\]/, function()
   {
      switch(arguments[1])
      {
         case 'cantarell'  : font = 'Cantarell'; break
         case 'cardo'      : font = 'Cardo'; break
         case 'crimson'    : font = 'Crimson Text'; break
         case 'droidsans'  : font = 'Droid Sans'; break
         case 'droidsansm' : font = 'Droid Sans Mono'; break
         case 'droidserif' : font = 'Droid Serif'; break
         case 'imfell'     : font = 'IM Fell English'; break
         case 'inconsolata': font = 'Inconsolata'; break
         case 'josefin'    : font = 'Josefin Sans Std Light'; break
         case 'lobster'    : font = 'Lobster'; break
         case 'molengo'    : font = 'Molengo'; break
         case 'neuton'     : font = 'Neuton'; break
         case 'nobile'     : font = 'Nobile'; break
         case 'oflsorts'   : font = 'OFL Sorts Mill Goudy TT'; break
         case 'oldstandard': font = 'Old Standard TT'; break
         case 'reenie'     : font = 'Reenie Beanie'; break
         case 'tangerine'  : font = 'Tangerine'; break
         case 'vollkorn'   : font = 'Vollkorn'; break
         case 'yanone'     : font = 'Yanone Kaffeesatz'; break
      }
```

```
    if (!window[font])
    {
       window[font]     = true
       gfonts[gfindex++] = font
    }

    S(thistag).fontFamily = font

    if (window.opera) setTimeout(function() // Required by Opera
       { document.body.style += "" }, 1)    // to redraw window
    } )
}
```

Text Middle (textmiddle)

This class centers text using the trick of setting the CSS `line-height` property to that of the containing object. This is easy enough to do in your CSS on a single-element basis, but because exact heights must be entered, this class is superior since it does the calculation for you.

For example, the `<div>` in Figure 30-13 has been set to 100 pixels in height, and the text within it has been vertically centered using this recipe.

Variables, Functions, and Properties

Px()	Function to add the suffix px to a string
lineHeight	Property containing the line height of the object

About the Class

This class looks up the height of the object and then sets the line height of its contents to the same as the object height, which has the effect of vertically centering the text.

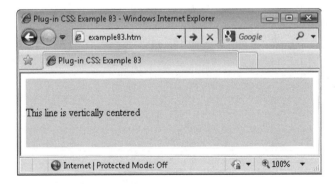

Figure 30-13   The text within the object has been vertically centered.

How to Use It

To vertically center text within an object, mention this class in its `class` argument like in this example, which first sets the object height to 100 pixels and the background to aqua, so you can clearly see the effect:

```
<div class='h[100] textmiddle aqua_b'>
   This line is vertically centered
</div>
```

The JavaScript

```
if (classname.search(/\btextmiddle\b/, 0) != -1)
{
   S(thistag).lineHeight = Px(H(thistag))
}
```

 ## Text Glow (textglow[#nnnnnn|#nnnnnn|n])

This class cycles between two colors over a time period you specify, providing a glowing effect. For example, in Figure 30-14 the text has been set to cycle from yellow to red over the course of a second, and then back again, and so on.

Variables, Functions, and Properties

cnamecopy	String variable copy of the class name
arguments[1]	JavaScript array element containing the first color
arguments[2]	JavaScript array element containing the second color
arguments[3]	JavaScript array element containing the animation duration
replace()	JavaScript function to replace one section of a string with another
ColorFade()	Function to constantly fade between two colors

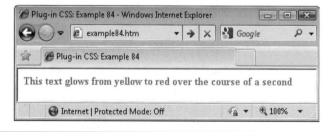

FIGURE 30-14 You can create a text glow effect with this class.

About the Class

This class calls the `ColorFade()` function (JavaScript Recipe 74) to constantly fade between two text colors. It uses the JavaScript `replace()` function to capture the values passed with the class, and then supplies them to `ColorFade()` via the `arguments[]` array.

How to Use It

To use this class, you must specify two six-digit hex color numbers, prefaced by # symbols, as well as a duration for the animation in milliseconds. These parameters should be separated by | symbols and placed within square brackets following the class name that is passed in a `class` argument, like this:

```
<div class='textglow[#ffff00|#ff0000|1000] b'>
   This text cycles from yellow to red over the course of a second
</div>
```

This example cycles between the colors yellow and red over the course of a second (1000 milliseconds), and then back over the same duration, at which point the animation begins again.

The JavaScript

```
if (classname.search(/\btextglow\b/, 0) != -1)
{
    cnamecopy.replace(/textglow\[([^\|]*)\|([^\|]*)\|([^\]]*)\]/,
       function()
    {
       ColorFade(thistag, arguments[1], arguments[2], 'text',
          arguments[3])
    } )
}
```

Background Glow (backglow[#*nnnnnn*|#*nnnnnn*|*n*])

This class is similar to the previous one, but it provides a glow effect to the background color property of an object, as shown in Figure 30-15. This is the same as the previous example, except that a background glow from lime green to blue over 1.5 seconds has been added.

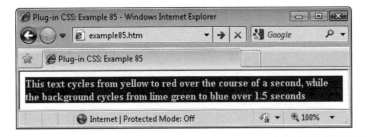

FIGURE 30-15   Combining background and foreground color glows

Variables, Functions, and Properties

`cnamecopy`	String variable copy of the class name
`arguments[1]`	JavaScript array element containing the first color
`arguments[2]`	JavaScript array element containing the second color
`arguments[3]`	JavaScript array element containing the animation duration
`replace()`	JavaScript function to replace one section of a string with another
`ColorFade()`	Function to constantly fade between two colors

About the Class

This class calls the `ColorFade()` function with slightly different arguments to constantly fade between two background colors. It uses the JavaScript `replace()` function to capture the values passed with the class, and then supplies them to `ColorFade()` via the `arguments[]` array.

How to Use It

To use this class, you must specify two six-digit hex color numbers, prefaced by # symbols, as well as a duration for the animation in milliseconds. These parameters should be separated by | symbols and placed within square brackets following the class name passed in a `class` argument, like this:

```
<div class='textglow[#ffff00|#ff0000|1000] b
   backglow[#00ff00|#0000ff|1500] b'>
   This text cycles from yellow to red over the course of a
   second, while the background cycles from lime green to blue
   over 1.5 seconds
</div>
```

This example cycles between the text colors yellow and red over the course of a second (1000 milliseconds), and then back over the same duration, at which point the animation begins again. At the same time, the background color cycles from lime green to blue over 1.5 seconds, and back again, and so on.

CAUTION *Due to the way the two color glow functions operate, they require six-digit hex color values, and will not accept three-digit or named color values.*

The JavaScript

```
if (classname.search(/\bbackglow\b/, 0) != -1)
{
   cnamecopy.replace(/backglow\[(([^\|]*)\|(([^\|]*)\|(([^\]]*)\]/,
      function()
   {
      ColorFade(thistag, arguments[1], arguments[2], '',
         arguments[3])
   } )
}
```

CHAPTER 31

Dynamic Interaction

The classes in this chapter are designed to offer features that could only otherwise be created using JavaScript. For example, both the HTML5 placeholder and autofocus attributes have been emulated as dynamic classes, so you can now offer these features on most JavaScript-enabled browsers.

Also, there is a powerful system for adding citations to a web page, and automatically creating a list of them all at the article end, giving you the ability to use names to refer to objects, which are then automatically converted into numbers you can use to create labels or captions such as Figure 1, Table 3, and so on. During this, the numbering is kept consistent even if you move the referenced objects about on the page.

Finally, there's a simple class for preventing casual users from trying to copy and paste the contents of your web page.

Placeholder (placeholder[*prompt*])

This class provides similar functionality to the HTML5 placeholder attribute for input fields. With it, you can specify default text you would like to appear in a field that has no input—for use as a prompt for the user—as shown in Figure 31-1.

In Figure 31-2, once the user starts entering data into the field, the placeholder is forgotten and will not reappear unless the data entered is deleted by the user.

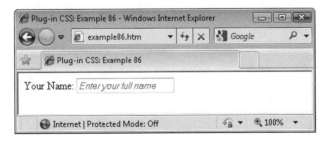

FIGURE 31-1   A placeholder prompt is displayed in an empty field.

Variables, Functions, and Properties

tagname	String variable containing the name of the current tag, such as input
origcname	String variable containing an exact copy of the class name before the class name is converted to lowercase
arguments[1]	JavaScript array element containing the placeholder text
replace()	JavaScript function to replace a section of text in a string with another
FieldPrompt()	Function to activate a placeholder in a field
placeholder	HTML5 Property containing any placeholder text

About the Class

This class uses the replace() function to pass the argument containing the placeholder text to the FieldPrompt() function (JavaScript Recipe 90), via the arguments[] array. The origcname string variable is used for the replace() function, rather than the usual cnamecopy string, since it retains any uppercase characters that should be used in the placeholder. But before applying the placeholder text to a field, it checks whether the browser already has an HTML5 placeholder value set, and if so, it does nothing, allowing that to override this class.

How to Use It

To insert a placeholder prompt in a field, place the prompt text within square brackets following the class name, in the class argument of an object, like this:

```
<input type='text' name='name' class='placeholder[Enter your name]' />
```

The JavaScript

```
if (classname.search(/\bplaceholder\b/, 0) != -1 &&
    tagname == 'input')
{
    origcname.replace(/placeholder\[([^\]]*)\]/, function()
    {
        if (thistag.placeholder == '' ||
            typeof thistag.placeholder == UNDEF)
            FieldPrompt(thistag, arguments[1])
    } )
}
```

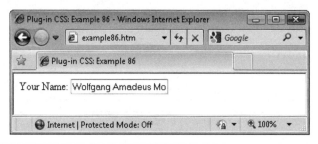

FIGURE 31-2   The placeholder prompt is removed when data is entered into the field.

Autofocus (autofocus)

With this class, you can specify which object should have focus when a page loads, in the same way that *google.com,* for example, automatically places the input cursor into the search field so it's ready for you to enter your search term.

In Figure 31-3, normally no field would have focus on page load, but by using this class the input field has been focused, and the text cursor is now displaying within it.

Variables, Functions, and Properties

`tagname`	Variable containing the tag name, such as `input`
`tagtype`	Variable containing the type of a tag, such as `hidden`
`focus()`	JavaScript function to provide focus to an object

About the Class

This class checks whether the tag name is one of `input`, `select`, `textarea`, or `button`, and proceeds only if it is. Next, it checks whether the tag type has the value `hidden`, and if so, it then uses the `focus()` function to give the tag focus.

How to Use It

To use this class, enter its name into the `class` argument of any `<input>`, `<select>`, `<textarea>`, or `<button>` object, like this:

```
<input type='text' name='name' class='autofocus' />
```

The JavaScript

```
if (classname.search(/\bautofocus\b/, 0) != -1 &&
    tagname == 'input'    || tagname == 'select' ||
    tagname == 'textarea' || tagname == 'button')
{
    if (tagtype != 'hidden') thistag.focus()
}
```

Figure 31-3 in browser window:

Plug-in CSS: Example 87 - Windows Internet Explorer

example87.htm — Google

Plug-in CSS: Example 87

Your Name: |

Internet | Protected Mode: Off   100%

FIGURE 31-3   Use this class to give focus to any object you choose

Cite (cite[*citation*])

Using this class, you can easily add citations as you create an article, which will then be automatically numbered, hyperlinked in superscript text, and referenced at the end of the article. For example, Figure 31-4 features a short biography of Sir Timothy Berners-Lee (inventor of the World Wide Web) that incorporates two references to articles on other sites, which have been marked as they occur in the text and detailed at the article end.

Variables, Functions, and Properties

origcname	String variable containing an exact copy of the class name before the class name is converted to lowercase
arguments[1]	JavaScript array element containing the citation details
cites[]	Array containing the list of citation details
cindex	Integer variable containing the number of citations
replace()	JavaScript function to replace a section of text in a string with another
Html()	Function to read or write the HTML contents of an object
InsVars()	Function for inserting one or more values into a string
verticalAlign	Property containing the vertical alignment of an object
textDecoration	Property containing the text decoration of an object, such as underline
fontSize	Property containing the font size of an object

About the Class

This class makes a note of all cite[] class references as they occur and places the citation details from each into the array cites[]. A superscript link is then made to the list of citations, which will appear once all have been processed. Using these links, you can jump directly to the matching citation later in the web page.

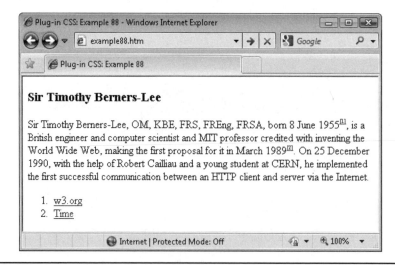

Figure 31-4   This class makes handling citations extremely easy.

How to Use It

To use this class, you need to include some citation details within the square brackets of a `cite[]` class argument, like this:

```
Global warming may be increasing<span class='cite[Wikipedia]'></span>.
```

Or you can include a link within the citation details if you prefer, like this:

```
Global warming may be increasing<span class="cite[<a href='
http://en.wikipedia.org/wiki/Global_warming'>Wikipedia</a>]"></span>.
```

In this case, the `class` argument is enclosed in double quotation marks so that the URL within it can be placed in single quotation marks.

Once you have placed all your citations in the article text, you must then place an object with the ID name of `citations` somewhere on your web page, which will then have the citation details placed in it once they have all been processed, like this:

```
<div id='citations'></div>
```

To see this work in practice, here is the HTML used for Figure 31-4:

```
<h3>Sir Timothy Berners-Lee</h3>

Sir Timothy Berners-Lee, OM, KBE, FRS, FREng, FRSA, born 8 June 1955<span
class="cite[<a href='http://www.w3.org/People/Berners-Lee/Longer.html'>
w3.org</a>]"></span>, is a British engineer and computer scientist and
MIT professor credited with inventing the World Wide Web, making the
first proposal for it in March 1989<span class="cite[<a href='http://205.
188.238.181/time/time100/scientist/profile/bernerslee.html'>Time</a>]">
</span>. On 25 December 1990, with the help of Robert Cailliau and a
young student at CERN, he implemented the first successful communication
between an HTTP client and server via the Internet.

<div id='citations'></div>
```

The JavaScript that Creates the Citation List

If you are interested in how this works, the following code runs after all the dynamic classes in a web page have been processed, but only if `cindex` has a value greater than 0 (indicating there is at least one citation):

```
if (cindex > 0)
{
   var html = '<ol>'

   for (index = 0 ; index < cindex ; ++index)
      html += InsVars('<a name=cite#1></a><li>#2</li>',
         index + 1, cites[index])

   if (typeof O('citations') != UNDEF) Html('citations', html + '</ol>')
}
```

It then creates an unordered list and iterates through the cites[] array extracting all the citations into the object that has been given the ID of citations (if it exists).

The code that first processes the cite[] class is shown next.

The JavaScript

```
if (classname.search(/\bcite\b/, 0) != -1)
{
    cnamecopy.replace(/cite\[(([^\]]*)\]/, function()
    {
        cites[cindex++]           = arguments[1]
        S(thistag).verticalAlign  = 'super'
        S(thistag).textDecoration = 'none'
        S(thistag).fontSize       = '50%'

        Html(thistag, Html(thistag) +
            InsVars("<a href='#cite#1'>[#1]</a>", cindex))
    } )
}
```

Reference (ref[*type*|*name*])

With this class, you can refer to sections of an article by using special names, and when the article is viewed by a user, all the references are changed to numbers, in the same way that figures in this chapter have numbers that run in order so as to easily identify them. This means you can relocate the references and sections to which they refer within an article without worrying about having to renumber them all.

For example, in Figure 31-5 there are two figures and one section that are referenced by the main text. Even though these objects do not appear in the same order in which they are referred, they have been given identifying numbers in the correct sequence.

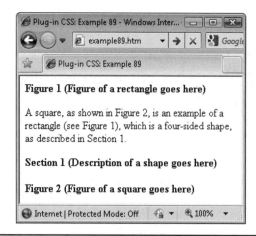

Figure 31-5   This class keeps track of referenced objects, renumbering them for you.

Variables, Functions, and Properties

cnamecopy	String variable containing a copy of the class name
arguments[1]	JavaScript array element containing the reference object type
arguments[2]	JavaScript array element containing the reference object name
a1 a2	Variable copies of arguments[1] and arguments[2] used as shorthand to simplify the code
refers[]	Array containing all the references
replace()	JavaScript function to replace a section of text in a string with another
Html()	Function to read or write the HTML contents of an object

About the Class

This class takes an object type and an object name and then keeps track of where these are used throughout a web page. They are then given numerical values according to the order in which they are encountered, such that (for example) the first figure object is given the value 1, the second is given the value 2, and so on.

How to Use It

To use this class, you must give every object you reference a unique name, so that whenever it is mentioned, the correct number can be placed with it. You also need to specify the type of each object so you can, for instance, have figures and tables, and as many other object types as you need.

So, for example, to announce that an object is a figure, you might use code such as this:

```
<b>Figure <span class='ref[fig|uniquename]'></span><br />
<img src='animage.jpg' />
```

In this case, the unique name is uniquename, and the object type is fig. To now reference this figure from anywhere in the web page, you would use code such as this:

```
(see Figure <span class='ref[fig|uniquename]'></span>)
```

Leave the contents of the <span> (or other object you use) empty because the class will place the number to display inside it, overwriting anything already there.

Once you have done this, you can move the figure and any references to it to any other places in the article and they will still correctly reference each other—and, if necessary, they will be renumbered should the figure be moved before or after another figure.

Here's another example that uses this class, and which creates the result seen in Figure 31-5:

```
<b>Figure <span class='ref[fig|rect]'></span>
(Figure of a rectangle goes here)</b>

<p>A square, as shown in Figure <span class='ref[fig|square]'></span>,
is an example of a rectangle (see Figure <span class='ref[fig|rect]'>
</span>), which is a four-sided shape, as described in Section <span
class='ref[sec|shape]'></span>.</p>
```

```
<b>Section <span class='ref[sec|shape]'></span>
(Description of a shape goes here)</b><br /><br />

<b>Figure <span class='ref[fig|square]'></span>
(Figure of a square goes here)</b>
```

I have highlighted the references in bold so you can quickly see them. Three objects in total are referenced:

- fig|rect
- fig|square
- sec|shape

Two of the objects are of type fig and the other is of type sec. What the class does is allocate the fig object numbers in the order in which they first appear in the document (and would do the same for the sec objects, except there is only one).

Therefore, if fig|square is encountered first, it will become Figure 1, but if fig|rect is the first one found, then *it* will be Figure 1. This means that all the objects will always be ordered correctly according to where they appear in an article (no matter where you move them to), making it easy for your readers to locate them.

You can use any names you want for the object types such as figure rather than fig, section rather than sec, or any other names, such as fred or wilma.

The JavaScript

```
if (classname.search(/\bref\b/, 0) != -1)
{
    cnamecopy.replace(/ref\[([^\|]*)\|([^\]]*)\]/, function()
    {
        var a1 = arguments[1]
        var a2 = arguments[2]

        if (typeof refers[a1] == UNDEF)
        {
            refers[a1]          = Array()
            refers[a1]['count'] = 1
            refers[a1][a2]      = 1
        }
        else if (typeof refers[a1][a2] == UNDEF)
            refers[a1][a2] = ++refers[a1]['count']

        Html(thistag, refers[a1][a2])
    } )
}
```

No Copy (nocopy)

Sometimes you want to prevent idle copying and pasting of your work, or simply wish to prevent the ugly effect that a highlighted section of text might have on your design. You can do so using this class, as shown in Figure 31-6, in which the first section of text can be copied, but the second cannot.

Variables, Functions, and Properties

`PreventAction()`	Function to prevent drag-and-copy actions

About the Class

This class prevents the use of drag and drop on an object. It works well on most browsers, but there is a bug in Internet Explorer in which you can commence a drag operation outside of an object that uses this class and the browser will allow you to continue the drag into it. However, IE does correctly prevent starting a drag operation from within objects using this class.

How to Use It

To prevent an object from allowing drag-and-copy operations, mention this class name in the object's `class` argument, like this:

```
<p class='nocopy'>This text is uncopyable</p>
```

However, due to the Internet Explorer bug, you will have the best results if you attach this class to the `<body>` section of a web page, like this (so that nothing on a web page can be copied):

```
<body class='nocopy'>
    ... Your web page contents
</body>
```

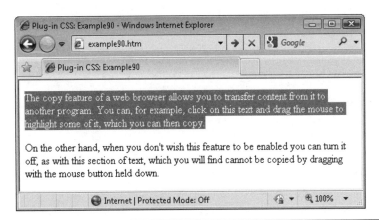

Figure 31-6   Prevent sections of text from being copied with this recipe

Here is the HTML used for Figure 31-6:

```
<p>The copy feature of a web browser allows you to transfer content
from it to another program. You can, for example, click on this text
and drag the mouse to highlight some of it, which you can then copy.</p>

<p class='nocopy'>On the other hand, when you don't wish this feature
to be enabled, you can turn it off, as with this section of text, which
you will find cannot be copied by dragging with the mouse button held
down.</p>
```

The JavaScript

```
if (classname.search(/\bnocopy\b/, 0) != -1)
{
    PreventAction(thistag, 'both', true)
}
```

CHAPTER 32

Incorporating JavaScript

Even if you are not a programmer, or not familiar with JavaScript, you can still make use of this powerful language using the classes in this chapter. With them, you can embed simple calculations or complex expressions within an object, just by placing them within a pair of special tokens.

You can also use these recipes to leverage the power of JavaScript for creating sections of conditional HTML, whether based on expressions of your choice, or using a special global keyword to identify the browser in use (such as Firefox, Internet Explorer, and so on).

Once you use these classes, you may find them so handy you'll wonder how you ever managed without them.

Embed JavaScript (embedjs)

Using this class, you can embed snippets of JavaScript within an object, without having to use `<script>` tags. This makes it easy for you to display the result of a calculation, or anything else that can be displayed by JavaScript.

For example, in Figure 32-1 a number of code snippets have been embedded within a paragraph of text, which have been evaluated, and the results then inserted in their place.

Variables, Functions, and Properties

`replace()`	JavaScript function to replace one section of text with another
`Html()`	Function to get or set the HTML contents of an object
`try ... catch()`	JavaScript to try an expression and, if there is an error, catch it quietly without throwing an error
`Eval()`	JavaScript function to evaluate an expression

About the Class

When this class is encountered, the object using it is parsed to see whether it has any sections embedded within `[[` and `]]` tags. If so, these sections are evaluated as JavaScript code, and the result returned by the evaluation is then substituted for the entire section from the opening `[[` to the closing `]]`.

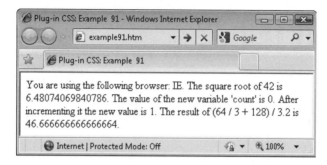

How to Use It

With this class, you have the ability to easily embed any JavaScript inline with text. For example, you might want to display the result of a simple calculation and can do so like this:

```
<div class='embedjs'>The result of 23.2 * 7 is [[23.2 * 7]].</div>
```

As you can see, you don't need to know anything about JavaScript to use this class to display the result of arithmetic calculations. You can also access the global variable BROWSER, which is used by the *WDC.js* file to keep track of the current browser type. It will have a value such as "IE", "Opera", "Firefox", and so on, and can be displayed like this:

```
<div class='embedjs'>Your browser is [[BROWSER]].</div>
```

You can also embed much larger sections of code by separating the expressions from each other with a semicolon, like this:

```
<div class='embedjs'> The multiplication table for the number 12 is
[[mystr = ''; for (myvar = 1 ; myvar &lt; 13 ; ++myvar) mystr += myvar
* 12 + ' '; mystr]]</div>
```

Or, if you prefer, you can format the contents like program code as follows (still ensuring that there are semicolons at the end of each statement except the final one, which is optional):

```
<div class='embedjs'>The multiplication table for the number 12 is
[[
    mystr = '';
    for (myvar = 1 ; myvar &lt; 13 ; ++myvar)
        mystr += myvar * 12 + ' ';
    mystr
]]
</div>
```

The output from this example is:

```
The multiplication table for the number 12 is 12 24 36 48 60 72 84 96 108
120 132 144
```

CAUTION *In the* `for()` *loop of this example, the* `&lt;` *entity is used instead of the* `<` *symbol because placing the* `<` *within HTML confuses browsers, which expect an HTML tag to follow it. Likewise, you must use the* `&gt;` *entity where you need a* `>` *symbol. The only way you can use the* `<` *and* `>` *symbols is if the entire JavaScript snippet is encased in quotation marks, like this:* `"[[76 < 83.3]]"`, *which will return the value* `true`.

Here's the HTML used for Figure 32-1, in which I have highlighted the embedded JavaScript snippets in bold:

```
<div class='embedjs'>
   You are using the following browser: [[BROWSER]]. The square root of
   42 is [[Math.sqrt(42)]]. The value of the new variable 'count' is
   [[count = 0]]. After incrementing it, the new value is [[++count]].
   The result of (64 / 3 + 128) / 3.2 is [[(64 / 3 + 128) / 3.2]].
</div>
```

As you can see, you can also create a new variable (such as count, in the preceding example), and then refer to it later in a web page (as long as you don't make it local by prefacing it with the var keyword, in which case it will work only in the current code snippet).

If you make a mistake, such as introducing a syntax error, an error message will be displayed in red, instead of the result you were expecting. For example, the following is invalid:

```
<div class='embedjs'>The result of 66 x 87 is [[66 x 87]].</div>
```

The problem is that the x symbol is not a valid operator in JavaScript, and it should be replaced with a * symbol. Therefore, because the parser was expecting a semicolon following the 66, the preceding snippet will generate an output similar to the following:

The result of 66 x 87 is [SyntaxError: missing ; before statement]

The JavaScript

```
if (classname.search(/\bembedjs\b/, 0) != -1)
{
   Html(thistag, Html(thistag).replace(/\[\[([^\]]*)\]\]/g,
      function()
   {
      arguments[1] = arguments[1].replace(/&lt;/g, '<')
      arguments[1] = arguments[1].replace(/&gt;/g, '>')

      try
      {
         return eval(arguments[1])
      }
      catch(e)
      {
```

```
            return "<span class='red'>[" + e + "]</span>"
      }
   } ))
}
```

If (if[*expr*])

If you've ever wished you could write conditional HTML, then you should find this class very handy, because with it you can display an object only if an expression evaluates to `true`. For example, in Figure 32-2, the screen grab was taken after midday; therefore, it displays the phrase "Good Afternoon".

Variables, Functions, and Properties

`replace()`	JavaScript function to replace one section of text with another
`Html()`	Function to get or set the HTML contents of an object
`Eval()`	JavaScript function to evaluate an expression

About the Class

This class evaluates the expression following the class name and then displays the object only if the expression evaluates to `true`. If it is `false`, to prevent the object's display it is simply encased within `<!--` and `-->` HTML comment tags.

How to Use It

Use this class when you want to display objects only when certain conditions are met. For example, the following object is displayed only after midday:

```
<span class='if[now = new Date(); now.getHours() > 11]'>Afternoon</span>
```

What is going on here is that a new object called `now` is created from the current date and time using the `Date()` function. Then, the `getHours()` method of the `now` object is used to return the current hour between 0 and 23. This value is compared with the number 11 and, if it is greater, the contents of the `<span>` is displayed, which in this case is the word "Afternoon".

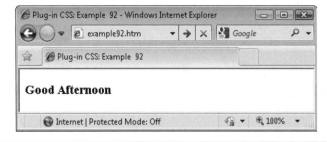

FIGURE 32-2 Using this class, you can display objects only when conditions are satisfied.

NOTE *Unlike its use in objects implementing the* embedjs *class, the direct use of the* > *symbol is acceptable in this case because the entire contents of the class argument are enclosed within quotation marks, and therefore the* > *cannot be mistaken for part of an HTML tag.*

Using the BROWSER Global Variable with this Class

Because they all work differently, the *WDC.js* library of JavaScript functions needs to know which browser is running, and therefore tweaks can be made to ensure all the functions have the same (or nearly the same) effect. You can use the global variable BROWSER that it creates for your own purposes, too.

For example, if you have written an application for the iPad tablet that you want to advertise, you could use the following code to display details about it only to people browsing your web page using that device:

```
<div class="if[BROWSER == 'iPad']">
   Check out our special app for iPad users...
   etc...
</div>
```

Table 32-1 lists all the values that BROWSER may have, in order of determination. For example, if an iPod Touch device is detected, then the string "iPod" is assigned to BROWSER, even though the browser running is a version of Safari.

Here is the code used for Figure 32-2:

```
Good
<span class='if[now = new Date(); now.getHours() < 12]'>Morning</span>
<span class='if[now = new Date(); now.getHours() > 11]'>Afternoon</span>
```

TABLE 32-1 The Possible Values of the BROWSER Variable	Value	Browser/Device Type
	IE	Internet Explorer
	Opera	Opera
	Chrome	Google Chrome
	iPod	Apple iPod Touch
	iPhone	Apple iPhone
	iPad	Apple iPad
	Android	Google Android
	Safari	Apple Safari
	Firefox	Mozilla Firefox
	UNKNOWN	No known browser type identified

PART IV

The JavaScript

```
if (classname.search(/\bif\b/, 0) != -1)
{
    origcname.replace(/(if|IF)\[([^\]]*)\]/, function()
    {
        if (!eval(arguments[2]))
            Html(thistag, '<!-- ' + Html(thistag) + ' -->')
    } )
}
```

If Not (ifnot[*expr*])

This class provides the inverse of the if[] class and is useful for implementing the equivalent of an if... else... block of code. For example, in Figure 32-3 this class is used in conjunction with the if[] class, and you can see the different results displayed in the Apple Safari browser and in Internet Explorer (the inset).

Variables, Functions, and Properties

replace()	JavaScript function to replace one section of text with another
Html()	Function to get or set the HTML contents of an object
eval()	JavaScript function to evaluate an expression

About the Class

This class evaluates the expression following the class name and then displays the object only if the expression evaluates to false. If it is true, to prevent the object's display it is simply encased within <!-- and --> HTML comment tags.

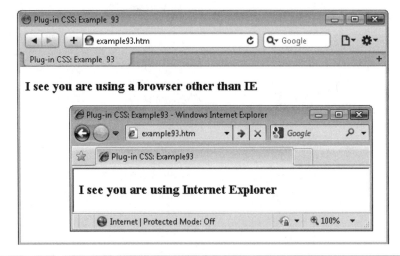

Figure 32-3   Using both the if[] and ifnot[] classes to target different browsers

How to Use It

You use this class in the same manner as the `if[]` class, except that the object will be displayed only if the result of the expression in the square brackets evaluates to `false`. For example, here is the code used for the screen grabs in Figure 32-3:

```
I see you are using
<span class="   if[BROWSER == 'IE']">Internet Explorer</span>
<span class="ifnot[BROWSER == 'IE']">a browser other than IE</span>
```

Of course, you could replace the second line with the following, in which the `if[]` class is used in place of `ifnot[]`, but with a modified expression:

```
<span class="if[BROWSER != 'IE']">a browser other than IE</span>
```

But the point of the `ifnot[]` class is that you don't have to rewrite an expression that was used in an `if[]` class; you can simply copy the entire expression and place it within an `ifnot[]` class to achieve the inverse effect of the original, which is very handy if the expression is quite complex.

NOTE *This completes all the dynamic classes in this book. In the next and final chapter, I'll show you how you can combine any of these classes together to create superclasses, which have the combined functionality of many classes at once.*

The JavaScript

```
if (classname.search(/\bifnot\b/, 0) != -1)
{
    origcname.replace(/(ifnot|IFNOT)\[([^\]]*)\]/, function()
    {
        if (eval(arguments[2]))
            Html(thistag, '<!-- ' + Html(thistag) + ' -->')
    } )
}
```

CHAPTER 33

Superclasses

Now that you have access to the almost 1800 classes from the previous chapters, this one focuses on combining them to make superclasses—single classes with the functionality of several classes at once. These superclasses include creating an RSS button, applying simple borders, handling rollovers, generating horizontal and vertical animated tabs, and more.

You'll also discover how easy it is to create your own superclasses using simple `<meta ...>` statements to help make building dynamic web pages the easiest it has ever been.

What Is a Superclass?

Superclasses are classes that contain groups of other classes. For example, the first superclass in this chapter, `clickable`, contains the `nooutline` and `pointer` classes (CSS Recipes 19 and 54).

Seven superclasses have been predefined for you in the *WDC.js* file (right at the end), and you can easily create your own using the `<meta ...>` tag, like this:

```
<meta http-equiv='sclass' name='clickable' content='nooutline pointer' />
```

In this example, the superclass `clickable` is created by placing the argument `http-equiv='sclass'` within a `<meta ...>` tag, followed by the argument specifying the name of the superclass, `name='clickable'`, and finally the classes to put in the superclass, `content='nooutline pointer'`.

Here's another example:

```
<meta http-equiv='sclass' name='yellowonblue' content='yellow blue_b' />
```

This creates the new superclass `yellowonblue`, which will set the foreground color of the object to which it applies to yellow and the background to blue.

NOTE *You can include as many classes in a superclass as you like, as well as any combination of normal and dynamic classes from this book, or even throw in your own classes created either within `<style>` tags or from a style sheet.*

Clickable (clickable)

The purpose of this class is to clearly indicate that objects, and buttons in particular, are clickable. It does this by removing any outline that may be placed around the object when it has the focus, and by turning the mouse cursor into a pointer when it hovers over the object.

In Figure 33-1, two rows of buttons have been created. The first row doesn't use this superclass, but the second does.

In the screen grab, you can clearly see the dotted outline that has been applied to the first Cancel button, but which will not appear over the second one. Also, the mouse cursor will change to a pointer when over the second row, but not the first.

Classes

`nooutline`	CSS Recipe 19: Prevents a dotted outline being placed over an object in focus
`pointer`	CSS Recipe 54: Turns the mouse cursor into a pointer when it hovers over the object

About the Superclass

By combining the effects of two other classes, this superclass helps to clearly indicate when an object is clickable.

How to Use It

To use this superclass, enter its name into the `class` argument of an object. For example, the following code was used to create the screen grab in Figure 33-1:

```
<button class='check_h'>Submit</button>
<button class='cross_h'>Cancel</button>
<button class='email_h'>Email Us</button>
<button class='star_h' >New Stuff</button><br />

<button class='check_h clickable'>Submit</button>
<button class='cross_h clickable'>Cancel</button>
<button class='email_h clickable'>Email Us</button>
<button class='star_h clickable' >New Stuff</button>
```

Try passing your mouse over the different rows and clicking various buttons to see the differences between them.

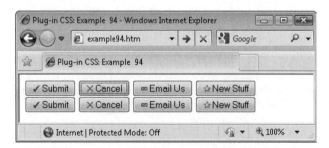

Figure 33-1   This superclass removes outlines and changes the mouse cursor to a pointer.

RSS Button (rssbutton)

This class creates a great-looking RSS button without the need for including an image. For example, Figure 33-2 shows it being applied to both a <button> and a <span> object in both the Chrome and Internet Explorer browsers. Although there are minute differences between them, all the buttons look quite respectable.

Classes

carrot1	CSS Recipe 4: Changes the background to the gradient carrot1
carrot2_a	CSS Recipe 5: Changes the background to the gradient carrot2 when the object is clicked
smallestround	CSS Recipe 8: Applies a two-pixel rounded border
b	CSS Recipe 21: Changes the font weight to bold
white	CSS Recipe 24: Changes the foreground color to white
yellow_h	CSS Recipe 24: Changes the hover color to yellow
smallbutton	CSS Recipe 33: Creates a button with a 75 percent font size and two pixels of padding
clickable	CSS Recipe 94: Indicates that the object is clickable

About the Superclass

This superclass brings together a large number of CSS rules from several different classes, even including the previous superclass, clickable, to create a dynamic, 3D-effect RSS button.

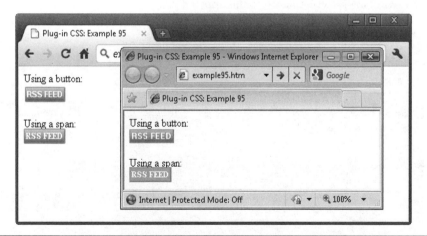

FIGURE 33-2   The RSS button superclass used on different objects in different browsers

How to Use It

To use this superclass, you will need to surround it with an `<a href='...'>` tag pointing to your RSS feed, like this:

```
<a class='n' href='myfeed.xml'>
   <span class='rssbutton'>RSS FEED</span>
</a>
```

The first line references the RSS feed and uses the n class to suppress the underline that would otherwise appear under the button. The middle line applies the `rssbutton` superclass to a `<span>` tag, and supplies the string "RSS FEED" to it.

You can also use the `<button>` tag by placing it in a form like this:

```
<form method='get' action='myfeed.xml'>
   <button class='rssbutton'>RSS FEED</button>
</form>
```

CAUTION *When using the `<button>` tag, Internet Explorer will submit the text between the `<button>` and `</button>` tags, while other browsers will submit the contents of its `value` attribute (if any).*

Border (border)

Often, you want to quickly add a border to an object, and this class will do the job for you without having to supply a set of CSS rules. For example, in Figure 33-3 a photograph is displayed twice, the second time using this superclass.

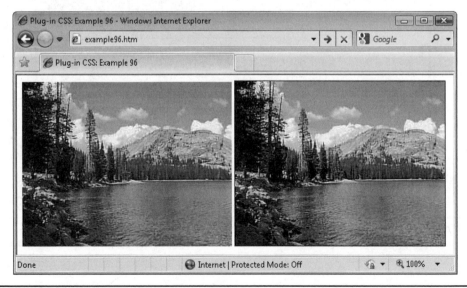

FIGURE 33-3   Displaying an image without, and with, the border superclass

Classes

bsolid	CSS Recipe 16: Sets the object's border to solid
bwidth1	CSS Recipe 17: Sets the object's border width to 1 pixel
bblack	CSS Recipe 18: Sets the object's border color to black

About the Superclass

This superclass uses all three border classes to create a simple, one-pixel black border around the object.

How to Use It

When you want to quickly add a border to an object, just enter this superclass name in its class argument, like this:

```
<img class='border' src='myphoto.jpg' />
```

Absolute Top Left (abstopleft)

Whenever you create a rollover or need to align objects on top of each other, the process is the same. All objects after the first one should be moved to the top-left corner of the containing object, and this class makes doing so quick and easy.

You can see this superclass in use in Figure 33-4, where the boat image has been superimposed over the photograph.

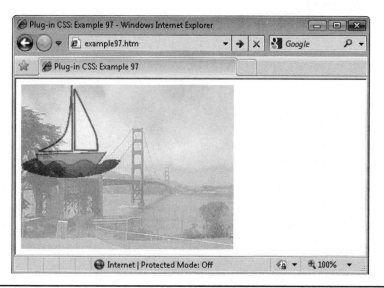

FIGURE 33-4   Use this superclass to lay objects over each other.

Classes

absolute	Recipe 1: Gives an object absolute positioning
totop	Recipe 13: Moves an object to the top of its container
toleft	Recipe 13: Moves an object to the left of its container

About the Superclass

This superclass applies three classes to give an object absolute positioning, and to move it to its containing object's top-left corner.

How to Use It

To use this superclass, you will need a container object with a position other than static in which to place your objects. Then, the second object onward must apply the superclass, as in the following example, which was used for Figure 33-4:

```
<div class='relative'>
    <img class='trans07' src='i2.jpg' />
    <img class='abstopleft trans06' src='boat.png' />
</div>
```

In this example, the larger image is given a transparency level of 7 and the boat a transparency of 6 and they have been superimposed over each other. Reasons you would want to do this include creating slide shows and rollovers, as in the following recipe.

Rollover (rollover)

This class makes it very easy for you to create rollover effects, as shown in Figure 33-5, in which two face images are displayed that, when moused over, turn from happy to sad, and vice versa.

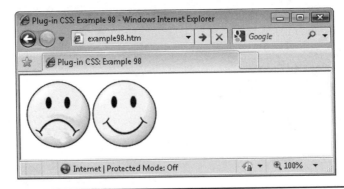

FIGURE 33-5   Creating rollover effects with this pair of superclasses

Classes

`trans00`	CSS Recipe 9: Sets the transparency of an object to fully visible
`trans00_h`	CSS Recipe 9: Sets the transparency of an object to fully visible when the mouse cursor passes over it
`trans10`	CSS Recipe 9: Sets the transparency of an object to completely invisible
`trans10_h`	CSS Recipe 9: Sets the transparency of an object to completely invisible when the mouse cursor passes over it
`abstopleft`	CSS Recipe 97: Gives an object absolute positioning and moves it to the top-left corner of its container

About the Superclasses

These two superclasses are intended to be used together. The `rollover` superclass should be applied to the first of a rollover pair of objects, and `rollover_h` to the second. Once implemented, whenever the mouse passes over the objects, the first one is set to transparent and the second to fully visible so the one you can see swaps. When the mouse is moved away, the first object becomes visible again and the second invisible.

In another illustration of superclasses being used as members of other superclasses, the `abstopleft` superclass is used as one of the members of this superclass pair.

How to Use Them

To use these superclasses, first create an object that has a positioning other than static, and then place two other objects within it, giving the first one the `rollover` superclass, and the second `rollover_h`, like this:

```
<div class='relative'>
    <img class='rollover'   src='frowney.gif' />
    <img class='rollover_h' src='smiley.gif'  />
</div>
```

The application of the relative class to the `<div>` ensures that it doesn't have a position of static, and therefore it will act as the containing object for the images within it. The `rollover_h` superclass makes use of the `abstopleft` superclass (among others), so there is no need to specify the positioning of the second image.

TIP *You are not restricted to only images by these superclasses, and can use any types of objects for the rollover pairs.*

Vertical Tab (vtab)

This class creates a tab that slides in from the left of the screen on browsers that support CSS transitions such as Opera 10, Firefox 4, Apple Safari 5, and Google Chrome 5 (or higher). Sadly, the smooth transition doesn't work on Internet Explorer, but it does degrade to a simple in or out animation.

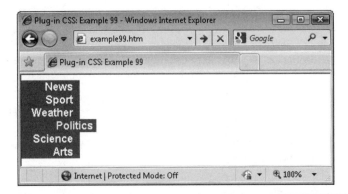

FIGURE 33-6   A number of pop-out tabs created using this superclass

In Figure 33-6, a number of tabs have been created using this superclass, and the mouse is currently hovering over the Politics tab, which has popped out.

Classes

`leftpadding10`	CSS Recipe 15: Applies 10 pixels of padding to the object's left side
`leftpadding40_h`	CSS Recipe 15: Applies 40 pixels of padding to the object's left side when it is hovered over by the mouse
`rightpadding5`	CSS Recipe 15: Applies 5 pixels of padding to the object's right side
`b`	CSS Recipe 21: Sets the object's font weight to bold
`transitionallfast_l`	CSS Recipe 51: Applies a linear transition of 0.3 seconds to any property changes that occur on the object (where supported by the browser)

About the Superclass

This is a great little superclass for creating a variety of animation and menuing effects. It works by changing the left padding of an object when the mouse passes over it. In conjunction with CSS3 transitions (on browsers that support them), the object will slide out and in smoothly over the course of 0.3 seconds. In Internet Explorer and other browsers that don't support transitions, the object will simply pop in and out.

How to Use It

To use this superclass, first create a container object by giving it a position other than static. For example, here is the HTML used for Figure 33-6:

```
<div class='relative red_b leftby20 arial w[100]'>
    <div class='vtab white red_b yellow_h right w[80]'>News</div>
    <div class='vtab white red_b yellow_h right w[80]'>Sport</div>
    <div class='vtab white red_b yellow_h right w[80]'>Weather</div>
    <div class='vtab white red_b yellow_h right w[80]'>Politics</div>
    <div class='vtab white red_b yellow_h right w[80]'>Science</div>
    <div class='vtab white red_b yellow_h right w[80]'>Arts</div>
</div>
```

In the first line of this example, the `<div>` is given relative positioning, a red background color, is moved to the left by 20 pixels (to send it past the screen edge), has its font family set to Arial, and is given a width of 100 pixels.

Inside it are six tabs, each of which uses the `vtab` superclass, and it is set to white text on a red background, which changes to yellow text when hovered over with the mouse. The text is also aligned to the right, and the width of each tab is set to 80 pixels.

When you pass your mouse over the tabs on a browser that supports CSS3 transitions, you'll see them sliding in and out in a pleasing and professional manner. Even on IE and other browsers that do not support transitions, the effect still happens, although instantly rather than over time.

All the example now needs is for `<a href='...'>` tags to be placed around each tab (possibly including the use of the n class to suppress any underlines) and the menu will be complete. When you do this, ensure that the `<a href='...'>` and `</a>` are placed around the `<div>` (or other container), not within it.

Horizontal Tab (htab)

This class is similar to the previous recipe, except that it creates dropdown tabs, as shown in Figure 33-7, where the Science tab is currently being hovered over and has therefore slid down.

Classes

`absolute`	CSS Recipe 1: Gives an object absolute positioning
`toppadding20_h`	CSS Recipe 15: Applies 20 pixels of padding to the object's top when it is hovered over by the mouse
`b`	CSS Recipe 21: Sets the object's font weight to bold
`center`	CSS Recipe 22: Centers the object's contents
`transitionallfast_l`	CSS Recipe 51: Applies a linear transition of 0.3 seconds to any property changes that occur on the object (where supported by the browser)

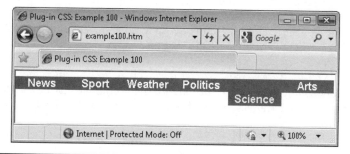

FIGURE 33-7   These pop-out tabs drop down vertically when hovered over.

About the Superclass

This superclass works by changing the top padding of an object when the mouse passes over it. In conjunction with CSS3 transitions (on browsers that support them), the object will slide down and up smoothly over the course of 0.3 seconds. In Internet Explorer and other browsers that don't support transitions, the object will simply pop down and back up again.

How to Use It

To use this superclass, you need to first create a container object by giving it a position other than static. For example, here is the HTML used for Figure 33-7:

```
<div class='red_b arial'>
    <span class='htab white red_b yellow_h w[80] x[0]'  >News</span>
    <span class='htab white red_b yellow_h w[80] x[80]' >Sport</span>
    <span class='htab white red_b yellow_h w[80] x[160]'>Weather</span>
    <span class='htab white red_b yellow_h w[80] x[240]'>Politics</span>
    <span class='htab white red_b yellow_h w[80] x[320]'>Science</span>
    <span class='htab white red_b yellow_h w[80] x[400]'>Arts</span>
</div>
```

In the first line of this example, the `<div>` is given a red background color, and its font family is set to Arial.

Inside it are six tabs, each of which uses the `htab` superclass. It is also set to white text on a red background, which changes to yellow text when hovered over with the mouse. The width of each tab is set to 80 pixels, and the horizontal location of each tab is moved in by 80 pixels from the previous one.

When you pass your mouse over the tabs on a browser that supports CSS3 transitions, you'll see them smoothly sliding down and up. In IE and other browsers, the tabs instantly pop down and up.

Summary

And there you have it, more than 300 different handcrafted recipes for PHP, MySQL, JavaScript, CSS, and Ajax, all contained in just three easy-to-access files (*WDC.php*, *WDC.js* and *WDC.css*). So now you can spend more time developing the new and exciting features you want on your web sites, and less time having to reinvent the wheel simply to provide standard features—because the chances are that there are recipes in this book for almost any project, whether server- or browser-based.

I hope you have found these recipes useful as well as time-saving, and have maybe even learned a few coding tricks from the examples. If you have any comments, ideas, or suggestions, please contact me via the *webdeveloperscookbook.com* web site, where I will be pleased to hear from you.

Index

K

L